ACCOUNTING INFORMATION SYSTEMS

Robert G. Murdick, Ph.D.
Thomas C. Fuller, CPA
Joel E. Ross, Ph.D.

*All from College of Business and
Public Administration
Florida Atlantic University*

Frank J. Winnermark, CPA

Peat, Marwick, Mitchell & Co.

ACCOUNTING INFORMATION SYSTEMS

Prentice-Hall Inc., Englewood Cliffs, New Jersey 07632

Library of Congress Cataloging in Publication Data

Main entry under title:
    Accounting information systems.

    Bibliography: p.
    Includes index.
    1. Information storage and retrieval systems—Accounting. 2. Accounting—Data processing. I. Murdick, Robert G.
Z699.5.A25A25   029'.9'657   77-17102
ISBN 0-13-002014-1

ACCOUNTING INFORMATION SYSTEMS
by Robert G. Murdick, Thomas C. Fuller,
Joel E. Ross, and Frank J. Winnermark

© 1978 by Prentice-Hall, Inc., Englewood Cliffs, N.J. 07632

All rights reserved. No part of this book
may be reproduced in any form or
by any means without permission in writing
from the publisher.

Printed in the United States of America

10 9 8 7 6 5 4 3

Cover photo by Marjorie Pickens,
courtesy American Institute of Certified Public Accountants.

PRENTICE-HALL INTERNATIONAL, INC., *London*
PRENTICE-HALL OF AUSTRALIA PTY. Limited, *Sydney*
PRENTICE-HALL OF CANADA, LTD., *Toronto*
PRENTICE-HALL OF INDIA PRIVATE LIMITED, *New Delhi*
PRENTICE-HALL OF JAPAN, INC., *Tokyo*
PRENTICE-HALL OF SOUTHEAST ASIA PTE. LTD., *Singapore*
WHITEHALL BOOKS LIMITED, *Wellington, New Zealand*

contents

part I
THE MANAGEMENT VIEW 1

1 accounting and information systems 3

2 management, information, and systems 27

part II
ACCOUNTING INFORMATION SYSTEMS FOR OPERATIONS 75

3 accounting and operating systems 77

4 internal control 107

5 reports 149

part III
ACCOUNTING INFORMATION SYSTEMS FOR DECISION MAKING 177

6 problem-solving and decision making 179

7 accounting information systems for major corporate decisions 208

part IV
DESIGN PROCESS AND CONCEPTS 245

8 accounting and management information systems development 247

9 techniques and tools for systems analysis and design 290

10 forms design, analysis, and control 341

11 hardware and software in AIS design 370

12 data base management systems 403

part V
CONTROL OF THE AIS 429

13 maintaining, controlling, and evaluating the AIS 431

14 auditing the AIS 455

appendix: CPA Examination Questions 480

index 493

foreword

The development of computers and computer-based information systems has presented the accounting profession with an enormous challenge and an impressive opportunity. Accounting has always been concerned with the recording and transmission of financial information. Computer-based information systems now make it possible to vastly expand the quantity and type of information recorded and transmitted.

Developing and managing these new information systems requires a special expertise. By virtue of his training, his broad systems experience, and his financial background the accountant is in an especially favorable position to assume control of this significant new technology.

To maintain his traditional leadership role in providing information for management decisions, the accountant must become involved in information systems design and the related information structure upon which management of the organization depends. To provide attestation for the financial statements drawn from the computer-based records, the independent accountant must understand the information system that forms the basis for those records. Moreover, the accountant must adapt to the significant societal, economic, and organizational changes that this information explosion is likely to produce.

The authors of this book have sought to provide a basic approach that will permit the accountant to deal with and capitalize on this important new development. The task is a difficult and important one; the authors are to be commended for embarking upon it.

SIDNEY DAVIDSON, CPA, Ph.D.
ARTHUR YOUNG,
Professor of Accounting
University of Chicago

preface

This is an accounting text which is designed for the accountant in a completely different role from that of the past. It is concerned with systems and with the managerial decision view. In today's organizations, these two perspectives are inseparable.

To avoid the necessity of extensive narratives to describe systems, many diagrams are presented to "show and tell." Some sections of the book present underlying philosophy and concepts for accounting contributions to managerial planning, control, and decision–making. Other sections deal with the practical aspects of "how to do it." Thus we have attempted to present good basic coverage of a new subject of vital importance to future practicing accountants. Supporting problems and cases are designed to make this an effective textbook.

The authors owe many debts for assistance in preparing this book. We wish to thank, in particular, Professors Dora R. Herring of Mississippi State University, James Kinard of Ohio State University, R. Keith Martin of Baruch College-CUNY, Randall W. Redenius of Comprehensive Accounting Services Co., and Arthur J. Schomer, a partner at Eisner & Lubin, CPA's, whose constructive reviews gave us many insights. Remaining deficiencies are ours alone. We thank also John C. Munson for preparing one of the most lucid chapters on data base management systems. Many companies and publishers kindly allowed us to use material which greatly enhances the reality of our illustrations.

Ronald P. Smith and Donna Gulin assisted us with many details of managing the manuscript preparation. We also wish to thank Emily Murdick, Carol Winnermark, and Kerry Ely for helping with the illustrations and typing chores.

THE MANAGEMENT VIEW

Preview:
This chapter introduces and defines accounting systems and their role in the MIS. The accountants' function as a member of the management team, as an auditor, and as a decision-maker are also examined.

CHAPTER ONE

accounting and information systems

Closely Related Chapters:
All chapters in this book are related to this chapter as it serves as a general introduction for all of the subjects we will discuss.

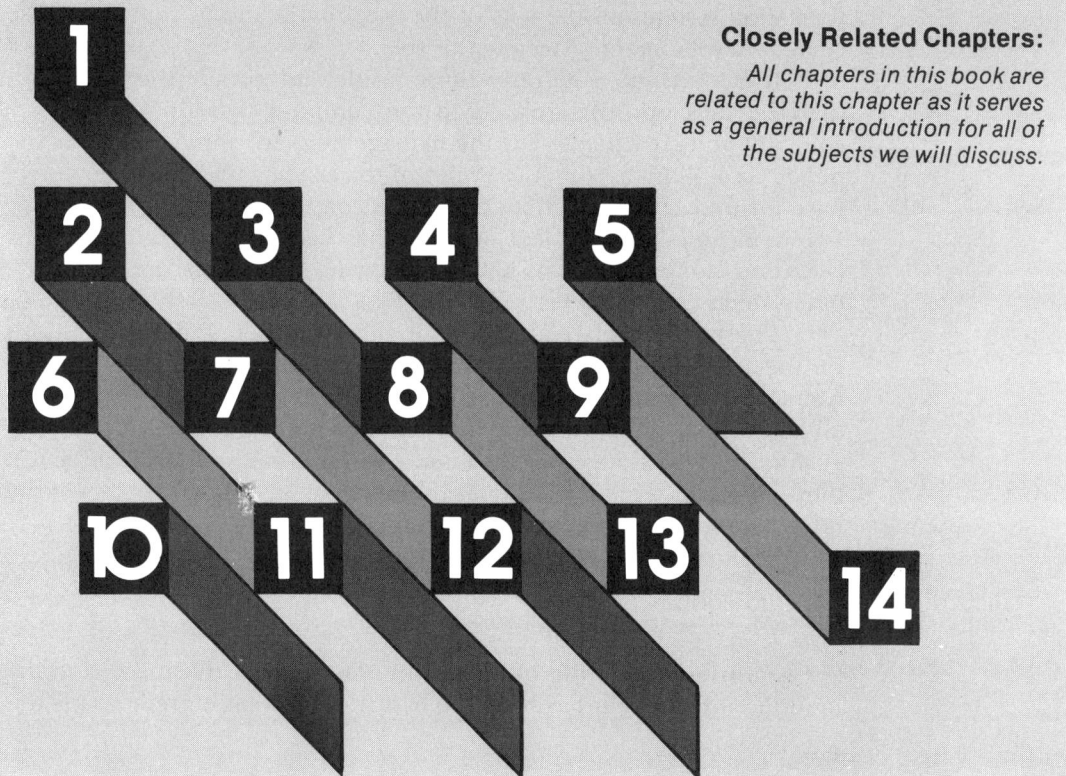

The objective of this book is to develop the reader's knowledge and appreciation of information systems in general and, more particularly, how the accelerating discipline of computer-based information systems has expanded the scope of the accounting profession and the functions of the accountant.

In this first chapter our purpose is to examine the impact of information systems on the role of the accountant and to summarize the current developments affecting this role.

It has become evident to those inside and outside the profession that the developments related to the computer have placed the accountant at a crossroads. For the management accountant, and for the public accountant as well, the events of the last few years may eventually have an impact greater than all of the cumulative events of the past. Foremost among these developments has been the emergence of the electronic computer and its natural offspring, computer-based information systems.

These computer-related developments raise a number of questions for the accounting profession. Should it broaden its activities to take advantage of information systems or should it rest comfortably in its traditional role? Logic argues for a broadened role. Because of his background, his knowledge, his training, and his broad systems experience, the accountant is in an excellent position to stand in the forefront of the information systems explosion that is now upon us.

INFORMATION AND ACCOUNTING

For centuries accounting has been the "language of business" and accounting information has been the basic information ingredient for the efficient management of the business organization. It would be difficult to explain how the modern organization could plan, coordinate, and control its multitude of activities without this information system.

Of all the functional specializations or professions, accounting may be affected the most by the emerging discipline of information systems. Certainly information is at the very core of the accounting profession. This conclusion was reached by the American Accounting Association's Committee to Prepare a Statement of Basic Accounting Theory:

> *Essentially, accounting is an information system. More precisely, it is an application of general theory of information to the problem of efficient economic operations. It also makes up a large part of the general information expressed in quantitative terms. In this context accounting is both a part of the general information system of an operating entity and a part of the basic field bounded by the concept of information.*
>
> Committee to Prepare a Statement of Basic Accounting Theory, "Statement of Basic Accounting Theory," American Accounting Association, 1966, p. 64.

Users of Accounting Information

The accounting system is the major quantitative information system in most companies and it is probably the most widespread in use today.

Table 1-1. Selected External Uses of Accounting Information

USER	INFORMATION NEEDS	ACCOUNTING SOURCE
Government (I.R.S. Social Security, Regulatory Agencies)	Profits & taxes, Wages earned, Taxes withheld, Operations	Government reporting requirements
Financial Community (Credit agencies, trade associations, underwriters, etc.)	Financial operations and creditworthiness	Special accounting reports
Customers	Billing data, Status of accounts	Sales orders, Accounts receivable
Suppliers	Credit reliability, Purchase requirements, Payment	Accounting reports, Purchase orders, Accounts payable
Employees	Financial and non-financial information, Wages and salaries	Accounting reports, Payroll

The users of this system can be conveniently classified as *internal* and *external*.

The needs of the *internal* users are normally met by the *managerial accounting system*, the one with which we are primarily concerned in this book. Internal users comprise the managers of the organization whose job it is to maximize the economic well-being of the organization. The managerial accounting system has two basic purposes: (1) to provide internal reports to managers for use in decision-making regarding plans, policies, and future operations, and (2) to provide internal reports to managers regarding the planning and control of current operations.

External users of accounting information are normally provided their requirements by the *financial accounting system*. These users are many and their information needs are varied. An indication of these users and their information requirements is shown in Table 1-1.

ACCOUNTING AND THE COMPUTER: THE CHALLENGE

The old adage that "necessity is the mother of invention" was never more true than in accounting. The discipline has always matched or led the increasing complexity of business. Few practitioners of business today can claim as rich a heritage as accountants.

The history of accounting can be traced back to about 5,000 B.C., when the temple priests of the Sumerian civilization developed the earliest form of writing. It is speculated that the managerial needs of this early civilization prompted the evolution of writing, an event which led to the first information revolution. At any rate, the earliest written documents in the world are the accounts of inventories of that period.

The growing need for accounting and managerial controls arising from increased commercial activity during the Renaissance and the Reformation gave rise to a second, and immensely important, event. In the year 1494 Luca Pacioli, a Venetian professor of mathematics, published *Summa de Arithmetica, geometrica, proportioni, et proportionalita*. This truly great classic in business literature was a treatise on double-entry bookkeeping and was of momentous impact. It provided businessmen with their credit and debit positions in general and in relation to specific persons or accounts. It was the first information system for management and provided: (1) a model of the firm, (2) quantitative methods for analysis, and (3) a fine management tool for decision-making.

Pacioli's information system of double-entry bookkeeping remained largely unchanged until the twentieth century. No subsequent improvement in accounting has approached the significance of his contribution. It is true that there have been refinements and improvements in financial reporting, cost accounting, and control systems, but none even matches Pacioli's double-entry bookkeeping *until the potential offered by the advent of the computer.* Indeed, the most significant external pressure in history to the accountant has come from the computer and computer-based information systems.

The Accountant's Stereotype

Although Karl Marx certainly overstated his case when he described accountants as "jackals of capitalism," it is probably true that the stereotype of modern accounting is something less than flattering, and something less than factual.

The popular view of the Certified Public Accountant is often one of a cold, aloof, impersonal individual wearing the traditional "green eyeshade." Among college students accounting is not normally thought of as an exciting subject and the profession itself is seen by the general public as a staid club that is a model for button-down, grey flannel decorum.

Accounting education, and the requirements of the profession frequently reinforce these notions. Reference to accounting texts will yield a list of accounting functions such as recording, processing, summarizing, reporting, and interpreting transactions. Inherent in each of these functions is the historical or "dead" transaction. To ascribe to the accountant *only* these historical transactions is to make him the unfriendly business undertaker. In public accounting many practitioners continue to emphasize that auditing consists almost solely of expressing an opinion on financial statements. This view is contrary to the acceleration of tax and management services, which are becoming an increasingly large part of public accounting revenues.[1]

Another problem is the so-called "one-for-one" changeover syndrome in systems design or conversion. Many accountants consider the computer as nothing more than a mechanical device to process the transactions that were formerly processed manually. The result is that the true capability of the computer to produce higher-order information is not being utilized. Clerical systems remain clerical systems instead of being upgraded during conversion from manual to computer based.

In precomputer days the data needed to generate the information required for accounting's purpose were generally considered to be those data relating to the assets and liabilities of the firm and to transactions af-

---

[1]From the excellent article by L. A. Robinson and M. J. Alexander, "Are Accountants Adjusting to Change?" *Management Accounting*, November, 1971.

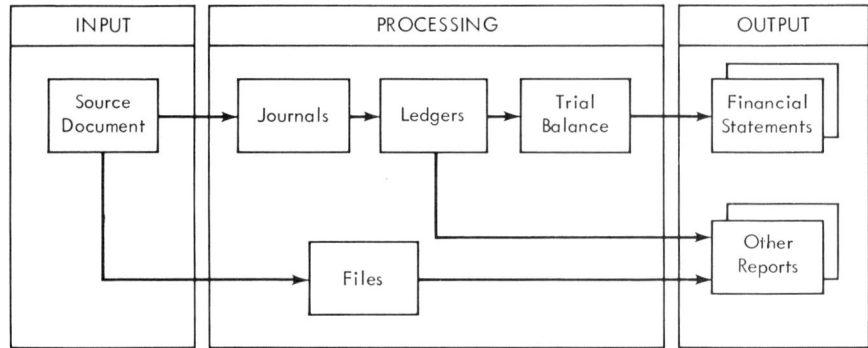

Fig. 1-1. The Accounting Data Processing Cycle

fecting those assets and liabilities. The accountant collected the data needed by the accounting system through the Day Book, gave it order by processing it through the Journal, and meaning and relationship by transferring these entries to the Ledger, according to the shifting principles and prejudices of the profession. The resulting information was communicated through the Balance Sheet, Profit and Loss Statement, and the supporting schedules. The entire process was historical and of little use in decision analysis.

The computer provides an added dimension for collecting, storing, and processing these data for higher-level purposes; i.e., decision-making, planning, and controlling operations. In general, however, this new dimension of the computer and its capability have not been fully utilized. Many accountants continue to conceptualize the data-processing cycle as shown in Fig. 1-1. This cycle is little more than mechanization of the manual system, and it overlooks: (1) the accounting system's interface with other systems (e.g., marketing, production) (2) the potential for upgrading the accounting system for higher-level purposes (e.g., order processing to sales analysis, general ledger to financial planning).

This suboptimization of computers has not gone unnoticed. A number of surveys have concluded that despite the spectacular advances in the capability of computer hardware, similar advances in systems design and utilization have been small by comparison.

Several years ago the National Association of Accountants (NAA) conducted a survey of hundreds of firms to determine the state of the art in management information systems. Their conclusion: "For the most part, what companies 'have done' shade into 'what we are now doing' which leads to 'what we plan to do' next year." The result of this approach has been called "islands of mechanization" or "the Band-Aid® approach."

The Answer: Education

Prior to the advent of the computer, management information systems education was largely accounting education because the formal business information system was the accounting system. Following the widespread adoption of the computer, education in information systems design and related topics has expanded enormously. Until recently, the accounting profession has not kept pace. Instead, the information system function has been taken over by line managers and information systems specialists.

As we enter the 1980s, the picture is changing considerably. The accounting profession has become vitally concerned with education for computer-based information systems, particularly as this discipline affects the accounting function.

The major professional associations[1] relating to accounting have all undertaken comprehensive efforts in this regard. All of them sponsor conferences relating to computers and information systems, provide continuing education programs, and organize special committees relating to the topic. In colleges and universities, it is almost a universal requirement for accounting education that the student's curriculum contain exposure to computers, information systems, and related topics.

DEVELOPMENTS AFFECTING INFORMATION SYSTEMS AND THE ACCOUNTING PROFESSION

It is an overworked phrase but nevertheless true that we are living in an era of unprecedented change. Many of these changes have or will have a significant impact upon the way that organizations are managed and the design of information systems to manage them. All of this will have an impact upon the accounting profession. Summarized in Table 1-2 are the more significant of these changes, all of which are now underway in various stages.

What are the implications of these changes? We have attempted in Table 1-2 to summarize the significance of these developments as they relate to the accounting profession. The readers can speculate for themselves what additional implications will be forthcoming in the future.

---

[1] Some of these are American Institute of Certified Public Accountants (AICPA), American Accounting Association (AAA), National Accounting Association (NAA), Financial Executives Institute, and so on.

Table 1-2. Developments Affecting Information Systems and the Accounting Profession

CATEGORY	DEVELOPMENT	SIGNIFICANCE FOR INFORMATION SYSTEMS

Sociopolitical	Increasing emphasis on social responsibility
	  Urban development
	  Health care
	  Education
	  Ecology
	  Information privacy
	  Increased negligence judgements related to computers
		1. Much of data measured in non-monetary terms.
		2. Detailed rather than summary data will be required.
		3. Increased use of planning and control models.
		4. Increased security meaures for information systems.

Economic	Increasing economic concentration Increasing firm size Increasing diversification Multinational trend Continuing inflation Skilled manpower shortage	1. Increased emphasis on external data for planning purposes. 2. New internal and external reporting requirements. 3. Reporting must be defined in terms appropriate for foreign firms. 4. Increased emphasis on forecasting models for sales, manpower, finance, technology, etc. 5. Change in management reporting under conditions of inflation. 6. Better reporting systems for human resources
Technical	Time sharing and telecommunications Improvements in software	1. Expansion of real time systems. 2. Greater interaction between user and the information system. 3. Increased use of programmed software packages.
Organizational Structure Change	Drift away from the classical functional organization structure designed as a result of inflexible information systems	1. Design of flexible information systems to accommodate organizational dynamics. 2. Demand for more better, faster information. 3. Increasing number of "programmed" decisions made by the information system. 4. Computerization of the programmed (bookkeeping) portion of the job of the accountant.
Increasing Organizational Complexity	Technology acceleration Product change Information explosion	Improved information systems to help manage complexity
Advances in Management Practice	Theory of information feedback systems Decision-making Management science	1. Focus on feedforward/predictive control system rather than historical. 2. Increased emphasis on programming decisions by decision rule. 3. Use of management science to manage complex operations and to design information systems that incorporate decision rules.
Changing "Mix" of the Economy	Growth of service sector, service institutions, and service departments within industry	Design of new and different types of information systems for planning and controlling the service type operation

WHAT IS AN INFORMATION SYSTEM?

Information systems are not new; only computerization of them is new. Before computers, information system techniques existed to supply information for accounting and other functional purposes. Today we have trouble with the concept.

Several years ago eighteen management science professionals, systems designers, academicians, computer technicians, consultants, and business executives held a symposium for the sole purpose of arriving at a definition of Management Information System (MIS).[2] The fact that they were unable to do so indicates the difficulty of accurately defining the terms "information system," "accounting information system," or "financial information system." Perhaps these are concepts rather than definitions. As one corporate controller said: "I can't define an information system but I know one when I see it."

The concept and purpose of the accounting and financial information systems can be better understood if we define Management Information System (MIS), the larger system of which accounting is a part.

Management Information System (MIS)

The scope and purpose of MIS is better understood if each part of the term is defined. See Fig. 1-2.

Management

Management has been defined in a variety of ways, but for our purposes it comprises the processes or activities that describe what managers do in the operation of their organization: plan, organize, initiate, and control operations. They *plan* by setting strategies and goals and selecting the best course of action to achieve the plan. They *organize* the tasks necessary for the operational plan, set these tasks up into homogeneous groups, and assign authority delegation. They *control* the performance of the work by setting performance standards and avoiding deviations from standard.

Because *decision-making* is such a fundamental prerequisite to each of the foregoing processes, the job of an MIS becomes that of facilitating decisions necessary for planning, organizing, and controlling the work and the functions of the business.

[2]*What Is a Management Information System?* Chicago: The Society for Management Information Systems, 1971.

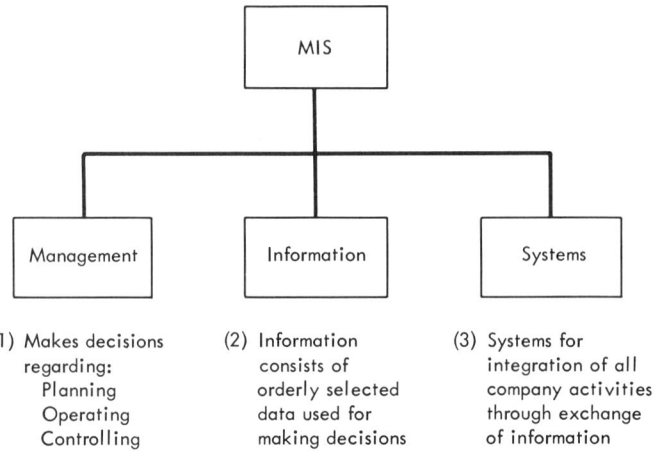

Fig. 1-2. The Basic Meaning of an MIS.

Information

Data must be distinguished from *information,* and this distinction is clear and important for our purposes. Data are facts and figures that are not currently being used in a decision process, and they usually take the form of historical records that are recorded and filed without immediate intent to retrieve for decision-making. An example would be any one of the supporting documents, ledgers, and so on, that comprise the source material for profit and loss statements. Such material would only be of historical interest to an external auditor.

Information consists of data that have been retrieved, processed, or otherwise used for informative or inference purposes, argument, or as a basis for forecasting or decision-making. An example here would also be any one of the supporting documents mentioned above, but in this case the data could be used by an internal auditor, the management services department of an external auditor, or by internal management for profit planning and control or for other decision-making purposes.

Systems

A *system* can be described simply as a set of elements joined together for a common objective. A subsystem is part of a larger system with which we are concerned. *All* systems are parts of larger systems. For our purposes the organization is the system and the parts (divisions, departments, functions, units, etc.) are the subsystems.

Whereas we have achieved a very high degree of automation and joining together of subsystems in scientific, mechanical, and factory manufacturing operations, we have barely scratched the surface of applying systems principles for organizational or business systems. The concept of synergism has not generally been applied to business organizations, particularly as it applies to the integration of the subsystems through information interchange. Marketing, operations, and finance are frequently on diverse paths and working at cross-purposes. The systems concept of MIS is therefore one of optimizing the output of the organization by *connecting the operating subsystems through the medium of information exchange.*

Summary:

The objective of an MIS is to provide information for decision-making on planning, organizing, and controlling the operations of the subsystems of the firm and to provide a synergistic organization in the process.

Accounting Information System

The accounting information system is a subset of the MIS and possesses all the characteristics of the MIS. The role of accounting in the total information system is discussed by the American Accounting Association:

> *The accounting function is one of the most important information systems in an organization. Clearly, it is not the whole or even the formal information system given (a) the diversity of data collected, processed, and distributed for the many different functions within the organization and (b) the expanded range of disciplines bearing on the information function. It is, however, difficult to conceive of accounting not being an integral part of the formal information system or accounting personnel not being a major force in information management.*
>
> *Accounting Review, op. cit.,* p. 191.

Until the advent of the computer, accounting was *the* information system of the organization. Today it still remains the most pervasive and is almost always the largest of the information subsystems in the firm. Of all the functional specializations or professions, accounting may be affected the most by the emerging discipline of information systems. Certainly information is at the very core of the accounting profession and accounting is an application of general theory of information to the problem of efficient economic operations.

Accounting: Information or Data?

What we are now witnessing in the accounting profession is a trend away from data and into information. Traditionally, accounting measurement has been made in terms of money—dollars and cents. When a significant event occurs (e.g., sales, inventory receipts, administrative expenses, etc.) it has only been recorded in the accounting records if it could be expressed in monetary terms. However, many significant events and a large number of managerial problems are not expressed, nor are they measurable in terms of dollars. Moreover, some events cannot be quantified. To illustrate the "nondollar" type of problem, consider some of those surrounding labor productivity, number of lost sales, or optimum assignment of maintenance crews. For the "nonquantifiable" event we have only to turn to those connected with labor turnover, morale, and public relations.

What does this distinction between data and information now mean to the accountant? It means two things: First, accountants should broaden the scope of their thinking. In addition to the traditional function of recording historical data, they should convert this data into information so that it can be utilized to improve decision-making and the management process. Second, accountants should extend the dimension of accounting by utilizing additional units of measurement. To illustrate how this may be done, we can take the example of the sales report which has historically been measured in units of product sold and prices of the sales. It doesn't take much imagination to see how the data on this report can be modified or converted to an item analysis by customer, territory, and salesman. Such conversion to "nondollar" units can provide a useful managerial or decision-making tool.

Accounting Information System: Concept and Definition

In general, accounting systems are concerned with two kinds of management information: (1) *financial* information, and (2) information generated from the processing of *transaction* data. Neither of these types is exclusive and both overlap in the use to which they are put. The accounting information system can be defined as the set of activities of the organization responsible for the preparation of financial information and the information obtained from transaction data for the purposes of: (1) internal reporting to managers for use in planning and controlling current and future operations, and (2) external reporting to stockholders, government, and other outside parties.

THE JOB OF THE ACCOUNTANT AND INFORMATION SYSTEMS

The scope of the accounting profession and the various types of duties that an accountant may perform is quite broad and continues to expand with the increasing complexity of organizations. The several professional or occupational routes that an accountant might take would include:

>Public Accounting
>>Auditing
>>Tax
>>Management Services
>
>Corporate Accounting
>>Management Accounting
>>Internal Control
>
>Government
>>Auditor and Management Accounting

The above list is not exhaustive; we show it to establish a framework for the approach to information systems taken in this book.

In this introductory chapter we will briefly examine the implication of these accounting functions for the design and use of information systems.

Managerial Accounting

The art of management has been defined as making irrevocable decisions based on incomplete, inaccurate, and obsolete information. This tongue-in-cheek definition is not very useful but it does point up the role of information in decision-making and the challenge of management accounting to provide such information.

The emphasis in accounting has historically been more on data collection, structuring, and processing than on analysis. This emphasis must change. Management is concerned with understanding alternative courses of action for decisions and for better planning and control of operations. This need represents both a challenge and an opportunity for accountants.

We will argue throughout this book that the role of the accountant has been broadened and includes not only a function of gathering information but also the considerably higher-level responsibility of participation with management in making of business decisions. This implies that managerial accounting should: (1) upgrade existing clerical systems, and (2) participate in the design of higher-level integrated information systems for decision-making. It is time for the accountant to advance from the firmly established clerical base of collecting data to one of making decisions on how the operations of the organization can be improved.

This view of the accountant's role is not a new one. However, the profession has not always been quick to take advantage of it. In the early fifties the accountants felt that they had the key to dominance in business decisions. Cost accounting was maturing and the discipline of financial planning (budgeting) buttressed by the return-on-investment (ROI) concept was emerging. This latter concept, pioneered by the DuPont Corporation, was based on the premise that the best way to plan and control the subsystems of the organization was through an analysis of variations in those elements or "profit centers" contributing to return-on-investment. The concept is summarized in the traditional chart as shown in Fig. 1-3. Presumably, the desired results could be forecast and controls installed to assure that results conformed to plan. Naturally, the accounting department would be "in charge" of the control system. Indeed, the controller had the only rational and continuing information system in the firm; the only game in town, so to speak.

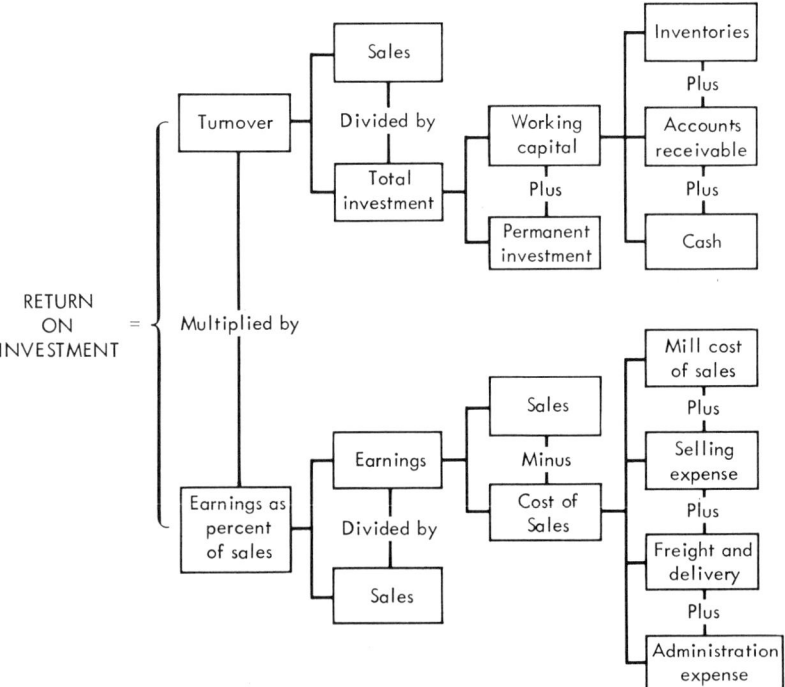

Fig. 1-3. The Traditional Return On Investment Concept

The above scenario was changed with the emergence of the computer. Technology provided an unlimited source of data storage that could be upgraded into information. Speed and costs were economical. Computers also gave entry into the office of the "science of abstraction-mathematics" in a multitude of applications. This led to the professionalization of a variety of information specialists who understood the world of information and made the transition from a record of transactions to integrated systems much wider in scope. While the systems analysts and line managers were advancing to the statistical analysis of the present and the mathematical computation of the future, many accounting departments were left to the arithmetical accounting of the past.

Accountants today have another opportunity to be in the forefront of information systems. The profession can rise above the common view of the accountant as a collector of historical data. The accountant can become the leader in the information revolution that is upon us.

The Management Accounting System

There are three facets to this information system and these have been identified by Horngren:

1. *Scorecard.* To answer the question: Am I doing well or badly?
   The accumulation of data. This aspect of accounting enables both internal and external parties to evaluate organizational performance and position.
2. *Attention-directing.* To answer the question: What problems should I look into?
   The reporting and interpreting of information that helps managers to focus on operating problems, imperfections, inefficiencies, and opportunities. This aspect of accounting helps managers to concern themselves with important aspects of operations promptly enough for effective action either through perceptive planning or through astute day-to-day supervision. Attention directing is commonly associated with current planning and control and with the analysis and investigation of recurring, routine internal-accounting reports.
3. *Problem-solving.* To answer the question: Of the several ways of doing the job, which is the best?
   This aspect of accounting involves the concise quantification of the relative merits of possible courses of action, often with recommendations as to the best procedure. Problem solving is commonly associated with nonrecurring decisions, situations that require special accounting analyses or reports.[3]

[3]Charles T. Horngren, *Accounting For Management Control* (Englewood Cliffs, N. J.: Prentice-Hall, 1974).

Public Accounting: Auditing

Maintaining the audit trail and performing the auditing function in a manual system are traditional and clearly understood procedures. However, since the advent of the computer, the process has become more complex depending upon the degree of sophistication of the design of the system being audited. To illustrate, let us identify and consider two types of applications: (1) the automation of a clerical system, and (2) an integrated or management information system (MIS).

Clerical Automation

In this type of system (e.g., payroll, inventory status reporting, accounts receivable) the computer is used for the most part as a piece of high-speed tabulating equipment. Despite the fact that this "clerical automation" approach yields minimum benefit in terms of information usage for managerial purposes, it remains the most frequently used type of accounting application. In this kind of system the audit trail parallels the information trail and exists as an appendage relatively separate from the computer system itself.

Figure 1-4 illustrates how the audit trail might exist in this type of system. We can see that the audit trail goes *to* the computer rather than *through* it. The input data are processed sequentially in batches and sequential files are accumulated after each step. In this system the files (tapes, disks, punched cards, etc.), provide a well-documented and easily-followed (sequential) information and audit trail from input to output. Auditing is not too much of a problem.

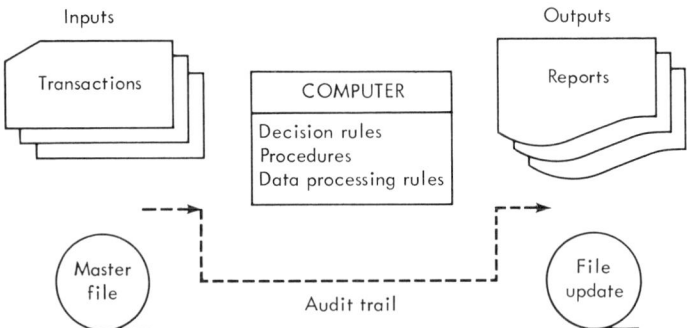

Fig. 1-4. Clerical Automation and the Audit Trail

Source: Joel E. Ross, "The Impact of Information Systems," *Management Accounting,* August 1974, p. 33.

Integrated Information System

As computer-based systems become more sophisticated and as integrated management information systems are designed with common data banks, the auditing function becomes increasingly complex. The audit trail is no longer a separable appendage but must become an integral part of the system. In other words, it is necessary to audit *through* the computer, not *to* the computer.

The expanded audit problem is illustrated in Fig. 1-5. In this case, input data, regardless of how they are introduced, update several files.

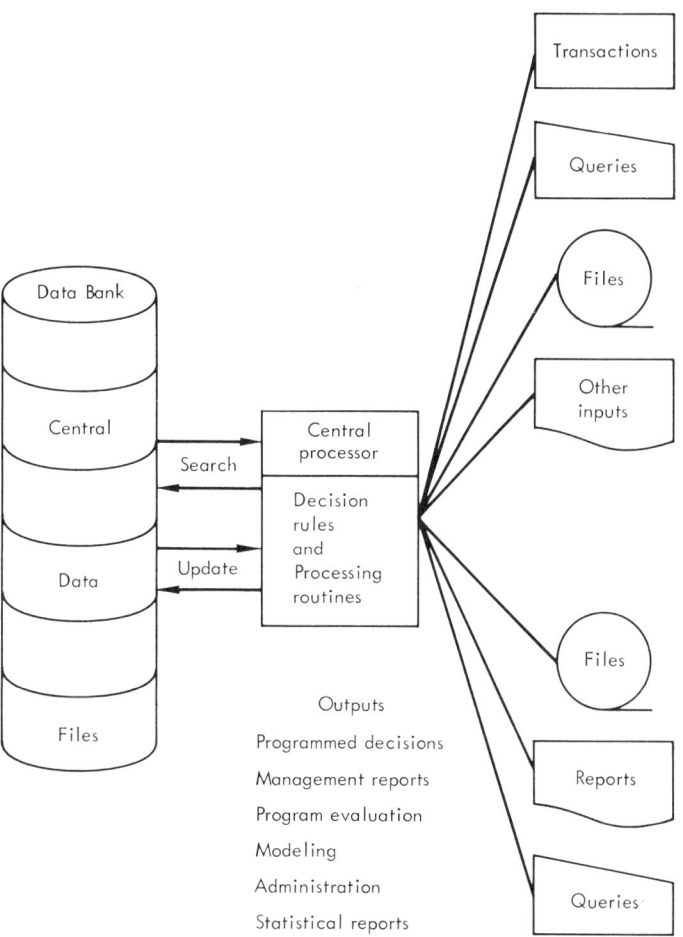

Fig. 1-5. The Integrated Information System and the Audit Trail

Source: Joel E. Ross, "The Impact of Information Systems," *Management Accounting,* August 1974, p. 34.

Moreover, a variety of outputs may be obtained in random fashion from the data bank. These outputs may not be in hard-copy form. The audit trail becomes an interwoven tangle of programmed relationships and while it still exists, it literally goes *through* the computer. Hence, the auditing function becomes considerably more complex and the accountant is required to understand the operation of the computer. Indeed, in more complex systems he may be required to actually be a systems designer himself; at the very least, he should be prepared to address the systems designer concerning systems considerations surrounding audit.

Source Documents in Electronic Form

Prior to the advent of computer systems, the auditor was accustomed to examining paper documents that contained information and transaction authorizations in "man-readable" form. However, the computer cannot accept "man-readable" inputs, which must, therefore, be converted to "computer-readable" form. This presents two new problems: first, the auditor usually cannot "read" the computer input document, and second, and more important, the computer input document is being replaced by source data that are initially recorded in the form of electronic impulses on some form of input device. Transaction authorizations are, thus, accomplished not by signature but by the use of a key to unlock the device, a plastic "credit card," a symbolic recognition code, or a combination of electronic "authorizations."

Management Services

Despite the fact that the billings for management services in some public accounting firms are approaching or exceeding fifty percent of total income, some individual auditors do not realize the potential in this area.

During an audit engagement, an auditor is sometimes asked to give an opinion or to resolve a management problem. The problem could range over the entire spectrum of management: pricing, costing, systems design, planning, or inventory valuation. The stereotyped auditor described previously in this chapter would recommend that his firm's management service department look into the matter. Although there is no particular criticism to this approach, one wonders what problems are left unsolved and what income is foregone because of the auditor's inability to sense the answer to such "systems" problems.

Fortunately the American Institute of Certified Public Accountants encourages its members to undertake such assignments. The policy of AICPA is clearly stated:

> *CPAs have historically been business consultants to their clients. The Council of the American Institute of Certified Public Accountants specifically encourages all CPAs to perform "the entire range of management services consistent with their professional competence, ethical standards and responsibility."*
>
> Statements on Management Advisory Services, New York: American Institute of Certified Public Accountants, Inc., 1974, p. 1.

The implications for information systems design are also rather clear, judging from the selected list of solutions to management consulting problems:

A management information system,
A sales reporting system,
A cost accounting system,
A work measurement program,
Improved production control,
An organization plan with statement of duties and responsibilities,
An electronic data processing system.[4]

The conclusion emerges that the management services function of the public accountant very clearly includes a familiarity with information systems.

Government Accountant

Since government expenditures now exceed one third of the nation's gross national product, it is logical to conclude that a substantial number of accountants will be employed in government related work. Although the "job description" of the government accountant is somewhat different from that of the public or corporate accountant, the basic principles of information systems still apply.

The number-one government accountant in the United States is the Comptroller General of the United States. He is also the Chief Executive of the General Accounting Office. A recent incumbent of that position, Elmer B. Staats, summarized his concept of the responsibility of the independent, external, auditor:

---

[4]*Statements on Management Advisory Services*, New York: American Institute of Certified Public Accountants, Inc., 1974, p. 11.

> 1. *Fiscal accountability*—*including fiscal integrity, disclosure, and compliance with applicable laws and regulations.*
> 2. *Managerial accountability*—*concerned with the efficient and economical use of personnel and other resources.*
> 3. *Program accountability*—*designed to assess whether programs are achieving their intended objectives and whether the best program options have been selected to achieve these objectives from the standpoint of total cost and outputs.*
>
> Elmer B. Staats, "The Role of the Accountant in the 70's," *Management Accounting*, April 1972, p. 13.

Internal Control

The increased complexity of the internal control function is due largely to the same considerations that surrounded the discussion of auditing. In other words, the control of documents and data, transactions, processes, and associated actions takes on a new dimension because control must now be maintained around and through the computer.

To aid in effecting the classical internal control procedures, the accountant has utilized these features: (1) separation of accountability from physical custodianship, (2) division of work, (3) assignment of direct responsibility, (4) rotation of duties, (5) internal audit and review, and (6) miscellaneous measures such as control totals, transmittal documents, and reconciliation points.

In the past these procedures were designed by the accountant and were generally sufficient for internal control. However, under the centralized type of computer organization where processing is accomplished centrally with data banks, the traditional control features have lost their effectiveness. It follows that if the accountant is to continue to discharge his traditional control and custodial functions, he will have to refocus his attention along the new channels of computer-based information. Indeed, internal control solutions must be reshaped around the data-processing center where information converges. This naturally implies a complete familiarity with management information systems and the subset of accounting information systems.

ACCOUNTING AND INFORMATION SYSTEMS: QUO VADIS?

What will be the role of the accountant in the future?

No one can provide an unequivocal answer to that question but we do know that the accounting profession stands at a crossroads. The accountant has two alternative directions to take. First, he can continue in his traditional role as auditor or as the organization's keeper of records and recorder of costs. Some predict that this route will lead to the elimination of the "accounting department" and the substitution of the "information department" staffed with a variety of information systems specialists such as "systems analyst," "operations researcher," "MIS manager," and the like. Another alternative for the accountant would be to enlarge the dominion of his decision-assisting function. He has honorably assisted the decisional process in the past. Can he not now embrace an increasing portion of the whole information structure?

Whatever the answer to these questions, the accountant of the future is going to have to be a systems analyst. He must become involved in accounting information systems design and the related information structure upon which management of the organization depends.

THE PLAN OF THIS BOOK: INTEGRATION OF THE ACCOUNTING INFORMATION SYSTEM

We have previously defined a system as a set of elements or components joined together for a common objective. This joining together of topics (components) is desirable if the subject matter of Accounting Information Systems is to be integrated. Although a serial or sequential approach in a system is difficult, we nevertheless attempt to introduce subject matter in a logical order and show how each topic relates to others. The overall relationship of subject matter is shown conceptually in Fig. 1-6. The five major parts of the book are summarized:

Part I *The Management View*
The management view describes how the computer and information systems are changing the role of the accountant and how information is the central element in the process of management.

Part II *Accounting Information Systems for Operations*
This part is a description of basic accounting information systems and reports that support the operating systems of the organization. It also treats the greatly expanded concept of internal control as it relates to computer-based systems.

Part III *Accounting Information Systems for Decision-Making*
Because the outputs and reports of most accounting information systems are ultimately used for making a decision, the process of decision-making is described as a prelude to an examination of how accounting information systems are used in major organizational and operational decisions.

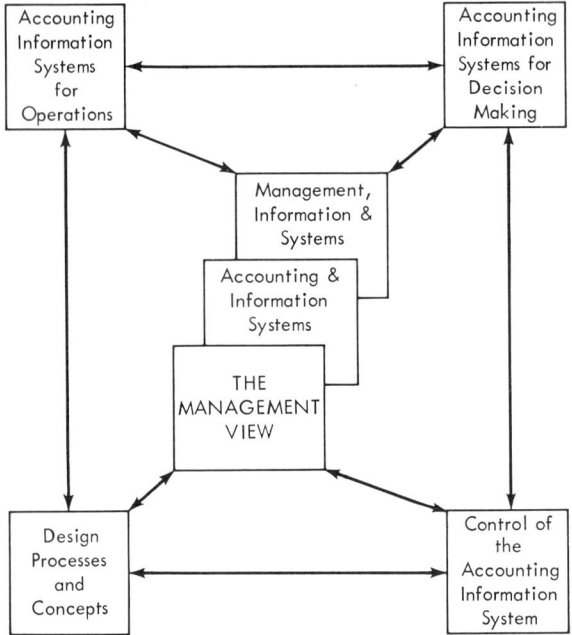

Fig. 1-6. Integration of Accounting Information Systems

Part IV *Design Process and Concepts*
The accountant is both a designer and a user of information systems. For this reason it is necessary to examine the topics related to the design process. These include the development process itself, as well as related tools and techniques. Forms design is similar to output design and is discussed as a related topic. Computer hardware and software, as well as the important subject of data bases, are treated from the user's and accountant's point of view.

Part V *Control of the Accounting Information System*
Accounting information systems, once designed and made operational, are dynamic and require continuing control. This maintenance and control are primary tasks of the accountant. Finally, the essential topic of auditing is discussed as that process is performed during the traditional audit function.

DISCUSSION QUESTIONS AND PROBLEMS

1. Discuss at least five environmental (external) developments affecting the AIS.

2. "The accountant plays no significant role in management's decision-making." Why has this statement been true in the past?
3. Discuss the accountant's function in relation to the following:
   a. EDP
   b. Data Collection
   c. Reporting
   d. Interpreting information
4. Discuss the AIS as an integral part of the MIS. What similarities exist? What differences?
5. What are the three components of the accounting data-processing cycle?
6. The organizational components in a manufacturing company usually include sales, production, finance, accounting, and so on. Do we need to integrate these organizational components into a system? If so, how do we do it?
7. Define:
   a. Data
   b. Information
   c. System
   Relate these terms to accounting.
8. List and discuss five major uses of the AIS and the information required by each.
9. South Florida has limited electrical generating capacity, virtually no raw materials, except phosphates, and the only economic transportation method is trucking. Further, there are increasing restrictions by cities and counties regarding the discharge of industrial waste into rivers and ocean out-falls. A South Florida manufacturing company is considering moving its existing plant facilities out of state. What role could the accountant play in determining the new plant location?
10. A small manufacturing firm has been dumping its industrial waste materials in a nearby river for several years. The Environmental Protection Agency has recently filed a suit against this company demanding that the waste be treated prior to disposal. What should the accountant's role be in assisting management in solving this problem?

Bibliography

Certificate in Management Accounting, Institute of Management Accounting, Examinations, 1972–75.

HORNGREN, CHARLES T. *Accounting for Management Control,* Englewood Cliffs, N.J.: Prentice-Hall, 1974.

ROSS, JOEL E. "The Impact of Information Systems," *Management Accounting,* August 1974.

"Statement of Basic Accounting Theory," American Accounting Association, Committee to Prepare a Statement on Basic Accounting Theory, 1966.

Statements on Management Advisory Services, American Institute of Certified Public Accounting, 1974.

Preview:
This chapter develops the systems view of management and explains the role of the manager in relation to the AIS.
–Planning
–Organization
–Control

CHAPTER TWO

management, information, and systems

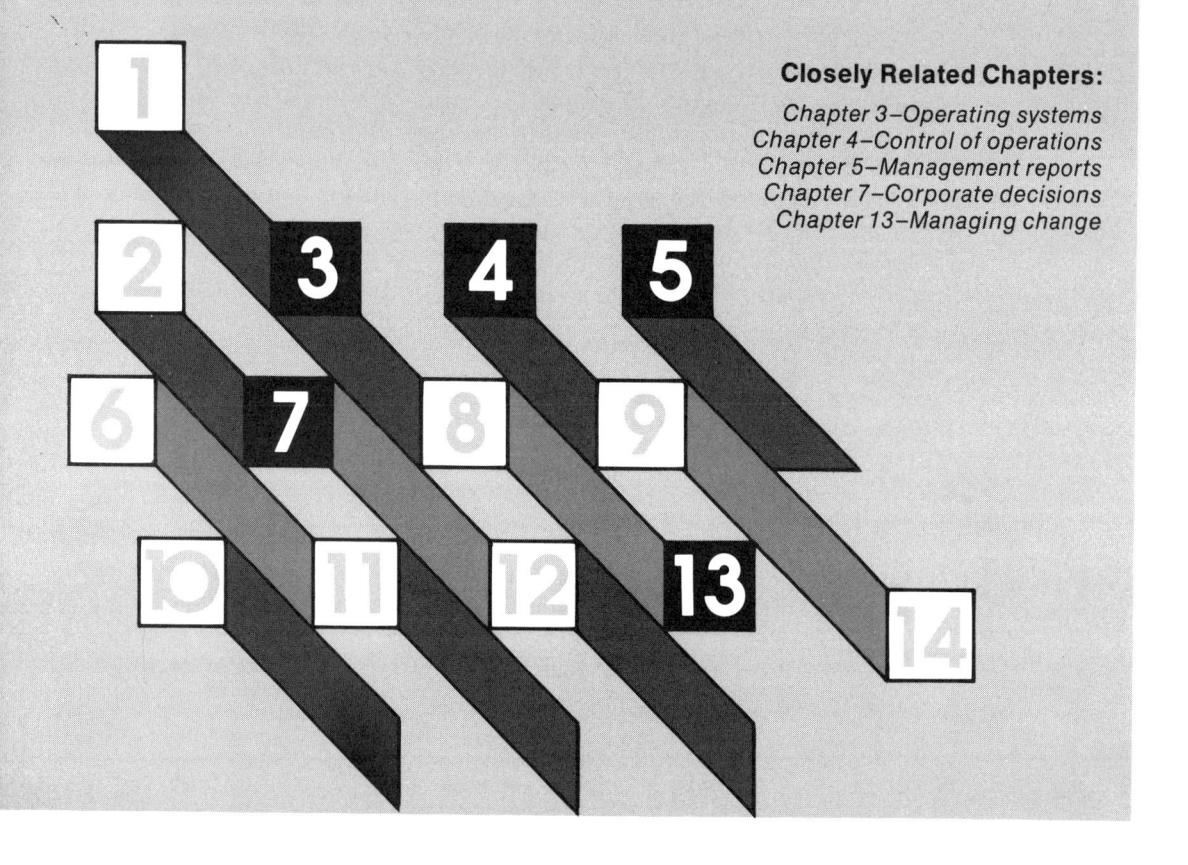

Closely Related Chapters:
Chapter 3–Operating systems
Chapter 4–Control of operations
Chapter 5–Management reports
Chapter 7–Corporate decisions
Chapter 13–Managing change

By itself, an accounting system is an accountant's information system. By its interaction with other functional systems, it becomes the basis for the total MIS.

A managed organization consists of two basic systems:

1. A structured behavioral system of people, and
2. An information processing system for problem-solving and decision-making.

Managed organizations form the basis for our society. Businesses, hospitals, retail institutions, government agencies, and nonprofit organizations (such as Common Cause or the Ford Foundation) are examples of managed organizations. Such organizations require a system of managers to establish basic objectives, obtain and allocate resources, and facilitate the activities of the organization. This is one reason that we present the functions and perspectives of managers to the accountant. Unless the accounting organization develops its information in a form useful to the systemic perspective of management, it will remain nothing more than a group of professional data collectors.

SYSTEMS VIEW OF MANAGING

At the operational level in a business, people carry out technical and functional activities, such as operating machines, cleaning offices, selling, designing products, accounting for transactions, training employees, and so on. In essence, they are implementing plans and procedures.

The work of the manager consists not of technical or functional activities but rather of acting upon company resources by:

Setting objectives
Planning
Organizing human and physical resources
Initiating action to be taken by other people
Controlling the processes of the business system
Communicating and providing communications channels throughout the organization

These activities are called the *processes* of managing. One very general activity required to carry out these processes is *decision-making*. Decision-making is so important that some people believe that it is the only managerial function. They believe that operational people and staff specialists *propose* while managers *dispose*. We feel that decision-making is central to all the specific processes that we have listed above, but is only a part of each process. Like the communications process, decision-making is an integrating activity that keeps the parts of the business functioning as a *system*. That is, when all parts of the system (company) are working cooperatively to obtain the best results for the system as a whole, we say that the parts are integrated.

In Fig. 2-1, you can see the systems view of the managerial process. Each process interacts with every other process. Thus when we plan, we plan objectives, we plan the organization of resources, we plan the means and timing of initiating action on plans, we plan our control methods, and we plan our communication process.

Follow each input in the first column of Fig. 2-1 across to see how it is related to each of the other managerial processes.

THE MANAGEMENT SYSTEM

Many organizations make the basic mistake of believing that a management *information* system can be designed or made operational without the backup of an adequate *management* system. An adequate management system includes organizational arrangements, structure and procedures for adequate planning and control, clear establishment of objectives, and all the other manifestations of good organization and management. Given this management structure and this framework of good management practices, an information system can be designed upon its foundation. Only then can the information system provide the manager with the information he needs in the form, place, and time that he needs it, in order to perform his job according to the specifications of the *management* system.

	SET OBJECTIVES	PLAN	ORGANIZE RESOURCES	INITIATE	CONTROL	COMMUNICATE
SET OBJECTIVES	D	Set objectives for the company	Match objectives to available resources	Develop objectives at the level of management	Develop key objectives for control	Set objectives for communication at each level of the organization
PLAN	Plan around basic objectives	E	Plan the company organization and allocation of resources	Plan the sequence and schedule of the organization of resources	Plan for standards and procedures for control	Plan procedures for communications throughout the organization
ORGANIZE RESOURCES	Organize the hierarchy of objectives	Organize for planning	C	Organize the system for action	Organize a control system	Organize resources to provide for communication
INITIATE	Take action to establish objectives	Initiate the planning process	Start the organization of human and other resources for conduct of the business	I	Start the control of objectives, plans, action, standards, and communication	Keep communications flowing freely at all stages and for all processes
CONTROL	Control the setting of objectives to suit the nature of the organization	Control the setting of plans to ensure plans are properly prepared on time	Control the mix of resources to achieve a balance	Control the process of directing action	D	Control the communication of standards. Control the communication performance for corrective action
COMMUNICATE	Communicate objectives to attain a unified sense of direction	Communicate plans in the proper detail to each person in the company	Communicate through organization charts, manuals, and reports: the distribution of resources	Communicate to initiate action at the proper time	Communicate standards of performance. Communicate performance to responsible individuals for corrective action	E

Fig. 2-1. The Systems View of the Managerial Processes

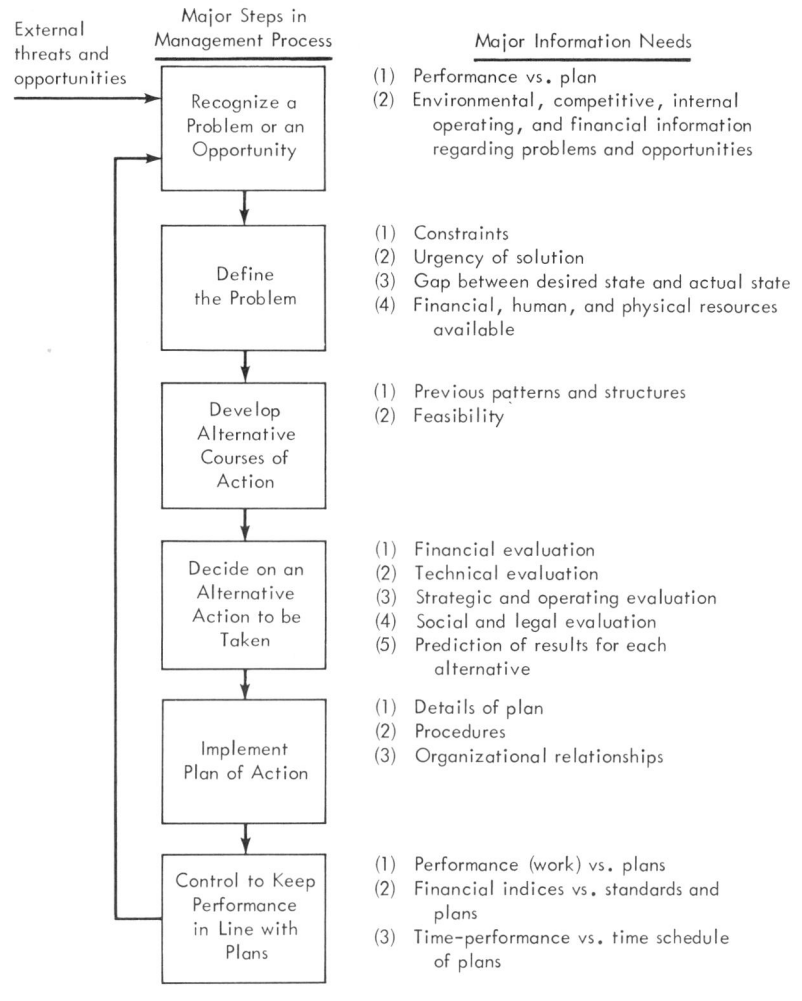

```
External            Major Steps in
threats and         Management Process              Major Information Needs
opportunities
                   ┌──────────────┐         (1) Performance vs. plan
         ────────▶ │  Recognize a │         (2) Environmental, competitive, internal
                   │  Problem or an│             operating, and financial information
                   │  Opportunity │             regarding problems and opportunities
                   └──────┬───────┘
                          │
                          ▼
                   ┌──────────────┐         (1) Constraints
                   │    Define    │         (2) Urgency of solution
                   │  the Problem │         (3) Gap between desired state and actual state
                   │              │         (4) Financial, human, and physical resources
                   └──────┬───────┘             available
                          ▼
                   ┌──────────────┐         (1) Previous patterns and structures
                   │   Develop    │         (2) Feasibility
                   │ Alternative  │
                   │  Courses of  │
                   │    Action    │
                   └──────┬───────┘
                          ▼
                   ┌──────────────┐         (1) Financial evaluation
                   │ Decide on an │         (2) Technical evaluation
                   │  Alternative │         (3) Strategic and operating evaluation
                   │ Action to be │         (4) Social and legal evaluation
                   │    Taken     │         (5) Prediction of results for each
                   └──────┬───────┘             alternative
                          ▼
                   ┌──────────────┐         (1) Details of plan
                   │  Implement   │         (2) Procedures
                   │Plan of Action│         (3) Organizational relationships
                   └──────┬───────┘
                          ▼
                   ┌──────────────┐         (1) Performance (work) vs. plans
                   │Control to Keep│        (2) Financial indices vs. standards and
                   │ Performance  │             plans
                   │ in Line with │         (3) Time-performance vs. time schedule
                   │    Plans     │             of plans
                   └──────────────┘
```

Fig. 2-2. The Management Process and Information Needs

The basic functions of the management system are (a) developing plans for achieving objectives set by managers, (b) organizing for implementation of plans, and (c) controlling performance of people and equipment so that plans are achieved on time and cost schedules. The role of information in performing these three functions is shown in Fig. 2-2. The first step, recognition of a problem or an opportunity, is usually prompted by either information about a threat or opportunity in the environment, information from the control process concerning a deviation from standard or by search and evaluation of those systems (environmental, competitive, internal) affecting the planning process. Definition of the problem, determination and evaluation of alternative courses of action, and selection of a course of action are fundamentally steps in the planning and decision-making process. Finally, once a decision is made or a plan developed, it is necessary to *implement* and *control* the solution. Implementation becomes a matter of organizing the necessary resources and directing them in the performance of the plan. Control involves the measurement of performance and correction of deviations. The process starts over again either by a recognition of the need for planning or by the appearance of a new problem arising from the control process or environment.

CROCKER'S TOM WILCOX: TOUGH MANAGEMENT FOR A STODGY BANK

As new CEO at San Francisco's Crocker National Corporation, the nation's 12th largest bank, Tom Wilcox has been shaking up a banking system that had reached a stage of near-paralysis.

Wilcox's first challenge at Crocker was merely finding out what was going on. The bank's management information system was so primitive that he could not even get answers to basic questions on costs, profitability, and management responsiblities. "I don't think those who designed the information system anticipated the requirement that management intercept the information flow," Wilcox said wryly.

The first key outsider Wilcox brought in was Arthur B. Hall, a specialist in management information systems at Touche Ross and Co., who became a Crocker vice-president in March 1974. "There was expense budgeting, but no profit planning. There was an incredible asset-liability mix problem, but no way to pinpoint it," Hall stated. "And the directors were receiving old-fashioned financial reports that were not particularly germane to this century."

Source: Business Week, Aug. 11, 1975 pp. 38–44.

In the rest of this chapter, we will study four aspects of the major managerial processes of planning, organizing, and controlling. First, we will give a definition and description of the process so that you will understand how the process is performed. Second, we will show how the *systems approach* to each managerial process differs from the traditional approach. Third, because managing requires a special information system for managers, we will describe how planning, organizing, and controlling are made possible by obtaining, processing, transmitting, and presenting selected *information*. Finally, we will describe briefly the role of *accounting/financial information systems* in the three managerial processes.

As a prelude to this discussion, we will introduce the concepts of the systems approach.

SYSTEMS APPROACH

The *systems approach* consists both of the way we look at the total set of activities under consideration and the method for studying, designing, or evaluating such a set. It starts with the concept that a "system" is the best form of design. A system consists of elements that work together so that the goals of every element (or subsystem) are subordinate to the goals of the system as a whole.

The systems approach is organized, creative, analytical, scientific, empirical-based, and pragmatic. These characteristics are briefly described:

1. *Organized.* The systems approach is a means for solving large amorphous problems whose solutions involve the application of large amounts of

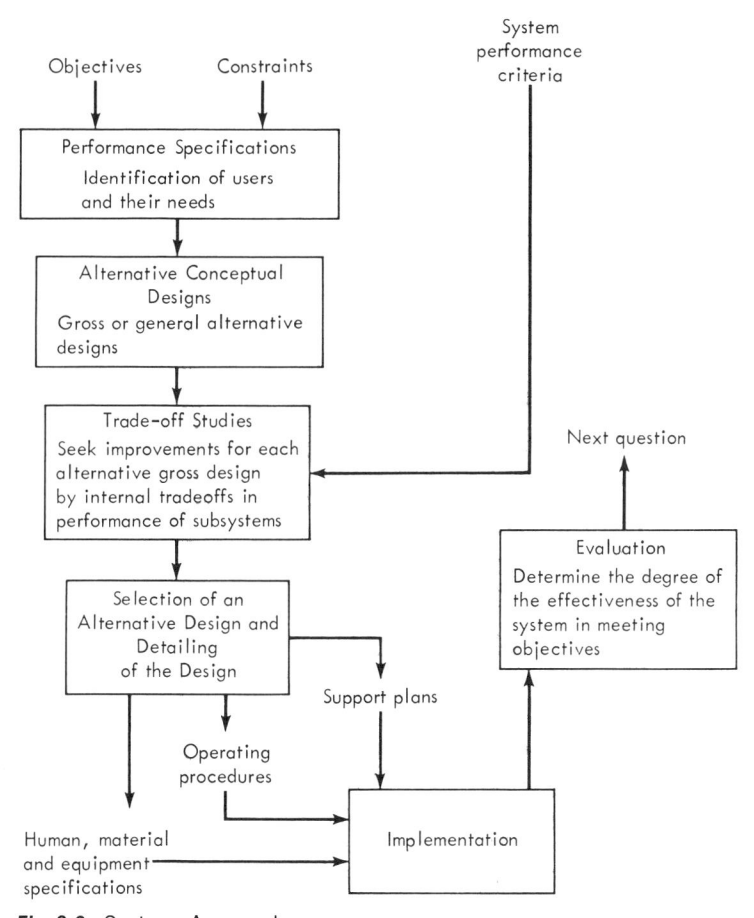

Fig. 2-3. Systems Approach

resources in organized fashion. The approach summarized in Fig. 2-3 consists of:
   a. Identification of users of the system and their needs.
   b. Identification of overall objectives of the *whole*, not just parts of the system.
   c. Specification of constraints upon the system design and performance criteria.
   d. Development of alternative conceptual or "gross" designs.
   e. "Tradeoff" studies to determine if *total system performance* can be improved by sacrificing the performance of some subsystems to the benefit of others.
   f. Detailed design of the most promising conceptual design.
   g. Implementation and evaluation of the final system design.

2. *Creative.* The systems approach must be creative because it focuses on goals first and methods second. The final system is greatly dependent on the originality and creativeness of the designers because:
   a. The problems are so complex and ill-structured that there is no unique formulation of solution.
   b. Much of the available data are so incomplete, uncertain, or ambiguous that imagination of a high order must be used to form a theoretical framework for the problem.
   c. Alternative solutions must be generated for subsystem problems, and, from among many solutions, selections must be made that yield an approximation of an optimal total system.
   d. Traditional functional and disciplinary barriers must be subordinated to the synthesis of the solution.

3. *Analytical.* The systems approach requires analysis of alternative concepts and analysis of tradeoffs among parts of a system. Analysis is also important in evaluation of the final system.

4. *Scientific.* Underlying the systems approach are both the methods and the knowledge of science. Principles from such diverse fields as communications theory, general semantics, mathematics, behavioral science, computer science, logic, economics, and management science may be drawn upon in the design of information systems.

5. *Empirical-based.* The search for empirical data is an essential part of the approach. Relevant data must be distinguished from irrelevant, and true data from false. Pertinent data generally include not only facts on the technical aspects but also facts on the practices, functions, interactions, attitudes, and other characteristics of organization in man-machine systems.

6. *Pragmatic.* For empirical or real systems, a crucial characteristic of the systems approach is that it yields an action-oriented result. The system must be feasible, producible, and operable. Systems activities are directed toward fulfilling a set of actual purposes or of real needs. The systems designers must therefore gain a good understanding of the organization for which the work is being done. Further, the personnel of the organiza-

tion must become involved in the process of diagnosis, development, and design.

In contrast, the inductive approach of the past relied heavily on intuition, trial and error, and using data to maximize performance of subsystems rather than the system as a whole. With this background, we may now cover the managerial functions.

PLANNING

The first and most basic management function is planning. All managers at all levels plan, and the successful performance of the other management functions depends on this activity. Planning is deciding in advance what has to be done, who has to do it, when it has to be done, and how it is to be done. It bridges the gap from where we are to where we want to go. Managers plan for the allocation of resources and the work of other people in contrast to the nonmanager, who plans only his own activities.

The past decade has witnessed a tremendous upsurge in formal planning by all types of organizations, both governmental and industrial. (See Table 2-1 for the results of one such survey.) Various causes have been advanced to explain this phenomenon. Steiner attributes the growth in the planning to six basic factors:

1. A changing philosophy, which insists that an organization can initiate trends and set its own course rather than sail on the tide of market conditions and business changes.
2. The rapid rate of technological change.
3. Increased complexity of management, owing to the growth in size and diversity of business.
4. Growing competition, resulting partly from product obsolescence and growth of new industries.

Table 2-1. Percent of Surveyed Corporations Preparing Annual Corporate Plans, 1965 Versus 1973

REVENUE ($)	NUMBER OF CORPORATIONS	1965	1973
10–50 million	7	14%	71%
50–150 million	7	0	71
150–350 million	6	33	83
350–1 billion	7	29	100
1–20 billion	7	57	100

Source: William E. Lucado, "Corporate Planning—A Current Status Report," *Managerial Planning*, Nov./Dec. 1974, p. 27.

5. The increasingly complex environment of business.
6. The lengthening span of time for which commitments must be made and the resultant need to forecast for longer periods of time in making today's decisions.[2]

DIMENSIONS OF PLANS

Plans occur throughout the company. They must be consistent, related to one another, and directed toward the objectives of the company as a whole (systems approach). Table 2-2 shows the classification of plans by key characteristic.

Table 2-2 shows how plans are integrated by characteristics. If we read across for time, we recognize that long-range plans shape or constrain intermediate plans and that intermediate plans shape short-range plans. A similar nesting or hierarchical arrangement exists for each of the other characteristics.

If we read down a column, we find that characteristics for a single column provide an integrated description of a particular type of plan. The type of planning illustrated in the first column is so important from an integrating systems view that we shall next focus on this type.

Table 2-2. Characteristics of Plans

CHARACTERISTIC	ILLUSTRATION		
Time	Long range (5–25 years)	Medium range (2–4 years)	Short range (1 week—1 year)
Level	Corporate	Divisional	Operational
Function	General management	Research and development	Advertising
Purpose	Strategy	Project or program	Task
Scope	Companywide	Division or product line	Quality control department

The Strategic Planning Process

The strategic planning process consists of two steps: (1) developing the *strategy* and (2) formulating the steps, timing, and costs required to

---

[2]George Steiner, *Top Management Planning,* Toronto: Collier-Macmillan Canada, Ltd., 1969, pp. 14–16.

achieve the strategy. The expression of these steps, timing, and costs is called the strategic plan (or often, the long-range plan).

Strategy is the desired configuration of the firm *at a future specified date*. This configuration, identity, or posture of the firm may be described in terms of:

1. Scope—products, customers, markets, price/quality relationships of products, and product characteristics.
2. Competitive edge—special market position or supply position, unique product advantages, special financial strength or credit lines, unique management or technical talents, or capacity for rapid response to competitive moves.
3. Specifications of targets—quantitative statements of acceptable and desired goals such as size of the company, market share, profitability, return on investment, assets, and trade-off between risk and reward.
4. Assignment of resources—allocation of long-term capital, investment and disinvestment, emphasis on particular activities such as marketing, engineering, production, management development, geographic regions, market segments, and so on.[3]

The strategic planning process consists of the following steps as shown schematically in Fig. 2-4.

1. *Analyze the environment.*[4] Identify those existing and future conditions in the environment that have an influence on the company. The objective in performing this step is to identify *new opportunities* for existing and new products and services to identify major future *risks* to market position and profit margins. Of primary interest would be economic, competitive, technological, governmental, and market conditions.
2. *Identify company strengths, weaknesses.* After an analysis of the conditions in Step 1 and an orderly review of products, markets, processes, personnel, and facilities, certain strengths and weaknesses will emerge. Such resource analysis will not only serve to highlight possible competitive advantages available to the company but will also tend to focus on opportunities and risks.
3. *Consider personal values of top management.* The aesthetic, social, religious, and personal values of top management and influential stockholders exert a significant influence on strategy. Additionally, the emerging constraints of social responsibility and consumerism are factors to consider. Personal values represent both guides and constraints upon the direction of the business.

---

[3]Robert L. Katz, *Management of the Total Enterprise,* Englewood Cliffs, N.J.: Prentice-Hall, 1970. See also J. Thomas Cannon, *Business Strategy and Policy,* New York: Harcourt, Brace & World, 1968.

[4]For a comprehensive treatment of this step in the strategic planning process, see Francis J. Aguilar, *Scanning the Business Environment,* New York: The Macmillan Co., 1967.

```
┌─────────────────┐   ┌─────────────────┐   ┌─────────────────┐
│   ANALYZE       │   │IDENTIFY STRENGTHS│   │ TOP MANAGEMENT  │
│ THE ENVIRONMENT │   │ AND WEAKNESSES  │   │ PERSONAL VALUES │
│                 │   │                 │   │                 │
│ Economic        │──▶│ Products        │──▶│ Economic        │
│ Technological   │   │ Markets         │   │ Ethical         │
│ Competitive     │   │ Processes       │   │ Social          │
│ Market          │   │ Management      │   │ Political       │
│ Governmental    │   │ Facilities      │   │ Management      │
│ Social          │   │   Production    │   │   Philosophy    │
│                 │   │   Finance       │   │                 │
│                 │   │   R&D           │   │                 │
└─────────────────┘   └─────────────────┘   └─────────────────┘
```

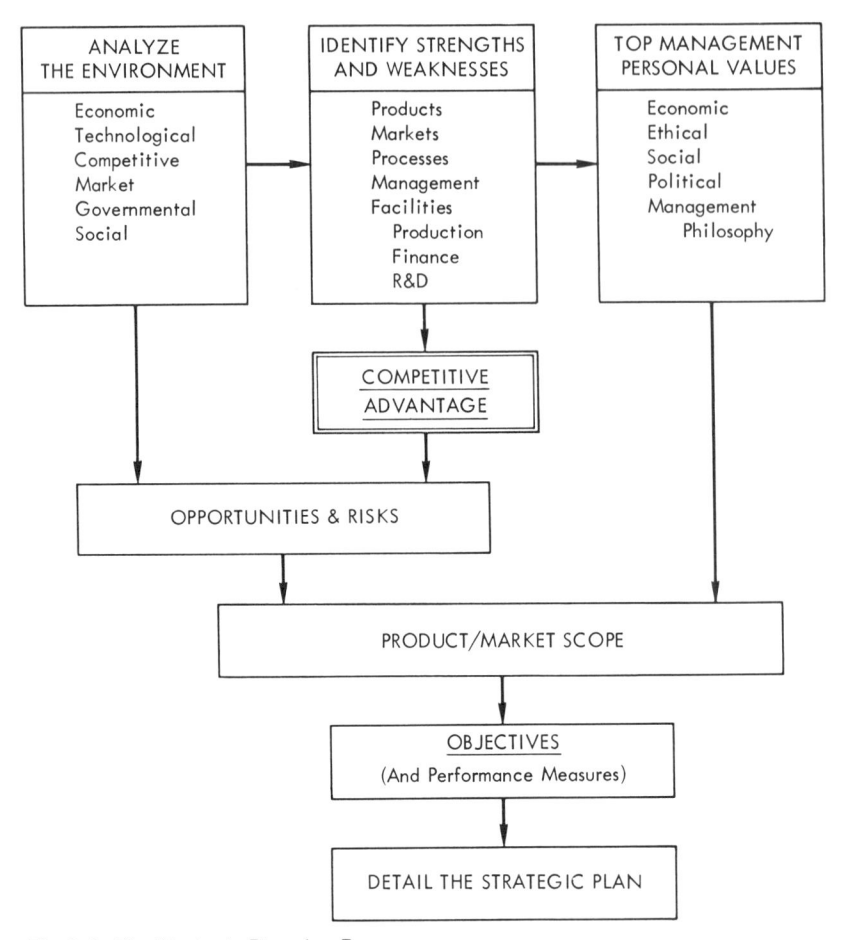

Fig. 2-4. The Strategic Planning Process

(flow continues to COMPETITIVE ADVANTAGE, OPPORTUNITIES & RISKS, PRODUCT/MARKET SCOPE, OBJECTIVES (And Performance Measures), DETAIL THE STRATEGIC PLAN)

4. *Identify opportunities and risks.* The company should, at this point, be able to identify opportunities in the environment to fill a unique niche. These opportunities occur when there are specific needs for products (or services) which the firm is uniquely able to supply because of its resources.

5. *Define product/market scope.* This involves the explicit definition of the future scope of the company's activities. The main idea is to concentrate on a very limited number of carefully defined product/market segments. These depend upon the analysis resulting from Steps 1 to 4 above.

   Careful identification of the product/market scope is advantageous because it (a) reduces time and complexity of decisions regarding acquisitions, new investments, and other elements of the development plan, (b) promotes integration of divisions and other organizational entities by providing a basis for their plans, (c) allows the company to focus on decisions and actions that take advantage of their competitive edge.

6. *Define the competitive edge.* This requires a careful evaluation of unique company skills, position, market advantages, and other competitive factors.
7. *Establish objectives and measures of performance.* Quantitative specifications are required to describe many characteristics of the firm and to provide a clear definition of strategy. Quantitative goals may be established for such parameters as annual rate of growth of sales, profits, return on investment; market share; number of employees; value of assets; debt; standing in the industry; and so on.[5]
8. *Determine deployment of resources.* Should resources be applied to growth from within or to acquisitions? What areas should the company focus its resources upon? Readjustment of application of resources is thus established in a manner similar to the grand-scale shifts of men and material in military conflicts. Conversion from one type of resource to another, as changing from labor-intensive to capital-intensive manufacturing, is also a part of such deployment.

Short-Range Planning

Short-range planning (frequently called operational or annual planning) is almost always heavily financial in nature; it states objectives and standards of performance in terms of financial results. The basic notion is to decentralize responsibility to "profit centers" or "cost centers," where sales, cost of sales, gross profits, or expenses may be established. These in turn are broken down into measurable and controllable elements, such as investment (fixed assets, inventory, accounts receivable, cash, and so on) and cost of sales (direct labor, overhead, selling, transportation, and administration).

In the traditional approach, financial planning is the integrating process. Its major failure is that emphasis is put on dollars instead of the work to be done.

On the basis of short-range plans, specific objectives may be established for each individual in the organization. The individual and his manager negotiate the objectives, their cost, their schedule, and level of desired quality of performance. Formal systems for feeding back information on actual performance are included in the MIS to detect problem areas. The individual and his manager meet regularly once a month or once a quarter to review progress and add new objectives. This focus on objectives by an individual worker is known as MBO (management by objectives).

---

[5] See, for example, Robert L. Katz, *Management of the Total Enterprise,* Englewood Cliffs, N.J.: Prentice-Hall, 1970; see also Edward P. Learned, C. R. Christensen, and K. R. Andrews, *Business Policy,* Homewood, Ill.: Richard D. Irwin, Inc., 1972; and [Steiner, *Top Management Planning.*]

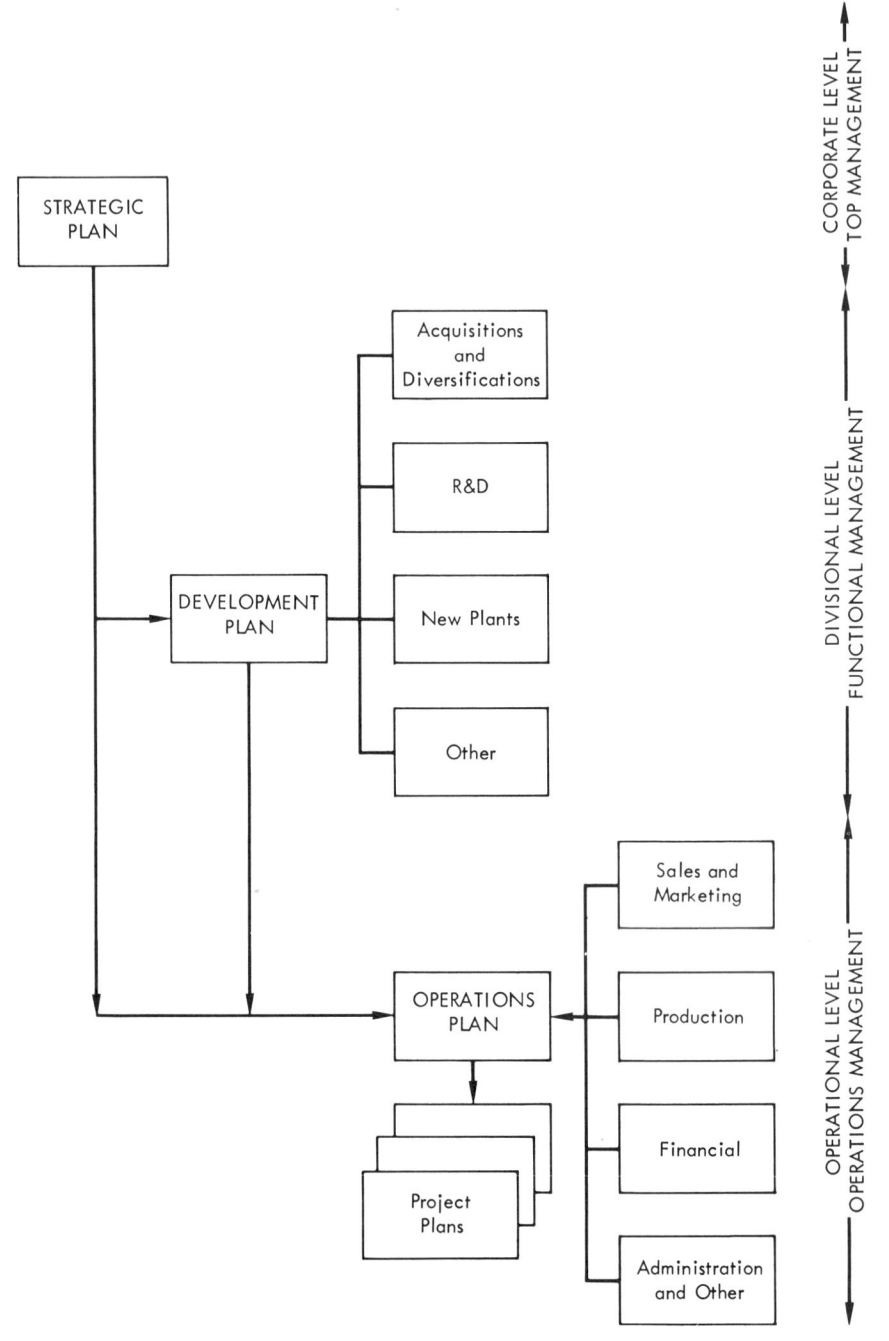

Fig. 2-5. Systems Approach to Planning

The Systems Approach to Planning

The systems approach to planning starts with the strategic plan as the framework. The strategic plan is specific but not detailed, because although specific goals may be established for the distant future, detailed methods for achieving these goals must be related to current environmental (including competitive) conditions. The distant-time goals of the strategic plan provide the constraints for setting intermediate and short-term goals. Therefore, as shown in Fig. 2-5, the strategic plan ties together the development plan (short-range plan). The development plan focuses on the growth of the company through internal or external expansion. The operations plan is the one-year play which links together in full detail the functional plans with project or program plans.

Information and Planning

It is evident that the first four steps in the planning process depend heavily upon the availability and utilization of critical information. It is hard to imagine the manager trying to develop any of the three major types of plans without first gathering the necessary planning premises that permit adequate evaluation of alternate courses of action to achieve the plan.

The planning information needs of an organization can be classified into three broad types: (1) environmental, (2) competitive, and (3) internal. Because these are so important in the planning process and in the design of an information system for planning, it is desirable that

ENVIRONMENTAL INFORMATION
  Politics and government
  Demographic and social trends
  Economic trends
  Technological environment
  Factors of production

COMPETITIVE INFORMATION
  Industry demand
  Firm demand
  Competition
  Past performance
  Present activity
  Future plans

INTERNAL INFORMATION

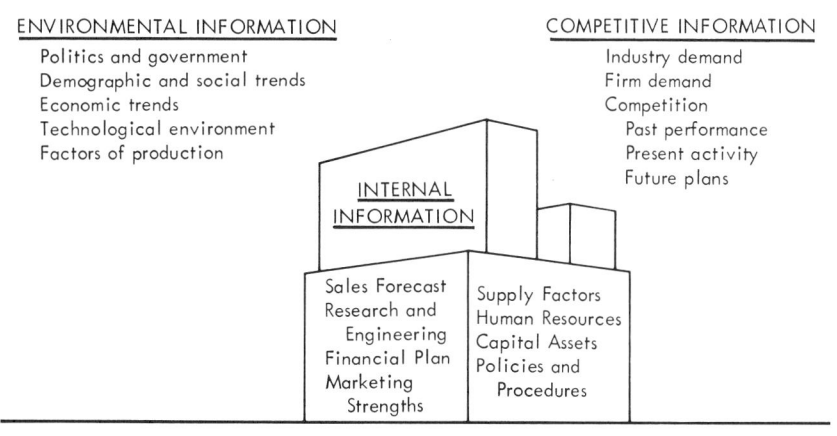

  Sales Forecast
  Research and Engineering
  Financial Plan
  Marketing Strengths

  Supply Factors
  Human Resources
  Capital Assets
  Policies and Procedures

Fig. 2-6. Planning Premises

each category be considered in some detail. Conceptually, planning premises can be viewed as shown in Fig. 2-6.

Environmental Information

Each company will have to determine specific information about the environment that is important to it. In addition, a system for "scanning" the environment or just trying to identify future threats and opportunities should be established. Descriptions of some general areas that companies should consider follow.

Political and Governmental Considerations

Some information on political stability, at whatever level of government, is important for forecasting plans. Additionally, the nature and extent of government controls and their effect on the organization must be taken into account. A third factor is the important role played by government financial and tax policies; they have a very significant effect on many planning decisions.

Demographic and Social Trends

The products, services, or outputs of most firms and organizations are affected by the totals, composition, or location of the population. Social trends and consumer buying behavior are important. It is necessary therefore to forecast trends for both the short and long run in this critical area.

Economic Trends

Included herein would be (a) the GNP level and trend and consumer disposable income, which are significant for almost all organizations; (b) employment, productivity, capital investment, and numerous other economic indicators that provide valuable planning information for those firms whose output is a function of these important variables; and (c) price and wage levels, whose effects are vital to almost all organizations regardless of product or service.

Technological Environment

Because of accelerating technical changes and their effect on new products and processes, it becomes necessary or desirable for many firms to forecast the technological changes in their industry and the probable effect on the firm. Firms like TRW, Inc., forecast key technological advances in all fields for a period of twenty years.

Factors of Production

These include source, cost, location, availability, accessibility, and productivity of the major production factors of (a) labor, (b) materials and parts, and (c) capital.

Competitive Information

The MIS should provide a formal approach to obtaining information about the industry as a whole and major competitors in particular. Since the company is bound so closely to the industry it serves, it should monitor the structure of the industry and trends that will affect the entire industry. Then, more specifically, forecasts and trends of sales for the industry should be monitored. The reason is that the company's sales will fluctuate with industry sales. In addition, total market potential for the industry should be estimated.

Other industry information of value would concern financial resources, profitability, pricing, promotional methods, new tactics, new products, and new channels of distribution.

When there are relatively few firms in the industry or a few dominant leaders, detailed information on these firms should be gathered continuously. Past performance, return on investment, share of the market, and breadth of product lines help to identify threats posed by competition. Such information also provides yardsticks for measuring your company's performance.

Internal Information

Because internal premises affect the planning decisions of so many levels in the organization, in some respects they are more important than the external information. Although the premises about the business environment and competition are very important, these categories of information are utilized by relatively few managers in a firm, mainly top managers and marketing managers.

As they relate to the total planning process, internal data are aimed at an identification of the organization's strengths and weaknesses. It is useful to think of internal premises as being of the following types.

1. Sales Forecast

This is perhaps the single most important planning document in the organization, because the allocation of the entire company's resources is a function of the sales plan. It sets the framework on which most other internal plans are constructed and can therefore be regarded as the dominant planning premise internal to the firm.

2. The Financial Plan

This plan, frequently called the budget, is second only to the sales forecast in importance. In many ways, the financial plan preempts the sales forecast because it represents a quantitative and time commitment of the allocation of the *total resources* of the company (manpower, plant, capital, materials, overhead, and general and administrative expenses). Properly constructed, the financial plan involves the entire organization and, when completed, provides subsidiary planning information for a variety of subplans throughout the company. It is a system that links all activities of the company together.

3. Supply Factors

Manpower, capital, plant and equipment, organization, and other supply factors are vital planning premises that provide constraints or boundaries within which planning takes place. These factors are controllable to a large extent by the firm, but their availability and limitations must be taken into account in developing the financial plan and subsidiary plans for achieving objectives.

4. Policies

Basic policies are relatively fixed for long-run purposes. To the extent that product, marketing, financial, personnel, and other basic policies are unchangeable in the short run, they provide constraints to planning in much the same way as do supply factors.

Table 2-3. Role of Accounting in Planning

STRATEGIC PLANNING	ACCOUNTING CONTRIBUTIONS
Scope	None
Competitive edge	a. Fund flow analysis for support of alternative competitive edge b. Cost analysis of alternatives
Specifications or quantitative targets	a. Development of acceptable and desired financial goals such as profitability, ROI, debt, cash, and numerous financial ratios b. Analysis of financial risk
Assignment of resources	a. Capital budgets b. Labor cost analysis
SHORT-RANGE PLANNING (OPERATIONS)	
Total company (system)	a. Pro forma statements b. Capital expenditure flow c. Cash flow projections
Marketing	a. Distribution cost analysis b. Budgets c. New production introduction expenses
Production	a. Variable budgets b. Projected cost of production by product c. Breakeven analysis d. Budgets
Engineering/research	a. Budgets
Administration	a. Cost schedules by type of worker b. Budgets

Role of Accounting in Planning

The accounting function is not concerned with *creating* strategic concepts such as product scope or competitive edge. It does provide a service, however, by *evaluating* the financial impact of the alternatives upon the economic performance of the company. Accounting does play a leading role in setting certain specifications for financial performance. It proposes financial ratios and projections which are feasible in terms of product scope and deployment of resources.

In short-range planning, in which objectives have been established specifically, accounting plays a much more significant role. It integrates the entire plan by means of budgets, cash flows, and pro forma operating statements.

In Table 2-3 we have summarized the contributions of accounting to planning.

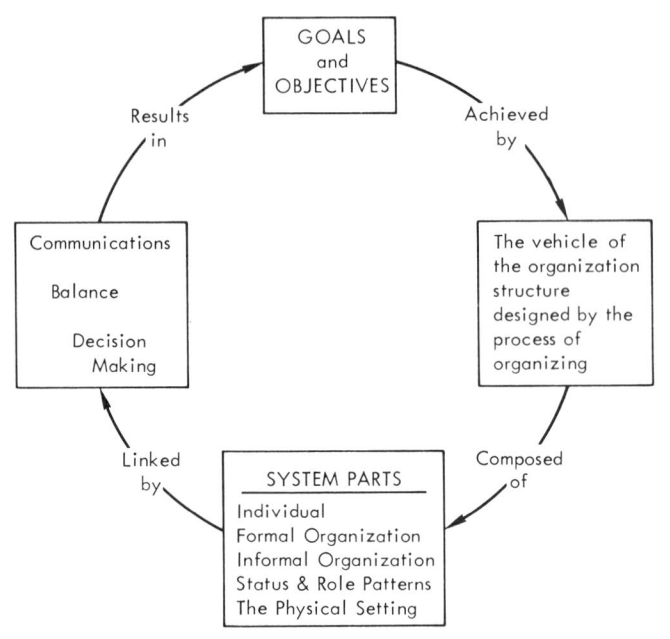

Fig. 2-7. Integration of the Organizational System Through the Organizing Process

ORGANIZING

Organizing human resources by managers is the method by which effective group action is obtained. A structure of roles must be designed and maintained in order for people to work together in carrying out plans and accomplishing objectives. This is the task of organizing. It involves the grouping of tasks necessary to accomplish plans, the assignment of work to departments, and the delegation of authority to obtain coordination. The structure provided by the function of organizing facilitates the operation of the organization as a system. This concept is shown in Fig. 2-7.

The Classical Organization Structure

The classical (bureaucratic or pyramidal) hierarchical organization structure is the most common form of the modern corporation. It

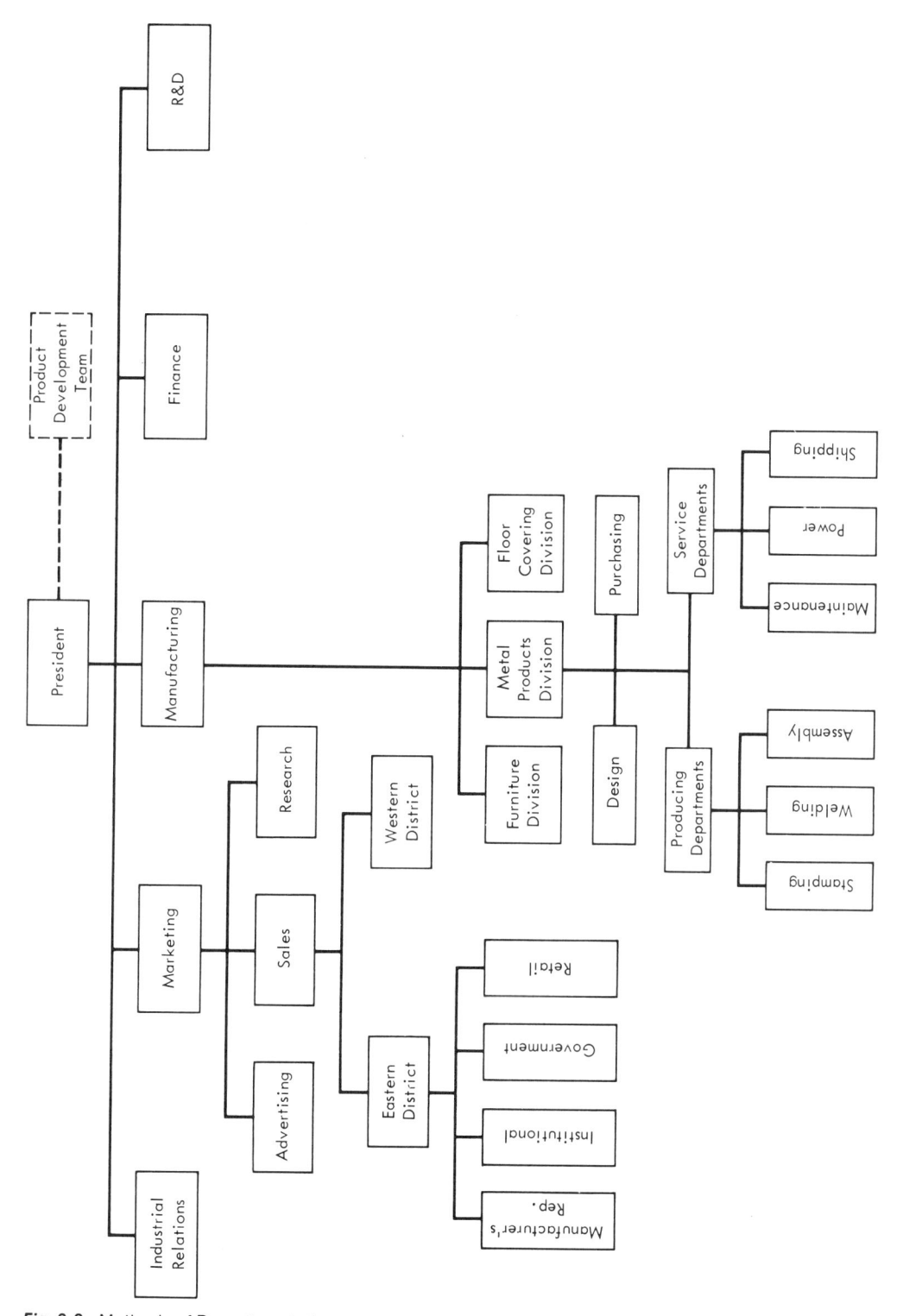

Fig. 2-8. Methods of Departmentation

provides the foundation upon which adaptations and modifications are constructed.

The key words are *structure* and *formal*. The basic tenets are: specialization of work (departmentation), span of management (supervision of a limited number of subordinates), chain of command (authority delegation), and unity of command (no subordinate has more than one superior). Because the classical format is so prevalent, we will examine the basic tenets of this form of organization.

Departmentation

Departmentation deals with the formation of organizational units. At the lowest level, homogeneous activities are grouped together. The activities form departments. Methods of departmentation that have proved logical and useful are: by function, by product, by territory, by customer, by process, and by project. An example of each of these methods of departmentation is illustrated in Fig. 2-8. For example, departmentation by *function* is shown at the top level by the common functions of marketing, personnel, operations, R & D, and finance. The breakdown of operations into the furniture division, the metal products division, and the floor-covering division is an example of product organization. The sales department is organized into eastern and western districts to establish a *territory* departmentation, and these territories are further departmented by the *customer* breakdown of retail, government, institutions, and manufacturer's representatives. The manufacturing operation in the metal products division depicts both *process* (assembly, welding, stamping) and *function* (maintenance, power, shipping). Finally, a special *project* team, organized for new-product development, reports to the president.

Functional departmentation is by far the oldest and most widely used form of grouping activities. In almost every organization there are three fundamental activities of producing, selling, and financing to be performed. These are the basic functions. As organizations grow, additional staff or service functions are added. Almost all organizations show some functional division of labor.

Product departmentation is common for enterprises with several products or services. The method is easily understood and takes advantage of specialized knowledge. Common examples are department stores (e.g., appliances, furniture, cosmetics) and banks (commercial, personnel).

Territory departmentation is frequently used by organizations that are physically dispersed. The rationale is that activities in a given area should be grouped and assigned to a manager. Such an approach takes advantage of economies of localized operation. The most frequent use of this method is in the sales force, where division by geographical region favors recruitment and training. Manufacturing and distribution may be organized by territory for similar reasons.

Customer departmentation may be used when the major emphasis is upon service to the customer or where it permits taking advantage of specialized knowledge. Sex, age, and income are common yardsticks for identifying customers. Examples of this type of organization include banks (loans to retailers, wholesalers, manufacturers), department stores (men's shop, teen shop, bridal salon), and aircraft manufacturers (government, foreign, domestic).

Process departmentation, most frequently used in manufacturing enterprises and at the lowest level of organization, is a logical method whereby maximum use can be obtained from equipment and special skills. Frequently the process matches an occupational classification, such as welding, painting, or plumbing.

Project departmentation, sometimes referred to as team or task force, is relatively new and growing in importance. This approach has gained much favor in defense-related industries because the work involved in research and development lends itself to identification in natural blocks or events. A major advantage of the project organization is the feeling of identification it gives its members.[6]

Span of Management

If it were not necessary to coordinate the activities of an organization, departmentation would permit its expansion to an indefinite degree. However, this coordinative need requires a structure composed of levels of supervision, a structure achieved by establishing these levels of supervision within the confines of the span of management—the number of subordinates that a manager can supervise. The importance of this factor can be appreciated if we consider that were it not for a supervisory limit, there would be no need to organize, since everyone in the organization would report to the president. Hence, one reason for organizing is to overcome the limitations of both human ability and time.

The basic question surrounding the span of management—stated two ways—is: (1) How many subordinates should be assigned to a supe-

---

[6] See *Project Manager's Handbook* (New York: Booz, Allen & Hamilton, 1967), Chap. 2, "Organization"; see also D. W. Karger and R. G. Murdick, *Managing Engineering and Research,* 2nd ed. (New York: Industrial Press, Inc., 1969), Chap. 9, "Project Management."

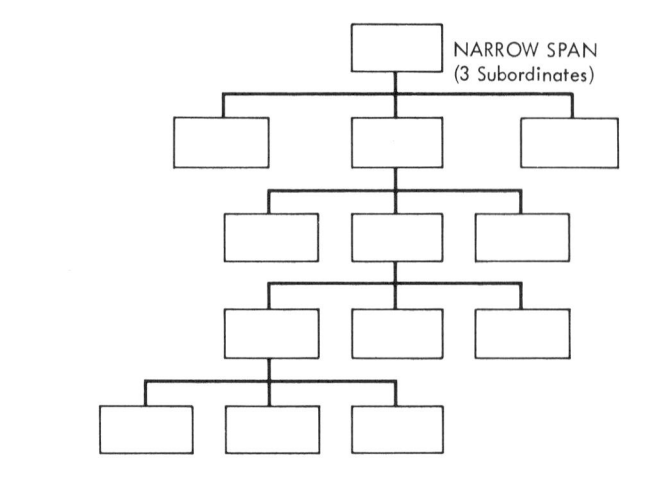

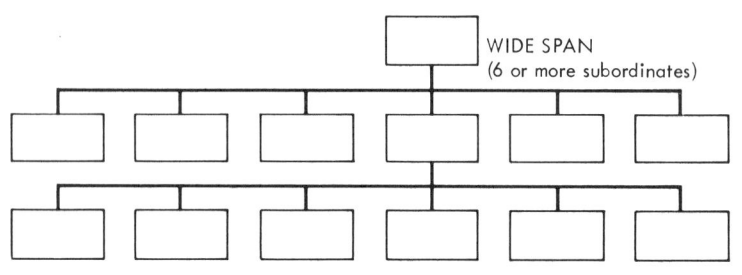

Fig. 2-9. Two Approaches to Span of Management

rior? and (2) Should the organization structure be "wide" or "narrow?" Figure 2-9 depicts the types of organizational structures involved in each instance, and Fig. 2-10 gives examples.

Generally speaking, the effort to identify a specific number or range of subordinates has not been productive. In practice the number varies widely. For example, former President Eisenhower was noted for his span of management of one—his chief of staff. To take another extreme, 750 Roman Catholic bishops report directly to the pope.

The span of management appears to depend on the manager's ability to reduce the time and frequency of subordinate relationships. These factors, in turn, are determined by: (1) how well the subordinate is trained to do his job, (2) the extent of planning involved in the activity, (3) the degree to which authority is delegated and understood, (4) whether standards of performance have been set, (5) the environment for good communications, and (6) the nature of the job and the rate at which it changes.

Kaiser Aluminum's new 'flat' management

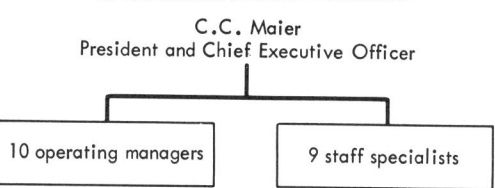

C.C. Maier
President and Chief Executive Officer

- 10 operating managers
- 9 staff specialists

Its old 'pyramid' structure

President
— 6 staff specialists

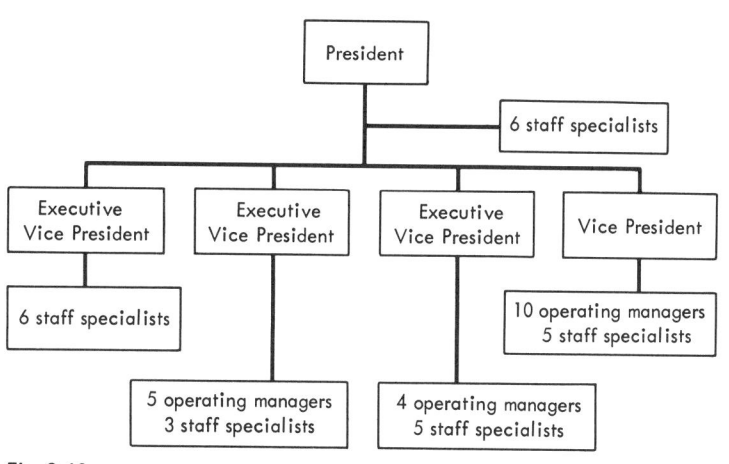

- Executive Vice President
  - 6 staff specialists
- Executive Vice President
  - 5 operating managers
  - 3 staff specialists
- Executive Vice President
  - 4 operating managers
  - 5 staff specialists
- Vice President
  - 10 operating managers
  - 5 staff specialists

Fig. 2-10.

Source: "Kaiser Aluminum Flattens its Layers of Brass," reprinted from the February 23, 1973 issue of *Business Week* by special permission. (c) 1973 by McGraw-Hill, Inc.

Authority Relationships

Without delegation of authority the formal organization would cease to exist; there would be only one department because the chief executive would be the only manager. It does no good to set up a structure of activities unless authority is delegated to the units within the structure to accomplish particular assignments.

The major determinant of a manager's ability to delegate authority is his temperament and personality, but other determinants are beyond his control. Some of these are: (1) cost—the more costly the decision, the more likely it is to be centralized; (2) uniformity of policy—the more uniform and centralized a policy (price, personnel) the less need there is to delegate authority surrounding it; (3) the established formal organization structure; (4) custom of the business—frequently the delegation philosophy and character of top management determine authority delegation; and (5) environment for good management—the availability in the company of managers and good management practices (including control techniques) that would encourage delegation.

Among the tools and techniques for communicating the delegation of authority and organization structure are the organization manual, organization charts, position descriptions, activity charts, and procedural flowcharts. Others are plans, policies, programs, budgets, and procedures.

Organizing and Systems Concepts

By its very nature, the systems philosophy of organizing creates several basic and valuable by-products. The first of these is integration of the many subsystems making up the total organization. We have seen how planning tends to put managers in the frame of mind for thinking of the organization as a system. This approach to organizing will accomplish similar results. Further, people will begin to understand how their jobs interact with others in the company. A second benefit is the enhancement of decentralization. Advantages of decentralization include greater economies of supervision, improved morale, better development of managers, and in general more awareness of the contribution that decentralized units make to the whole. The systems approach and computer-based information systems give us many new and different capabilities for organization and management of a business, especially more centralized and more automated control of major portions of operations.[7] It is this *centralized control* that permits *decentralized operations*.

The greatest impact will come in the organization structure itself. Traditional organizational practice and theory have emphasized structure and authority. Under the systems approach the concept of the organization is changing from one of structure to one of process.

Advanced technology, the information explosion, increasing complexity—these require an organization structure that will accommodate change. We are fitting increasingly sophisticated techniques to a primitive vehicle, the bureaucratic structure. By adopting the systems approach to organizing, we emphasize integration of the parts as well as design of a vehicle that will accommodate accelerating change.

Equally important is the emphasis that the systems approach places upon the *systems* as opposed to the *functions* of organizations. The typical business has been organized along functional lines (sales, finance, production) at the top, and by other methods (customer, process, territory, etc.) at lower hierarchical levels. This emphasis on organization structure has frequently overlooked the interrelationship of the parts and the programs, projects, and processes that the parts were designed to produce.

Another systems aspect of organization that has received little attention is the interrelationship of structure, strategy, and control. As companies grow large, their strategies tend to change from single product to vertical integration and then to diversification. The structure of the companies and their control systems change to follow strategy. A study of over 200 of the *Fortune* 500 largest companies and of 100 top companies in Europe led to the system relationships among the managerial functions shown in Table 2-4.

Emerging Concepts: The Team Approach

If we are to take the systems approach to organizing, the tasks involve integrating the subsystems of the organization and accommodating to change. There is a growing recognition that some form of task force or team approach can achieve these goals. Warren Bennis sees the key word describing the systems approach as "temporary." He says, "There

---

[7] Victor Z. Brink, "Top Management Looks at the Computer," *Columbia Journal of World Business*, January–February 1969, p. 78.

Table 2-4. The Three Stages of Organizational Development

COMPANY CHARACTERISTICS	STAGE I (SMALL)	STAGE II (INTEGRATED)	STAGE III (DIVERSIFIED)
Product line	Single product or single line	Single product line	Multiple product lines
Distribution	One channel or set of channels	One set of channels	Multiple channels
Organization structure	Little or no formal structure; "one-man show"	Specialization based on function	Specialization based on product-market relationships
Product-service transactions	Not applicable	Integrated pattern of transactions A → B → C → Markets	Nonintegrated pattern of transactions A B C → Markets
R&D organization	Not institutionalized; guided by owner-manager	Increasingly institutionalized search for product or process improvements	Institutionalized search for *new* products as well as for improvements
Performance measurement	By personal contact and subjective criteria	Increasingly impersonal, using technical and/or cost criteria	Increasingly impersonal, using *market* criteria (return on investment and market share)
Rewards	Unsystematic and often paternalistic	Increasingly systematic, with emphasis on stability and service	Increasingly systematic, with variability related to performance
Control system	Personal control of both strategic and operating decisions	Personal control of strategic decisions, with increasing delegation of operating decisions through policy	Delegation of product-market decisions within existing businesses, with indirect control based on analysis of "results"
Strategic choices	Needs of owner versus needs of company	Degree of integration; market-share objective; breadth of product-line	Entry and exit from industries; allocation of resources by industry; rate of growth

Source: Bruce R. Scott, "The Industrial State: Old Myths and New Realities," *Harvard Business Review,* March–April, 1973, p. 137.

will be adaptive, rapidly changing *temporary* systems. These will be task forces organized around problems to be solved.[8]

Matrix Project Management

This form of task force gets it name from the fact that several project managers exert planning, scheduling, and cost control supervi-

[8] Warren F. Bennis, "The Coming Death of Bureaucracy," in David I. Cleland and William R. King, eds., *Systems, Organizations, Analysis, Management: A Book of Readings,* New York: McGraw-Hill Book Co., 1969, p. 11.

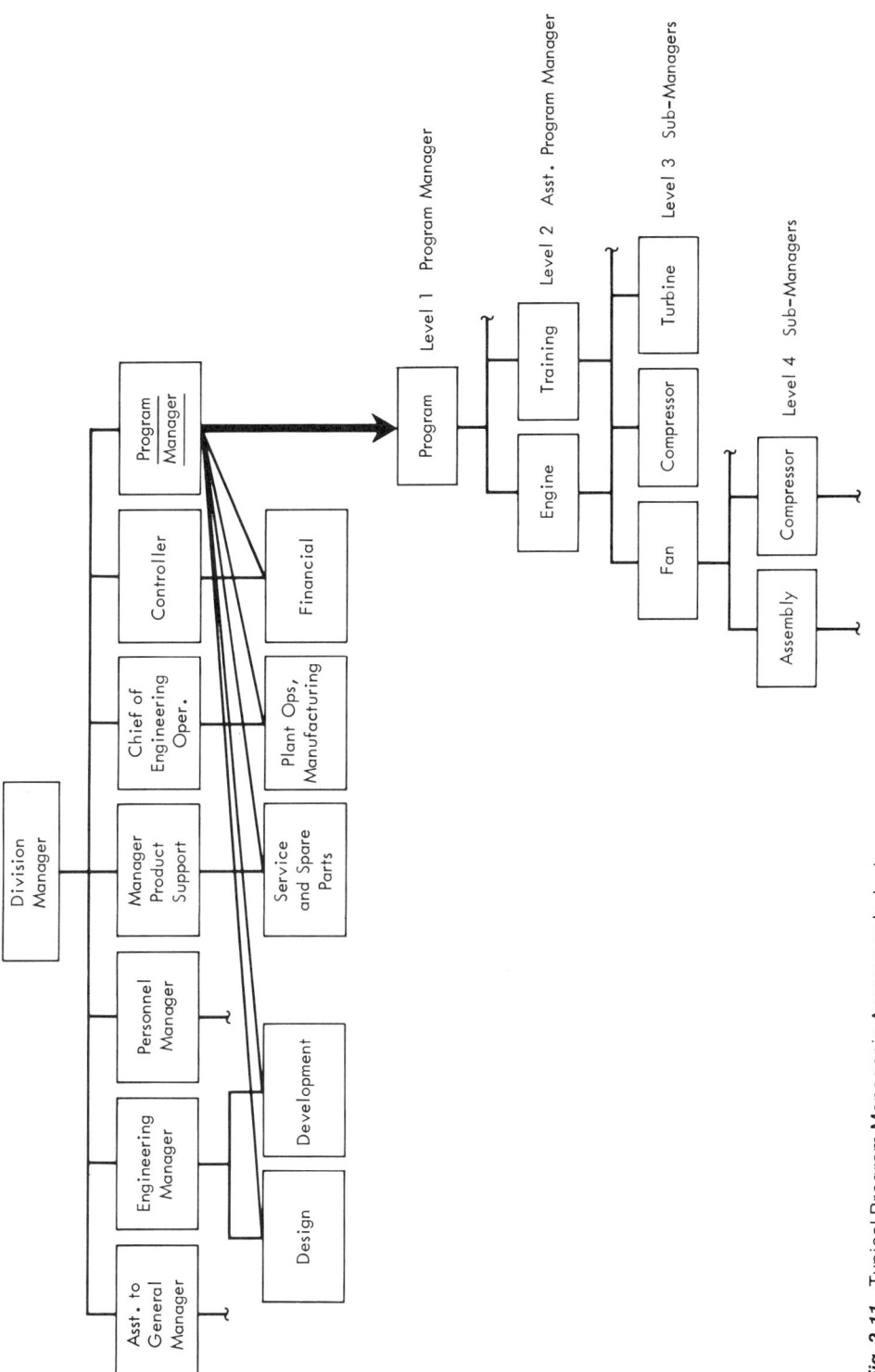

Fig. 2-11. Typical Program Manager in Aerospace Industry

sion over people who have been assigned to their projects while the functional managers exert line control. Thus there is shared responsibility for the worker and he must please two superiors. The organization of a typical project in a major aerospace firm is shown in Fig. 2-11. The program manager is essentially a "contractor" who hires his personnel from the line or functional organization.

Line Project Management

In this form of project management organization, each employee has only one home: the project to which he is assigned (or to an auxiliary service group). Usually a number of projects are active in different stages of their life cycles. As new projects begin and build up, people are transferred from other projects that are approaching completion.

The line project manager has complete responsibility for resources of both money and men. He contracts for auxiliary services. He is held accountable for meeting planned time, cost, and technical performance goals. A typical organization chart is shown in Fig. 2-12.

Venture Teams

More and more multinational, multidivisional, multiproduct companies are beginning to realize that the traditional *functional* organizational structure cannot accommodate risk, innovation, and new ventures or products. They are turning to the venture team, a recent organizational innovation that resulted from the need to meet the demand for a breakthrough in product marketing.

The venture team resembles the project manager type approach in

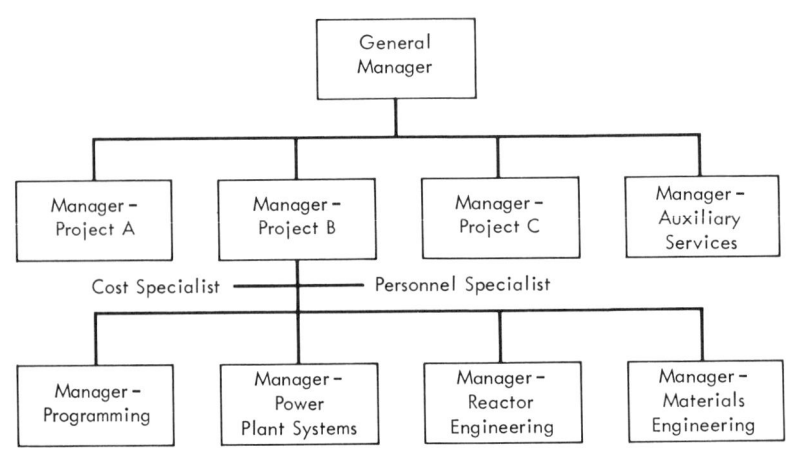

Fig. 2-12. Line Project Management

that its resources and personnel are obtained from the functional departments. Other similarities include organizational separation of team members, multidisciplinary composition of personnel, and the goal-directed effort of a single project; in this case the development and introduction of a new product.

Information and Organizing

Organization structure and information needs are inextricably interwoven. In an analogy between an organization and the human body, the organization *structure* can be compared to the human anatomy and the *information* to the nervous system.

The systems view of the organization takes into account the integrative nature of information flows. This concept is demonstrated in Fig. 2-13, where each organizational entity is seen as an information system with the components of input, process, and output. Each is connected to the others through information and communication channels, and each organizational entity becomes a decision point.

Information also affects organizing by the manner in which in-

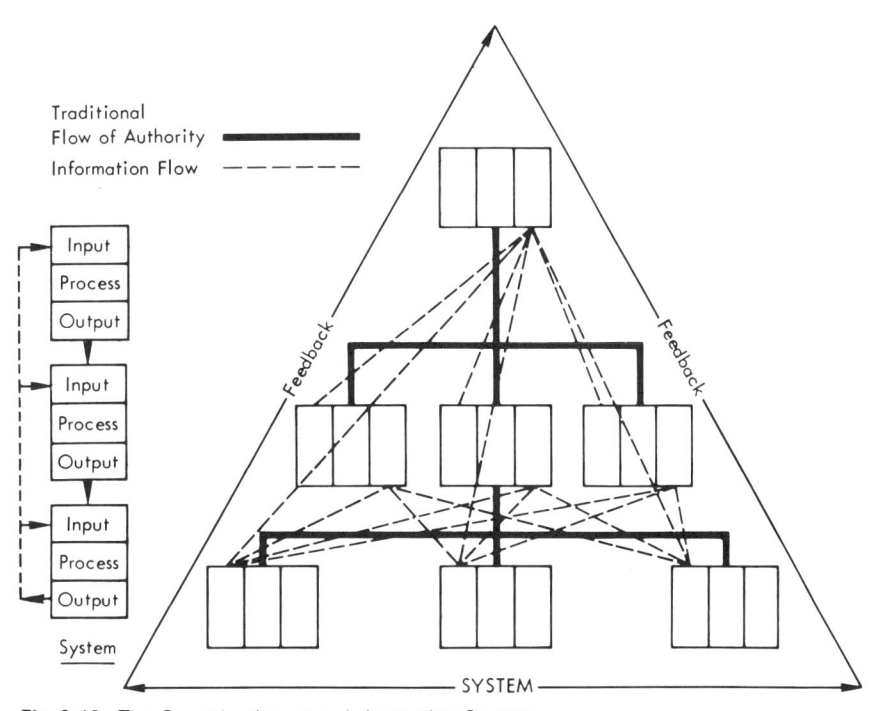

Fig. 2-13. The Organization as an Information System

formation systems are designed. These should conform to the organizational structure and the delegation of authority within the company. Only then can each organizational unit's objective be established and its contribution to companywide goals be measured. This means that organizations must be designed around information flow and those factors of information chosen to plan and control performance. Frequently organizational structure and performance reporting do not coincide. In these cases information systems cannot truly reflect plans and results of operations.

Another major cause of organizational and information mismatch is the lag between organizational changes and information systems to facilitate them. As needs, structure, and managers change, the information system should be changed to support them. Rarely does one find a change in informational systems matching a change in organizational responsibilities and the needs of managers. The result is often an "information lag."

Accounting and Organizing

In nonfinancial and large diversified companies, the impact of accounting on the managerial process of organizing is not large. The accountant's influence is limited to the organization for control of financial transactions and assets.

In financial institutions such as banks, the accounting/financial group has a significant impact on the organization. The organization must be built around financial information systems and the predominant financial transactions. Therefore, organization for efficient operation and careful control of cash, credit, and other financial instruments is of paramount importance. The computer injects both simplicity in operations and complexity in control into organizational development.

CONTROLLING

If the manager could depend upon the flawless execution of plans by a perfectly balanced organization, there would be no need for control because results would invariably be as expected. However, plans and operations rarely remain on course, and control is needed to obtain desired results. The real test of a manager's ability is the result he achieves.

Control is a basic process and remains essentially the same regardless of the activity involved or the area of the organization. The fundamental process consists of three steps: (1) setting standards of performance, (2) measuring performance against these standards, and (3) correcting deviations from standards and plans.

Standards of Performance

Setting standards of performance involves defining for personnel in all levels of the organization what is expected of them in terms of job performance. Hence, standards are criteria against which results can be measured. These criteria can be quantitative (e.g., 10 percent increase in sales) or qualitative (e.g., maintain high level of morale). A frequently used definition of standards of performance is *a statement of conditions existing when a job is performed satisfactorily.*

A discussion of standards can be better understood when related to actual examples. Table 2-5 illustrates the basic components of a very im-

Table 2-5. Standards of Performance for Controlling the Financial Plan

FINANCIAL PLAN	CRITERIA			ILLUSTRATION OF STANDARD
	Cost	Time	Quantity	Quality
Sales	x	x	x	Sales quota during time period at standard cost
Cost of goods sold				
Raw materials	x		x	Unit usage rate at standard cost
Direct labor			x	Hours per unit of output
Manufacturing expense	x	x	x	Maintenance cost per machine-hour
Total				
Gross margin on sales	x		x	Percent of sales
Less:				
Distribution expense	x			Percent of sales
Administrative expense	x	x	x	Budgeted amount
Total				
Operating income	x		x	Percent of sales
Federal income tax				
Net income	x		x	Return on investment

portant operation plan—the financial plan. Note that a standard of performance is indicated for each of these major items.

The usual standards of performance for an activity are related to: cost, time, quantity, and quality. For example, in Table 2-5 the *cost* of raw materials for manufacturing a product can be controlled in terms of cost per unit, and this standard would apply in the purchasing operation. *Time* is a standard for the sales force when performance is measured in terms of meeting sales quotas during established time periods (e.g., weeks, months). In manufacturing, the direct labor hours per unit of output in a process operation is a common *quantity* measure. *Quality* is a common measure in judging the acceptability of such factors as product specification, grades of products sold, and reject rates in quality control.

The foregoing are yardsticks, not areas of activity to be measured. Ideally, everyone in the organization should have some standard so that he understands what is expected of him.

Types of critical standards have been identified:[9]

1. *Physical.* The fundamental nonmonetary measurements so common at the operating level. They may reflect quantitative performance (units per man-hour, raw material usage rate) or quality (color, hardness).
2. *Cost.* Monetary measurements that attach value to the cost of operations. These are usually cost ratios as, for example, overhead cost per unit of output.
3. *Revenue.* Monetary values that are attached to sales, expressed in ratios such as average sales per customer.
4. *Program.* Unlike ongoing operations, programs are one-time processes and performance is measured in terms of time to complete events, meeting program specifications, or cost.
5. *Intangible.* These are standards that are not ordinarily expressed in quantitative terms because they are hard to measure. Examples are advertising, employee morale, industrial relations, and public relations.

In addition to operating standards, there are critical areas of overall company performance that are the concern of top management. Is the company achieving its objectives? Are its strategies paying off? Indeed, by appraising overall company performance in these areas, the company evaluates its progress toward its basic purposes and objectives. These areas include:

1. Profitability.
2. Market standing.
3. Productivity.
4. Innovation and product leadership.

[9] Adapted from Koontz and O'Donnell, *Principles of Management,* pp. 649–50.

5. Employee and managerial attitudes and development.
6. Public responsibility.
7. Use of resources.
8. Balance between short-range and long-range objectives.

Measuring Performance

Once standards have been established, it is necessary to measure performance against the expectation of the standards. The statement of measurement, and of any differences, is usually in the form of a personal observation or some type of report—oral or written.

Increasingly, control and performance reporting is in written form, owing in part to the accelerating use of computer-based information systems and related reporting. The written report has the advantage of providing a permanent record, subject to periodic review by the manager and subordinates. This method of measuring performance may take a variety of forms. Among the most common is the statistical report, which presents statistical analysis of performance versus standard, either in tabular or chart form. Special or one-time reports are frequently made in problem areas as they arise. A significant portion of written reports are operational in nature and concern performance against standards for the financial plan.

Correcting Deviations

It does little good to set standards of performance and measure deviations from standard unless corrections are made to get the plan back on course to achieve the objective. Methods and techniques for correcting deviations can be described in terms of the functions of management:

Plan—Recycle the management process: review the plan, modify the goal, or change the standard.
Organize—Examine the organization structure to determine whether it is reflected in standards, make sure that duties are well understood, reassign people if necessary.
Staff—Improve selection of subordinates, improve training, reassign duties.
Direct—Provide better leadership, improve motivation, explain the job better, manage by objectives, make sure that there is manager-subordinate agreement on standard.
Control—Provide organizational structure that channels the flow of in-

formation on performance to managers and others who have the responsibility for taking corrective action.

Control and Systems Concepts

The concept of control lies at the very heart of the systems approach. Indeed, no system could exist for very long without control. Unlike our classical notion of control as a process of coercion, or "compelling events to conform to plan," control in a cybernetic sense or systems sense views the organization as a self-regulating system. The key idea underlying control is *feedback*.

An example of feedback is the heating system. A thermostat maintains the temperature at a predetermined level by making or breaking an electrical circuit that starts or stops the heating system. Another example is the case of raw materials inventory. When inventory exceeds the accepted standard, a reduction in orders occurs until the inventory level is within standard. These examples illustrate the major characteristics of cybernetic systems: (1) a predetermined equilibrium to be maintained, (2) a feedback of changes in environment to the system, causing changes in its state, (3) a transfer of information from the external environment to the system, and (4) a device that prompts corrective action when the output of the system oscillates beyond desired limits.

The objective of control is to maintain the output that will satisfy the system requirements. This necessitates the building of control into the system. In the case of information systems, control is a major consideration of systems design and may take the form of a programmed decision rule. The steady state of the system (organization) is maintained by feedback of information concerning the functioning of the system within allowable limits.

Information and Control

Control systems depend upon information systems, because the rapidity and appropriateness of corrective action—the end result of the control process—depends on the kind of information received.

Information required to perform control is different in both type and characteristic from information needed for planning. Planning places greater emphasis on structuring the future; control is based more on the immediate past, present, and specific trends.

To control the business organization, we may divide the business into five groups of subsystems and control each of these subsystems. The first set consists of the management-level subsystems. The top-management level is concerned with strategy and its performance as a whole should be kept in line with measures established by the board of directors. Middle management, as a system of managers concerned with short-range planning and operations, must be subject to control in terms of productivity and efficiency. Similarly, first-line management represents the system for conducting day-to-day transactions. This system must also contain information feedback and be subject to control.

A second set of subsystems which make up the business is the resources set. Human resource, capital asset, materials, liquid assets, and credit line subsystems must be kept within control limits established by the responsible managers.

Another set of subsystems over which all companies seek to maintain control are the functional subsystems. Control information required in this instance more specifically, is:

Marketing information concerning the progress of the sales plan: quotas, territories, pricing, and the like. In other words, market information is basically that required to measure performance against the sales forecast. In addition, control information may be obtained in other areas of the marketing plan, such as product acceptance, advertising, market research, and distribution costs.

Manufacturing information concerning quantity and quality of direct labor, materials, overhead, and inventories. Control is also concerned greatly with the time aspect in the production system.

Personnel information concerning profiles and performance of personnel, recruiting reports, staffing reports, training reports, etc.

Accounting information such as the financial master plan, financial reports, variances, cash flow forecasts, etc.

Research, development, and engineering information giving performance, cost, and time for projects and periodic reports of variances from project plans.

Another set of subsystems for which control information is required is the product set. Each product line must be controlled by supplying information to product managers or product division managers. Such information as sales, profitability, trends, competition, marketing/manufacturing/accounting information for product planning and control is required.

Finally, the operating phase subsystems must be controlled by providing information to managers and key people. These operating-phase subsystems are forecasting, financing, designing, material handling and processing, costing, and selling.

The different characteristics of planning and control data reflect

Information and Control—The Systems Approach

The traditional approach to control has several shortcomings:

1. *Performance standards* were usually related to short-run financial planning and frequently overlooked the measurement of progress toward overall company objectives.
2. The *control process* took on a restrictive meaning, and the process became the overriding concern instead of the work that was to be controlled.
3. *Control reports* were viewed as a tool of subordinate measurement, not as a tool to improve operations.
4. *Lateness* was a characteristic of variance reporting. The lapse of time between a deviation and its discovery precluded corrective action until it was too late.

In order to overcome these objections and to achieve a greater degree of integration in the organization, a modern control system should be constructed around four central ideas:

1. *Integrate planning and control.* The central idea of IPC (information, planning, and control) is that each level of plans provides the standards of performance (objectives) for the next lower level of operations.
2. *Relate the control system to the organization structure.* The information system has usually been built around a financial chart of accounts, not decision centers. Moreover, the organization has not achieved synergism because the parts (functions or organizational elements) have not been related to a whole unified set of objectives or to the other parts. See Fig. 2-14.
3. *Design the system for decision-making,* not after-the-fact reporting. The manager-user must define systems in terms of information demands for decision-making.
4. *Timely information is essential.* The ideal control system is one that provides information in sufficient time to correct a deviation *before* it occurs.

A basic requirement of any control system is feedback. For the most part, existing control systems rely on feedback *after* deviation from desired performance and managers are being frustrated by discovering too late that actual accomplishments are missing the desired goals. They have been dependent upon accounting data and information systems that are historical in nature.

A modern business control system will utilize *feedforward* control. It will anticipate the lags in feedback systems by monitoring inputs and predicting their effects on outcome variables. In so doing, action can be taken to change the input and thereby bring the system output into equilibrium with desired results *before* the measurement of the output discloses an historical deviation from standard.

Accounting and Managerial Control

Accounting reports, properly prepared and promptly distributed, may provide management with early warning symptoms of performance variances. This applies both to strategic activities and daily operations. The skilled manager can interpret financial ratios, financial performance figures, and trends just as a symphony conductor can detect a flawed note among the many. Not many managers possess great financial skill, however, and the accounting manager may play a very significant role in managerial control by analyzing and interpreting data to provide *information* to the manager.

The accounting group should develop a system of "responsibility reporting" in which each operating manager receives information aggregated and appropriate to his level of management. Associated with this concept are "profit centers" and "cost centers" for which individual managers are responsible. An example for a hospital is shown in Table 2-6.

Such accounting and financial reporting for control would not be possible, however, if the accounting/financial systems were not integrated into the basic operating systems. Fig. 2-15 summarizes the sweep of the accounting/financial systems throughout an organization in relation to both planning and control.

Summary

Although we have attempted to examine information as it affects each of the major management functions of planning, organizing, and controlling, these functions cannot be separated; they are linked both functionally and by a common system of information. These systems characteristics of integration and linkage are shown in Fig. 2-16. It can be seen that although the inputs of planning and of control information

Plant Level Reports

COST DETAIL, PLANT NO. 14 NEW AUSTIN GRAVEL PLANT

	Period 1	Period 2	Period 3	Period 4	Period 5
FIXED COSTS:					
DIRECT LABOR	0	137280			
DEPRECIATION	0	221286			
TOT FXD COST	0	358566			
VAR COSTS:					
OPER SUPPLIES	0	1847			
KILN BRICK	0	9233			
ELEC POWER	0	23294			
REPAIRS	0	33237			
ROYALTY	0	51702			
SHOP CHARGES	0	7386			
GRAVEL PURCH	0	80876			
MISC EXP	0	7386			
TOT VAR COST	0	214961			
TOTAL COST	0	573527			

PLANT INCOME, PLANT NO. 14 NEW AUSTIN GRAVEL PLANT

	Period 1	Period 2	Period 3	Period 4	Period 5
SALES:					
SAND	0	167918	176415	185341	194720
GRAVEL	0	204422	214767	225633	237049
FILL MATRL	0	58559	61522	64635	67906
TYPE I SACK	0	91260	95878	100729	105826
I C GRAVEL	0	199555	209653	220261	231406
TOTAL SALES	0	721714	758235	796599	836907
DEDUCTIONS	0	0	0	0	0
NET SALES	0	721714	758235	796599	836907
FIXED COSTS	0	358566	334573	314700	298487
VRBLE COSTS	0	214961	226862	239454	252771
TOTAL COST	0	573527	561435	554154	551258
OPRTG INCM	0	148187	196800	242445	285649

Area Level Summary Report

OPERATING SUMMARY, AREA 01 AUSTIN

	Period 1	Period 2	Period 3	Period 4	Period 5
PLANT 01	280211	251442	266468	280805	294453
PLANT 03	30657	32730	35611	41317	43245
PLANT 04	201112	0	0	0	0
PLANT 06	117611	134145	149651	162477	171631
PLANT 10	16606	17144	19173	22299	22793
PLANT 12	0	0	0	0	0
PLANT 14	0	148187	196800	242445	285649
TOT OPR INC	646197	583648	667703	749343	817771
AR SPRT COST					
ADMIN+SALES	228161	233655	240433	250649	261595
TOT AD+SL EX	228161	233655	240433	250649	261595
TOT AR INC	418036	349993	427270	498694	556176
OPR RATIOS					
INC/SALES	17	14	16	17	17
PLANT ASSETS	3569915	3419370	3297306	3220333	3174439
OVHD ASSETS	62471	62934	66620	70265	73164
TOT ASSETS	3632386	3482304	3363926	3290598	3247603
AVG ASSETS	2533934	3557345	3423115	3327262	3269101
PERCH R O A	16.5	9.8	12.5	15.0	17.0

Fig. 2-14. Capitol Aggregates, Inc. Relates Control to Planning by Information Appropriate to Organizational Level

Source: Robert E. Engberg and Roger L. Moore, "A Corporate Planning Model for a Construction Materials Producer," *Management Adviser*, January–February 1974.

CAPITOL AGGREGATES CORPORATE OPERATING SUMMARY

	Period 1	Period 2	Period 3	Period 4	Period 5
OPERATING INCOME:					
...AREA .01	418036				
...AREA .02	1947960				
...AREA .03	97451				
TOTAL	2463447				
GEN+ADMN	238989				
EXPLORATION	14207				
OTHR INC+EXP	(37015)				
PRFT SHRING	264334				
TOT ADMN EXP	480515				
OPER INC	1982932				
INTEREST	485042				
INC BEF FIT	1497890				
FED INC TAX	718987				
INVEST CRT	(331722)				
NET INC	1110625				
PERCENTAGES:					
NT INC/SALES	11				
PERC R O A I	17				
NET INC/EQTY	18				
EQTY/T ASSET	47				
AVG ASSETS	12013204				

CAPITOL AGGREGATES CORPORATE CASH FLOW SUMMARY

	Period 1	Period 2	Period 3	Period 4	Period 5
NET INCOME	1110625				
DEPRECIATION	948047				
SHT TRM DEBT	0				
DEPLETION	6080				
NEW L T DEBT	3354000				
TOTAL AVLBLE	5418752				
ASSET REPLMT	448890				
PRPSED ASSET	4290000				
SHT DEBT RTR	300000				
SCH DEBT RTR	1087846				
REC REQRMNTS	477280				
INV REQRMNTS	(97734)				
LAND INVESTM	0				
OTHER ASSETS	0				
ACCTS PAYBLE	335271				
TAX LIABLTS	0				
TOTAL REQRMNT	6841553				
NET CASH FLW	(1422801)				
DEBT/ASSETS	.53				
TOTAL DEBT	6960254				
POLICY DEBT	6717607				
AVAILABLE	(242647)				

CAPITOL AGGREGATES CORPORATE BALANCE SHEET

	Period 1	Period 2	Period 3	Period 4	Period 5
CASH	(1122801)				
RECEIVABLES	1566772				
INVENTORIES	420477				
CURR ASSETS	864448				
PLT+EQUP	13637602				
ACUM DPRCTN	3941461				
NET PLT+EQUP	9696141				
LAND	2016370				
OTHER ASSETS	593920				
TOTAL ASSETS	13170879				
SHT TERM DEBT	0				
CRR PORT LTD	1168440				
ACCTS PAYBLE	664729				
FIT PAYBLE	0				
CURR LIABLTS	1833169				
LNG TRM DEBT	5127085				
TOTL LIABLTS	6960254				
OWNERS EQTY	6210625				
LIABLTS+EQTY	13170879				
CURRENT RATIO	.5 / .47				

Corporate Level Reports

CAPITOL AGGREGATES CORPORATE OVERVIEW REPORT

	Period 1	Period 2	Period 3	Period 4	Period 5
CURRENT RATIO	.5	.9	1.5	1.9	2.4
EQTY/ASSETS	.47	.30	.35	.38	.45
TOTAL ASSETS	13170879	25191364	25247775	28770269	28953701
NT CASH FLOW	(1422801)	819801	476423	1129449	1329290
AREA 01 P/L	418036	349993	427268	498695	556177
PERC R O A I	17	10	13	15	17
AREA 02 P/L	1947960	1550535	3495365	3978810	4356416
PERC R O A I	25	11	17	19	20
AREA 03 P/L	97451	106518	112772	116939	116016
PERC R O A I	242	148	190	219	227
NET INCOME BEF INT+TAXS	1982932	1664312	3438134	3904374	4262708
R O A I BEF INT+TAXS	17	9	14	14	15
NET INCOME	1110625	1205395	1114257	1603144	1552675

Fig. 2-14. cont.

are basically different, the planning that results affects subsequent control, and the action and information processing resulting from control in turn provide a feedback that affects the planning process.

Figure 2-16 represents the three subsystems of planning, operating, and controlling integrated into the system of management. Shown also is the basic flow of information for operation of the integrated system. The planning system receives as input the planning premises and objectives, from which we get the output of management plans. These plans in turn provide the input to the operating system, which utilizes them as premises for the organization that attempts to achieve the plans. A basic output of the operating system is performance against plan, and information concerning this performance is in turn provided as input to the control system.

Feedback on performance is obtained through the control system, which monitors the operating system and furnishes feedback information to it as well as to the planning system. Decisions are made within each system based upon information, and within each system there is a flow of information to implement changes and correct deviations based on feedback from other systems. It is evident that the key to success in

Table 2-6. Revenue and Costs by Center

CENTER	REVENUE	COSTS	NET REVENUE (COST)
Service Centers			
Operating rooms	$ 200,074	$ 230,925	$ (30,851)
Delivery rooms	27,360	75,836	(48,476)
Anesthesia	21,200	20,086	1,114
X-ray	177,039	124,078	52,961
Laboratory	182,533	146,026	36,507
Blood bank	16,889	15,351	1,538
Physical therapy	118,512	109,774	8,738
Inpatient Centers			
Inpatients	904,248	830,526	73,686
Nursery	60,000	66,893	(6,893)
Outpatient Centers			
Outpatients	123,352	106,544	16,808
Emergency	26,015	23,786	2,229
Totals	$1,857,222	$1,749,861	$107,361

planning, organizing, and controlling lies in the information–decision system. It follows that success in achieving the goals and objectives of the organization lies similarly in performing these managerial functions through the vehicle of properly designed management information systems.

The concept of how a management information system operates in the context of a "total system" of the organization is depicted in Fig. 2-17. *Notice that the information flow for the information system is integrated with the four other resource flows (money, manpower, materials, and machines and facilities) to provide a system of planning and control for the entire organization.* Both the planning information and the data for the specific system provide inputs that are transformed by the processor into an output whose objective is to provide information for planning and control.

Sensors must be developed to measure the attributes of the output as well as the attributes of the transformation process. We will call these sensors *control*. A part of the control component contains management reports that track the status of the output relative to a predetermined standard of performance for the transformation process.

If the results being achieved in the organizational system (as opposed to the information system) do not conform to standard, this information is fed to the *planning analysis and control* component, which makes decisions regarding one or both of two actions: (1) alternative resource allocations are made as system imput changes or (2) modifications are made in the transformation process. Either or both of these decisions may be taken based upon decision rules or data stored in the central data base.

OPERATING SYSTEMS

MARKETING
- Order Entry
- Billing
- Sales Analysis
- Forecasting
- Distribution Statistics
- Demand History
- Stock Availability
- Sales Quota Control

PRODUCT DEVELOPMENT AND ENGINEERING
- Engineering Standards
- Cost Estimating
- Pricing
- Bill of Material
- R&D Control
- Project Planning and Control

OPERATIONS
- Requirements Planning
- Purchase Commitments
- Accounts Payable
- Inventory Costing
- Direct Labor Budgets
- Manufacturing Expense Control
- Capacity Planning
- Job Performance & Costs
- Variances

FINANCE & ACCOUNTING
- Financial Planning
- Cost Accounting
- General Ledger
- Asset Accounting
- Budgets
- Accounts Receivable
- Payroll

FINANCIAL REPORTING AND MANAGEMENT INFORMATION FOR PLANNING AND CONTROL

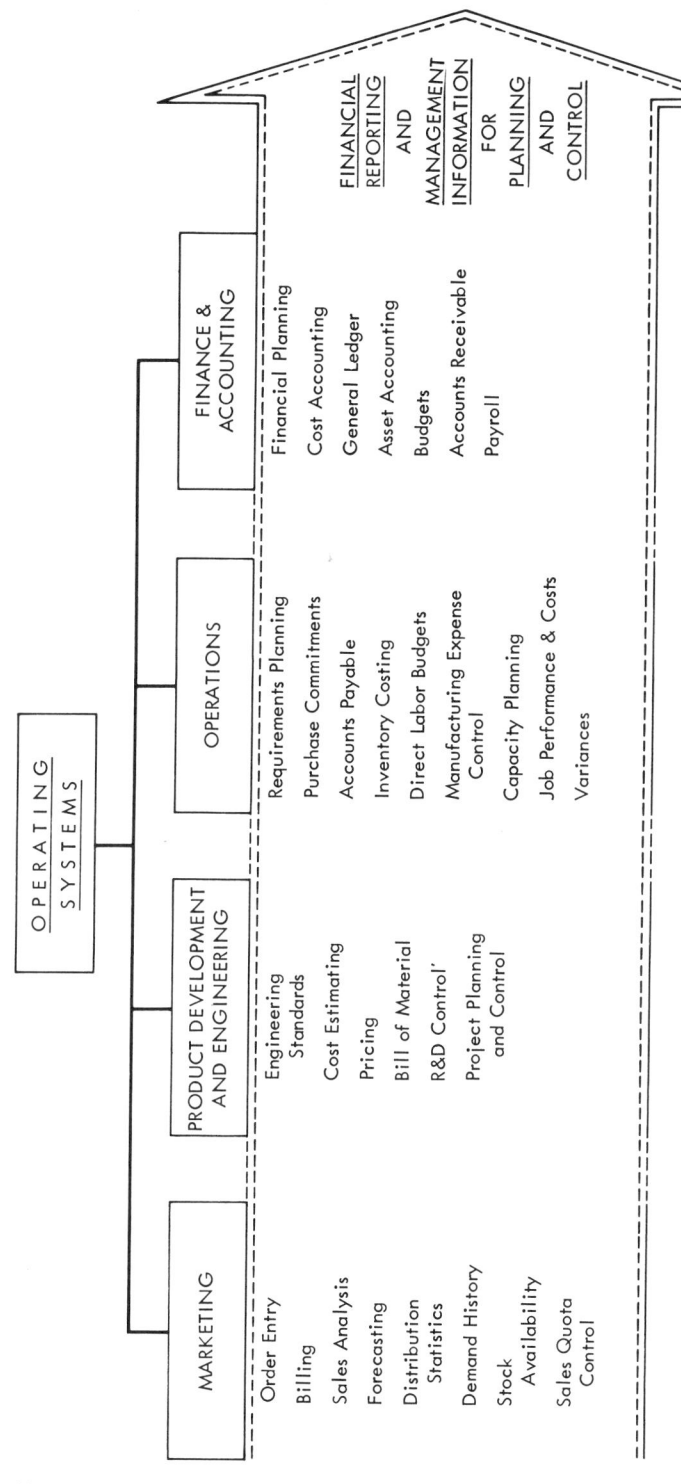

Fig. 2-15. Integration of Operating Systems with Accounting and Financial Information Systems

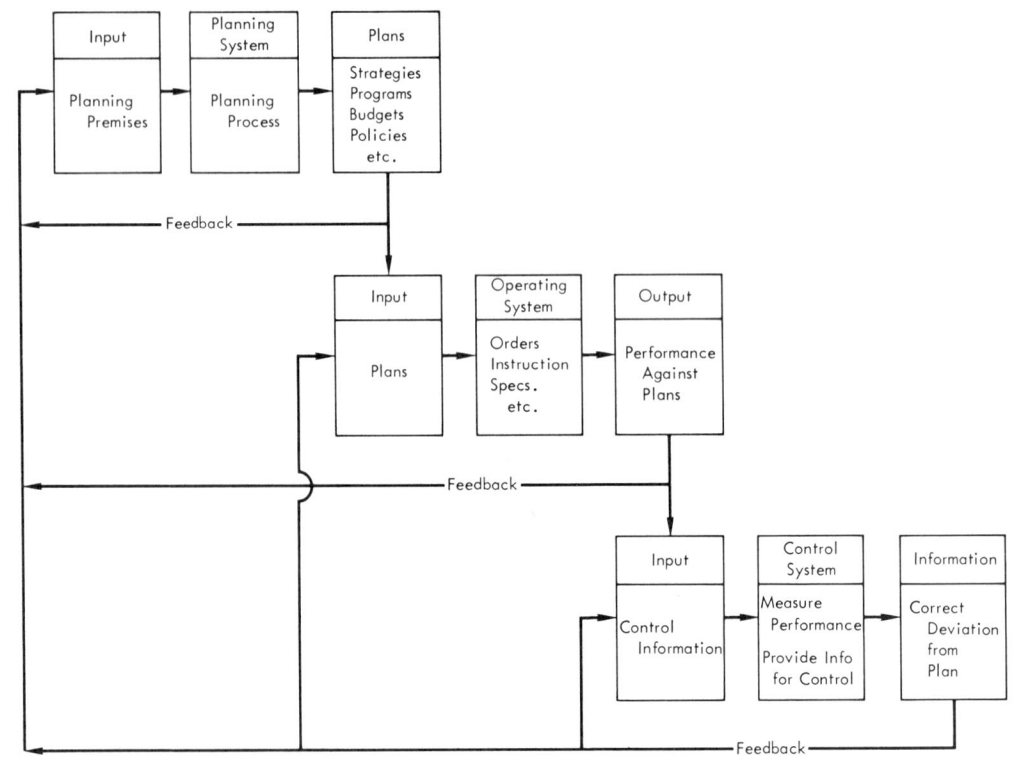

Fig. 2-16. Information Flow in the Management Process (Planning System, Operating System, Control System)

DISCUSSION QUESTIONS AND PROBLEMS

1. Who should the Internal Audit Staff report to for the following areas of responsibility?
   a. a total audit
   b. audit of accounts payable
   c. audit of EDP
   d. audit of Production Control
2. Encouraged by Secretary of Defense McNamara and the head of the U.S. Air Force, the armed forces changed substantially from a functional type of organization in the 1960s to a systems type, with headquarters and subordinate commands organized around "weapons systems" (e.g., Polaris, Nike, Apollo, Strategic Air Command). This concept provided for the design and development of a weapons system as well as for its ultimate operation and evaluation in the field over its life. A similar type of organization, providing

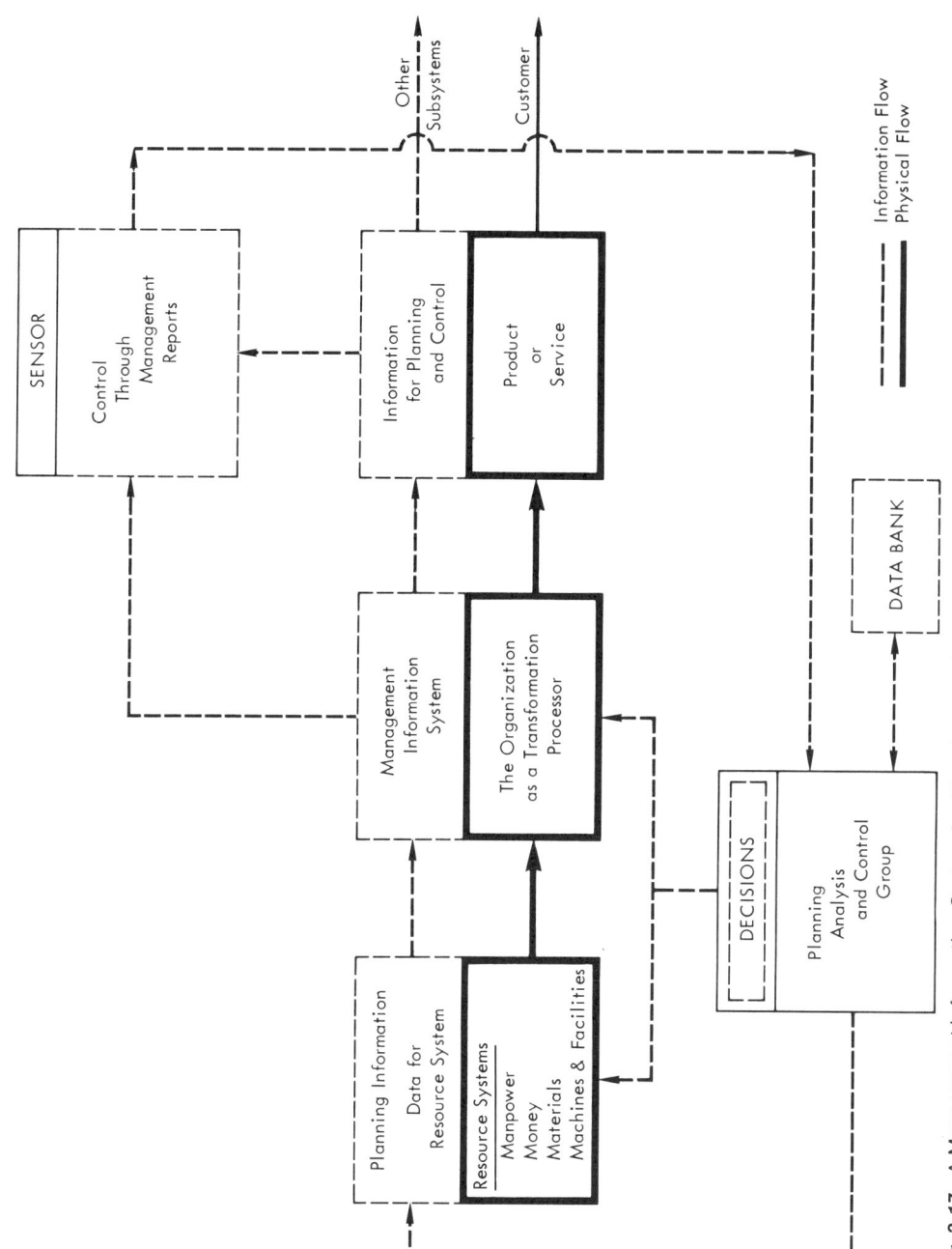

Fig. 2-17. A Management Information System for Planning and Control

for product managers, has been developed in recent years by several multiproduct companies.

Following the lead of the armed forces, most defense contractors have moved to the weapons system or project type of organization, partly to accommodate the interface between the contractor and the particular defense organization for which the system is being produced, and partly because experience has shown that such an organization is preferable to the old-style functional approach.

Questions:

a. Construct an organization chart showing how a functional type of organization might adapt to the weapons system or product approach.
b. How might the functions (e.g., finance, personnel, marketing, production) be affected by such an organizational change?
c. How might the functions of management (e.g., planning, organizing, controlling) be affected by such an organizational change?
d. Which type of organization would be preferable in Sears Roebuck? In General Electric? In IBM? In the Bell Telephone System? Support your answers.

3. In the 1960s and early 1970s, there was an upsurge in the growth of light electronic manufacturing in the South Florida area. Among the major firms that established plants there was United Aircraft, International Telephone and Telegraph, Radio Corporation of America, Westinghouse, and International Business Machines. Because transportation costs in these industries were such a small part of total costs, and because jet travel made sales and service available nationwide, plant location was largely independent of transportation factors. Additional arguments for selecting this area for plant location included availability of unskilled labor and lack of militant unions. However, the major advantage was the climate. For example, it was much easier to recruit urgently needed engineers and scientists for relocation to South Florida than to the Northeastern states.

In 1971, the executive committee of the Computer Components Corporation (CCC) decided that expansion to an additional plant was necessary and tentatively agreed to examine the West Palm Beach area for a location site. CCC, headquartered in Boston, was a manufacturer of custom computer components.

Questions:

a. In a systems approach to the plant location project, what would be the major parts of the system and how would these interact?

    b. How would information problems be compounded by location of the additional plant?
    c. If you were put in charge of the move, what information would you need?
    d. What "people" problems might arise from such a move?
 4. How would the accounting organization fit into the organizational chart for the following firms?
    a. Manufacturing
    b. Hospital
    c. Bank
    d. Insurance Company
    e. A widely diversified multidivision company
 5. Discuss the concept of "feedback" in the accounting information system and list at least four transactions that show elements of this concept. For example, what types of feedback would be involved in the generation of a purchase order?
 6. List and discuss the functions of a manager.

    If a bright young cost accountant wishes to become an effective manager, will his technical background be sufficient to prepare him for his desired management role? Discuss in terms of the functions of the two positions.
 7. Define the "systems approach."
    Discuss the six characteristics of the systems approach.
 8. Define strategic planning. Define strategy and list at least five elements to be considered in developing a strategy for the firm.
 9. How does the Accounting Information System aid in planning?
10. Will systems changes impact the organizational structure of the firm.
11. Discuss the accountant's role in the three steps involved in control.

Bibliography

BLUMENTHAL, SHERMAN C. *Management Information Systems: A Framework for Planning and Development,* Englewood Cliffs, N.J.: Prentice-Hall, 1969.

EMERY, JAMES C. *Organizational Planning and Control Systems,* New York: Macmillan, 1969.

LAWLER, EDWARD E., III, and JOHN GRANT RHODE. *Information and Control in Organizations,* Pacific Palisades, Cal.: Goodyear, 1976.

MURDICK, ROBERT G., "MIS for MBO," *Journal of Systems Management,* March, 1977.

SCHODERBEK, PETER P., ASTERIOS G. KEFALIS, and CHARLES G. SCHODERBEK. *Management Systems: Conceptual Considerations,* Dallas, Texas: Business Publications, 1975.

SIEGEL, PAUL. *Strategic Planning of Management Information Systems,* New York: Petrocelli, 1975.

THACKER, RONALD J., and RICHARD L. SMITH. *Modern Management Accounting,* Englewood Cliffs, N.J.: Prentice-Hall, 1977.

ACCOUNTING INFORMATION SYSTEMS FOR OPERATIONS

Preview:
This chapter outlines the chain of operations for businesses and related functions of the AIS.
–Banking systems
–Hospitals
–Cities
–Developing an A/R system

CHAPTER THREE

accounting and operating systems

Closely Related Chapters:

Chapter 3–Management needs
Chapter 4–Build in controls
Chapter 5–Reporting requirements
Chapter 7–Corporate decisions
Chapter 12–Data base requirements

Although management is concerned first with aggregate and long-range planning before disaggregating to accounting and operating systems, we will take the reverse approach. We have used this approach in order to go from the specific to the general.

In this chapter we will describe accounting and operating systems. We continue in the next chapter with a discussion of transactions and the control of them. We next present the output reports of the AIS. We then proceed to the use of AIS for strategic problems. If this book were addressed to experts in systems, we would take just the opposite approach. Since this is a text for students who are building their knowledge block upon block, a discussion of strategy would be meaningless to such students unfamiliar with the underlying accounting and operating systems.

FUNDAMENTAL OPERATIONS OF ORGANIZATIONS

Organizations in society include a wide range of basic missions. Business firms—that is, profit-seeking firms—may engage in such activities as:

- Agriculture
- Extraction of resources from the environment
- Construction
- Manufacturing
- Transportation services
- Communication services
- Utility services
- Wholesale and retail trade

Finance, insurance, and real estate
Services of many kinds, such as land development, health care, consulting, entertainment, advertising agencies, and so on

In addition to business organizations, there are not-for-profit organizations (such as research labs, unions, and foundations) and municipal, state, and federal agencies.

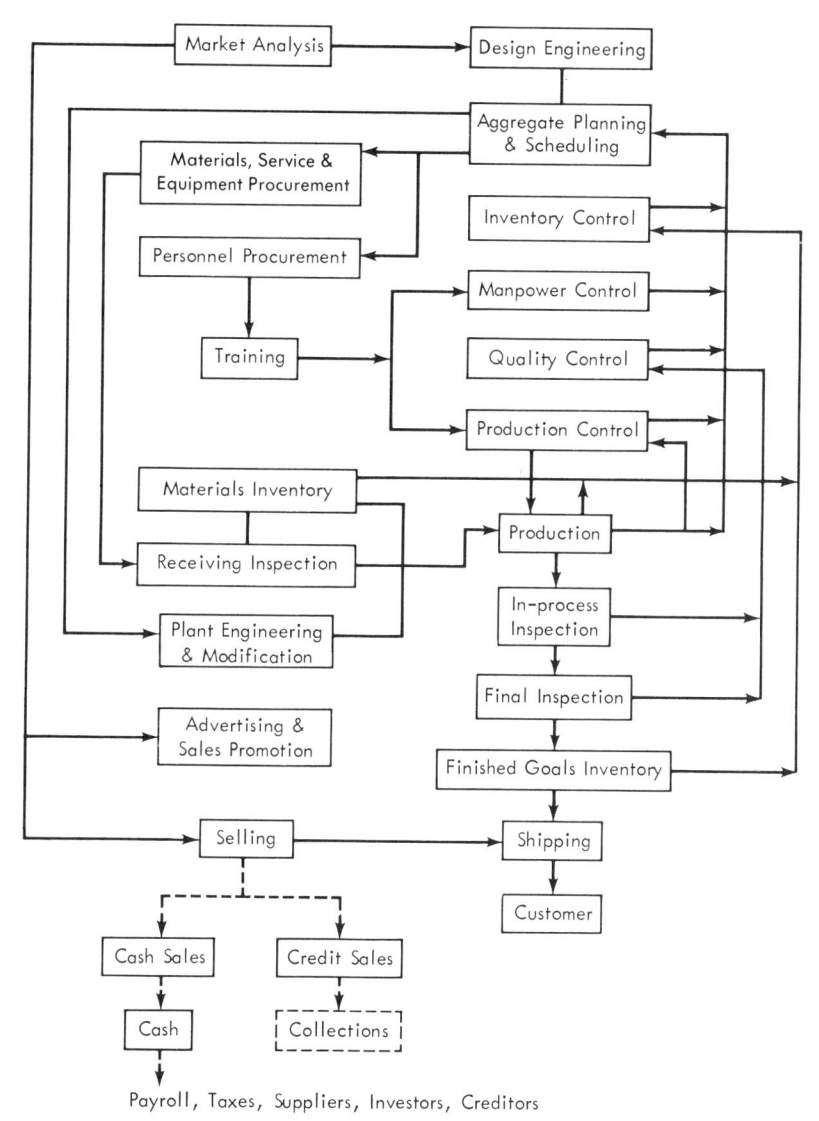

Fig. 3-1. Manufacturing Company Operating System (See text discussion on p. 81)

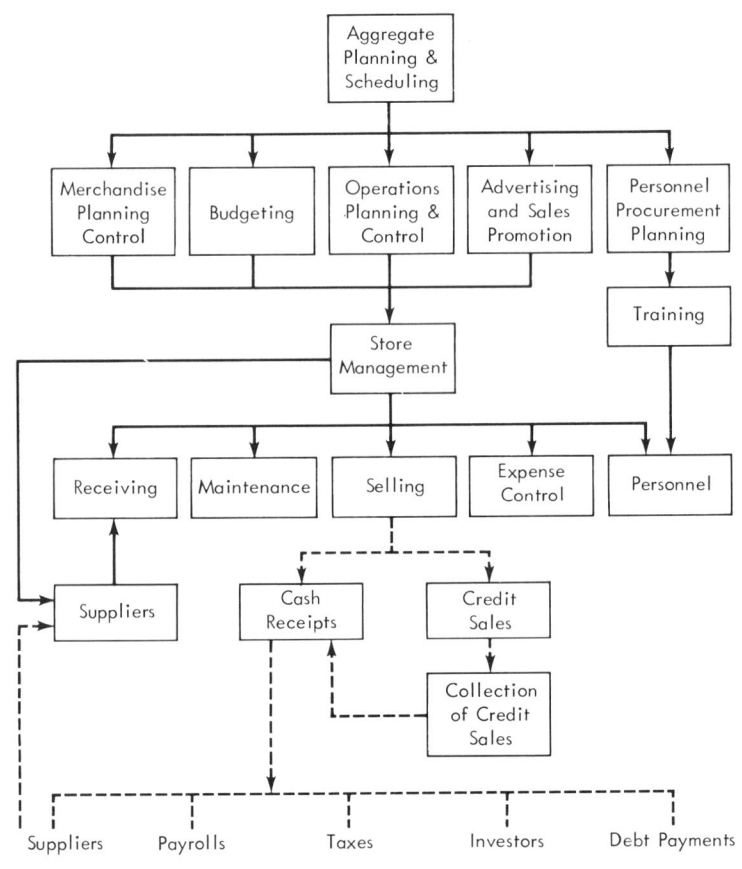

Fig. 3-2. Operations Flowchart For a Department Store (See text discussion on p. 81)

Since we cannot cover all of these organizations, we will focus primarily on manufacturing firms with examples from retailing, banking, and health care. The concepts from manufacturing may be converted to all other types or organizations, but such analogies may not be readily apparent. The sample applications of AIS in other types of organizations will provide helpful bridges.

Fundamental Chain of Operations

Each type of organization has a fundamental chain of operations which characterizes the mission of the organization. Below we have listed these chains for the various types of organizations:

80

Accounting and Operating Systems

ACTIVITY CHAINS	TYPICAL ORGANIZATIONS
Design a service * * Provide the service	Not-for-profit and government agencies
Design * * Sell * * Provide the service	Service companies and some not-for-profit organizations
Purchase * * Store * * Sell * * (Ship)	Retail and wholesale firms, some not-for-profit organizations
Sell * * Design * * Purchase * * Store * * Manufacture * * Store * * Ship	Custom manufacturers, shipbuilders, military defense components, manufacturers, machine tool manufacturers
Design * * Purchase * * Store * * Manufacture * * Store * * Sell * * Ship	Mass production and batch production; manufacturers of consumer goods

Functional System Models of Organizations

Within any particular type of organization, the above operations do not occur in sequence, but rather as a complex network of interrelated activities. An expansion for a manufacturing firm is shown in Fig. 3-1. For a retailing organization, see Fig. 3-2. Then for comparison with a bank and a hospital, see Figs. 3-3 and 3-4.

ACCOUNTING SYSTEMS

We define the AIS as the system that authorizes and executes transactions, records expenses, disbursements, and receipts in the day-to-day operation of the business. The various subsystems of the AIS provide control and yield data from which managerial planning, controlling, and decision-making reports are developed. Although variations appear, many organizations have the same basic accounting subsystems:

   Accounts receivable
   Accounts payable
   Supplies, inventory control, and purchasing
   Payroll, personnel, and labor costing
   Fixed asset/property accounting
   Cash control and investment
   General ledger
   Auditing

Bank Services Performed	BANK OPERATIONS

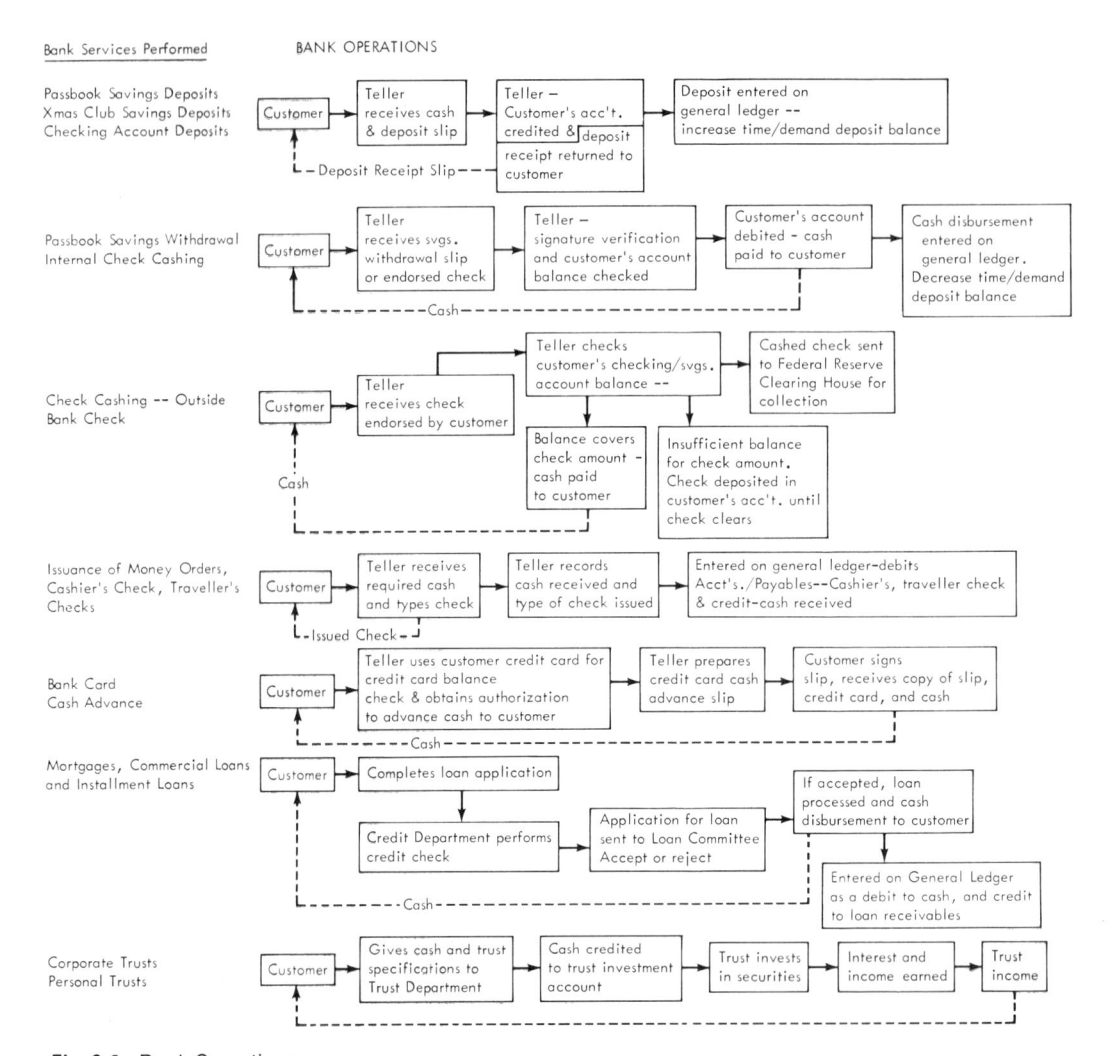

Passbook Savings Deposits
Xmas Club Savings Deposits
Checking Account Deposits
→ Customer → Teller receives cash & deposit slip → Teller — Customer's acc't. credited & deposit receipt returned to customer → Deposit entered on general ledger -- increase time/demand deposit balance
└ — Deposit Receipt Slip — —

Passbook Savings Withdrawal
Internal Check Cashing
→ Customer → Teller receives svgs. withdrawal slip or endorsed check → Teller — signature verification and customer's account balance checked → Customer's account debited - cash paid to customer → Cash disbursement entered on general ledger. Decrease time/demand deposit balance
└ — — — Cash — — —

Check Cashing -- Outside Bank Check
→ Customer → Teller receives check endorsed by customer → Teller checks customer's checking/svgs. account balance --
  → Balance covers check amount - cash paid to customer
  → Insufficient balance for check amount. Check deposited in customer's acc't. until check clears → Cashed check sent to Federal Reserve Clearing House for collection
└ — Cash — —

Issuance of Money Orders, Cashier's Check, Traveller's Checks
→ Customer → Teller receives required cash and types check → Teller records cash received and type of check issued → Entered on general ledger-debits Acct's./Payables--Cashier's, traveller check & credit-cash received
└ — Issued Check — ┘

Bank Card Cash Advance
→ Customer → Teller uses customer credit card for credit card balance check & obtains authorization to advance cash to customer → Teller prepares credit card cash advance slip → Customer signs slip, receives copy of slip, credit card, and cash
└ — — — Cash — — —

Mortgages, Commercial Loans and Installment Loans
→ Customer → Completes loan application → Credit Department performs credit check → Application for loan sent to Loan Committee Accept or reject → If accepted, loan processed and cash disbursement to customer → Entered on General Ledger as a debit to cash, and credit to loan receivables
└ — — — — Cash — — —

Corporate Trusts
Personal Trusts
→ Customer → Gives cash and trust specifications to Trust Department → Cash credited to trust investment account → Trust invests in securities → Interest and income earned → Trust income

Fig. 3-3. Bank Operations

These subsystems are outlined by the flowcharts in Fig. 3-5, except for auditing. Auditing will be studied in Chapter 14.

Figure 3-5 presents these subsystems as distinct elements of the total AIS. However, it is important to note that these subsystems are totally integrated in a well-designed AIS. Transactions flow through the AIS in a cyclical pattern, usually crossing several departmental lines between the time a transaction is authorized and when it is finally recorded. For example, the "revenue cycle" of transactions would include sales, accounts receivable, shipping, and cash receipt. The "pur-

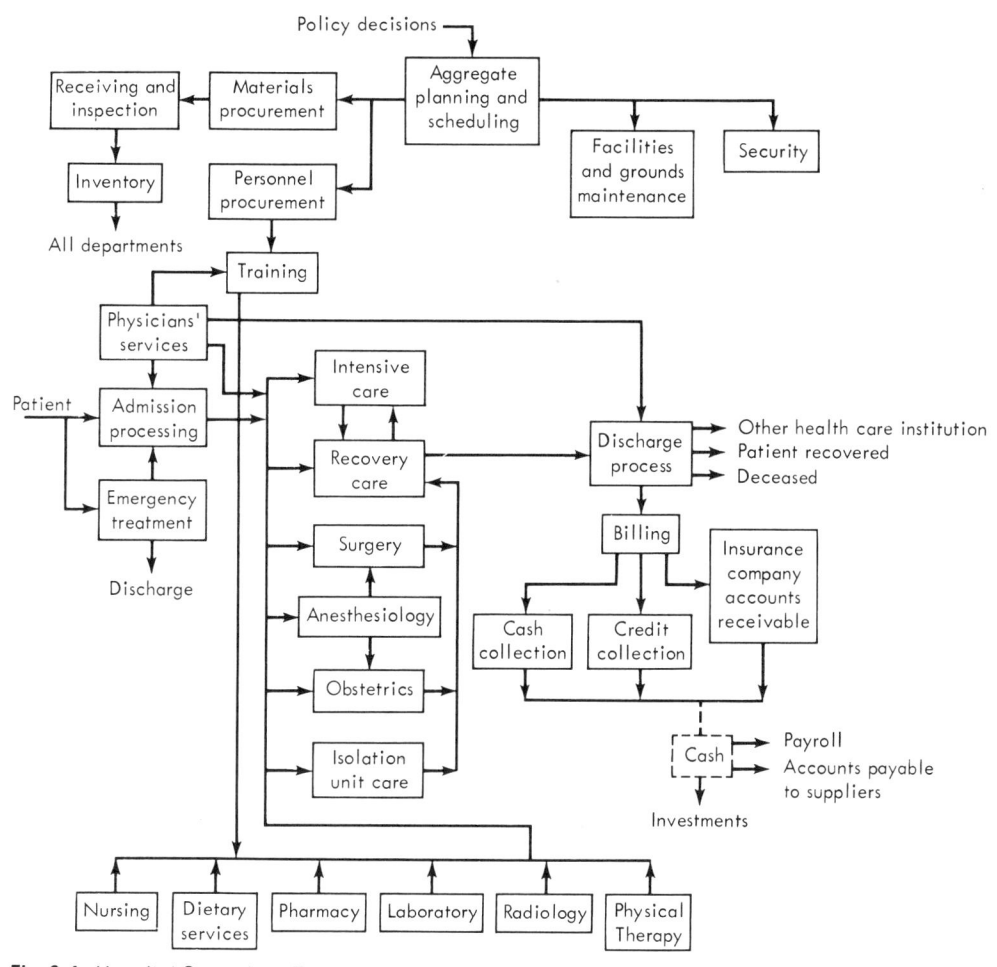

Fig. 3-4. Hospital Operations Flowchart

chasing cycle" would include purchasing, receiving, accounts payable, and cash disbursement. The relationship between the accounting and operating systems will be discussed later in the chapter.

For a hospital, we should add the claims preparation system. This system is concerned with gathering data for preparation of claims to be presented to insurance companies. The insurance companies have a different accounting system, the claims processing system, for responding to claims.

In banks and savings and loan companies, the basic commodity is money. Therefore, the principal systems are accounting systems. Other types of systems such as building maintenance, marketing, and perhaps

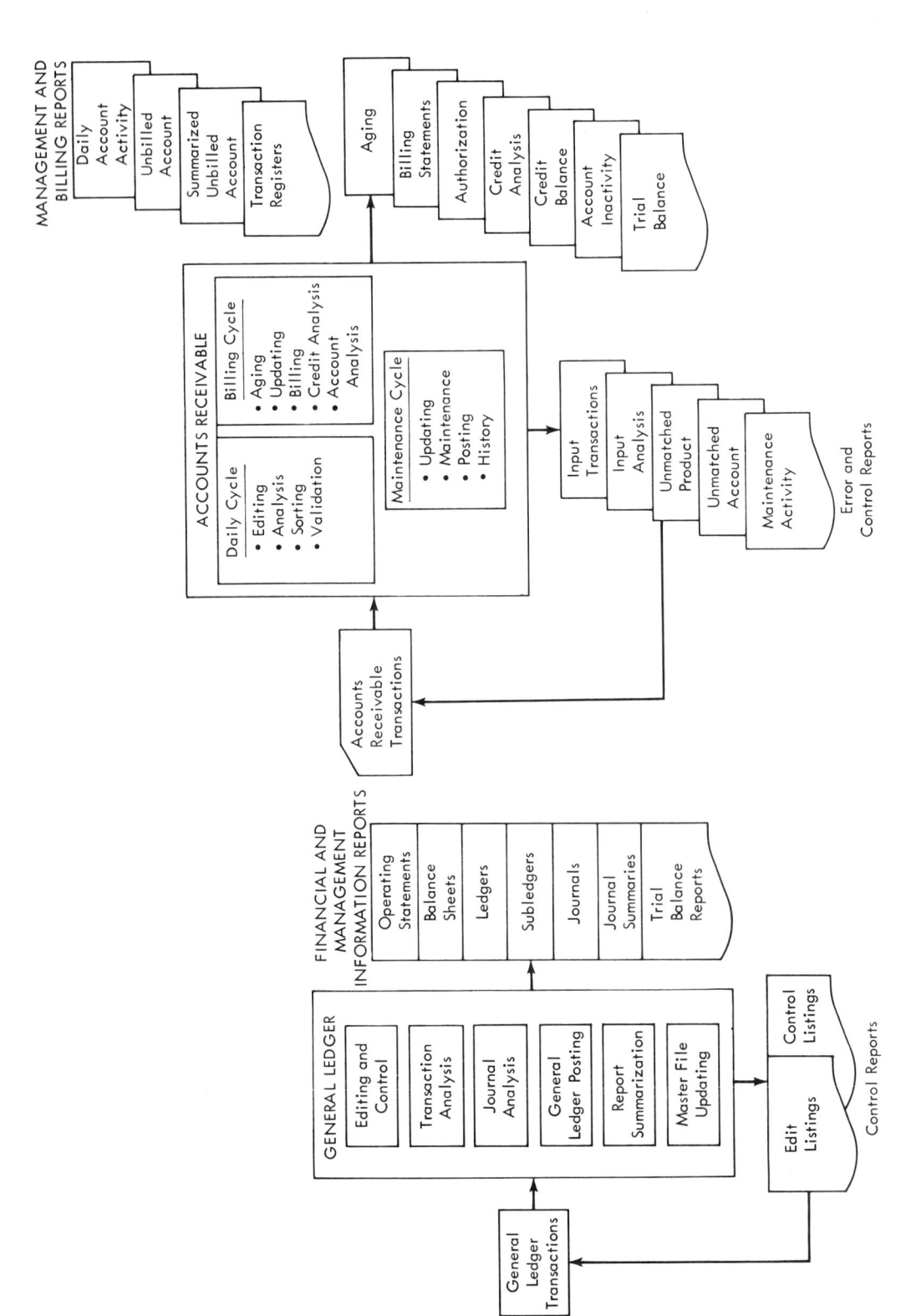

MANAGEMENT AND BILLING REPORTS

- Daily Account Activity
- Unbilled Account
- Summarized Unbilled Account
- Transaction Registers

- Aging
- Billing Statements
- Authorization
- Credit Analysis
- Credit Balance
- Account Inactivity
- Trial Balance

ACCOUNTS RECEIVABLE

Daily Cycle
- Editing
- Analysis
- Sorting
- Validation

Billing Cycle
- Aging
- Updating
- Billing
- Credit Analysis
- Account Analysis

Maintenance Cycle
- Updating
- Maintenance
- Posting
- History

Error and Control Reports
- Input Transactions
- Input Analysis
- Unmatched Product
- Unmatched Account
- Maintenance Activity

Accounts Receivable Transactions

FINANCIAL AND MANAGEMENT INFORMATION REPORTS

- Operating Statements
- Balance Sheets
- Ledgers
- Subledgers
- Journals
- Journal Summaries
- Trial Balance Reports

GENERAL LEDGER

- Editing and Control
- Transaction Analysis
- Journal Analysis
- General Ledger Posting
- Report Summarization
- Master File Updating

Control Reports
- Edit Listings
- Control Listings

General Ledger Transactions

84

Fig. 3-5. The Accounting Functions

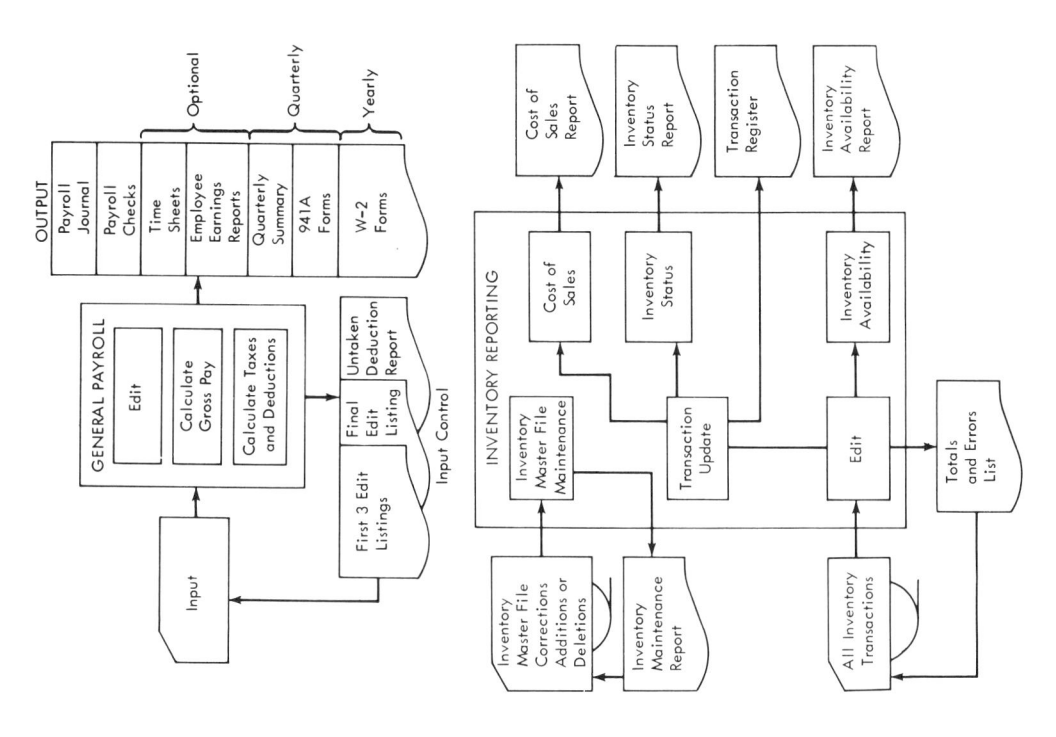

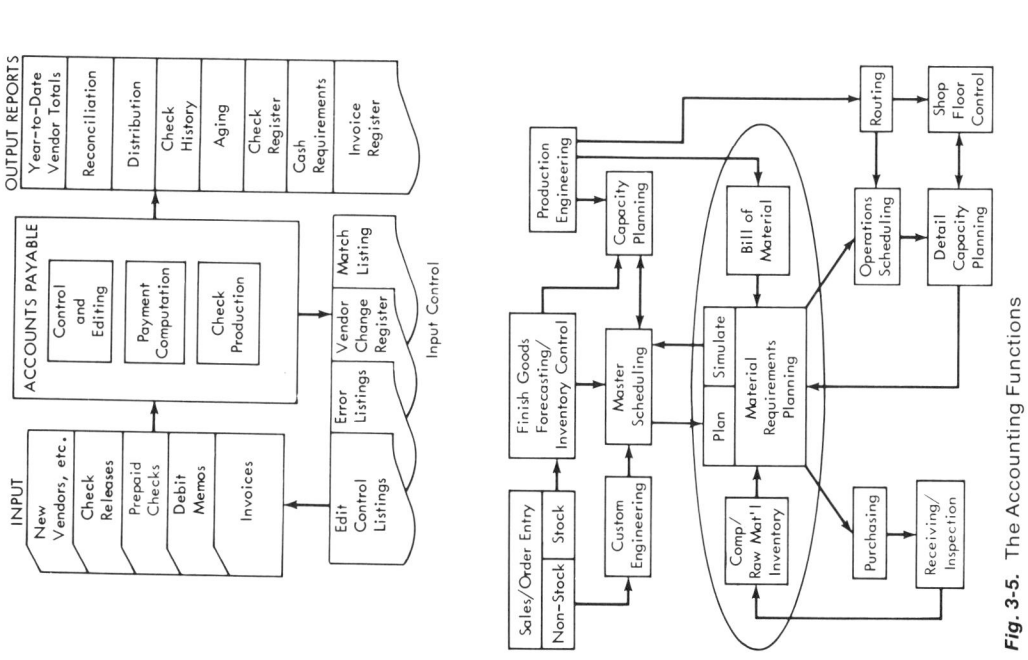

Source: W. W. McKee, "Small Businesses Can Be Computerized," *Management Accounting,* April 1972.

data processing are supporting systems. Figure 3-3 shows the flowcharts for the accounting systems of a typical bank.

There are enough differences in municipal accounting systems to include a flowchart for such. We have done this in Fig. 3-6.

Detailing a System (Accounts Receivable)

Detailing a particular accounting system requires that we specify the organizational structure for staffing purposes, the office layout, the work flow, a narrative description of the system, the equipment used, the files and their contents, flowcharts of information flow, software programs, and output reports.

The heart of this type of description deals with information flows and files. Software International of Andover, Massachusetts, is one of a number of companies that have developed software programs for accounting systems. Software International has kindly allowed us to include a portion of their extensive description of their Accounts Receivable system as follows.

In support of the narrative description, three flowcharts and a table of application programs are shown in Figs. 3-7 through 3-9 and Table 3-1.

MMS ACCOUNTS RECEIVABLE SYSTEM SYSTEMS NARRATIVE[1]

The MMS Accounts Receivable System has three basic cycles. They are: a posting cycle; an "as required" cycle; and a period ending cycle.

During the posting cycle, invoices, memos, adjustments, transfers, cash, and maintenance transactions are validated and processed by the system producing various audit, control and exception reports. The transaction source can be from card, tape or disk depending upon the environment. The system contains several audit and control features to provide complete control of transactions processed during the cycle.

In the edit phase, due dates, discount dates, and discount amounts can be calculated based upon user specified terms if not supplied by the originating source. All necessary editing is performed on each transac-

[1]Courtesy of Software International. *Accounts Receivable System* (Andover, Mass.: Software International, 1976).

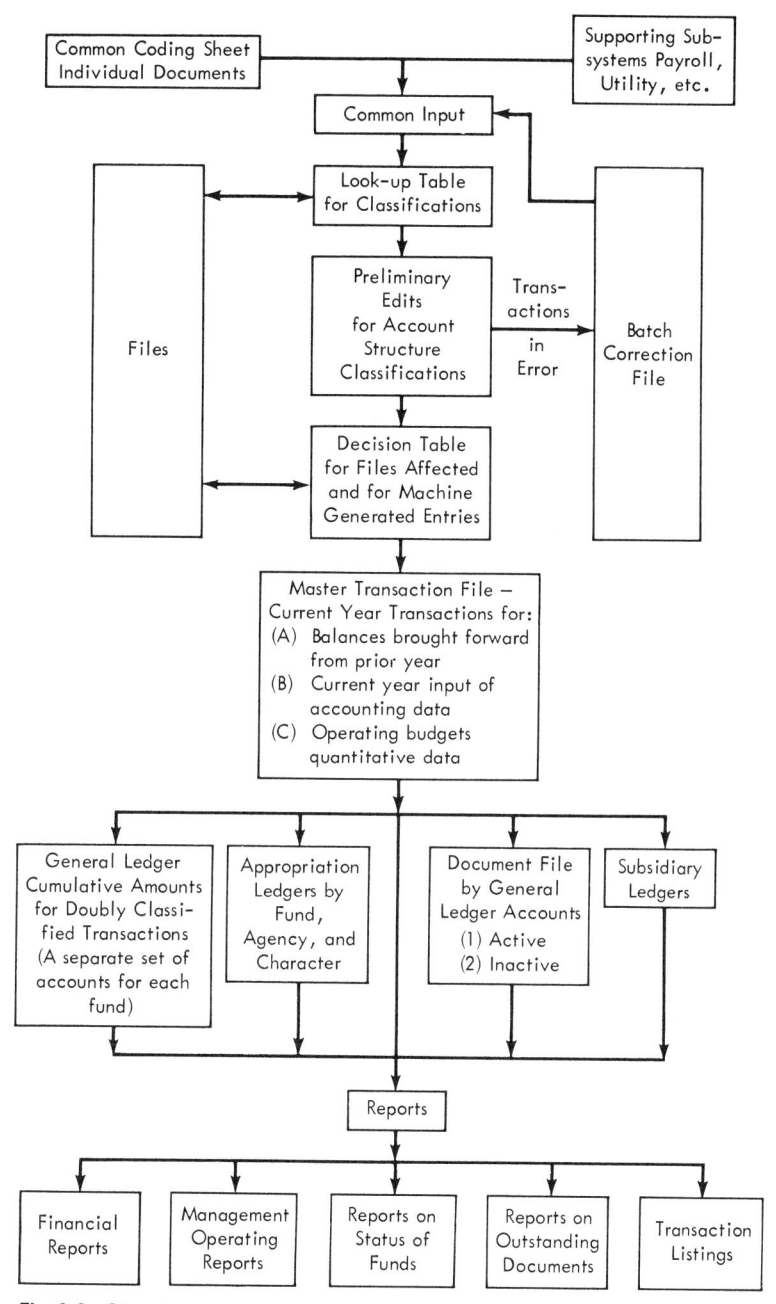

Fig. 3-6. City of Fort Lauderdale: Overview of the Computerized System

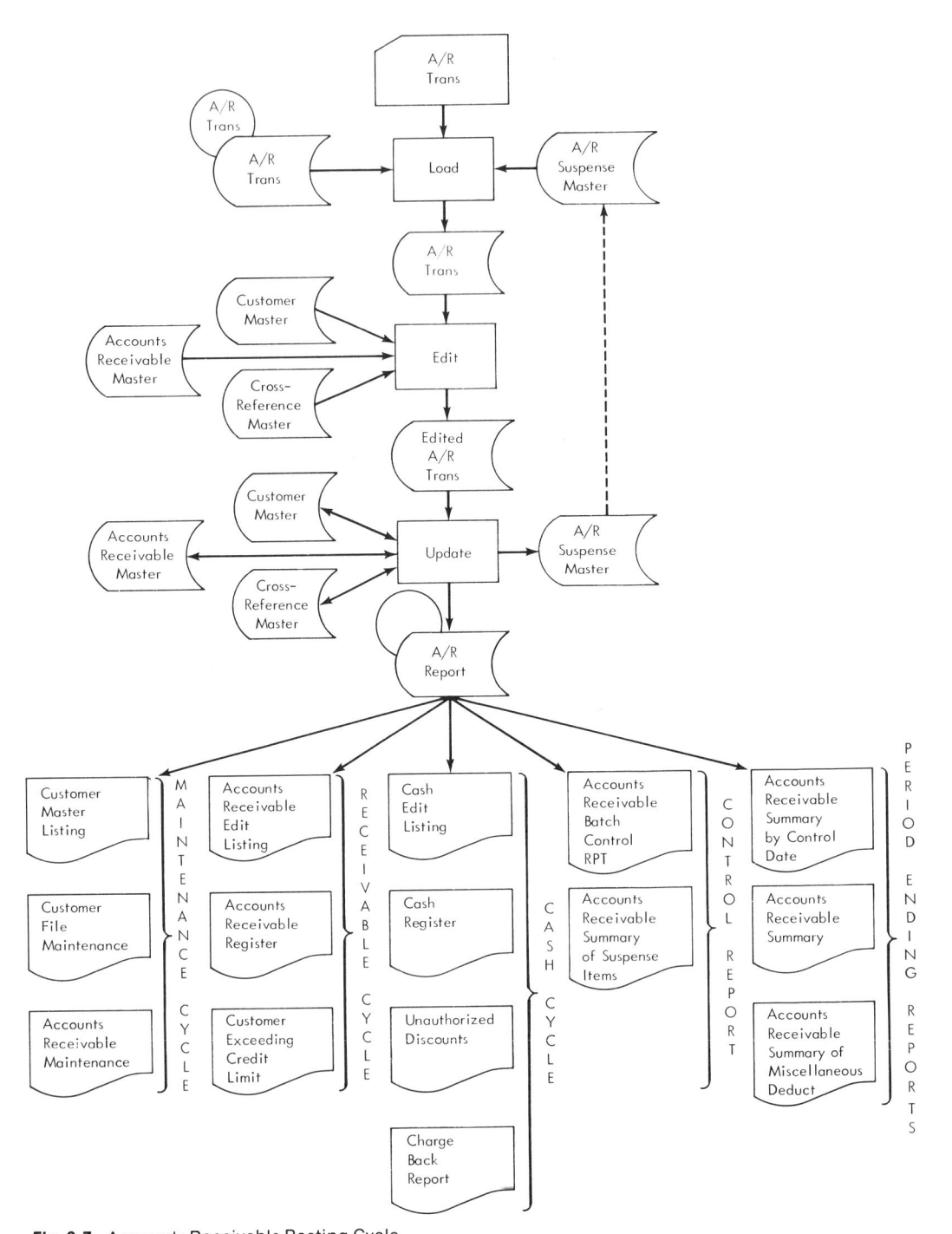

Fig. 3-7. Accounts Receivable Posting Cycle

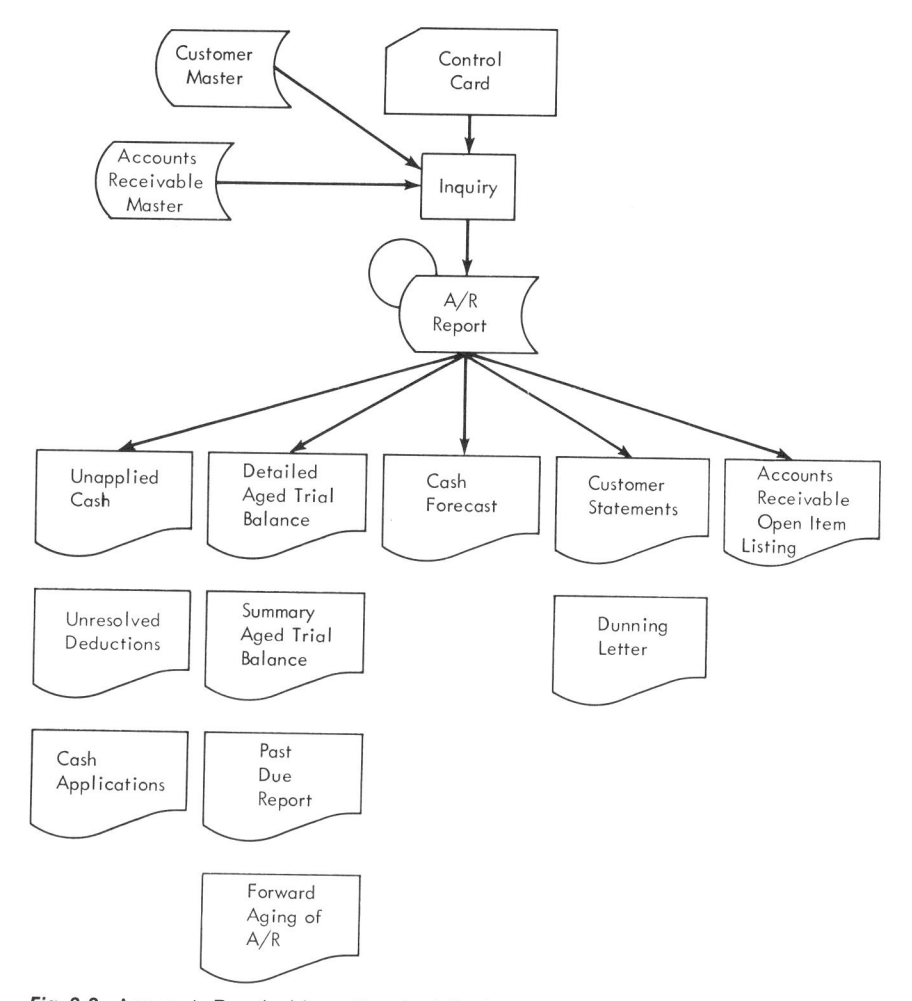

Fig. 3-8. Accounts Receivable as Required Cycle

tion to insure that only transactions containing valid data are posted by the system. For example, invoices or memos containing invalid transaction numbers, or improper customer numbers, or invalid dates and amounts will cause the transaction to be rejected. Individual transactions or entire batches containing errors can be retained by the system on a suspense file if desired, until corrective action is taken.

During the update phase, a record for each invoice, memo and cash transaction (accepted by the edit) will be added to the Accounts Receivable Master. Also, the accounts receivable balance, sales, or remittance history is updated for the appropriate account on the Customer Master. A corresponding entry is made to the Cross-Reference Master for each record added to the Accounts Receivable Master. The Cross-

Reference Master provides the edit phase with an efficient vehicle to detect duplicate invoice or memo numbers and supply cash transactions with missing customer numbers when just the invoice number has been provided. Specific transactions or all transactions can be transferred between accounts during the cycle. Charge-back transactions can automatically be generated for short-payments, over-payments, and service charges if desired.

Exception reports are generated during the report phase when unearned discounts, unauthorized deductions, service charges, and credit limit exceeded conditions are detected. The Accounts Receivable Register and Cash Register provide the user with a detailed audit trail of

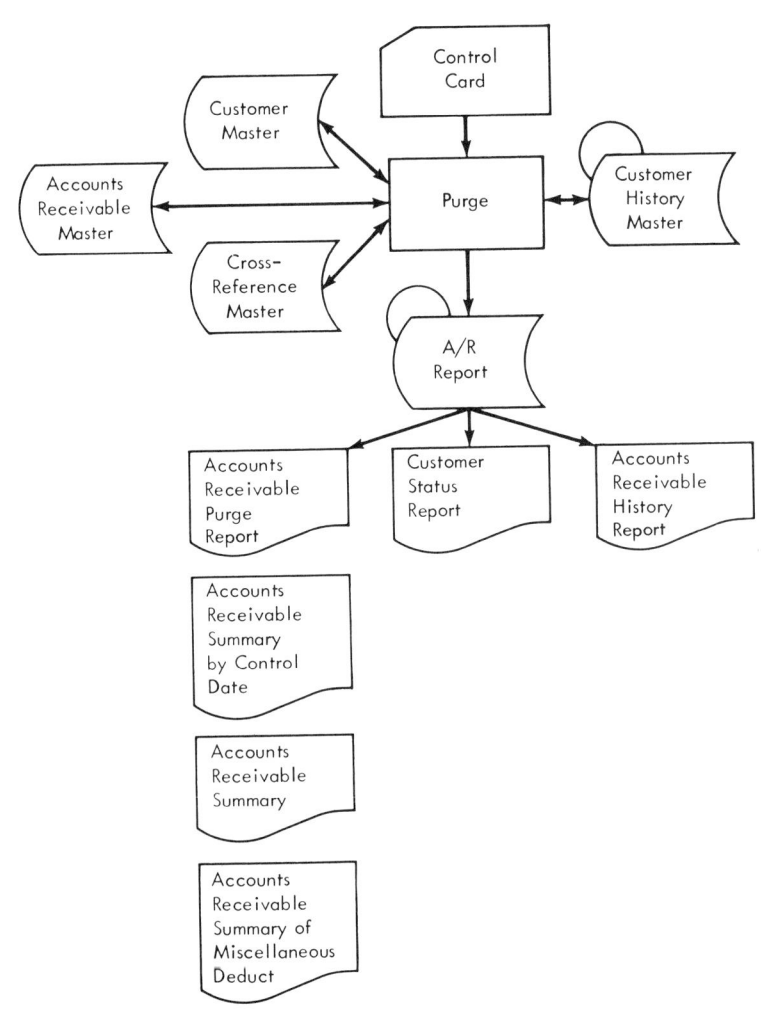

Fig. 3-9. Accounts Receivable Period Ending Cycle

Table 3-1. Program Categories

1. *File Creation Cycle*
   A. Customer Master
   B. Accounts Receivable
   C. Cross-Reference Master
2. *Customer File Maintenance Cycle*
   A. Customer Maintenance Transaction Load
   B. Customer File Maintenance
   C. Print Customer File Maintenance Report
   D. Print Customer File Maintenance Report
   E. Reorganize Customer Master
3. *Posting Cycle*
   A. Load Accounts Receivable Transactions
   B. Accounts Receivable Batch Editing
   C. Edit Accounts Receivable Transactions
   D. Update Accounts Receivable Transactions
   E. Update Transfer Transactions
   F. Distribute Accounts Receivable Transactions
   G. Recreate Cross-Reference Master
   H. Print Accounts Receivable Maintenance Report
   I. Print Accounts Receivable Edit Listing
   J. Print Accounts Receivable Register
   K. Print Customer Exceeding Credit Limit Report
   L. Print Cash Edit Listing
   M. Print Cash Register
   N. Print Unauthorized Discount Book
   O. Print Charge Back Report
   P. Print Accounts Receivable Batch Control Report
   Q. Print Accounts Receivable Summary of Suspense Items
4. *Backup and Restore Cycle*
   A. Backup Accounts Receivable Master
   B. Restore Accounts Receivable Master
5. *As Required Cycle*
   A. Accounts Receivable Inquiry
   B. Create Accounts Receivable Master Report File
   C. Print Unapplied Cash Listing
   D. Print Unresolved Deductions Listing
   E. Print Cash Application Document
   F. Print Detailed Aged Trial Balance Report
   G. Print Summary Aged Trial Balance Report
   H. Print Accounts Receivable Past Due Report
   I. Print Forward Aging of Accounts Receivable Report
   J. Print Cash Forecast
   K. Print Customer Statements
   L. Print Dunning Letter
   M. Print Accounts Receivable Open Item Listing
6. *Period Ending Cycle*
   A. Strip Accounts Receivable Summary Control Records
   B. Print Accounts Receivable Summary by Control Date Report
   C. Print Accounts Receivable Summary Report
   D. Print Accounts Receivable Summary of Miscellaneous Deductions
   E. Strip Accounts Receivable Records
   F. Purge Accounts Receivable File
   G. Print Accounts Receivable Purge Report
   H. Update Accounts Receivable Detail History
   I. Print Accounts Receivable History Report
   J. Update Customer Accounts Receivable Summary History
   K. Print Customer Status Report

transactions posted by the system. Reports such as the Accounts Receivable Maintenance, Accounts Receivable Edit, Accounts Receivable Batch Control Report, and Accounts Receivable Summary of Suspense Items reflect the transaction control, and highlight conditions requiring corrective action.

During the "as required" cycle, reports can be produced for the entire Accounts Receivable File or can be run selectively through inquiry control reflecting the current status of each account. The reports are normally generated at period end, but as the cycle name implies, can be requested based upon the user's requirements. Detailed and Summary Aged Trial Balance Reports are produced with flexible aging capability through seven aging periods. If desired, a Past Due Aged Trial Balance and a Forward Aging of the Accounts Receivables can be printed. Reports such as the Unapplied Cash Listing, Unresolved Deduction Listing, Customers Exceeding Credit Limit, Unauthorized Discount, and Accounts Receivable Open Item Listing will highlight the exception conditions. The cycle provides a Cash Application Document for posting cash and a Cash Forecast Report projecting how much and when cash can be expected to be received. Statements and/or dunning letters can be issued to customers on an exception basis.

The system at period end produces a report by control date and a report by department or division reflecting summary totals for each type of Accounts Receivable transaction processed for the period. Also, a summary of allowed deductions by type of deduction is reported. The main function of the cycle is to purge the Accounts Receivable Master of records containing a zero balance amount due, because of payment or adjustment entries. The Accounts Receivable Purge Report provides an audit trail of records removed by the system. All purged records are retained on a Detailed History File under user control and can be printed on the Accounts Receivable History Report if desired. In the final phase of the cycle, a Customer Status Report can be generated and history data on the Customer Master will be transferred to the Customer Summary History File as required.

Major Features of MMS Accounts Receivable System

1. *Detailed and Summary Audit Trails*
   The Accounts Receivable Register and Cash Register provide the user with a detailed audit trail of transactions posted by the system. The Accounts Receivable Purge Report is a detailed listing of transactions removed by the system. The Accounts Receivable Edit and Cash Edit indicate input error conditions requiring corrective action. Period end summary reports include totals for each transaction type posted by control date.

2. *Complete Batch Control and Validation of Input*

   All necessary editing is performed on each transaction. Individual transactions or entire batches containing errors may be held in suspense until corrective action is taken. The Batch Control Report provides an analysis of the posting cycle, indicating out of balance and error conditions.

3. *Customer Historical Analysis Available in Detail or Summary Form*

   The Accounts Receivable History Report provides the user with a detailed list of all transactions past and present to answer customer inquiries. A summary of customer activity is provided on the Customer Status Report giving management the tools necessary for credit analysis.

4. *Open Item and Balance Forward Methods are Used*

   Customers requiring Open Item or Balance Forward Processing can be inter-mixed.

5. *Statements and Dunning Letters Produced Selectively*

   The above reports and other period end reports can be generated for the entire Accounts Receivable File or selectively through inquiry or exception control.

6. *Customer Records are Constantly Up To Date and Available for Inquiry*

   All Accounts Receivable transactions are automatically posted to the Customer Master File when added to the Accounts Receivable File. Therefore, the Customer Master File contains current information if inquiry is desired.

7. *Cash Application Document*

   This document can be used by the Accounts Receivable Department for the application of cash, eliminating the laborious task of preparing a keypunch form.

8. *Multi-Company Capability*

   The system has the ability to report, control, and maintain Accounts Receivable entries for multiple companies within the same file.

9. *Automatic Discount and Due Date Calculations If Required*

   The system will automatically calculate discount amount, discount date, and payment due dates based upon term codes on the input document or Customer Master File. The user may override the standard terms by entering the information on the invoice.

10. *Exception Reports Highlight Customer Abuses*

    Exception reports are produced for unauthorized deductions, unearned discounts, and credit limit violations detected by the system during the posting cycle.

11. *Automatic Charge-Back Feature*

    The system will automatically generate charge-back transactions on the Accounts Receivable File for short-payments and over-payments if desired. The system can also automatically create penalty or service charges for late payments.

12. *Statements are Customized to User's Requirements*

    Customer Statements are tailored to the specifications of the user with aging totals and special messages provided.

13. *Flexible Aging Capability*
    The system allows the user to age all outstanding Accounts Receivable transactions through seven aging periods on the Detailed and Summary Aged Trial Balance Report. Aging can reflect individual company requirements.
14. *Cash Projection*
    The Cash Forecast Report provides management with a summary report indicating how much and when cash can be expected based upon individual customer payment habits.
15. *On-Line Cash Application and Credit Inquiry (Optional Feature)*
    The system is capable of providing the user with on-line cash application and customer status inquiry for credit analysis. Payments, when submitted on-line, will be balanced for both batch and deposit totals. They will then be retained on a remittance file until the items to be paid have been identified or the remittance considered as payment on account. Once identification has been established, corresponding transactions for the remittance will be generated as input to the accounts receivable posting cycle utilizing the system's audit and control features. The credit inquiring function can provide the user with an up-to-date summary or detailed status of each account requested. Complete credit information can be displayed similar to that reflected by the Customer Status Report.

Master File Descriptions

The *Accounts Receivable Master File* will contain one record for each invoice, memo, adjustment, and cash transaction posted by the system. All transactions pertaining to a customer will be linked to the customer master providing an unlimited number of transactions per customer. The records in this file will contain the following data fields:

1. Customer number
2. Date of transaction
3. Invoice, credit memo, or debit memo number
4. Transaction type
5. Terms code
6. Memo type
7. 'As of' date
8. Discount date
9. Date transaction is due
10. Amount subject to discount
11. Authorized discount amount
12. Apply to number

Accounting and Operating Systems

13. Last batch number posted
14. Date last activity
15. Net amount due
16. Remittance data
    A. Date of last remittance
    B. Last remittance number
    C. Remittance amount
    D. Discount amount taken
    E. Deduction amount allowed
    F. Type of deduction
17. 12 optional fields available for information or control

The *Customer Master File* will contain one master record for each customer. The record contains a disk address that provides linkage to all associated transactions on the Accounts Receivable File. The record may contain the following data fields.

1. Customer number
2. Customer name
3. Customer address
4. Zip code
5. Terms code
6. D & B code
7. Duns Number
8. Credit Limit
9. High Balance
10. Current accounts receivable balance
11. Date customer record established
12. Date last activity
13. Last remittance data
    A. Date
    B. Number
    C. Amount
14. Payment History
    A. Number of payments
    B. Average number of days outstanding
    C. Number of late payments
    D. Maximum number of days late
    E. Number of discounts taken
    F. Discount amount taken
    G. Number of unearned discounts taken
    H. Unearned discount amount taken
    I. Number of deductions taken
    J. Deduction amount taken
    K. Number of payments

L. Payment amount received
   M. Interest paid
   N. Amount written-off
15. Sales & Returns History
   A. Month to date
   B. Year to date
   C. Last year
   D. Date last sale
16. Accounts Receivable Status
   A. Current amount
   B. Past due amount
   C. Open credit amount
17. Report Control
   A. Statement account number
   B. Statement code
   C. Customer short name
   D. Dunning code
   E. Aging override code
18. 19 optional fields available for information or control data

The *Cross-Reference Master File* will contain one record for each record on the Accounts Receivable Master File. The records contain the transaction number, transaction type, customer number, and disk address of the corresponding accounts receivable record. The file is used to maintain invoice integrity and to enhance the application of cash.

The *Accounts Receivable Transaction File* is used to enter invoices, memos, and adjustment transactions into the accounts receivable system via tape or disk from various sources such as order entry and billing systems. Optional data fields are available in the record for information and control as determined by the user.

RELATIONSHIPS BETWEEN ACCOUNTING AND OPERATING SYSTEMS

Organizations have many operating systems, that is, systems designed to achieve some objectives of the organization. Some objectives and related systems fall within organizational components. For example, the sales promotional system falls within the marketing organization and the engineering drawing systems fall within the engineering organization.

The majority of systems in today's complex organization, however, tend to cut across organizational lines. That is, people from different organizations participate in the functioning of the system. Consider the

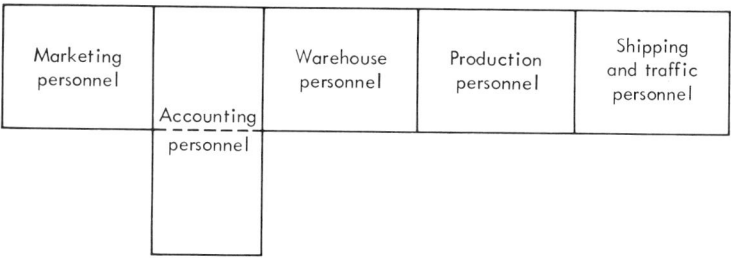

ORDER PROCESSING SYSTEM

Marketing personnel		Warehouse personnel	Production personnel	Shipping and traffic personnel
	Accounting personnel			

(a) Participating

STAFFING SYSTEM

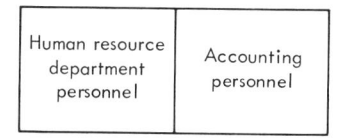

Human resource department personnel	Accounting personnel

(b) Related

Fig. 3-10. The Accounting System as a Participating and as a Related System

order processing system. Marketing is responsible for taking orders and monitoring the system to achieve the objectives of getting the correct products to the customer promptly. Accounting is responsible for billing the customer and collecting payments. Manufacturing or warehousing is responsible for getting the product ready for shipping. There may be a separate shipping and receiving or traffic department responsible for the actual shipping.

Accounting is a part of many systems, but it also interacts with *all* systems, whether or not accountants participate directly in achieving the goals of the system. We have just described how accounting actually participates in the order processing system. Contrast this with the staffing system. Accountants do not take part in the process of recruiting, selection, and hiring. However, accountants do interact with this system by preparing budgets for management's approval, recording costs, and providing statistical analyses for management. (Figure 3-10 shows the difference in relationships.)

Operating Systems in a Manufacturing Company

We will select a few operating systems in a manufacturing company first and show the interaction with accounting. Operating systems typically

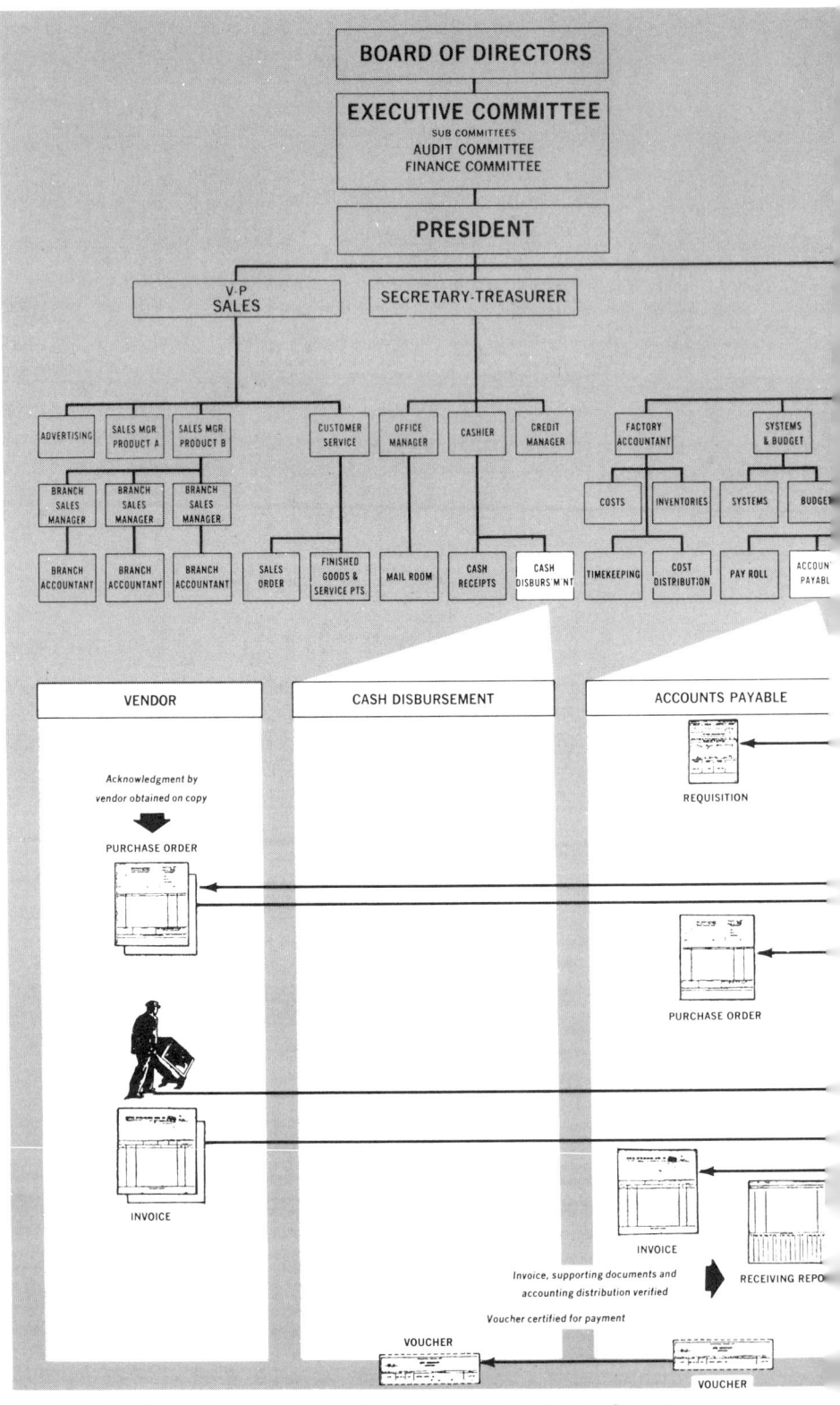

Fig. 3-11. Purchases Procedural Flow Chart Shown in Relation to Organization Chart to Portray the Control Obtained Through Segregation of Functional Responsibility

PURCHASES

PROCEDURAL FLOW CHART SHOWN IN RELATION
TO ORGANIZATION CHART TO PORTRAY
THE CONTROL OBTAINED THROUGH SEGREGATION
OF FUNCTIONAL RESPONSIBILITY

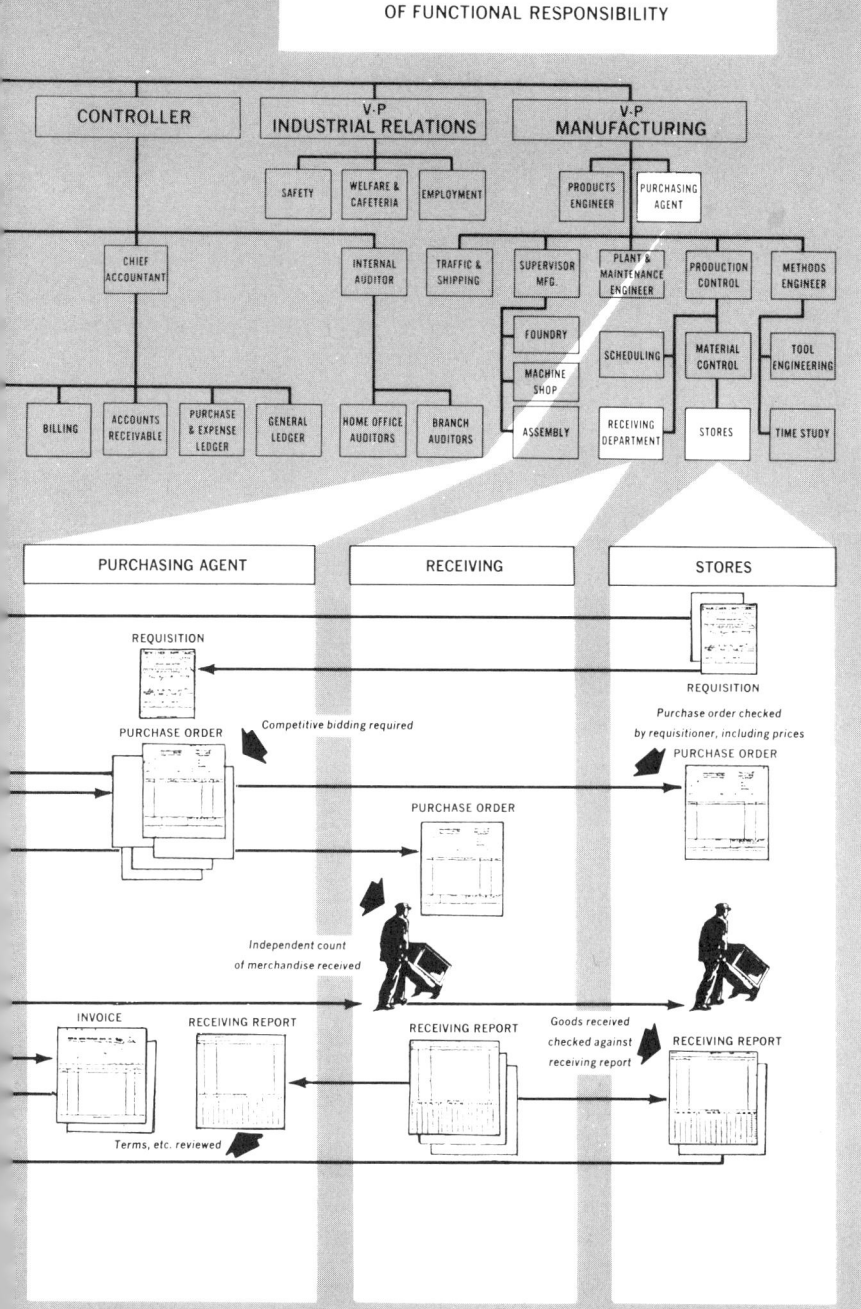

(FROM *Internal Control*, AICPA)

Howard F. Stettler, Systems Independent Audit, (Englewood Cliffs, N.J.: Prentice-Hall, found in manufacturing companies (excluding financial/accounting systems) are:

Product planning
Sales forecasting
Selling
Advertising and sales promotion
Order processing
Warehousing
Credit and adjustments
Logistics (traffic management)
Customer service
Engineering design
Engineering change and data control
Bill of materials
Laboratory testing
Production planning
Purchasing
Inventory management
Tooling planning and control
Maintenance and equipment replacement
Order scheduling and release
Plant monitoring and control—shop floor control
Plant maintenance
Materials handling
Receiving
Manpower planning and inventory
Recruiting
Wage and salary administration
Employee benefits
Plant security
Safety
Data base management system
EDP operations
EDP security

Let us take as our first example the purchasing system. In Fig. 3-11 we have an elaborate pictorial representation of this system. We note that accounting takes an active part in achieving the objectives of the system. Accounting pays for the purchase and also checks to see that the payment matches the purchase order, the invoice, and the receiving report.

In the production system, in contrast, accounting does not take part in the operation. Accounting, as an external system, may assist with budgets and record costs. A very simplified version of production and its relationship to the accounting system is shown in Fig. 3-12.

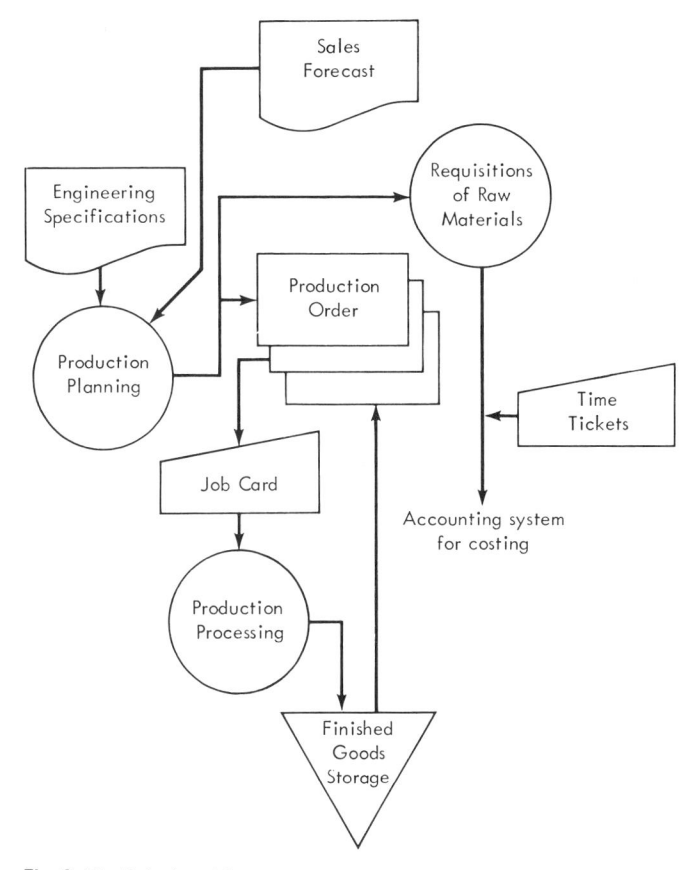

Fig. 3-12. Relationship of Production System to Accounting System

HISTORICAL REPORTING AND STATISTICAL ANALYSIS

The accounting systems, as we mentioned at the beginning of the chapter, have been defined for the purpose of this text as those which gather and record data in the day-to-day operations of the business. These data are assembled, classified, and presented to operating employees to aid in working with others and to help them control their own performance. Classified data are also presented in reports to all levels of management. For example, the P & L statement presented to the president at the end of the year is a classification of historical data. Chapter 5 has treated most such straightforward reports.

Statistical analysis represents a manipulation, as well as organization, of data. For accounting systems, in contrast to financial planning, such statistical analyses serve control purposes. These reports, which are made available to the operating individual and the supervisor, provide measures of performance. They highlight problem areas when they appear.

Manufacturing Organization

Let us look at two examples to illustrate the use of statistical reports. In Fig. 3-13, a portion of a "distribution-by-value" report is presented. This report has arranged the list of products sold by a company according to sales in dollars. Examination of such a report will allow the salespeople and sales supervisors to answer such questions as:

> Which products are providing the most revenue? (It can be seen in Fig. 3-13 that about 1% of the items provide over 17% of the revenue.)
> Which products are providing negligible revenue?
> What percentage of products provide 80% of dollar volume?
> Are there any products which are not selling at all?
> Are there a few products that produce practically all of the sales revenues?
> Are any significant changes occurring in the distribution-by-value from the last period?

As another example, assume that a large well-managed company owns a large number of expensive machine tools. Such machines vary in cost from $20,000 to $300,000. Some are special-purpose machines that have no other application than that of making the company's products. Others are general-purpose items such as lathes and milling machines. The company keeps a master file with a record for each machine. Items in the record include (a) source, cost, and date of purchase, (b) annual depreciation schedule, (c) annual and cumulative operating costs, (d) annual and cumulative maintenance costs, (e) estimated cost of replacement (updated), (f) estimated salvage or scrap value (updated), and (g) estimated remaining life.

With the foregoing data, accounting may establish routine annual statistical reports to show the average age of capital equipment, average cost per unit, and the corresponding trends. The average investment in equipment per worker, average increases in cost of replacement, average operating cost per machine, and average maintenance cost per machine may also be developed if these are useful figures. Comparisons of similar machines purchased from different vendors may be made to aid purchasing.

Distribution-by-Value Report

Item No	Cumulative Count - Rank by $ Sales	%	Annual Units	Unit Cost	Annual $ Sales	Cumulative Sales $	%
411045	1	.2	104,578	.966	101,023	101,023	3.8
411118	2	.4	375,959	.246	92,486	193,509	7.3
411063	3	.5	40,602	2.012	81,693	275,202	10.4
411075	4	.7	69,570	1.123	78,128	353,330	13.3
411176	5	.9	133,534	.490	65,432	418,762	15.8
411381	6	1.1	106,651	.510	54,392	473,154	17.8
411368	110	20.0	90,191	.073	6,584	1,886,385	71.0
411425	111	20.2	7,513	.800	6,011	1,892,396	71.2
411263	112	20.4	1,820	3.286	5,983	1,898,379	71.4
411503	113	20.5	10,611	.553	5,868	1,904,247	71.6
411444	545	99.2	813	.145	118	2,657,997	100.0
411465	546	99.4	4,227	.022	93	2,658,090	100.0
411243	547	99.6	90	.715	65	2,658,155	100.0
411516	548	99.8	4	2.916	12	2,658,167	100.0
411541	549	100.0	0	0	0	2,658,167	100.0

Distribution-by-Value with Item Movement Activity

LAURENTIAN INDUSTRIES, INC.
ANALYSIS OF INVENTORY ACTIVITY

12 MONTH PERIOD ENDING 7/1/--

STOCK LOCATION	STOCK NUMBER	DESCRIPTION	UNIT	DATE OF LAST ACTIVITY	NET ISSUES FOR PERIOD — NUMBER OF TRANS	QUANTITY	AVERAGE PER MONTH	BALANCE ON HAND — QUANTITY	MONTHS SUPPLY	VALUE
2715-237	127205	LIGHT RECEPTACLE	EA	7/-	2	4	.3	16	53.3	$ 4.32
2715-420	247389	SOLENOID, HEATER	EA	7/--	1	1	.1	7	70.0	4.48
2715-267	111462	SWITCH, STARTER	EA	8/--	1	4	.3	4	13.3	8.64
2715-601	896124	PINION STUD	EA	9/--	4	16	1.3	84	64.6	9.24
2716-234	59827	GASKET, MANIFOLD	EA	11/--	2	12	1.0	16	16.0	7.52
2716-320	614	WASHER, RUBBER	DZ	12/--	1	3	.2	14	70.0	2.52
2717-086	6213	BOLT, CARRIAGE	DZ	12/--	1	2	.2	27	135.0	32.40
2717-742	1032	BEARING, CLUTCH	EA	1/--	1	1	.1	9	90.0	34.83
2717-748	148722	AXLE	EA	3/--	1	1	.1	3	30.0	24.60
2719-147	2642	BRUSH, GENERATOR	EA	3/--	3	9	.7	42	60.0	7.14
2719-382	222649	REGULATOR	EA	3/--	4	4	.3	3	10.0	3.78

Courtesy of IBM Corporation.

Fig. 3-13. Inventory Management Reports

There are literally hundreds of statistical analyses that accounting may establish for control purposes in the organization. A small sampling over several departments, in addition to the two suggested above are:

Human resources management
   Cost of recruiting by class of worker
   Average training cost per person
   Average fringe benefits cost

Engineering
    Cost per square foot of engineering drawing
    Square feet of drawings per draftsman
    Support costs per engineer

Marketing
    Spare parts sales by product
    Sales by salesperson and region
    Average salesperson's expense per month
    Returns from customers, classified and ranked by dollar value

Manufacturing
    Average work week
    Overtime hours and costs per week
    Materials cost per production batch
    Value of inventories

Retailing

Because of the need for rapid response to change by retailing organizations, weekly, and even daily, statistical analyses are very important. For example, if several gross of a new type of ladies' lingerie arrive for sale, sales-per-day records are very important. Possible returns to the manufacturer, price mark-downs, or reordering may require immediate action.

Sales per square foot of floor space must be carefully watched for change so that reallocation of selling space may be made. If sales per square foot are uniformly decreasing, then purchasing or floor salespeople should be investigated. Better selection of goods or retraining may be indicated. Shrinkage and bad check losses are other items of interest.

Banking

Banking requires a wide variety of statistical analyses for the purpose of monitoring the health of the bank. Some examples are:

    Number of account transactions
    Average account size
    Average number and average value of loans
    Average number of credit card holders
    Interest rate fluctuations
    Average cash on hand daily

Hospitals

Hospitals also require a large number of statistical reports to monitor administrative and health activities. In the administrative area, some reports might be:

Distribution of days of patient stays
Revenues by special service centers
Room occupancy rate by day of week and by month
Average nurse/patient ratio per month
Number of meals served per day, per week, per month, and per year
Average inventory by department
Classification of patients by type of illness
Number of errors in treatment (food, medicine, diagnoses, etc.), by type

Generally, all statistical analyses have a cost or revenue aspect that involves the accounting department.

Summary

This chapter surveys operations and financial systems. The flowchart descriptions introduce the reader to the general nature of accounting systems and their relationships to the operating systems. In addition, an understanding of these systems is necessary for the accountant who will develop, design, or participate in financial/accounting systems. These latter deal with managerial planning, control, and decision-making, i.e., the future, as opposed to historical data gathering.

DISCUSSION QUESTIONS AND PROBLEMS

1. List and describe the activity chains for:
   a. hospitals
   b. banks
   c. restaurants
   d. funeral homes
   e. real estate firms
2. Discuss the statistical analysis for evaluation that could be developed for the following areas:
   a. engineering
   b. marketing

c. production
   d. personnel
3. List several areas in the production department where accounting information is:
   a. used
   b. collected
4. Design a month-end routine for an accounts payable program.
5. Describe the data elements that should be collected for an accounts payable subsystem.
6. List and discuss several subsystems of the AIS emphasizing the differences for the following types of firms:
   a. manufacturing
   b. bank
   c. CPA firm
   d. retailer
   e. construction firm
7. Draw an operations flowchart for the following:
   a. a small job-order print shop
   b. a real estate sales office
   c. a doctor's office
   d. a grocery store

Bibliography

BLUMENTHAL, SHERMAN. *Management Information Systems,* Englewood Cliffs, N.J.: Prentice-Hall, 1969.

DALTON, EDWARD F., JOHN S. MORRISON, and ROBERT E. DIGGS. *Hospital Financial Management System Concepts,* White Plains, N.Y.: IBM, 1975.

Forms for the 9 Key Operations of Business (No location). Moore Forms, Inc. (Undated).

General Ledger and Financial Reporting System, Andover, Mass.: Software International (undated).

General Ledger System (and related software packages) (9th ed.), Atlanta, Ga.: Management Science America, Inc., 1976.

GROSS, PAUL E., and ROBERT D. SMITH. *Systems Analysis and Design for Management,* New York: Dun-Donnelly, 1976. (See p. 186.)

How Order Information Serves Apparel Management, American Apparel Manufacturer's Association, 1974.

SHITZKER, DAVID R., "A Proposal to Computerize the Accounting System," *Management Accounting,* September 1969.

Preview:
This chapter defines internal control and discusses the flow of transactions concept. We will also look at the impact of EDP on internal control.
—AICPA definition
—Managers role in I/C
—Systems security
—EDP controls

CHAPTER FOUR
internal control

Closely Related Chapters:
Chapter 2—Control of operations
Chapter 3—Define operations
Chapter 8—Project control
Chapter 10—Documentation
Chapter 11—EDP control
Chapter 12—Data base control
Chapter 13—Contolling change

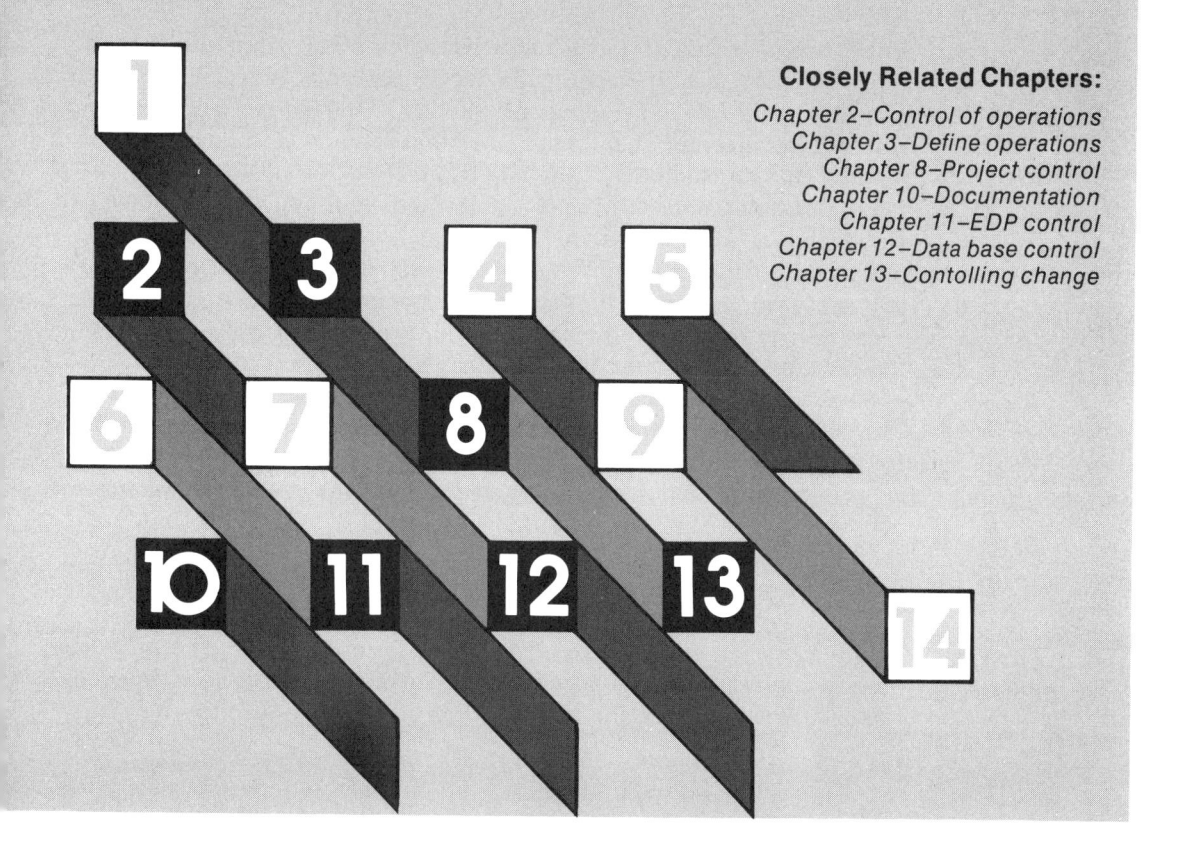

INTERNAL CONTROL IN THE AIS

The management information system (MIS) must rely on the quality of information to function effectively. Chapter 6 will point out that the quality of information is a function of: (1) relevance, (2) verifiability, (3) freedom from bias, and (4) quantifiability. This chapter is concerned with the verifiability of information. Management must be reasonably assured that decisions are made and transactions are performed according to the stated policies of the organization. Additionally, there must be reasonable assurance that the accounting information system (AIS) is providing reliable "internal" reports for management decision-making and accurate "external" reports for the benefit of interested outsiders such as investors, lending institutions, and regulatory agencies. The vehicle used to attain these objectives is generally referred to as internal control.

Before we develop a formal definition of internal control, consider for a moment the nature of internal control as it relates to the MIS. The accounting information system, as a subsystem of the MIS, is similar to a maze of city streets. In a typical city street system there are main thoroughfares that must accommodate high volumes of traffic, and there are infrequently traveled side streets that are, nevertheless, essential to the efficient operation of the system. All of the streets together accomplish the objective of the system: to transport vehicles quickly and safely through the city. The "main streets" of the accounting information system are the major transaction cycles or groups of related activities in the system. Typically these cycles are the purchasing cycle (purchasing, receipt of goods, inventory, accounts payable, and cash disbursements) and the sales cycle (sales, shipping of goods, accounts receivable, and cash receipts). In the case of a manufacturing concern there would also be a production cycle. Through these major cycles flow the highest volume of accounting data which must be efficiently and accurately converted into management information. Just as the city streets (even the main streets) must intersect at numerous points throughout the city, so must the major elements of the accounting information system. Even the major transaction cycles cross numerous departmental lines. There must be some method to monitor the flow of information as it travels through the system.

In order to reduce the number of traffic accidents and backups, the city uses traffic control devices such as stoplights for major intersections and stop or yield signs for side streets where the volume of traffic is lower. A highly integrated accounting information system must use similar traffic control mechanisms to assure that the incidence of error does not exceed acceptable levels. These traffic control mechanisms in the AIS are internal controls.

Two further extensions of this "city street" analogy are worthy of comment. The city maintains a staff of policemen not only to enforce the formal control mechanisms at busy intersections, but to provide a mobile control for side streets where such control mechanisms are not as necessary. In the accounting information system this additional control is provided by the internal audit department. The function of the internal auditors, as an element of the internal control system, is to monitor the formal internal control strengths in major transaction cycles and to act as a "mobile" control to monitor accounting activity in areas where control is less formal. The procedures used in this internal audit function will be discussed in Chapter 14. Finally, when the city outgrows its system of streets, a freeway is usually constructed to provide rapid transportation of vehicles through the city. The "freeway" in the accounting information system is the computer. When the organization outgrows its manual accounting system, a computerized accounting system is usually installed to facilitate the processing of information. However, just as the building of a freeway can change minor fender benders into multicar fatal accidents, the installation of a computer system can, if not properly monitored, change occasional errors in a manual system into a monumental AIS disaster! Accordingly, the internal control system must be modified to accommodate the computerized AIS.

With these concepts in mind, let us develop a more formal definition of internal control and then see how this control is specifically adapted to a computerized system.

DEVELOPING A DEFINITION

The most widely accepted source for clarification of accounting terminology is the American Institute of Certified Public Accountants (AICPA). This body issues certain statements on accounting and auditing matters to provide accountants with standardized accounting principles and auditing standards that are generally accepted throughout the profession. In Section 320 of the AICPA's Statement on Auditing Standards No. 1, internal control is defined as a two-part set of controls as follows:

Administrative control includes, but is not limited to, the plan of organization and the procedures and records that are concerned with the decision processes leading to management's authorization of transactions. Such authorization is a management function directly associated with the responsibility for achieving the objectives of the organization and is the starting point for establishing accounting control of transactions.

Accounting control comprises the plan of organization and the procedures and records that are concerned with the safeguarding of assets and the reliability of financial records and consequently are designed to provide reasonable assurance that:

a. Transactions are executed in accordance with management's general or specific authorization.
b. Transactions are recorded as necessary to (1) permit preparation of financial statements in conformity with generally accepted accounting principles or any other criteria applicable to such statements and (2) maintain accountability for assets.
c. Access to assets is permitted only in accordance with management's authorization.
d. The recorded accountability for assets is compared with the existing assets at reasonable intervals and appropriate action is taken with respect to any differences.

The most notable element of this definition is the emphasis placed on transactions. Previous definitions of internal control have only extended to the safeguarding of assets and reliability of financial records for external reporting purposes. This "transaction-based" definition more clearly demonstrates the integration of internal controls into the accounting information system. The basic components of business operations are transactions, hence these transactions are the primary subject matter of internal control. As noted earlier, the majority of critical accounting transactions are usually included in the main transaction cycles (purchasing, sales, and production). In each of these cycles, the AIS is concerned with the authorization, execution, and recording of transactions and the accountability for resulting assets. Therefore, it is in these areas of concern that we must integrate the internal controls to insure the reliability of the AIS. Now let us consider how these transactions and transaction cycles of the AIS relate to the two elements of the AICPA's definition of internal control.

Administrative Control

Management is continuously going through decision processes leading to authorization of transactions. For example, decisions must be made relative to sales prices based on costs and required margins. Still other decisions are made essentially apart from the output of the accounting system, such as negotiations for long-term debt. There are many other decision-making areas, but it is clear that these types of decisions are critical to the operations of the organization. Therefore, an organizational plan with stated policies and procedures must exist to provide internal control over these decision-making processes. Failure to provide control over these processes can result in serious problems for the organization. For example:

Company A is a conglomerate with numerous subsidiaries engaged in the vegetable canning business. This business is highly competitive and a few cents difference per case could mean a loss of significant sales opportunities. One of the major elements of cost is the cans used in the production process. In order to better control the purchase discount on cans (which is significant) the parent company pays the can invoices for all subsidiaries. The discount on these invoices is negotiated between the parent company's chief executive and the can company on an annual basis. The parent company does not pass on these discounts to the subsidiary companies because for income tax purposes it is more beneficial to recognize this discount as income to the parent. Consequently, the vegetable canning subsidiaries never know the extent of their can discount. However, their competitors are keenly aware of their own discounts and consistently underbid Company A in sales competition. Administrative controls must be established to allow the purchase discount information to be disseminated to the applicable subsidiaries to be included in their decision-making process for setting sales prices.

Company B's vice-president of finance negotiated a long-term loan with a bank. Included in the loan agreement was a restriction on capital expenditures during the period of the loan. No one was assigned the responsibility of assuring that the restrictions of the debt agreement were not violated. Consequently, at the end of the year, the external auditors informed the company that capital expenditures exceeded the restrictions in the debt agreement, and the debt was considered to be in default, hence, due and payable immediately. The related disclosure in the company's annual report caused a major decrease in the company's stock price. This unnecessary damage to the interest of the stockholders could have been avoided by a simple administrative control requiring current review of items such as restrictions included in long-term debt.

These two examples point out the serious consequences of poor internal administrative controls. However, closely related to the administrative controls are the accounting controls which insure the reliability of financial information used in the decision-making processes.

Accounting Control

The time to consider internal accounting controls is when the AIS is being developed (a subject more fully discussed in Chapter 8). As we develop the accounting information system, we must identify those areas most requiring control. In doing so we should answer the following ten questions:

1. What are the most critical outputs of the system, and how can we assure that such outputs are reliable?
2. What are the primary inputs to the system, and how can we ascertain that these inputs are accurately entered into the system?
3. At what point are transactions executed, and how can we determine that such transactions are executed in accordance with management's general or specific authorization?
4. When are transactions recorded, and what controls do we need to assure that they are recorded correctly?
5. At what points in the system must control be exercised to restrict access to assets in accordance with management's authorization?
6. What are the "busy intersections" in the system where the probability of error is highest? How can we reduce the probability of such an error going undetected?
7. What are the "side streets" in the system where the activities are more mundane and demand less formal controls?
8. How can we best use the internal audit department to test the effectiveness of the formal controls and still provide a mobile form of control for those areas not subject to more formal controls?
9. Where in the system should we insist on specific segregation of duties to avoid one person performing incompatible duties (such as one person being responsible for and having control over cash receipts and accounts receivable)?
10. At what points in the system must we have reasonable assurance that no errors go undetected, and at what points, if any, must we have absolute assurance that no errors go undetected?

In order to answer these questions properly, the accountant must develop a clear understanding of the system. This requires some form of documentation and analysis. Chapter 9 will examine the tools and techniques the accountant uses to perform this function. Table 4-1 represents an example of the accounting flow of a purchase/production/sales system. This example shows how the accountability for assets and responsibility for input to record transactions crosses departmental lines as the assets flow through the firm.

As our internal accounting control system begins to take shape, we must concentrate on three particular areas: (1) execution and recording of transactions, (2) segregation of duties, and (3) reasonable assurance versus absolute assurance.

Table 4-1. Accountability Function Following the Change-custody as Assets Flow Through the Firm

EVENT	CHANGE IN CUSTODY	RECORD ENTRY	COMMENTS
Purchase of raw materials	A. Inventory control assumes custody of raw materials B. Treasurer's office is relieved of custody of cash upon completion of payables cycle	A. Debit: Raw materials inventory 　　Credit: Accounts payable B. Debit: Accounts payable 　　Credit: Cash	The firm exchanges assets with a party outside the entity
Production control requisitions raw materials	Production control assumes custody of a portion of raw materials	Debit: Work in process Credit: Raw materials inventory	Inventory detail records should be adjusted accordingly
Completion of production function	Material transferred to finished goods inventory, production control relieved of responsibility	Debit: Finished goods inventory Credit: Work in process	Record entries will reflect the addition of direct and indirect changes
Sale of finished product	A. Transfer from finished goods inventory to shipping department B. Transfer from shipping department to common carrier or customer C. Cash received from customer	A. Debit: Accounts receivable 　　Credit: Sales B. Debit: Cost of goods sold 　　Credit: Finished goods inventory C. Debit: Cash 　　Credit: Accounts receivable	Entries A & C are made at selling price. Entry B is made at cost plus freight. The firm has again exchanged assets with a party outside the entity

Execution and Recording of Transactions

Transactions should be executed by persons acting within the scope of their authority. This authority may be specific or general in nature, that is, authority to execute a specific transaction, or general authority to conduct certain types of transactions as set forth in company policy or job descriptions. Procedures should be established to insure that these transactions are executed in accordance with stated control policies. An example would be a purchasing system where purchase orders are compared to receiving reports and vendor's invoices before payment. The authorization for the purchase should be established and the approvals noted on (a) the receiving report, (b) the purchase order, and (c) the voucher requesting payment. The lack of these documents or lack of approval on them may be a serious internal control weakness.

Control over the recording of transactions centers around the accuracy of three items: (a) amount, (b) time period, and (c) account classification. If transactions are recorded in the correct amounts, within the period executed, and posted to the correct accounts, then the control system is functioning properly.

Segregation of Duties

It should be noted that any system of control is dependent upon people. The success of a control system will be directly related to the competence and integrity of the people employed, their independence, and the segregation of their duties. The proper segregation of accounting functions prohibits individuals from participating in conflicting activities, and minimizes the opportunities for concealment of errors or defalcations. Any employee who has access to the records of the firm, and also has access to assets, would be in a position to perpetrate irregularities and also conceal his misdeeds. For example, if an employee had access to both the cash and the account receivable records, he would have the opportunity to lap checks or write off receivables to conceal embezzlements.

Reasonable Assurance

A system should be designed to provide reasonable, but not absolute, assurance that transactions will be authorized, executed, and recorded in accordance with management's policies. Management is concerned with profitability and should not be concerned with insignificant errors. This is not to say that management is not concerned with the reason the error occurred. The fact that an error is present means that the system failed to detect and correct the error in the normal course of activities. The reason for the error should be determined and appropriate action taken. However, in no way should the control system's costs exceed the benefits derived from the system.

The foregoing discussion has attempted to show some of the major areas of concern related to internal control. In summary, it can be said that an adequate system of accounting control includes the following characteristics.:

1. delegation of authority to specific individuals and checks to assure that transactions have proper authorization.
2. proper physical control of assets.
3. documentation that provides independent cross-checking.
4. segregation of conflicting accounting functions.
5. personnel having ability and training commensurate with their responsibilities.
6. proper control over system input and output.
7. proper control in those areas where there is a high volume of critical accounting data.
8. proper utilization of internal audit personnel.
9. reasonable, but not absolute, assurance that errors do not go undetected.
10. adequate administrative control policies.

It can be seen that internal controls are not isolated procedures and practices, but rather an integrated system of controls designed to safeguard the assets, allow for the efficient production of reliable financial information, and provide reliable input for the management decision-making processes. These concepts of internal control apply to both computerized and manual accounting information systems. However, due to the particular control problems in a computerized system, specific EDP internal control procedures must be considered.

INTERNAL CONTROLS IN A COMPUTERIZED AIS

A common mistake in analyzing internal controls is to say, "Well, now that we've looked at the controls in the manual system, let's look at the controls on the computer." There is indeed only one accounting information system. Although some segments of the AIS may be computerized, we must visualize the total system (or transaction cycle) as one continuous operation from the initiation of the transaction to its final recording. Figure 4-1 demonstrates the integration of the computer into a simplified sales cycle of the AIS.

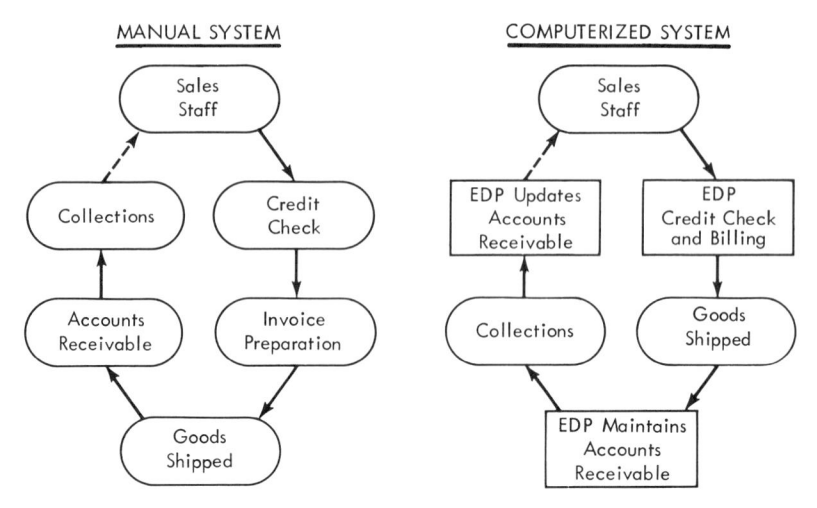

Fig. 4-1. AIS Sales Cycle

Figure 4-1 points out the cyclical pattern of the flow of information from the initiation of a sales transaction to the final collection of the related account receivable. By using the concepts discussed earlier in this chapter, we could integrate a series of internal controls into this cycle to determine that: (1) only reliable information is transferred through the cycle and (2) related assets are properly safeguarded. We would be greatly assisted in the task by the obvious departmental segregation of duties in the manual system.

By introducing the computer into this sales cycle, we have eliminated the segregation of duties by department. Although we still have a complete sales cycle, we must now cope with the concentration of incompatible activities (sales and accounts receivable) in one department. Therefore, the system of internal controls must be modified to still provide reasonable assurance that the AIS is operating in accordance with management's policies. This modification is accomplished by adding specific EDP controls to the internal control system.

There are two general categories of EDP controls: (1) general controls and (2) application controls. General controls are environmental in nature and span most or all of the accounting applications. Application controls relate specifically to each accounting cycle or flow of information. The types of controls typically included in these two categories are as follows.

General Controls
1. Preinstallation controls
2. Organizational controls
3. Development controls

Application Controls
1. Input controls
2. Processing controls
3. Output controls

Figure 4-2 shows the relationship of general controls, application controls, and controls within the user departments in the AIS.

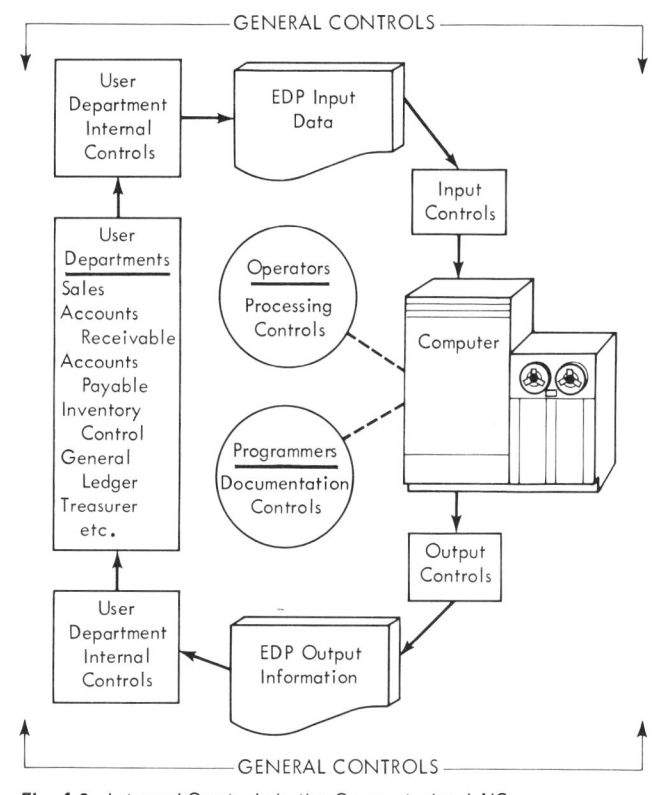

Fig. 4-2. Internal Controls in the Computerized AIS

GENERAL CONTROLS

General controls relate to the environment of the computerized AIS as opposed to controls that are concerned with specific accounting applications. The importance of these general controls cannot be overemphasized because serious weaknesses in general controls usually negate even the most sophisticated application controls. For example, if the general controls allow computer programmers to actually operate the computer, then these programmers could alter the computer programs during processing to bypass application controls. However, this weakness could be mitigated by other general controls such as external reviews of processing, not permitting the EDP department to initiate transactions, isolating the EDP function from any responsibility for safeguarding assets (other than those assets of the EDP department itself), and effective user department controls. Thus the integrity of a computerized AIS relies extensively on strong general controls. Further, time to consider the structure and extent of general controls is before the system becomes operative.

Preinstallation Controls

Preinstallation controls should determine that a computer is integrated into the AIS only if it will produce greater benefits than the existing system or other possible modifications of the existing system. A management team should be charged with the responsibility of determining the information processing requirements of the AIS. The procedures used in this determination are extensive and will be fully discussed in Chapter 8. It is imperative, however, that the systems processing requirements be clearly identified before the decision is made to install a computer. Once this decision has been made, appropriate computer facilities and services must be selected.

The first step in acquiring suitable computer facilities and services is to identify the types of processing tasks to be performed by the computer. Once identified, these requirements should be submitted to potential suppliers. The management team then must evaluate each of the suppliers' proposals to determine the best source for the required facilities and services. Preinstallation decisions and contractual arrangements with suppliers should undergo extensive review by top management. Many an organization has regretted entering into long-term contracts for computer facilities and services which either failed to meet current processing requirements or quickly became obsolete due to organizational changes or technological improvements. As the new computer system is integrated into the AIS, organizational controls must be established to accommodate the concentration of activities in the EDP department.

Organizational Control

The organizational plan must establish the structure within which the EDP processing procedures will operate in order to ascertain the reliability of computerized AIS information. The most essential element of this organizational structure is effective separation of incompatible duties. As was noted earlier, separation of duties is a characteristic of a well-controlled manual or computerized AIS. However, this control objective is particularly significant in a computerized system due to the concentration of information processing in the EDP department. There are two separate elements in the concept of proper separation of duties: (1) the separation of the EDP department from incompatible functions within the AIS and (2) proper separation of duties within the EDP department.

The EDP department should act as a service center for other departments in the organization. Accordingly, no initiation of transactions should take place within the EDP department. Source documents should be initiated and approved by the user departments. In a sophisticated EDP environment, there will usually be some violations of this control objective. For example, the computer may perform the customer credit-checking function prior to printing a sales invoice. If a perpetual inventory system is maintained, then the computer may also initiate a purchase transaction when inventories fall below predescribed levels. In these types of situations, other general controls, such as external review, controls in the user departments, and separation of duties within the EDP department, become even more significant.

Isolating the EDP Department

The overall management of the EDP department must also be separated from other incompatible departments within the organization. The EDP department should report directly to a vice-president of information who is not directly responsible for the accounting or finance functions. Proper separation of duties requires that the EDP department be independent from the accounting function.

Equally important as the isolation of the EDP function from incompatible departments in the organization, is the separation of duties within the EDP department. There are three primary objectives in acheiving proper separation of duties within the EDP department. These are: (1) separation of the responsibility for controlling EDP input and output from the actual processing of this information, (2) separation of the responsibility for maintaining the ongoing EDP "master files" from other EDP functions, and (3) separating the functions of system design and programming from computer operations.

EDP Input and Output Control Group

The EDP department organizational plan should include a separate control group to monitor EDP input and output and to provide a liaison with user departments. The control group should be responsible for scheduling computer input and output and controlling the flow of information through the department. This allows the operators to concentrate on the operational aspects of the computer and also serves to limit contact between the computer operators and the user departments. The control group should record all input data in a control log, noting any control totals that will be used for subsequent balancing. The group should insure that: (1) output reports are timely, (2) output reports reconcile to control totals recorded on receipt of the input, and (3) such reports are properly distributed in accordance with stated guidelines. One additional funcion of the control group is to determine that input errors rejected by the computer are communicated to the appropriate user department, corrected, and reentered into the system under the same controls as original input.

Implementation of the AIS

One of the first steps in the implementation of a computerized AIS is the consolidation of data into master files. One example would be the accounts receivable master file which contains information on each customer's account, such as name and address, credit limits, sales totals, current balance, customer payments, and discounts taken. Each time the accounts receivable computer programs are processed, this master file is updated. The information contained in this master file is critical to the operations of the company, therefore it is important to restrict access to the master file to only authorized EDP personnel. To accomplish this objective, a file "librarian" system is usually established within the EDP department. In a sophisticated EDP environment this "librarian" control system is expanded to also control the access to computer programs.

In a well-designed EDP organization, the system designer and programmer develops, implements, and maintains the computer systems, while the computer operator processes the data using the files and computer programs. If the computer programmer is permitted to perform the processing function, he could take advantage of his programming knowledge to bypass critical application controls. Many organizations exist under a "one-man shop" system where the computer programmer is also the operator. Therefore, separation of duties is not practical. In such organizations other internal controls must be enhanced to insure the reliability of EDP output. The most significant control to consider in these circumstances is external review by the user departments. Procedures must be established and enforced in the user departments to determine that accounting information is processed by the EDP department in accordance with predescribed guidelines. One other critical control in a "one-man shop" EDP environment is not permitting the EDP department to either initiate transactions or have access to the assets of the organization.

Figure 4-3 presents a typical EDP department organizations structure in a medium to large installation.

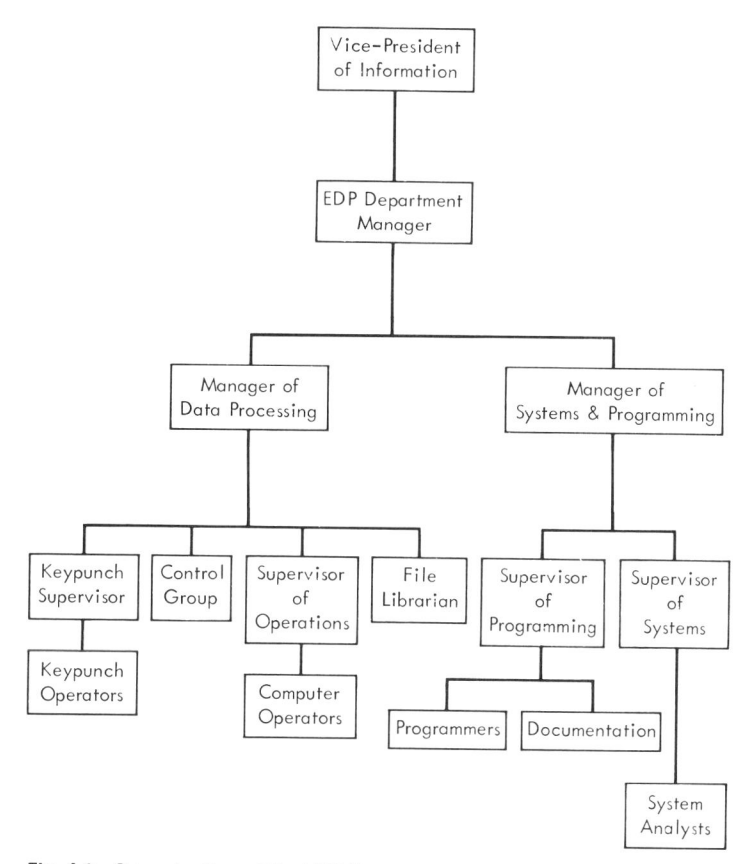

Fig. 4-3. Organization of the EDP Department

This organization chart is representative of a medium to large EDP installation. For smaller installations, many of the duties presented above are performed by a limited number of personnel. As the formal separation of duties within the EDP department diminishes, the need for strong user department controls becomes imperative.

Developmental Controls

As the organizational plan for the EDP department is being designed to achieve the control objectives mentioned above, consideration must be given to controls over the development of specific systems. The two critical internal control objectives in systems development are documentation of the system and testing of the system.

Proper system documentation starts with a precise "problem definition" or statement of AIS requirements for each processing application. The design of a computer system can only be controlled if such processing requirements are clearly stated. As the computer system is designed, proper documentation must be developed to provide all interested departments with a clear understanding of the system's objectives, methods, information flow, data files, and output. Computer programs developed to process data within such systems must also be fully documented. Adequate computer program documentation includes program specifications and narrative descriptions, diagrams of program logic, input and output formats, master file formats, and operating instructions. The operating instructions should be developed into an operations manual covering all EDP applications. A well-developed operations manual can significantly reduce the level of operator error during processing. There must also be adequate documentation of file control instructions to be used during the processing. These file control procedures should specify, at a minimum, the file name, updating cycle, file backup instructions, and reconstruction procedures in case of file destruction. Finally, user department instructions should be documented for each system and distributed to the appropriate departments.

Once a system is developed and fully documented, it must be tested to insure that information will be processed in accordance with AIS requirements. This testing procedure is usually performed by developing a set of input data, processing this data through the system and reviewing the resulting output to determine that the system is operating as designed. The system may also be tested by processing actual AIS data on a parallel basis with the manual or previous EDP system and comparing the output. Whichever method is used, it is important that the test data and output be retained for review by someone independent of the development of the system. This review function may be performed by the internal audit department in a large organization or by the appropriate user departments in a "one-man shop" environment.

Once an effective system of general controls has been established, the organization should develop a set of specific application controls to monitor the flow of information through the various systems. These individual application controls remain, however, a subsystem of the general controls. Therefore, if general controls are inadequate, then application controls will rarely provide the reliability required by a computerized AIS.

APPLICATION CONTROLS

The purpose of application controls is to provide reasonable assurance that no undetected errors occur in: (1) the recording and summarizing of properly authorized transactions, (2) the updating of the system's master files, and (3) the presentation of processing results. Specific application control procedures are designed for each application of the computerized AIS (e.g., accounts receivable, accounts payable, inventory). These procedures are not necessarily performed solely within the EDP department. They may be performed by the user departments, the EDP control group as discussed earlier, supervisory personnel within the EDP department, computer operators, the computer itself, or a combination of any of these. Therefore, once again we must envision the computerized AIS as a continuous operation transcending numerous departments within the organization. The EDP department rarely exists as an island in the organization separately performing all necessary control functions. The most sophisticated controls within the EDP department can be completely negated by internal control weaknesses in the user departments. For example:

> *A large national bank has a very sophisticated computerized accounting system. One of the functions of this system is to provide for automatic transfers between a customer's savings account and checking account. Extensive specific application controls are used within the EDP department to insure that each automatic transfer is processed through the computer with no undetected errors. These application controls are: (1) checking for a code which signifies customer authorization of such transfers, (2) verification of the customer account number with the appropriate master file, (3) verification of specific transaction codes which signify the type of transfer, and (4) reconciliation of control totals to assure that all transfers are processed for the right amount. However, the input form which generates an automatic transfer requires no second party review and authorization. Indeed all that is required is for the customer to telephone the bank and request that such a transfer be made. A clerk then completes the input form and forwards it to the EDP department. Unfortunately for the bank, a dishonest clerk generates an automatic transfer between a customer's savings account and her own checking account. Just before leaving for Buenos Aires the next day, the clerk cashes a check against her new balance causing a significant loss and unnecessary embarrassment to the bank. In this case the sophisticated application controls within the EDP department only served to insure that the embezzlement, once perpetrated, was properly recorded in the accounts.*

Conversely, weaknesses within the EDP department can negate internal control strengths in the user departments. For example:

A medium sized manufacturing company has a very limited budget for the EDP department, and accordingly, cannot afford to hire a separate EDP operator. The system programmer performs all operating duties.

One of the key controls in the purchasing transaction cycle is a specific application control within the computer program that allows only properly approved vouchers to be paid. However, when the system was designed, management realized that the programmer could override this control and permit payment of bogus vouchers. Therefore, additional applications controls were established in the accounts payable department. Before any checks are mailed, the control total from the cash disbursements system is reconciled to the control total taken of the approved vouchers sent to the EDP department. Unfortunately management failed to realize that if the programmer could alter the vouchers payable programs, he could also alter the cash disbursements programs generating the control total used in the user department reconciliations. Two weeks after the programmer unexpectedly resigned, it was discovered that $50,000 of bogus vouchers were paid, and this amount was excluded from the cash disbursements control total.

The central theme of both of these examples is that when we are considering the internal controls of a specific application, we must evaluate the entire system. Now let us discuss three categories of specific application controls: (1) input controls, (2) processing controls, and (3) output controls.

Input Controls

The first objective of input controls is to ascertain the completeness of input data. If transactions are processed that contain erroneous information or not all transactions initiated are processed, then input controls are inadequate. The most commonly used type of "completeness" control is control or batch totals. User departments establish these control totals before data are forwarded to the EDP department for processing. The output totals from the EDP department are then reconciled by the user department to the original control totals. Such control totals are usually taken by: (1) adding the totals of dollar value amounts, (2) using hash totals (the sum of any numeric item on the input form such as dates or account numbers), and (3) counts of the total number of transactions or documents. The computer may also be programmed to check these control totals at various points during the processing of the information. If computer control totals do not agree with input control totals an error report should be generated and used to identify the errors causing the difference. This report can also be used to control the reentry of the corrected data into the system.

Another type of completeness control is the verification by the computer of information on the input form. The computer can be programmed to verify that essential information is not omitted from the input form. For example, in an accounts receivable application, the system should verify that the invoice number, quantities, unit prices, and other critical information are not omitted from the input forms. If such an error is detected, the entire record should be rejected from processing and included on an error report for appropriate follow-up.

Input controls should also determine that no errors occur when data is converted to machine-readable form. The most common example of this conversion is the keypunching into computer cards of manually prepared input forms. This process is generally controlled by using control totals. If the input data are correct, but keypunched incorrectly, the resulting output control totals will not agree with control totals established prior to keypuncing. This procedure is valid regardless of the means used to convert data to machine-readable form. However, when data are keypunched, an important control procedure to consider is the "key-verifying" of significant information on the input form. "Key-verifying" is when a second person rekeypunches a card to determine that the original keypunching is correct.

Finally, input controls should ascertain that transactions are properly authorized before they are processed. This authorization can range from a general authorization to process a group of transactions to specific authorization of individual transactions. In the example presented earlier concerning the automatic transfers in a bank, the probability of embezzlement taking place would be significantly reduced by requiring specific authorization of each transfer by an officer of the bank.

Processing Controls

Processing controls take advantage of the computer's ability to efficiently perform logical checks during the processing of data. The objectives of processing controls are to ascertain that: (1) input data are complete, (2) the information included on input forms is reasonable, and (3) the accuracy of data is maintained throughout processing.

We have already discussed the computer's ability to monitor control totals during processing and to produce an error report when differences occur. These control total checks are an essential component of processing controls. Without them, errors would go undetected throughout the processing function and only be discovered if adequate user department control totals are maintained.

In order to ascertain that the input included on input forms is reasonable, a computer can be programmed to verify that the data do not conflict with predescribed norms. The following are examples of such computer checks to verify the reasonableness of input:

> Limit tests. For example, cash disbursements in excess of a predescribed amount are printed on a separate output for immediate follow-up and verification.
>
> Specific amount or account tests. For example, in processing a sales journal, all debits must be posted to accounts receivable or sales discount accounts.
>
> Self-checking numbers. For example, assume that the inventory item number 16251 is a self-checking item number, and the last digit is the check digit. During processing the check digit would be verified by dividing the first four digits by a constant, 8 (1625 ÷ 8 = 203 with a remainder of 1). The check must equal the remainder for processing to continue.
>
> Codes or account numbers may be verified by checking them against a master file of authorized codes or numbers. For example, vendor identification codes for cash disbursements are checked against a master file of authorized vendors before processing continues.

Once the computer has accepted the data as complete and reasonable, additional procedures should be instituted to determine that such accuracy and completeness is maintained throughout processing. The computer should perform record count, control, and hash total checks on a run-by-run basis. Transaction files and master files used during processing should be checked to determine that: (1) files are entered in the proper sequence, (2) correct files are used in processing (by using "header" labels at the beginning of a file to identify the file's purpose), and (3) the date of the file is appropriate for current processing. Still other checks that can be performed by the computer during processing are:

> Dual reading of input and comparison of data before continuing processing.
>
> Read-after-write routines to provide an additional check when output is on magnetic tape.
>
> Echo checks whereby data entered are echoed back for comparison with original input.
>
> Double arithmetic computations which perform all calculations twice and compare answers for a zero difference.

After the input and processing of data are effectively controlled, we must consider specific application controls over the output of the system.

Output Controls

The objectives of output controls are to ascertain that: (1) output data are complete and reasonable and (2) output is distributed in accordance with stated policies. As we previously discussed, reconciliation of output control totals with user department control totals is a significant internal control strength in a computerized AIS. Although this procedure will verify the completeness of the output, it will provide little comfort as to the reasonableness of the output. For example, control totals in an inventory pricing system might verify that all inventory items were priced but would not identify a pricing error, such as using the wrong unit of measure. To accomplish this "reasonableness of output" objective, the user department must review the output in addition to checking control totals. When processing involves continuous updating of a master file, (such as in an accounts receivable system) the master file should be periodically printed out and reviewed for reasonableness.

For each application, those persons designated to receive specific output should be clearly identified. Many output reports are confidential (such as product cost data, marketing strategy, and executive payroll), and should only be distributed to clearly identified users. Other reports are critical to the decision-making processes of the organization and must be channeled to the appropriate person on a timely basis. Still other reports serve as additional internal control checks and must be carefully distributed to avoid undermining such controls. Effective output controls should provide a well-structured framework for distribution of system output in accordance with management's policies.

AUDIT TRAILS AND MANAGEMENT TRAILS

Internal controls in the AIS should provide reasonable assurance that transactions are authorized, executed, and recorded in accordance with stated policies. However, one additional objective of an effective internal control system is to provide a method to identify and locate the component documents used in the processing of a transaction. This function is necessary to provide a basis for independent verification of the transactions and to satisfy requirements of governments and other regulatory groups.

The procedures and documents used to provide this service are usually referred to as the audit trail. However, the predetermined routes whereby data can be traced through the transaction cycles are more often used by management to solve problems that occur during the processing of data and to maintain the systems. Although the system must leave a sufficient audit trail to provide a basis for independent verification, the primary goal of the system is to serve the needs of management. What the system should provide is an effective "management trail" that also meets the requirements of an audit trail. Some of the most common uses of the management trail are:

> Identifying and correcting errors produced by the system.
> Analyzing data for management information purposes.
> Replying to customer or supplier queries.

A good audit trail is a by-product of an effective internal control system. In most cases, a well developed system of internal controls coupled with an effective management trail will provide a basis for independent verification. Chapter 14 will discuss the methods used to audit the computerized AIS.

INTERNAL CONTROLS FOR AN OUTSIDE SERVICE BUREAU

For many organizations the extent of computerized applications within the AIS does not justify the cost of maintaining an EDP department. These companies usually contract with an outside EDP service bureau to perform the data processing function. When selecting a service bureau, the organization should determine that the same internal controls required for an "in-house" EDP installation are present in the service bureau.

Once the organization has selected a service bureau, data are forwarded on a regular basis to the installation, processed, and returned to the organization. There is usually no direct involvement in the operations of the service bureau by the organization's management. Therefore management cannot insure the day-to-day enforcement of internal controls within the service bureau. For this reason, the development of strong user department controls (batch totals, review of output for reasonableness, etc.) becomes even more important when a service bureau is used for the processing function. If the organization has an internal audit department, the auditors should make periodic inspections of the service bureau to ascertain the existence of "advertised" internal controls.

INTERNAL CONTROLS IN ON-LINE SYSTEMS

With the advent of on-line data base systems, the user departments can now input data, modify master files, and obtain output information through remote terminals located in the user departments. In this type of a system, most internal control concepts previously discussed still apply. However, due to special control problems caused by an on-line system, other control procedures should be added to the normal general and application controls.

Remote access terminals are often used to transmit data rather long distances over telephone lines. Due to the complicated nature of this transmission system, specific "completeness" controls must be added to the system. In addition to item counts and control totals, "dual transmission" procedures should be used. Dual transmission controls require the data to be transmitted two times. The data are then compared and any differences will cause the transaction to be rejected from processing.

On-line systems also present certain problems relative to the security of data. Physical security must be maintained over the remote terminals to prevent their use by unauthorized persons. Additionally, the computer system itself should determine that only authorized personnel are operating the terminals. This is usually accomplished by the use of operator identification codes. Before the operator is permitted to access the system, the computer checks the operator's identification code to a file of authorized codes. The operator's access to the system should be limited to those applications necessary to perform the duties of the operator. By using various types of identification codes, the computer can properly restrict access on a "need-to-know" basis. For example, the operator identification code AP408 would only permit access to the accounts payable system and another code AR650 would permit that operator to access the accounts receivable system. The system should also preclude operators from performing certain transactions that would compromise the integrity of the system. For example, in a bank a separate file of employee account numbers would be maintained and on-line access to these accounts would be restricted to a limited number of authorized persons.

Finally, when using an on-line system a second party review should be performed on a regular basis. Transaction listings summarized by terminal and user should be forwarded to authorized personnel for review. Also, printed reports of unauthorized attempts to gain access to the system should be generated by the system for review and appropriate follow-up.

Summary

Our purpose in this chapter was to present internal control concepts and show how these concepts are integrated into the AIS. Accordingly, we have not attempted to list all possible internal controls (however, a rather detailed EDP internal control checklist is presented in the appendix to this chapter). Each accounting information system is unique (if for no other reason, due to the "people" element) and a set of internal controls must be specifically tailored for each system to provide reasonable assurance that AIS activities are conducted in accordance with management's policies. General and application controls in the computerized applications of the AIS must be effectively coupled with the total systems administrative and accounting controls to provide this reasonable assurance.

DISCUSSION QUESTIONS AND PROBLEMS

1. a. Define "internal control."
   b. Define "administrative control."
   c. Define "accounting control."
2. This chapter lists ten questions to be answered in developing the AIS. Relate these questions to the development of the AIS for the following firms:
   a. bank
   b. manufacturing firm
   c. CPA firm
   d. hospital
3. List and discuss the major cycles for the AIS that would be found in the followings firms:
   a. bank
   b. manufacturing firm
   c. CPA firm
   d. hospital
4. Develop a chart similar to Table 4-1 for the purchase of municipal bonds by the treasurer, and the subsequent sale of the bonds one year later.
5. a. What three items are most important, in terms of accuracy, in the recording of transactions?
   b. Give examples where each of the three could cause serious misstatement in the reports to management.
6. Define "segregation of duties" and list at least five conflicts that could occur within the general accounting department.
7. List and discuss the ten characteristics of a system of accounting control and give an example of each.
8. a. Define "audit trail" and "management trail."
   b. What are the major differences between them?

9. Discuss the two classifications of EDP controls and give examples of each subgroup.
10. The computer may assist in maintaining certain types of controls. Give examples in which this would be true for the following:
    a. input
    b. processing
    c. output
11. How does the concept of internal control relate to:
    a. AIS objectives?
    b. AIS design?
    c. AIS reports?

Bibliography

AICPA, *Codification of Statements on Auditing Standards.* Chicago, Ill.: Commerce Clearing House, Inc., 1977.

ARENS, ALVIN A., and JAMES K. LOEBBECKE. *Auditing: An Integrated Approach,* Englewood Cliffs, N.J.: Prentice-Hall, 1976.

Canadian Institute of Chartered Accountants. *Computer Control Guidelines,* Toronto, 1972.

CUSHING, BARRY E., *Accounting Information Systems and Business Organizations,* Reading, Mass.: Addison-Wesley Publishing Company, 1974.

MEIGS, WALTER B., E. JOHN LARSEN, and ROBERT F. MEIGS, *Principles of Auditing,* (6th ed.), Homewood, Ill.: Richard D. Irwin, Inc., 1977.

Peat, Marwick, Mitchell & Co. Technical Material.

STETTLER, HOWARD, F. *Auditing Principles,* (4th ed.), Englewood Cliffs, N.J.: Prentice-Hall, 1977.

APPENDIX
SAMPLE AUDIT PROGRAM AND QUESTIONNAIRES
Notes On Use

The attached sample audit program and questionnaires illustrate a format which may be helpful in organizing the field work and resulting working papers. The content is generalized and is intended to serve as a guideline. Not all of the questions will be appropriate in every examination, and in certain examinations, additional questions may be required, depending upon the circumstances of the examination. The sample audit program and questionnaires are not intended to deal with detailed reviews and compliance or substantive testing of the EDP portion of significant accounting systems; rather they are intended to provide a base to build upon should such reviews and tests be performed.

In completing the questionnaires, care should be taken to record clearly the extent of work performed in answering the questions. In the case of answers supplied by clients with no additional examination performed by the auditor, for example, a "C" can be indicated in the scope column of the questionnaire provided for this purpose. Similarly, an "A" can be used to identify documentation developed by the auditor, and a "CA" can be used to identify information or documentation acquired from the client and confirmed by the auditor.

This appendix is divided into the following sections:

1. Index.
2. Audit program.
3. Background information schedules.
4. General controls questionnaire.
5. Application controls questionnaire.

SAMPLE INDEX OF WORKING PAPERS

Reference

Summary memorandum and conclusions

Preliminary review audit program

EDP department background information

General controls questionnaire

Review of the _____ application
- Questionnaire
- Flow of transaction documentation
- Control point documentation

Review of the _____ application
- Questionnaire
- Flow of transaction documentation
- Control point documentation

SAMPLE PRELIMINARY REVIEW AUDIT PROGRAM

                                                                       Reference   Done by/Date

1. Arrange for the preparation and completion of the EDP department background information schedules.
2. Identify significant accounting applications.
3. Determine the extent of use of EDP within each significant accounting application.
4. Complete the General Controls Questionnaire.
5. Based upon the results of the review of general controls, assess whether these controls appear to provide a basis for reliance.
6. Document the flow of transactions through the EDP portion of each significant accounting application.
7. Describe the basic structure of accounting controls within each significant accounting application.
8. Complete the Application Controls Questionnaire.
9. Based upon the results of the review of application controls, assess whether controls within the EDP portion of each significant accounting application appear to provide a basis for reliance.
10. Develop an audit program for subsequent audit activities taking into account the results of the preliminary review.

EDP DEPARTMENT BACKGROUND INFORMATION SCHEDULES

Notes On Use

The schedules included in this section are designed to provide information which will be helpful in gaining an overall perspective of the EDP Department and the work it performs.

It is expected that the schedules can be prepared by the client's staff. Such schedules should be reviewed by the auditor before performing other preliminary review procedures.

If information requested in any of the schedules is already prepared and available in another format, attach this information and indicate its attachment on the appropriate schedule.

EDP DEPARTMENT BACKGROUND INFORMATION SCHEDULES

SCHEDULES
PREPARED BY: _____

SCHEDULES
REVIEWED BY: _____

DATE: _____

DATE: _____

1. Name of company _____

2. Location(s) of EDP department _____

3. Name of individual in charge of the EDP department_____

4. Attach a copy of the EDP organization chart starting one level above the EDP department manager.

5. Indicate the number of personnel (by level) within each area of the EDP department. *

	Data Entry	Data Control	Systems and Programming	Operations and Scheduling
Managers/supervisors				
Systems analysts				
Programmers				
Operators				
Key transcription				
Control clerks				
Librarians				
Clerical assistants				
Other				
Total				

* Indicate on the reverse side the number of personnel (by level) performing EDP functions in departments other than EDP.

Appendix to Chapter 4

6. Describe the major duties and responsibilities for each key individual or section within the EDP department.

KEY INDIVIDUAL OR SECTION	SIZE OF GROUP	MAJOR DUTIES AND RESPONSIBILITIES

7. Identify EDP equipment used. For each entry, indicate manufacturer, model number and quantity unless otherwise indicated.

	Configuration 1	Configuration 2	Configuration 3
Location	_____	_____	_____
Central processor: CPU	_____	_____	_____
Internal storage size	_____	_____	_____
External storage units:			
Magnetic tape drives	_____	_____	_____
Magnetic disc drives	_____	_____	_____
Other units	_____	_____	_____
Input-Output units:			
Card readers	_____	_____	_____
Card punches	_____	_____	_____
Line printers	_____	_____	_____
On-line terminals	_____	_____	_____
Remote-batch entry terminals	_____	_____	_____
Data entry devices	_____	_____	_____
Other units	_____	_____	_____

8. Identify operating system(s) used.

	Configuration 1	Configuration 2	Configuration 3
Name and version	_____	_____	_____
Release number	_____	_____	_____
Number of partitions generally used	_____	_____	_____
Size of partitions generally used	_____	_____	_____
System utilization:			
Shifts per week	_____	_____	_____
Days per week	_____	_____	_____
Hours per month (CPU meter time)	_____	_____	_____

Appendix to Chapter 4

9. Indicate the applications which utilize EDP and the extent of use. CPU hours shown in the schedule below are for the month of _____.

If exact times are not readily available, estimates may be used and indicated as such with an (E) on the schedule.

Application	Automated Yes	Automated No	CPU Hours Production	CPU Hours Rerun	CPU Hours Test	Programs Number	Programs Language(s)
A—Payroll:							
1—Salary							
2—Hourly							
3—Distribution							
4—Taxes and benefits							
5—Other _____							
B—Sales and receivables:							
1—Sales orders and backlog							
2—Invoicing							
3—Sales analysis							
4—Accounts receivable							
5—Cash receipts							
6—Other _____							
C—Costs and payables:							
1—Purchase orders							
2—Receiving							
3—Cost distribution							
4—Accounts payable							
5—Cash disbursements							
6—Other _____							
D—Inventory:							
1—Perpetual inventory							
2—Inventory control							
3—Other _____							
E—Production:							
1—Production orders							
2—Machine scheduling							
3—Status reports							
4—Efficiency reports							
5—Costs							
6—Material availability							
7—Other _____							
F—Forecasting:							
1—Sales							
2—Production							
3—Financial and accounting							
4—Other _____							

Application	Automated		CPU Hours			Programs	
	Yes	No	Production	Rerun	Test	Number	Language(s)
G—Properties:							
1—Depreciation, depletion, and amortization							
2—Insurance and taxes							
3—Other _____							
H—Operating statements:							
1—Departmental							
2—Divisional							
3—Company							
4—Other _____							
I—General Accounting:							
1—General ledger							
2—Trial balance							
3—Other _____							
J—Other accounting applications:							
Total of other applications (nonaccounting)							
Month totals							

Appendix to Chapter 4

10. Indicate the nature of documentation developed and maintained by the EDP department.

	Included		
	Always	Sometimes	Never
GENERAL:			
Table of contents			
Revision sheets			
Description of system			
Overall system flowchart			
System test plan			
INPUT:			
Sample input forms			
Instructions for completion of input			
Key transcription instructions			
Input record layouts and file definitions			
PROCESSING:			
Pertinent segment of system flowchart			
Description of job control and parameter cards			
Description of job setup procedures			
Description of special processing requirements			
Data control and error correction procedures			
File and report disposition procedures			
OUTPUT:			
Sample reports			
Output control and distribution procedures			
Output record layouts and file definitions			
PROGRAM:			
Narrative program description			
Program flowchart or decision table			
Error detection and correction procedures			
Source program listing			

GENERAL CONTROLS QUESTIONNAIRE

Notes On Use

This questionnaire is intended to provide the information regarding general EDP controls in sufficient depth to allow the auditor to make an assessment of these controls as discussed in Paragraph 26 of SAS-3. A copy of this questionnaire should be completed for each separate EDP location.

QUESTIONNAIRE
PREPARED BY: _____

QUESTIONNAIRE
REVIEWED BY: _____

DATE: _____

DATE: _____

Name of company _____

Location of EDP Facility _____

Organization controls:

1. Does the company's organizational structure and its division of duties appear to provide for adequate supervision and segregation of functions within the EDP department and between EDP and user departments?

    Yes _____   No _____

In assessing organization controls the auditor should consider the following:	Contributes to Possible Reliance Yes	Contributes to Possible Reliance No	Source of Information (C, A, or CA)	Comments And/Or Reference
• Separation of programming, systems analysis and operations functions				
• Application of management techniques to planning and reviewing the department's work				
• Data control function separate from user and operations functions				
• Regular rotation of duties				
• Independence of EDP department				
• Internal audit involvement in EDP				

Operations controls:

2. Are the general controls over computer operations sufficient to provide reasonable assurance as to the accuracy and completeness of processing results?

Yes _____   No _____

In assessing operations controls the auditor should consider the following:	Contributes to Possible Reliance		Source of Information (C, A, or CA)	Comments And/Or Reference
	Yes	No		
• Supervision of operations personnel and review of all computer activities on a periodic basis				
• Precluding EDP personnel from authorizing or initiating transactions				
• Restricting access to systems and program documentation				
• Adequate operating instructions				
• Limiting operator intervention				
• Scheduling computer work load				
• Restricted access to computer facilities and data files				
• General housekeeping and orderly work flow in EDP facility				

Documentation controls:

3. Are the general controls over all levels of documentation for EDP systems sufficient to ensure (for audit purposes) that documentation is adequate, complete and up to date?

Yes _____ No _____

In assessing documentation controls, the auditor should consider the following:	Contributes to Possible Reliance		Source of Information (C,A, or CA)	Comments And/Or Reference
	Yes	No		
• Formal documentation standards				
• Formal management review and acceptance of documentation				
• Documentation prepared concurrently with system and program development and maintenance				
• Separate levels of documentation for the users, systems, programming, operational and data control functions				
• Access to each level of documentation restricted to authorized individuals				

Systems development and programming controls:

4. Are the general controls over system development, program development, and maintenance activities sufficient to ensure that applications are properly developed, implemented and maintained?

Yes _____ No _____

In assessing systems development and programming controls, the auditor should consider the following:	Contributes to Possible Reliance		Source of Information (C, A, or CA)	Comments And/Or Reference
	Yes	No		
• Development of formal systems and program specifications				
• User approval of systems and program specifications				
• Supervisory review of detail program coding				
• Formal systems and program test plans including user approval of plans and results				
• Formal implementation plans (including parallel testing)				
• Formal controls over the authorization, documentation, testing and implementation of system and program changes				

Hardware and systems software controls:

5. Are the general controls over hardware and systems software sufficient to ensure that errors are detected and that EDP resources are used only as authorized?

    Yes _____   No _____

In assessing hardware and systems software controls, the auditor should consider the following:	Contributes to Possible Reliance Yes	No	Source of Information (C, A, or CA)	Comments And/Or Reference
• The existence of automatic hardware error detection				
• Periodic maintenance of all hardware				
• Formal procedures to recover from hardware errors				
• Authorization and control over implementation of and changes to systems software				

Access and library controls:

6. Are the general controls relating to the physical safeguards of the computer facility and its records sufficient to ensure that access to EDP resources is appropriately restricted and that data and programs are properly identified and used only for authorized purposes?

    Yes _____   No _____

In assessing access and library controls, the auditor should consider the following:	Contributes to Possible Reliance Yes	No	Source of Information (C, A, or CA)	Comments And/Or Reference
• Formal authorization and control procedures over the release, use and return of data media				
• Controls over access to, and use of the computer and its related equipment				
• Controls over access to, and use of, operational programs and related documentation				
• External labelling of computer files				
• Library function independent of operations and programming				

APPLICATION CONTROLS QUESTIONNAIRE

Notes On Use

The attached questionnaire for the preliminary review of an accounting application is intended to provide information regarding the internal controls within the EDP portion of the application to permit the auditor to make the assessment required by Paragraph 26 of SAS-3. In assessing application controls, the auditor should consider the effect of any weaknesses in general controls.

A copy of the questionnaire should be completed for each significant accounting application.

QUESTIONNAIRE
PREPARED BY: _____

QUESTIONNAIRE
REVIEWED BY: _____

DATE: _____

DATE: _____

Name of company_____

Application _____

Input controls:

1. Are there input controls within the EDP portion of this application that appear to provide a basis for reliance?

    Yes _____   No _____

    In answering the above question, the auditor should consider several questions with respect to input controls.

    a. Are there controls to ensure that input data is authorized?

    Yes _____   No _____

Examples of appropriate control techniques may include the following:	Contributes to Possible Reliance		Source of Information (C, A, or CA)	Comments And/Or Reference
	Yes	No		
• Initials or signature of individual authorized to approve input				
• Use of standard forms or distribution stamps				

Appendix to Chapter 4

b. Are there controls to ensure that input data is not lost, added to, or otherwise improperly changed?

Yes ____   No ____

Examples of appropriate controls may include the following:	Contributes to Possible Reliance		Source of Information (C, A, or CA)	Comments And/Or Reference
	Yes	No		
• Pre-numbered transmittal forms				
• Pre-numbered source documents				
• Batches of reasonable size				
• Batch totals on critical fields				
• Hash totals				
• Item counts				
• Cancellation of source documents to prevent resubmission				

c. Are there controls to ensure that conversion of input into machine-sensible form is performed accurately?

Yes ____   No ____

Examples of appropriate control techniques may include the following:	Contributes to Possible Reliance		Source of Information (C, A, or CA)	Comments And/Or Reference
	Yes	No		
• Verification of important information by the key transcription section				
• Control ledger for the data control and key transcription functions				

d. Are there controls to ensure that transactions containing errors identified during processing are properly investigated, corrected and resubmitted?

Yes ____   No ____

Examples of appropriate control techniques may include the following:	Contributes to Possible Reliance		Source of Information (C, A, or CA)	Comments And/Or Reference
	Yes	No		
• Error control logs				
• Error transmittal lists				
• Error suspense files and periodic listings				

Processing controls:

2. Are there processing controls within the EDP portion of this application that appear to provide a basis for reliance?

    Yes _____   No _____

    In answering the above question, the auditor should consider several questions with respect to processing controls.

    a. Are there controls to ensure that data submitted for processing is subjected to adequate programmed editing, validation and error detection procedures?

    Yes _____   No _____

Examples of appropriate techniques may include the following:	Contributes to Possible Reliance Yes	No	Source of Information (C,A, or CA)	Comments And/Or Reference
• Range and reasonableness checks				
• Alphabetic vs. numeric tests				
• Self-checking numbers				
• Listing of all errors				
• Validation of input by comparison to existing information in master files or tables				

   b. Are there controls to ensure that processing is complete and accurate?

    Yes _____   No _____

Examples of appropriate techniques may include the following:	Contributes to Possible Reliance Yes	No	Source of Information (C,A, or CA)	Comments And/Or Reference
• Control totals report showing in or out-of-balance condition				
• Listing of additions, deletions and changes to records in the master files				
• Programmed run-to-run control totaling and balancing				
• Controls over machine-generated transactions				
• File identification procedures for all files				

Output controls:

3. Are there output controls within the EDP portion of this application that appear to provide a basis for reliance?

    Yes ____   No ____

    In answering the above question, the auditor should consider several questions with respect to output controls.

    a. Are there controls to ensure that the results of processing, either machine-readable data or reports, are complete and accurate?

    Yes ____   No ____

Examples of appropriate techniques may include the following:	Contributes to Possible Reliance		Source of Information (C, A, or CA)	Comments And/Or Reference
	Yes	No		
• Output totals agreed to input and processing control totals				
• Overall review of reports for reasonableness and completeness				
• Machine-generated data files adequately labeled and physically controlled				

   b. Are there controls to ensure that output is distributed only as authorized and is not lost or improperly altered?

   Yes ____   No ____

Examples of appropriate techniques may include the following:	Contributes to Possible Reliance		Source of Information (C, A, or CA)	Comments And/Or Reference
	Yes	No		
• A report distribution list indicating those authorized to receive the output				
• A report distribution log indicating when and to whom output was distributed				
• Special handling procedures for classified, sensitive or negotiable documents and reports				

Preview:
This chapter explains the use of external and internal reports and discusses the users needs, as well as report preparation.
–Role of the treasurer
–Role of the controller

CHAPTER FIVE

reports

Closely Related Chapters:
Chapter 2–Management reports
Chapter 3–Management needs
Chapter 7–Corporate decisions
Chapter 8–Report definition
Chapter 10–Report forms
Chapter 11–EDP reports
Chapter 13–New requirements

The objective of the accounting information system is to provide information to those who need it, whether they are inside or outside the organization. The form of this information may vary but can generally be referred to as AIS reports. Some of these reports only provide information, while others provide information and require action. These INFORMATION and ACTION reports will be discussed separately for both inside and outside users of the system.

This chapter deals with the various types of reports that the system must be capable of generating. The starting point in any systems design is the definition of information needs. This definition is most exactly accomplished if all output reports are compiled and reviewed for compliance with reporting requirements. First we will discuss the major requirements for external users.

EXTERNAL USER REQUIREMENTS

The largest single group of external users is the stockholder/investor group. This includes present stockholders, bond holders, and potential investors. The organization must produce certain statements for these external users on at least an annual and sometimes a quarterly basis. Although these statements are the responsibility of management (and indeed they are *management's* statements) they are usually audited by a firm of Certified Public Accountants. The CPA firm is only expressing an opinion on the financial statements, including footnotes, and is not actually involved in the creation of the underlying data. The responsibility for the underlying data rests with management, as does the responsibility for establishing and maintaining an effective system of internal control to provide reasonable assurance as to the reliability of this data (see Chapter 4).

The audited financial statements provided to investors generally do not show the types of financial analysis that this group of external users rely upon for decision-making. Investors often use interest coverage ratios, current ratios, and price/earnings ratios in their investment decisions. These ratios are seldom provided in the audited statements and therefore must be computed by the user. The financial statements aggregate similar accounts and make detailed interpretations difficult due to the complexity of the principles used in this aggregation. The footnotes are used to describe these functions but they may be unintelligible to the lay reader. The appendix to this chapter presents a complete set of audited financial statements. Particular attention should be given to the detail presented in the footnotes.

In addition to annual and quarterly financial statements, a publicly held company, under the jurisdiction of the Securities and Exchange Commission, must file several types of reports. A partial list follows:

1. A Form 10-K must be filed annually, if applicable, based on SEC regulations. Together with the Form 10-K is a complete set of financial statements of information normally not included in the annual report, expanded information concerning management and ownership of the firm, a five-year summary of earnings and other detailed information. The form and content of the financial statements and related schedules is set out in SEC Regulation S-X.
2. A Form 10-Q is filed quarterly when applicable. The financial information included with this form is less detailed than with the Form 10-K. The purpose of this form is to provide the external users with current data during the year regarding the financial condition of the company.
3. A Form 8-K is filed when required by SEC regulations to notify external users of any unusual or significant events or transactions on a current basis.
4. Form S-1 and Form 10 are required (among others) for the issuance of securities.

In addition to these SEC reports, many companies must now file "Line-of-Business" reports with the Federal Trade Commission. These reports are quite detailed and are difficult to file, because most businesses are not organized in a manner that allows these types of subconsolidation.

Many companies must also file reports with local, state, and federal regulatory agencies. Most regulatory agencies have been established to provide regulation in lieu of competition. For purely economic reasons, several industries have little or no competition within a geographic region and therefore regulation of these "licensed monopolies" is necessary. In most cases, the regulation takes the form of rate setting, although some regulation of the timing of service and quality may also be appropriate. Other regulations may relate to quality control or standardization of reporting. Some of the types of organizations most affected by such regulation are: (1) utilities, (2) airlines, (3) insurance companies, (4) hospitals, and (5) banks. Let us consider some of the reporting requirements of each of these types of organizations.

Utilities

In addition to the Federal Power Commission, most power-generating utilities must file reports with the state and local agencies claiming jurisdiction. Most of the reports are of a monitoring nature. However, when a utility requests a rate increase, the request must be accompanied by lengthy, detailed reports on financial position and income from operations. Further, it may be necessary to project the effect of the increase on the economy of the area. The report will usually require projections of the effect of the increase on the financial reports of the company.

Telephone service is generally provided by only one company within a given area, therefore regulation of this monopoly is also necessary. The Federal Communications Commission has jurisdiction at the national level over radio, television, microwave, and telephone companies. Most of these reports relate to quality control and rate-setting procedures. The majority of rate-setting reports are filed with state and local agencies.

Airlines

Airlines report technical matters to the Federal Aviation Administration and financial service matters to the Civil Aeronautics Board. The FAA has jurisdiction over the airworthiness of aircraft and dictates maintenance schedules, aircraft modifications, crew qualifications, and safety standards. Compliance reports must be timely. The CAB has jurisdiction over routes to be flown and rates that may be charged. By carefully monitoring the revenue passenger miles flown, the CAB may increase or decrease the number of flights servicing airports or alter the flight mix of an individual carrier to allow their continued profitable operation. The level of detail of required reports almost approaches the detail required for internal operations.

Insurance Companies

Insurance companies (just as airlines and utilities) must report to investors. Further, they must report to the insurance industry regulatory commission in the state in which they are domiciled (some states require reports for all companies operating within the state). These special reports differ from those provided to other outsiders in that they are prepared on a policy-year basis rather than a fiscal or regular calendar year. The policy year is defined as the calendar year in which the policy attaches (becomes effective). The policy may continue to be in effect for several months after the end of the calendar year, but for reporting purposes it will be reflected back to the year of attachment. Premiums must be reported as (1) received, (2) earned, and (3) unearned. Claims are reported as (1) incurred, (2) reported, (3) outstanding, and (4) paid. For any one policy year, several (if not all) of these special reporting features may be present. An example should help show the differences.

DATE	EVENT	REPORT FEATURES
10-1-77	Policy attaches	Premium received
12-27-77	Major insured loss incurred	Not reported at 12-31-77, complete earned premium
12-31-77	Year-end for insurance company	Estimate losses incurred/not reported
1-6-78	Loss reported	Establish loss revenue (estimate)
9-30-78	Policy expires, not renewed	All premium now earned
12-31-78	Year-end for insurance company	No premium written, no loss paid
2-15-79	Loss settled	Loss must be reflected back to policy year 1977 for actual payment, loss revenue reduced to zero

The year of 1977 now shows the premium written in that year and the claims settled against that income. This allows for meaningful analysis by the appropriate insurance commissioner for the establishment of rates. This rate-setting function would be more difficult if he had to rely on only the regular calendar year statements, because it would be impossible to relate premiums to corresponding claims.

Hospitals

Many hospitals are now operating under a "draw" or "allowance" system when reporting to medicare. Under this arrangement, the hospital is allowed to receive periodic funding rather than have individual medicare-covered expenses reported and processed. There also must be a reconciliation made for all reported claims versus all "draws." Other hospitals must still file for separate reimbursement for each claim. In addition to these filing requirements, each hospital must support its claimed amounts together with cost justification reports. These reports show justifications for each expense and require timely updating of cost formats and careful projection of anticipated future costs.

Preparation of External Reports

As discussed earlier, most external reports are prepared in a predefined format, and many are audited. This gives the preparer very little flexibility to exercise creativity. It does, however, mean that most external reports should be useful to those who receive them. The audited reports provided to investors are not precisely defined but are structured under guidelines established by the accounting profession. These guidelines permit certain alternatives for some situations and are constantly being revised and clarified. The Financial Accounting Standards Board issued fourteen statements in its first three years, and there are now seventeen statements on auditing standards.

The preparation of external reports should be done with the utmost care. The report in the hands of outsiders may be their only contact with the firm, and therefore it should be prepared with great attention to detail. Clerical accuracy, pleasing format, and concise language are all basic considerations, however the most important consideration is the quality of information presented in the report. In Chapter 3 we discussed the various accounting systems that provide the data for the report. In Chapter 4 we discussed the internal control procedures used to provide reasonable assurance that this data is reliable. All the concepts in these chapters should be considered when designing a system to produce quality external reports. The same concepts, of course, relate to the generation of internal reports.

INTERNAL USER REQUIREMENTS

Reports given to regulatory agencies and investors comprise only a minority of the total reporting requirements of the firm. The majority of the required reports given to the different levels of management differ in form, function, level of detail, and purpose. We shall discuss each of these very important report elements separately. Refer to Fig. 5-1 as an aid.

Fig. 5-1. Integrated Report Structure

Higher Level Managers (e.g., president, vice presidents and managers of major functions)	Narrative summary of current major projects and activities, such as capital expenditures and research programs Income statement, comparing budgeted with actual values Statement of profit earned by each product line and organizational segment Balance sheet, comparing last period with current period Cash flow statement, comparing projection with actual Control reports, comparing budgeted with actual expenses for each major unit and function Measures of key performance and success factors relating to entire firm and to major functions and divisions Long-range forecasts and planning reports, including relevant information relating to environment
↓	↑
Middle Level Managers (e.g., plant managers, division managers, purchasing agents, sales managers, chief cost accountants)	Cost accounting operating summaries Statement of profit earned (or) loss incurred (assuming the existence of profit centers) Control reports, comparing budgeted with actual expenses for each department or activity at the lower level Status or exception reports concerning inventories, maintenance, spoilage, product quality, idle time, facility utilization, personnel, etc. Measures of key performance factors relating to responsibilities Analyses of sales, of orders, of products, of purchases, etc. Medium-range planning reports and schedules
↓	↑
Lower Level Managers (e.g., foremen, supervisors, department heads, sales branch managers)	Cost accounting operating reports Control reports, comparing budgeted with actual expenses Labor distribution and efficiency reports Measures of key performance factors relating to responsibilities Short-range planning reports and schedules

Joseph Wilkinson, "Effective Reporting Structures," *Journal of Systems Management*, Nov., 1976.

Elements of Internal Reports

As presented in Figure 5-1, the bottom of the organization chart is representative of the lowest level or first-line management. The top of the chart represents top-level management. The lower levels of management generally receive reports that are action oriented rather than informative. Usually the purpose of reports at lower levels of management is to cause future or corrective actions. As we move up the chart, reports become less action oriented and more informational. Of course, upper levels of management will always receive crisis action reports. However, for the most part, they will concentrate on summaries of operation reports for control and decision-making.

Action reports should contain sufficient detail to allow the manager to identify problems. First-line managers have responsibility for very limited areas and consequently are able to respond in detail to complicated requirements. As we go up the chart, higher-level managers deal with wider ranges of management problems, and their needs turn more to aggregated reports and less to detail.

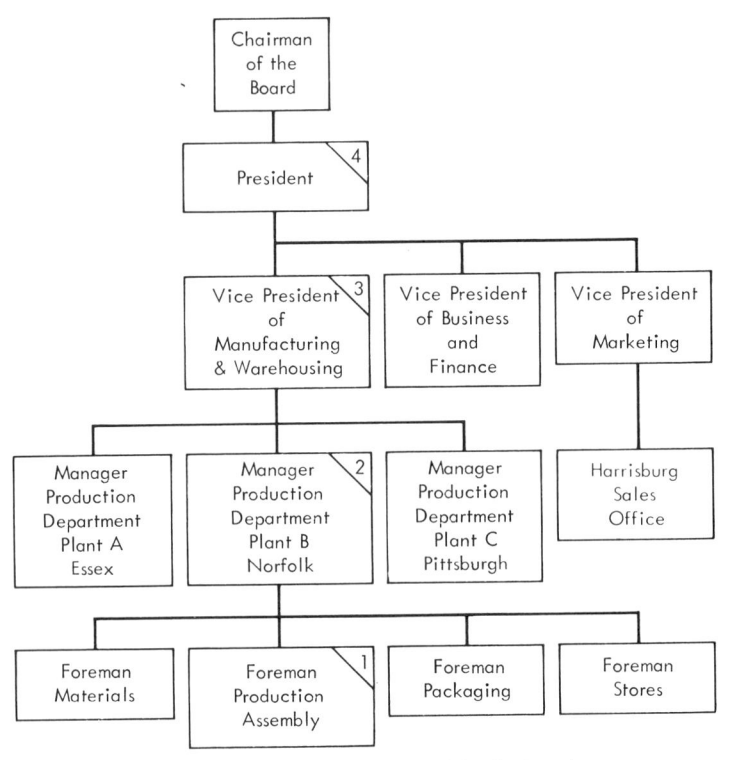

Fig. 5-2a. Responsibility Reporting Relationships by Levels

```
┌─────────────────────────────────────┲┓
│ President                         4 ┃│
│                                     │
│ Controllable Costs      3/31/74     │
│                                     │
│   Marketing          $    xx,xxx    │
│   Administration          xx,xxx    │
│   Manufacturing          447,221    │
│   O  O  O  O                 xxx    │
│   O  O  O  O                 xxx    │
│                       $2,224,103    │
└─────────────────────────────────────┘
```

```
┌─────────────────────────────────────┲┓
│ Vice President of Manufacturing   3 ┃│
│ & Warehousing                       │
│                                     │
│ Controllable Costs      3/31/74     │
│                                     │
│   Plant A (Essex)    $      xxx     │
│   Plant B (Norfolk)      119,099    │
│   Plant C (Pittsburgh)      xxx     │
│   O  O  O  O                xxx     │
│   O  O  O  O                xxx     │
│                        $447,221     │
└─────────────────────────────────────┘
```

```
┌─────────────────────────────────────┲┓
│ Manager, Production Department    2 ┃│
│ Plant B (Norfolk)                   │
│                                     │
│ Controllable Costs      3/31/74     │
│                                     │
│   Materials          $      xxx     │
│   Assembly               41,747     │
│   Packaging                 xxx     │
│   Stores                    xxx     │
│   O  O  O  O                xxx     │
│   O  O  O  O                xxx     │
│                        $119,099     │
└─────────────────────────────────────┘
```

Note: The design of responsibility reports should be tailored by the user. The responsible person needs to take an active role in preparing his own budgets and standards.

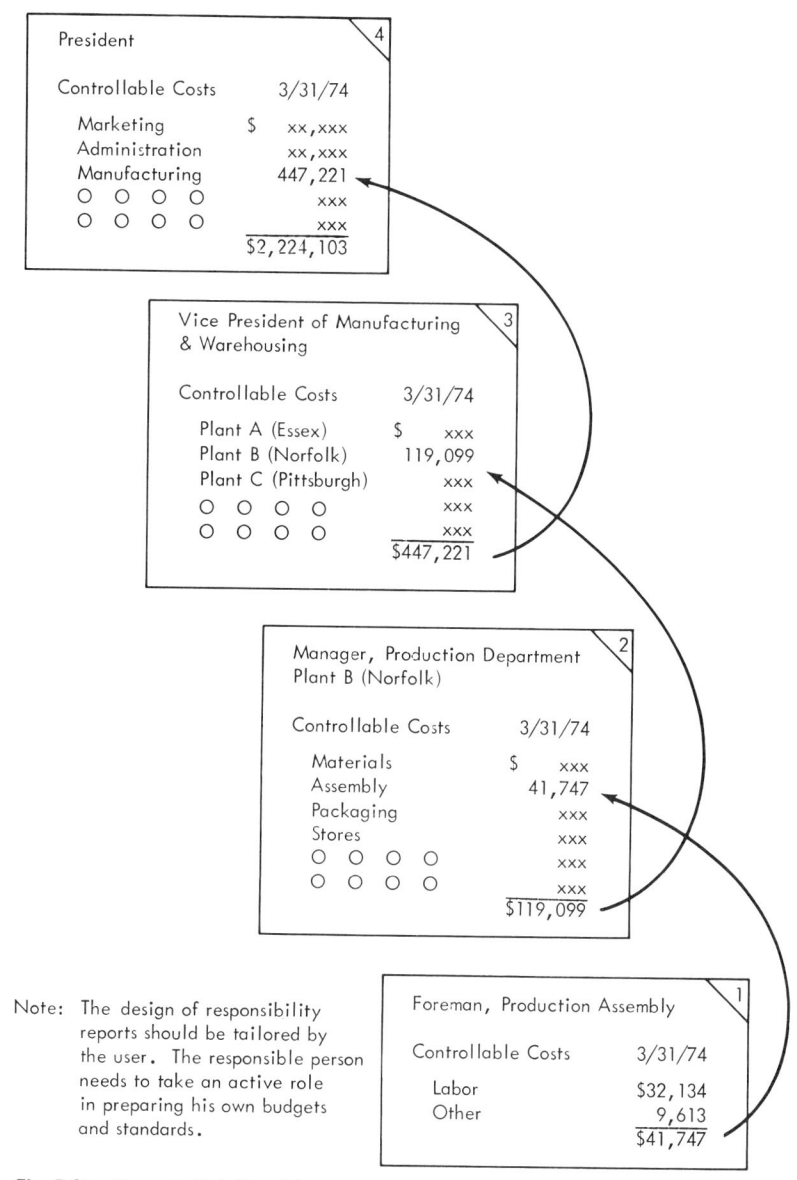

```
┌─────────────────────────────────────┲┓
│ Foreman, Production Assembly      1 ┃│
│                                     │
│ Controllable Costs      3/31/74     │
│   Labor                 $32,134     │
│   Other                   9,613     │
│                         $41,747     │
└─────────────────────────────────────┘
```

Fig. 5-2b. Reports Relationships

Source: *MSA General Ledger System,* Courtesy of Management Science of America, Inc.

157

First-level managers spend much of their time controlling the activities under their area of responsibility. This function of control demands detailed, timely reporting in order to identify and correct problems. The overall planning function is generally performed by upper-level personnel. To accomplish the planning function, managers usually need overall reports, not necessarily detailed analysis. The planning function needs not only historic reports but future projections for decision-making. These projections must cover a wide range of activities including cash flow, sales, capital budgeting, and staff requirements. Figure 5-1 shows the different areas that often concern each level of management. It should be noted that planning is done at each level of management, however the time devoted to planning increases as you move upward on the organization chart.

An example of this reporting by levels of responsibility is presented in Fig. 5-2. The first part of the figure presents the organization structure of the company. The second part of the exhibit shows how manufacturing costs are reported from the lower levels of the organization to the president of the company. At each stage of the reporting process, the information necessary to perform the managerial functions is included in the reports at that level.

Generating Internal Report Information

The AIS should be capable of generating all information required for reports from a common data base. In order to accomplish this, the data base must contain all the data that will be needed for each report. Most of the data will initially be captured on source documents in the traditional manner. Other data, particularly projected data, must be collected by other means, and great care should be exercised to insure that they maintain the same level of integrity as internal data. Several outside data sources are used every day in business; some are informally and some are formally introduced into the system.

Competitors' actions are a prime concern to management, as are such things as demographic changes in their marketing areas, changes in the cost of borrowing money, unemployment, and changes in gross national product. It is important to management that the measurement of these variables be consistent and reliable. Further, it takes considerable effort on the part of management to decipher which variables should be accorded more importance. Constant monitoring of the system, in-depth knowledge of possible simulation formulas, and a method of verifying the data are all inherent in a viable system.

It is important that the system perform in a consistent manner. Because people must be relied on to gather and interpret data, monitoring the people performing these tasks is necessary. The data gathered and interpreted must be afforded similar treatment if the results are to be meaningful. Businesses use several indicators to predict the value for a single variable and balance changes in indicators before changing a variable. Long-range plans must be made in stages with milestones to measure performance against the overall plan. As the variables that helped formulate the plan change, it may be necessary to change the plan even though the milestones may show that progress is in line with the plan. For example, a five-year plan started in 1972 could well be obsolete in any year after that due to inflation, unemployment, or interest rates. If inflation continues to run over a stated percent, almost all plans that used earnings or cash position as a significant measuring point will have to be revised. Net income, when computed using historic cost depreciation, must be incorrect by at least the inflation rate. This is explained by the fact that depreciation should be an allocation of cost against current income to allow for the replacement of the asset at the end of its useful life. With inflation constantly increasing the cost to replace assets, the depreciation expense charged to income will not be adequate to provide for replacement.

Another example, humorous to some, will show the error of following the lead of others without analyzing the potential impact. Imagine a small manufacturing firm that was in very aggressive competition with another local and somewhat larger company. The president of the small firm was asked how he set prices for his goods, and his answer was simple: He charged the same price as his competitors! He had no system to accurately report his cost of goods manufactured. Unfortunately, neither did the larger firm. They went bankrupt at about the same time.

The moral of the story is, of course, that the *accuracy* of input may be close to perfect but the *validity* completely false. Following the lead of competitors is only one way to incorporate accurate, yet misleading, data. Other possible pitfalls are:

1. Buying from the same vendor without checking prices with other vendors.
2. Selling a majority of manufactured goods to a single buyer who may come to dictate prices.
3. Expanding because the competition is expanding.
4. Diversifying into areas without competent management experience.

This list is not exhaustive, but merely shows that there can be several areas where outside data sources may prove unreliable or unusable. Great care should be taken when choosing outside data sources.

The data selected should be tested and continually monitored for change.

Preparation of Internal Reports

After carefully selecting the outside data to be included in internal reports, it will be necessary to interpret the data and convert it to a format that will be usable when combined with internally generated data. The internally generated data are the subject of other chapters, and we will assume that the data are sufficient at this point. The single most important step in internal reporting is identifying the information needs of the users of the system. This should be done in consultation with the user/managers and their superiors, as well as those responsible for the creation of the data. It is not uncommon to find a communication gap between data handlers and data users. The one group blindly collects and processes data, and the other group uses whatever they receive in the way of information, assuming that it is both correct and complete. The report to be designed should be designed by both groups and then tested to insure that report is not duplicated elsewhere in the system. There is no need to develop entire new reports just to introduce a few new data fields. However, this is often the reason used to expand the number of reports generated or received.

THE ROLE OF THE TREASURER AND CONTROLLER

We have discussed the flow of informational reports from the AIS to the various levels of operations management. Two individuals in the organization have a particular role in the generation of reports and subsequent relations with internal and external users. These individuals are the treasurer and the controller.

The Role of the Treasurer

The treasurer is generally considered by most firms to be the chief financial officer and as such maintains a functional position at the vice-president level. In addition, the treasurer often serves as chairman of the finance committee. The functions of the treasurer with which this chapter is concerned lie in areas of reporting to parties outside the business entity. The controller is responsible for extracting the necessary information from the data base for the preparation of the reports, but it is primarily the concern of the treasurer to format and explain the contents of the report.

As chief financial officer, the treasurer has several functions that relate to working capital and cash. Providing adequate cash for operations and capital acquisitions is of prime importance. This function is related closely to several of the other functions shown in Table 5-1. The granting of credit and collection of receivables, along with maintaining good banking relationships, constitute the main sources of cash for the firm. As a functional manager, the treasurer is a user of the AIS with the objective of predicting the timing and quantity of cash demands. Capital and expense budgets, together with dividend policy, cover most of the expected cash outlays.

The Role of the Controller

The controller can be characterized as being the top-level systems manager. This position requires supervision of all aspects of data collection and storage as well as data extraction for both internal and external reports. The last decade has seen the EDP installation of the firm move out of the controller's department and into a new area called Information Systems. This is a beneficial move from the internal control point of view in that it provides for better separation of incompatible functions (see Chapter 4). Although the computer, the programmers, and the data

Table 5-1. Functions of the Treasurer and Controller

TREASURER	CONTROLLER
1. Stockholder and Investor Relations	1. Data Collection and Storage for all operations
2. Provides insurance	2. Control of documentation for cash receipts and disbursements
3. Credit and collections	3. Control of N/R records
4. Banking arrangements	4. Control of inventory records
5. Provides cash for operations	5. Preparation of internal operating reports and schedules
6. Short and long-range planning, primarily for working capital	6. Tax Administration
7. Investments	7. Payroll administration
8. Custodian of cash and cash-like assets	8. Processing of data for the preparation of external reports
9. Tax planning	

base administrator (see Chapter 12) have been physically removed from the controller's department, the responsibility for information control and documentation remain with the controller. Again refer to Table 5-1 for a list of the controller's duties.

Summary

External reports are prepared for numerous regulatory agencies and other interested outsiders. However, the majority of AIS reports are prepared for internal users. The type of information included in these reports will vary depending on the needs of the user. External reports usually must comply with predescribed guidelines imposed by the external users. Internal reports should contain information that is relevant to the internal user. All reports, whether internal or external, should contain quality information generated with reasonable assurance by a properly designed and controlled AIS.

Bibliography

AICPA, *Codification of Statements on Auditing Standards*, New York, 1977.
Canadian Institute of Chartered Accountants, *Computer Control Guidelines*, Toronto, 1972.
Peat, Marwick, Mitchell & Co., Technical Material.

DISCUSSION QUESTIONS AND PROBLEMS

1. Define the objective of the AIS.
2. List at least five users of external reports for the following firms:
   a. manufacturing firm with international sales
   b. interstate trucking firm
   c. oil exploration firm
   d. hospital
3. a. List and describe at least five action reports.
   b. How would these reports be refined to become higher management level information reports?

4. a. Define the types of internal reports that the treasurer would receive.
   b. What types of internal reports would he prepare?
   c. What types of external reports would he prepare?
5. a. Define the type of internal reports that the controller would receive.
   b. What types of internal reports would he prepare?
   c. What types of external reports would he prepare?
6. List and give an example of each of the functions of the treasurer and controller.
7. List at least ten reports, internal and external, for a manufacturing firm and discuss the factors that would determine the frequency and distribution of each.
8. Prepare a table of contents for an annual report to stockholders for the following firms:
   a. book publisher
   b. trucking firm
   c. airline
   d. hospital
   e. bank
   f. large retailer, such as Sears, Roebuck & Co.
9. The president of your firm has asked you to design a summary annual report on the status of the AIS, with particular emphasis on a review of internal controls. Develop a list of topics that should be included in your report.
10. Refer to the audited financial statements in the Appendix to this chapter. List the various statements and exhibits and discuss why each is important in the decision–making process of managers.

APPENDIX TO CHAPTER 5

Balance Sheet
International Finance Corporation

June 30, 1976 and June 30, 1975
Expressed in United States Dollars—*See Notes to Financial Statements, Exhibit F*

	1976	1975
Assets		
DUE FROM BANKS—*Note B*	$ 4,213,547	$ 1,599,814
INVESTMENTS		
Short-term obligations of governments (At cost or amortized cost, which approximates market) — $ 14,187,455		7,458,022
Accrued interest — —		36,766
	14,187,455	7,494,788
LOAN AND EQUITY INVESTMENTS (At Cost)—*Note A (See Exhibit D)*		
Investments held for the Corporation — $778,933,748		658,974,932
Less—Undisbursed investments — 256,090,611		197,040,402
Disbursed and outstanding — $522,843,137		461,934,530
Less—Reserve against losses—*Note A* — 30,700,000		24,500,000
	492,143,137	437,434,530
ACCRUED INCOME ON LOANS—*Note A*	9,256,267	9,034,114
RECEIVABLE FROM PURCHASERS OF LOAN AND EQUITY INVESTMENTS SOLD OR AGREED TO BE SOLD — $ 61,729,391		76,113,398
Less—Undisbursed investments sold or agreed to be sold — 58,148,586		74,576,955
	3,580,805	1,536,443
OTHER ASSETS	326,477	530,414
TOTAL	$523,707,688	$457,630,103

Exhibit A

	1976	1975
Liabilities, Capital and Surplus		
LIABILITIES AND DEFERRED INCOME		
Accrued charges on borrowings	$ 6,749,356	$ 5,351,582
Accounts payable and other liabilities	1,459,487	1,194,145
Deferred income	1,614,987	—
	$ 9,823,830	6,545,727
BORROWINGS—*Note C*		
Loans from the International Bank for Reconstruction and Development	$501,943,192	443,391,438
Less—Undrawn	179,792,928	175,511,936
Withdrawn and outstanding	$322,150,264	267,879,502
Loan from the State of the Netherlands	5,000,000	5,000,000
	327,150,264	272,879,502
CAPITAL AND SURPLUS		
Capital stock		
Authorized 110,000 shares of $1,000 par value each		
Subscribed 108,324 shares—1976, 107,331 shares—1975	$108,324,000	107,331,000
Payment on account of pending subscriptions	—	155,000
General reserve—*Note A*	78,409,594	70,718,874
	186,733,594	178,204,874
TOTAL	$523,707,688	$457,630,103

Statement of Income

International Finance Corporation

Exhibit B

For the Fiscal Years Ended June 30, 1976 and June 30, 1975
Expressed in United States Dollars—*See Notes to Financial Statements, Exhibit F*

		1976	1975
Operating Income			
Income from obligations of governments..................................		$ 271,756	$ 243,754
Income from loan and equity investments and standby and underwriting commitments:			
Interest...	$33,997,043		26,073,474
Dividends and profit participations........................	7,036,429		5,955,288
Commitment charges..................................	1,592,013		1,582,907
Commissions..	582,606		303,077
		43,208,091	33,914,746
Other operating income.......................................		(186,429)	58,326
		$43,293,418	$34,216,826
Operating Expenses			
Charges on borrowings......................................	$22,096,703		$16,905,583
Administrative expenses[1]..................................	11,399,504		10,446,809
		33,496,207	27,352,392
Income from Operations.....................................		$ 9,797,211	$ 6,864,434
Realized Gain on Sales of Loan and Equity Investments..........................		4,260,415	5,106,885
Provision for Losses—*Note A*................................		(6,366,906)	(6,576,112)
Net Income—Transferred to General Reserve—*Note A*..........................		$ 7,690,720	$ 5,395,207

[1] The International Bank for Reconstruction and Development is charging the Corporation an annual "Service and Support Fee" which for the year ended June 30, 1976 was fixed at $1,485,000 ($1,455,000—1975).

Statement of Changes in Financial Position

International Finance Corporation

Exhibit C

For the Fiscal Years Ended June 30, 1976 and June 30, 1975
Expressed in United States Dollars—*See Notes to Financial Statements, Exhibit F*

	1976	1975
Funds Provided		
Net income	$ 7,690,720	$ 5,395,207
Items not requiring current outlay of funds:		
Provision for losses on investments	6,366,906	6,576,112
Changes in accrued income and expenses	1,128,191	(626,463)
Other	(5,351)	(51,777)
Funds provided from operations	$ 15,180,466	$ 11,293,079
Capital subscriptions	993,000	111,000
Loans from the International Bank for Reconstruction and Development	65,719,008	101,717,337
Repayment of loans	32,675,607	26,497,716
Sales and participations	102,446,888	59,117,978
Other	1,665,943	166,692
TOTAL FUNDS PROVIDED	$218,680,912	$198,903,802
Funds Used		
Disbursements on loan and equity investments	$199,703,574	$184,419,286
Repayments on loans from the International Bank for Reconstruction and Development	9,634,172	8,350,138
TOTAL FUNDS USED	$209,337,746	$192,769,424
Increase in Cash and Short-Term Obligations of Governments	$ 9,343,166	$ 6,134,378

Statement of Loan and Equity Investments
International Finance Corporation

June 30, 1976
Expressed in United States Dollars (in thousands)—*See Notes to Financial Statements, Exhibit*

COUNTRY and Obligor	Type of business	Original commitments	Loans	Equity	Total loans and equity (at cost)
Afghanistan					
Industrial Development Bank of Afghanistan	Development financing	$ 322	$ —	$ 322[1]	$ 322
Argentina					
Celulosa Argentina, S.A.	Pulp and paper	12,500	5,905	—	5,905
Dalmine Siderca, S.A.I.C.	Steel products	17,000	14,200	—	14,200
Calera Avellaneda, S.A.	Cement	5,500	4,591	—	4,591
		TOTAL	24,696	—	24,696
Bolivia					
Plasmar, S.A.	Plastic products	400	207	100	307
Banco Industrial, S.A.	Development financing	550	—	550	550
Banco Hipotecario Nacional	Capital market development	338	—	338	338
		TOTAL	207	988	1,195
Brazil					
Champion Papel e Celulose, S.A.	Pulp and paper	4,000	2,589	(*Note 2*) 163	2,752
Aços Villares S.A.	Steel	9,926	—	3,408	3,408
Papel e Celulose Catarinense, S.A.	Pulp and paper	7,192	—	3,408	3,408
Ultrafértil, S.A.—Indústria e Comércio de Fertilizantes	Fertilizers	11,250	—	2,945	2,945
Petroquímica União, S.A.	Petrochemicals	8,380	2,087	2,046	4,133
Poliolefinas, S.A. Indústria Comércio	Petrochemicals	8,377	2,902	2,000	4,902
Oxiteno, S.A. Indústria e Comércio	Petrochemicals	6,040	3,737	1,240	4,977
Indústria de Celulose Borregaard, S.A.	Pulp	4,900	4,165	—	4,165
CIMINAS—Cimento Nacional de Minas, S.A.	Cement	32,340	4,256	3,200	7,456
Companhia Siderurgica da Guanabara (Cosigua)	Steel	73,500	11,572	6,500	18,072
Capital Market Development Fund (FUMCAP)	Capital market development	5,000	5,000	—	5,000
Industrias Villares, S.A.	Elevators and industrial equipment	6,000	2,824	—	2,824
Fábrica de Tecidos Tatuapé, S.A.	Textiles	31,000	7,750	—	7,750
Capuava Carbonos Industriais, Ltda.	Carbon black	7,262	2,480	1,082	3,562
Oxiteno Nordeste, S.A.	Petrochemicals	10,000	10,000	—	10,000
Santista Industria Textil do Nordeste, S.A.	Textiles	7,450	6,450	1,000	7,450
Tecanor S.A. Textil Catarinense do Nordeste	Textiles	6,000	6,000	—	6,000
		TOTAL	71,812	23,584	95,396
Cameroon					
Bata Société Anonyme Camerounaise	Shoes	399	—	399	399
Chile					
Empresa Minera de Mantos Blancos, S.A.	Copper mining	4,337	—	1,237	1,237
Fideos y Alimentos Carozzi, S.A.	Food products	1,654	—	154	154
Minera Sagasta, S.A.	Copper mining	10,900	7,803	450	8,253
		TOTAL	7,803	1,841	9,644
China					
Asia Cement Corporation	Cement	4,219	600	1,087	1,687
Oriental Chemical Fiber Corporation	Synthetic fibers	5,625	2,407	612	3,019
		TOTAL	3,007	1,699	4,706
Colombia					
Corporación Financiera Colombiana	Development financing	2,024	—	1,012	1,012
Corporación Financiera Nacional	Development financing	2,042	—	604	604
Compañia Colombiana de Tejidos, S.A.	Textiles	2,126	—	63	63
Corporación Financiera de Caldas	Development financing	812	—	701	701
Industria Ganadera Colombiana, S.A.	Livestock	1,581	—	580	580
Enka de Colombia, S.A.	Synthetic fibers	7,605	4,000	2,505	6,505
Corporación Financiera del Norte	Development financing	454	—	454	454
Corporación Financiera del Valle	Development financing	431	—	235	235
Pro-Hoteles, S.A.	Tourism	1,019	590	139	729
Corporación Colombiana de Ahorro y Vivienda	Capital market development	455	—	455	455
Cementos Boyaca, S.A.	Cement	1,500	1,500	—	1,500
Cementos del Caribe, S.A.	Cement	3,600	3,600	—	3,600
Minera Las Brisas S.A.	Asbestos mining	6,000	6,000	—	6,000
		TOTAL	15,690	6,748	22,438

Exhibit D

COUNTRY and Obligor	Type of business	Original commitments		Loans	Equity	Total loans and equity (at cost)
Cyprus						
Cyprus Cement Company, Ltd.	Cement	$ 2,884		$ 1,743	$ 544	$ 2,287
Dominican Republic						
Cementos Nacionales, S.A.	Cement	7,380		6,000	1,380	7,380
Ecuador						
La Internacional, S.A.	Textiles	3,963		1,188	—	1,188
Ecuatoriana de Desarrollo, S.A. (Compañia Financiera)	Development financing	338		—	338	338
Sociedad Agricola e Industrial San Carlos, S.A.	Sugar	5,000		5,000	—	5,000
			TOTAL	6,188	338	6,526
Egypt, Arab Republic of						
Arab Ceramic Company, S.A.	Ceramics	5,652		4,725	927	5,652
El Salvador						
Hoteles de Centro América Sociedad Anónima	Tourism	934		437	233	670
Ethiopia						
Cotton Company of Ethiopia, S.C.	Textiles	4,815		1,161	837[1]	1,998
Ethiopian Pulp and Paper, S.C.	Pulp and paper	1,909		—	1,209	1,209
H.V.A.—Metahara, S.C.	Sugar	9,045		2,484	1,622	4,106
			TOTAL	3,645	3,668	7,313
Greece						
"Titan" Cement Company, S.A.	Cement	1,526		50	—	50
National Investment Bank for Industrial Development, S.A.	Development financing	719		—	102	102
General Cement Company, S.A.	Cement	3,500		700	—	700
Aluminium de Grèce, Société Anonyme Industrielle et Commerciale	Aluminum production	8,653		958	577	1,535
Hellenic Food Industries, S.A.	Food products	1,132		928	132	1,060
			TOTAL	2,636	811	3,447
Guatemala						
Exploraciones y Explotaciones Mineras Izabal, S.A.	Nickel mining and refining	15,000		15,000	—	15,000
India						
Mahindra Ugine Steel Company, Ltd.	Steel products	12,797		10,050	830	10,880
Lakshmi Machine Works, Ltd.	Textile machinery	1,312		—	314	314
Indian Explosives, Ltd.	Fertilizers	11,462		890	2,263	3,153
Zuari Agro Chemicals, Ltd.	Fertilizers	18,911		9,113	3,040	12,153
Escorts Limited	Engine parts	6,600		6,600	—	6,600
			TOTAL	26,653	6,447	33,100
Indonesia						
P. T. Primatexco Indonesia	Textiles	4,801		2,701	801	3,502
P. T. Unitex	Textiles	3,300		750	800	1,550
P. T. Semen Cibinong	Cement	26,816		12,820	4,500	17,320
P. T. Kabel Indonesia—Kabelindo	Cable manufacturing	3,172		1,238	372	1,610
P. T. Daralon Textile Manufacturing Corporation	Textiles	6,000		3,375	1,125	4,500
P. T. Jakarta International Hotel	Tourism	11,000		4,000	—	4,000
P. T. Private Development Finance Company of Indonesia	Development financing	483		—	483	483
P. T. Monsanto Pan Electronics	Electronic products	900		800	—	800
P. T. Kamaltex	Textiles	3,000		2,400	600	3,000
			TOTAL	28,084	8,681	36,765
Iran						
Sherkate Sahami Aam Navard Va Luleh Ahwaz	Steel	7,739		960	263	1,223
Kaghaz Pars Sherkat Sahami Aam	Pulp and paper	14,193		9,447	1,944	11,391
Sherkate Sahami Carbon Iran, Sahami Khass	Carbon black	3,553		2,281	432	2,713
			TOTAL	12,688	2,639	15,327
Israel						
Makhteshim Chemical Works, Ltd.	Chemicals	10,500		8,750	1,750	10,500

Appendix To Chapter 5

Statement of Loan and Equity Investments (continued)
International Finance Corporation

June 30, 1976

Expressed in United States Dollars (in thousands)—*See Notes to Financial Statements, Exhibit F*

COUNTRY and Obligor	Type of business	Original commitments	Loans	Equity	Total loans and equity (at cost)
Ivory Coast					
Banque Ivoirienne de Développement Industriel, S.A.	Development financing	$ 204	$ —	$ 204	$ 204
Jamaica					
Pegasus Hotels of Jamaica, Ltd.	Tourism	2,913	1,298	669	1,967
Jordan					
Jordan Ceramic Industries Company, Ltd.	Ceramics	1,826	1,350	226	1,576
Jordan Fertilizer Industry Company, Ltd.	Fertilizers	3,064	—	3,064	3,064
	TOTAL		1,350	3,290	4,640
Kenya					
Kenya Hotel Properties, Ltd.	Tourism	5,877	3,791	715	4,506
Panafrican Paper Mills (E.A.), Ltd.	Pulp and paper	17,582	7,706	3,903	11,609
Tourism Promotion Services (Kenya), Ltd.	Tourism	2,420	1,590	—	1,590
Rift Valley Textiles, Ltd.	Textiles	9,070	5,300	2,769	8,069
	TOTAL		18,387	7,387	25,774
Korea					
Korea Development Finance Corporation	Development financing	18,869	8,900	796	9,696
Honam Silk Industry Company	Textiles	1,677	840	277	1,117
Korea Investment and Finance Corporation	Capital market development	1,394	—	1,394	1,394
Gold Star Company, Ltd.	Electronic products	27,677	13,000	1,677	14,677
Korea Securities Finance Corporation	Capital market development	5,581	5,000	581	5,581
Hae Un Dae Development Company, Ltd.	Tourism	3,450	2,750	700	3,450
Tong Yang Nylon Company, Ltd.	Textiles	9,000	6,929	2,071	9,000
Korea Zinc Company, Ltd.	Zinc refinery	19,008	15,000	4,008	19,008
Chonju Paper Manufacturing Co., Limited	Pulp and paper	5,532	5,000	532	5,532
	TOTAL		57,419	12,036	69,455
Lebanon					
Lebanon Textiles (Libtex) S.A.L.	Textiles	3,900	3,400	—	3,400
Bank of the Near East S.A.L.	Capital market development	1,250	—	1,250	1,250
	TOTAL		3,400	1,250	4,650
Liberia					
Liberia Bank for Industrial Development and Investment	Development financing	250	—	249	249
Malawi					
David Whitehead & Sons (Malawi) Ltd.	Textiles	6,000	6,000	—	6,000
Malaysia					
Malayawata Steel, Berhad	Steel	3,693	615	—	615
India-Malaysia Textiles, Berhad	Textiles	1,498	890	248	1,138
	TOTAL		1,505	248	1,753
Mauritius					
Dinarobin Inns and Motels, Ltd.	Tourism	615	262	—	262
Mexico					
Fundidora Monterrey, S.A.	Steel	23,741	1,104	1,419	2,523
Industria del Hierro, S.A.	Construction equipment	1,962	—	361	361
Celanese Mexicana, S.A.	Textiles	12,000	7,571	—	7,571
Promotora de Papel Periódico, S.A. de C.V.	Pulp and paper	25	—	25	25
Cementos Veracruz, S.A.	Cement	10,500	5,856	—	5,856
Cancún Aristos Hotel	Tourism	1,240	976	264	1,240
Mexinox, S.A.	Steel	15,603	12,000	3,603	15,603
	TOTAL		27,507	5,672	33,179
Morocco					
Banque Nationale pour le Développement Economique	Development financing	1,496	—	852	852
Compañia Industrial del Lukus, S.A.	Food processing	1,388	—	398	398
Société des Ciments de Marrakech, S.A.	Cement	1,353	—	1,353	1,353
	TOTAL		—	2,603	2,603

Exhibit D

COUNTRY and Obligor	Type of business	Original commitments	Loans	Equity	Total loans and equity (at cost)
Nepal					
Soaltee Hotel, Ltd.	Tourism	$ 3,107	$ 2,700	$ 407	$ 3,107
Nicaragua					
Textiles Fabricato de Nicaragua, S.A.	Textiles	2,071	400	—	400
Propiedades Azucareras de Nicaragua Limitada	Sugar	6,500	6,500	—	6,500
Posada del Sol, S.A.	Tourism	900	700	200	900
		TOTAL	7,600	200	7,800
Nigeria					
Arewa Textiles, Ltd.	Textiles	1,575	3	442	445
Funtua Cottonseed Crushing Company, Ltd.	Cottonseed oil and byproducts	1,580	1,064	—	1,064
Nigerian Aluminium Extrusions, Ltd.	Aluminum	1,328	1,002	326	1,328
Lafiagi Sugar Estate	Sugar	117	—	117	117
		TOTAL	2,069	885	2,954
Pakistan					
Gharibwal Cement, Ltd.	Cement	5,668	449	418	867
Pakistan Industrial Credit and Investment Corporation, Ltd.	Development financing	520	—	483	483
Crescent Jute Products, Ltd.	Textiles	1,950	230	—	230
Packages, Ltd.	Paper products	3,152	465	605	1,070
Pakistan Paper Corporation, Ltd.	Paper	7,401	4,836	2,019	6,855
Dawood Hercules Chemicals, Ltd.	Fertilizers	3,923	—	2,923	2,923
		TOTAL	5,980	6,448	12,428
Panama					
Corporación de Desarrollo Hotelero, S.A.	Tourism	1,472	1,133	266	1,399
Paraguay					
FINAP, S.A.	Lumber products	5,400	4,400	1,000	5,400
Peru					
Cemento Andino, S.A.	Cement	2,461	—	192[1]	192
Compañia de Cemento Pacasmayo, S.A.	Cement	1,605	—	117	117
Southern Peru Copper Corporation	Copper mining	15,000	15,000	—	15,000
		TOTAL	15,000	309	15,309
Philippines					
Private Development Corporation of the Philippines	Development financing	19,359	6,465	—	6,465
Manila Electric Company	Electric power	8,000	2,868	—	2,868
Meralco Securities Corporation	Electric power	4,000	—	3,639	3,639
Philippine Long Distance Telephone Company	Utilities	4,500	3,477	—	3,477
Mariwasa Manufacturing, Inc.	Construction materials	1,193	128	239	367
Philippine Petroleum Corporation	Lubricating oil refinery	8,000	5,270	1,800	7,070
Marinduque Mining and Industrial Corporation	Nickel mining and refining	15,000	14,375	—	14,375
Victorias Chemical Corporation	Chemicals	2,196	1,586	346	1,932
Filipinas Synthetic Fiber Corporation	Synthetic fibers	1,500	1,421	—	1,421
Maria Cristina Chemical Industries, Inc.	Ferroalloys production	1,986	1,550	436	1,986
RFM Corporation	Food products	1,200	1,137	—	1,137
Philippine Polyamide Industrial Corporation	Synthetic fibers	7,000	7,000	—	7,000
Philagro Edible Oils, Inc.	Vegetable oils	2,838	2,650	188	2,838
		TOTAL	47,927	6,648	54,575
Rwanda					
Société d'Investissement Rwandaise du Thé S.A.R.L.	Tea	535	535	—	535
Senegal					
Société Industrielle d'Engrais au Sénégal	Fertilizer	3,460	614	810	1,424
Bud Senegal, S.A.	Agribusiness	868	—	701	701
Société Financière Sénégalaise pour le Développement Industriel et Touristique	Development financing	237	—	237	237
		TOTAL	614	1,748	2,362
Spain					
Industrias de Tableros y Derivados de la Madera, S.A.	Construction materials	5,251	4,386	865	5,251

Statement of Loan and Equity Investments (continued)
International Finance Corporation

June 30, 1976

Expressed in United States Dollars (in thousands)—*See Notes to Financial Statements, Exhibit F*

COUNTRY and Obligor	Type of business	Original commitments	Loans	Equity	Total loans and equity (at cost)
Sudan					
Khartoum Spinning and Weaving Company, Ltd.	Textiles	$ 2,212	$ 195	$ 273	$ 468
Cotton Textile Mills, Ltd.	Textiles	9,976	8,715	1,261	9,976
		TOTAL	8,910	1,534	10,444
Thailand					
Siam Cement Co., Ltd.	Cement and steel	32,082	12,413	2,042	14,455
Tunisia					
Banque de Développement Economique de Tunisie	Development financing	1,208	—	1,208	1,208
Compagnie Financière et Touristique, S.A.	Tourism financing	10,248	6,845	2,248	9,093
Société Touristique et Hotelière Rym, S.A.	Tourism	1,930	1,557	298	1,855
Société d'Etudes et de Développement de Sousse Nord	Tourism	3,162	2,530	633	3,163
Industries Chimiques du Fluor, S.A.	Chemicals	640	—	640	640
		TOTAL	10,932	5,027	15,959
Turkey					
Turkiye Sinai Kalkinma Bankasi, A.S.	Development financing	63,416	15,000	1,345	16,345
Sentetik Iplik Fabrikalari, A.S.	Textiles	4,568	984	555	1,539
Viking Kagit ve Seluloz, A.S.	Pulp and paper	3,169	1,719	669	2,388
Anadolu Cam Sanayii, A.S.	Glass	11,583	6,713	1,583	8,296
Nasas-Aluminyum Sanayii ve Ticareti, A.S.	Aluminum products	9,946	6,387	1,372	7,759
Akdeniz Turistik Tesisler, A.S.	Tourism	603	235	268	503
Borusan Gemlik Boru Tesisleri, A.S.	Steel pipes	4,036	3,600	436	4,036
AKSA Akrilik Kimya Sanayii, A.S.	Textiles	10,000	10,000	—	10,000
Kartaltepe Mensucat Fabrikasi T.A.S.	Textiles	1,300	1,300	—	1,300
Sasa Sun'i ve Sentetik Elyaf Sanayii, A.S.	Chemicals	15,000	7,500	—	7,500
Aslan ve Eskihisar Muttehit Cimento ve su Kireci Fabrikalari A.S.	Cement	10,600	5,600	—	5,600
Doktas Dokumculuk Ticaret ve Sanayii, A.S.	Steel	8,676	7,500	1,176	8,676
Asil Celik Sanayi ve Ticaret, A.S.	Steel	15,403	12,000	3,403	15,403
		TOTAL	78,538	10,807	89,345
Uruguay					
Fabrica Uruguaya de Neumaticos, S.A.	Tires	3,800	3,800	—	3,800
Venezuela					
Sociedad Financiera Valinvenca S.A.	Capital market development	351	—	351	351
Sociedad Financiera Promotora del Mercado de Capitales, C.A.	Capital market development	701	—	701	701
		TOTAL	—	1,052	1,052
Yugoslavia					
International Investment Corporation for Yugoslavia	Development financing	2,000	—	2,000	2,000
Zavodi Crvena Zastava/Fiat, S.p.A.	Automobiles	13,000	4,000	7,400	11,400
Tovarna Avtomobilov in Motorjev Maribor/Klöckner Humboldt-Deutz, A.G.	Commercial vehicles	9,598	6,375	1,399	7,774
Fap-Famos Belgrade/Daimler-Benz, A.G.	Commercial vehicles	15,348	11,040	2,097	13,137
Sava-Semperit	Tires	5,520	3,500	1,179	4,679
Belisce-Bel Tvornica Papira, Poluceluloze I Kartonaze—Belisce	Pulp and paper	13,259	10,683	—	10,683
ZP Slovenske Zelezarne Zelezarna Jesenice	Steel	10,000	10,000	—	10,000
Salonit Anhovo Industrija Gradbenega Materiala	Cement	10,000	2,500	—	2,500
Rudarsko Metalurski Kombinat Zenica	Steel	50,000	5,000	—	5,000
		TOTAL	53,098	14,075	67,173
Zaire					
Société Financière de Développement	Development financing	756	—	756	756
Zambia					
Zambia Bata Shoe Company, Ltd.	Shoes	2,278	643	228	871
Century Packages, Ltd.	Packaging materials	1,035	775	260	1,035
Development Bank of Zambia	Development financing	545	—	545	545
		TOTAL	1,418	1,033	2,451

Exhibit D

COUNTRY and Obligor	Type of business	Original commitments	Loans	Equity	Total loans and equity (at cost)
Regional Investments					
Africa					
SIFIDA Investment Company, S.A.	Development financing	$ 680	$ —	$ 680	$ 680
Latin America					
ADELA Investment Company, S.A.	Development financing	10,000	8,200	—	8,200
TOTAL			8,200	680	8,880

Investments held for the Corporation (including undisbursed balances)

	Loans	Equity	Total
INVESTMENTS HELD FOR THE CORPORATION			
Total	$626,545	$152,389	$778,934
Undisbursed balances	225,470	30,621	256,091
Disbursed balances	$401,075	$121,768	$522,843
INVESTMENTS HELD BY THE CORPORATION FOR PURCHASERS AND PARTICIPANTS			
Total	$293,807	$ 2,536	$296,343
Undisbursed balances	56,776	1,372	58,148
Disbursed balances	$237,031	$ 1,164	$238,195
TOTAL INVESTMENTS HELD FOR THE CORPORATION AND FOR PURCHASERS AND PARTICIPANTS			
Total	$920,352	$154,925	$1,075,277
Undisbursed balances	282,246	31,993	314,239
Disbursed balances	$638,106	$122,932	$ 761,038

Note (1): IFC's equity investment has been the subject of acquisition procedures by the Government; the matter of payment is pending.
Note (2): Equity investment in this company was acquired at no cost.
General: The operational investments are represented by loans and equity, as stated. In addition, in certain investments, the Corporation has the right to acquire shares and/or participate in the profits of the enterprise.

Statement of Cumulative Gross Commitments

Exhibit E

International Finance Corporation

June 30, 1976

Expressed in United States Dollars (in thousands)—*See Notes to Financial Statements, Exhibit F*

COUNTRY	Number of Enterprises	Cumulative Gross Commitments (including exchange adjustments)	COUNTRY	Number of Enterprises	Cumulative Gross Commitments (including exchange adjustments)
Afghanistan	1	$ 322	Malaysia	4	$ 8,691
Argentina	8	53,210	Mauritania	1	20,007
Australia	2	975	Mauritius	1	615
Bolivia	3	1,287	Mexico	13	69,921
Brazil	23	276,316	Morocco	3	4,237
Cameroon	1	399	Nepal	1	3,107
Chile	5	21,191	Nicaragua	3	9,471
China	2	9,844	Nigeria	5	6,000
Colombia	22	36,200	Pakistan	9	30,224
Costa Rica	1	589	Panama	1	1,472
Cyprus	1	2,884	Paraguay	1	5,400
Dominican Republic	1	7,380	Peru	7	23,980
Ecuador	3	9,302	Philippines	14	78,980
Egypt, Arab Republic of	1	5,652	Rwanda	1	535
El Salvador	2	1,074	Senegal	3	4,565
Ethiopia	3	15,768	Spain	4	18,761
Finland	4	3,148	Sri Lanka	1	3,250
Greece	6	16,129	Sudan	2	12,188
Guatemala	2	15,200	Tanzania	1	4,657
Honduras	2	453	Thailand	3	32,766
India	12	58,403	Tunisia	6	20,688
Indonesia	9	59,472	Turkey	13	158,302
Iran	7	42,536	Uganda	2	4,618
Israel	1	10,500	Uruguay	1	3,800
Italy	1	960	Venezuela	8	32,121
Ivory Coast	1	204	Yugoslavia	9	128,724
Jamaica	2	3,137	Zaire	1	756
Jordan	2	4,890	Zambia	3	3,858
Kenya	4	34,948			
Korea	10	97,188	Regional:		
Lebanon	4	7,280	Africa	1	680
Liberia	1	250	Latin America	1	10,000
Malawi	1	6,000	TOTAL	271	$1,505,465

Summary

	June 30 1976	June 30 1975	Increase
Investments held for the Corporation	$ 778,934	$ 658,975	$119,959
Principal repayments to the Corporation	142,084	109,409	32,675
Loan and equity investments sold or agreed to be sold	479,346	391,576	87,770
Cancellations	98,152	97,041	1,111
Investments written off	6,198	6,031	167
Revaluation of disbursed non-US dollar loans	751	(1,003)	1,754
Total Commitments	$1,505,465	$1,262,029	$243,436
Revaluation of undisbursed non-US dollar commitments made in prior years			1,869
Commitments—Fiscal Year 1976			$245,305

Notes to Financial Statements
International Finance Corporation

Exhibit F

June 30, 1976 and June 30, 1975

Note A—Significant Accounting Policies

Translation of Currencies—Equity investments disbursed in currencies other than United States dollars are expressed in United States dollars at the exchange rates which applied at the time of disbursement. Other assets and liabilities not denominated in United States dollars are expressed in terms of United States dollars at approximate market rates prevailing at the fiscal year-end. Exchange gains and losses are credited or charged to income as they occur.

Reserve Against Losses—The Corporation charges income directly with a provision for losses on investments with a corresponding credit to the Reserve Against Losses. The annual charge is based on the Corporation's historical loss experience, the amount of investments in respect of which a significant and relatively permanent decline in value is recognized and the amount of investments in respect of which losses cannot yet be identified.

Net income remaining after the above charge to income has been transferred to Surplus and allocated to a General Reserve. Losses on investments when written off are charged directly to the Reserve Against Losses. Changes in the Reserve Against Losses are summarized as follows:

	Fiscal Year Ended June 30	
	1976	1975
Balance beginning of period	$24,500,000	$20,000,000
Provision charged to income	6,366,906	6,576,112
Investments written off	(166,906)	(2,076,112)
Balance end of period	$30,700,000	$24,500,000

Investment Transactions—Investments are recorded at the date an investment commitment is made and are reflected as assets when disbursed. The market value of equity investments in the Corporation's portfolio is estimated to exceed the cost of such investments. Gains or losses on sales of investments are measured against the average cost of the investments sold. Gains on investments are credited directly to income when realized and losses are provided for as described in the preceding paragraph.

Revenue Recognition—Dividends, profit participations and commissions are recorded as income when received. Interest, commitment and other charges on loans are recorded as income on an accrual basis except that the Corporation does not currently accrue interest where collectibility is in doubt.

Staff Retirement Plan—The International Bank for Reconstruction and Development has a contributory retirement plan for its staff which also covers the staff of the Corporation. All contributions to the Plan and all other assets and income of the Plan are held by the Bank separately from the assets of the Bank and the Corporation and can be used only for the benefit of the participants in the Plan and their beneficiaries. The total cost of the Plan includes amortization of unfunded liabilities. The Bank and the Corporation's policy is to fund pension costs accrued. The cost of the Plan to the Corporation for the fiscal year ended June 30, 1976 was $1,142,541 ($1,004,243 —1975) which included amortization of unfunded liabilities over periods from 15 to 40 years.

Note B—Amounts Due Within One Year

Asset balances due the Corporation within one year are summarized as follows:

	As at June 30 ($ thousands)	
	1976	1975
Due from banks	$ 4,214	$ 1,600
Short-term obligations of governments	14,187	7,495
Principal instalments on loans	40,136	26,501
Accrued income on loans	9,256	8,580
Receivable from purchasers of loan and equity investments sold	2,185	227
Other	195	139
Total	$70,173	$44,542

The amount shown as due from banks at June 30, 1976 includes $1,691,150 ($1,220,171—1975) which is temporarily restricted as to use or as to conversion into other currencies.

Note C—Borrowings

The Corporation's long-term borrowings comprise the following:

(1) Loans totaling $502 million ($443 million—1975) from the International Bank for Reconstruction and Development. A commitment charge is payable on the undrawn balances of the loans at the rate of ¾ of 1% per annum. The loans are repayable in semi-annual instalments summarized below:

Principal Amount ($ millions)		Interest Rate Per Annum	Maturity Dates
1976	1975		
$176	$184	7%	1976 to 1989
$206	$209	7¼%	1976 to 1994
$120	$ 50	8½%	1978 to 1996

The principal amounts repayable during the fiscal years ending June 30, 1977 and 1978 are $11.5 and $14.7 million, respectively.

The proceeds of these loans may only be used by the Corporation in its lending operations.

(2) A loan of $5 million from the State of the Netherlands repayable in equal semi-annual principal instalments commencing on June 1, 1979, and having a final maturity date of December 1, 2000 with an interest rate equal to the rate of cash dividend, if any, paid by the Corporation on its capital stock. The Corporation may use the proceeds of this loan in any operation authorized by its Articles of Agreement.

Report of Independent Accountants

Financial Statements Covered by the Foregoing Report

 1801 K Street, N.W.
 Washington, D.C. 20006
 July 30, 1976

To
International Finance Corporation
Washington, D.C.

In our opinion, the accompanying financial statements present fairly, in terms of United States currency, the financial position of International Finance Corporation at June 30, 1976 and 1975, the results of its operations and the changes in financial position for the years then ended, in conformity with generally accepted accounting principles consistently applied. Our examinations of these statements were made in accordance with generally accepted auditing standards and accordingly included such tests of the accounting records and such other auditing procedures as we considered necessary in the circumstances.

 PRICE WATERHOUSE & CO.

Balance Sheet
Statement of Income
Statement of Changes in Financial Position
Statement of Loan and Equity Investments
Statement of Cumulative Gross Commitments
Notes to Financial Statements

ACCOUNTING INFORMATION SYSTEMS FOR DECISION MAKING

Preview:
This chapter defines the nature of problems as well as the development of the problem-solving process.
–Value of information
–Factors that shape decisions
–Management's role
–Accountant's role

CHAPTER SIX

problem-solving and decision making

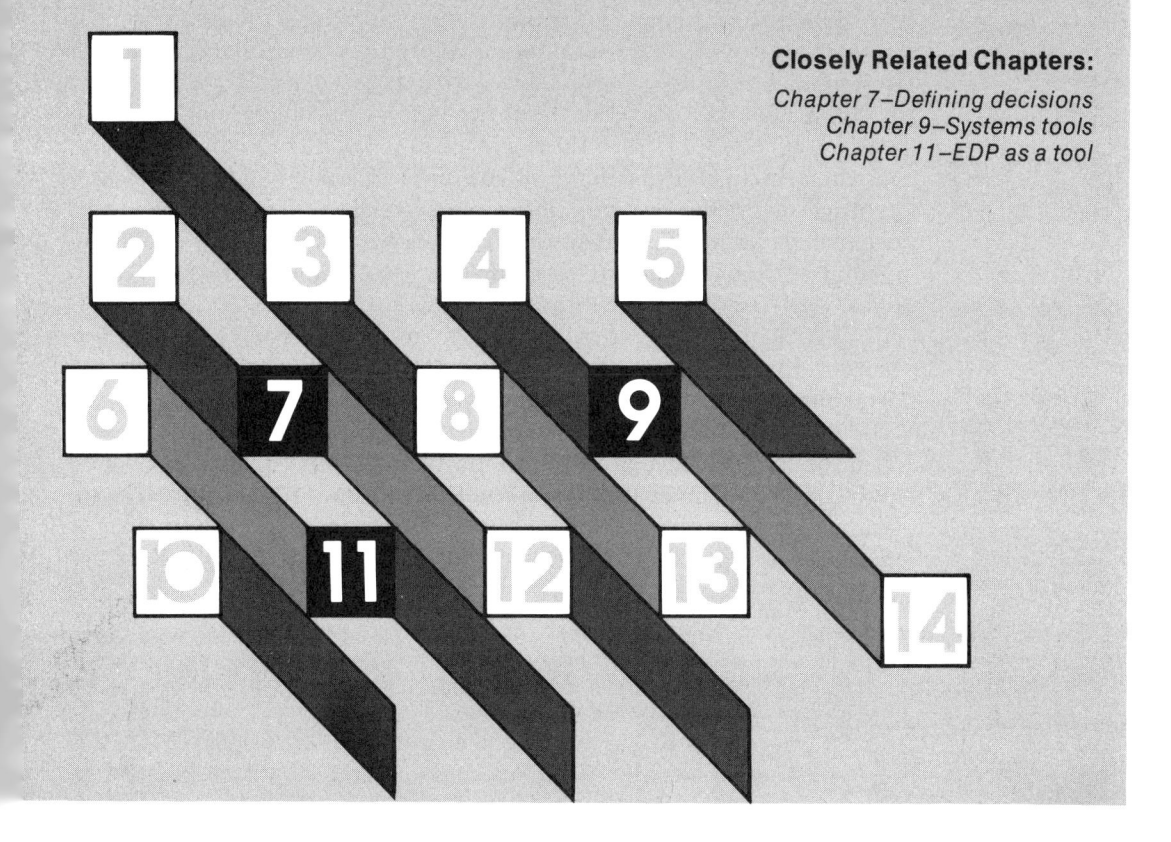

Closely Related Chapters:
Chapter 7–Defining decisions
Chapter 9–Systems tools
Chapter 11–EDP as a tool

Economics is the study of the principles for allocating scarce resources to competing wants. Land, capital, labor, management, and time are the basic scarce resources.

A society thrives in proportion to its efficient use of its resources. In our economic system, therefore, there is an economic side, or set of economic criteria, for all problems and decisions. While at times other criteria may seem to dominate, in the last analysis it is the cost and the benefit in terms of resources that must be considered. For this reason, the skilled dispassionate quantitative analysis which the accountant is trained to provide is essential to managerial problem-solving and decision-making.

This chapter discusses the formulation of problems and decision-making. The emphasis on these processes is from the managerial view. We then discuss the accountant's role in economic evaluation and comparative economic evaluation for managerial planning, allocation of resources, and measuring for control. Following this, we give six fundamental economic concepts to guide the accountant in making evaluations.

Problem-solving, in its essential form, is the *seeking of answers to a question*. Decision-making is the *cutting off* of further consideration of the problem, the elimination of all alternatives but one; it is a commitment to action. The solving of applied problems usually involves a means-end chain of subproblems. For each subproblem, alternatives are developed and a decision is made to follow a course of action, which requires the solution of another subproblem. Thus, decisions are made at a number of points in the sequential problem-solving process, as for example:

1. Decisions as to goals. These involve both values and empirical considerations.
2. Decisions as to subgoals and means in means-ends chains of action.
3. Decisions as to ranges of input values.
4. Decisions as to the selection from among alternate means-ends chains.

5. Decisions regarding basic assumptions.
6. Decisions regarding available data. Should they be accepted or rejected, or should a search for further data be carried out?
7. Decisions on final action to implement the selected solution to the problem.

It is the initial selection of goals and of the general strategy to be followed in solving means-ends chains that is usually referred to as executive decision-making.

THE NATURE OF PROBLEMS

Although managers spend much of their time in solving problems, one of their most important and often overlooked responsibilities is recognizing that a problem exists or impends. Too often managers remain unaware of problems until a crisis is reached or affairs have gone beyond the point of no return. Perhaps they have been misled by the naive idea that a problem exists only when something "bites" them. The manager must look further and discover what will "bite" him if he does not start solving problems in advance. With this in mind, we can say that major symptoms of present or impending problems are:

1. Performance is *presently* not meeting present objectives.
2. It is *anticipated* that at some future time performance will not continue to achieve present objectives.
3. Objectives of the present *are going to be changed* and *present* operating procedures will not result in the achievement of the new, future objectives.

A problem is, therefore, a felt need, a deviation between *that which is* (or is anticipated) and *that which is desired,* or between *that which is known* and that which is *desired to be known.* It is an indeterminate situation in which doubt or uncertainty is felt and a stimulus presses for a solution.

In business, or other innovative institutions, major problems appear in a four-stage cluster of problems. These broad problem types are:

1. The *problem of searching* for and identifying the primary problem to be solved. Consider, as an example, a company that produces fertilizers and chemicals. Symptoms of declining sales, declining prices, and stiff competition indicate that fundamental problems are present. What are the problems? Is one of them an overproduction of phosphates? Have technical innovations made entry into the industry so easy that the industry is overcrowded? Have substitute chemical fertilizers been found? Is the company's marketing program at fault? Has world demand declined?

2. The problem of *diagnosing the situation to determine the primary problem* (or problems) in the presence of many symptoms of problems. For the fertilizer company, the diagnosis showed that the industry was overcrowded, production too high, and prices unrealistically low for the current world demand.
3. The *primary problem itself.* Solution of the primary problem requires the development of alternative courses of action and selection of the best course. One alternative might be to increase demand by arranging financing for countries that urgently need fertilizer but lack the foreign exchange to pay for it. The fertilizer company adopted another strategy, however: it diversified into other chemicals; it eliminated uneconomical and geographically undesirable facilities; and finally, it introduced greater efficiency into its remaining operations.
4. *Secondary problems* connected with the first three classes of problems. They may be problems of method or of a subsidiary nature. One of the problems arising from falling sales and profits might be an attempted takeover by another company. Another might be a shortage of working capital at some time.

The primary and secondary problems cited are *decision problems,* because the objective of finding feasible solutions is to select and implement one. In the case of the fertilizer company, we note that for the decision problems, there was a decision-maker who had a problem, an outcome or goal of reversing the sales and profit trends, several alternative courses of action that might achieve the goal, uncertainty as to which course to follow, and a set of environmental conditions and constraints of time and resources. Criteria for a solution are also usually defined, although none were given in our case. Such a set of elements is usually present in all business decision problems.

FORMULATION OF THE PROBLEM

The way in which a problem is formulated, that is, stated and described, is apt to determine the nature of the solution. In complex business situations, verbalization, discussions, and reflection can do much to refine a problem, leading to its formulation and thereby ultimately contributing to its solution. It is also true that some problems are never solved because they are not formulated correctly. The right answer to the wrong problem may be more damaging than no solution at all.

Well-structured problems may be formulated quite precisely by means of mathematical models. The formulation, again, will be valid if the model describes the true problem. Formulation in this case requires that all variables, parameters, and constants be defined. Complex problem situations in which the problems themselves are not readily identifiable nor describable are called ill-structured problems. Here, formulation plays a much larger part in the development of a solution.

In each of these two extreme cases, formulation requires a statement of the elements of the problem, the present state and the desired state, the constraints involved in solving the problem, and the criteria the solution must meet. The elements are the factors that are relevant to describing the various states and the relationships among the factors. Consider the fertilizer company again. We might list the elements of the problem, the states, constraints, and criteria as:

Elements

1. Company resources
2. Competition
3. Chemical makeup of fertilizer
4. Pricing activities in the market
5. Current demand and potential demand for fertilizer
6. Availability and cost of raw materials
7. Efficiency of production
8. Efficiency and effectiveness of the marketing program

Present State

1. Company has faced declining sales of 10 percent per year for three years.
2. Profits have dropped 5 percent per year in the last two years
3. Production is conducted in widely scattered plants
4. Eight new companies have gone into production in the past two years

Desired State

1. A major role in the industry
2. Higher prices
3. Steadily increasing sales and profits

Constraints

1. No capital expansion funds available for one year
2. Diversification to be accomplished internally rather than through acquisition
3. New research authorization not to exceed $100,000

Criteria for the Solution

1. As a major factor, obtain at least 25 percent of the market
2. Price per unit of fertilizer to be at least $2.25
3. Sales to increase each year at a rate of at least 3 percent
4. Profits to increase each year at a rate of at least 5 percent

In practice, formulation of the problem facing the fertilizer company would be a lengthy one, partly verbalized and partly quantified. The greater the degree to which actual numbers may be attached to items describing the states, constraints, and criteria, the clearer the problem formulation.

There are four common, basic approaches for developing a good formulation of a problem:

1. Start with the general, vague statements characteristically employed to describe complex and amorphous situations. "The problem appears to be a marketing problem, somehow related to our production scheduling, our distribution system, and something that our competitors are either doing better or convincing the customers that they are. Of course, it may lie in our product. At any rate, sales have become more variable from month to month."
Ask questions about the meanings of statements, particulary about goals to be achieved. Redefine the problem over and over until it is clearly described by elements, present and desired states, constraints, and criteria for solution.
2. Start with the usual broad statement, then reformulate the problem very specifically as a narrow one, expand again to a broad problem, and thus oscillate in scope and specificity until you have zeroed in on the problem. Let us examine the hypothetical case of a company that has decided it will diversify, and its problem is, "Into what?" Analysis of its resources and of market opportunities suggests that the problem should be "How do we get into the food distribution business?" This is too broad a problem statement, because there are thousands of kinds of food businesses. The problem is reformulated, "How do we get into the franchised snack business?"

This is too narrow for a company of our size and we enlarge the scope of the problem. "Our problem is the determination of whether to become a franchiser or an operator of a chain of snack-type food outlets or of low-variety restaurants." Of course, the complete formulation of the problem should follow the pattern we have previously described.

3. Start with a problem symptom and define a very narrow, specific problem, then expand by steps to include all aspects of the total problem. A production manager notices that he is exceeding standard costs consistently on a certain type of product. He enlarges the scope of the problem as one of production control. This is expanded to include the training of operators and quality control personnel as well. This problem is expanded further to a consideration of priority of orders and to improved recruiting, selection, and assignment procedures.

4. Start with objectives to be achieved, rather than with the symptoms of the problem. Redefine objectives until they are clearly expressed and quantified as much as possible. Then specify other parts of the problem that are related to the achieving of these objectives. With this method, the relevance of problem elements, current state of the situation, constraints, and criteria for the solution may be determined as each factor is analyzed. In the fertilizer company, the goals may be set as part of long-range plans. Possible goals in terms of marketing objectives might be established for classes of products—agricultural, industrial, and consumer. Specific quantitative goals might then be developed for the agricultural line by first breaking it down into feed ingredients and pesticides, to meet identified needs for plant nutrition, plant health, animal health, and flavor enhancement. Similar development of industrial and consumer product lines could be established. Company resources, market position, future environmental conditions, and constraints would then be developed in terms of these goals.

This fourth method of problem formulation is used to develop plans that may solve anticipated problems by advance problem solving (refer to Chapter 2).

Because problem formulation is crucial in systems design, many resources are usually devoted to this stage before entering the stages of detailed design and implementation of systems. The further along the systems work has progressed, the more costly to the industry is the lack of a good definition of the problem. Management systems have been established that have not solved the really relevant problems because the real problems were not formulated initially.

The accountant's contribution to formulating management problems lies in:

a. Evaluating the present costs and financial situation
b. Recommending desired financial conditions
c. Uncovering economic constraints
d. Developing economic and financial criteria for possible solutions.

THE PROBLEM-SOLVING PROCESS

Once a problem has been formulated, we proceed to solve it. We have all come across a wide range of problems that we found difficult to solve. Further, methods of solution seem to diverge widely. Contrast the solving of a plane geometry problem with the solving of some complex accounting systems problem. In the first case, any approach that achieves the objective is satisfactory. In the second case, we may have to *decide* among several courses of action, none completely satisfactory, to reach only a partial solution.

A Pragmatic Approach

The pragmatic approach to problem solving in business firms, which has proved effective throughout the years, is clarified by means of the model in Fig. 6-1. The general approach is "handling" the problem to avoid the intellectual process of creating an original solution except as a last resort. This is because it is simply more economical to either bypass the problem, find someone who has solved similar problems (an expert), or find a published solution.

Let us follow through some of the principal steps in Fig. 6-1. Obviously, if the problem is overlooked, it is not solved. This is not necessarily bad, because only a limited number of problems may be solved with the resources available. If it is a critical problem and is overlooked, disaster may result. MIS should be designed to provide information so that critical problems will be identified.

If the problem is obviously unsolvable, we try to avoid it. In a sense, this *is* a solution. We run around a barrier if we can't get over it. If we use cyclamates in our diet drink and the government orders us to stop production, the problem of maintaining production is unsolvable. We do not determine that we can get the government to change its mind, nor do we intend to bootleg the product. We avoid the problem by concocting a new beverage or substitute.

Block C indicates that a solution may be useless; i.e., too late, too costly, or perhaps illegal. Again we try to avoid the problem itself.

When we cannot avoid a problem that appears to have some sort of useful solution (Block D), we proceed to Block E, gather information. Information is gathered by asking other people—experts and operational people—consulting the literature, or passing the problem itself on

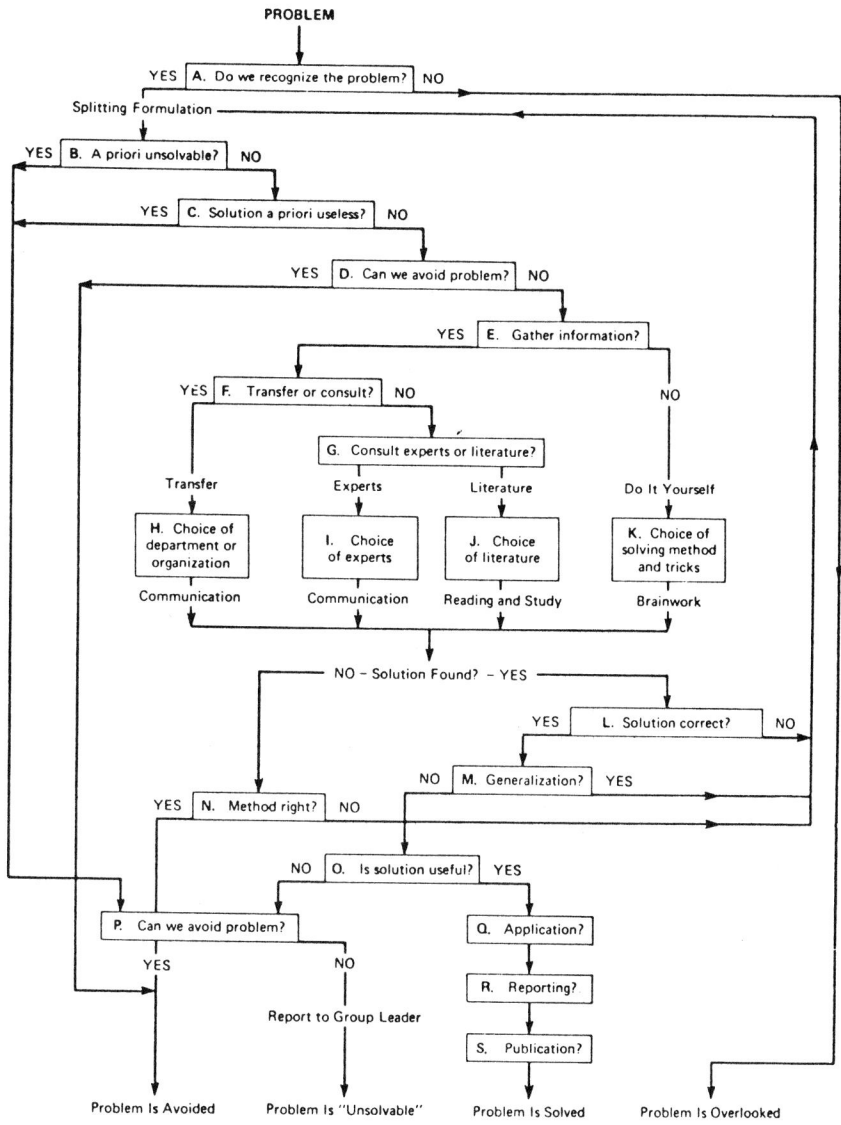

Fig. 6-1. Problem-Solving Decisions in an Organization

Source: Dr. Ir. A. H. Boerdijk, "Step-by-Step Guide to Problem-Solving Decisions," reprinted from *Product Engineering.* Copyright 1963 by McGraw-Hill, Inc.

to people who have the expertise (Block H). If the problem is completely novel, or no one else is available to work on it, or we ourselves are the experts, we attempt to solve it ourselves (Block K). From here on, if the problem is unsolvable we avoid it; if it is solvable, we use the solution and try to generalize it for future problems of a similar nature.

A Procedure for Solving Ill-Structured Problems

Block K of Fig. 6-1, Do It Yourself, leaves a lot to the imagination. We will try to fill out this block with a discussion of a method of solving ill-structured problems. The solution of well-structured problems in his own field is familiar to the accountant.

Ill-structured problems in business are both common and difficult to attack. They are called ill-structured because the objectives to be achieved are not defined, the symptoms may lead to various formulations of what may be different control problems, the current situation is muddled and difficult to describe, and procedures for solving the problem are not self-evident.

In order to attack such problems, we must first study and analyze the system in which the problems exist. Next, we step outside the system to ask, "What are management's problems in making this system work?" And then we formulate the research whose outcome will provide the solutions to management's problems. This problem formulation we call Phase I. Phase II is the attempt at solution. It requires searches for data, relationships, and alternative solutions. Let us detail these phases:

Phase I, The Formulation Process

A. Analyze the functions of the system, its components, its operation, and the information system that controls it. This step clarifies the structure in which the problem is imbedded.
   1. Identify and trace each channel of communication that links components (humans, machines, facilities) in the system.
   2. Identify each transformation of data in the system.
   3. Identify each operation performed in the system.
   4. Locate control (decision) points in the system. Generally, a control point is associated with either a manager or a checkpoint that controls on a routine basis (such as an individual operator or a machine).
   5. Drop from consideration each operation or transaction that has no effect on the objectives of the system.
   6. Group together the operations performed between every pair of control points.
   7. Prepare a flowchart showing:
      a. Control points and kind of decisions made at each control point.
      b. Information that flows between every connected pair of control points.
      c. Materials, if any, that flow between every connected pair of control points.
      d. Times required for flow of information and flow of materials in (b) and (c).

B. Formulate management's problems.
   1. Identify decision-makers and the decision-making procedure.
   2. Determine the decision-makers' relevant objectives.
   3. Identify other participants and the channels of their influence on a solution.
   4. Determine objectives of the other participants.
   5. Determine alternative courses of action available to decision-makers.
   6. Determine counteractions available to other participants.
   7. Establish criteria for evaluation of solutions.
C. Formulate the research problems that are most likely to lead to a solution of management's problems.
   1. Edit and condense the relevant objectives.
   2. Edit and condense the relevant courses of action.
   3. Define the measure of effectiveness to be used.
      a. Define the measure of efficiency to be used relative to each objective.
      b. Weigh objectives (if qualitative) or units of objectives (if quantitative).
      c. Define the criterion of best decision as some function of the sum of the weighted efficiencies (e.g., maximum expected return, minimum expected loss).[1]

Phase II, The Search Process

The search process consists of uncovering data and transformations that bring the problem-solver closer to his final goal. If the final goal is undefined in the problem formulation, the search also involves the development of trial goals along with alternative chains of means-ends.

The construction of all possible alternative paths that link the present state of affairs with the desired state of affairs is usually impossible. Even if many alternatives could be constructed, evaluating all of them to find the best is too difficult. Therefore, general, heuristic rules, either objectively framed or so complex that they are internalized in his mind, guide the problem-solver in a sequential series of steps or among major strategies. The following steps can only crudely represent this search process.

A. Gather data that seem relevant to the specific research problem to be solved. Find conditions imposed on the problem. Look for trends in data.
B. Classify the data. Draw charts, diagrams, and tables if they will help to organize the data. Look for conflicting data.

---

[1] See C. West Churchman, Russell L. Ackoff, and E. Leonard Arnoff, *Introduction to Operations Research*, New York: John Wiley & Sons, Inc., 1957, p. 132.

C. Devise a plan of attack.
   1. Hypothesize complete broad solutions to be detailed subsequently.
   2. Devise an incremental approach whereby a small part of the problem is solved first, the remainder is studied, and another small part is solved. This way we arrive at a solution by a step-by-step or means-end approach.
   3. Design research to answer specific questions that, when answered will make a set of solutions evident to the decision-maker.
D. Carry out the plan of attack by employing reflective processes and systematic questioning.
   1. Find relationships among the variables of the problem.
   2. Draw upon experience and creative reflection to develop hypotheses (trial solutions) to be tested.
   3. Search for analogies, differences, inversions, substitutions, and similar past problems that may produce hypotheses for solutions.
   4. Start with the desired state of affairs and work backward to determine what is required to achieve the goals.
   5. Develop tests, if possible, to check out parts of the tentative solution or the entire solution. At this stage, models or simulation may be helpful.
   6. Evaluate test results and iterate the first five steps to the extent that modification is indicated.
   7. Evaluate the alternative solutions in terms of criteria established in the formulation of the management problem.

Organizational and Individual Problem-Solving

Observation of problem-solving in large institutions such as business corporations reveals that there is a spectrum of problem situations and problem-solving. At one end of the spectrum is the individual who solves a problem completely independently and implements the solution. At the other end is the solving of the organizational problem of viability, to which everyone contributes on a continuous basis. It is very probable that the janitor solves more problems independently than does the president of a large corporation. The president deals with problems of such breadth that he must seek guidance, counsel, and evaluation at every step of the problem-solving process. Although he may make some lonely major decisions, the development of alternatives that offer him a decision situation is a shared process.

Organizational problem-solving is affected by conflicting values and interests of organizational members. Conflict and compromise are mixed with rationality. A comparison of individual and organizational problem-solving activities in greatly abbreviated form is shown in Table 6-1.

Table 6-1. Problem-Solving: Individuals and Groups

	INDIVIDUALS	GROUPS
Goal-setting	A. Task demands B. Personality C. Establish operational hypothesis	A. Task demands B. Group vs. individual conflicts C. Establish operational plan to problem
Search	A. Invoke basic strategy B. Recall and manipulate information C. Consider information in light of the hypothesis	A. Development—seek discussions B. Summarizing—seek discussions C. Consider supporting and opposing discussions
Hypothesis testing (proposed solution)	A. Suggest solution as "correct" B. If no solution, use feedback to develop another hypothesis C. Repeat, if necessary D. If (A) is correct problem solved	A. Agree to solutions as "correct" B. If not, try different planning of problem on feedback basis C. Repeat, if necessary D. If (A) is correct, problem solved

Source: Marcus Alexis and Charles Z. Wilson, *Organizational Decision Making*, Englewood Cliffs, N.J.: Prentice-Hall, 1967, p. 75.

The institutionalization of problem solving is becoming more firmly established by the development of management systems and management information systems. For the programmed problem-solving process, computerized systems are rapidly taking over. For the more ill-structured problems, man-machine systems are being developed in which information and the computer are featured.

THE DECISION PROCESS

The detailed decision process is a function of information and behavioral and environmental factors that shape the process. An exhaustive presentation of the processes of decision-making would require separate treatment for decisions made by (1) an individual, (2) a small group, and (3) large, complex organizations. A description of the process of decision-making in a large organization might astound the inexperienced student because of the large number of people who may be involved. Let us consider a company that wishes to buy jet engines for an advanced airplane it is developing. It must choose among a number of proposals put forth by outside companies. The decision to select a certain proposal may depend upon engineering approval, legal approval, accounting evaluation, manufacturing evaluation, top management approval, and even governmental approval, if it is a defense contract. Conceivably, more than 100 people could contribute to and influence the decision.

In this chapter we cover primarily the general aspects of decision-making. Group interaction, bargaining, compromise, conflict, and other forms of negotiation are beyond the scope of this book.

Decision-Making and Information

We have precisely defined an MIS as a processor of information (input) to yield decisions (output). The quality, quantity, rate of flow, and timing of information supplied by the MIS to the decision-makers are critical to effective operation of the company. The function of the system must be to seek out, evaluate, select, and manipulate information and disseminate it to decision-makers within the organization.

The *quality* of information may be measured by the criteria of the American Accounting Association: (1) relevance, (2) verifiability, (3) freedom from bias, and (4) quantifiability.[2] With regard to the *quantity* of information supplied to decision-makers, the inexperienced person may believe that the more information disseminated, the better the decision that results. But there are several points that contradict this view. Decisions in practical affairs face deadlines, and the cost of additional information to be supplied in a short time rises rapidly. Also, the quantity of information that humans can handle per unit of time is limited; although humans may be able to detect and transmit to the brain millions of bits per second of sensory information, they can handle only a small fraction of them in the form of concepts or signs.[3] Therefore, it is possible to overload the decision-maker with too much information and consequently obtain poorer decisions than with little information.

The systems designer must be concerned with the *timing* of information as well as the *rate*. If the information is transmitted too soon, the decision-maker may forget it. Also, information that is sent too early may become obsolete, so that the decision-maker either employs out-of-date information or is interrupted again for a new transmission. On the

---

[2] Gerald A. Feltham, *Information Evaluation (Studies in Accounting Research #5)*, Sarasota, Fla.: American Accounting Association, 1972, p. 26.

[3] See George A. Miller, "The Magical Number Seven, Plus or Minus Two: Some Limits on Our Capacity for Processing Information," *Psychological Review*, March 1956, pp. 81–97; and Alfred Kuhn, *The Study of Society, A Unified Approach*, Homewood, Ill.: Richard D. Irwin, Inc., 1963, pp. 178–79.

other hand, information that is transmitted at a time beyond the decision deadline is useless. There is a natural tendency for people in an organization to fear sending incomplete or inaccurate information to decision-makers; so high is the aversion to such risk that suppliers of information often take time to check and recheck. There must instead be a mutual understanding between the information collector and the decision-maker on the degree of risk of faulty information. Unverified information received on time is better than volumes of perfect information received too late to be used.

Very often, better information may be obtained within a given time span if we are willing to pay the price. The cost of additional information in terms of dollars, time, and risk size of outcome of the decision should be estimated before purchasing it. We must remember one of the basic rules of information management: information is the measure of the value (worth) of a message to a decision-maker in a specific situation.

The reception of information is affected to a great degree by the perception or "filtering" process of the receiver and the format of the presentation. The systems designer and the manager-user must therefore consider carefully the format of information presentation to reduce distortion. For example, visual media such as charts may be effective in communicating to marketing executives, whereas tables and schedules may be more meaningful to accounting and financial personnel. Flowcharts and raw computer output may be most appropriate for computer and management scientists in the organization, while verbal communication may be most effective among operative workers and their first-line supervisors.

Factors that Shape the Decision Process

Managers often say, "Get me the facts and then I'll make the decision." This implies that once the facts are available, they will be able to make well-reasoned, objective decisions. In reality, decisions by managers are influenced by a wide variety of factors, most of which they are not even aware of. These may be classified as:

1. Rational factors
2. Psychological characteristics of the decision-maker
3. Social influences
4. Cultural influences

These factors provide constraints in the design of MIS.

Rational Factors

Rational factors are those that the manager consciously employs to arrive at a decision—such as cost, time, management principles, and forecasts. To him, they are *measurable* things.

Systems designers tend to focus on the rational aspects of decision-making, with the result that sometimes the system cannot be implemented. Rational choice implies complete information, the establishment of objective goals, the development of objective standards and measures, the availability of all feasible alternatives, and the means for selecting the optimum alternatives. In practice, of course, we have only incomplete information for complex problems. Though objective standards and measures in the form of dollars, share of the market, turnover rate, or number of units per month are often available, there are usually many other criteria that cannot be measured. Goodwill, employee morale, air pollution, quality of management, or company image are examples of factors that may affect decisions and are difficult to define, let alone measure.

Humans engaged in solving complex problems are able to consider only a limited number of alternatives within the restraints imposed by time. They search among the limited number to find one or a few that appear to meet at least minimum requirements. Considerable effort may then be expended in selecting from among these few. Generally, it may be said that if an optimum solution may be found in a real-world situation, the problem may be solved by a machine or computer, because it is of such limited scope that logic, objective criteria, and measurement are sufficient to reach a decision.

Psychological Factors

Rational factors represent common methods and criteria for decision-making, but psychological factors are not interpersonal. Psychological factors are what the individual brings to the decision process; they involve his personality, capabilities, experience, perceptions, his values and aspirations, and his perceived role. There is, of course, considerable overlap among psychological, social, and cultural influences, because it is a rare individual who stands apart from his society and culture in terms of his behavior processes.

Attempts to develop a theory of decision-making based on psychological factors have been based largely on the "utility" curve of the individual. The utility function represents the values, aspirations, and risk aversion of the individual, perhaps to the greatest degree. The development of utility functions depends upon stated preferences of the individual and certain assumptions regarding the ordering of preferences. Unfortunately, either humans cannot discriminate well

Rational Factors

Rational factors are those that the manager consciously employs to arrive at a decision—such as cost, time, management principles, and forecasts. To him, they are *measurable* things.

Systems designers tend to focus on the rational aspects of decision-making, with the result that sometimes the system cannot be implemented. Rational choice implies complete information, the establishment of objective goals, the development of objective standards and measures, the availability of all feasible alternatives, and the means for selecting the optimum alternatives. In practice, of course, we have only incomplete information for complex problems. Though objective standards and measures in the form of dollars, share of the market, turnover rate, or number of units per month are often available, there are usually many other criteria that cannot be measured. Goodwill, employee morale, air pollution, quality of management, or company image are examples of factors that may affect decisions and are difficult to define, let alone measure.

Humans engaged in solving complex problems are able to consider only a limited number of alternatives within the restraints imposed by time. They search among the limited number to find one or a few that appear to meet at least minimum requirements. Considerable effort may then be expended in selecting from among these few. Generally, it may be said that if an optimum solution may be found in a real-world situation, the problem may be solved by a machine or computer, because it is of such limited scope that logic, objective criteria, and measurement are sufficient to reach a decision.

Psychological Factors

Rational factors represent common methods and criteria for decision-making, but psychological factors are not interpersonal. Psychological factors are what the individual brings to the decision process; they involve his personality, capabilities, experience, perceptions, his values and aspirations, and his perceived role. There is, of course, considerable overlap among psychological, social, and cultural influences, because it is a rare individual who stands apart from his society and culture in terms of his behavior processes.

Attempts to develop a theory of decision-making based on psychological factors have been based largely on the "utility" curve of the individual. The utility function represents the values, aspirations, and risk aversion of the individual, perhaps to the greatest degree. The development of utility functions depends upon stated preferences of the individual and certain assumptions regarding the ordering of preferences. Unfortunately, either humans cannot discriminate well

Table 6-1. Problem-Solving: Individuals and Groups

	INDIVIDUALS	GROUPS
Goal-setting	A. Task demands B. Personality C. Establish operational hypothesis	A. Task demands B. Group vs. individual conflicts C. Establish operational plan to problem
Search	A. Invoke basic strategy B. Recall and manipulate information C. Consider information in light of the hypothesis	A. Development—seek discussions B. Summarizing—seek discussions C. Consider supporting and opposing discussions
Hypothesis testing (proposed solution)	A. Suggest solution as "correct" B. If no solution, use feedback to develop another hypothesis C. Repeat, if necessary D. If (A) is correct problem solved	A. Agree to solutions as "correct" B. If not, try different planning of problem on feedback basis C. Repeat, if necessary D. If (A) is correct, problem solved

Source: Marcus Alexis and Charles Z. Wilson, *Organizational Decision Making,* Englewood Cliffs, N.J.: Prentice-Hall, 1967, p. 75.

The institutionalization of problem solving is becoming more firmly established by the development of management systems and management information systems. For the programmed problem-solving process, computerized systems are rapidly taking over. For the more ill-structured problems, man-machine systems are being developed in which information and the computer are featured.

THE DECISION PROCESS

The detailed decision process is a function of information and behavioral and environmental factors that shape the process. An exhaustive presentation of the processes of decision-making would require separate treatment for decisions made by (1) an individual, (2) a small group, and (3) large, complex organizations. A description of the process of decision-making in a large organization might astound the inexperienced student because of the large number of people who may be involved. Let us consider a company that wishes to buy jet engines for an advanced airplane it is developing. It must choose among a number of proposals put forth by outside companies. The decision to select a certain proposal may depend upon engineering approval, legal approval, accounting evaluation, manufacturing evaluation, top management approval, and even governmental approval, if it is a defense contract. Conceivably, more than 100 people could contribute to and influence the decision.

In this chapter we cover primarily the general aspects of decision-making. Group interaction, bargaining, compromise, conflict, and other forms of negotiation are beyond the scope of this book.

Decision-Making and Information

We have precisely defined an MIS as a processor of information (input) to yield decisions (output). The quality, quantity, rate of flow, and timing of information supplied by the MIS to the decision-makers are critical to effective operation of the company. The function of the system must be to seek out, evaluate, select, and manipulate information and disseminate it to decision-makers within the organization.

The *quality* of information may be measured by the criteria of the American Accounting Association: (1) relevance, (2) verifiability, (3) freedom from bias, and (4) quantifiability.[2] With regard to the *quantity* of information supplied to decision-makers, the inexperienced person may believe that the more information disseminated, the better the decision that results. But there are several points that contradict this view. Decisions in practical affairs face deadlines, and the cost of additional information to be supplied in a short time rises rapidly. Also, the quantity of information that humans can handle per unit of time is limited; although humans may be able to detect and transmit to the brain millions of bits per second of sensory information, they can handle only a small fraction of them in the form of concepts or signs.[3] Therefore, it is possible to overload the decision-maker with too much information and consequently obtain poorer decisions than with little information.

The systems designer must be concerned with the *timing* of information as well as the *rate*. If the information is transmitted too soon, the decision-maker may forget it. Also, information that is sent too early may become obsolete, so that the decision-maker either employs out-of-date information or is interrupted again for a new transmission. On the

[2] Gerald A. Feltham, *Information Evaluation (Studies in Accounting Research #5)*, Sarasota, Fla.: American Accounting Association, 1972, p. 26.

[3] See George A. Miller, "The Magical Number Seven, Plus or Minus Two: Some Limits on Our Capacity for Processing Information," *Psychological Review*, March 1956, pp. 81–97; and Alfred Kuhn, *The Study of Society, A Unified Approach*, Homewood, Ill.: Richard D. Irwin, Inc., 1963, pp. 178–79.

other hand, information that is transmitted at a time beyond the decision deadline is useless. There is a natural tendency for people in an organization to fear sending incomplete or inaccurate information to decision-makers; so high is the aversion to such risk that suppliers of information often take time to check and recheck. There must instead be a mutual understanding between the information collector and the decision-maker on the degree of risk of faulty information. Unverified information received on time is better than volumes of perfect information received too late to be used.

Very often, better information may be obtained within a given time span if we are willing to pay the price. The cost of additional information in terms of dollars, time, and risk size of outcome of the decision should be estimated before purchasing it. We must remember one of the basic rules of information management: information is the measure of the value (worth) of a message to a decision-maker in a specific situation.

The reception of information is affected to a great degree by the perception or "filtering" process of the receiver and the format of the presentation. The systems designer and the manager-user must therefore consider carefully the format of information presentation to reduce distortion. For example, visual media such as charts may be effective in communicating to marketing executives, whereas tables and schedules may be more meaningful to accounting and financial personnel. Flowcharts and raw computer output may be most appropriate for computer and management scientists in the organization, while verbal communication may be most effective among operative workers and their first-line supervisors.

Factors that Shape the Decision Process

Managers often say, "Get me the facts and then I'll make the decision." This implies that once the facts are available, they will be able to make well-reasoned, objective decisions. In reality, decisions by managers influenced by a wide variety of factors, most of which they are not aware of. These may be classified as:

1. Rational factors
2. Psychological characteristics of the decision-maker
3. Social influences
4. Cultural influences

These factors provide constraints in the design of MIS.

enough or they change their minds, so that ordering rules run into difficulty.[4]

A general description of psychological criteria for decision-making is given by Herbert Simon. The decision-maker does not try to maximize his satisfactions but settles for satisfactory solutions that "suffice." Finding solutions that both satisfy and suffice is therefore called "satisficing" by Simon. This means that the manager searches for the optimal alternative but discontinues his search and evaluation when a reasonable choice is found.[5]

What is satisfactory depends on the decision-maker's level of aspiration, and according to numerous studies, the aspiration level depends on past experience. If the decision-maker has achieved his goals in the recent past, his level of aspiration will rise. If he has not fully achieved past goals, he lowers his level of aspiration.

Social Factors

Decisions in an organization must be made with due regard to acceptance by members of the organization, otherwise implementation will suffer. The decision-maker must therefore consider not only his own values, but the values and goals of the individuals affected. Thus, "participative" decision-making is often employed to reach a decision that will be accepted by the group, or in the case of manager-subordinate situations, by the subordinate.[6]

Decisions involving great or sudden change in organizational structure are usually avoided by experienced managers unless it is obvious that everyone in the organization benefits immediately, Instead, decisions are limited to incremental changes over a period of time so as to reduce resistance to what is really a major decision. The use of committees often helps to diffuse responsibility for decisions among organizational members so that acceptance is achieved more readily.

Cultural Factors

Cultural factors are learned behavior patterns. For business organizations in the United States, three cultural influences predominate:

[4] For a further discussion of applied decision-making, see Arthur D. Hall, *A Methodology for Systems Engineering,* Princeton, N.J.: D. Van Nostrand Co., Inc., 1962.

[5] Herbert Simon, *Administrative Behavior,* 2nd ed., New York: The Macmillan Co., 1958, p. xxiv.

[6] For a discussion of this topic, see Aaron Lowin, "Participative Decision-Making: A Model, Literature Critique, and Prescriptions for Research," *Organizational Behavior and Human Performance,* February 1968.

the culture of the particular firm, the culture of the geographical region in which the firm is located, and the culture of the American people.

Let us give an example of a cultural influence from each of these classes. The learned behavior in an R&D-oriented firm is one of innovation, aggressive change, and search for new ideas, whereas in the United States shipbuilding industry, there is resistance to technological changes and a desire to retain old ways. Regional cultural differences are most evident to those who have worked in the frenetic, competitive pace of New York City and then in firms in the South where activity is more moderate.

National cultural differences are great. In the United States, the workday differs from that of many countries; some countries have a long siesta period and the workday ends later. In the United States, there is a greater opportunity for young men to exercise a voice in corporate affairs, whereas in many countries, firms are dominated by single families and elderly leaders. In United States firms, continuing education is a strong cultural characteristic rarely found in other countries. Many other differences could be listed that distinguish the culture of United States firms from those in other particular countries.

Besides the more obvious cultural differences in firms in different countries, there are some that most of us are not aware of. These are internalized and rarely verbalized differences in values and thought processes. For example, we behave as if youth were the most valuable attribute of people, whereas in some countries the elders are held in high esteem. We believe that Americans have the best management, the most advanced technology and the greatest "know-how," and this unspoken assumption is often reflected in our dealings with businessmen from other countries and in our decisions. We believe our system of ethics is superior to that of others, and yet we often engage in business practices abroad that we would not condone in the United States. Our decisions are influenced by the reasoning processes we have learned in our schools. Without realizing it, our approach to problem-solving and decision-making is quite different from that of people in other cultures.

Management and the Decision Process

We would like now to tie information and decision factors into management from a systems view. Fig. 6-2 does this by picturing management and the management system as an information processor for planning and controlling to achieve objectives. Management is represented as the decision-maker in this figure.

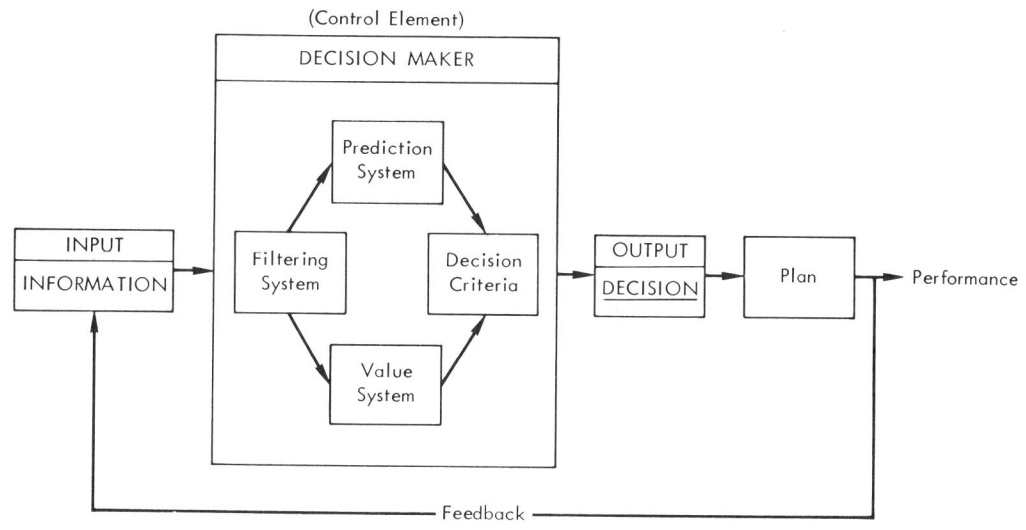

Fig. 6-2. Management and the Decision System

ANATOMY OF CHOOSING

To a great extent, the process of actually making the choice is hidden in a "black box," the Decision-Maker block in Fig. 6-2. Whereas psychologists attempt to explore the psychological process, management scientists attempt to develop normative methods. The systems designer must use the more objective, rational approaches to decision-making in MIS design. We start, then, by describing the rational decision process.

First, we note that information about the real world is the starting point, as shown in Fig. 6-2. So either the MIS system must supply information or the manager must search for and recall it. The information is then filtered by the manager to select what he believes is most useful to him in the solution of his problem. This filtering is the selection of the key variables to be used in a model of the problem.

The model of the problem provides the predictive system. The decision-maker can vary the inputs to the model so that the model can predict the alternative outcomes. Decision criteria must be established to provide objective evaluation of the alternative input and outputs. Let us now examine the process of choice in a more specific and rigorous fashion.

The elements of the process are:

1. Objectives of the decision-maker
2. Decision criteria and decision rules
3. Possible states of nature (a state of nature is simply the real-world situation.

Often our focus is on a single key variable whose value is said to represent a "state" or condition)
4. Outcomes of research, each of which predicts the likelihood of various states of nature occurring
5. Alternative actions that may be taken

The relationships among these elements are indicated approximately by Fig. 6-3. We note that at the top of the diagram we must formulate objectives, establish criteria that our choice must satisfy, and establish decision rules for making the choice once we have the information that predicts alternative outcomes. Outcomes of research, such as market research, indicate the probable states of nature. The reliability of such indicators depends upon a combination of the future we assume and random events in the world in which we operate. Outcomes are sometimes called premises, which state, "If we do this, then that will happen," or, "If this event in the environment occurs, then such and such a condition of the environment will result." Outcomes of research constitute the information that, when processed through the decision rules and criteria, leads to a choice.

A simplified concrete application of the decision-making model of Fig. 6-3 is as follows. Suppose the objective of a company is to introduce a new product, and several products are then developed. Only one may be brought out in the current year because of limited company resources. The company establishes certain criteria for inclusion in its decision rule. These might be the requirements that profit exceed 20 percent of sales, that return on investment before taxes exceed 30 percent, that present excess manufacturing capacity be utilized, and that the product fit into the current channels of distribution.

Possible states of nature might consist of a large sales potential, a medium sales potential, or little sales potential. Market research

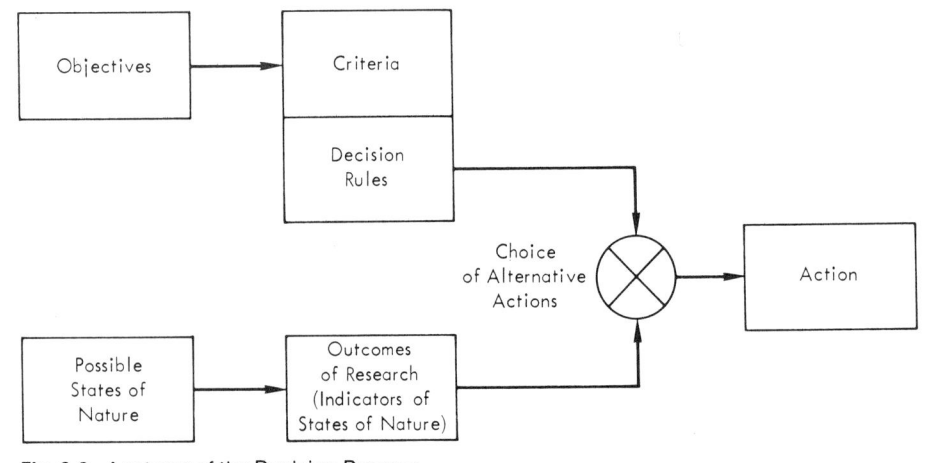

Fig. 6-3. Anatomy of the Decision Process

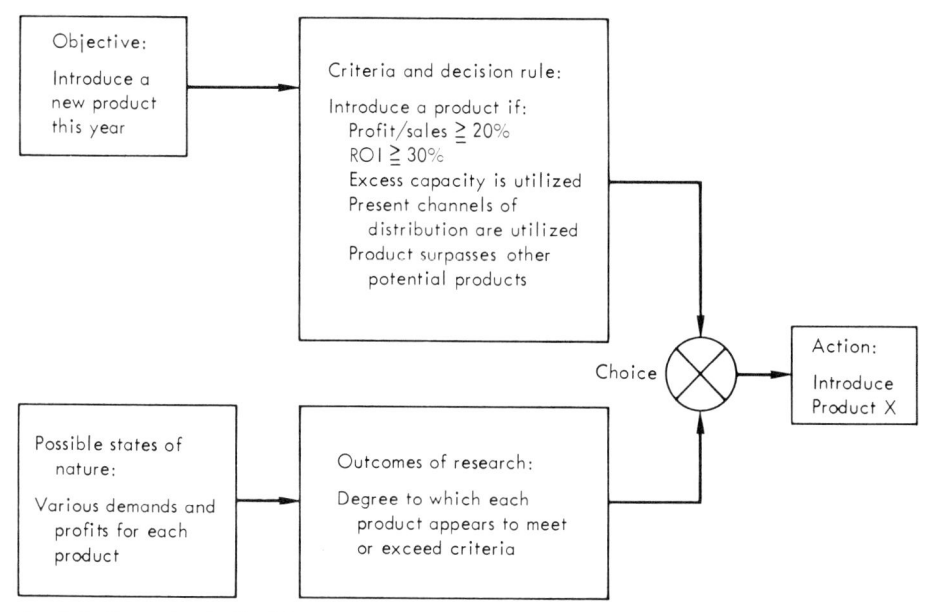

Fig. 6-4. Example of a Decision

provides indications of the market potential for each product. The reliability of such indicators depends, of course, on the extent (and hence costs) of the research.

Alternative actions consist of marketing alternative products on a local and expanding basis, a regional basis, or an immediate national basis. The entire process derived from Fig. 6-3 is shown in Fig. 6-4.

Simplifying the Choice Process for Complex Decision Problems

The complexity of our environment is such that the abstraction of management science models removes too much of reality. The decision-maker must find some way of selecting important elements and evaluating them to reach a decision. Some of the ways in which complexity is handled are suggested by William T. Morris.[7]

1. Rules of thumb based on past experience are employed to narrow the search for alternatives. Examples: Three-year payback for capital investment. Hire only experienced salesmen. Keep thirty days of inventory on hand. Allow an annual increase in payroll of only 6 percent.
   Often these rules are poor guides to choice, and their only merit is that they lead to a choice in a short time.

[7] William T. Morris, *Management Science, A Bayesian Approach,* Englewood Cliffs, N.J.: Prentice-Hall, 1968, p. 15.

2. Categorization of guidelines provides general guidance and rules. Company operating and policy guides, standard operating instructions, procedures manuals, and administrative memos and circulars circumscribe behavior to limit choice to a great degree.
3. Suppression of intangible values such as employee morale, customer goodwill, ethical considerations, public welfare, and industry relationships simplifies the choice process greatly. The focus is on economic units, profits, costs, number of employees, and efficiency.
4. Adoption of a short-range view is common. It is much easier to make a choice if the ramifications of the art beyond today, next week, next year, or the next five years are not taken into consideration.
5. Suppression of risk or a rough estimation of the total risk has sufficed in the past. Deterministic estimates of sales, costs, and new-product profits are still common. Management science and the computer have steadily introduced more and more subjective risk estimates into the choice process in recent years.
6. Quasi-resolution of conflict has simplified organizational decision-making. Goals of different departments are treated as independent constraints. Problems are broken into parts and treated separately. Different goals and aspirations of individuals are treated at different times in order to reduce conflict. Compromises and "satisficing" are employed to find mutually agreeable decisions.
7. An indifference approach is taken to making small decisions. Where two choices are apparent and the import of the action is obviously not significant, a snap judgment is made to eliminate the time-consuming effort of evaluating all the tangible and intangible aspects of each choice.
8. "Muddling through" is a common approach to complex situations in which the organizational decision-makers face a very complex problem with greatly significant consequences attached to the total series of acts required to resolve the problem. They make an initial decision on a first act and observe the consequences. Sequential decisions are made on a similar trial-and-error basis so that considerable maneuverability is maintained at all times. This approach is precisely the opposite of making a clear-cut decision on long-range objectives and plans.

THE ACCOUNTANT'S CONTRIBUTION TO MANAGERIAL PROBLEM-SOLVING AND DECISION-MAKING

The accountant plays an important role in assisting management in the three important functions of planning, allocating resources, and measuring/controlling. The accountant assists with the quantitative aspects of problem formulation and evaluation of solutions. It is often because of accounting reports to management that problems first become evident. Variances from plans, financial trends, changes in financial ratios, company-industry comparison information, and pro-forma financial statements are examples of the relevant information the modern accountant brings to the attention of management.

While management generally conceives of alternative solutions to strategy and operating problems, the experienced accountant may suggest alternatives such as acquisition or divestment of divisions that will yield capital gains, reduce losses, or create significant tax advantages.

With regard to the allocation of resources to alternative projects, or simply the evaluation of a current operation, the accountant supplies indispensable information. The dominant criteria in such cases are usually of an economic nature. The focus may be on such classes of costs and revenues as:

ORGANIZATION COSTS	SOCIAL COSTS
Capital costs	Cost to community
Human costs	Cost to environment and ecology
Operating costs	Cost to the population at large
Taxes	
Image—building costs	

REVENUES
Capital gains
Operating revenues
Royalties and commissions
Interest and dividends

ECONOMIC CONCEPTS FOR ACCOUNTING ANALYSIS

There are seven economic concepts that the accountant should be familiar with for managerial decision analysis. The data for application of these concepts are normally not available from traditional accounting information systems. The design of a modern accounting information should be based upon providing information as required by these economic concepts.

Relevancy

"Bygones are forever bygones." Only those costs and revenues which will occur in the future are relevant to decision-making. Consider the following alternatives for our company, which has just spent $10 million building a new textile plant. A new process has just appeared such that cloth may be produced at five times the rate at which our plant produces. A competitor will have a plant in operation using the new process within two years.

Basic Data
Cost of plant is $10,000,000
Present value of future cash flows from the project are $500,000 because the price of the textile will be noncompetitive when the competitor's plant goes on-stream. The sale value of our plant will be about $3,000,000 two years from now.
Market value of the $10,000,000 plant is estimated at $4,000,000 for land, building, and machinery sold as scrap.
Alternative A: Hang on to the plant because you have $10,000,000 sunk in it.
Alternative B: Sell the plant.

Is the cost of the plant relevant? No! Only future costs and revenues are relevant. The $4,000,000 that can be obtained from selling our plant now is greater than the $3,500,000 we may obtain from operating our plant for two years and then selling it.

"Relevant" costs also means that only those costs which differ for the alternatives should be considered. One important application will be discussed below under incremental reasoning. Another instance is when certain manufacturing processes have joint costs up to a point and then separate costs are incurred. Only costs after the split-off are relevant.

If two alternatives are being considered which have the same fixed costs, only the variable costs should be considered as relevant.

Incremental Reasoning

Incremental reasoning says that we should look at the net change caused by a decision. It applies to questions such as: Shall we take on an additional contract or order? Shall we add plant capacity? Shall we hire additional people? Shall we double our advertising?

A decision is profitable if *net* revenue is increased by causing:

a. Revenue to increase more than costs
b. Costs to be reduced more than revenue
c. Decreasing some costs by an amount more than other costs are increased
d. Increasing some revenues by an amount more than other revenues are decreased

Consider a simple problem of a printing firm that is considering taking on a new order which will bring in $20,000 in *additional revenue*.

The costs of filling the order are:

Labor	$ 9,000
Materials	6,000
Overhead (at 100% of labor)	9,000
Full cost	$24,000

From the traditional full-cost view, our printer would not take on this order. Suppose, however, that he has idle capacity so that the order may be worked into the schedule over a five-week period. Little added administrative costs, power, and wear on machinery will occur. Some workers who would be idle between other jobs will be assigned to this. The *incremental costs* of taking on the order are:

Labor	$ 7,000
Materials	6,000
Overhead	2,000
Total incremental cost	$15,000

Instead of a *loss* of $4,000, incremental reasoning shows that we would have a *gain* of $5,000 and that we should take on the order.

Opportunity Cost and Economic Profit

Decisions are based upon "economic" profits. The economic profit considers normal accounting costs plus opportunity costs. The opportunity cost of a decision is the sacrifice of the gain from the best alternative course of action. Some examples will help explain this:

a. The opportunity cost of a $100,000 per year movie star might be the $6,000 per year he could earn as a dishwasher. His economic profit is therefore $94,000 so he should stick to acting.

b. A certain woman may earn $30,000 per year as a corporation executive. She is considering going into business for herself and estimates that she would earn $20,000 per year. Her opportunity cost for self-employment is $30,000 and her economic profit would be −$10,-000. From an economic consideration only, she should not follow a course of action yielding a negative economic gain.

c. A firm is producing a line of wrenches on a machine which has been fully depreciated and has no resale or salvage value. Revenues and expenses for next year are:

Revenues from sales		$25,000
Expenses		
Utilities	$ 300	
Materials	5,000	
Labor	10,000	
Total expenses		15,300
Accounting profit		$ 9,700

The company is considering modifying the machine so as to produce more complex, higher quality wrenches that would bring in revenues of $30,000 per year. The economic profit is determined as follows:

Revenue		$30,000
Expenses		
Utilities	$ 300	
Materials	6,000	
Labor	12,000	
Conversion expense	700	
Opportunity cost	9,700	
Total economic cost		28,700
Economic profit		$ 1,300

Since there is an economic profit rather than loss, we should convert the machine.

Segregation of Costs According to Behavior

Segregation of costs into variable and fixed for break-even analysis and contribution reporting is one example of segregating costs according to objective. Assessment of make or buy alternatives or product line additions or deletions requires organization of costs on a direct costing basis.

Time Value of Money

Although bankers are well aware of the time value of money, managers in manufacturing and service industries often ignore it. Even on an annual budget, postponement of many costs for only a few months may result in significant return on invested assets. Large companies have cash managers, but often no planning to postpone cash payments as long as possible.

Another consideration today is inflation. Not only is there a premium for one dollar today versus one dollar received a year hence, but one dollar received a year hence may have less purchasing power. Thus "present dollar accounting" becomes especially important for capital equipment replacement.

Expected Monetary Value

Future inflows of cash may be reduced because of unforseen adversity such as bankrupt customers. Therefore, such flows should be discounted on the basis of estimated risk. Thus a dollar which is expected to be revenue received five years hence needs to be discounted to the present to reflect risk, time, and inflation.

Diminishing Marginal Productivity and Equimarginal Allocation

As units of labor are added to increase production, eventually each unit added yields less output per unit. The same is true of capital added. Maximum productivity per dollar invested is achieved when the productivity per dollar of labor equals the productivity per dollar of capital. This is evident because, with diminishing returns from each resource, any change in balance (equality of marginal productivity) will reduce total output.

The accountant will not find such marginal productivity curves for resources in his bag of accounting data, but must develop such data for decisions.

Summary

Problem-solving is finding answers to a question. Decision-making consists of evaluating alternative solutions and selecting a preferred one based upon prior established criteria.

Problems are well structured if they are clearly defined, if the data are adequate and valid, and if the methods of solutions are well established. A problem is said to be ill-structured if it is not well defined; if data are missing, inaccurate, or unreliable; and if known approaches to solving it are not available. Well-structured problems may be solved by programmed models and evaluation of solutions may be carried out to obtain a programmed decision. Nonstructured problems require interaction between the manager and the MIS.

The accountant may contribute both to proposals of solutions and to economic evaluations. Such evaluations require a different perspective and different data than historical accounting provides. Decision-making is concerned with future costs and revenues and employs the economic concepts of (a) relevancy of data, (b) incremental reasoning, (c) opportunity cost and economic profit, (d) segregation of costs according to application or behavior, (e) time-value of money, (f) expected monetary value, and (g) equimarginal allocation of resources.

As a final statement, the entire problem-solving and decision process depends upon the flow and processing of information. The MIS, the various information systems, and the financial information system, in particular, are all of prime concern to the accountant.

DISCUSSION QUESTIONS AND PROBLEMS

1. Discuss the major symptoms that might be indicative of problems in the following areas:
   a. accounts receivable
   b. accounts payable
   c. production
   d. inventory control
2. Discuss the four approaches to formulating a problem and develop an example for each.
3. Discuss the accountant's role in formulating management problems.
4. Identify the key steps in defining an ill-structured problem.
5. Two rug companies in upper New York State merged. This resulted in duplication of several VP positions. The individuals in each pair of jobs were of like competence. The purpose of the merger was to consolidate operations. How may the accountant assist in developing the performance measurements to be used in the decisions to be made regarding their continuing employment?
6. How may the quality of information be assessed?
7. What are the decision elements to be considered for a plant manager who is going to replace a number of individual machine units with a single $200,000 numerical control unit.

8. List and discuss the factors that shape the decision process.
9. Discuss several methods of simplifying decisions and give an example of each.
10. A national firm wishes to become an international company. Develop a list of subproblems and means for simplifying the choice process.
11. A company measures its managers' productivity against a standard return on investment of 6%. What is the economic flow in this reasoning?
12. Discuss the role of the accountant in assisting management in decision-making and problem-solving.

Bibliography

BOMBLATUS, RICHARD L. "Decision-Making in Middle Management," *Management Accounting,* August 1974.

DRIVER, MICHAEL J., and THEODORE J. MOCK. "Human Information Processing, Decision Style Theory, and Accounting Information Systems," *Accounting Review,* July 1975.

FELTHAM, GERALD A. *Information Evaluation* (Studies in Accounting Research #5), Sarasota, Florida: American Accounting Association, 1972.

GREGORY, CARL E. *The Management of Intelligence,* New York: McGraw-Hill Book Co., 1967.

HAYES, W. WARREN, and WILLIAM R. HENRY. *Managerial Economics* (3rd ed.), Dallas, Texas: Business Publications, Inc., 1974.

LACEY, JOHN M. "Replacement Cost Accounting: Another Answer," *The CPA Journal,* March 1976.

RAWCLIFFE, G. A. "Accounting Concepts for Managerial Decision-Making," *Management Accounting,* April 1972.

TROWBRIDGE, MARTIN. "Managing in Crisis Situations," *International Management,* September 1972.

Preview:
This chapter shows several major corporate decisions and ways in which the AIS can assist in defining and solving problems.
—Strategic planning
—Operational planning
—Master budget
—Capital investment alternatives
—Cost allocation

CHAPTER SEVEN

accounting information systems for major corporate decisions

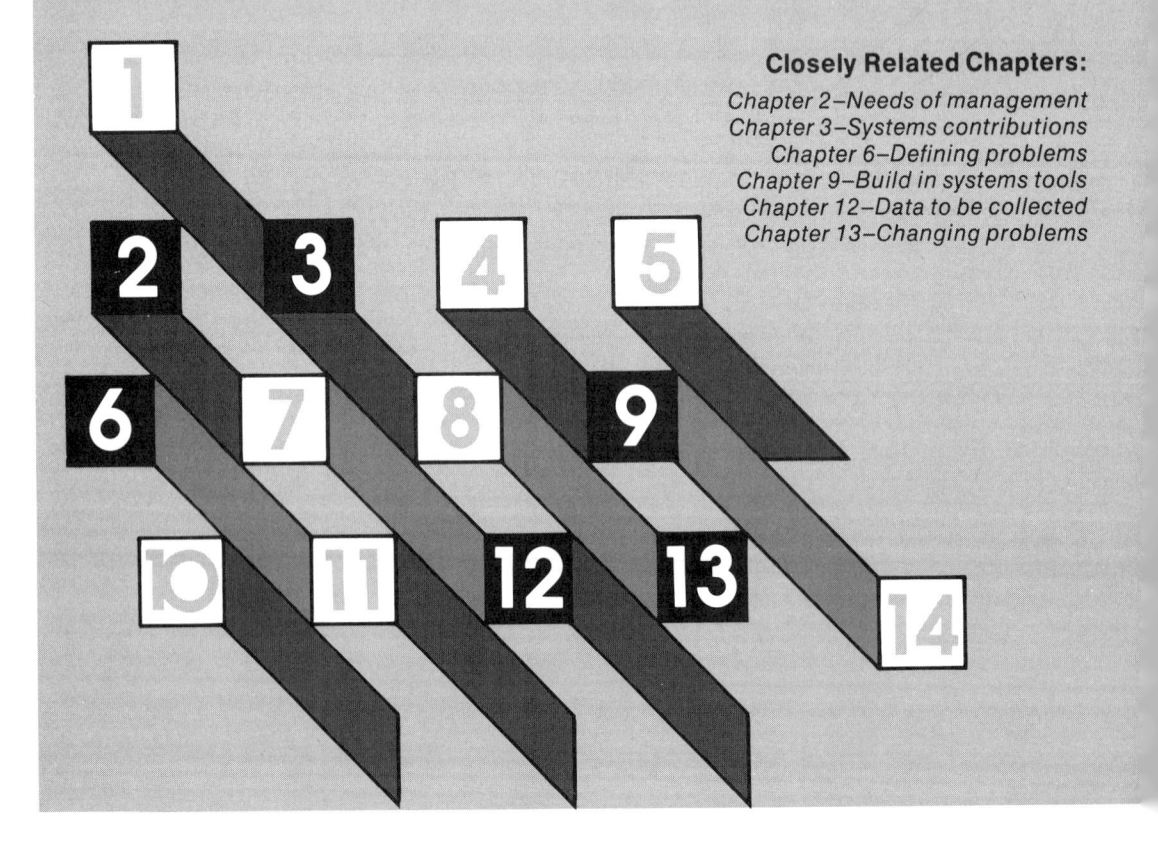

Closely Related Chapters:
Chapter 2—Needs of management
Chapter 3—Systems contributions
Chapter 6—Defining problems
Chapter 9—Build in systems tools
Chapter 12—Data to be collected
Chapter 13—Changing problems

In the previous chapter, we related the accounting information systems to the daily operations of the organization. The role of the accounting information systems for gathering and recording data was examined. We will now look at the role of accounting information systems (or perhaps more accurately, financial information systems) as they deal with important *future* courses of action. Strategic planning, the annual operating plan, and major decisions involved in developing and implementing a strategy are now considered.

How can formal accounting information systems aid management in these areas? The presentation of the complete accounting information system that is required is too lengthy for this introductory text. Therefore, we will discuss the nature and source of information required and illustrate some subsystems by means of flowcharts.

Our view is broader than the usual writer's. It is common to view accounting information systems as *reporting* systems. We view these systems as *interacting* with management information systems. That is, there is constant interchange of information between professional accountants and management in the development of strategic and operating plans and in evaluation of major alternatives for decision-making.

STRATEGIC PLANNING

In Chapter 2 we treated the nature and procedure for strategic planning from the managerial viewpoint. We will now indicate how the AIS provides support for the development of strategy.

Accounting Information for Developing Corporate Strategy

The AIS relates to the components of strategy which we called corporate scope, competitive edge, specifications, deployment of resources, and risk. These factors are developed, we recall, by analyzing opportunities in the environment and our internal capabilities and resources. Analysis of opportunities for new products, new markets, and expansion of the company require a thorough economic evaluation. The financial data, both internal and external, for such evaluations are supplied by the accounting and the finance departments. In addition, accounting should develop cost allocation and analysis models that, with the aid of the computer, permit management to review many alternatives.

Analysis of internal financial resources includes the capacity for raising capital and generating cash. The AIS should provide the model and data to yield information in a variety of forms for management. For example, management may raise such "What if" questions as "What if we sell off our paper products division?," or "What if we liquidate all obsolescent inventory?," or "What if we dispose of all company-owned

EXTERNAL INFORMATION

Inflation trends

Price trends of alternative products

Costs of raw materials and trends

Costs of energy and trends

Valuations of potential acquisitions

Cost of money and capital

Trends in risks of doing business with customers, vendors, etc.

Tax laws and regulations and government policy trends

Liability trends – products, management, patent, etc. Insurance rates

INTERNAL INFORMATION

Product costs

Prices and price elasticities

Gross margins

Administrative costs

Selling costs

Support costs

Support cost per engineer, per manager, etc.

Cash flow and credit lines

Capital assets and master file

Depreciation and retention value

Human resource costs and evaluation

Investment per worker

Accounting and financial planning → Financial feasibility of opportunities, Corporate strengths and weaknesses, Scope, Competitive edge, Specifications, Deployment of resources, Risk (exposure)

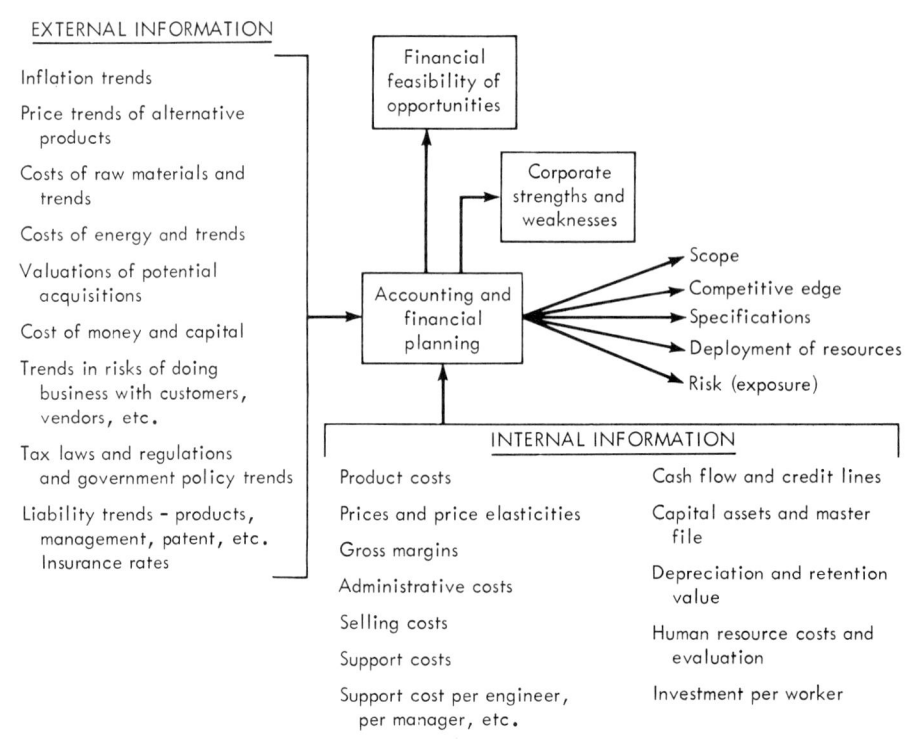

Fig. 7-1. The AIS for Formulation of Strategy

retail outlets?" The AIS should be able to contribute the financial implications in answers to these questions. It should be emphasized that marketing considerations play an equal part in reaching decisions on such questions of strategy.

In Fig. 7-1, a simplified view of the AIS in strategy formulation is shown.

Evaluation of Strategic Alternatives

One characteristic of a good AIS is that it routinely makes data available so that special research for data is not required every time a business problem is identified. Entry into a new field of endeavor, however, may require expert searching for financial data by the accounting department. However, the costing of alternative deployment of resources, or the comparison of owning vs. leasing retail outlets may be made using data already available within the company. The *procedure* for requesting such analyses and the reporting of results are part of the AIS.

Long-Range Planning

More and more companies are preparing long-range plans and revising them annually. These long-range plans show the major events and activities required to achieve the company's strategic objectives (i.e., to implement strategy). As we all recognize, there are many paths through a forest. Similarly, there are many alternative chains of activities to go from the present strategic posture to the new strategic definition of the firm.

Managers and the corporate planner must prepare a schedule of activities and *costs* over the next three-to-five years as part of the long-range plan. Alternate capital investments, alternative methods of financing, alternative tax-benefit tactics, and alternative timing of expenditures must be evaluated. The *system* that automatically brings the accountants into such evaluations is the AIS. Without such a financial information system, financial evaluation for long-range planning could be sporadic and superficial.

The AIS should be carefully structured to deal with new product project alternatives. A flowchart based upon that of Gulf Energy and En-

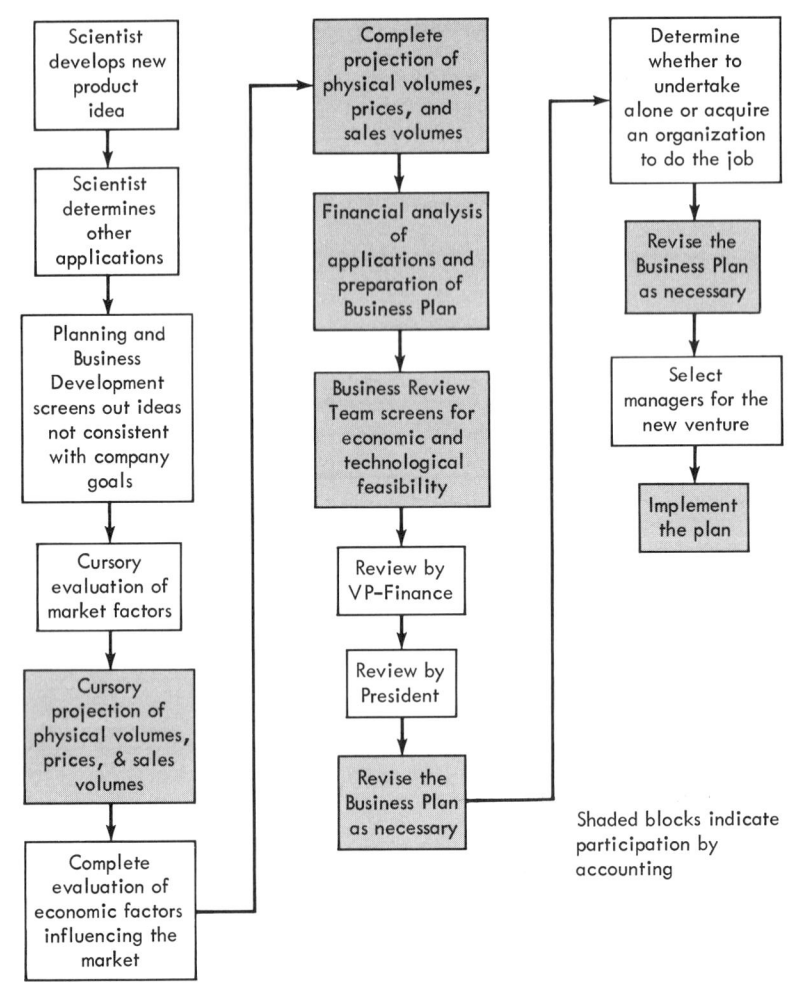

Fig. 7-2. Activities for New Product Ventures

vironmental Systems, Inc., is shown in Fig. 7-2. This flowchart shows the new-product evaluation process with the shaded boxes indicating formal participation by accounting.

The AIS places a major role in the evaluation of alternative capital expenditure projects. A typical information flow system is shown in Fig. 7-3. Operating data, capital items proposed, and maintenance data are supplied by line management. Line management also proposes replacement equipment, priorities, and timing. The financial system develops costs and contribution information. It also shows alternative schemes of budgets that fall within financial resource limitations.

Flexibility in long-range planning depends heavily upon methods

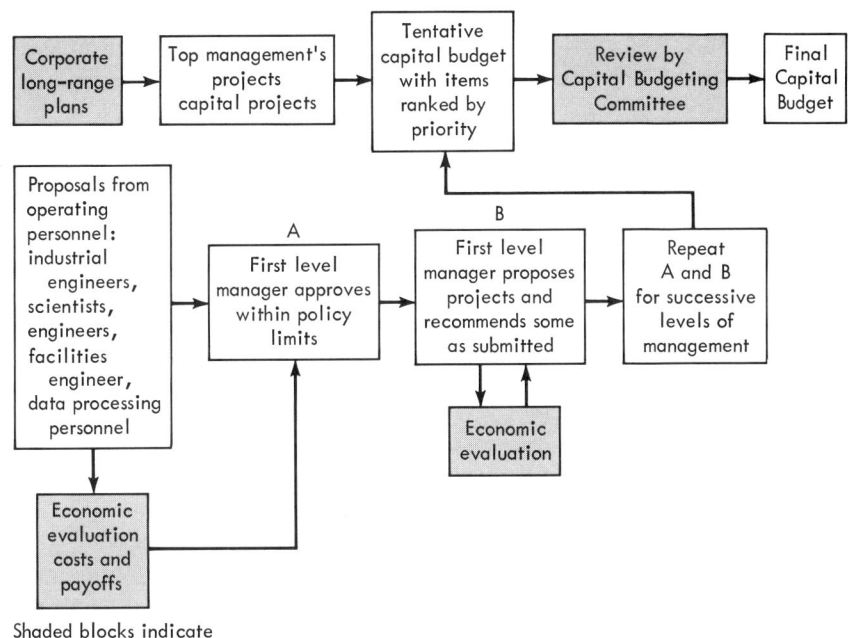

Fig. 7-3. Information Flow System for Capital Budgeting

of raising capital. Debt financing or stock issues must be evaluated by the financial information system models and accounting input data. As a part of such studies and planning, cash flow projections become a part of the long-range plans.

OPERATIONAL PLANNING

Operational planning is the annual plan for the business for the next year. It is a detailing of the first year of the long-range plan. As such, the financial analysis is much more detailed and refined than for the following years. We may show the relationship of the AIS to operating plans and long-range plans by means of two diagrams and an exhibit.

In the first diagram, Fig. 7-4, we show the step-down, or *disaggregation,* of a long-range plan to the annual profit plan. In Fig. 7-5, we show a more detailed development of annual operations and financial planning evolving from the long-range plans. In Fig. 7-6, a portion of a long-range plan is presented. The importance of the financial aspect is readily apparent.

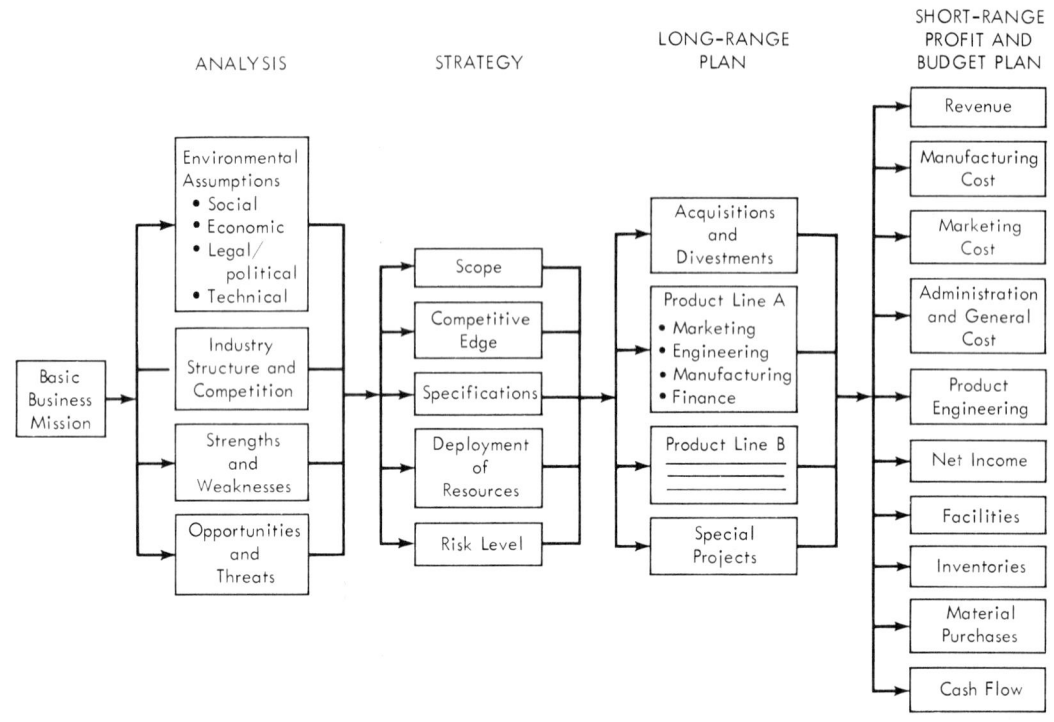

Fig. 7-4. Information Disaggregation From Long-Range Plan to Short-Range Profit Plan

Organizational Operating Plans and the AIS

Annual operating plans are usually prepared for each functional organization as well as for each division and for the company as a whole. That is, there are usually engineering plans, marketing plans, manufacturing plans, human resource plans, accounting (organization) plans, and other miscellaneous function plans. In addition, there are operating plans for identifiable cost centers such as laboratories or mail rooms, for profit centers such as retail branches or mail order services, and for some special organizational segments. A part of each of these plans is the financial plan that is developed by the AIS.

If we examine a particular plan in a little detail, we may see more clearly how the AIS relates to operating plans. In particular, let's look at the marketing plan. Remember that a tentative plan must be prepared and then analyzed by accounting to determine if expenditures fall within the guidelines issued by top management.

The preparation of a tentative plan would lead to the development of a summary as shown in Table 7-1 and associated product expense

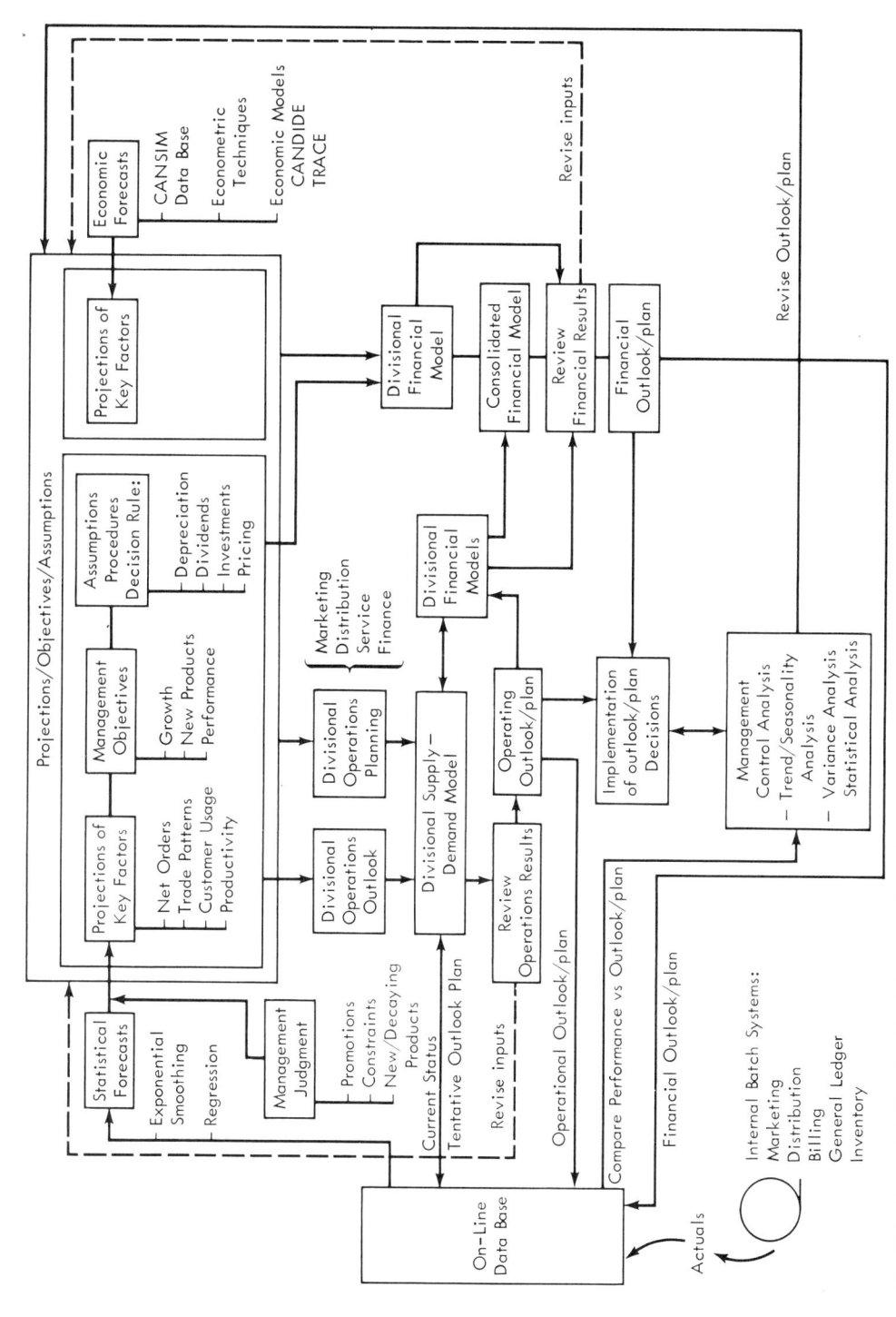

Fig. 7-5. Financial Planning Evolving from Long-Range Planning

Source: Ronald A. Seaberg and Charlotte Seaberg, "Computer Based Decision Systems in Xerox Corporate Planning," *Management Science*, December 1973.

Forecast Data in Thousands of Constant 1974 U.S. Dollars (Local Currency)	DIV./PLANT: (name) PROGRAM NUMBER: 001 PROGRAM RANKING: 1 OF 7 TYPE OF PROGRAM: Product Engineering PRODUCT LINE: (name)

TITLE: [Program Title]

OBJECTIVE AND SCOPE:
Standardize design of lever hoists marketed worldwide. Price the new design competitively while maintaining 20 percent net profit. New design will meet OSHA requirements and will be developed to metric standards. Project will require both division and corporate research center participation.

BUSINESS JUSTIFICATION:
Program will provide incremental sales of $388 in 1977 and $876 in 1979. Incremental profits in the same years will be $78 and $175. Return on incremental capital employed in the mature year will be 14 percent. Over a longer-term basis, [the company's] market share will continue to decline by about 1-2 percent per year unless this program providing for a redesign of the product line is approved.

INCREMENTAL INVESTMENT FORECASTS:

YEAR	CAPITAL REQUIREMENTS ANNUAL	CUMULATIVE	PROGRAM EXPENSES ANNUAL	CUMULATIVE	QUARTERLY R AND D EXPENSE FORECAST QUARTER	AMOUNT
Prior	$ —	$ —	$ —	$ 35	3/74	$ 20
1974	150	150	67	102	4/74	35
1975	53	203	25	127	1/75	17
1976	—	—	—	—	2/75	—
1977	—	—	—	—	3/75	—
1978	—	—	—	—	4/75	—
1979	—	—	—	—		
Beyond	—	—	—	—		

Probability of program success through capital spending __90__ %
MATURE YEAR INCREMENTAL AVERAGE CAPITAL EMPLOYED: Net Plant and Equipment $ 177
Working 100
Total $ 277

INCREMENTAL (DECREMENTAL) SALES AND PROFIT:

FIRST YEAR OF INTRODUCTION 1975 ANTICIPATED SALES $ 75

	TARGET YEARS 1977		1979		MATURE YEAR 1978	
	SALES	PROFIT	SALES	PROFIT	SALES	PROFIT
ATTRITION PREVENTED	$ 95	$ 19	$ 246	$ 49	$ 150	$ 30
PRESENT PRODUCT INCREASE	395	79	882	176	583	117
NEW PRODUCT	—	—	—	—	—	—
COST REDUCTION	XX	—	XX	—	XX	—
TOTAL PRODUCT LINE IMPACT	$490	$ 98	$1128	$ 225	$ 733	$ 147
CONFIDENCE OF SUCCESS	85%	80%	75%	70%	80%	75%
TOTAL AFTER DISCOUNTING FOR CONFIDENCE FACTOR	$368	$ 74	$ 846	$ 169	$ 550	$ 110
RETURN ON DISCOUNTED SALES	20 %		20 %		20 %	

MATURE YEAR RETURN ON INCREMENTAL AVERAGE CAPITAL EMPLOYED .... 40 %

GENERAL MANAGER	(DATE)	PROGRAM MANAGER	(DATE)

Fig. 7-6. Action Program Identification Form, With Illustrations—a Capital Goods, Automotive, and Consumer Products Company

Source: Rochelle O'Connor, *Corporate Guides to Long-Range Planning,* New York: The Conference Board, Inc., 1976.

Table 7-1. Product Marketing Plan Summary

SALES, YEAR ENDING 12/31/79
TREND FORECAST FOR 1980
SALES INCREMENTS FOR 1980 PROFIT PLAN

    I Major Problem Areas—Improvement Increment
       a. Field sales management
       b. Repair service time
       c. Trade shows

    II Low Performance—Improvement Increment
       a. Eastern U.S.
       b. Latin America
       c. France

    III Expansion Planning—Increment
       a. Technical improvements in packaging
       b. Standardized advertising media mix
       c. Improved market segmentation and product targeting
       d. Winter direct mail campaign
       e. Improved inventory control to reduce stockouts

Total Volume Added by Incremental Plan

Total Sales ($) Added by Incremental Plan

Trend Forecast for 1980

Total Sales ($) Budget for 1980

budgets. For each product the product expense budget shown in Table 7-2 would be prepared by the accounting organization in collaboration with the marketing organization.

The procedure for developing the Master Marketing Plan and Budget would be as follows.

    I. Top management provides long-range planning guides and tentative budgeting constraints to the marketing manager.

    II. The marketing manager and his product managers go over new product opportunities and "momentum" growth for present products. Engineering is called in to advise on product development and improvement possibilities and costs. The product mix is then formulated.

    III. The Product Managers prepare preliminary marketing plans and review them with sales and promotion executives. Accounting is called upon to prepare cost estimates and budgets.

    IV. The marketing manager then reviews the plans for adequacy of objectives, sales volume, profit, ROI, market share, channel relationships, and distribution of costs.

    V. The marketing manager consolidates the products and combines with other marketing support costs as determined by the accounting department. These support costs include test marketing, opening new offices, training personnel, etc.

VI. The marketing manager then reviews the Master Marketing Plan and Budget relative to the long-range plan. If no changes are required, the manager submits it to the president for consolidation and reconciliation with other functional activities.

Table 7-2. Product Expense Budget

Sales Budget for 1980

Cost of Sales

Gross Profit

Variable and Programmed Expenses
  Sales Planning
    Salesmen's Salaries
    Salesmen's Commissions
    Travel & Entertainment
    Mgmt. & office salaries
    Tel. & Tel.
    Marketing Research

  Services
    Installation
    End-of-year check of condition

  Ad & Promotion
    Publication advertising
    Direct mail
    Catalogs and sales aids
    Dealer & distrib. help
    Exhibits, shows, conventions
    Administration and other
    Public relations
      Total Variable and Prog. Expenses

Fixed Expenses
  Insurance
  Depreciation
  Taxes
    Total Fixed Expenses

Grand Total of Expenses

Net Profit Contribution of Product Sales
  % of Product Sales
  1979 Product Profit Contrib. % of Sales

Consolidated and Pro Forma Profit Plans

The consolidated profit plan and pro forma plans for the second and third years in the future lend themselves to computerized modeling. Once the basic operational plans of the divisions and international subsidiaries have been prepared in detail, they become inputs to the AIS model. For companies with few products and stability of product mix, computerized models are especially useful in preparing future profit plans. One example of such an industry is the shipping industry. The sources of revenues are clearly identifiable as are the principal costs which are easily established. The risk of wide variations in revenue and in certain costs make it desirable to prepare pro forma statements for different sets of premises. Figure 7-7 indicates the relationship of financial planning to basic information systems.

In a similar manner, the oil industry may utilize a computerized AIS to prepare its profit plan. For comparison with Fig. 7-7, see Fig. 7-8 for a typical oil marketing company.

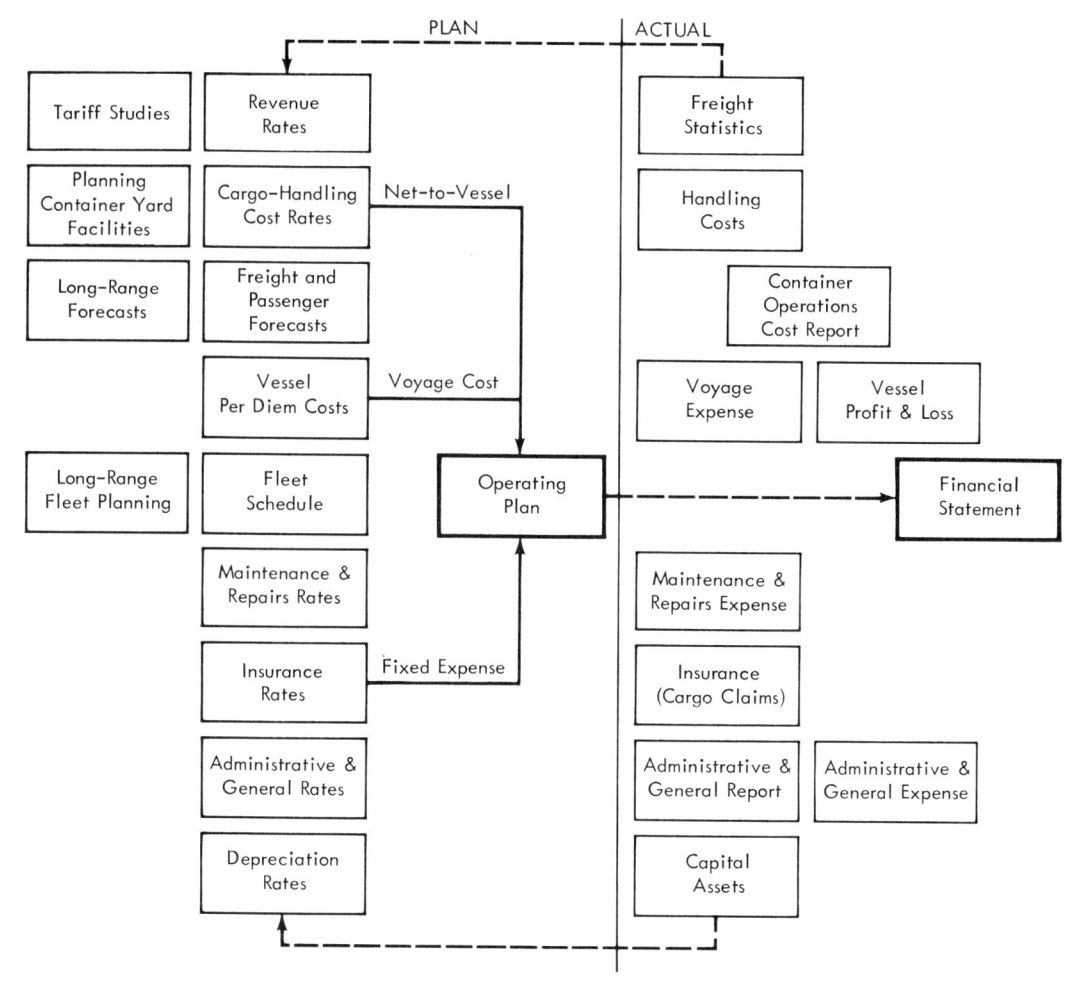

Fig. 7-7. Information Processing Functions in Relation to Financial Planning

Source: Lyle F. Hughes and Charles A. Olson, "Computer Assisted Financial Planning," *Management Accounting*, April 1969.

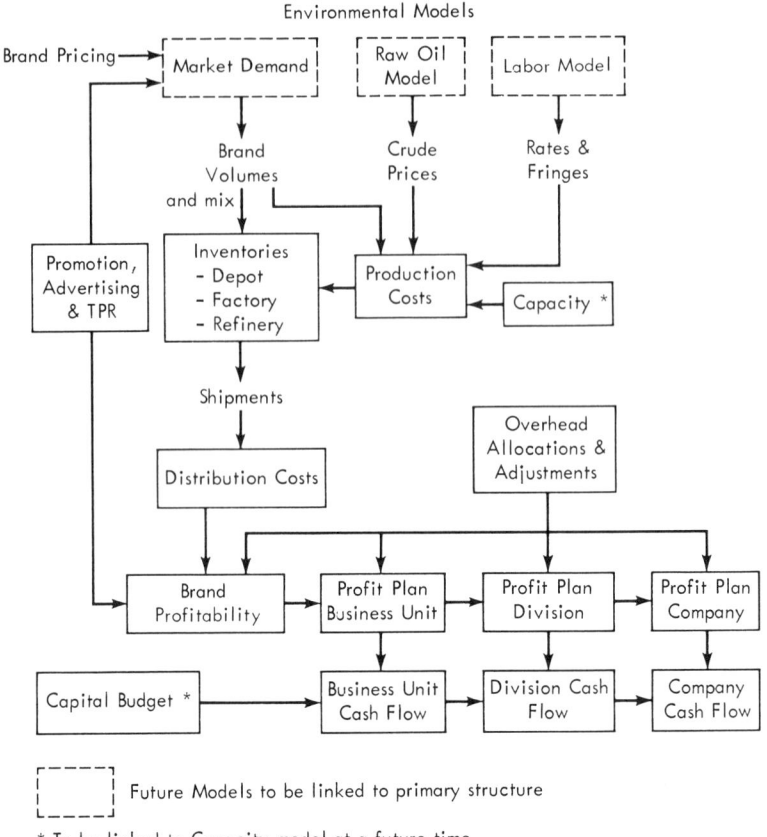

Fig. 7-8.

Source: James J. Boulden, "Computerized Corporate Planning," *Long Range Planning*, June 1971.

Project Plans and AIS

Project planning is required for complex, expensive one-of-a-kind developments such as design of a submarine, launching of a new product, or development of a management information system. Performance (work tasks), cost, and time must be closely integrated. Usually critical path networks such as PERT and CPM are utilized for planning and control purposes. The accounting information system is tightly locked into such project planning and control.

Basically, the total job is broken down into major tasks. These are divided into subtasks, and so on. The hierarchical structure of work requirement is called Work Breakdown Structure (WBS). Costs are calculated for the smallest work elements, work packages, and consolidated into task and project costs. In addition to costing by tasks, costing must

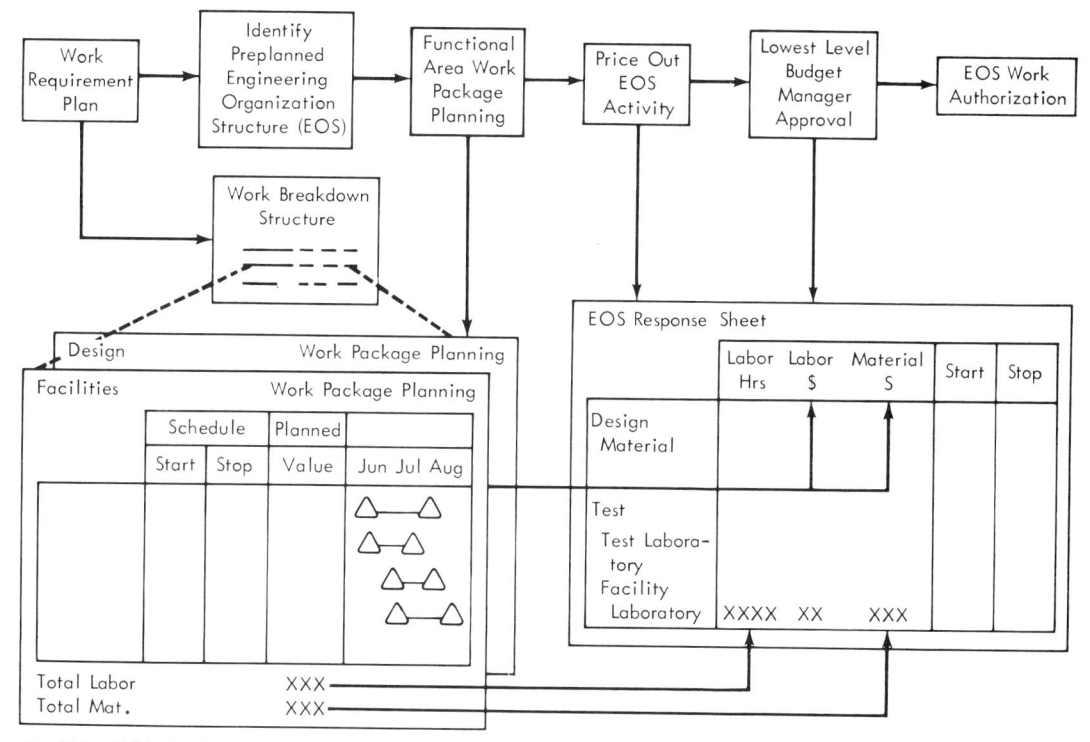

Fig. 7-9. AIS in Project Planning and Control

be carried by organizational component (fund owner) and fund performers. Figure 7-9 summarizes the activities of the accounting organization in project planning. By reporting costs and variances of tasks, fund owners, and fund users, the accounting information system participates in project control.[1]

Master Budget

The purpose of a budget is to plan for and control three variables, namely, *performance, cost,* and *time.* A schedule of any one or two of these unrelated to the third is meaningless. The Master Budget consists of a consolidation of an organization's plan for one year plus all backup budgets. The principal, but not the only, components of the Master Budget are therefore:

---
[1] For a fuller treatment of engineering project budgeting, see D. W. Karger and R. G. Murdick, *Managing Engineering and Research,* New York: Industrial Press, 1969.

1. Operating budget
   a. Sales budget
   b. Production budget (in manufacturing companies)
   c. Cost-of-goods sold budget (for both manufacturing and merchandising companies)
   d. Selling expense budget
   e. Administrative expense budget
2. Financial budget
   a. Cash budget: receipts and disbursements
   b. Budgeted balance sheet
   c. Budgeted statement of sources and applications of funds.

The Master Budget shows budgeted amounts for each month, as well as totals. By means of such devices as three-month rolling forecasts, the budgets are used to track expenditures and potential variances for

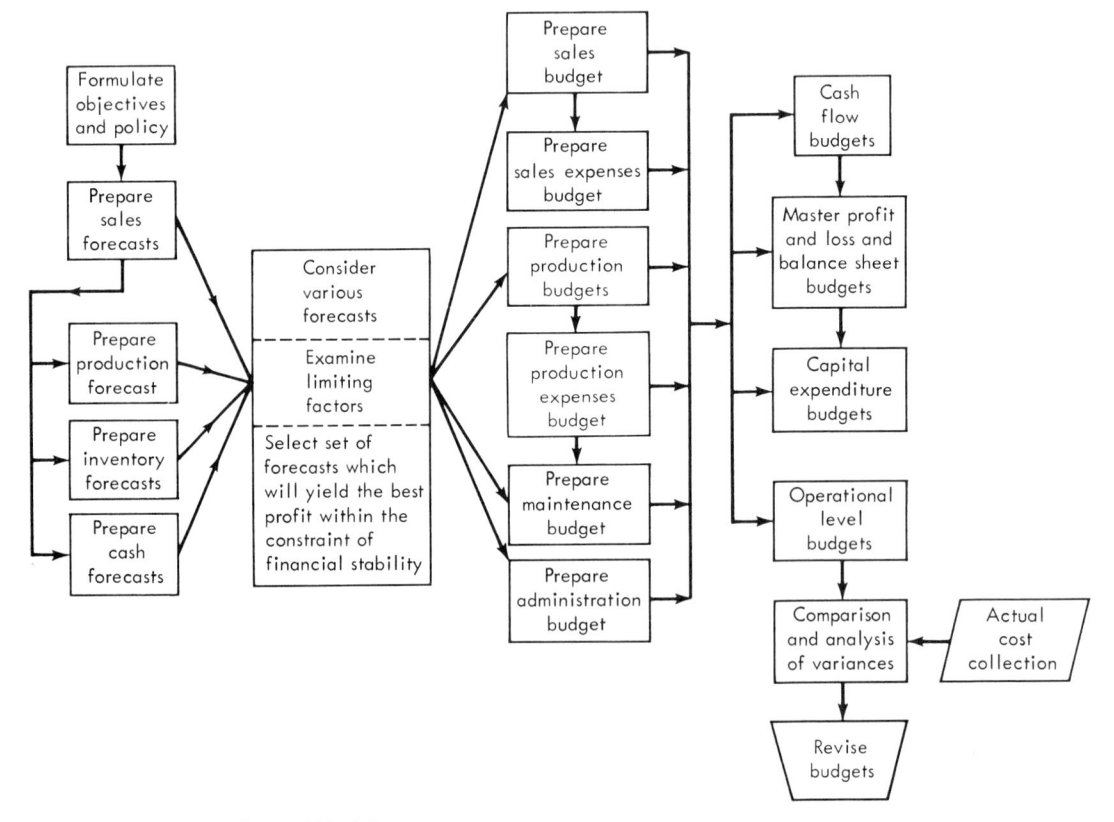

Fig. 7-10. Budgetary Control Model
Source: G. W. Radley, *Management Information Systems*, New York: Intext, 1973.

the year as a whole on a month-to-month basis. Such a three-month rolling forecast shows, each month:

a. Expenditures to date
b. Anticipated monthly expenditures for each of the next three months
c. New estimate of expenditures for the year
d. Variance of estimate from original amount budgeted for the year.

All budgets must be based upon the sales forecast as a premise. The subsequent steps in the development of budgets is presented in the flowchart of Fig. 7-10.

ACCOUNTING ANALYSIS FOR CORPORATE AND OPERATING DECISIONS

There are a number of types of major decisions which must be made from time to time for corporate planning. They are major in that they involve commitment of resources, avoidance of losses, or control of resources which are of significant size for the company. Traditional accounting systems deal with historical data and are deficient for such decisions for the following reasons:

1. They do not always show the opportunity costs of decisions. Opportunity costs vary as economic conditions vary.
2. They often ignore implicit costs such as overtime work of managers, the labor costs of the single proprietor, or time value of money (in the budgetary process).
3. They utilize accounting classifications which do not measure incremental costs or escapable costs required in decision analysis.
4. Overhead allocation procedures often confuse the real issues and values of economic analysis for decision-making.

The controller should make sure that the AIS is designed to fulfill its decision-making role. The controller accomplishes this objective by organizing the accounting function so that accountants with proper expertise are assigned responsibilities for modeling, estimating economic values, and making economic analyses. Further, the AIS should have an intelligence capability built into it to obtain data and information from the environment as input to decision analyses.

We will examine briefly some major decision problems of companies to illustrate more specifically the role of the AIS.

II. INVESTMENT AND RETURN

A. INITIAL INVESTMENT

26	INSTALLED COST OF PROJECT	$ _____			
	MINUS INITIAL TAX BENEFIT OF	$ _____	(Net Cost)	$ _____	26
27	INVESTMENT IN ALTERNATIVE				
	CAPITAL ADDITIONS MINUS INITIAL TAX BENEFIT	$ _____			
	PLUS: DISPOSAL VALUE OF ASSETS RETIRED BY PROJECT*	$ _____		$ _____	27
28	INITIAL NET INVESTMENT (26-27)			$ _____	28

B. TERMINAL INVESTMENT

29 RETENTION VALUE OF PROJECT AT END OF COMPARISON PERIOD
(Estimate for Assets, if any, that cannot be depreciated or expensed. For others, estimate or use Mapi charts.)

Item or Group	Installed Cost, Minus Initial Tax Benefit (Net Cost) A	Service Life (Years) B	Disposal Value, End of Life (Percent of Net Cost) C	MAPI Chart Number D	Chart Percentage E	Retention Value $\left(\frac{A \times E}{100}\right)$ F
	$					$

	ESTIMATED FROM CHARTS (Total of Col. F)	$ _____		
	PLUS: OTHERWISE ESTIMATED	$ _____	$ _____	29
30	DISPOSAL VALUE OF ALTERNATIVE AT END OF PERIOD*		$ _____	30
31	TERMINAL NET INVESTMENT (29-30)		$ _____	31

C. RETURN

32	AVERAGE NET CAPITAL CONSUMPTION $\left(\frac{28-31}{P}\right)$	$ _____	32
33	AVERAGE NET INVESTMENT $\left(\frac{28+31}{2}\right)$	$ _____	33
34	BEFORE-TAX RETURN $\left(\frac{25-32}{33} \times 100\right)$	_____ %	34
35	INCREASE IN DEPRECIATION AND INTEREST DEDUCTIONS	$ _____	35
36	TAXABLE OPERATING ADVANTAGE (25-35)	$ _____	36
37	INCREASE IN INCOME TAX (36× TAX RATE)	$ _____	37
38	AFTER-TAX OPERATING ADVANTAGE (25-37)	$ _____	38
39	AVAILABLE FOR RETURN ON INVESTMENT (38-32)	$ _____	39
40	AFTER-TAX RETURN $\left(\frac{39}{33} \times 100\right)$	_____ %	40

*After terminal tax adjustments.

Fig. 7-11. Investment and Return
Source: Copyright 1967, Machinery and Allied Products Institute

Capital Investment Alternatives

A well-managed company will have more capital projects than it can either manage or finance. The problem it faces is identifying the best projects in terms of ROI, market share expansion, time, time horizon of the projects, time value of money, and maintaining financial reserves so that it may take advantage of better unforeseen projects which may come along.

General methods used by companies for evaluating capital projects are, however, relatively unsophisticated such as present value of the project, discounted cash flow, or MAPI.[2] The major tasks involved in utilizing these methods are gathering relevant cost data and forecasting net operating profit for a number of years in the future. Let us look at the role of the AIS for the MAPI method where assumptions about future profits are built into a choice of models.

Figure 7-11 shows one of several tables and charts employed by the MAPI method. Basically, the method permits comparison between a present project and a new project. From a decision point of view, as discussed in Chapter 6, only incremental costs and incremental income should be considered. Past history of the current project is irrelevant. Depreciation is relevant only as it affects the cash flow of taxes. The AIS should have the procedure for making the calculation of after-tax return available, preferably on a computer program. The AIS should provide for the availability of internal information for lines 26, 29, 35, and 36, and external information for lines 27, 30, 35, 36, 37.

Most well-managed companies have prepared procedures which are to be followed for capital budgeting decisions. For example, Xerox Corp. includes seven pages of instruction in its Controller's Manual to cover the analysis required to complete an Appropriation Request form. Table 7-3, which shows the first two pages of the instruction, indicates the nature of the accounting and financial information required. Fig. 7-12 shows the summary form. Obviously, the AIS should be designed to supply input data and prepare information as capital and expense requirements for the five years shown on the form.

Acquisition, Divestment, and Merger Analysis

Both large and small companies are likely to face acquisition, divestment, or merger (ADM) decisions. The small companies are more likely to be faced with the merger question or being acquired by another com-

---

[2] See George Terborgh, *Business Investment Management,* Washington, D.C.: Machinery and Allied Products Institute, 1967.

Table 7-3. Xerox Controllers Manual

A. **GENERAL**: A Capital/Lease Appropriations Request will be processed and approved in accordance with the guidelines of this manual before an expenditure or commitment is made for the acquisition, disposition or exchange of capital assets. This includes the sale, dismantlement or phase-out (including the premature termination of a lease) of any facility.

Lease or rental expenditures for non-facility assets (office machines, automobiles or material handling equipment) will require CAR approval when the intended use is for a period of more than six months. If the planned use is for a period of less than six months, a CAR will not be required. In cases where the item is leased on a month-to-month basis but is retained beyond the six month period, a CAR for the approval of the entire proposed leased expenditure will be required at the end of the six month period.

The originator of a CAR will ensure that the CAR is prepared in accordance with the guidelines of this manual. Every CAR will include an executive summary, concurrence and approval signatures, a financial data summary and detailed back-up as necessary to support the CAR. In addition, the originator will:

1. Notify the Manager of Capital Investment Analysis - ISG, during the initial formulation of projects or CAR's expected to require approval of the ISG President.

2. Consult and obtain the advice of the Manager of Capital Investment Analysis - ISG regarding formulation of the project, evaluation techniques and alternative considerations (lease vs. purchase, make vs. buy, etc.).

3. Discuss with the Manager of Capital Investment Analysis - ISG, and agree upon, the basic assumptions required to evaluate the project (volumes, labor costs, overhead, etc.).

Historically, CAR's have been processed on a project basis. In a few cases, especially for office furniture, the program CAR concept has been used successfully in processing total requirements. The program CAR concept should also be used for Branch/ASO expansion and relocation facility actions when feasible.

B. **EXECUTIVE SUMMARY**: The Executive Summary provides a discussion of the salient factors and other information in sufficient detail to permit Management to make a decision on the proposal. This summary includes:

1. **Highlights** - A section which indicates general information about the request including identification of the organization presenting the proposal, capital and expense funds involved and commitments being made.

2. **Proposal** - A brief description of what is being proposed, either purchased, leased, rearranged, or renovated, including the location, size or special features.

3. **Budget Status** - An indication whether or not the costs were included in the expense and capital budgets. If not covered in the budgets, an explanation of how funding will be provided is required.

4. **Justification** - This section provides background information on events or management actions leading to the request and should address the question as to why the proposal represents a viable approach to a sound business objective. The justification should cover the risks and alternatives considered.

5. **Financial** - A financial summary which covers the capital investment, operating costs, increased revenue or cost savings, discounted cash flow analysis, return on investment, payback period, sensitivity analysis, and comparisons to similar approved programs or situations.

6. **Recommendation** - The course of action recommended to management.

The Executive Summary should follow the format outlined in Exhibit C of the Appendix.

C. **CONCURRENCE/APPROVAL**: Appropriate levels of management reviewing the CAR will indicate their concurrence, approval or comments as appropriate on the Capital/Lease Appropriation Request Form, Exhibit A of the Appendix. The form contains, for the benefit of management, summary capital and expense data which indicates the financial impact of the approval action.

D. **FINANCIAL DATA SUMMARY**: The CAR form identifies data which is necessary for establishing project control on a financial basis and is the source for verifying the budgeted and non-budgeted status of the project.

E. **DETAILED BACK-UP**: The detailed back-up in the CAR provides the information which supports the Executive Summary and will normally be required by the reviewing staff. The arrangement of the detailed information will be similar to the Executive Summary but will deal with issues in depth. The following items, although not all-inclusive, should be considered:

1. **Description** - A description or identification of the major comments of investment and/or items of equipment required, the capacity, special design features, and location should be included.

2. **Justification** - The proposal should be discussed with specific reference to the mandatory, cost savings, and strategic implications of the project. The capacity aspects of the proposal, taking into account such items as future expansion, technical risk and the impact of reasonable changes to the volume projections should be evaluated.

    If the proposal is for manufacturing space, refurbishing space, distribution space or warehouse space, the volume and new product projections used for determining requirements should be identified. Specific assumptions contained in the Operating and Long Range Plans should be used whenever possible and applicable. Any assumed changes to relevant factors in the approved plans should be explained in detail.

    If excess capacity has been built into the proposal, discuss the relative costs of providing for the excess as opposed to adding capacity at some later date.

    If the proposal is for office space, include a standard ISG Field Facility Planning Manpower/Space Requirement Plan. If space requirements have not been developed in accordance with space standards, explain the reason for not using accepted standards.

    List and discuss the favorable and unfavorable factors and all risk aspects associated with approval or rejection of the proposed investment.

    Discuss alternate proposals which would appear to warrant consideration and discuss the logic leading to the rejection of those alternatives.

3. **Financial Evaluation** - There is no single criterion for evaluating an investment proposal. The analytical methods for project evaluation in order of preference at Xerox are:

    - Discounted Cash Flow (DCF) Rate of Return.
    - Average Annual Return on Investment
    - Payback Period on a Net Cash Flow Basis
    - Net Present Value at a Predetermined Discount Rate.

    Proper financial evaluation of a project must address all three elements associated with a business venture: REVENUE, EXPENSE and INVESTMENT. It is understood that not all programs/projects can be clearly and directly associated with revenue, expenses and investment. There are cases in which the criterion is one of minimizing cash outflows among several options. In cases where no revenue is involved, the evaluation must thoroughly analyze alternative courses of action to seek the most advantageous cash outflow. The discounted method of evaluation should be applied to the net cash flow difference between the most advantageous situations (i.e., a lease/buy analysis).

    a. Definitions:

        Discounted Cash Flow (DCF) Rate of Return - The discount rate at which the net present value of a stream of cash flows is equal to zero (commonly referred to as the actual rate of return). It can be obtained by graphic solution or interpolation of the net present value as a function of the discount rate used.

        Average Annual Return on Investment - Annual Net Profit after tax divided by the cumulative gross investment during the years and averaged over the life of the project.

        Payback Period - The time period required for an investment to generate cash inflow equal to the cash outflow (i.e., the cumulative cash flow or sum of net annual cash flows is equal to zero). The discounted payback period at a given rate is obtained in a similar manner but using annual cash flows discounted at the prescribed rate.

        Net Cash Flow - The cumulative sum of incremental cash receipts and disbursements occurring during a specified time period (years) and solely attributable to the project or investment under consideration. It is equal to the sum of net profit after tax plus depreciation less investment during the years (life of the project).

        Net Present Value - The present dollar value of a future stream of net annual cash flows discounted at a given rate. It is obtained by adding the discounted cash flows. It can be positive, negative or zero.

Table 7-3. (cont'd)

Risk - The degree of exposure to less-than-satisfactory performance or loss inherent in the proposed project. Good business judgement requires a relatively large return on projects having greater risks to compensate for the possibility of failure to achieve objectives.

Maximum Cash Exposure - The largest negative value of cumulative cash flow. It provides an indication of the apparent cash risk associated with a project which may have to be terminated prematurely due to unforeseen circumstances. It is not the maximum risk since additional financial risks may exist due to commitments, cancellations, etc.

Project Life - The best estimate of the economic life of the project.

Sensitivity Analysis - A parametric evaluation of the effect that changes in key variables and critical assumptions would have on the discounted cash flow rate of return or on the average annual return on investment. Sensitivity analysis should be used whenever possible since it is a valuable aid for Group and Corporate Management in identifying factors that are most important and which therefore should be closely monitored or controlled.

b. General Evaluation Approach:

A financial analysis should be provided for all proposals including those which involve:

- Make or buy decisions
- Purchase or lease and sale-leaseback arrangements
- Differences between timing or magnitude of anticipated cash flows between operationally viable alternatives.

It is essential that the financial implications of a proposed project are identified and carefully evaluated as an integral part of an overall business decision. This is required to provide proper financial perspective.

Economically justified projects must be justifiable on the basis of a DCF rate of return. No cut-off point can be used as a yardstick since the risk associated with investment proposals is not the same in all cases. It is a prerogative of management to decide if the stated rate of return of an investment proposal is sufficient to justify the risk involved.

The Net Present Value should also be calculated in evaluating economically justified projects when evaluating project alternatives with similar investments and life (i.e., alternative purchase arrangements or lease option). It is necessary that the analysis be constructed so that each alternative accomplishes the same objectives over the same period of time.

Specific financing arrangements for asset acquisitions will be determined at Group or Corporate Management level. The asset(s) will be purchased if the DCF rate of return indicated for the acquisition is deemed reasonable in relation to the inherent risks. Otherwise, the asset(s) will be procured externally (leased, sales-lease-back, etc.).

All analyses should include the following information for each alternative considered:

- A summary of all assumptions such as project life, depreciable life and depreciation method for each type of asset, volumes, location, labor and overhead rates, etc. which have been reviewed and approved by the Operating Group.

- A summary of financial highlights containing total investment including working capital, DCF rate of return, payback period in years, maximum cash exposure and point in time at which it occurs.

A statement of cash flows should be included with each CAR requiring Group or Corporate approval. The statement of cash flows should be prepared in a manner similar to the sample shown in Exhibit D of the Appendix. The example provided is not intended to be all-inclusive and is given only as a guideline.

A lease versus buy analysis should be prepared when these options are among the preferred alternatives. The analysis should be prepared in accordance with the format outlined in Exhibit E of the Appendix. As the schedule indicates, a net cash flow after tax should be prepared for the buy and the lease option. Maintenance costs, lease cost, amortization of leasehold improvements are examples of the type of costs that should be included in the lease option. The buy case should include depreciation, taxes, insurance and other owner costs. In addition, the capital investment cash flows for the lease case should be subtracted from the annual cash flows for the buy (or build) option. The difference should be discounted until a DCF rate is found. This is the rate of return on the investment for the acquisition or construction of the facility.

The useful life of the asset(s), method of depreciation and salvage value (if any) should follow the guidelines outlined in Controllers Manual, Volume I, Policy 305.

For purposes of project evaluation and investment analysis, the lower of book value or salvage value is recovered at the end of the project's life. If salvage is less than book value, the book loss is carried as a pre-tax depreciation expense.

When determining the present value or DCF rate, the continuous stream discount tables included in Exhibit F of the Appendix should be used.

F. **FACILITY RELATED CAR**:

1. **Approval**: Corporate approval is required for all acquisitions and dispositions of land, buildings and building additions. Corporate Facilities concurrence is required on all lease CAR's as an integral part of implementation.

    The sale, dismantlement or closedown of a facility, including the termination of a lease which involves a cancellation payment, requires approval through the CAR procedure. If the proposed disposition of a fixed asset is related to an acquisition of a fixed asset, both considerations may be stated in the same CAR. If the disposition does not relate to a current investment decision, it will be addressed in a separate CAR. For purposes of CAR approval levels, the book value of the disposed asset (write-off or cancellation payment) is the governing factor.

2. **Lead Time**: The lead time required from submission of a facility related CAR to anticipated occupancy will vary depending on the construction, remodeling or rearrangements necessary for occupancy. Since circumstances will vary with individual projects, the lead time schedule will be determined by agreement of the CAR originator, Group Facilities Planning Manager and Group Capital Investment Analysis Manager.

3. **Funding**: If final approval by Corporate of a facility related CAR authorizes a method of procuring the space (i.e., buy instead of lease), which is different from the approach recommended in the CAR, budget adjustments will be requested from Corporate.

    Where the decision to lease is clear, the CAR should be processed based on estimated lease costs prepared by Corporate Real Estate. However, the lease versus purchase question must be addressed when appropriate and the documentation must include a discounted cash flow analysis. In evaluating the lease versus buy situation, the book value of the facility, if it is owned by Xerox, should be recovered at the end of the project's life.

4. **Feasibility Study**: When an Operating Executive identifies a probable need for construction of any facility, a feasibility study will be prepared. This study is to identify: (a) major parameters and specifications; (b) environmental health and safety features, including pollution control implications where appropriate; (c) preliminary architectural design features; (d) the construction schedule; (e) cost estimate.

    The basis for preparation of the feasibility study will be the project requirements. The expense associated with the feasibility study should be provided for in the Expense Operating Plan of the sponsoring organization.

    Based on the feasibility study, the facility CAR will be prepared to provide funding for the costs of design and construction. A copy of the study will be incorporated as a part of the CAR documentation to substantiate cost and scheduling data.

5. **The Facility CAR Package**: In addition to and within the context of Section I of this manual, the facilities CAR package must include the following:

    a. Business Proposal - If a proposal was prepared for the project, a copy of the approved business proposal should be furnished with the CAR. A proposed new facility action or upgrade not included in the approved Facility Plan will require a business proposal.

    b. Feasibility Study - A copy of the feasibility study prepared for new construction projects must be furnished with the CAR or appropriate data summarized and referenced to the study.

    c. Request for Marketing Facilities - A copy of the request must be furnished with the CAR. This document is to be prepared in accordance with instructions contained in the ISG

Table 7-3 (cont'd)

     Field Facilities Standards and Guidelines. A copy of the Corporate Project Manager's response reflecting the CAR estimate and preliminary project schedule should also be furnished.

   d. Manpower/Space Requirements Plan - The standard ISG Field Facilities Manpower/Space Requirements Plan, Exhibit B of the Appendix, will be required for showing manpower projections and space requirements for office facilities.

   e. Furniture and Equipment Cost Estimate Schedule - Facility CAR's will include provision for office furniture and fixtures required to equip the building for the manpower level at the time of occupancy. No provision will be made for growth requirements – even though the facility may have been sized for increased manpower levels. All office furniture and equipment with a unit value of less than $300 will be expensed (without regard to total aggregate value); that portion to be expensed will be identified in the CAR as "program associated" expense.

   f. Associated/Operating Expense Estimates - The Financial Data Summary section of the CAR form requires identification of associated and operating expenses. Associated expenses are the one-time expenses related to the facility action such as moving or telephone installation costs. Operating expenses are those continuing costs that are directly related to the new facility or additional space and include utilities, taxes, maintenance, guard service, groundskeeping, amortization, etc.

   g. Present and Proposed Comparison - The Executive Summary should include a complete comparison of present and proposed facility arrangements. This comparison should include the square foot, cost per square foot, identification of expense elements such as gas, electricity, maintenance and guard service included in the cost, etc.

G. **SUPPORT RELATED CAR:**

  1. **Definition**: Any CAR that is not facility related will be considered as support related within ISG.

  2. **The Support CAR Package**: In addition to and within the context of Section I of this manual, the Support CAR package should address the following:

   a. Substantiation of Need - An explanation of where the machinery, equipment, tools or furniture will be utilized with a discussion of the causal factors such as machine activity, supplies volume, manpower growth, replacement, etc. This substantiation must clearly show why present assets are not adequate.

   b. Lease vs. Buy - Any evaluation of the lease versus buy question must be included for the acquisition of machinery and equipment, particularly material handling, demo vans and other vehicular items.

   c. Disposition of Replaced Equipment - Disposition of equipment being replaced with the proposed acquisition must be clearly explained.

   d. Adaptability to Other Uses - If equipment is designed for a particular use, the adaptability of the required items to other programs or general use should be addressed as a risk in recognition of changes which can occur in product program direction.

   e. Model Calculations - Where estimating models are used, the assumptions and mechanics of the calculation should be explained.

   f. Other Data - Factors, standards or ratios employed in formulating the CAR should be explained clearly and concisely.

   g. Associated/Operating Expense Estimates - The Financial Data Summary section of the CAR form requires identification of associated and operating expenses. Associated expenses are the one-time expenses related to the asset acquisition and generally do not exist with support related CAR's. Operating expenses are those continuing costs that are directly related to the asset and generally consist of depreciation, maintenance and repair.

XEROX CAPITAL/LEASE APPROPRIATION REQUEST

DATE: _____

OPERATING GROUP	PROJECT NO.	PROJECT TITLE	ORIGINATING MANAGER

	CAPITAL			ASSOCIATED EXPENSE	LEASE PER YEAR	LEASE TOTAL
	BUDGETED	NOT BUDGETED	TOTAL			
PRIOR APPROVALS	$	$	$	$	$	$
THIS REQUEST						
FUTURE REQUESTS						
TOTAL PROJECT	$	$	$	$	$	$

CASH FLOW THIS REQUEST:

	19	19	19	19	19	TOTAL
CAPITAL	$	$	$	$	$	$
EXPENSE						

CONCURRENCE OR APPROVAL	SIGNATURE	DATE
OPERATING GROUP		
DIVISION/DEPT.: ORIGINATOR		
LEVEL 4 MANAGER		
LEVEL 3 MANAGER		
LEVEL 2 MANAGER		
DIVISION/DEPT. STAFF		
DIVISION/DEPT. CONTROLLER		
DIVISION/DEPT. MANAGER (Region, Country or Subsidiary Manager)		
GROUP: GROUP CONTROLLER		
GROUP FACILITY MANAGER		
GROUP PRODUCT PROGRAM MANAGER		
GROUP PRESIDENT		
CORPORATE: CORPORATE STAFF		
CORPORATE STAFF		
CORPORATE VICE PRESIDENT FINANCE		
EXECUTIVE VICE PRESIDENT		
PRESIDENT/CHAIRMAN OF THE BOARD		

COMMENTS/QUALIFICATIONS:

Form 51394 (1/73) Printed in U.S.A.

Fig. 7-12

FINANCIAL DATA SUMMARY

PROJECT NO. 　　　PROJECT TITLE

CAPITAL ITEMS

ITEM NO.	DESCRIPTION	APPROVED BUDGET TO DATE	AUTHORIZED TO DATE	THIS REQUEST	ANTICIPATED FUTURE	TOTAL ITEM
	TOTAL CAPITAL ▶					

LEASE AND ASSOCIATED EXPENSES

BUD. CTR. / ACCT. NO.	DESCRIPTION	EXPENSES PRIOR YEAR	CURRENT YEAR BUDGET	CURRENT YEAR EXPENSES	FUTURE ANNUALIZED EXPENSES	EXPENSE OVER LEASE PERIOD
	LEASE EXPENSE					
	ASSOCIATED EXPENSE (ONE TIME)	NOT APPLICABLE			NOT APPLICABLE	
	TOTAL LEASE AND ASSOCIATED EXPENSES ▶					

OPERATING EXPENSES (ANNUAL)

	TOTAL OPERATING EXPENSES (ANNUAL) ▶					

Fig. 7-12. (cont'd)

pany. The impact of both quantitative and qualitative information on the ADM decision must be analyzed by the accountant. The AIS should be designed so that (1) internal relevant data are stored in the data base to be available and (2) intelligence methods are established to gather external data for the controller's analysis and evaluation.

Since this is not a text on the subject of ADM, we only suggest a few items and their classifications as shown in Table 7-6 in order to indicate that the AIS has a specific role in aiding management with ADM decisions.

Table 7-4. Typical AIS Information for Acquisition, Divestment and Merger Analysis

	INTERNAL	EXTERNAL
QUANTITATIVE	Own Balance Sheet and P & L reports Impact on stock price and stockholders Tax impact Cost of combining and duplicating executive positions if a policy of attrition rather than firing is followed	Other company's Balance Sheet and P & L reports Impact on stockholders Minority interests Capital structure and debt analysis Executive compensation Taxes
QUALITATIVE	Evaluation of marketing, manufacturing, and research synergy gains Impact on own vendor relationships	Evaluation of quality of items of other company's financial statements such as assets, facilities, inventories, contracts with customers, and leases Union contracts Impact on vendors Lines of credit Patents Good will

Cost Allocation

Cost is probably a major factor in all major corporate decisions. Surprisingly, the costs that are really relevant to the decision are frequently not available to management. The typical accounting system is directed toward gathering historical data for the necessary historical reports.

Some types of costs that the AIS should attempt to provide are marginal costs, incremental costs, costs of "cost centers," the separation of controllable and uncontrollable costs for profit and cost center managers, contribution costs, and cost behavior as a function of internal and external as well as controllable and noncontrollable variables.

The accountant, in designing the AIS, should make sure that data are captured and computer application programs are developed for flexibility in costing according to circumstances or policy. As a simple example, suppose that a subsidy for the telephone system on a university campus is withdrawn. The system must increase charges to various users based upon both costs and policies desired by the administration. In particular, costs and charges for use of a number of extensions by a large fraternity house are at issue. The administrator considers that it may cost and charge on:

1. An incremental basis for the local switchboard, two operators, and equipment
2. The basis of cost of distance of the lines to the main switchboard and the rental cost of the instruments
3. The basis of the number of extensions, only
4. The basis of the number of calls per day through the switchboard
5. The basis of the average number of students in the fraternity house per month.

Further, the administration would like an analysis on each of the above bases to determine what proportion of total campus costs each method would carry. Can the AIS readily retrieve and segregate current costs on the above base? Can it project future charges in each case based on a number of variables such as usage, number of students, and leasing costs?

Although the above is a simple case, large companies face a continuing multitude of decisions which require a variety of costing approaches. Managment cannot wait while AIS is patched up or special studies are made to gather data that should have been available in the data base. If the AIS is not capable of supplying the information promptly in the form needed, management must often make riskier decisions.

Contribution Analysis and Segment Evaluation

Two related decision areas are contribution analysis and the evaluation of "segments." A segment is any operation or subsystem of the business for which separate determination of costs and revenues are desired. Contribution analysis relates to those costs under the control of the segment manager. Uncontrollable costs for the segment manager are those such as overhead or corporate assessments applied to the segment. The AIS should be designed to aid the segment manager with planning and control and aid higher management with evaluating the segment manager.

In addition, since the performance of the segment as an economic unit differs from the performance of the segment manager, the AIS should also be capable of assisting with the economic analysis of the unit.[3]

Contract Bidding

There are two basic types of contracts upon which a company may bid. The first is a one-of-a-kind purchase, service, or product. The second involves repetitive production of a product or service. In the first case, the large oil company may bid to purchase or lease oil rights or an industrial company bids to produce a space satellite or fuel processing plant. In the second case, a company bids for a contract to manufacture a number of units of a special product such as 15 tanks, 100,000 computer subassemblies, or 200 duplexes in a building development.

For the unique, one-of-a-kind contract, the intelligence gathering activity and the selection of data which should and can be collected for costing and bidding are extremely important. For example, competitive bidders should be identified and their costs estimated as closely as possible. Such costs depend upon present utilization of their plant, for example. If a firm produces large steam turbines, has few orders currently in progress, unused plant capacity and idle labor, their incremental costs for a single large order are greatly reduced.

The AIS should also be capable of handling less tangible intelligence factors in its development of a bid price for such unique projects. What are the probabilities of follow-on contracts of various sizes? What are the advantages of bidding low to gain experience in the technology or of increasing prestige or market share?

With regard to bids for production of batches of a product, both costs and intangibles likewise enter into the decision. The major feature of costing in this case is the development of the "manufacturing progress function." To obtain the cost of production of, say 150 units of a new product, accountants tend to research the cost of the first unit and then multiply by 150. Industrial engineers have long been aware that each consecutive unit produced costs less. This is due to such factors as learning gains of labor, better management planning and control, minor manufacturing and engineering changes, and lower costs of vendors' components as vendors reduce their own production costs.

[3] For a more detailed discussion of the accounting concepts required, see Chapter 11 of Charles T. Horngren, *Accounting for Management Control* (3rd ed.), Englewood Cliffs, N.J.: Prentice-Hall, 1974.

Suppose, for example, that Company A bids on a Navy contract to produce five vessels at $400 million each for a total of $2,000 million. Company B, with the same cost structure, recognizes that costs will decline 10% every time production is doubled. It calculates that price should follow cost and calculates it should therefore bid $1,736 million.[4]

The AIS should have appropriate bidding models available and means for systematically evaluating the parameters used in the model. There should also be a formal intelligence system for obtaining external data required for inputs to the model. Such intelligence data relates to customers' and competitors' characteristics.

Tax Planning

It is obvious today that the company that focuses on making profits and then calculates and pays taxes subsequently and mechanically is a poorly managed company. Tax planning should start before investment, before production, and before financing. Once an operating decision is implemented, tax management may be too late.

The controller, once again, is a critical component of the AIS. He must have access to top management to participate in the early stages of planning. He provides input to the AIS for analysis and evaluation of the tax impact of major decisions. This is particularly important for long-range planning.

The AIS must be designed to monitor tax laws and rulings both in the U.S. and foreign countries. Early warning signals of impending changes may affect the location of a major plant, the flow of currency and earnings, or the import of components in manufacture. Therefore, the *formal* gathering of information as provided by the AIS is a necessity to avoid costly oversights.

Executive and Nonexecutive Compensation Plans

The role of the accountant in the development of compensation plans is a critical one. Further, these plans require continual review as factors in the business environment keep changing. Traditionally, the accountant has simply evaluated and reacted to compensation plans proposed by the

---

[4] For development of experience models and tables for unit and cumulative values of the manufacturing progress function, see W. J. Fabrycky, P. M. Ghare, and P. E. Torgersen, *Industrial Operations Research,* Englewood Cliffs, N.J.: Prentice-Hall, 1972.

human resources department. The accountant's objective was to hold down compensation costs regardless of other factors because this policy led directly to greatest earnings. Or so it seemed, at any rate. The modern accountant, educated in the systems approach, behavioral science, and managerial accounting now takes a much broader view.

The entire range of variables entering into the compensation packages must be viewed in terms of system interaction, the system being the business firm as a whole. The compensation package must not be viewed just as a cost but as a dynamic force for attracting, keeping, and modifying behavior of the best possible executives and individual workers.

The accountant, in the systems view, must be concerned with estimating benefits in terms of marginal costs devoted to human resources. The human resources department will play the principal role in creating alternatives, and accounting will play the principal role in evaluating alternatives. Both groups will work together to evaluate impact of alternatives on profits of the company. Factors to be considered are:

1. Salary structure
2. Level of compensation structure relative to that of local competitors and the industry as a whole
3. Fringe benefits such as paid vacations and holidays, pensions, medical benefits, insurance, illness and personal leave time
4. Flexitime
5. Commissions
6. Bonuses
7. Stock ownership plan
8. Executive bonuses
9. Executive stock options
10. Other executive perquisites such as company car and aircraft.

If possible, the AIS should include a model of the impact of various mixes of compensation factors. This will permit management to ask "What if" questions as environmental data indicate that the total compensation plan may need revision.

CONTROLLER'S MANUAL

The controller's manual, or its equivalent financial manual, provides a means for obtaining consistency in company operations. It represents a set of corporate decisions which guide future decisions. In addition, it specifies procedures for processing business transactions. While many companies believe that they benefit from the orderliness brought about by the Controller's Manual, others believe that the cost of updating such a manual makes it impractical. There is an answer to this objection, however. It consists simply of limiting the manual to a relatively few important policies and procedures.

Preparation of Policies and Procedures

The controller's manual should typically be prepared by the accounting department. Because the formulation of the wording of a policy requires that the author be highly skilled in writing, the accounting department is usually assisted by a management staff expert. Responsibility for maintenance of the manual must be assigned specifically.

The controller's manual replaces a hodgepodge of memos. It is a reference for long-time employees and a guide for new employees. It both aids decision making and provides controls for all levels of the organization. As an information source, it is a key part of the AIS.

The chart of accounts is the starting point for the preparation of a new manual. An examination of memoranda dealing with accounting-related policies will suggest policies to be prepared first. At this time, consistency and clarity should be sought. It also is a good time to review procedures thoroughly before they are prepared for the manual.

A policy is usually prepared in draft form by the interested department or manager. It is then edited and put into correct format by a staff writer. The draft will then be sent to managers who will be affected so that they may make comments. Top management (the controller) will then advise the staff writer regarding incorporation of comments. The final policy statement will be approved by management (according to a policy for approval) and copies circulated to holders of the controller's manual.

Physical Characteristics of the Manual

Manuals are loose-leaf so that revised policies and procedures may be inserted to replace obsolete ones. Durable simulated leather or smooth vinyl binders with tab indexes are common. Reproduction of policies must be clear so that good mimeograph, dry-copy processes, offset printing, and letter press are satisfactory. Letter press is probably too expensive for small companies where the number of manuals is rela-

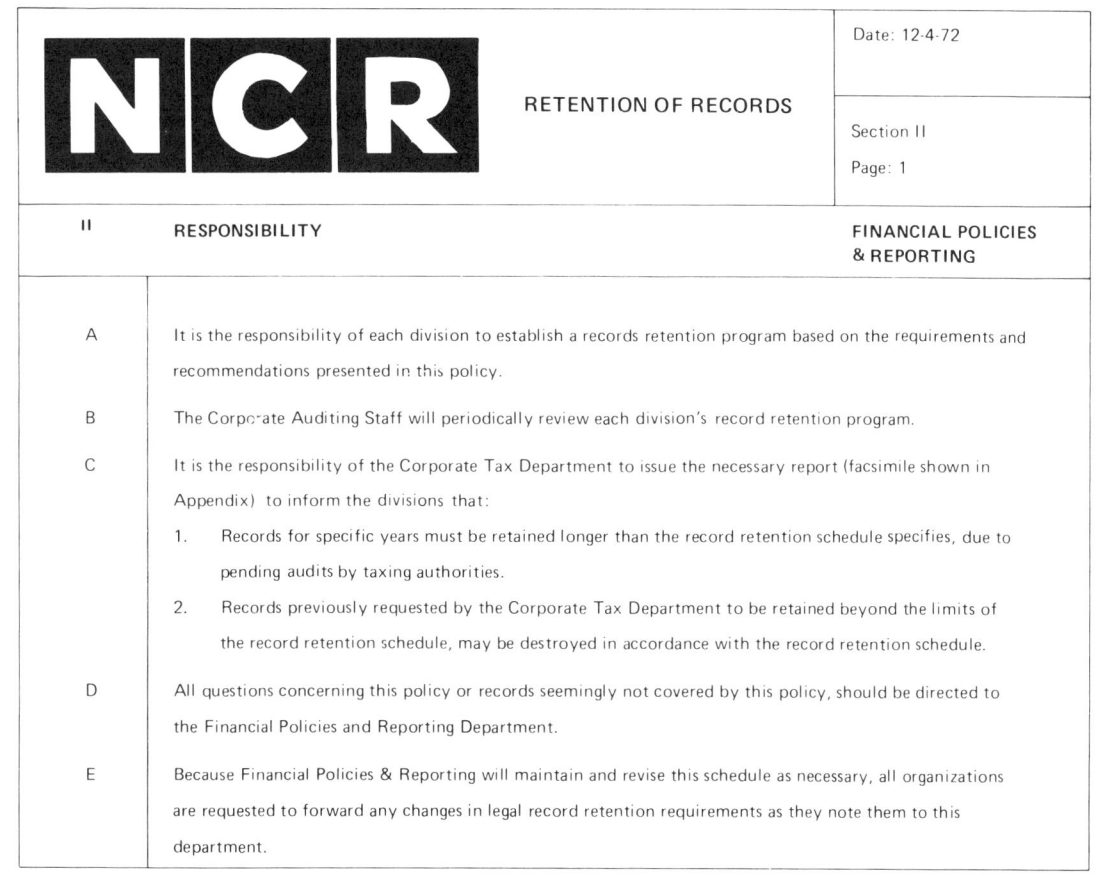

NCR	RETENTION OF RECORDS	Date: 12-4-72
		Section II
		Page: 1
II	RESPONSIBILITY	FINANCIAL POLICIES & REPORTING

A	It is the responsibility of each division to establish a records retention program based on the requirements and recommendations presented in this policy.
B	The Corporate Auditing Staff will periodically review each division's record retention program.
C	It is the responsibility of the Corporate Tax Department to issue the necessary report (facsimile shown in Appendix) to inform the divisions that:
	1. Records for specific years must be retained longer than the record retention schedule specifies, due to pending audits by taxing authorities.
	2. Records previously requested by the Corporate Tax Department to be retained beyond the limits of the record retention schedule, may be destroyed in accordance with the record retention schedule.
D	All questions concerning this policy or records seemingly not covered by this policy, should be directed to the Financial Policies and Reporting Department.
E	Because Financial Policies & Reporting will maintain and revise this schedule as necessary, all organizations are requested to forward any changes in legal record retention requirements as they note them to this department.

Fig. 7-13. Courtesy of NCR

tively small. The page formats may be preprinted on letter press in more cases since the same format is used for all policies.

A sample page of a manual is shown in Fig. 7-13.

Topics In the Manual

Manuals may have over a hundred or so policies and classifications vary widely. We give an example of a classification of topics below:

1. Organization and administration
2. Financial controls
3. The accounting system

4. Chart of accounts and coding
5. Capital expenditures and leases
6. Cash management
7. International accounting
8. Transfer pricing
9. Cost allocation
10. Profit planning and control
11. Accounting reports
12. Internal control
13. Forms and records control
14. Auditing
15. Taxes
16. Insurance.

Other systems may simply organize the manual to parallel the principal operating statement and balance sheet. We can only say that companies issue policies for topics they consider require them most.

Summary

This chapter has dealt with the AIS as an aid to decision-making by management. It deals with major decision areas, namely long-range planning, operating and financial (accounting) plans, and key classes of corporate decisions. For this function, the AIS involves not only capturing, storing, and manipulating internal data but building in an intelligence capability. This intelligence activity is a formal systematic approach to scanning the environment and capturing relevant data for the AIS.

Since some types of decisions are made periodically with changing input data and changes in parameters, the AIS should include a bank of models. Such models permit rapid analyses and provide prompt answers to management questions in many cases.

In the long-range planning activity, the AIS interacts with, or is considered a part of, the management information system. It assists with the presentation of the consequences of various alternative strategies. The accounting portion provides one of the major bases for control subsequent to planning.

For short-range (one to three year) operating plans, the financial plan is an integral part. The financial plan presents a quantitative picture of deployment and usage of resources to guide employees and measure performance. The AIS must provide rapid response to out-of-bound performance as the operating plans are implemented.

Finally, some important decision problems which require high-level and sophisticated treatment by the AIS are identified. These problems are important ones which occur in planning and control and are generally critical to the success of the company.

DISCUSSION QUESTIONS AND PROBLEMS

1. Discuss several reasons why accounting systems of the past have not been satisfactory for analyzing major corporate decisions.
2. a. What is the time-frame for strategic planning?
   b. Could it be different for various firms?
3. Relate the level of accounting detail to the planning horizon.
4. a. What is the time-frame for operational planning?
   b. What is the origin of the operational plan?
5. What three factors are meant to be controlled by the budget?
6. List and discuss the components of the master budget.
7. Discuss the master budget as an input and/or output of the AIS.
8. Discuss the reasons that historical accounting information is deficient for managerial decision-making.
9. Develop a chart similar to Figure 7-4 for:
   a. capital investment decisions
   b. contract bidding decisions
   c. tax planning
   d. executive compensation plans
10. Draw flowcharts showing the data sources, inputs to the decision-makers, and outputs from the decision-making based on the information developed in Question 9.
11. List and discuss several types of situations where contract bidding would be appropriate.
12. List and discuss several factors to consider when designing compensation plans.
13. Prepare a report format to show the types of information needed to evaluate a segment of a business.
14. Accountants must constantly make decisions dealing with the classification of costs. Develop a chart to show typical information that would be used to determine if an item should be classified as overhead or direct cost and the allocation method to be used.

Bibliography

ALLIO, R. J. "The Corporate Road Map—Planning at Babcock and Wilcox," *Long Range Planning,* December 1972.

BOULDER, JAMES B. "Computerized Corporate Planning," *Long Range Planning,* June 1971.

BRUNS, W. J., JR. "Accounting Information and Decision-Making: Some Behavioral Hypotheses," *The Accounting Review,* July 1968.

CHAMBERS, JOHN C., and SATINDER K. MULLICK. "Determining the Acquisition Value of a Company," *Management Accounting,* April 1970.

CHANDRA, GYAN and SURENDRA SINGHVI (eds.), *Budgeting for Profit,* Oxford, Ohio: The Planning Executives Institute, 1975.

CHEN, KUANG-CHIAN. "A Conceptual Structure of Corporate Strategic Planning Information Systems," *Managerial Planning,* September–October, 1977.

DAVEY, PATRICK J. *Financial Manual,* New York: The Conference Board, 1971.

DERMER, JERRY. *Management Planning and Control Systems,* Homewood, Ill.: Irwin, 1977.

DEW, R. BERESFORD and K. P. GEE. "Management's Use of Budgeting Information," *Management Accounting* (England), March 1970.

DICKE, HOWARD W. "Management Accounting for Research and Development Projects," *Management Accounting,* May 1969.

EDWARDS, JAMES DON. "Financial Planning and Control," *Managerial Planning,* November/December 1975.

FAIRAIZL, ALAN, F., and SATINDER K. MULLICK. "A Corporate Planning System," *Management Accounting,* December 1975.

FERRARA, WILLIAM L. "Accounting for Performance Evaluation and Decision-making," *Management Accounting,* December 1976.

GEDRICH, S. F. "Business Planning at Sperry Rand," *Long Range Planning,* April 1976.

HALL, THOMAS W. "Post-completion Audit Procedure," *Management Accounting,* September 1975.

HAMILTON, WILLIAM F., and MICHAEL A. MOSES. "A Computer-Based Corporate Planning System," *Management Science,* October, 1974.

HAYNES, W. WARREN, and WILLIAM R. HENRY. *Managerial Economics* (3rd ed.), Dallas, Texas: Business Publications, Inc., 1974.

HORNGREN, CHARLES T. *Accounting for Management Control* (3rd ed.), Englewood Cliffs, N.J.: Prentice-Hall, 1974.

IRVINE, PETER. "Mergers and Acquisitions," Parts I, II, III, *Executive,* November and December 1976.

LUH, MARTIN J., JR. "Forecasting and Budgeting in a Research Firm," *Management Accounting,* June 1972.

MCCARTHY, DANIEL J., and CHARLES A. MORRISSEY, "Using the Systems Analyst in Preparing Corporate Financial Models," *Financial Executive,* June 1972.

MURDICK, ROBERT G., et al. *Business Policy: A Framework for Analysis,* (2nd ed.), Columbus, Ohio: Grid, Inc., 1976.

MURDICK, ROBERT G., and DONALD D. DEMING. *The Management of Capital Expenditures,* New York: McGraw-Hill Book Co., 1968.

MURPHY, RICHARD C. "A Computer Model Approach to Budgeting," *Management Accounting,* June 1975.

PERRY, CLYDE. "Computerized Estimating," *Management Accounting,* January 1975.

REDMAN, LOUIS N. "Planning & Control and Accounting: Divide and Conquer," *Managerial Planning,* July/August 1976.

SIMMONS, DAVID A. *Medical and Hospital Control Systems,* Boston: Little, Brown and Company, 1972.

SWIERINGA, ROBERT J. and ROBERT H. MONCUR. *Some Effects of Participative Budgeting on Managerial Behavior,* New York: National Association of Accountants, 1975.

WELSCH, GLENN A. *Budgeting: Profit Planning and Control* (4th ed.), Englewood Cliffs, N.J.: Prentice-Hall, 1976.

IV

DESIGN
PROCESS
AND
CONCEPTS

Preview:
This chapter shows the process for the development of the AIS and it's relationship to the MIS. We shall look at the components of the AIS and will show the steps involved in developing the AIS.
–State objectives
–Identify contracts
–Project proposals
–Preliminary design
–Detailed design

CHAPTER EIGHT

accounting and management information systems development

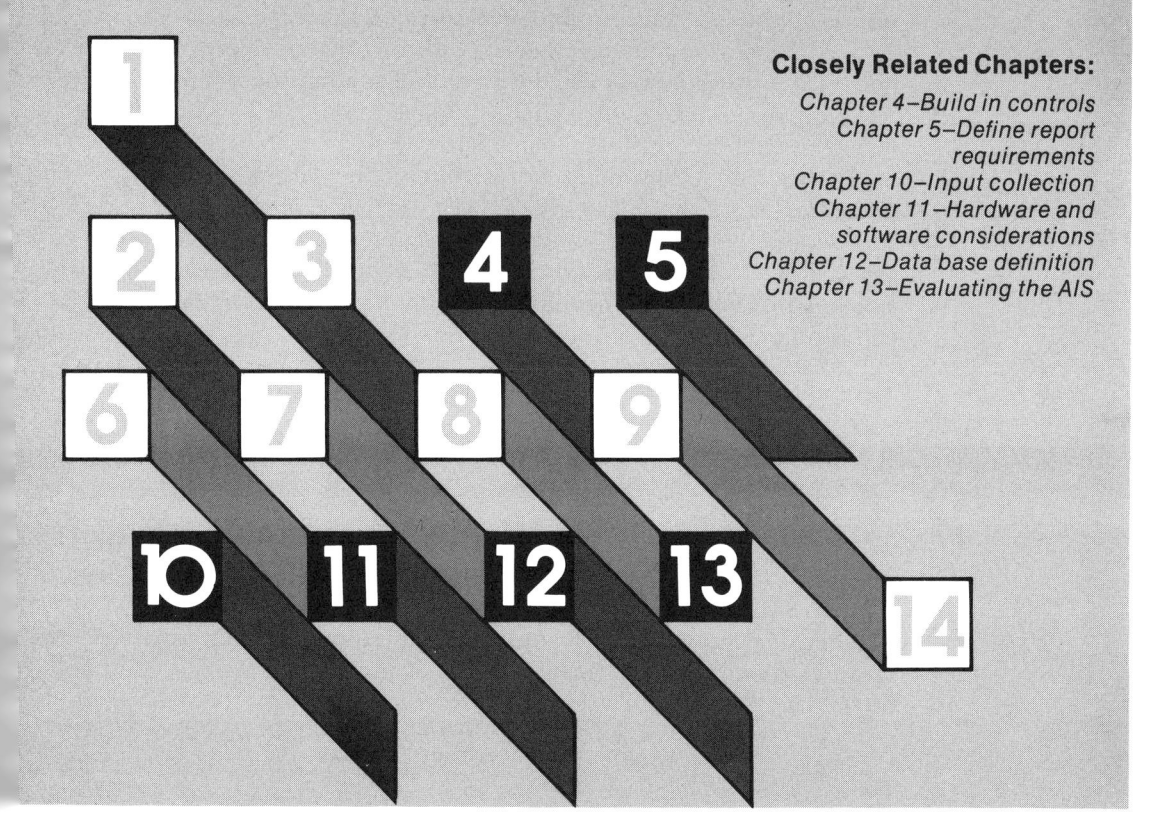

Closely Related Chapters:
Chapter 4–Build in controls
Chapter 5–Define report requirements
Chapter 10–Input collection
Chapter 11–Hardware and software considerations
Chapter 12–Data base definition
Chapter 13–Evaluating the AIS

The development of the accounting information system is similar to the development of a management information system. In fact, the development of the AIS should properly be a part of the development of the MIS. The AIS is a part of every operating system since it is a system for collecting cost data and revenue data and reporting such data to responsible individuals throughout the organization (Fig. 8-1).

AIS reports to management are in the form of selective information such as variances, unusual events, and summaries. In addition, the AIS supplies to the organization the budgets and guidelines prepared by management for control of the financial resources of the organization.

Since the AIS is designed as part of the MIS we will outline a procedure that encompasses both but gives special attention to the AIS. This chapter utilizes the concepts of Chapters 2 and 3. The detailed aspects of AIS development will be expanded upon in specialized discussions in Chapters 9 through 15. Chapters 4 through 7 describe the end results that we are trying to achieve.

ORGANIZATION FOR AIS DESIGN

The development of the MIS is carried out by the company's systems design group or by an *ad hoc* working committee. The accounting organization should be represented on the design team or the committee. A number of people in the accounting organization will likely be assigned responsibilities for the MIS which affects accounting activities and for the AIS itself.

The manager of accounting or the controller should clearly have overall responsibility for the AIS development. Other managers and technical specialists within the accounting organization will actually prepare proposals, flowcharts, and other documents as the design progresses.

COMPONENTS OF THE AIS

The components of the AIS may be viewed in several ways. First, we may view it in terms of outputs, which in one sense represent the ultimate purpose of the AIS. These are:

1. External reports (earnings statements, balance sheets, 10K and 10Q reports, regulatory reports required by the federal and state governments including insurance, FCC, ICC, FAB, and FPC reports)
2. Audit trail capabilities and procedures
3. Internal control system for ensuring the fairness of the above outputs
4. A data base for the use of other information systems.

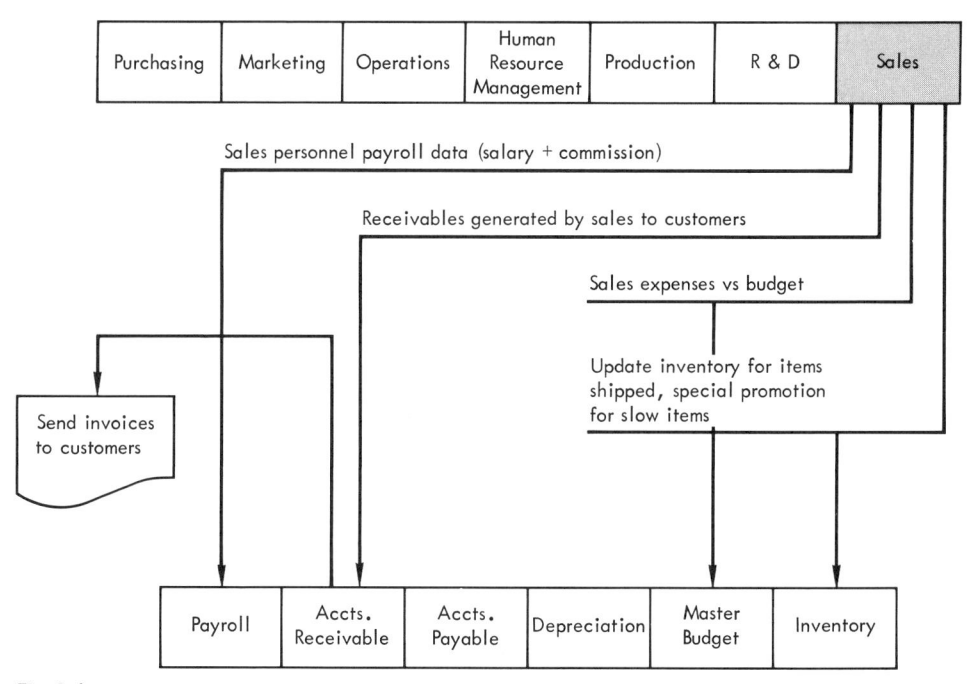

Fig. 8-1.

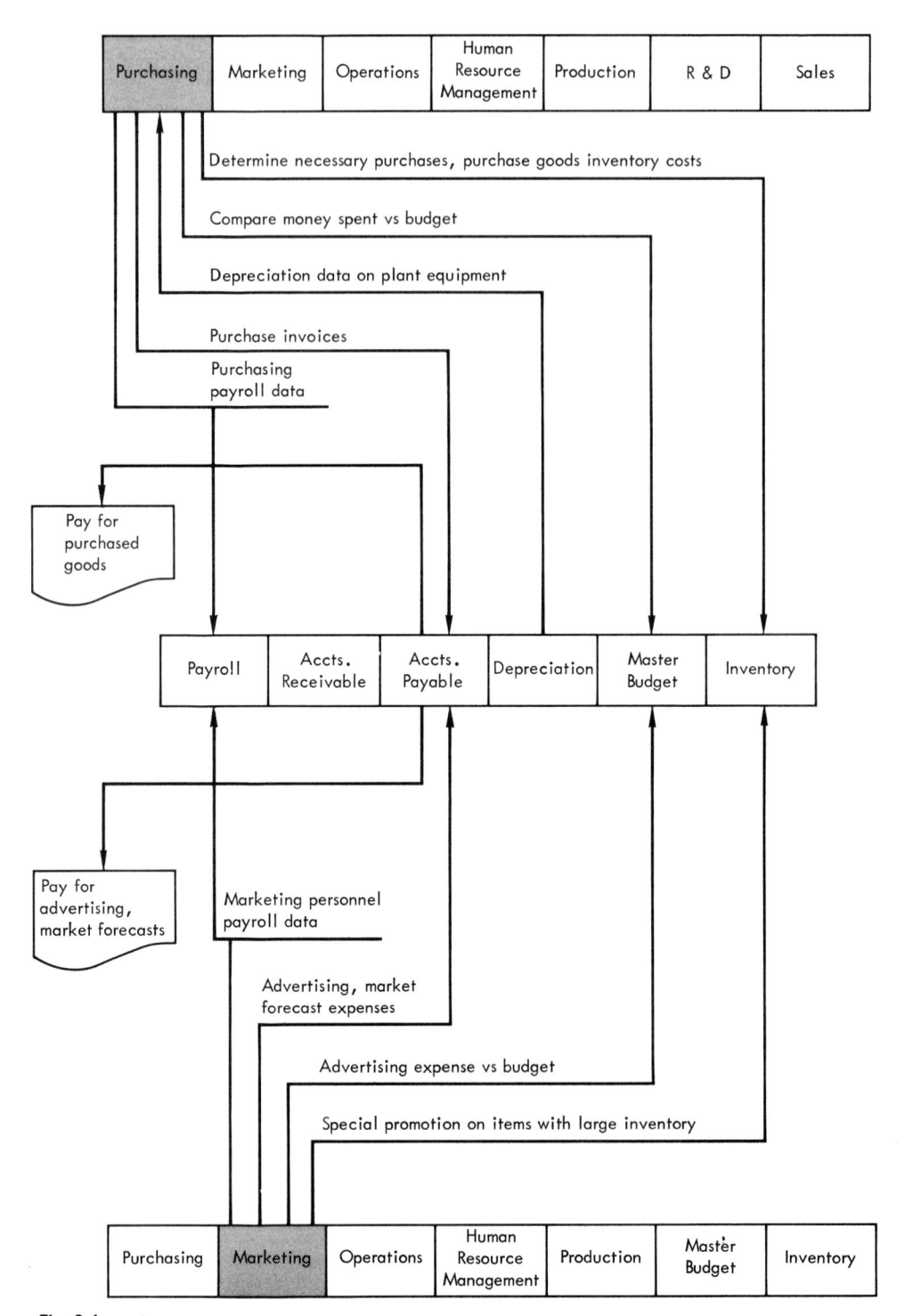

| Purchasing | Marketing | Operations | Human Resource Management | Production | R & D | Sales |

- Determine necessary purchases, purchase goods inventory costs
- Compare money spent vs budget
- Depreciation data on plant equipment
- Purchase invoices
- Purchasing payroll data

Pay for purchased goods

| Payroll | Accts. Receivable | Accts. Payable | Depreciation | Master Budget | Inventory |

Pay for advertising, market forecasts

- Marketing personnel payroll data
- Advertising, market forecast expenses
- Advertising expense vs budget
- Special promotion on items with large inventory

| Purchasing | Marketing | Operations | Human Resource Management | Production | Master Budget | Inventory |

Fig. 8-1. cont.

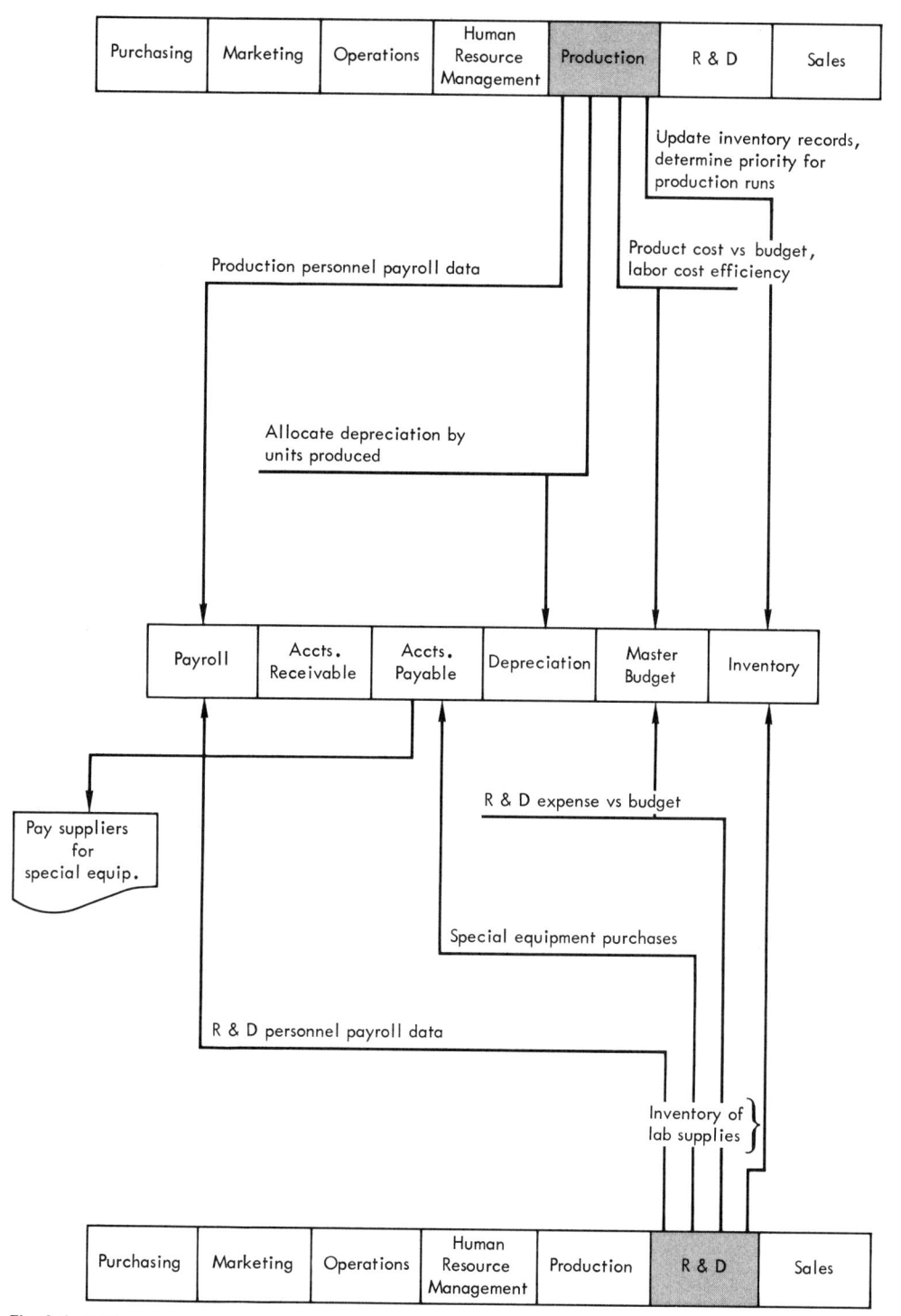

Fig. 8-1. cont.

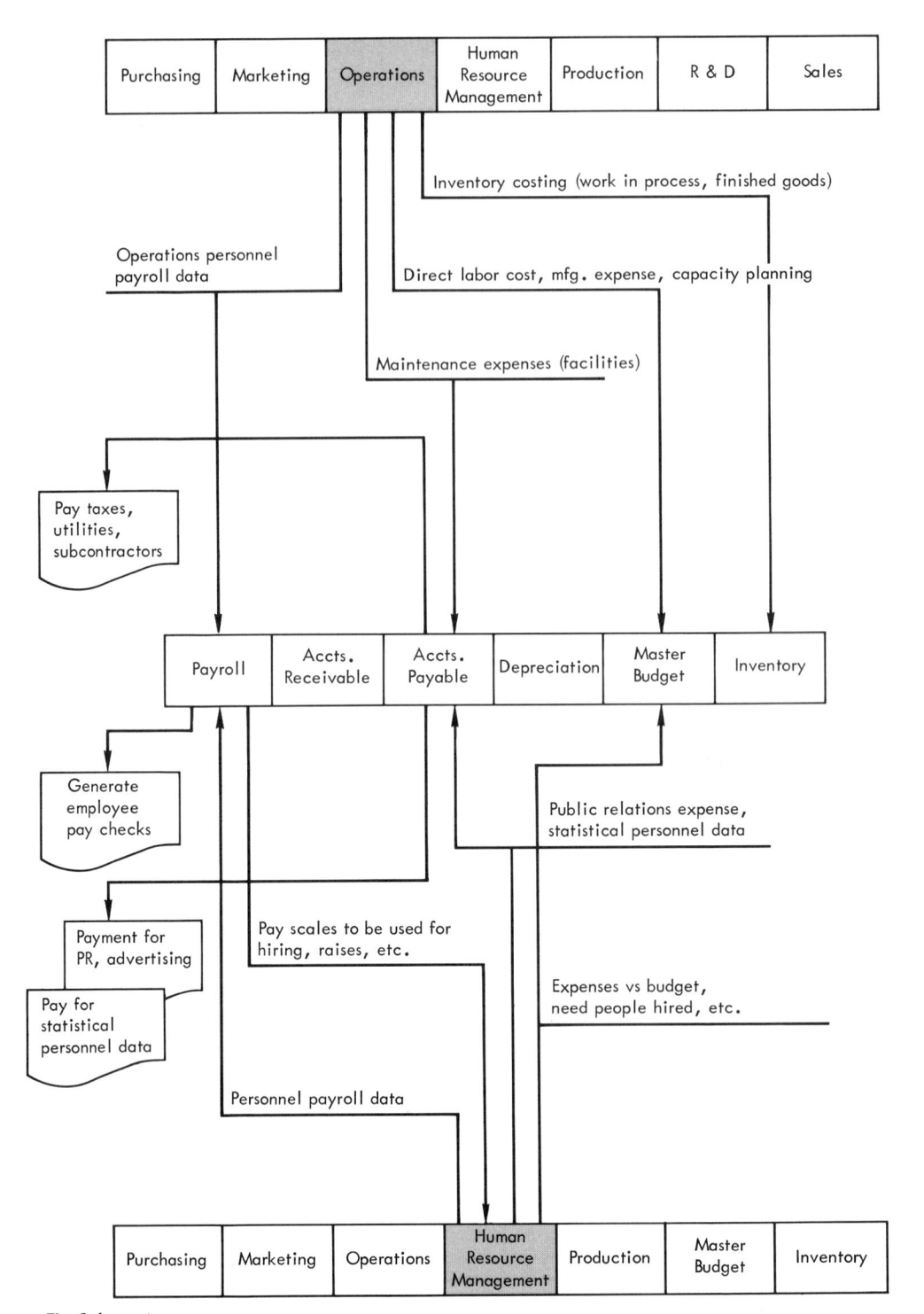

Fig. 8-1. cont.

Another way to look at the AIS is to identify the subsystems. In a manufacturing firm, these are typically:

1. General ledger and financial reporting system
2. Accounts receivable system
3. Accounts payable system
4. Materials and inventory planning system
5. Payroll system
6. Cost of production system
7. Capital budgeting system
8. Operations budgeting system.

Typical flowcharts of these systems are shown in Figs. 8-2 through 8-9.

For comparison, we note the AIS subsystems for a hospital, as outlined by flowcharts, are as shown in Fig. 8-10 through 8-11.

For each organization, variations of "standard" AIS are possible. Particularly, the detailing of the AIS depends upon the ingenuity of the designer to develop work flows and utilize people and equipment in combinations to achieve accounting/financial objectives.

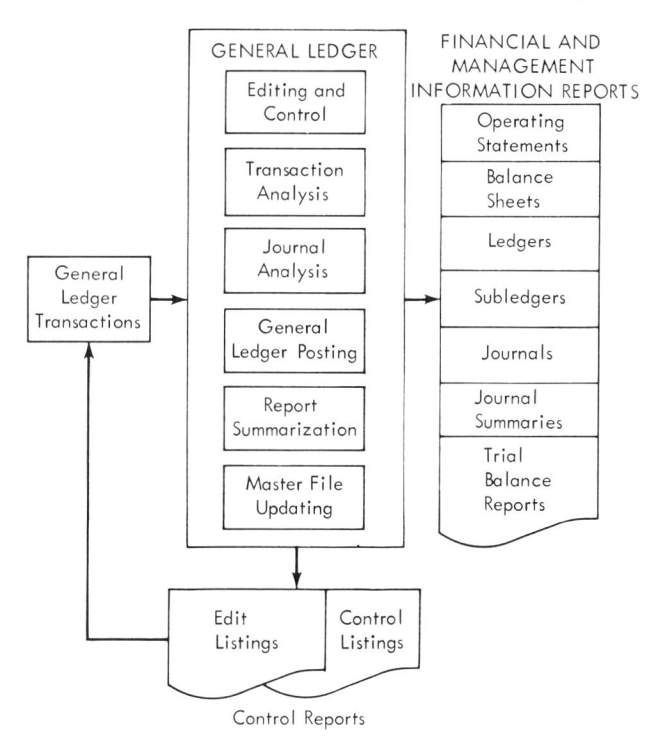

Fig. 8-2. General Ledger and Financial Reporting System

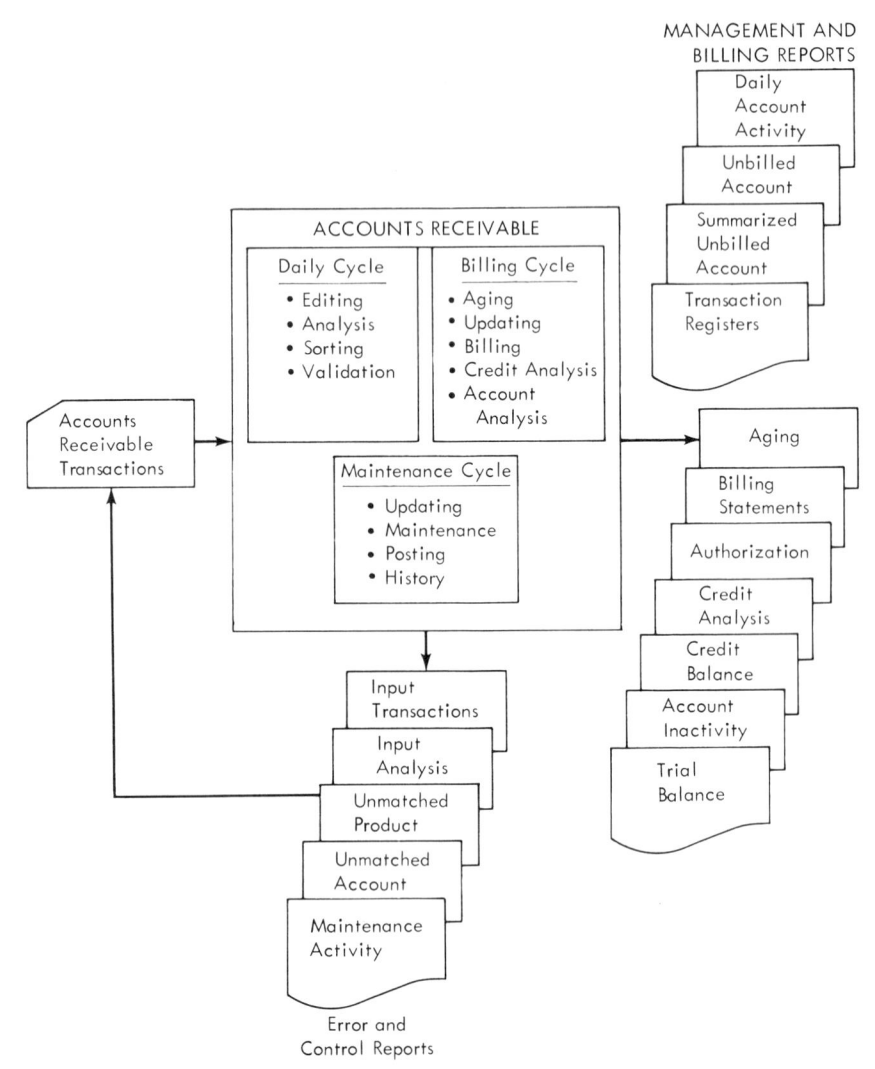

Fig. 8-3. Accounts Receivable System

Source: Wayne W. McKee, "Small Business Can Be Computerized," *Management Accounting,* April 1972.

STEPS IN DEVELOPMENT OF INFORMATION SYSTEMS

We will assume that management is considering the development of a new MIS and AIS. This is the case when companies are overhauled because of poor management or when long-range planning is put into effect. At other times, projects may be undertaken to revise parts of these key information systems. In any case, the general procedure is much the

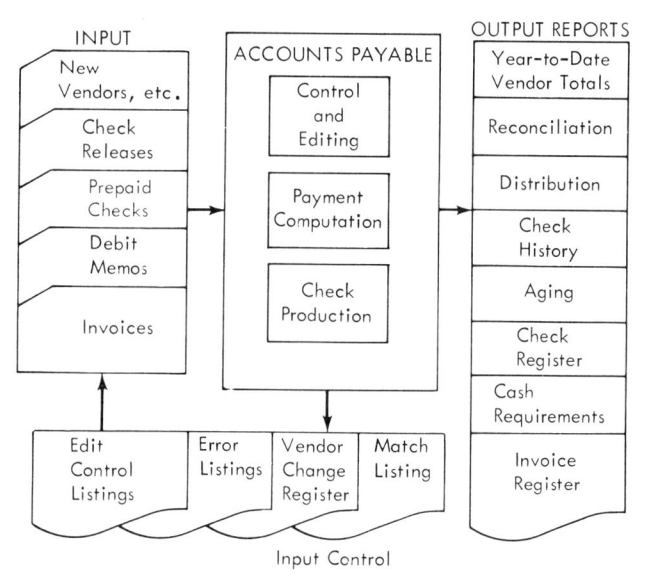

Fig. 8-4. Accounts Payable System

Source: Wayne W. McKee, "Small Business Can Be Computerized," *Management Accounting*, April 1972

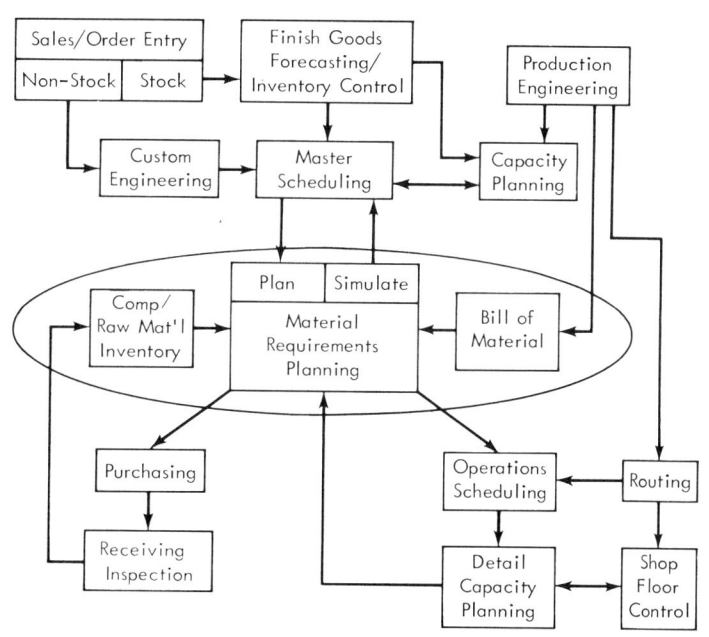

Fig. 8-5. Materials and Inventory Planning System

Courtesy of Software International

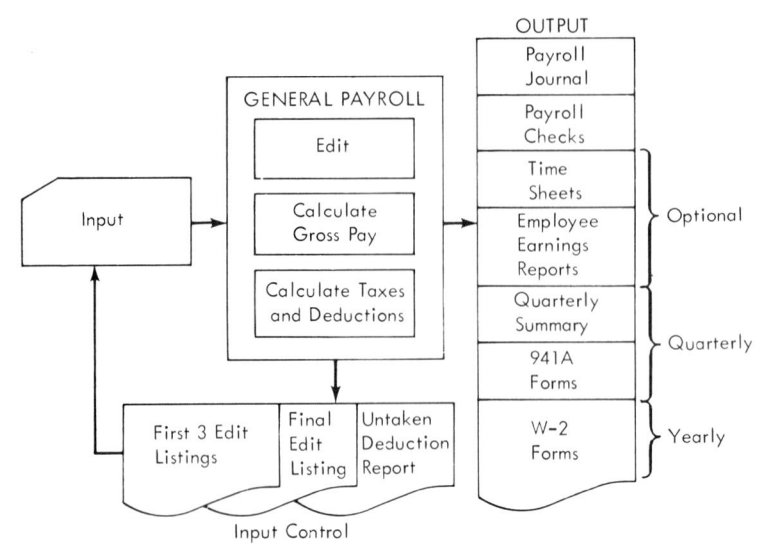

Fig. 8-6. Payroll System

Source: Wayne W. McKee, "Small Business Can Be Computerized," *Management Accounting,* April 1972.

same. We will describe the development of the MIS since the AIS is included in this type of project.

Generally, the development consists of studying information needs, resources available, and constraints upon system design. Then objectives are established and a plan is prepared which covers tasks, time, and cost. Next, the MIS/AIS is roughed out in the form of a conceptual or "gross" design. This is an attempt to sketch a feasible system that will achieve the objectives of the project within the limitations previously laid out. The next step is to expand upon the gross design by developing all the detailed parts. This detailing may uncover a need to revise or modify the gross design. Generally, the gross design provides the structure and guide for the many people who may be involved with the detailed design.

When the design appears to be completed, it may be tested as a whole or by parts. The AIS, in particular, should be tested prior to acceptance of the new system.

The above general approach is divided into specific steps as follows.

Analyze the Management and Operating Problems

The systems team usually begins by studying current operations. This may require preparing organization charts if none are available and

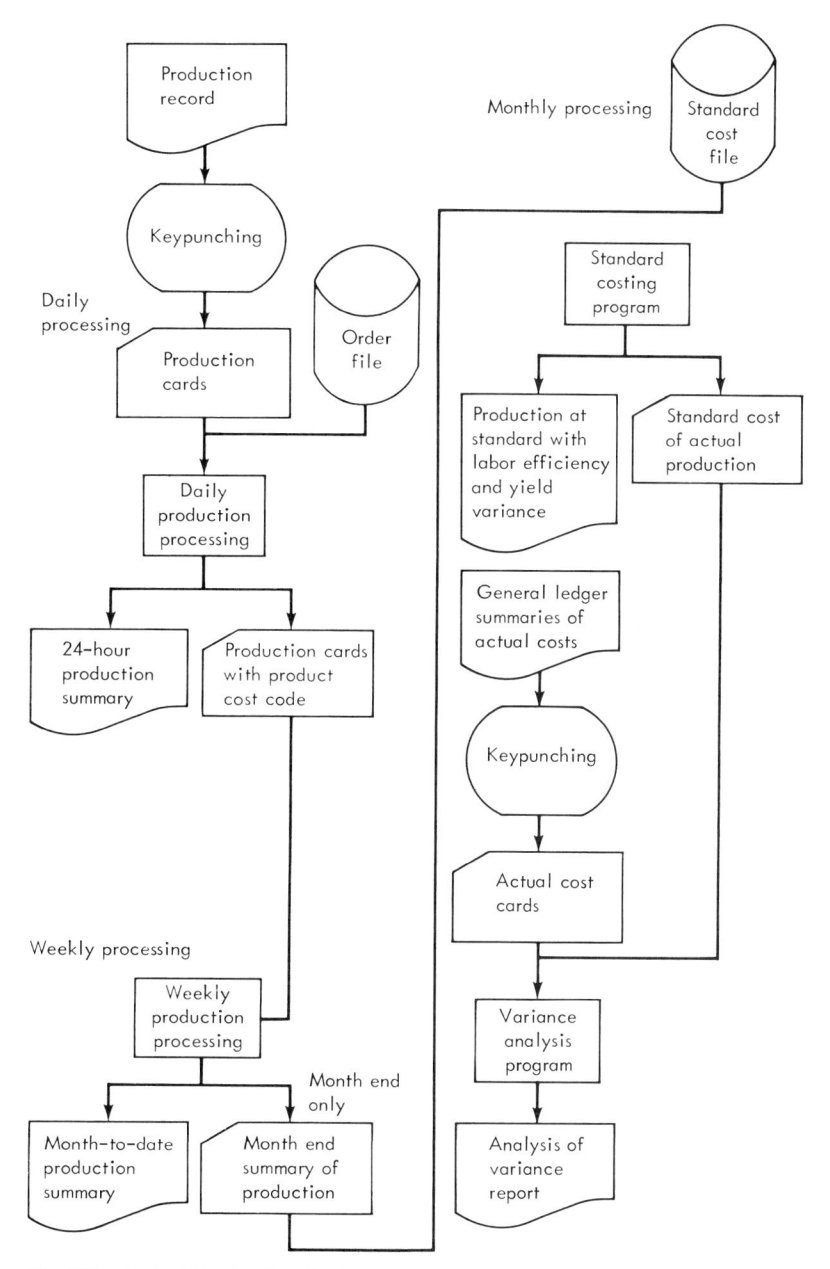

Fig. 8-7. Cost of Production System

Source: J. P. Guequierre, "A Need for a Non-Redundant System," *Management Accounting,* June 1972.

Fig. 8-8. Capital Budgeting System

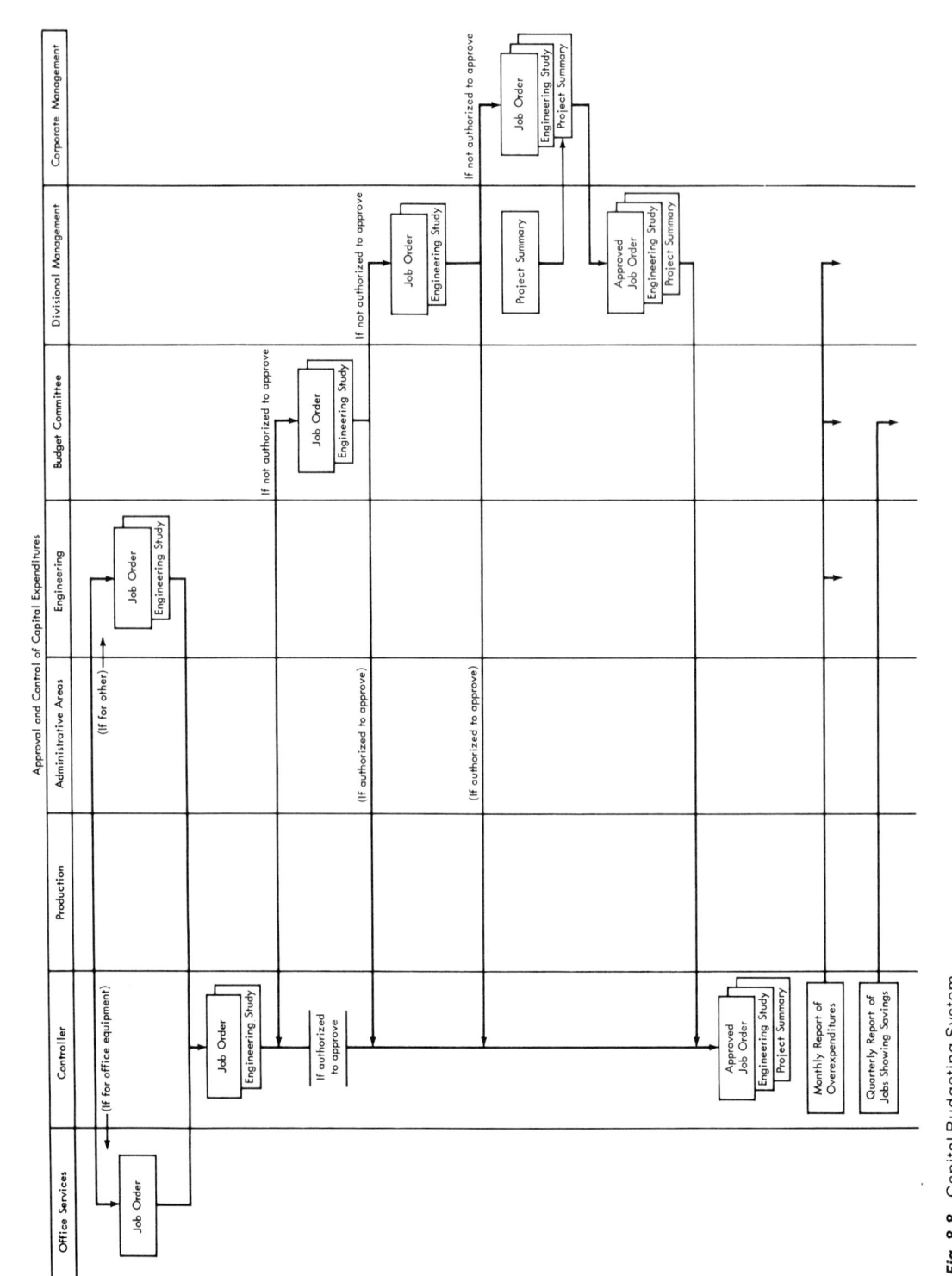

Source: Robert G. Murdick and Donald D. Deming, *The Management of Capital Expenditures*, New York: McGraw-Hill Book Co., 1968, p. 169.

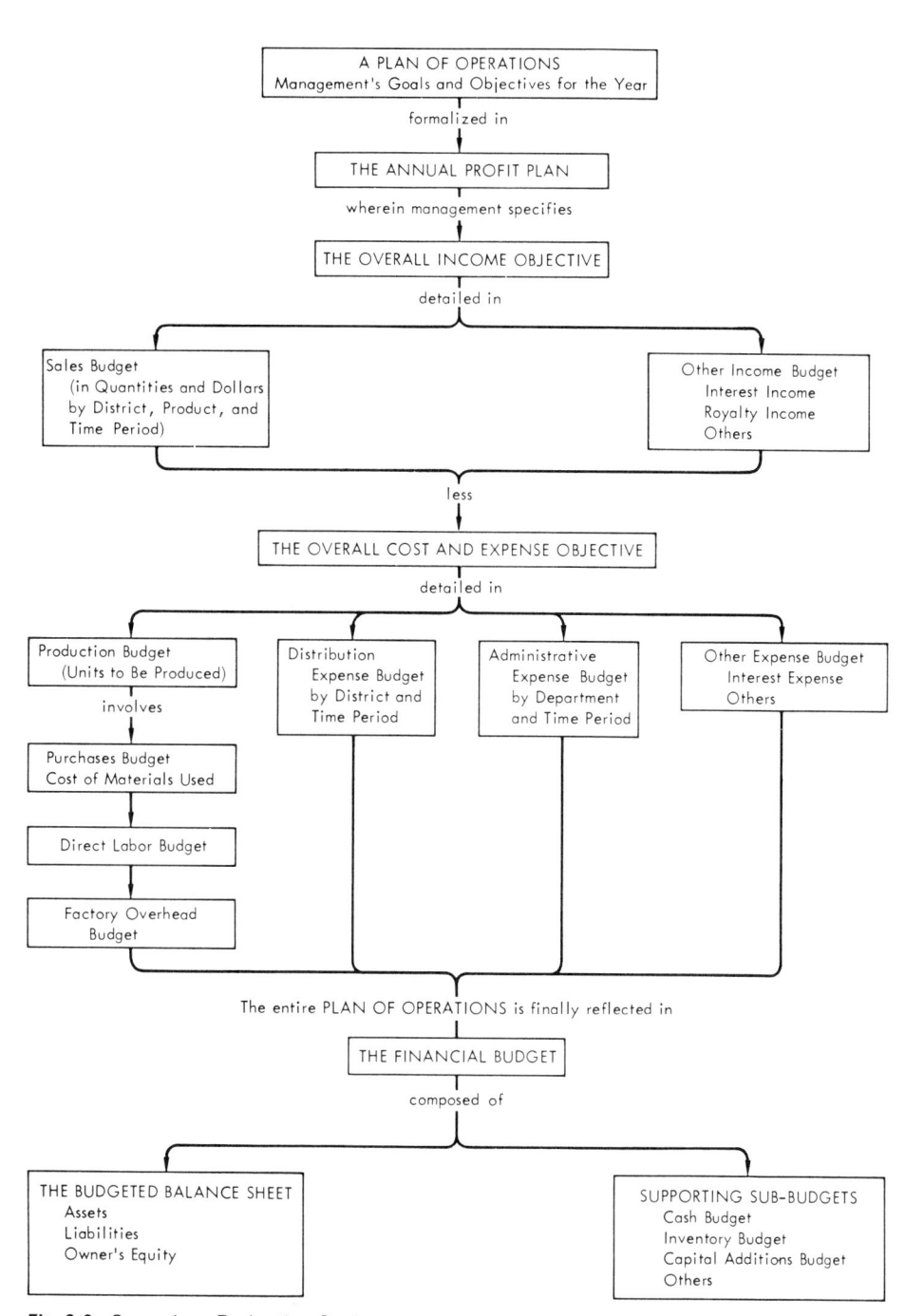

```
┌─────────────────────────────────────────┐
│         A PLAN OF OPERATIONS            │
│ Management's Goals and Objectives for the Year │
└─────────────────────────────────────────┘
                    │ formalized in
                    ▼
        ┌──────────────────────┐
        │ THE ANNUAL PROFIT PLAN │
        └──────────────────────┘
              │ wherein management specifies
              ▼
        ┌──────────────────────────┐
        │ THE OVERALL INCOME OBJECTIVE │
        └──────────────────────────┘
                    │ detailed in
    ┌───────────────┴────────────────┐
┌─────────────────┐            ┌──────────────────┐
│ Sales Budget    │            │ Other Income Budget │
│ (in Quantities  │            │ Interest Income  │
│ and Dollars by  │            │ Royalty Income   │
│ District, Product,│          │ Others           │
│ and Time Period)│            │                  │
└─────────────────┘            └──────────────────┘
                    │ less
                    ▼
   ┌──────────────────────────────────┐
   │ THE OVERALL COST AND EXPENSE OBJECTIVE │
   └──────────────────────────────────┘
                    │ detailed in
   ┌────────┬───────┴────────┬────────────┐
┌──────────┐ ┌──────────┐ ┌──────────┐ ┌──────────────┐
│Production│ │Distribution│ │Administrative│ │Other Expense │
│ Budget   │ │ Expense   │ │ Expense   │ │ Budget       │
│(Units to │ │ Budget    │ │ Budget    │ │ Interest     │
│ Be       │ │ by District│ │ by Department│ │ Expense    │
│ Produced)│ │ and Time  │ │ and Time  │ │ Others       │
│          │ │ Period    │ │ Period    │ │              │
└──────────┘ └──────────┘ └──────────┘ └──────────────┘
     │ involves
     ▼
┌──────────────────┐
│ Purchases Budget │
│ Cost of Materials Used │
└──────────────────┘
     │
     ▼
┌──────────────────┐
│ Direct Labor Budget │
└──────────────────┘
     │
     ▼
┌──────────────────┐
│ Factory Overhead │
│ Budget           │
└──────────────────┘

The entire PLAN OF OPERATIONS is finally reflected in
                    ▼
        ┌────────────────────┐
        │ THE FINANCIAL BUDGET │
        └────────────────────┘
                    │ composed of
    ┌───────────────┴────────────────┐
┌──────────────────────┐      ┌──────────────────────┐
│ THE BUDGETED BALANCE │      │ SUPPORTING SUB-BUDGETS │
│       SHEET          │      │   Cash Budget        │
│   Assets             │      │   Inventory Budget   │
│   Liabilities        │      │   Capital Additions Budget │
│   Owner's Equity     │      │   Others             │
└──────────────────────┘      └──────────────────────┘
```

Fig. 8-9. Operations Budgeting System

Source: Glenn A. Welsch, *Budgeting: Profit Planning and Control*, (2nd ed.), Englewood Cliffs, N.J.: Prentice-Hall, 1970.

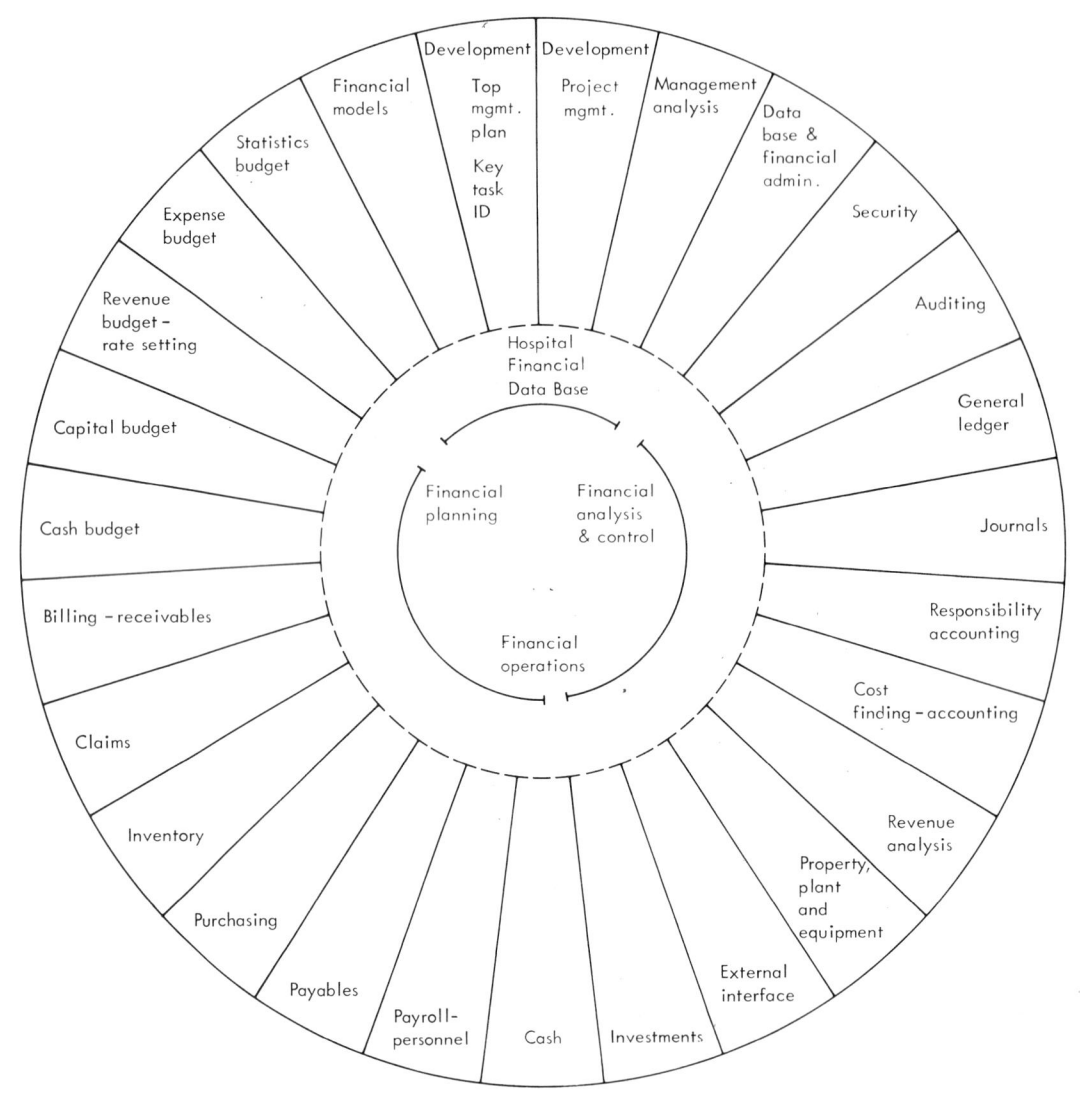

Fig. 8-10. Hospital Financial Management System
Source: *Hospital Financial Management System Concepts,* IBM, 1975.

flowcharting activities as they currently function. A list of all financial reports to management should be obtained and studied.

Copies of all forms used by the organization should be obtained and examined in connection with the flowcharts. Data processing as related to system activities and forms usage should also be studied.

After the systems' team has become familiar with current operations, it is in a position to conduct "needs research." That is, it should

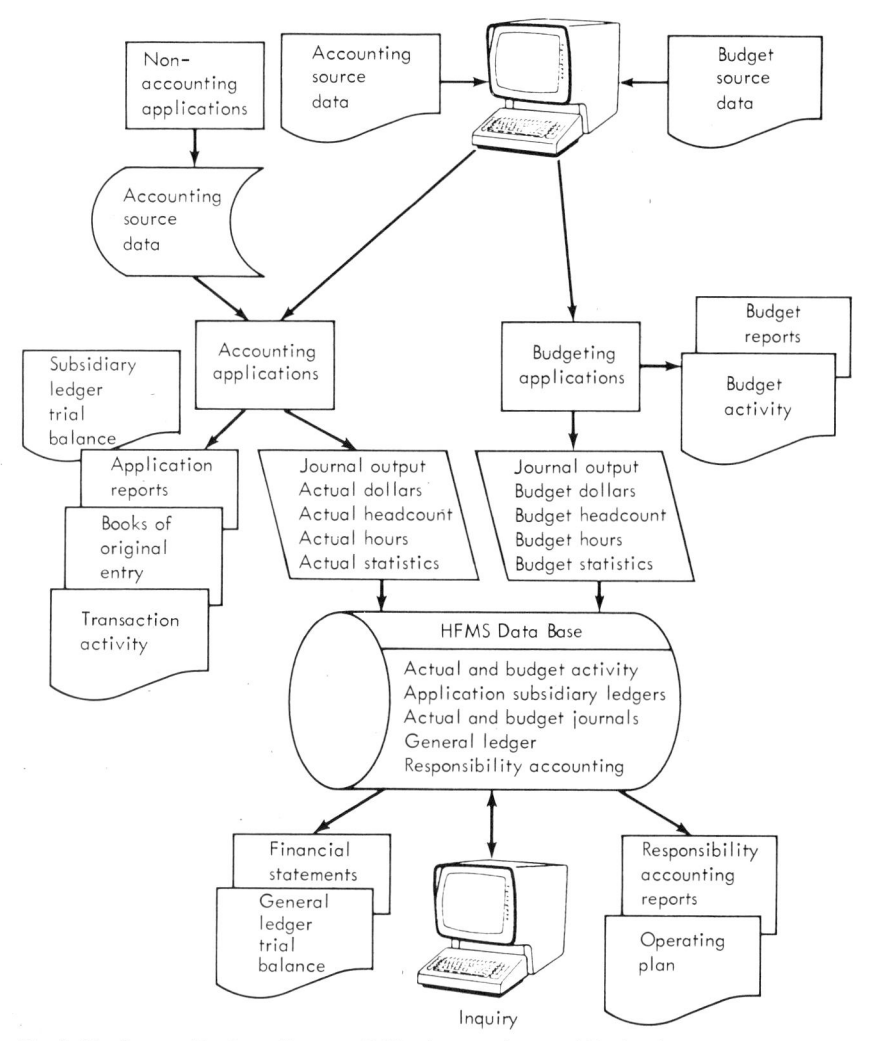

Fig. 8-11. General Ledger, Responsibility Accounting, and Budgeting
Source: *Hospital Financial Management System Concepts*, IBM, 1975.

study management's and workers' information needs in order to set objectives for new MIS/AIS. Information needs are based upon

1. Planning activities conducted within the company (long and short range)
2. Control activities
3. Decision problems typically found in the organization
4. Current special areas of difficulty.

Rather than attempting to give a complete directory of possible problems, we list a few typical ones below:

Order processing delays
Unreliable cost data for forward pricing
Billing errors
Lack of information on dollar value of inventories by product
Poor cash management
Loose capital budgeting and control
No expense variance reports
Inaccurate cost accounting
Inadequate rework and scrap cost data
Monthly rolling forecasts of expenses supplied to management three weeks after closing
Frequent payroll errors
No financial ratio analysis supplied to management
No profit center and cost center reports to management
No breakdown of advertising costs by product, media, and campaign
Too many accounts for a small company.

Determine Information Needs

Before the installation of the first computer for business purposes in the United States, Ralph Cordiner, then chairman of the board of General Electric, made a prophetic comment on the need for information in systems design:

> *It is an immense problem to organize and communicate the information required to operate a large, decentralized organization. This deep communication problem is not solved by providing more volume of data for all concerned, by faster accumulation and transmittal of conventional data, by wider distribution of previously existing data, or by holding more conferences. Indeed, the belief that such measures will meet the . . . [management information] challenge is probably one of the great fallacies in business and managerial thinking. What is required, instead, is a far more penetrating and orderly study of the business in its entirety to discover* what specific information is needed at each particular position in view of the decisions to be made there.[1] [Roman added.]

A clear statement of information needs is fundamental and necessary to good systems design. Too many companies spend lavish sums on hardware and software to perpetuate existing systems or build sophisticated data banks without first determining the real information needs of management: information that can increase the perception of managers in critical areas such as problems, alternatives, opportunities, and plans.

[1] Ralph J. Cordiner, *New Frontiers for Professional Managers,* New York: McGraw-Hill Book Co., 1956, p. 102. Used by permission of the McGraw-Hill Book Company.

Unless managers can provide the specifications for what they want out of an information system, the design effort will produce less than optimum results. If, on the other hand, the manager-user can define his objectives and spell out the items of information that are needed to reach the objective, he is then at least halfway home in systems design. Failure to be specific on these two steps probably accounts for the downfall of more design efforts than any other factor. If systems design begins without such clear-cut statements by the manager, the systems analyst or technician will provide *his* objectives and *his* information needs.

Yet it is not easy for a manager to spell out the specific information requirements of his job, and therein lies a basic frustration in the improvement of systems. In an attempt to get a clear statement of information needs, the analyst frequently meets with an interviewing situation somewhat like this typical exchange:

Analyst: Could you tell me what the objectives of this cost accounting system are, as you see them?

Financial Manager: Sure . . . to get the reports out faster . . . to do something about keeping the costs in line . . . to keep management informed. . . .

Analyst: Yes, I understand . . . let me put it another way. What are your responsibilities as you see them?

Financial Manager: Whatta you mean? I'm in charge of the accounting department.

Analyst: Yes, I know; we need to get a better statement of your department's objectives, how the cost accounting system can further these objectives, and what information is needed to do this.

Financial Manager: Well, we need the information we've been getting, but we need it faster and with a lot more accurate input from those fellows in operations.

This hypothetical conversation reflects the difficulty of getting managers to be specific about information needs. One approach, sometimes used by consultants, is to get top management to require in writing from subordinate managers a statement containing: (1) a list of four or five major responsibilities for which the manager believes himself to be accountable and (2) the four or five specific items of information that are required to carry out the responsibilities. These requirements could be framed in terms of duties performed or decisions made; the idea is to get the manager to think of information needs. If this can be done, the information system is well on the way to being designed.

Another approach is avoidance of the direct question: What information do you need? Instead, the designer requests that the user describe what occurs in the decision-making process; then the designer concerns himself with the identification of the questions that are to be resolved in the activity for which the system is being designed. This approach is also a good one for the manager-user, because he is intimately familiar with his operation and presumably with the difficult decision operations in it.

One way of determining what managers do *not* need in the way of information is to cease issuing selected periodic reports or reduce their circulation list. If a manager really uses a report, he will complain, and his name may be restored to the circulation list.

A manager needs information for a variety of reasons concerned with the management process. The type of need that he will have at various times and for various purposes depends largely upon two factors that we shall examine briefly: the personal managerial attributes of the individual manager, and the organizational environment in which decisions are made.

Personal Attributes

Knowledge of Information Systems

If the manager is aware of what computer-based systems can do, his information requests will probably be more sophisticated and more specific. His knowledge of capabilities and costs places him in a much better position to aid in the design of a good system.

Managerial Style

A manager's technical background, his leadership style, and his decision-making ability all affect the kind and amount of information he requires. Some prefer a great amount of detail; others like to decide with a minimum of detail and prefer personal consultation with subordinates.

Manager's Perception of Information Needs

"You tell me what I need to know" and "Get me all the facts" represent two opposite perceptions of information needs. This dichotomy is due partly to the fact that many managers are ignorant of what information they need. Another dimension of the problem is the widely differing views of managers regarding their obligation to disseminate information to subordinates and to groups outside the firm. The manager who cannot or will not delegate authority is likely to keep information closely held.

Organizational Environment

Nature of the Company

Problems in communication and in controlling operations seem to be a function of the company's size and the complexity of its organization. The larger, more complex firms require more formal information systems, and the information needs of these systems become more critical to operations.

Level of Management

We outlined in Chapter 2 the three levels of management (i.e., strategic planning, management control, operational control) and the varying needs for information at each. Each level needs different types of information, generally in different form. Top levels need the one-time report, the summary, the single inquiry. The management control level needs the exception report, the summary, and a variety of regular reports for periodic evaluation. The operational control level requires the formal report with fixed procedures, the day-to-day report of transactions, in order to maintain operational control of actions as they occur. Managers at *all* levels have changing information needs depending on the nature and importance of the particular decision.

Structure of the Organization

The more highly structured the organization, the easier it is to determine the information needs. Where authority and responsibility are clearly spelled out, relationships understood, and decision-making areas defined, the information needs of managers can be determined more easily.

Returning to our illustrative subsystems, some information needs might be stated:

SUBSYSTEM	INFORMATION NEEDS
Inventory	Daily report on items that have fallen below minimum inventory level, in order that expediting action can be taken.
Accounts Payable	Incoming invoices coded according to "days to due date," because invoices should be paid no sooner than two days prior to due date in order to conserve cash.
Purchasing	The performance of each individual buyer, indicated by comparing actual purchases with hypothetical purchases at base or standard prices.
Production Control	Exception report to identify by shop order and lot number the variances in cost and quantity that are over or under by 5%.
Project Control	Weekly report on progress against plan for the events in critical path. Also need to know where float exists in other events so that resources may be shifted.

Propose System Objectives

The development of objectives for systems that cut across all functional areas of the business is not easy. The AIS must not only serve objectives of other functional information systems, but it also must fulfill the key objectives of the MIS. We should therefore start with objectives for the MIS and AIS as defined by managers.

Unlike the *technician* who turns to topics such as file structure, efficiency of computer time, and quantity of output, the *manager* must define system objectives in terms of decision information related to basic objectives of the organization. Data processing analysts (and computer salespersons) tend to stress processing efficiency. Similarly, first-line functional supervisors commonly believe that their objective is to "complete the report of their activities on time for management use." This view disregards the real objective of the systems design—*management effectiveness*. The value of systems lies in the benefits to their users, not in mere efficiency of transactions. We have witnessed the design of information systems in several government agencies in which the system objective was the automation of hundreds of reports, without regard to management of the many tasks related or to functional or resource subsystems represented by the reports (e.g., training, employee relations, safety, recruitment, staffing, etc.). Such focus on the automation of records or the processing of existing data overlooks the true objectives of the operational entity represented by the subsystem.

Yet it is not an easy matter to determine the real objectives of an information system any more than it is easy to determine the objectives of the operational system served by it. A common fallacy in stating objectives is to emphasize the obvious or to state objectives in vague terms; "reduce costs," "improve efficiency," "keep accurate records," "meet the production schedule." When asked for his objectives, a university president may reply, "Provide quality education," and a government bureaucrat may say, "Provide more jobs for the unemployed"; yet in neither case is the objective stated in terms specific enough to provide a measure of performance of the system or to design an information system to help achieve the objective.

Despite its difficulty, being specific is necessary. System objectives must ultimately be stated in terms of the objectives of the department, group, function, or manager to be served or in terms of the functions the information system is to perform. In other words, system objectives should be expressed in terms of what managers can do after their information requirements have been met. Such expression may use descriptive statements, flowcharts, or any other means that will convey to management the objectives that the systems designer must meet in order to develop the system. If possible, the objectives should be stated in

Table 8-1. Objectives of Material Control System: Major Electrical Manufacturer

SUBSYSTEM	OBJECTIVE
Routings	Capture routing information and time values that can be used by manufacturing for cost of completed work, labor status by contract, effect of changes by rerouting, etc.
Status	Establish a system that can be used by manufacturing to determine workload in shop, effect of accepting additional work, overload in various cost centers, status of self-manufactured work in process, etc.
Tools	Capture all tool information that can be used by manufacturing to determine tool status *prior* to release of work to shop, and maintain a tool inventory by contract for auditing purposes both by the company and the government on government contracts.
Cost Control	Establish an overall system that can be used by manufacturing to very quickly determine labor costs, material costs, tool costs, overruns, etc., by contract.
Scheduling	Determine effect of engineering changes, lack of material, tool shortages, etc.
Make or Buy	Make decisions on those items to subcontract, based on cost, load, schedule, etc.
Request for Proposal Information	Establish a system that can be used by manufacturing to produce immediately the necessary information needed for customer requests and requests for proposals.
Elapsed Time	Analyze, improve, and prepare an orderly procedure that can be used by manufacturing to report elapsed time, if required by contractual obligation.

quantitative rather than qualitative terms so that alternative system designs as well as system performance can be measured for effectiveness. That is, a statement of objectives should include exactly what it is that the system is supposed to accomplish and the means by which it will subsequently be evaluated. Table 8-1 shows an example of such a statement. This table contains a statement of objectives for the material control system of one of the nation's major electrical manufacturers. Notice how specific objectives are defined.

In Table 8-2 we have listed another group of functional subsystems and statements of possible objectives for each. We will use these for illustrations as we go along.

Identify System Constraints

The iterative nature of the systems design process is easily understood when we consider the third step in the process—establishing constraints. Sometimes called *problem boundaries* or *restrictions*, constraints enable the designer to stipulate the conditions under which objectives may be at-

Table 8-2. Illustration of Objectives

SUBSYSTEM	OBJECTIVE
Inventory	Optimize inventory costs through the design of decision rules containing optimum reorder points, safety stock levels, and reorder quantities, each capable of continuous and automatic reassessment.
Accounts Payable	Pay 100 percent of invoices before due date.
Purchasing	Provide performance information on buyer's price negotiations with suppliers in order that purchase variance can be controlled within set limits.
Production Control	Identify cost and quantity variances within one day in order to institute closer control over these variables.
Project Control	Identify performance against plan so that events, costs, and specifications of the project can be met.

tained and to consider the limitations that restrict the design. To state it another way, constraints, which are provided by the manager-user or the designer himself, limit freedom of action in designing a system to achieve the objective. It is clear then that a constant review of objectives is necessary when considering system constraints. Indeed, the two steps of setting objectives and establishing constraints may be considered together as one.

Although identification of constraints appears at first to be a negative limitation on design, there is a positive benefit as well. Establishing constraints will help ensure that the design is realistic.

Constraints may be classified as internal or external to the organization. This concept is shown in Fig. 8-12 which forms the basis of the following discussion.

Internal Constraints

If *top management support* is not obtained for the systems concept and for the notion that computer-based information systems are vital for management planning and control, the type of design effort discussed in these chapters cannot be implemented. A good environment for information systems must be set, and one essential ingredient is the approval and support of top management. This constraint definitely influences the kind of system the manager-user may design.

Organizational and policy considerations frequently set limits on objectives and modify an intended approach to design of a system. The structure of the organization and the managers occupying various positions

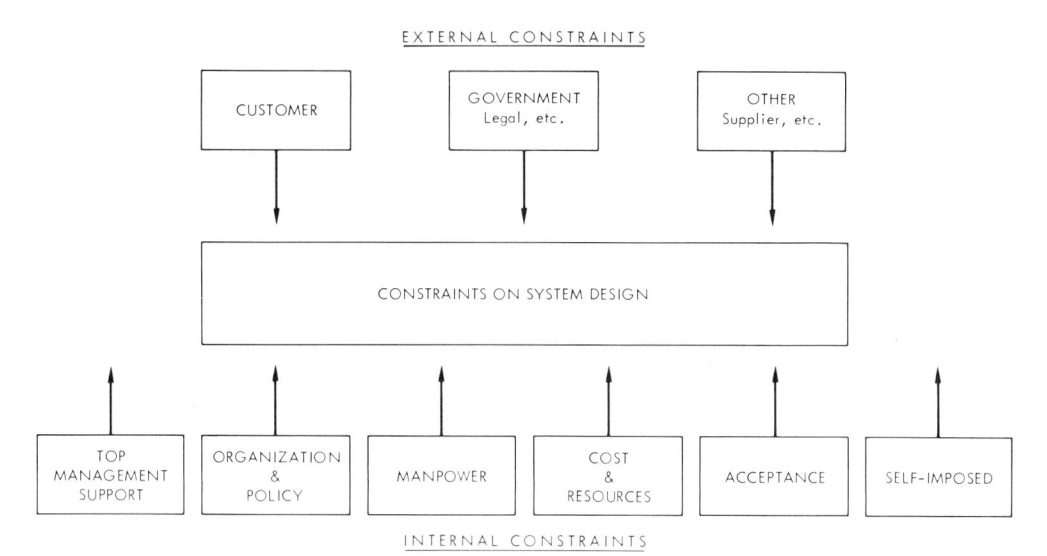

Fig. 8-12. Constraints on MIS/AIS Design

influence information flow and use of system outputs. In a decentralized multiplant organization with a wide product line, the design of common systems in cost accounting or production control is obviously less acceptable than in a more centralized organization with fewer products. An additional organizational difficulty is related to the turnover of managers. More than one head of computer operations has stated that his major difficulty is the abandonment or redesign of systems due to the turnover among manager-users. Also, company policies frequently define or limit the approach to systems design. Among these are policies concerned with product and service, research and development, production, marketing, finance, and personnel. For example, a "promote from within" personnel policy would have an impact on the type of systems design to build a skills inventory. Other important considerations in design are those concerning audits.

Manpower needs and personnel availability are a major limiting factor in both the design and utilization of information systems. Computer and systems skills are among the most critical in the nation; rare indeed is the manager who admits to having sufficient personnel to design, implement, and operate the systems he desires. Additional considerations concern the nature of the work force and the skill mix of users. Elaborate and sophisticated systems are of little value if they cannot be put to use.

Perhaps the most significant constraint of all is the one concerning *people*. "People problems" is probably the factor most often mentioned where failure to achieve expected results is concerned. Here we have the difficulties associated with the natural human reaction to change, the antagonism, and the lack of interest and support frequently met in systems design and operation. Automation, computer systems, and systems design often call for the realignment of people and facilities, organizational changes, and individual job changes. Therefore, these reactions are to be expected and should be anticipated in designing systems to achieve the objective.

Cost is a major *resource* limitation. The cost to achieve the objective should be compared with the benefits to be derived. You do not want to spend $20,000 to save $10,000. Although a cost-benefit analysis is frequently difficult, some approach to priority setting must be undertaken. Considerations similar to those surrounding cost apply also to the use of other resources. *Computer capacity* and other facilities relating to operation of data-processing systems should be utilized in an optimum way.

Self-imposed restrictions are those placed on the design by the manager or the designer. In designing the system to achieve the objective, he may have to scale down several requirements in order to make the system fit with other outputs, equipment, or constraints. Usually, he will also restrict the amount of time and effort devoted to investigation. For example, he may want to design a pilot or test system around one product, one plant, or one portion of an operation before making it generally applicable elsewhere. Functional requirements also define constraints placed on the system by its users. The data requirements, the data volumes, and the rate of processing are constraints imposed by the immediate users. More remote users impose constraints by the need to integrate with related systems.

External Constraints

Foremost among the considerations surrounding the external environment are those concerning the *customer*. Order entry, billing, and other systems that interface with systems of the customer must be designed with his needs in mind. If certain outputs from the system are not acceptable to the customer, a definite limitation must be faced up to. He may require that bills be submitted in a form that provides input to his system of accounts payable. For example, standard progress-reporting and billing procedures are among the requirements imposed for processing data under many military procurement programs.

A variety of additional external constraints should be considered in addition to the customer. The *government* (federal, state, local) imposes certain restrictions on the processing of data. Among these are the need to maintain the security of certain classes of information (e.g., personnel) in order to comply with law and regulation in the conduct of business (e.g., taxes, reporting), and to meet certain procedures regarding record keeping and reporting to stockholders (e.g., outside audit). *Unions* can and do affect the operation of systems involving members in matters such as compensation, grievances, and working conditions. *Suppliers* are also an important group to be considered when designing information systems because these systems frequently interface with that group.

In summary, it is important to recognize the constraints that have an impact on systems design. Having recognized them and made appropriate allowance in the design function, the manager will then be in a position to complete the remaining steps toward the design of an operating system that will achieve the objective he has previously determined.

The nature of constraints is illustrated here by stating a hypothetical constraint for each of our selected functional subsystems, as shown in Table 8-3.

Table 8-3. Example of Constraints

SUBSYSTEM	STATEMENT OF CONSTRAINT
Inventory	Regardless of reorder points and reorder quantities, the supplier will not accept orders for less than carload lots for raw materials 7 and 12.
Accounts Payable	The individual who prepares the check for payment of invoices must not be the same individual who approves payment.
Purchasing	It is not necessary to negotiate purchases in amounts under $500.
Production Control	System output for shop control will be identified by department only and not by the individual worker or foreman.
Project Control	We are required to report weekly to the U.S. Department of Defense any slippages in time or cost exceeding 10% of any event in the project control critical path.

Prepare a Project Proposal

At this point, we are ready to prepare a proposal for an MIS/AIS project. A formal project proposal must be prepared for management's decision. The purposes of the project proposal are:

1. To present objectives of the project
2. To identify both tangible and intangible benefits from implementation of the project
3. To estimate resources required for project development
4. To estimate total life costs of implementation and operation of the MIS and AIS

5. To inform managers and other users about the approach to design and the role that they will play in the development.

In Table 8-4, an outline which could form the basis for the Table of Contents of a project proposal is given.

Table 8-4. MIS Project Proposal Outline

1. Introduction
   a. A brief, clear statement of the problem or technical requirement.
   b. Purposes of the proposed MIS.
   c. Conservative estimate of the performance of the proposed system, its limitations, its life, and its cost.
   d. Premises and assumptions upon which the MIS is to be developed. These give organizational limitations, special requirements imposed by managers, vendors, or customers, environmental restrictions, or other ground rules.
2. What Is Offered
   a. Description of present method of operation and its weaknesses and problems.
   b. Information requirements, present and future. General description of proposed data base.
   c. Hardware, present and future, available within the company.
   d. Alternative approaches to the information-decision-operational systems. A brief summary of each approach is given and the advantages and disadvantages of each are discussed to show why the proposed system is being offered.
   e. A somewhat more detailed description of the proposed MIS is given. The general plan of action, the budget estimate, and the schedule are provided.
   f. Management action required for adoption of the proposal and for planning and implementing the MIS are stated.
3. Method of Approach
   An outline of the plan of attack on the gross design, detailed design, and implementation. This demonstrates that the project manager has a practical approach for planning and executing the project.
   a. Method of data-gathering and analysis.
   b. Personnel assignments.
   c. Programming techniques to be used for the project.
   d. Project reports and review. A description of the type and frequency of reports to keep management abreast of progress on the MIS project.
4. Conclusion
   This is not usually required. If an MIS project looks especially good from a highly technical viewpoint, the conclusion may summarize the strong points to give additional emphasis.
5. Appendixes
   Organization charts, schedules, flowcharts, quantitative analyses, and other detailed substantiating data of a technical or detailed nature that will aid management or technical staff personnel in evaluating the proposal.

Prepare a Plan and a Reporting System for the Project

For very small projects, common sense techniques for planning and documenting the plans for the MIS project are sufficient. We will discuss here the most elaborate techniques for planning for larger projects. Most of these techniques and tools have been borrowed from engineering project-management theory and practice, where they originated.

Techniques exist for a rational approach to planning the design and implementation of large systems. A basic premise is that the assignment of project management to a project manager with wide responsibilities is an important factor in increasing the probability of success of a project. The project manager must control all funds required for the project. However, the project manager may direct the activities of a program without having direct-line command over all persons involved in the program. He achieves this by means of a clearly defined work breakdown structure for the project.

Work Breakdown Structure

A fundamental concept in project management is the work breakdown structure, which starts with the total end result desired and terminates with the individual detailed tasks. The project breakdown structure is a natural *decomposition* of the project end result. It is created in a level-by-level breakdown from:

1. System to subsystem
2. Subsystem to task
3. Task to subtask
4. Subtask to work package.

The manner in which the project is broken down into tasks is illustrated in Table 8-5.

Table 8-5. Standard Task List of the Work Breakdown Structure for Project Control

I. Study Phase
    Task 1   Study organization goals and problems.
      Subtask 1.1 Interview managers and study internal documents.
      Subtask 1.2 Survey operating problems.
      Subtask 1.3 Study informational problems.
    Task 2   Study company resources and opportunities.
      Subtask 2.1 Evaluate company resources.
      Subtask 2.2 Study needs of the market and environmental trends.
      Subtask 2.3 Evaluate competitive position.
    Task 3   Study computer capabilities—equipment and manpower skills.
    Task 4   Prepare proposal for MIS design study.
II. Gross Design Phase
    Task 1   Identify required subsystems.
      Subtask 1.1 Study work flow and natural boundaries of skill groupings and information needs.

Table 8-5 (cont'd)

      Subtask 1.2   Develop alternative lists of subsystems.
      Subtask 1.3   Develop conceptual total-system alternatives based upon the lists of subsystems.
      Subtask 1.4   Develop scope of work to be undertaken based on need of the company and estimated resources to be allocated to the MIS.
      Subtask 1.5   Prepare a reference design showing key aspects of the system, organizational changes, and computer equipment and software required.

III. Detailed Design Phase
    Task 1   Disseminate to the organization the nature of the prospective project.
    Task 2   Identify dominant and principal trade-off criteria for the MIS.
    Task 3   Redefine the subsystems in greater detail.
      Subtask 3.1   Flowchart the operating systems.
      Subtask 3.2   Interview managers and key operating personnel.
      Subtask 3.3   Flowchart the information flows.
    Task 4   Determine the degree of automation possible for each activity or transaction.
    Task 5   Design the data base or master file.
      Subtask 5.1   Determine routine decisions and the nature of nonroutine decisions.
      Subtask 5.2   Determine internal and external data required.
      Subtask 5.3   Determine optimum data to be stored in terms of cost, time, cross-functional needs, and storage capacity.
    Task 6   Model the system quantitatively.
    Task 7   Develop computer support.
      Subtask 7.1   Develop computer hardware requirements.
      Subtask 7.2   Develop software requirements.
    Task 8   Establish input and output formats.
      Subtask 8.1   Develop input formats (design forms).
      Subtask 8.2   Develop output formats for decision-makers.
    Task 9   Test the system.
      Subtask 9.1   Test the system by using the model previously developed.
      Subtask 9.2   Test the system by simulation, using extreme value inputs.
    Task 10   Propose the formal organization structure to operate the system.
    Task 11   Document the detailed design.

IV. Implementation Phase
    Task 1   Plan the implementation sequence.
      Subtask 1.1   Identify implementation tasks.
      Subtask 1.2   Establish interrelationships among tasks and subtasks.
      Subtask 1.3   Establish the performance/cost/time program.
    Task 2   Organize for implementation.
    Task 3   Develop procedures for the installation process.
    Task 4   Train operating personnel.
    Task 5   Obtain hardware.
    Task 6   Develop the software.
    Task 7   Obtain forms specified in detail design or develop forms as necessary.
    Task 8   Obtain data and construct the master files.
    Task 9   Test the system by parts.
    Task 10   Test the complete system.
    Task 11   Cut over to the new MIS.
    Task 12   Debug the system.
    Task 13   Document the operational MIS.
    Task 14   Evaluate the system in operation.

The work breakdown structure, referred to as WBS, starts with a word description of the entire project and is then decomposed by word descriptions for each element of each subdivision. The organizational structure should have no influence on the development of the WBS. The primary question to be answered is, What is to be accomplished? Next, an acceptable way of classifying the work must be found. The classification should be such that natural systems and components are identified and milestone tasks for accomplishing their design are related. Neither gaps nor overlaps must be allowed, yet the structure should interlock all tasks and work packages.

The smallest element in the WBS, usually appearing at the lowest level, is the work package, a paragraph description of the work that is to be done to achieve an intermediate goal. Requirements of time, resources, and cost are listed, including definite dates for starting and completing the work—a short duration compared to that of the total project. The breakdown of the project into work packages, each assigned to a single responsible manager, provides the means for control of the entire project. A typical list of items of information contained in a work package form is given in Table 8-6.

Table 8-6. Work Package Information Checklist

1. Project identification, title, and number
2. Title and number of work package
3. Responsible organization and manager
4. Interface events and dates
5. Start and end date for work package
6. Dollar and labor estimates, projections of dollars and labor on a weekly or monthly basis, and a schedule of actual application of resources maintained as current
7. Contract or funding source identification
8. Account charge number
9. Work order or shop order, to be opened when authorization is obtained to expend a specified amount of money under a particular account number

Sequence Planning

The relationships among tasks must be set forth by a chronological ordering, starting with the terminal task of the project and working backward. As each task is set down, it is necessary to determine what immediately preceding tasks must first be completed. When a network of events has been established, estimates of the time required to complete each event, based upon the work package information, may be entered.

There are a number of time paths through a network that run from the starting event to the terminal event. The longest is called the *Critical Path.* On the basis of management decisions, resources may be added or redeployed to change the length of time of a current Critical

Path to yield a new one, thus gaining time by a trade-off involving increased costs. The final network is sometimes called the *Master Project Network Plan.*

Master Program Schedule

The Master Program Schedule (MPS) is a management document giving the *calendar dates* for milestones (major tasks and critical-path minor tasks), thus providing the control points for management review. The MPS may be in the form of a Gantt chart for small MIS projects or in machine (computer) printout for large projects whose networks have been programmed for computer analysis and reporting. In the latter case, the MPS is derived from the network schedule by establishing a calendar date for the starting event.

Budgeting

The establishment of cost and resource targets for a planned series of periods in advance is project budgeting. Although cost constraints may be applied in a top-down fashion during planning, such constraints must be reconciled with a *bottom-up* approach through the work breakdown structure. Reconciliation is accomplished by either (1) allocating more funds or (2) narrowing and reducing the scope of the work and redefining the objectives of the project.

Cost and resource targets must be established for a work package by:

1. Performing organization
2. Funding organization
3. Elements of cost: labor, materials, and facilities

Only direct costs are included in the project budget, because they are the only costs over which the project manager has control.

Cushioning should not be added to the resource costs because meaningful measures of control depend upon realistic goals. However, because experience has shown that project cost overruns are far more common than underruns, a contingency fund should be budgeted to cover unanticipated problems. The project manager's use of the contingency fund is also a measure of his performance.

Reporting and Controlling

Control of the project means control of performance/cost/time (P/C/T). These elements, P/C/T, must be reported in a way that ties them all together, otherwise the report is meaningless. Consider, for instance, a project in which performance and costs are on target. It is possible for such a project to be behind and in trouble from the time standpoint. On the other hand, a project may show an overrun of costs as of a particular date, yet if the work performance is ahead of schedule, this is good news instead of bad news.

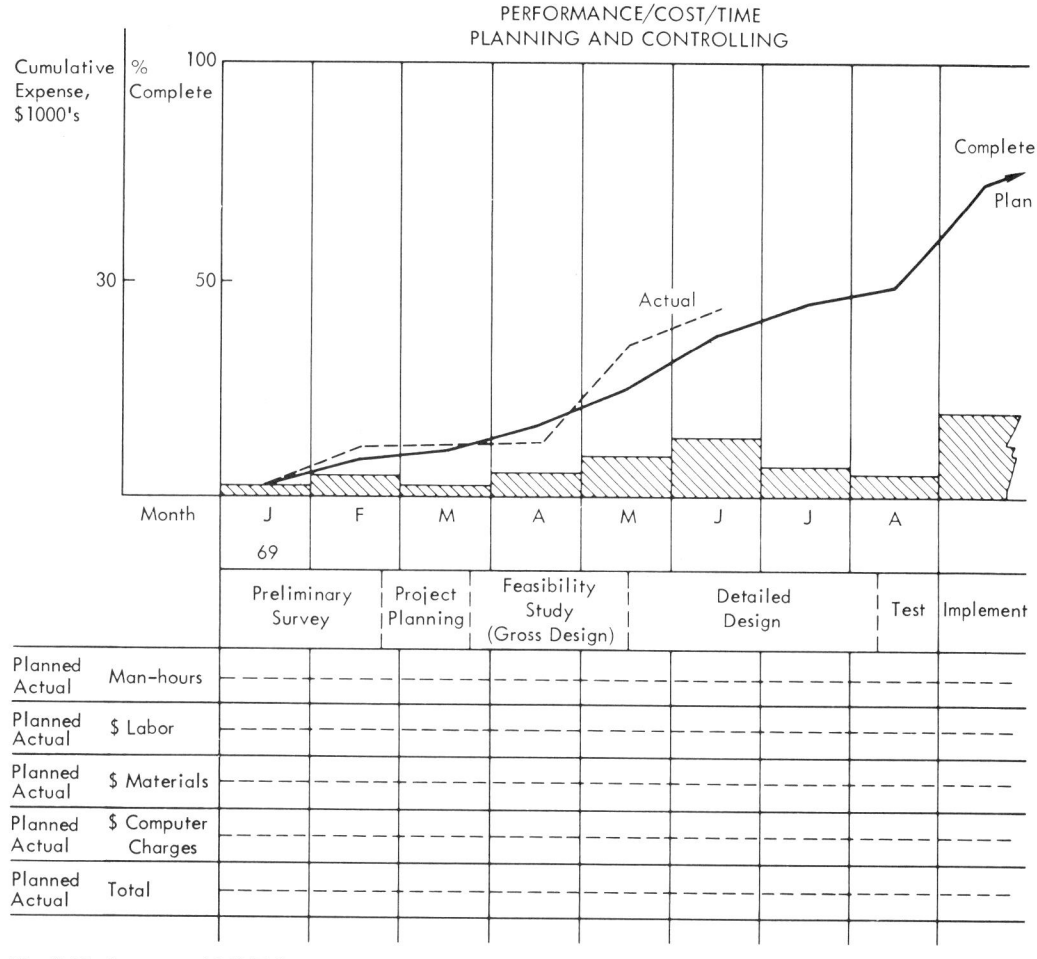

Fig. 8-13. Integrated P/C/T Chart

Reporting Techniques

The reporting system for a project is its own MIS. Some methods of project reporting are:

1. Integrated P/C/T charts as shown in Fig. 8-13
2. Financial schedules and variance reports
3. Time-scaled network plans and computerized reports based on them
4. Problem analysis and trend charts
5. Progress reports
6. Project control room and computerized graphic systems
7. Design review meetings and "reference designs." A common "reference design" must provide a formal description of system specifications and goals at any particular time. All designers work on the basis of assumptions about parts of the system other than theirs. If they are not working on the same assumptions, chaos results. The reference design may change with time, and the design review meeting of all key personnel is a good time to make formal changes.

Reporting Problems

Control is difficult if the only reports are written narratives requiring interpretation by management. At the other extreme, reams of computer data reports are equally poor. Managers prefer graphic displays which reduce large amounts of complex information into easily understood pictorial form. Comparisons and trends of major variables are also effective in communicating. Graphic display must be designed to guard against too gross a level of reporting, however, or else growing problems may be obscured.

Other problems in reporting are the use of complex grammatical structure; high "fog index" of writing; excessive and unexplained abbreviations, codes, and symbols; and too much technical jargon.[2] Projects may fail if the project manager and his technical specialists do not make clear to management what is happening and how the money is being spent.

[2] Robert Gunning, *The Technique of Clear Writing*, New York: McGraw-Hill Book Co., 1952. Fog index = 0.4 (average number of words per sentence) + 0.4 (average number of three-syllable words excluding capitalized words and words made up of easy words). Use several samples of about 100 consecutive words.

Control Through "Completed Action"

A manager in a chain of command cannot divest himself of accountability for a task that is delegated to him. Responsibility for a work package may be delegated to the lowest level in the organizational hierarchy, but each manager up the line is evaluated on the basis of completed action on the work package. The worker who has responsibility for a work package should be supplied with adequate reports of P/C/T. As variances are reported to the responsible performer, the burden is on him to take corrective action. His ultimate responsibility is "completed action," the presentation of a completed job to his manager. Only in emergencies and cases of wide variances from planned action should the managers at various levels in the organization step in to reclaim delegated responsibility. The control in a well-run project is essentially self-control, based upon a good reporting system.

Prepare a Preliminary Design

The preliminary (or "gross") design structures the MIS/AIS design by defining subsystems, showing the interrelationships among subsystems, identifying information sources, outlining the data base (listing files), and proposing a hardware configuration.

The core subsystems (general ledger, etc.) for the AIS are fairly well standardized in the traditional business organizations as indicated in the early part of this chapter. As health care, land development, fast food, motel-recreation, conglomerate, and quasigovernmental organizations have developed uniquely, even these core subsystems require creative modification. In addition, special accounting and financial information subsystems beyond the core subsystems must be developed. In every case, we must start with objectives of the company or agency, identify management information needs, and then specify a system that will both provide needed service and information outputs for management.

The AIS subsystems may be defined for the preliminary design by narratives which specify:

- Outputs to managers
- Outputs going to other subsystems
- Objective and process performed
- Input data/information and source

In Fig. 8-14 we show a schematic definition of the accounts payable

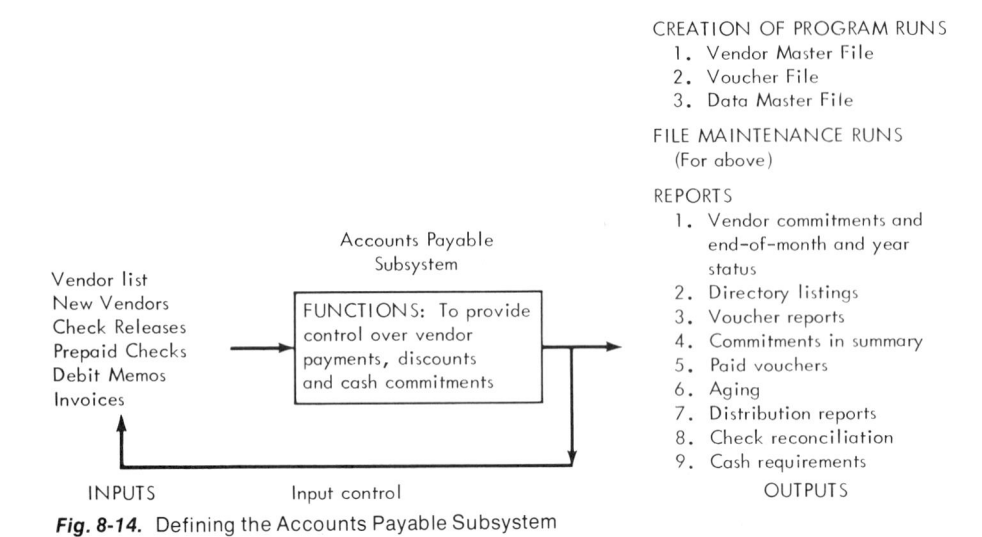

```
                                                    CREATION OF PROGRAM RUNS
                                                      1. Vendor Master File
                                                      2. Voucher File
                                                      3. Data Master File
                                                    FILE MAINTENANCE RUNS
                                                      (For above)
                                                    REPORTS
                          Accounts Payable            1. Vendor commitments and
                            Subsystem                    end-of-month and year
Vendor list                                              status
New Vendors          ┌─────────────────────┐          2. Directory listings
Check Releases       │ FUNCTIONS: To provide│         3. Voucher reports
Prepaid Checks   ──▶ │ control over vendor  │  ──▶    4. Commitments in summary
Debit Memos          │ payments, discounts  │         5. Paid vouchers
Invoices             │ and cash commitments │         6. Aging
                     └─────────────────────┘          7. Distribution reports
                                                      8. Check reconciliation
                                                      9. Cash requirements
   INPUTS              Input control                      OUTPUTS
```

Fig. 8-14. Defining the Accounts Payable Subsystem

subsystem which may be used as an alternative to the narrative description.

The flow of information from source to manager or other user may be shown by a flowchart or by a matrix. The flowchart is, perhaps, a more effective method since the role of the computer and data base as intermediaries may be more easily seen. Since examples of information flowcharts appear throughout the book, we simply show an illustration of an information input/output matrix in Fig. 8-15. The computer must be shown as an input source and output receiver.

The amplification of the flowchart requires a list of forms and a list of files. Forms will be specified to store and transmit data and to present information as needed to meet subsystem functions. The business data which is to be made available for system functioning and for transformation to user information needs to be grouped and classified into files at this time. The detailed development of the data base is carried out after the preliminary design has been approved. Chapter 12, Data Base Systems, will discuss in more detail the development of the data base.

At this point, the systems designers should document the preliminary design and seek review by key staff and management. A typical organization of the report is shown in Fig. 8-16.

Develop the Detailed Design

When management has approved the preliminary design, the costly and time-consuming job of developing the details of the MIS/AIS begins. The objectives of this stage are to

MANAGER \ FILE	Customer	Accounts Payable	Accounts Receivable	Orders – Completed	Orders – In Process	Sales	Manufacturing Costs	Market Costs	Purchasing Costs	Shipping Costs	Competitor Operations	Engineering	Inventory	Payroll	Authorized Personnel	Employee	Job Schedule
Order Department	•			•	•	•			•								•
Controller	•	•	•			•	•						•				
Accounting	•	•	•				•		•				•				
Payroll					•								•			•	
Roof Truss Fabrication				•		•						•	•				•
Saw Department				•								•					•
Table Leaders																	•
Shipping Roof Truss										•							•
Connector Plate Fabrication				•		•						•	•				•
Plate Fabrication												•					•
Plate Application												•					•
Steel Department				•								•					•
Tool and Die				•								•					•
Shipping and Receiving	•			•						•							•
Support Operations	•			•	•			•				•					•
Parts Department				•								•					•
Duplication Services							•										
Mailroom	•									•							
Purchasing				•				•	•	•		•	•				•
Security															•	•	
Custodial																	
Sales	•			•	•	•	•	•		•	•	•					•
Chief Engineer (R&D)				•	•		•	•	•		•	•					•
Drafting and Engineering				•	•						•	•					•
Research				•	•							•					
Development											•	•					
Computer Operations																	
New Product Testing											•	•					•

Fig. 8-15. Management-users and Data Sources

1. Specify in detail the flow of information
2. Specify in detail the inputs and outputs including their format, media, frequency, and level of aggregation
3. Provide a complete specification of the data base system
4. Specify the computer configuration
5. Specify the organization and facilities required to operate the system.

At this stage, a new project plan and control system are required. This is the most costly and complex stage to control. A general network diagram as shown in Fig. 8-17 may be helpful in integrating and controlling the project.

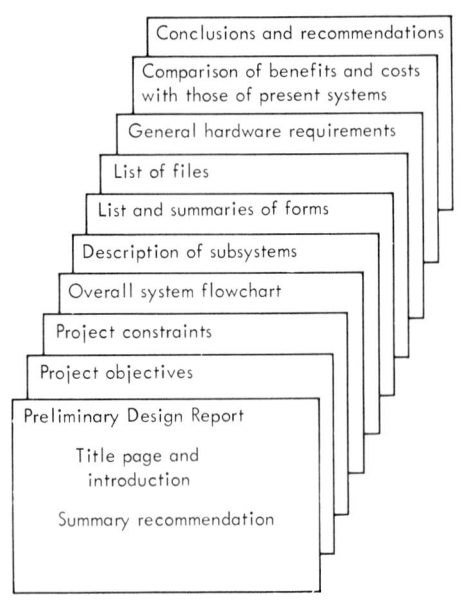

Fig. 8-16. Preliminary Design Report

The detailed design is tied in closely to the various operating systems. Conceptually, we may represent this relationship by a network of activities with their inputs, outputs, and processes as shown in Fig. 8-18. The information is the focus of our attention in this book so that our diagrams and descriptions omit the underlying related flows of materials, people, and energy.

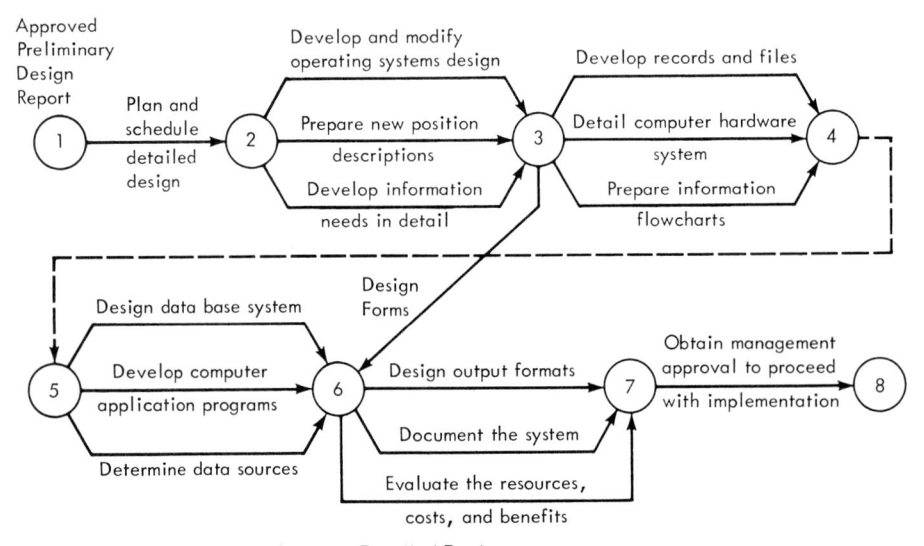

Fig. 8-17. Network Activity Plan for Detailed Design

282

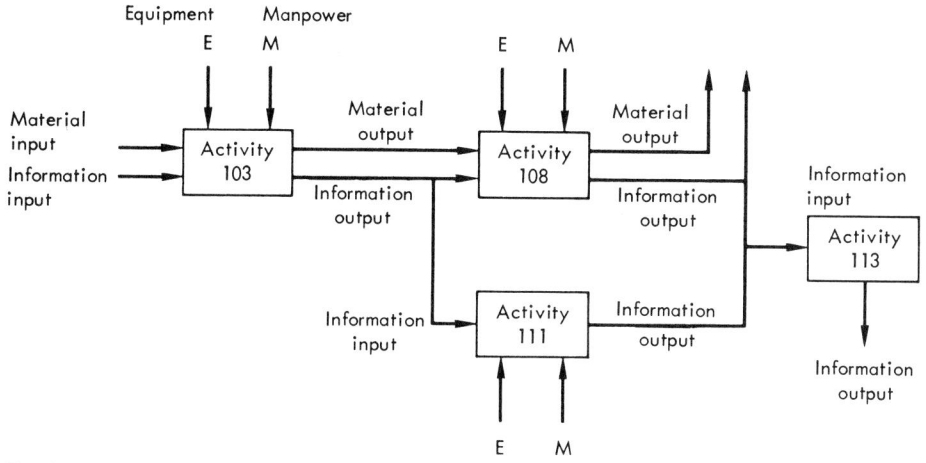

Fig. 8-18. Interrelating Activities

The techniques for developing the detailed design specifications are covered in the next chapter. The major problems in achieving detailed design objectives do not lie so much in techniques as in integration of all the subsystems to achieve optimum, balanced system performance. That is, the design of any one subsystem often affects the performance of other subsystems. It is necessary to trade off the high performance of one subsystem to bring up the performance of another subsystem so that the total system is improved. For instance, reducing the number of models of a company's product from 302 to 26 may reduce sales and revenue, but the manufacturing costs may be lowered so greatly that total company profitability is increased. In one case, a department store in London eliminated all internal accounting systems and operated on a cash basis. The tradeoff here was that the reduction in accounting control costs more than offset pilferage by employees.

Documentation

The end of the detailed design project is production of the documents that specify the system, its operation, and its design justification. Documentation consists of:

1. A summary flowchart
2. Detailed flowcharts
3. Operations activity sheets showing inputs, outputs, and transfer functions
4. Specification of the data base or master file
5. Computer hardware requirements

Table 8-7. Documentation Manual

TOPIC	PURPOSE	FORMS	TABLES	DIAGRAMS	NARRATIVE
I. Total MIS					
A. System objectives	Defines what the system is supposed to achieve				X
B. Performance specifications	States each requirement of the system, preferably in quantitative terms		X		X
C. Conceptualization	Describes the gross design or arrangement of subsystems			X	X
D. System flowchart	Shows flow of information through the MIS as well as relationships with the operating systems			X	
E. Data base					
1. File organization	Describes the file organization and retrieval method	X			
2. Data element descriptions	Defines and describes data elements	X			
3. File interrelationships			X		
F. Model base description	Lists models, applications, and presents the models in detail		X		X
G. Output description	Describes the medium, the format, the frequency, and the uses of each MIS output	X	X	X	X
II. System Operation					
A. Work flowchart	Shows the sequence of operations of the operating system and the forms that accompany the work from station to station			X	
B. Processing instructions	Gives step-by-step procedures for processing data before it goes into the computer, during, and after	X	X	X	X
C. Other instructions	Defines special actions required for MIS operations				X
III. Computer programs					
A. Identification	Shows program number and subsystem identification	X	X	X	
B. Input definition	Defines the medium (cards, tapes, optical reader, etc.) and formats of input	X	X		
C. Processing	Describes the computer logic for the MIS programs		X	X	
D. Output definition	Defines the medium and format of output reports and displays	X			X
IV. User's manual					
A. System description	Defines the objectives of the system, the arrangement of subsystems, and the general flow of work and information			X	X

Table 8-7. Documentation Manual (cont'd)

TOPIC	PURPOSE	FORMS	TABLES	DIAGRAMS	NARRATIVE
B. Data preparation	Gives instructions on how to prepare and edit data entering the MIS		X		X
C. Error correction procedures	Explains how to correct errors made in operating the MIS which yield error messages			X	
D. Linear responsibility chart	Specifies the specific tasks and roles of each person in the MIS (in matrix form)		X		
E. Glossary of terms	Defines terms and abbreviations used in the MIS		X		

6. Software (programs)
7. Personnel requirements by type of skill or discipline
8. Final (updated) performance specifications
9. Cost of installation and implementation of the system
10. Cost of operating the system per unit of time
11. Program for modification or termination of the system
12. An executive digest of the MIS design. This is a report that top management can read rapidly in order to get the essence of the system, its potential for the company, its cost, and its general configuration. We point out that a high-level MIS official at General Electric remarked, "If the MIS can be justified on the basis of cost savings, it isn't an MIS." The executive digest should be directed toward showing how the system will aid managers' decision-making by gains in information or in time.

Some documentation should be on standardized forms. Input–output–activity diagrams or listings are an example. Obviously, standard symbols should be used on flowcharts and guidelines should be established for flowchart format. Some documentation is unique to a project, such as the data base, and the format and classification of items should be determined by the needs of the particular user. Other documentation should simply follow good reporting style.

An illustration of the nature of the contents of the documentation of the MIS/AIS is shown in Table 8-7. Typical means for presenting sections of information are given in the four right-hand columns. These subjects may be organized in report form in a manner indicated by Fig. 8-19. This report is called the *specification report, design report,* or *docu-*

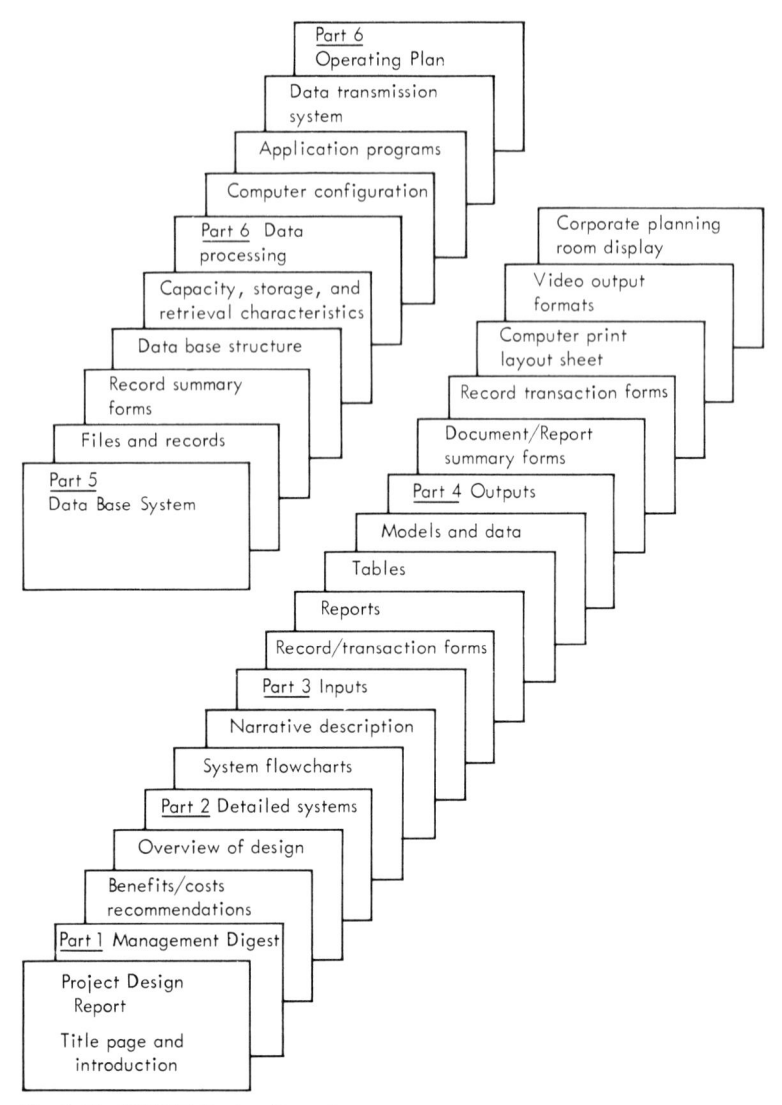

```
                              Part 6
                              Operating Plan
                              Data transmission
                                system
                              Application programs
                              Computer configuration
                         Part 6 Data
                         processing                            Corporate planning
                                                                 room display
                         Capacity, storage, and               Video output
                         retrieval characteristics              formats
                      Data base structure                    Computer print
                                                               layout sheet
                   Record summary                          Record transaction forms
                     forms
                Files and records                        Document/Report
                                                           summary forms
         Part 5                                       Part 4 Outputs
         Data Base System
                                                   Models and data
                                                Tables
                                             Reports
                                          Record/transaction forms
                                      Part 3 Inputs
                                   Narrative description
                                System flowcharts
                             Part 2 Detailed systems
                          Overview of design
                       Benefits/costs
                         recommendations
                   Part 1 Management Digest
                 Project Design
                   Report
                 Title page and
                   introduction
```

Fig. 8-19. MIS/AIS Design Report

mentation manual. A typical table of contents for the AIS subsystem design report is shown in Table 8-8.

Summary

Financial and accounting information systems must be integrated with all the functional and operating systems of the organization.

Table 8-8. Table of Contents

Section I
  History and Background
  Letter of Engagement
  Letter of Transmittal

Section II
  Existing Organizational Chart
  Revised Organizational Chart

Section III
  Duties and Job Descriptions of Officers and Management

Section IV
  Chart of Accounts
  Consolidated Balance Sheet Format
  Income Statement Format
  Explanation

Section V
  Revised and Proposed Forms:
    Purchase Order
    Receiving Report
    Telephone Orders Form
    Journal Sheet

Section VI
  Flow Charting Symbols and Abbreviations
  System Overview
  Forms Flow Charts

Furthermore, the AIS plays a key role in providing management with vital planning, control, and decision information.

The accounting organization is not only responsible for developing the traditional accounting information systems, but it must participate in the development of the MIS. One or more representatives of the accounting department will usually work continually with the MIS design team throughout the project.

The development of the AIS follows the same procedure as the development of the MIS and is usually a part of the MIS project. The principal steps in MIS/AIS development have been given in this chapter. Basically, information systems design consists of

1. Activities analysis
2. Information needs research
3. Setting objectives
4. Developing the gross or preliminary design
5. Defining and detailing the design
6. Developing an implementation plan
7. Documenting the system.

DISCUSSION QUESTIONS AND PROBLEMS

1. a. Should the accounting group develop the AIS independently of the MIS?
   b. What is actually done in practice?
2. List a typical set of subsystems for a
   a. Manufacturing firm
   b. Large department store
   c. Bank
   d. Hospital
   e. CPA firm
3. a. What is the accountant's role in analyzing management's problem?
   b. What is the accountant's role in analyzing operating problems?
   c. Is it necessary to have an accountant on the MIS development team?
4. Give an example of an accounting information need in:
   a. long-range planning activities
   b. short-range planning activities
   c. control activities
   d. typical major decision problems
   e. a special problem area (merger, environmental input, bankruptcy)
5. A manager said, "The information needs for a work station should remain the same without regard to the individual occupying the position." Discuss.
6. Discuss reasons for different individuals requiring different information to accomplish the same managerial function.
7. Why should the identification of management's information needs be one of the first steps in the analysis of information systems?
8. List and discuss several internal and external constraints on AIS design.
9. What are the purposes of the project proposal?
10. Write a three-page project proposal for a new AIS design for a company that has recently doubled its sales, gone from one product to five product lines, and has undergone several complete reorganizations.
11. On the basis of question 10, identify eight to ten major tasks in the development of the AIS. Show a feasible schedule for the accomplishment of these tasks.

12. a. Define and discuss "work structure breakdown."
    b. What is the objective of a "work package"?
    c. What should the work package contain?
13. Discuss the objectives of developing the detailed design.
14. a. List and discuss the documentation that should be generated during the detailed design.
    b. Is it necessary to have this documentation prior to implementation?
15. Give reasons why project planning and control are necessary in developing AIS.
16. Relating to Fig. 8-7:
    a. What information should be contained in the production record?
    b. Who utilizes the 24-hour production summary?
    c. What information is contained in the analysis of variance report and who uses it?
    d. What is the purpose of this subsystem?
17. Develop a matrix similar to Fig. 8-15 for the manager/users of a company assigned by the instructor:
    Manager/user   *Data sources*

Bibliography

ALEXANDER, M. J. *Information Systems Analysis,* Chicago: Science Research Associates, 1974.

BOWER, JAMES B., ROBERT E. SCHLOSSER, and CHARLES T. ZLATKOVICH. *Financial Information Systems, Theory and Practice,* Boston: Allyn and Bacon, 1969.

BURCH, JOHN G., JR., and FELIX R. STRATER, JR. *Information Systems: Theory and Practice,* Santa Barbara, Cal.: Hamilton Publishing, 1974.

BYRNE, BRENDAN, ALAN MULLALLY, and BRIAN ROTHERY. *The Art of Systems Analysis,* London: Business Books, Ltd., 1976.

CUSHING, BARRY E. *Accounting Information Systems and Business Organizations,* Reading, Mass.: Addison-Wesley, 1974.

DAVIS, GORDON B. *Management Information Systems: Conceptual Foundations, Structure, and Development,* New York: McGraw-Hill Book Co., 1974.

KINDRED, ALTON R. *Data Systems and Management,* Englewood Cliffs, N.J.: Prentice-Hall, 1973.

MURDICK, ROBERT G., and JOEL E. ROSS. *Information Systems for Modern Management,* Englewood Cliffs, N.J.: Prentice-Hall, 1975.

MURDICK, ROBERT G., and JOEL E. ROSS. *Introduction to Management Information Systems,* Englewood Cliffs, N.J.: Prentice-Hall, 1977.

Preview:
This chapter will show several types of techniques that may be employed in various steps of systems design.
–Projects planning and control
–PERT
–Flow charting
–Data-flow matrices
–Job station analysis
–Decision tables
–Data gathering
–Simulation

CHAPTER NINE

techniques and tools for systems analysis and design

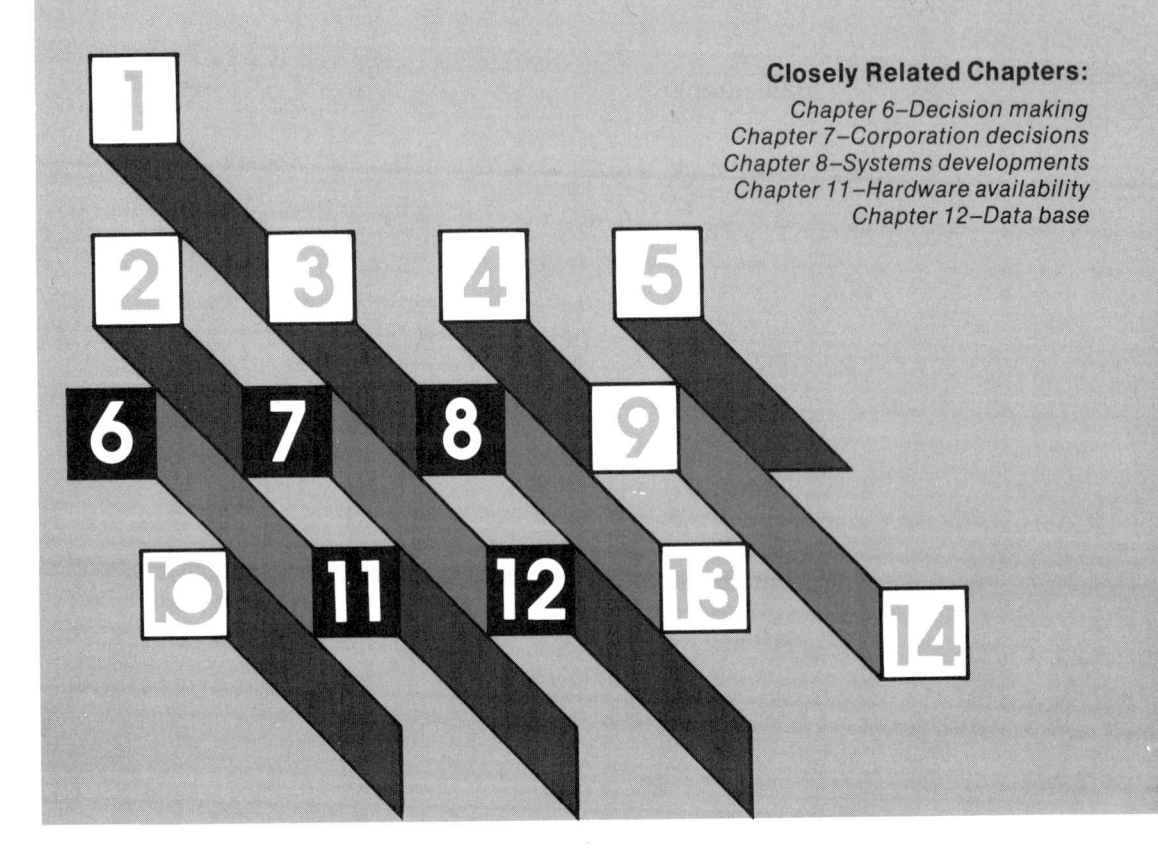

Closely Related Chapters:
Chapter 6–Decision making
Chapter 7–Corporation decisions
Chapter 8–Systems developments
Chapter 11–Hardware availability
Chapter 12–Data base

Chapter 8 presented the major steps in the design of an AIS. If we had gone into details of the techniques used throughout, the basic ideas would have been lost in a maze of digressions. Also, some specialized techniques may be used for various major steps according to the nature of the AIS project. For these reasons, we have brought the techniques and tools together in one chapter for the student to utilize where they are appropriate. The project planning/control technique with which we start is especially important for AIS design.

PROJECT PLANNING AND CONTROL

Without the serious application of project planning and control techniques, actual costs and time for projects have ballooned to three or four times their original estimates. *Planning and control are critical to the success of a project.*

A project is a unique well-defined effort to produce specified results at a particular point in time. Good project planning is required, therefore, to

1. Provide a basis for control of time, cost, and performance
2. Make sure that objectives are established
3. Make sure that key tasks are identified
4. Establish procedence relationships among tasks
5. Establish costs and prepare budgets related to time and performance of tasks
6. Organize and assign personnel to ensure that tasks will be performed.

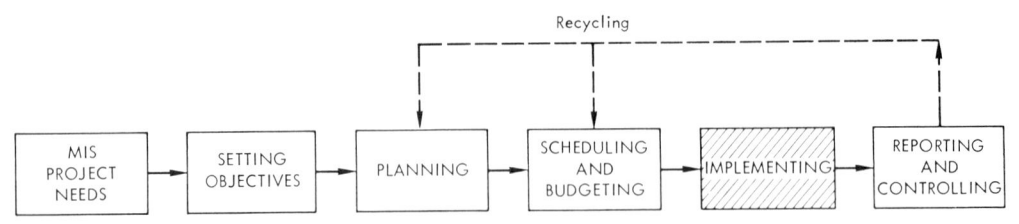

Fig. 9-1. The Planning-Controlling Cycle for Project Management

In Fig. 9-1 we show the planning and control cycle for the AIS project. Before engaging in design work, we should first determine the most pressing needs of the organization. Then, as shown in Fig. 9-1, the objectives of the project are established. These are sometimes called the *performance specifications* because they tell us what the AIS should do when it is designed and installed. The planning continues with the establishment of a work breakdown structure. This is the hierarchy of tasks required to achieve project objectives as discussed in the previous chapter.

A commonly used technique, PERT (Program Evaluation Review Technique) or CPM (Critical Path Method) is employed to relate the timing of tasks to each other and to the project finish date. These techniques have evolved until they are essentially the same. Generally, they are referred to as critical path network methods. The bare bones idea of critical path network will next be given in a series of tables. The reader should refer to entire books devoted to the fine points for further information.

Basic Network Concepts and the Critical Path

PERT requires the selection of specific identifiable *events*. An event is essentially the completion of an *activity*. The events are sequenced relative to each other. Estimates of times required to carry out an activity are prepared.

Let us take the A/R project with the necessary activities shown in Fig. 9-2. The network is constructed by identifying the end event, completion of the A/R design, and then determining the last tasks that *must* be done to finish the design. There are three such tasks or activities shown in Fig. 9-2. These are 3-5, 4-5, and 2-5. For each event immediately preceding event 5, the same process is repeated. We determine that event 2 and event 3 must occur before event 4 can occur. And event 3 cannot occur until event 2 has occurred. Finally, event 2 cannot occur until event 1, start the project, has occurred. By this

PROJECT: Design a new A/R System

ACTIVITIES:
Specify the requirements
Design the information flow
Establish the organization and equipment
Develop the forms
Specify the data base
Design the management reports

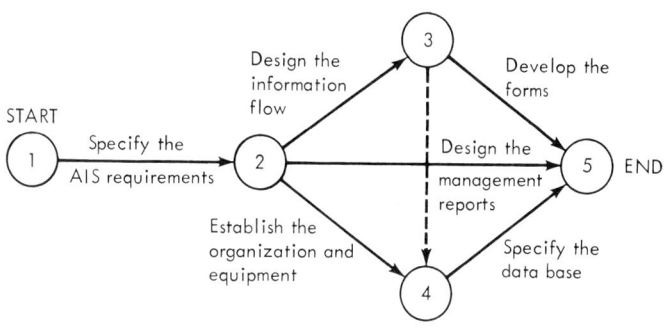

Fig. 9-2. Precedence Network

method, we set up precedence relationships shown by the *network* diagram of Fig. 9-2.

Note that there is no "activity" associated with the arrow from event 3 to 4. The dotted arrow means that event 4 cannot occur until after activities 2–3 and 2–4 have been completed. Since two arrows joining the

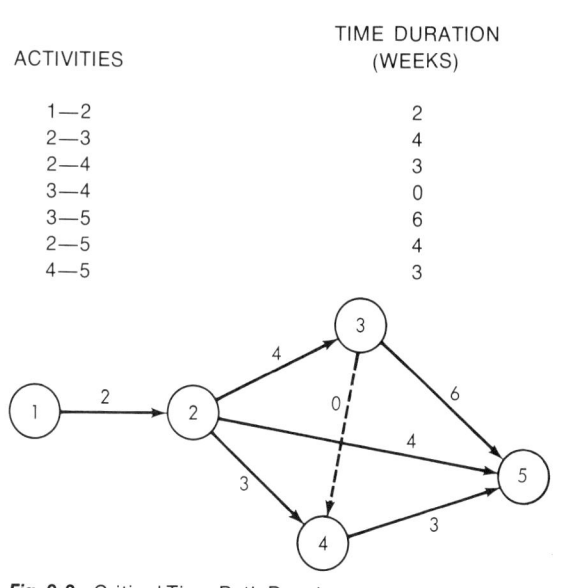

ACTIVITIES	TIME DURATION (WEEKS)
1—2	2
2—3	4
2—4	3
3—4	0
3—5	6
2—5	4
4—5	3

Fig. 9-3. Critical Time Path Development

same two events are not allowed by PERT, the activity 3–4 is a "dummy" activity required to establish that event 3 must precede event 4.

Next look at Fig. 9-3. We have shown the expected time required to carry out each activity and placed it on the corresponding arrow in the network. Note that the following chains of events exist from start to finish:

1-2-3-5	12 weeks
1-2-3-4-5	7 weeks
1-2-5	6 weeks
1-2-4-5	8 weeks

In three of the paths, time slippages could occur and the paths could still be carried out in less than 12 weeks. In the 12-week path, any time slippage means the end-event will occur later. This *longest time path* is therefore called the *critical path*. The AIS project manager must therefore monitor and control the chain of activities in this path very closely.

The difference between time for any complete path and the critical path is called the *slack time*. The slack for the critical path is obviously zero. By means of routine calculation, the slack time for completion of intermediate events may be calculated. Since standard computer programs exist for these calculation methods, we refer the interested reader to specialized books on PERT.

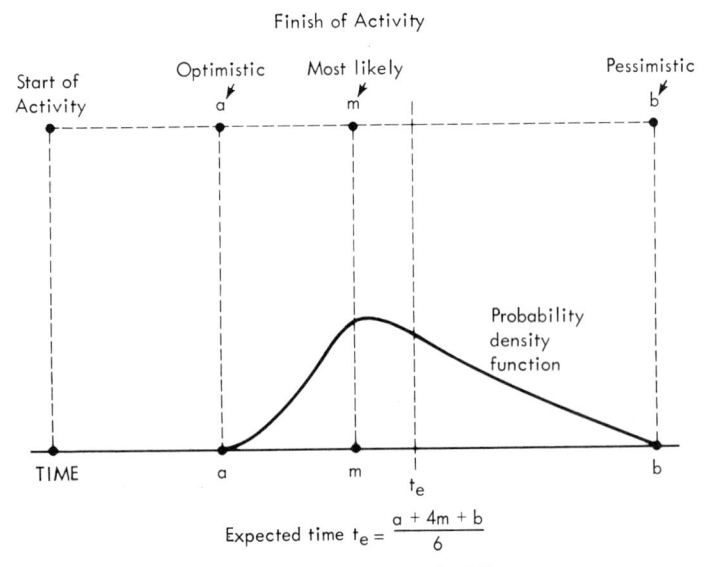

Fig. 9-4. Estimating Expected Time for an Activity

Expected time $t_e = \dfrac{a + 4m + b}{6}$

Time Estimates

The judgment of the length of time to complete an activity is difficult to make. Variability is produced by random unforeseen causes and by the experience, optimism, or pessimism of the person making the estimate. For these reasons, the estimated time to complete an activity is assumed to be a variable following a probability distribution.

The person responsible for completing a task estimates the minimum time for the activity, the maximum time the task will take if bad breaks occur, and the *most likely time*. These times are designated a, b, and m respectively (see Fig. 9-4). The expected times shown in Fig. 9-3 were based on estimates,

$$t_e = \frac{a + 4m + b}{6}:$$

a	m	b	t_e
1.0	1.95	3.2	2 weeks
3.0	3.75	6.0	4 weeks
2.5	1.90	4.0	3 weeks
4.4	5.85	8.2	6 weeks
2.6	4.10	5.0	4 weeks
1.0	3.25	4.0	3 weeks

A typical computer output report for a large scale project using PERT is shown in Fig. 9-5.

Fig. 9-5. PERT Network Printout

EVENT Preceding	Following	ACTIVITY	Est. Time Weeks	PL	ES	EF	LS	LF	SE	TF	FFE	FFL	IF
1	2	Define site	2	0	0	2	30	32	2	30	0	30	0
*1	4	Employ manager	6	0	0	6	0	6	6	0	0	0	0
1	17	Select computer	4	0	0	4	3	7	4	3	0	3	0
2	3	Prepare site	10	32	2	12	32	42	12	30	0	0	0
3	20	Dummy	0	42	12	12	42	42	42	30	30	0	0
*4	5	Employ programmers	4	6	6	10	6	10	10	0	0	0	0
4	10	Employ analysts	6	6	6	12	17	23	12	11	0	11	0
4	12	Employ operators	3	6	6	9	25	28	17	19	8	19	8
*5	6	Train programmers	6	10	10	16	10	16	16	0	0	0	0
*6	7	Write programs	16	16	16	32	16	32	32	0	0	0	0
*7	8	Develop test data	4	32	32	36	32	36	36	0	0	0	0
8	9	Complete documentation	4	36	36	40	38	42	40	2	0	2	0
*8	14	Dummy	0	36	36	36	36	36	36	0	0	0	0
9	20	Dummy	0	42	40	40	42	42	42	2	2	0	0
10	11	Write detailed procedures	5	23	12	17	23	28	17	11	0	0	0
11	12	Dummy	0	28	17	17	28	28	17	11	0	0	0

Fig.9-5 cont.

EVENT Preceding	EVENT Following	ACTIVITY	Est. Time Weeks	DATES PL	DATES ES	DATES EF	DATES LS	DATES LF	DATES SE	FLOATS TF	FLOATS FFE	FLOATS FFL	FLOATS IF
11	15	Design forms	4	28	17	21	30	34	21	13	0	2	0
12	13	Train operators	4	28	17	21	28	32	21	11	0	0	0
13	14	Convert files	4	32	21	25	32	36	36	11	11	0	0
*14	20	Test and debug programs	6	36	36	42	36	42	42	0	0	0	0
15	16	Order forms	2	34	21	23	34	36	23	13	0	0	0
16	20	Await forms	6	36	23	29	36	42	42	13	13	0	0
17	18	Order computer	4	7	4	8	7	11	8	3	0	0	0
18	19	Await delivery	30	11	8	38	11	41	38	3	0	0	0
19	20	Install computer	1	41	38	39	41	42	42	3	3	0	0
*20	21	Run parallel	8	42	42	50	42	50	50	0	0	0	0

Legend:
PL — latest date of preceding event
ES — earliest starting date
EF — earliest finishing date
LS — latest starting date
LF — latest finishing date
SE — earliest date of succeeding event
* — critical path

TF — total float
FFE — free float early
FFL — free float late
IF — independent float

LF — ES — A
SE — ES — A
LF — PL — A
SE — PL — A

Output in sequence by preceding event and following event.

Source: Alton R. Kindred, *Data Management and Systems,* (Englewood Cliffs, N.J.: Prentice-Hall, Inc. 1973).

FLOWCHARTING

Flowcharts are diagrams representing the sequencing of activities or operations and/or the flow of data or information, or logical concepts. Elements, concepts, activities, documents, or logic decisions are usually represented by geometric forms such as rectangles, and the flow relationships are indicated by connecting lines with arrowheads.

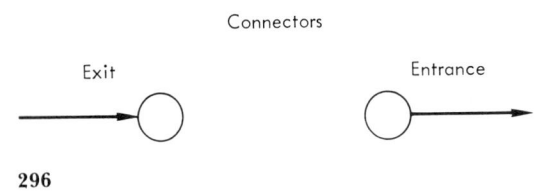

The basic system flowchart and program flowchart symbols are:

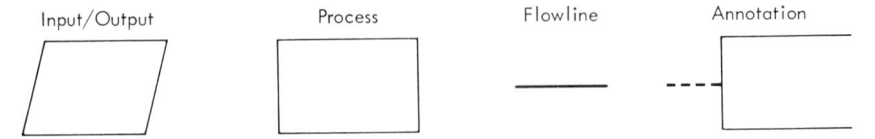

Input/Output   Process   Flowline   Annotation

Two additional symbols that permit connecting a flowchart from one page to the next are:

Connectors

Exit   Entrance

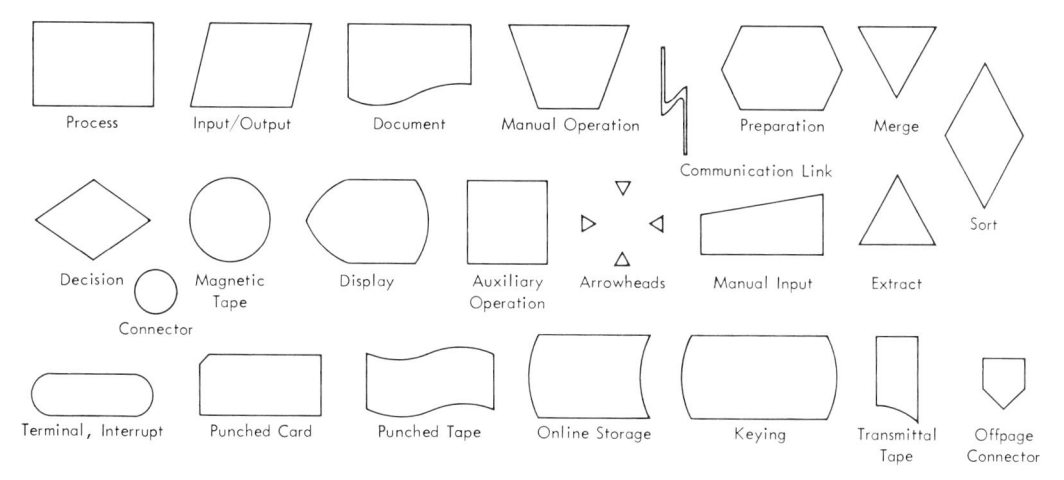

Fig. 9-6. Program and System Flowchart Symbols

Additional and specialized symbols are shown in Fig. 9-6, Flowchart Symbols. These are adequate for the MIS designer. The important point is that *standardization within the company is essential.*

Guidelines to Flowcharting

The expert systems analyst will develop his own approach to creating flowcharts. Flowcharting is indeed a creative problem-solving process, so that no method can be completely prescribed. Some guidelines that may help the novice are:

1. Specify the objective of the flowchart.
2. Establish the level at which you are going to flowchart.
3. If a completely new system is being developed, start with a high level of aggregation and block out major subsystems.
4. Proceed from the known to the unknown. That is, identify subsystems that you know must appear and develop the subsystems that must relate to them.
5. Use standardized symbols and a template, a plastic device with symbols cut out. Templates are available from computer vendors or office equipment stores.
6. Chart the main line of data flov in the system or program first.
7. Begin flowcharting at the top of each page. The charts should run from top to bottom or left to right.
8. Each page should have a heading or caption that clearly identifies the project, the chart, the date (of revision, if any), the author, and the page number.

9. Write within the symbols, using as few words as possible. Use the annotation symbol to describe data more fully.
10. Collect incoming flows so that the flowlines shown actually entering a symbol are kept to a minimum. Similarly for outgoing flowlines.
11. Leave blank space around major nonconvergent flows.
12. For many flowlines on complex charts, use connectors to reduce their number.
13. Avoid intersecting (crossover) flowlines.
14. Be neat. Put yourself in the place of the reader and ask if the diagram can be quickly and clearly read.

Types of Flowcharts and Examples

Examination of numerous flowcharts developed in companies leads to the classification below. For each class we show a typical flowchart although there are variants even within the classes.

1. Block diagram of general relationships within a system. These are used early in the design process (Figs. 9-7 and 9-8).

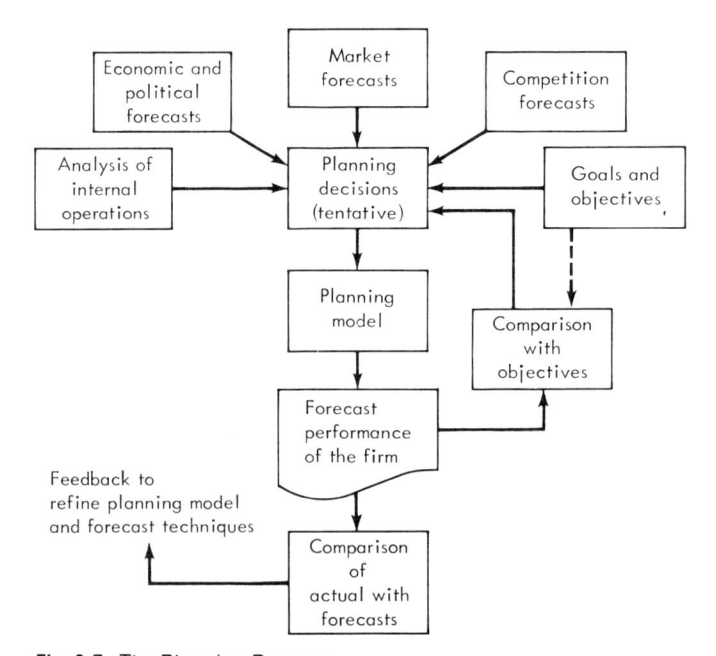

Fig. 9-7. The Planning Process
Source: R. H. Sprague, Jr., "System Support for a Financial Planning Model," *Management Accounting,* June 1972.

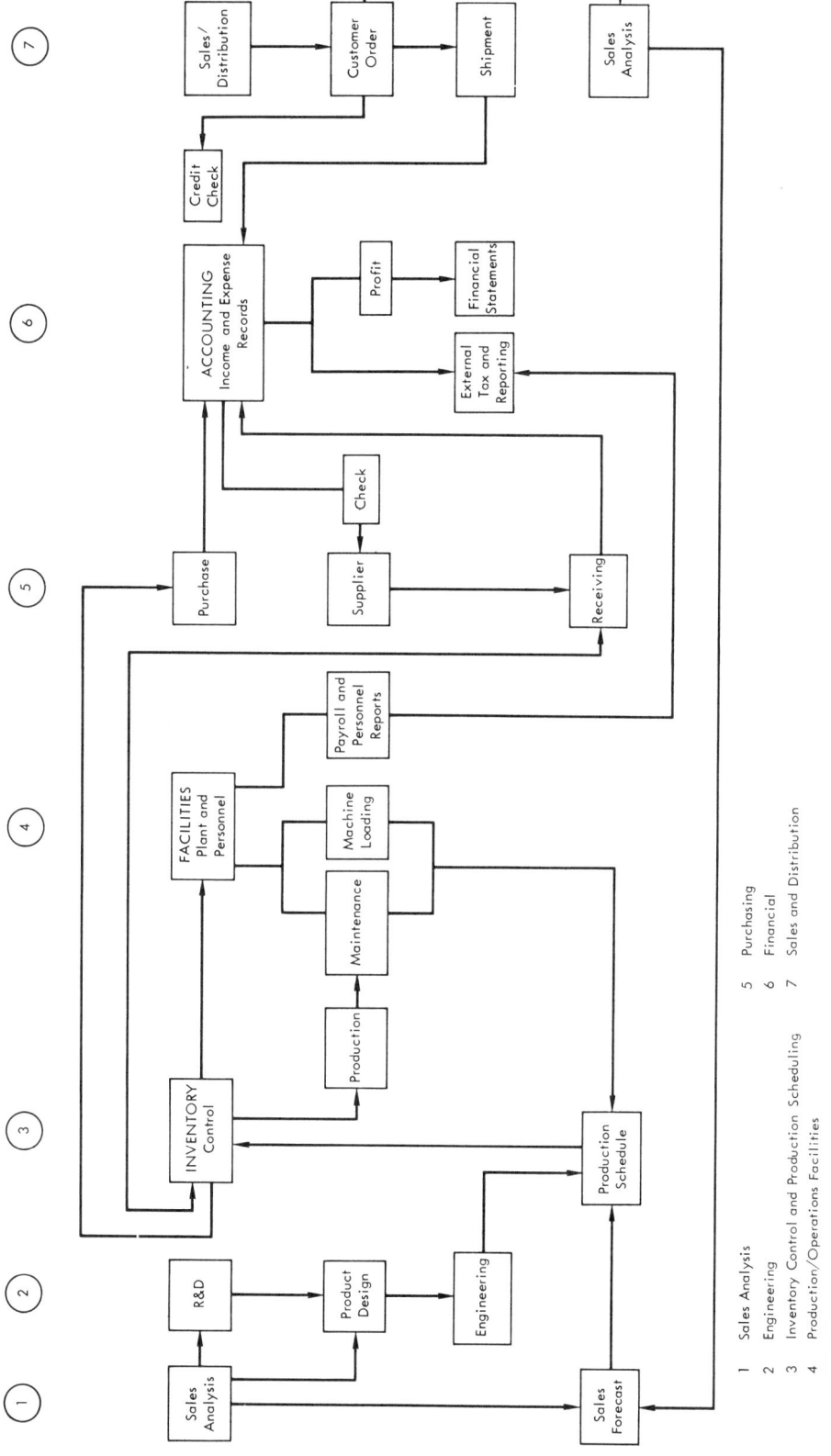

Fig. 9-8. Integration of Subsystems Through the Information Flow in the Production/Operations System

1 Sales Analysis
2 Engineering
3 Inventory Control and Production Scheduling
4 Production/Operations Facilities
5 Purchasing
6 Financial
7 Sales and Distribution

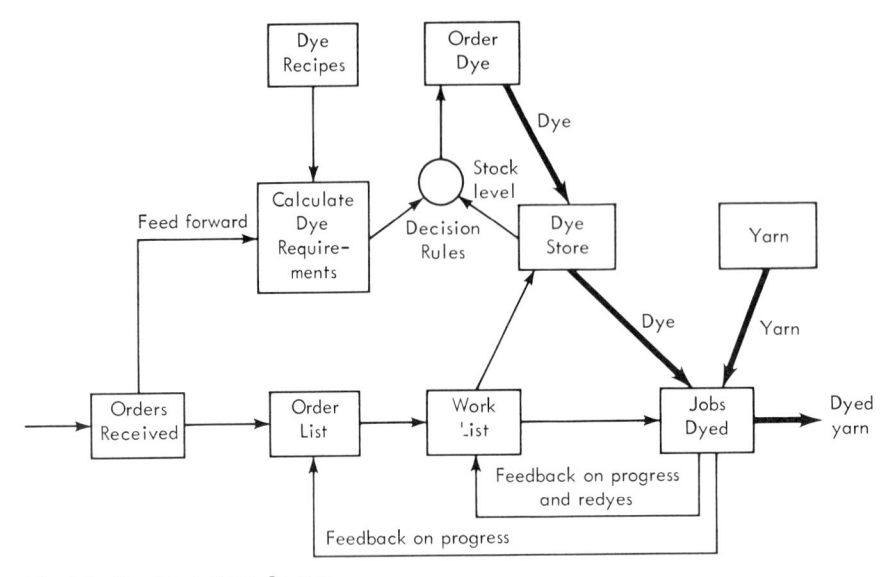

Fig. 9-9. Dye Operations System

Source: Ian Duff and Malcolm Henry, "Computer-Aided Management: A Case Study," *Management Decision*, Winter 1971.

2. Block diagrams of operating and information systems (Fig. 9-9).
3. Process flowchart. These charts are useful for analyzing the kinds and number of operations for a complete procedure. By recording other data such as number of storages and number of inspections, the systems analyst may be led to more efficient and better controlled procedures (Fig. 9-10).
4. Detailed system flowchart. These more complex charts are useful in the detailed design phase (Fig. 9-11).
5. Forms flowchart. This chart shows the number of copies of each form when initiated and the distribution of the copies of the forms for a particular system (Fig. 9-12).
6. File relationships. In this case, the flow of data may follow alternative paths after an initiating transaction. This chart tracks only the movement of data from one storage file to another and operations must be inferred (Fig. 9-13).
7. Data base relationships. A wide variety of flowcharts are possible for this class. Fig. 9-14 shows a file input/output process in a data base system. Fig. 9-15 shows a file updating process in a data base management system.
8. Program logic flowchart (Fig. 9-16). This provides the logic for a computer program. The program is then written in detail at the computer compiler language level.
9. Detailed computer program flowchart. This shows the detailed instructions to the computer (Fig. 9-17).

FLOW PROCESS CHART

No. 765B
Page 1 of 1
Job Complete Expense Acct.
Man ☐ Mat'l ☒ Form
Chart begins _____
Chart ends _____
Charted by B. Davis
Date 7/27

	Present		Proposed		Difference	
	No	Time	No	Time	No	Time
Operations	4		2		2	
Transportations	4		2		2	
Inspections	2		1		1	
Delays	6		3		3	
Storages	0		0		0	
Distance Travelled	1560'		1525'		35'	

#	OPER TRANS STORE INSP DELAY	Dist.	Time	(PRESENT) Details of (PROPOSED) Method
1	○⇨△☐D			Expense account form written (4 copies) by employee
2	○⇨△☐D			In basket awaiting interoffice mail pickup
3	○⇨△☐D	1500'		To accounting office
4	○⇨△☐D			Waiting on accounting officer's desk
5	○⇨△☐D			Examined by accounting officer
6	○⇨△☐D			Approved by accounting officer
7	○⇨△☐D	25'		To accounting clerk's desk
8	○⇨△☐D			On desk waiting for preparation of check
9	○⇨△☐D			
10	○⇨△☐D			
11	○⇨△☐D			
12	○⇨△☐D			
13	○⇨△☐D			
14	○⇨△☐D			
15	○⇨△☐D			
16	○⇨△☐D			
17	○⇨△☐D			
18	○⇨△☐D			

COMMENTS:

Fig. 9-10. Flow Process

Source: Arthur C. Laufer, *Operations Management,* Cincinnati, Ohio: South-Western Publishing Company, 1975, p. 306.

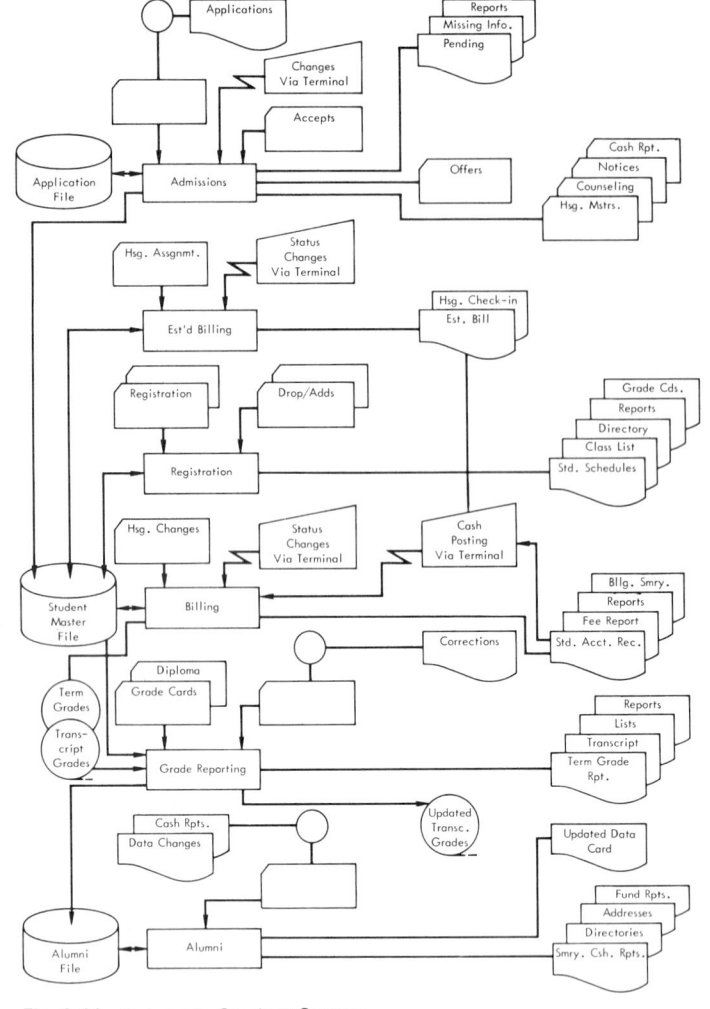

Fig. 9-11. University Student System
Source: Alton R. Kindred. *Data Systems and Management*, Englewood Cliffs, N.J.: Prentice-Hall, 1971.

DATA-FLOW MATRICES

Matrices (tables) showing various relationships among data and between data and other system components are very helpful in systems analysis, design, and documentation. Often such tables are a good substitute for some types of flow diagrams. The tables serve as a basis for gathering information during interviews with managers and nonmanagers. They also provide an integrated view of some aspects of the AIS.

The following matrices are helpful:

1. Reports vs. data required (Fig. 9-18)
2. Reports vs. data sources (Fig. 9-19)

302

Fig. 9-12. Forms Distribution Flowchart

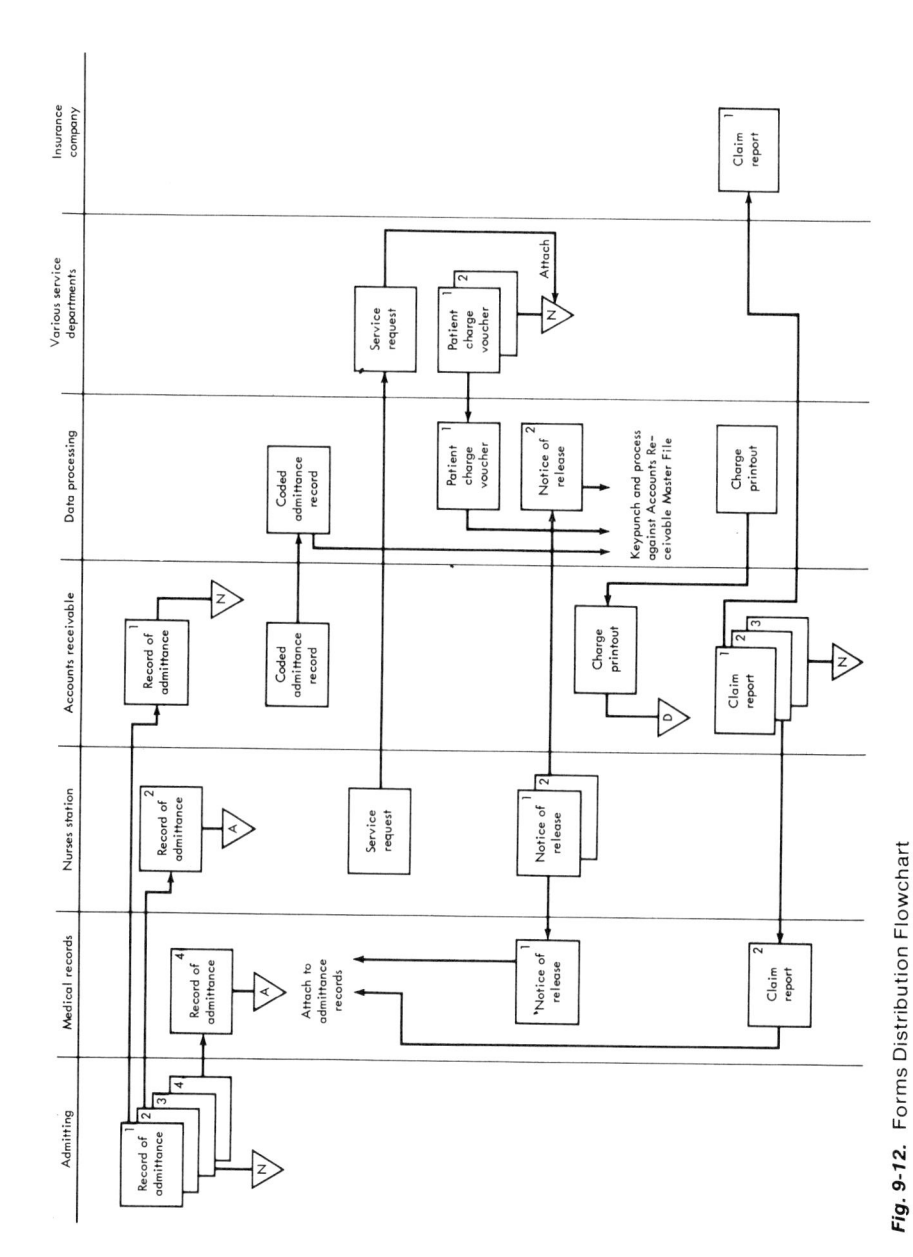

Source: Barry E. Cushing, *Accounting Information Systems and Business Organizations*, Reading, Mass.: Addison-Wesley, 1974.

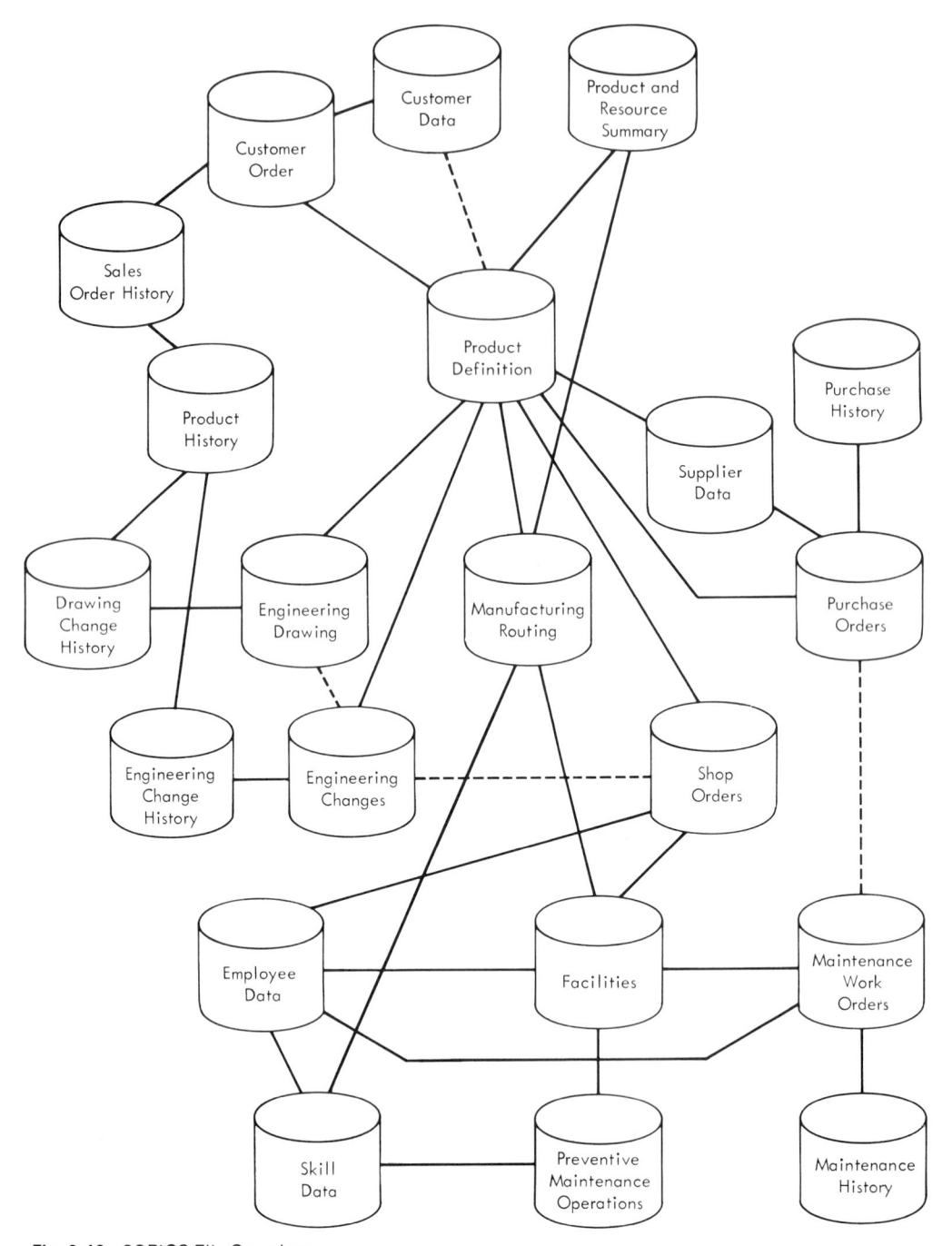

Fig. 9-13. COPICS File Overview
Source: *Communications Oriented Production Information and Control System,* IBM, 1972, p. 42.

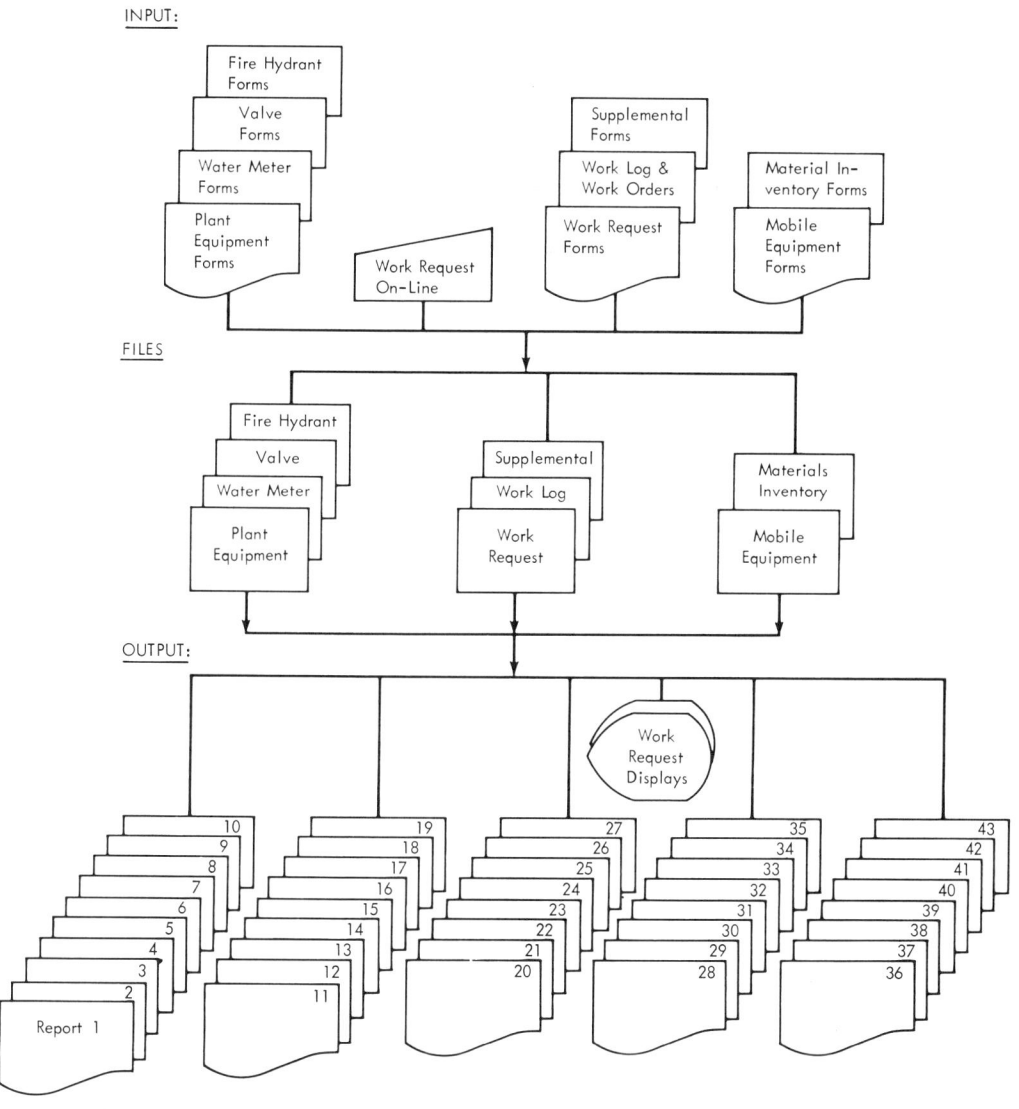

Fig. 9-14. Schematic of Input, Files and Output

    3. Documents vs. distribution
    4. Subsystems vs. data input (Fig. 9-20)
    5. Subsystems vs. data output
    6. Information input/output (information user vs. information transmitter)
    7. Computer application (program) vs. departmental user (Table 9-1)
    8. Report vs. user (Table 9-2)
    9. File vs. user (Table 9-3).

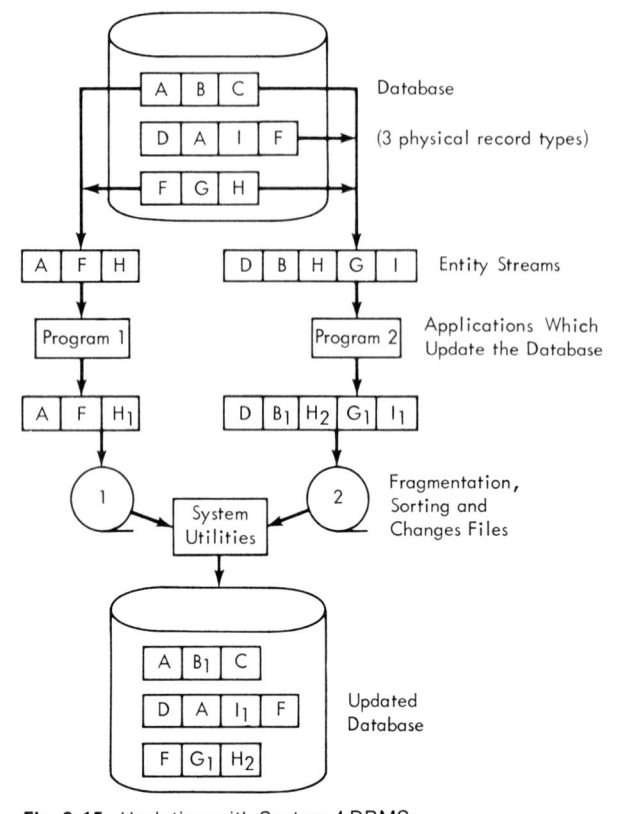

Fig. 9-15. Updating with System 4 DBMS

Source: Ian Palmer, *Data Base Systems: A Practical Reference*, Wellesley, Mass.: Q.E.D. Information Sciences, Inc., 1975, pp. 4–36.

Illustrations of most of the above matrices are shown in the referenced figures.

JOB STATION ANALYSIS

Study of the current AIS will show the way to potential benefits of a revised system. Job station analysis is a technique for uncovering problems or inefficiencies at the "nodes" of the system. The documentation of the job station analysis should be carefully planned so that comparisons among similar stations, costs and benefits, necessity for the station, and efficiency may be examined easily. The steps in job station analysis are outlined next.

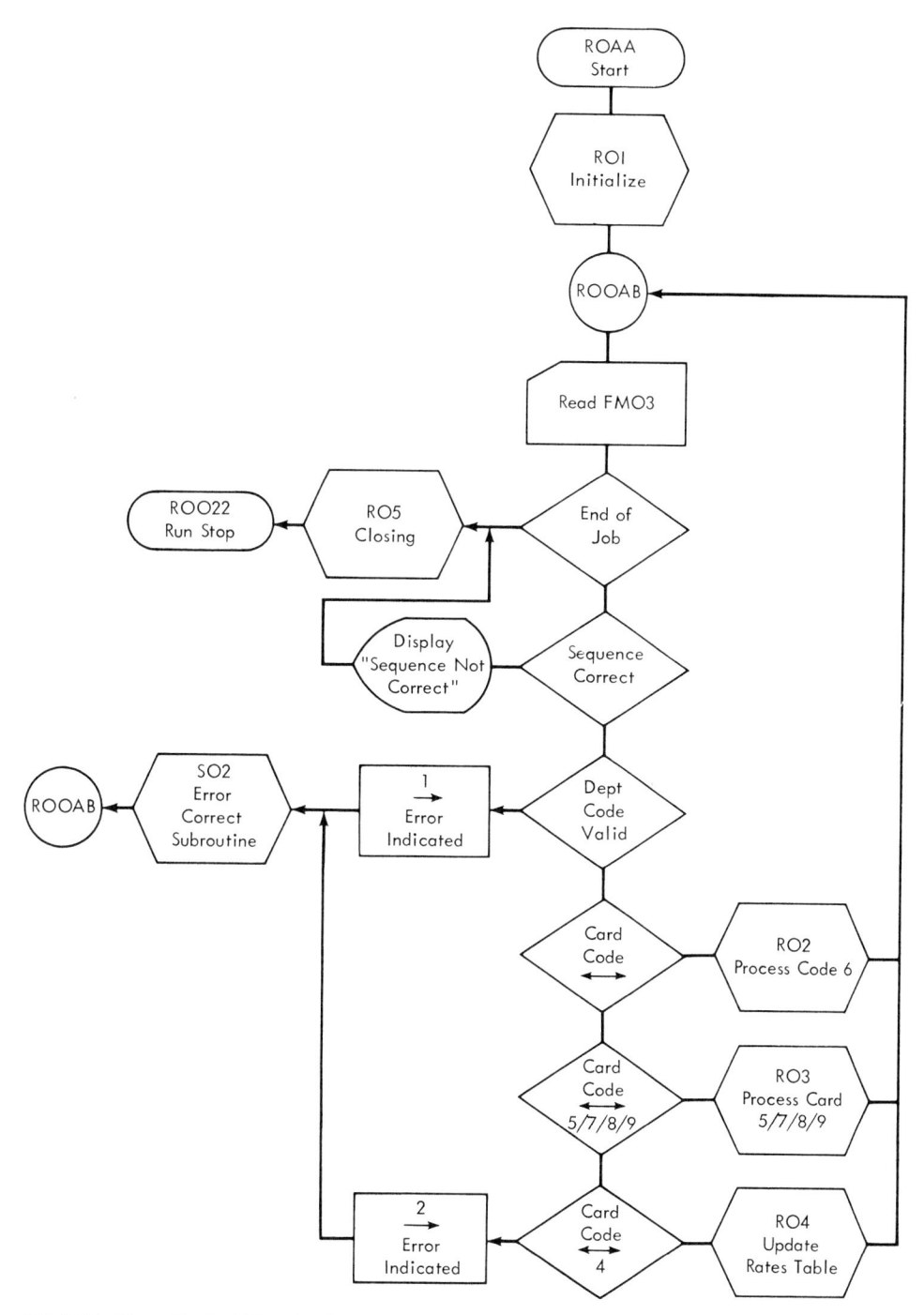

Fig. 9-16. Wage Control Flowchart

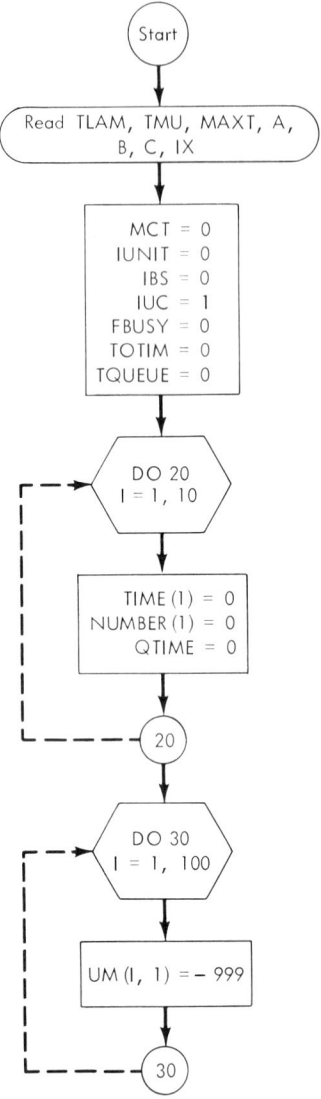

Fig. 9-17. Program for Single Channel Queuing Simulator

Source: J. W. Schmidt and R. E. Taylor, *Simulation and Analyses of Industrial Systems*, Homewood, Ill.: L Richard D. Irwin, 1970.

Title and Position Description

Titles of all positions should be listed and compared for consistency. For example, why is one position in accounts receivable called a specialist or analyst while a very similar position in accounts payable is called a clerk?

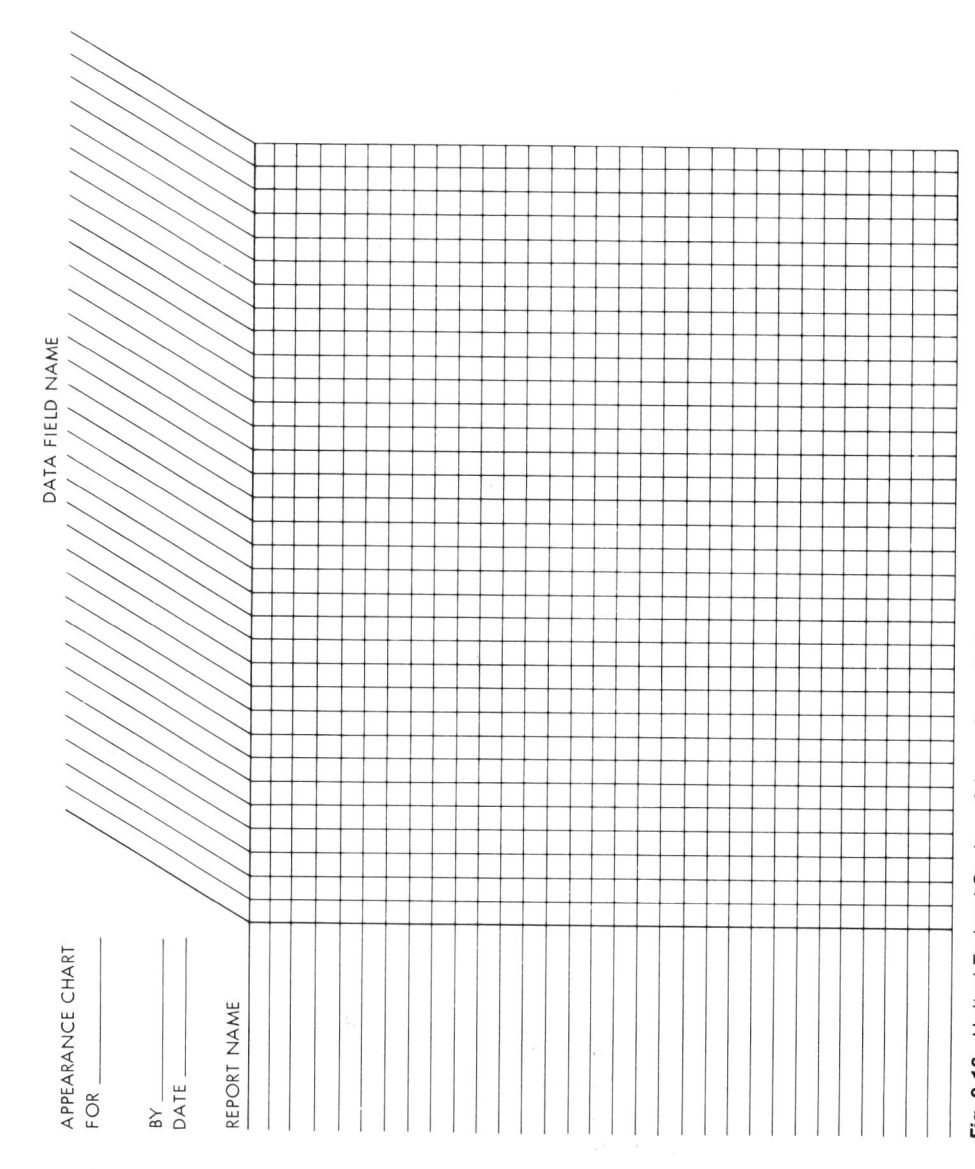

Fig. 9-18. United Federal Savings & Loan Association

PURCHASE ORDER PROCESSING

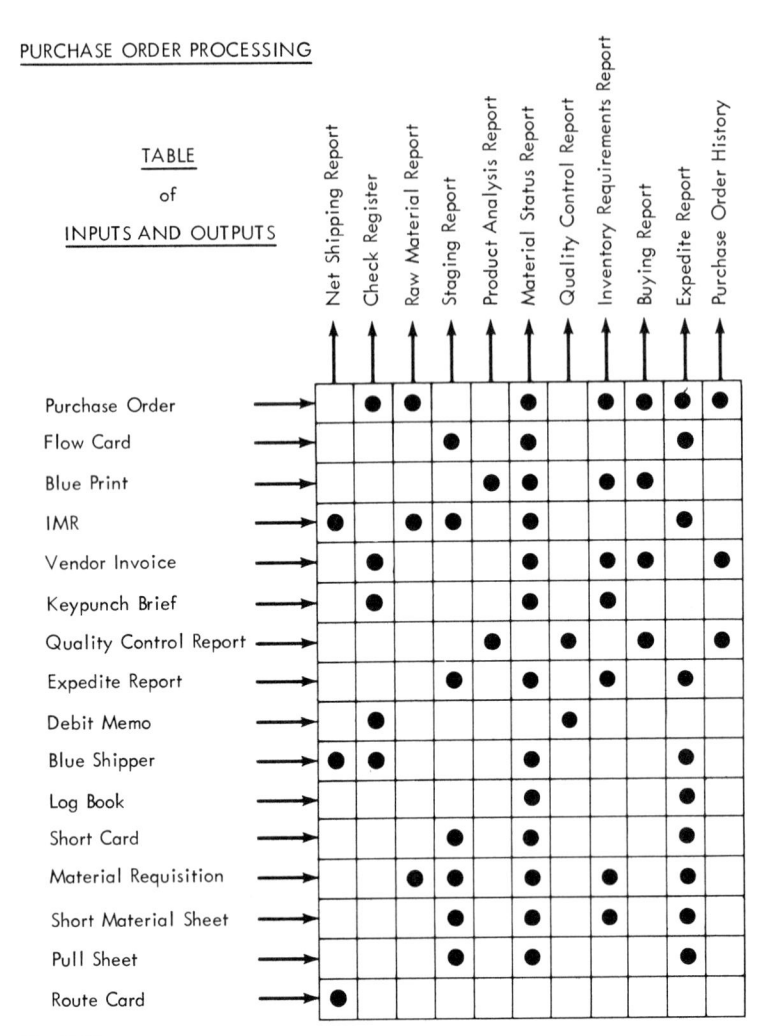

TABLE of INPUTS AND OUTPUTS

Input \ Output	Net Shipping Report	Check Register	Raw Material Report	Staging Report	Product Analysis Report	Material Status Report	Quality Control Report	Inventory Requirements Report	Buying Report	Expedite Report	Purchase Order History
Purchase Order		●	●			●		●	●	●	●
Flow Card				●		●				●	
Blue Print					●	●		●	●		
IMR	●		●	●		●				●	
Vendor Invoice		●				●		●	●		●
Keypunch Brief		●				●	●				
Quality Control Report					●		●		●		●
Expedite Report				●		●		●		●	
Debit Memo		●					●				
Blue Shipper	●	●				●				●	
Log Book						●				●	
Short Card				●		●				●	
Material Requisition			●	●		●		●		●	
Short Material Sheet				●		●		●		●	
Pull Sheet				●		●				●	
Route Card	●										

Fig. 9-19.
Courtesy of Airpax Inc.

Do titles reflect both work content and level of the position?

Position descriptions in the accounting department should also be consistent and reflect the objectives, the responsibilities, and the duties of the job. Although the human resource department generally works with employees and managers in accounting, everyone should understand the construction of position descriptions. They should not be inflated fantasies, but rather they should represent the actual characteristics of the position. In Table 9-4 and Figs. 9-21 and 9-22, we show a position description for a manager and two individual contributors.

Codes:
1- Usually on Order
2- On Order or Generated at in House Order Writing
3- Internal Information

SOURCE DATA	CODE	FINANCIAL INFORMATION														MARKETING INFORMATION									DISTRIBUTION				MANUFACTURING											
		CREDIT		PLANNING								CONTROL																												
		Order Acceptance	Projected Cash Collections	Projected Sales	Projected Profit Contrib.	Projected A/R	Backlogs	Projected Purchases	Projected Mfg. Requirements	Projected Distrib. Cost	Projected Cash Required	Plan vs Act. Sales	Plan vs. Act. Profit	Commission Expense	Inventory Balance	Forecasting	Item Avail. Delv. Control	Sales Follow-Up	Mailing List	Unusual Activity List	Customer Correspondence	Territory Sales Analy.	Salesmen Sales Analy.	Mark Down Control	Order Handling	Selection	Shipping	Allocation	Piece Goods Allocation	Trimmings Allocation	Machine Loading	Production Scheduling	Production Order Writing	W.I.P. Control	Materials Procurement	Materials W'housing	Manpower Planning	Production Planning	Facilities Planning	Materials Inventory
ORDER INFORMATION																																								
Date Written	1	×																							×			×												
Date Entered	3			×		×																						×												
Customer Order No.	1	×				×	×														×				×		×													
Our Order No.	3																				×				×		×	×												
Confirmation Status	3																								×															
CUSTOMER INFORMATION																																								
Customer Name & Address	1	×	×			×					×		×					×	×		×				×		×	×												
Ship To: Name & Address	1	×																×	×		×				×		×													
Buyer Name & Dept.	2																	×	×		×				×		×													
Customer Priority	3																								×			×												
Credit Rating (Limit)	3																	×																						
PRODUCT INFORMATION																																								
Lot Identification																																								
• Style - Name/No.	1			×	×		×	×	×	×		×	×		×	×	×	×		×	×				×	×	×	×	×	×	×	×	×	×	×					×
• Color - Name/No.	1				×		×	×	×				×		×	×	×	×		×	×				×	×	×	×	×	×			×	×	×					×
• Size	1				×		×	×	×				×		×	×	×	×		×	×				×	×	×	×					×	×						
Quantity Ordered	1	×	×	×	×	×	×	×	×	×	×				×	×	×	×		×	×				×	×	×	×	×	×	×	×	×	×	×	×	×	×	×	×
Unit Price	2	×	×	×	×	×	×				×	×												×																
SHIPPING INFORMATION																																								
Factory Name/No.	3																																							
Requested Delv. Date	1															×	×	×							×		×	×			×	×	×	×			×	×		×
Routing	2									×															×		×													
Cancellation Date																									×		×	×												
SALES INFORMATION																																								
$ Amount of Order	2	×		×			×							×								×	×																	
Salesmen Codes	3													×				×			×	×	×																	
Terms	2	×	×																		×																			
Discounts	2	×	×	×	×		×			×				×							×							×												
Season	2															×									×															
Territory																		×			×	×	×		×			×												

Fig. 9-20. Data Relationship Grid

Source: How Order Information Serves Apparel Management. American Apparel Manufacturers Association, 1974.

Table 9-1. Current and Proposed Computer Applications Departmental Users

Application	Building	City Clerk	Civil Service	Engineering	Finance	Fire	Planning	Police	Public Works	Recreation	Traffic Eng.	Utilities
Personnel	X	X	X	X	X	X	X	X	X	X	X	X
Budget Analysis	X	X	X	X	X	X	X	X	X	X	X	X
Budget Preparation	X	X	X	X	X	X	X	X	X	X	X	X
City Planning	X	X	X	X	X	X	X	X	X	X	X	X
Cost Accounting	X	X	X	X	X	X	X	X	X	X	X	X
Equipment Analysis	X	X	X	X	X	X	X	X	X	X	X	X
Inventory	X	X	X	X	X	X	X	X	X	X	X	X
Bldg. Code & Zoning												
Adm.	X			X			X					
Sign Renewal				X								
Payroll	X	X	X	X	X	X	X	X	X	X	X	X
Inspection Scheduling	X					X						
Cost Accounting	X	X	X	X	X	X	X	X	X	X	X	X
Street Analysis	X			X			X	X	X		X	X
Traffic Analysis				X			X				X	X
Special Assessments				X	X							
Water & Sewer				X								X
Traffic Adm.				X								
Engineering Calculations				X								
Construction Bids				X								
Purchasing					X							
Revenue					X							
Fire Incident						X						
Computer Aided Dispatching						X		X				
Intelligence								X				
Vehicle Reg.								X				
Police Reporting								X				
Traffic Enforcement								X				
Traffic Adm.								X			X	
Police Records								X				
Resource Allocation								X				
Traffic Citations								X				
Recreation								X		X	X	
Sanitation												X
Utility Billing												X
Periodic Main.									X			

Table 9-2.

REPORTS \ USERS	Credit & Lending	Investment	Audit	Operations	Bookkeeping	Accounting	Demand Deposits	Installment Loans	Commercial Loans	Budget	Board of Directors	President	Asst. President	Operations Mgr.	V.P. Loans	Bank Bookkeeping	Customer Service	Customer Books	V.P. Comm. Loans	Asst. V.P. Inst. Loan	Consumer Credit
Demand Account Overdrafts				■	■		■							■		■					
Return Item List				■	■		■							■		■					
Statement of Condition					■	■								■		■					
Payments on Past-Due Loans	■				■			■													
Report of Past-Due Loans	■							■													
Income & Expense Report				■		■				■	■	■		■		■					■
Statistical Comparison of Earn				■						■	■										
Securities Report		■			■						■			■							
Detailed Income & Exp. Report				■	■					■				■							
Past-Due Loans	■			■	■			■													
Daily Average Balance													■								

List of Operations, Filings, and Transports

A list of operations actually performed at the work stations is prepared. Interviews and observation may be used as cross checks. This list may be checked further against the position description.

In addition to performing operations, the incumbent may file, and remove from file, documents as part of the job. The incumbent may also transport records or documents from one work station to another. The

Table 9-3. Manager Input into File Matrix

MANAGER \ FILE	Accounting File	Customer Master File	Invoice Master File	Representative Master File	Receivables Master File	Order Hold File	Customer History File	Invoice History File
Production Supervisor	X							
Distribution Manager	X	X	X			X		X
Warehouse Manager	X							
Material and Inventory Mgr.	X					X		
Manufacturing Manager								
National Ind. Sales Mgr.		X		X			X	
National Auto. Sales Mgr.		X		X			X	
National Sales Coordinator		X	X			X	X	X
Vice Pres. of Sales/Marketing								
Chief Accountant	X	X	X		X		X	X
Assistant Controller								
Controller								
Non Prod. Purch. Corp. Services	X							
Director Info. Systems								
Director Personnel Adm.	X							
Vice President Administration								
Director Research/Develop								
Executive Vice President								

─────── No Input

Table 9-4. Job Description

TITLE: Controller

ORGANIZATION RELATIONSHIPS: Reports to President

PRIMARY FUNCTIONS: To protect the company's assets and provide adequate working capital to meet the needs of the business.

SPECIFIC DUTIES:
1. Devise and maintain adequate accounting records.
2. Plan, take, and calculate the physical inventory.
3. Oversee credits and collections of accounts receivable.
4. Oversee merchandise budgeting and control in cooperation with the merchandising division.
5. Oversee expense budgeting and control.
6. Prepare reports for general management.
7. Oversee insurance coverage and lease arrangements.
8. Assure safekeeping of all records prepared by or furnished to him.
9. Maintain familiarity with and compliance with governmental rules and regulations—local, state, and federal.
10. Prepare reports for governmental and other agencies.

process chart mentioned earlier is a useful tool in this phase of work station analysis.

Inputs and Outputs

Inputs of all forms (documents, verbal, video, and so on) and outputs to the work station should be tabulated for analysis. Content, format, frequency, source, and destination should be considered.

Equipment Used

Equipment used at accounting work stations may consist of desk computers, computer video terminals, typewriters, file tubs, special telephones, reproduction machines, and mechanical stamping devices. Any redesign of a work station must take into account not only the process but the equipment.

Work Relationships with Other Work Stations

By means of flowcharts or matrices, the interactions among work stations should be described. Frequency of contact and physical distance between stations are important considerations for office layout.

Fig. 9-21. Job Description for a Supervisor

Job Description

JOB TITLE: Assistant Treasurer and Bookkeeping
DEPARTMENT: OPERATIONS
SOURCE OF SUPERVISION: Vice President–Treasurer

JOB DUTIES AND METHODS:

Supervision of 3 departments (General Ledger and Bookkeeping Up and Downstairs)

All Monthly, Quarterly, Semi-Annual and Annual Reports

Closing of Community Federal and Comfed books annually

Back up on General Ledger and Payroll postings

Assembling of Accrual and Prepaid Accounts

Checking of expense bills being paid

Doing various statistical schedules and Reports for the Board of Directors and Associations.

Daily report-validate daily business

Post daily business to General Ledger

Check bank balances of each account each morning and report to officer

Do trial balance on General Ledger weekly and microfilm it.

Make up journal entries for each department and approve them

Must be available to answer questions that arise from any department

F.I.C.A. report every three months

Participation reports—S.W.D., Hawaii, Eustis, Waterbury

Does Board of Directors reports each month, quarter, and year.

Closing of the books (C.F.S. and Comfed)

Assists treasurer on all accrual and deferred accounts, Monthly & Quarterly.

In contact with computer center on any daily report problems.

Assistant Security Supervisor for Main Office alarm system, Monthly.

Set up furniture, fixture, and equipment depreciation cards.

Customer problems

Occasional job interview

Transfer funds from time deposit in F.H.L.B.

Notary Public

Give approval on checks for cash return

Helping with inter-office problems

Secondary Duties:

Set up new employee material

Check loans in process interest

In charge of Cash count—Monthly (Only if person in charge is not available)

Sells travelers cheques and bonds

Set up new share loans

Fig. 9-22a. Position Description for an Individual Worker

Data Processing Control Clerk

Reports to: Operations and Systems Supervisor

Department: Data Processing

Job responsibilities are as follows:
1. Receives input data from various departments and users; reviews input for acceptability; maintains log of all input activity.
2. Distributes input to keypunch and/or computer operations.
3. Sees that work is punched on cards and checked for proper format.
4. Controls work flow and schedule from keypunch to computer operations.
5. Supervises the keypunch operators in the absence of the Keypunch Supervisor and/or Lead Keypunch Operator.
6. Reviews output for acceptability.
7. Balances reports to control totals.
8. Checks for obvious errors; reports all suspected discrepancies and possible causes.
9. Maintains list of departments and individuals for receipt of input from and output to.
10. Responsible for the distribution of reports to the various departments—and/or individuals.
11. Maintains log of output distributed.
12. Notifies supervisor of schedule delays and all inadequacies.

Fig. 9-22b. Position Description for an Individual Worker

Senior Accounts Receivable Clerk

Report to: Accounts Receivable and Billing Supervisor

Department: Finance

Following are the duties performed:
1. Post cash receipts to customer accounts
2. Analysis of customer accounts
3. Type and send letters to clarify payments
4. Interpret promotions for correct cash application
5. Train new Account Receivable Clerks
6. Maintain distribution sheets for control and entry of cash application for preparation of monthly journal entry
7. Assist Accounts Receivable and Billing Supervisor in the supervision of the Accounts Receivable section of the Department.

Methods and Time Studies

Although the stopwatch time study in the office is certainly a rarity, methods for performing routine or repetitive operations are applicable. The basic principles of work methods such as placing materials close to their point of usage and the principles of finger, hand, and arm motions from industrial engineering are equally valid in the office. Predetermined time standards for motions may be used to establish a standard time for each task. If tasks are not repetitive, average time for a complete process (even involving several work stations) may be determined on the basis of a series of measurements of the entire process time.

Work Sampling

If there are many similar work stations or the cost of maintaining a certain work station is very high, the systems analyst may resort to the work sampling technique to find out how much of his/her time is spent on operations of various kinds, resting, telephoning, walking about, and so on. Work sampling requires hundreds of random-time observations of the incumbent and is somewhat expensive.

DECISION TABLES

A decision table (DT) is a visual means for showing how a rule (or set of rules) applies to repetitive situations. Table 9-5 demonstrates a simple example of a rule. An order for the company's product is received by a clerk. She examines the order and finds that the order comes from someone with whom the company has never done business. She therefore sends the order to the credit department. (If the order had come from a regular customer, she would have sent it to the shipping department.) The decision table shows the two possible conditions as statements. The two columns on the right each represent a rule. A rule says, "If conditions A, B, C, . . . exist, then take Action 1." In essence, the rule when applied to a specific case yields a *decision* on action to be taken.

One purpose of the MIS is to relieve managers from routine decision-making. Quite complex decision rules may be structured by the use of decision tables. *If a decision table can be formulated, the decision can be programmed for the computer to make!*

Another purpose of the DT is to force the decision-maker to clarify the basis of his decisions on objective rather than subjective grounds.

Table 9-5. Decision Rule

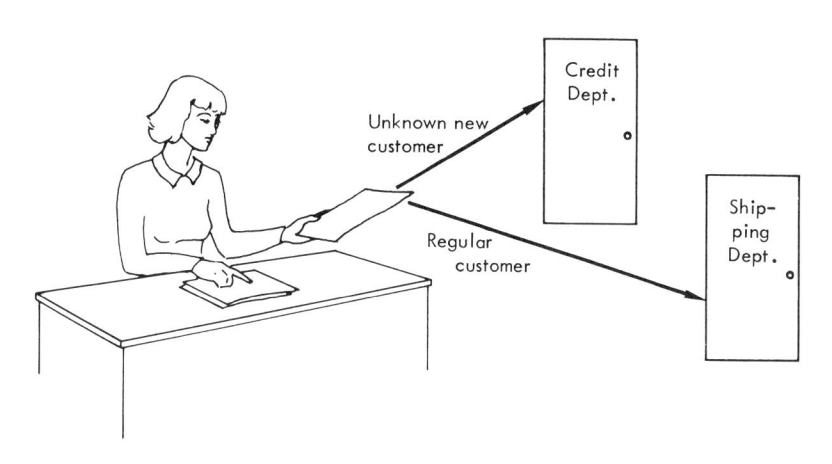

Conditions	Rules	
	1	2
Order from new customer	Yes	No
Order from regular customer	No	Yes
Action: Send to Credit Dept.	Yes	-
Action: Send to Shipping Dept.	-	Yes

Once this has been done, *consistency* of decision-making will result, even though several different people deal with the repetitive situations. In fact, if it is economical, the decision-making may again be turned over to the computer.

A further use of the DT is to facilitate communication between the manager and the systems analyst or programmer. The logic flowchart of the programmer can be converted to DT for the manager. On the other hand, the manager can represent his decision process through DT to the systems analyst in a form that can be readily converted to flow diagrams for computer programming.

Finally, the DT is a method of documentation in MIS that is easily prepared, changed, and updated.

Definitions

Decision tables are visual representations of a decision situation consisting of:

1. *Conditions*—factors to consider in making a decision.
2. *Actions*—steps to be taken when a certain combination of conditions exists.
3. *Rules*—specific combinations of conditions and the actions to be taken under those conditions.

We refer now to Table 9-6. In this table, C1 refers to condition 1, A1 refers to action 1; Y and N stand for Yes or No, the condition exists or it doesn't; X indicates the action to be taken. Rule 2, indicated as R2, says that C1 exists but C2 does not, so the credit should be approved.

Table 9-6. Simple Example of Limited Entry Decision Table

Credit Order Approval Procedure

		R1	R2	R3
C1	Pay experience favorable	—	Y	N
C2	Order is within credit limit	Y	N	N
A1	Approve credit	×	×	—
A2	Return the order to sales	—	—	×

Note: Check to see that latest credit information is used.

The parts that make up this table are shown in Table 9-7. The description of each part is:

1. *Condition statements*—statements that introduce one or more conditions.
2. *Condition entries*—entries that complete the condition statements.
3. *Action statements*—statements that introduce one or more conditions.
4. *Action entries*—entries that complete the action statements.
5. *Rules*—unique combinations of conditions and the actions to be taken under those conditions.

Table 9-7. Components of a Decision Table

Header		
		Rule identifiers
Action condition identifiers	Condition Statements	Condition entries
	Action statements	Action entries
Notes		

6. *Header*—a title and/or code identifying the table.
7. *Rule identifiers*—codes uniquely identifying each rule within a table.
8. *Condition identifiers*—codes uniquely identifying each condition statement/entry.
9. *Action identifiers*—codes uniquely identifying each action statement/entry.
10. *Notes*—comments concerning the contents of the tables. Notes are not required, but might be used to clarify some items recorded in the table.

Types of Decision Tables

There are three types of decision tables: limited entry, extended entry, and mixed entry. Table 9-6 is a limited entry table because the entries give simple "yes" and "no" answers to condition and action statements.

In an extended entry table, the wording of all statements carry over into the condition and action entries. Table 9-8 gives us an example. The third type of table, mixed entry, is one in which there are some limited entries and some extended entries.

Open tables are tables wherein the last action of each rule tells you to go to another table and gives the name and number of this next table.

Closed tables are those which don't tell you where to go when the table is completed. Control remains with the original table, which sends you to a closed table. When the closed table has been executed, you return to the original table.

Guidelines for Constructing a DT

When beginners start to make decision tables, they tend to make them too large. Often several small tables are better than one large table be-

Table 9-8. Extended Entry Decision Table

	Policy Coverage			
C1	Miles driven per year	<8000	<15,000	≧15,000
C2	Age of youngest driver	>24	>24	≦24
C3	Driving record	Good	Good	Fair
C4	Major use	Pleasure	Pleasure	Business
A1	Type of policy	A	D	J
A2	Policy limit	100/300	75/50	25/50

cause the decision may be made in the first table, or at worst, by the use of two small tables. The size that best facilitates communication should be sought.

In constructing tables, keep the following points in mind:

1. All possible rules must be presented.
2. Every rule must have an action entry associated with it. That is, a rule must state the action to be taken under a given set of conditions.
3. Tables can be mere action tables consisting of a single rule; i.e., the only condition satisfied is that the table is entered. Such a table is illustrated in Table 9-9. The condition "enter" implies that a decision-maker/reader has entered the table from somewhere outside the table. That being the case, the indicated actions are then taken.
4. Rules are unique and independent—they do not duplicate or contradict one another. Therefore, only one rule will apply in any given situation.
5. The sequence of rules is immaterial, because only one rule can satisfy the conditions in a given situation.
6. Within a rule, an "and" relationship exists among applicable conditions and actions. That is, for a rule to be satisfied, the first applicable condition *and* the second applicable condition *and* the third must exist. Likewise, all of the applicable actions must be taken.
7. Within a rule an "if-then" relationship exists between conditions and actions. That is, a rule implies that *if* certain conditions exist *then* certain actions are to be taken.

Some rules for constructing a DT are:
Rule 1—Define specific boundaries for the decision problem.

   a. Define the objective. For example, a firm may have the option of answering a sales inquiry by personal telephone call, sending out a salesman, writing a letter, or ignoring it. The objective of the decision table would be to provide a decision for the order-inquiry dispatcher.
   b. Identify the variables. In our example, customer characteristics, size of order, and timing might be the variables that affect the decision.

Table 9-9. Single-Rule Action Table

Morning Routine

		R1
C1	Enter	Y
A1	Check sales report	×
A2	Call shipping on delayed sales	×
A3	Make scheduled sales calls	×

c. Set limits and ranges on the variables. Thus, orders between $2000 and $5000 might be a range that would influence the decision heavily toward making a personal telephone call. Orders over $500 might be the limit set to trigger off sending a salesman, *provided* some other condition statements such as credit rating were favorable.

Rule 2—Enumerate individual elementary decisions. Rarely are real-world decisions simply "yes" or "no." Often, decisions call for further steps and decisions.

Rule 3—Define all alternative outcomes.

Rule 4—Develop the set of value states (conditions) that yield each outcome.

Rule 5—Assign a decision to each outcome.

DATA GATHERING

The accounting systems analyst quickly learns that data gathering is a complex process. It does not consist of simply asking questions and receiving expertly formulated and responsive answers. Rather, data gathering consists of using a number of techniques to help piece together the total situation.

Methods of Data Gathering

Our emphasis here with regard to data gathering is in the operational and managerial problems at the operational, tactical, and strategic levels. The AIS analyst must be careful not to restrict his search simply to apparent financial areas. Financial and accounting data are so closely interrelated with operating systems (such as order processing or production planning) and with functional management (such as marketing) that analysts must obtain a broad view of the business as a whole. Without this view, his perceptions and evaluations may be dangerously distorted.

Methods of data gathering are:

1. *Search* for and examine records such as organization charts, files, reports and report forms, flowcharts, system descriptions, position guides of managers, and records of major decisions. Plans and problems reported with implementation of plans should be sought, as should correspondence that indicates customer complaints, vendor complaints, or other indicators of company problems.

Table 9-10. General Questionnaire

POSITION TITLE: DATE:

1. What are the major problems you anticipate facing over the next two years?
2. What information would you like to have to help you solve such problems, that is not available to you under present circumstances?
3. What repetitive problems do you face that you feel could be resolved by the development of a set of rules (decision table) or model (mathematical relationship) to yield the "best" answer?
4. What reports do you receive that you don't have time to read at all?
5. What reports do you receive so frequently that you read one only once in a while?
6. What reports do you receive that are much more detailed than you need?
7. If you had more time, what operations or systems for which you are responsible do you feel could be significantly improved?

---

2. Utilize *questionnaires* to obtain from managers their ideas of their information needs. The questionnaires may be loosely structured by asking broad questions (see Table 9-10) with regard to problems, types of information they would like to receive, frequency, and detail. On the other hand, the systems designer, *in a particular company and organizational situation,* may elect to develop more detailed questionnaires tailored to each individual manager (see Table 9-11 for example).

3. *Interview* managers and key personnel.

4. *Sample* inputs, outputs, or status. For example, take a sample of sales orders, customers, complaints, inspection reports, and employee grievances to determine where problems may be occurring. Sample machine down time, records of ages of machines, computer center log, back orders, or even scrap containers. In particular, sample opinions of operating employees. *Statistical* sampling allows fairly rigorous conclusions to be drawn in many cases concerning needs or problems.

5. Utilize job station analysis.

6. *Estimate* cost savings or revenue gains due to changes in the present MIS and concurrent changes in operations. Such estimates are, of course,

Table 9-11. Structured Questionnaire

POSITION TITLE: MARKETING MANAGER   DATE:

1. What information would you like to have to help you estimate market potential and forecast sales?
2. Would you like information on structural change of our industry such as mergers, new competitors, etc., besides what you are now getting?
3. What information would help you with pricing decisions?
4. What additional information about customers do you desire?
5. What additional information would help you to find, evaluate, and select new products for your company?
6. What additional information do you need to make product decisions on mix, lines of products, warranties, price/quality combination, etc.?
7. What additional information do you need to control sales operations?
8. What type of information would help you in making major promotional decisions?
9. Are you obtaining adequate information on new technological developments? Government and legal actions?
10. Do you need more information on channels of distribution? Physical distribution?

extremely crude at the information-gathering stage but may suggest priority of emphasis in gathering further information.

Guides for Data Gathering

We recall that managers make strategic decisions, tactical decisions, and implementation decisions. Under these headings we would seek accounting and financial data that would assist managers in:

1. Identifying opportunities for the company in the marketplace
2. Describing the long-range goals and strategies of the company
3. Evaluating goals and strategies
4. Developing marketing systems, manufacturing systems, financial, and other systems within the company which are related to the total operational system of the company
5. Developing standards of performance, methods of measurement, and methods of control over long-range and operational activities
6. Achieving greater effectiveness (reaching goals) and greater efficiency (decreasing costs)
7. Preventing disasters.

Elaboration of Interview Techniques

The AIS systems analyst will eventually interview job station employees, professional staff people, and managers. If the project is oriented toward a management AIS, the analyst will probably start with the highest level of management user and work down. This will present a hierarchy of management needs.

If the particular project is oriented toward improved efficiency and the generation of more timely and better reports within the existing MIS, the AIS analyst will likely interview managers after he has gained a thorough understanding of the system details. The analyst is then in a position to discuss changes in the AIS from the management view.

Here are important guides to effective interviewing:

Prepare a Plan Ahead of Time

Study the situation by examining available documents ahead of time. Make sure that you understand the *scope* and *objective* of the AIS project. Find out about the nature of the person you will interview.

Schedule the Interview

The interviewer should establish a schedule for his interviews. No interviews should be scheduled just before lunch, or late in the afternoon (or on Friday afternoon, if possible), because interviewees are apt to be tired or anxious to get away from the office. The systems analyst should remind the manager several days in advance of the forthcoming interview.

Approval

The systems designer should not enter a department for any interview without obtaining permission from the department manager.

Selling a Service

Outside investigators coming into a department are usually viewed with suspicion and distrust. In the initial interview, the systems analyst must gain the trust and confidence of the respondent. To do this, he must present his role as a *service* to the respondent. He must not come on strong as an efficiency expert. An informal manner and a sincere desire to uncover problems he can help with through the AIS are important. The first interview should be short; the objectives of the study and the involvement of all personnel in the study should be brought out. Broad questions may be raised so that both parties will think about their elaboration before subsequent meetings.

Conducting the Interview

The systems analyst should try to obtain a location where there will be no distractions. He should attempt to keep the interview on the subject to make the most of the time the manager has allocated to him. Questions that can be answered "yes" or "no" should be avoided because they may elicit snap judgments or easy agreements. In fact, the interviewer should encourage "thinking time" before answers.

The systems analyst is at the interview to learn. He should avoid any intimation of criticism. Rather he should encourage the idea that every healthy organization constantly seeks new ideas and ways to improve.

The systems analyst must be interested and show interest in what the respondent is saying at all times. He should never contradict or express disagreement with the interviewee; he is there to *get* information, not give it or stifle it.

Note-taking may slow down the interview and make it difficult for the systems analyst to probe more deeply into problems. If possible, a tape recorder should be used. This requires agreement with the interviewee in advance as to how tape will be used.

Interviews should be brought to a close when the respondent shows signs of fatigue or restlessness. The interview should not be terminated abruptly, however. A review of key ideas, followed by a brief interval or pause, may cause an important idea to surface at this time.

Investigation Questions

Investigation questions for managers may deal with such topics as suggested below or as appropriate for the problem at hand. Possible questions are:

1. What are your principal responsibilities, goals, and problems, as *you* see them?
2. What programs are you now administering?
3. What are your sources of information?
   a. What reports or documents do you receive—how frequently, and how timely?
   b. What action do you take with the documents?
   c. What information do you find it necessary to request because it is not supplied to you routinely?
   d. What other information do you receive periodically or by request through other modes (telecommunications, video, staff meetings, etc.)?
   e. What documents or formal transmittals of information do you prepare, and to whom do these go?
4. What information do you receive that is unnecessary for your job?
5. What information would you like to receive to aid you with planning, implementing, and controlling?
6. What files do you maintain in your office?
7. What information in your files is also stored in other files?
8. What suggestions do you have for rearranging responsibilities, relationships, and work systems to form an integrated system for your department and all components to which your department relates?
9. Describe how you feel toward the computer center as providing a systems type of service for the company.
10. How do you feel about using a computer terminal in your office to ask "What if . . . ?" questions for planning?
11. How do you feel about all managers becoming familiar with the use of computer terminals through short workshop programs?

SIMULATION

Simulation means to "make like" the real system in process, in the context of AIS. Simulation will not provide optimization except by trial and error. It will provide comparisons of alternative systems or show how a particular system works under specified conditions. It requires a representation of the system and/or a representation of the inputs to the system. Thus we can:

1. Use the actual AIS and introduce the kind of job mixes and timings that we think will occur in actual practice. Representative job mixes are called "benchmarks."
2. Use the actual job mixes and timings and run them through a simplified version of the system, a portion of the system, or a computerized model of the system.
3. Use the kind of job mixes and timings we think will occur and run them through a computerized model.
4. Use extreme values of the job mix and run them through a computerized model.

In real life, we find that work (input) usually arrives in a random fashion. For example, invoices reach a clerk's desk or customer orders by the day. (An exception, of course, is the paced mass production line.) When it arrives at a desk or work station it must wait its turn in line to be serviced. Also, the length of time it takes a person or "work station" to service a work unit (such as preparing a customer's order, a purchase order, assembling a component, starting a computer run, or preparing a report) varies randomly. The complexity of many random arrivals and random transactions (servicings) in a system and the complex relationships with the system can only be handled economically with a computer.

Components of Simulation

Simulation depends upon four basic concepts. These are probability distributions of arrivals of units to be serviced, probability of service times, a model that represents the flow of work and/or information, and a computer.

Example

Now that we have told you how complex it is to simulate a system, we will show you several simulations of a very simple system as done with pencil and paper. In practice, the computer may perform hundreds or thousands of simulations to obtain probability distributions of the output rate.

In Figure 9-23, a and c in our case are based upon historical rela-

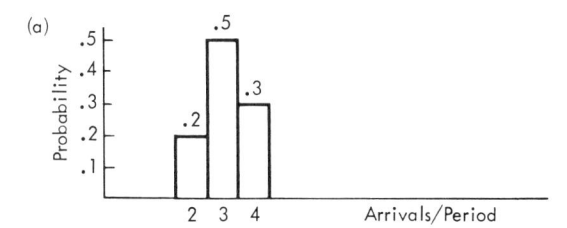

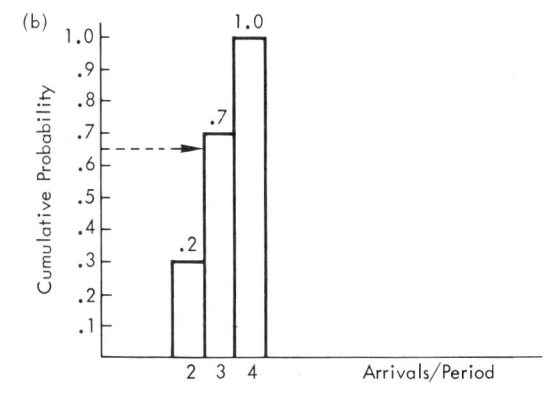

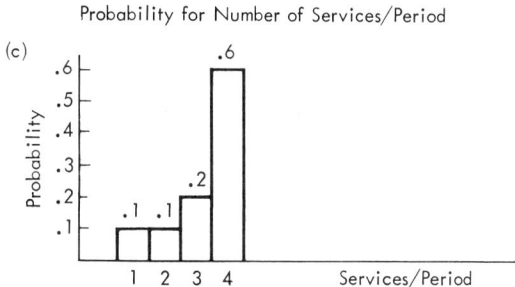

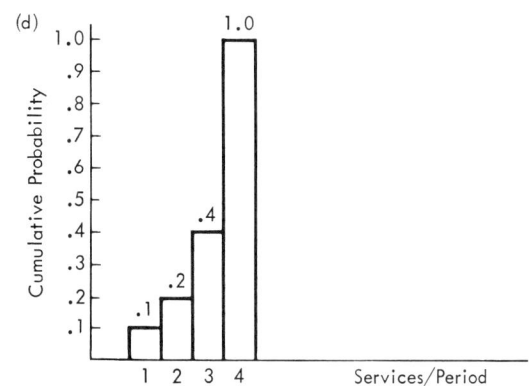

Fig. 9-23. Probability Distributions

329

tive frequencies or estimates by the system designer. Figure 9-23 b and d are the corresponding cumulative probability distributions.

In our example, we assume that nothing happens in the first period as the employee sets up his work. The simulation procedure is as follows:

1. Set up table headings to represent the time and position characteristics of each item in the system as in Table 9-12.
2. Obtain a table of random numbers (found in most statistic texts or math tables). A portion of a table of such unrelated numbers is shown in Table 9-13.
3. Select a row and column, *and then* proceed to the RN table. We selected the first and second column to start and decided to read *down*. Enter the RN in the table representing the system. The number was .63 for the first column and .17 for the second column.
4. Go to the first cumulative probability chart (b), find .63 on the vertical scale. Draw a horizontal line to the bar it first meets. This is the 3 arrivals/period bar. Enter 3 in the table in the appropriate column.
5. Go to the second cumulative probability chart and find .17 on the vertical scale. Draw a horizontal line to the bar it first meets. This is the 2 units serviced/period bar. Enter 2 in the appropriate column in the table.
6. Units arriving minus units serviced in the period gives a surplus of one waiting to be serviced in the next period.
7. Repeat steps 3 through 5, keeping track of units left over to be serviced in each following period, *if any*.

Note that no matter how complex the system may be, simulation consists of examining the inputs, waiting lines, services, and output at one particular time period. Then the "clock" is moved up one time period and the system is examined again. After hundreds of simulations, breakdowns in the system may be noted or average waiting periods or average total service times through many different transactions may be found, or idle times may be noted.

Besides statistically varying inputs, systems designers like to know how the system will respond to sudden surges in the quantity of inputs

Table 9-12. Simulation of Customer Order Processing for Three Periods

PERIOD	RN	UNITS ARRIVING DURING THE PERIOD	RN	UNITS SERVICED DURING THE PERIOD*	UNITS IN LINE WAITING TO BE SERVED AT END OF PERIOD
1	—	0	—	0	0
2	.63	3	.17	2	1
3	.87	4	.03	1	4
4	.11	2	.42	3	3

*These would proceed to the next station.

Table 9-13. Portion of a Table of Random Numbers

6317	5497	5736	9468
8703	0234	2454	6094
1142	9821	6650	2749
5613	9681	9971	0081

(step functions), steady and more gradual increases in input (ramp functions), or oscillating inputs. Simulation may provide answers in all cases.

When inputs consist of representative job mixes, the simulation is called "benchmark simulation."

Advantages and Disadvantages

The advantages of simulation are:

1. When a model has been constructed, it may be used over and over to analyze all kinds of different situations.
2. Simulation allows modeling of systems whose solutions are too complex to express by one or several grand mathematical relationships.
3. Simulation requires a much lower level of mathematical skill than do analytical (mathematical) models.
4. Simulation is usually cheaper than building the actual system and testing it in operation.

The disadvantages of simulation are:

1. Simulation models may be very costly to construct and program for the computer.
2. Running a simulation program often requires hundreds of simulations and consequently much computer time. This may be very costly.
3. Because it is so easy to carry out the steps of developing a simulation model, people tend to employ simulation when analytic (mathematical modeling) techniques are better and more economical.

Simulation Languages

If a simulation of a system were to be programmed in FORTRAN, a great deal of effort would be required to include all the detail, much of the effort being repetitive in nature. Therefore, simulation languages have been developed that allow the system designer to write down *characteristics* of the system components so that the built-in computer program will take over from this description. Programming of elemental time steps is not required.

We present here only enough to give the reader the flavor of two of these languages. To know that they exist is enough to know to seek your local computer programmer.

GPSS

In GPSS (General Purpose Systems Simulation), a system is described by terms of four types of entities:

1. Dynamic
2. Statistical
3. Equipment
4. Operational

Each entity is described by its own standard numerical attributes (SNA). For example, suppose a series of invoices arrive at the accounting department for processing and payment. These "dynamic" entities are described by "transit time" (accumulated time in the system waiting and being processed) and priority relative to others in the system. The accounting department is an "equipment" entity and is called a "facility."

A simple queueing system is represented by the block diagram in Fig. 9-24. The first block indicates that the computer program will generate the arrival of invoices according to a uniform (equal) probability distribution with mean of 12 time periods and range of 12 ± 4 periods. Equally spaced arrival times or other probability functions may be specified in GPSS. In the second block, the invoice is told to enter waiting line 1. Block 3 tells the invoice to attempt to be serviced in FACILITY 1. When FACILITY 1 is available, the invoice departs from the waiting line as instructed by Block 4 and enters the FACILITY. Block 5, ADVANCE, provides the random time interval for servicing the invoice. Block 6 releases the FACILITY for further processing. Block 7 says to tabulate certain information which the user of the simulation desires and has previously specified on card 70. Finally, the transaction (invoice) is TERMINATED and leaves the system.

This example shows only a few of 43 specific block types available in GPSS.

Simscript II

SIMSCRIPT II is a language that is divided into essentially five levels. Level 1 is a very basic programming language for teaching

(1)	GENERATE 12,4 A,G,F	Create transaction into system A,G,F fields not used Average time is 12 and range is 12 ± 4 periods
(2)	QUEUE 1	Transaction enters queue number 1
(3)	SEIZE	Transaction attempts to get facility 1
(4)	DEPART 1	Leave queue 1 when facility is taken
(5)	ADVANCE 10,3	Average time delay for processing of transactions is 10 and range is 10 ± 3 periods
(6)	RELEASE 1	Release facility 1 for further processing
(7)	TABULATE 70	Collect transit time information as specified in TABLE card #70 supplied by user of the simulation
(8)	TERMINATE 1	Leave system

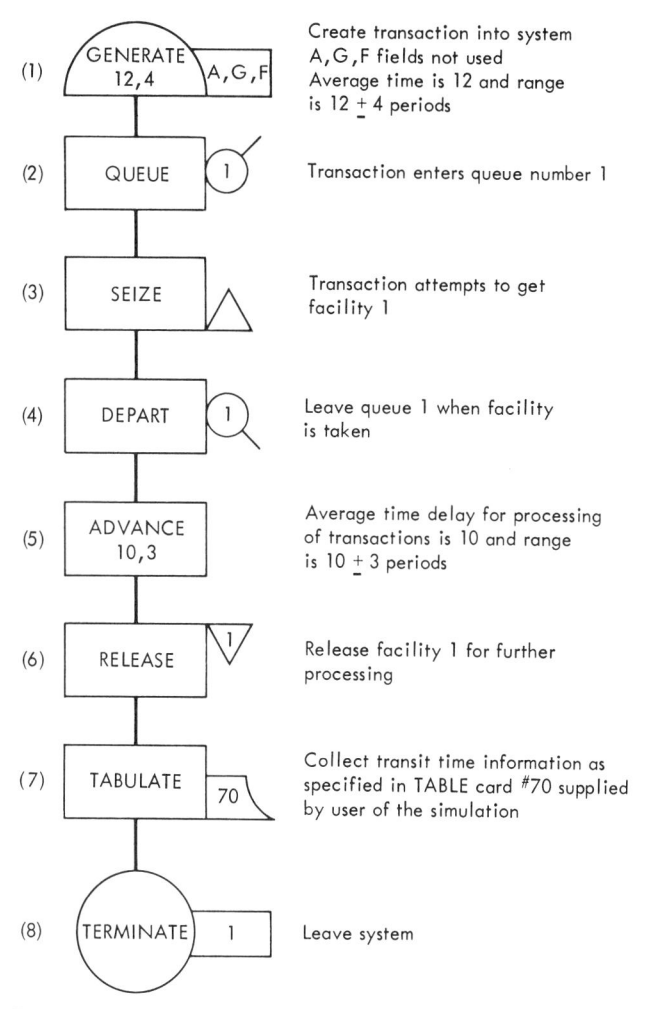

Fig. 9-24. GPSS Flowchart of the System for Processing an Invoice

programming concepts. The highest, Level 5, introduces the simulation features such as time-advance routines, event and activity processing, process generation, accumulation and analysis of statistical information.

The concepts used in SIMSCRIPT are

> *Entities*—things that exist in the simulated world
> > Temporary—such as a job which passes through for processing and then leaves the system
> > Permanent—receipt times of a service facility, types of machines, types of personnel, etc.
>
> *Attributes*—characteristics of entities such as number of each type of machine, age of each type of machine, number of each type of personnel

Sets—sets to which entities belong or are made up of

Events
{ *Exogenous*—events that arise from outside the simulation process such as the addition of new machines into the system
Endogenous events which are caused by prior occurrences in the simulation }

DOCUMENTATION

Documentation is one of the most important steps in AIS design and is the one most inadequately performed. Documentation is the physical record, generally in written or printed form, describing the structure of, operation of, method for testing, and method for revising the AIS. It provides descriptions of the system from the most general nature down to the finest detail, if it is carried out properly. *The AIS has not been completely designed until the documentation has been completed.*

Purposes of Documentation

Documentation of the AIS may save a company hundreds of thousands of dollars. Some companies have depended on a key individual who has kept the information flows and programs in his head, only to have him leave the company. The only choice of the company was then to restudy the entire system and document it or design a new system. Some of the reasons, then, that *good* documentation is important are:

1. Turnover of key personnel. If the AIS designer failed to document the system or did an inadequate or piecemeal job, his successor must restudy the system to solve problems or make modifications.
2. The AIS will require modification, either for improvement or because of changing conditions. Even if there is no personnel turnover, it is very unlikely that systems analysts can retain all details of the AIS in their heads over a period of time.
3. The increasing complexity of the fourth- and fifth-generation computer systems and data transmission systems will require documentation so that the original systems designers will not have to keep refamiliarizing themselves with equipment as the AIS design progresses.
4. Equipment conversion will require new flowcharts and new programs. Good documentation will make this much easier to carry out.
5. Documentation will reveal poor design features and lack of standards so that corrective action may be taken.

Specification, Standardization, Presentation, and Preservation

The four components of good documentation are specification, standardization, presentation, and preservation.

Specification

Specification means a clear, sufficiently detailed description. At the beginning of the AIS design process, *performance* specifications are prepared that describe objectives of the system. During the detailed design process, *design* specifications should be prepared that describe the systems. Then *operating* specifications should be prepared that describe the functions and activities of personnel who run the system. Finally, *test* specifications describe the tests and their conduct for checking out the system.

Standardization

The use of standardized procedures and standardized documentation provides a basis for clear, rapid communication, for less costly training of analysts, for reduced filing costs, and for assessing performance of the analysts and the AIS.

Standardization means that standard symbols are used in all flowcharts, that procedures manuals are prepared to prescribe standardized AIS and operating procedures, and that standardized forms are used for documentation.

Sources of standards are:

1. American National Standards Institute (ANSI) and International Standards Organization (ISO)
2. Industry users
3. Manufacturers
4. Published articles and books
5. Internal company staff organizations.

Maintenance of standards is achieved by publication of a manual of standards and proper training and control.

Documentation

Documentation of the AIS should be combined into a *documentation manual*. Table 9-14 suggests the possible contents of such a manual.

Table 9-14. Documentation Manual

Topic	Purpose	Forms	Tables	Diagrams	Narrative
I Total MIS					
A. System objectives	Defines what the system is supposed to achieve				X
B. Performance specifications	States each requirement of the system, preferably in quantitative terms		X		X
C. Conceptualization	Describes the gross design or arrangement of subsystems			X	X
D. System flowchart	Shows flow of information through the MIS as well as relationships with the operating systems			X	
E. Data base					
1. File organization	Describes the file organization and retrieval method	X			
2. Data element descriptions	Defines and describes data elements	X			
3. File interrelationships			X		
F. Model base description	Lists models, applications, and presents the models in detail		X		X
G. Output description	Describes the medium, the format, the frequency, and the uses of each MIS output	X	X	X	X
II System Operation					
A. Work flowchart	Shows the sequence of operations of the operating system and the forms that accompany the work from station to station			X	
B. Processing instructions	Gives step-by-step procedures for processing data before it goes into the computer, during, and after	X	X	X	X
C. Other instructions	Defines special actions required for MIS operations				X
III Computer programs					
A. Identification	Shows program number and subsystem identification	X	X	X	
B. Input definition	Defines the medium (cards, tapes, optical reader, etc.) and formats of input	X	X		
C. Processing	Describes the computer logic for the MIS programs		X	X	
D. Output definition	Defines the medium and format of output reports and displays	X			X
IV User's manual					
A. System description	Defines the objectives of the system, the arrangement of subsystems, and the general flow of work and information			X	X
B. Data preparation	Gives instructions on how to prepare and edit data entering the MIS		X		X

Table 9-14. Documentation Manual (cont'd)

Topic	Purpose	Forms	Tables	Diagrams	Narrative
C. Error correction procedures	Explains how to correct errors made in operating the MIS which yield error messages			X	
D. Linear responsibility chart	Specifies the specific tasks and roles of each person in the MIS (in matrix form)		X		
E. Glossary of terms	Defines terms and abbreviations used in the MIS		X		

The reasons for poor documentation stem from the attitude of management. When management constantly presses for new developments and new jobs, documentation receives a low priority. Documentation is a tedious detailed job at best, and systems designers are only too glad to turn to new, more exciting work. If management wants good documentation, it must rate the documentation manual as the completion event of design. Until the manual has been published, the AIS project manager must retain responsibility for an unfinished project.

Summary

We have provided information on a number of techniques utilized in the design of accounting information systems. The discussion of each topic is limited in scope to provide a starting point for the practicing accountant. The accountant who specializes in system design will need to refer to specialized texts on each of the topics covered.

DISCUSSION QUESTIONS AND PROBLEMS

1. Why is project planning needed for AIS development?
2. Define the terms: PERT, CPM, Events, Activity, Expected Time, Slack Time.
3. What are the advantages and disadvantages of using PERT/CPM for project control?

4. List the various types of flowcharts and distinguish among system block diagrams, forms flowcharts, and process flowcharts.
5. Develop a process flowchart showing the logic you used from the time you left home today until you arrived on campus.
6. Prepare a system flowchart for:
   a. student registration
   b. accounts receivable system for a retail store
7. a. Define: "Work Station Analysis."
   b. Relate this technique to flowcharting.
   c. Develop a work station analysis for a bank teller.
8. Discuss "Decision Tables." Include uses on purposes and comparison with alternatives.
9. List and discuss six or more methods of data collection used in developing AIS.
10. Design an interview program you could use to interview a manager of the accounts payable department.
11. a. List and discuss the advantages and disadvantages of using simulation for an order processing system
    b. By simulating the job station inputs and processing times, would it be possible to develop a useful simulation of the order processing system? Give reasons for your conclusion.
12. List and discuss several reasons for documenting the system.
13. Relative to Table 9-14, why is more than one documentation technique being used to describe several of the topics in the AIS?

Bibliography

PROJECT PLANNING AND CONTROL

ARCHIBALD, RUSSELL D. and RICHARD L. VILLORIA. *Network-based Management Systems,* New York: Wiley, 1967.

BRANDON, DICK H. and MAX GRAY. *Project Control Standards,* New York: Brandon/Systems Press, 1970.

GUNDERMAN, JAMES R. and FRANK W. MCMURRY, "Making Project Management Effective," *Journal of Systems Management,* February 1975.

LISTON, DAVID M., JR. and MARY L. SCHOENE, "A Systems Approach to the Design of Information Systems," *Journal of the American Society for Information Science,* March–April 1971.

METZGER, PHILIP W. *Managing a Programming Project.* Englewood Cliffs, N.J.: Prentice-Hall, 1973.

SHAW, JOHN C. and WILLIAM AKINS. *Managing Computer System Projects.* New York: McGraw-Hill Book Co., 1970.

Wiest, Jerome K. and Ferdinand K. Levy. *A Management Guide to PERT/CPM*, Englewood Cliffs, N.J.: Prentice-Hall, 1969.

Willoughby, Theodore C. "Origins of Systems Projects," *Journal of Systems Management*, October 1975.

FLOWCHARTING

Burch, John G., Jr. and Felix R. Srater, Jr. *Information Systems: Theory and Practice*, Santa Barbara, Cal.: Hamilton Publishing, 1974.

Kindred, Alton R. *Data Systems and Management*, Englewood Cliffs, N.J.: Prentice-Hall, 1973. (See Chapter 5, "Systems Flow Charting.")

Murdick, Robert G. and Joel E. Ross. *Introduction to Management Information Systems*, Englewood Cliffs, N.J.: Prentice-Hall, 1977.

DATA-FLOW MATRICES

Arlington, Va., "How Order Information Serves Apparel Management," American Apparel Manufacturers' Association, 1974.

Chen, Hui-Chuan and Russell C. Kick, Jr., "A Computer-Based Financial Management System for Small Business," *Management Adviser*, November–December 1973.

Murdick, Robert G. and Joel E. Ross. *Introduction to Management Information Systems*, Englewood Cliffs, N.J.: Prentice-Hall, 1977.

"Small Business," *Management Adviser*, November–December 1973.

Stults, Fred C. "Data Information, and Decision Making," *Journal of Systems Management*, June 1971.

JOB-STATION ANALYSIS

Buffa, Elwood D. *Basic Production Management*, New York: Wiley, 1971. (See Chapter 11, "Design of Jobs and Work Methods.")

Maynard, H. B. (ed.). *Handbook of Business Administration*. New York: McGraw Hill Book Co., 1967. (See Chapter 6, "Office Work Measurement.")

Neuner, John J. W., B. Lewis Keeling and Norman F. Kallaus. *Administrative Office Management*, Cincinnati, Ohio: South-Western, 1972. (See Chapter 18, "Analyzing Office Jobs.").

Schatz, Harvey E. "The Uses of Work Management." *Management Services*, November–December 1969

DATA GATHERING

Collard, Albert F. "Sharpening Interviewing Skills," *Journal of Systems Management*, December 1975.

Gross, Paul, and Robert D. Smith. *Systems Analysis and Design for Management*, New York: Dun-Donnelly, 1976. (See pp. 222–241.)

Hartman, W., H. Matthes, and A. Proeme. *Management Information Systems Systems Handbook*, New York: McGraw-Hill Book Co., 1968. (See section 6-3, "Data Gathering.")

Koudrey, Herbert J. "Techniques of Interviewing," *Journal of Systems Management*, May 1972.

Rubin, Martin L. *Introduction to the System Life Cycle,* Princeton, N.J.: Brandon/Systems Press, 1970. (See pp. 62–66.)

Video Assisted Instruction Guide to System Analyst Training. Elk Grove Village, Ill.: Advanced Systems, Inc., 1971.

SIMULATION

Kiviat P. J., R. Villanueva and H. M. Markowitz. *The Simscrpt II Programming Language,* Englewood Cliffs, N.J.: Prentice-Hall, 1969.

Schmidt, J. W. and R. E. Taylor. *Simulation and Analysis of Industrial Systems,* Homewood, Ill.: Richard D. Irwin, 1970.

GPSS/360 *Introductory User's Manual,* IBM Corp.

GPSS/360 *User's Manual,* IBM Corp.

DOCUMENTATION

Bingham, J. E. and G. W. Davies. *A Handbook of Systems Analysis,* New York: Wiley, 1972.

Glans, Thomas N., et al. *Management Systems,* New York: Holt, Rinehart and Winston, 1968.

"Systems Documentation," *Journal of Systems Management,* December 1970.

Preview:
Forms are a critical part of data collection and great care must be exercised in designing forms properly. This chapter discusses many considerations for establishing good communication.
−Cost
−Classification
−Forms analysis
−Forms design

CHAPTER TEN

forms design, analysis, and control

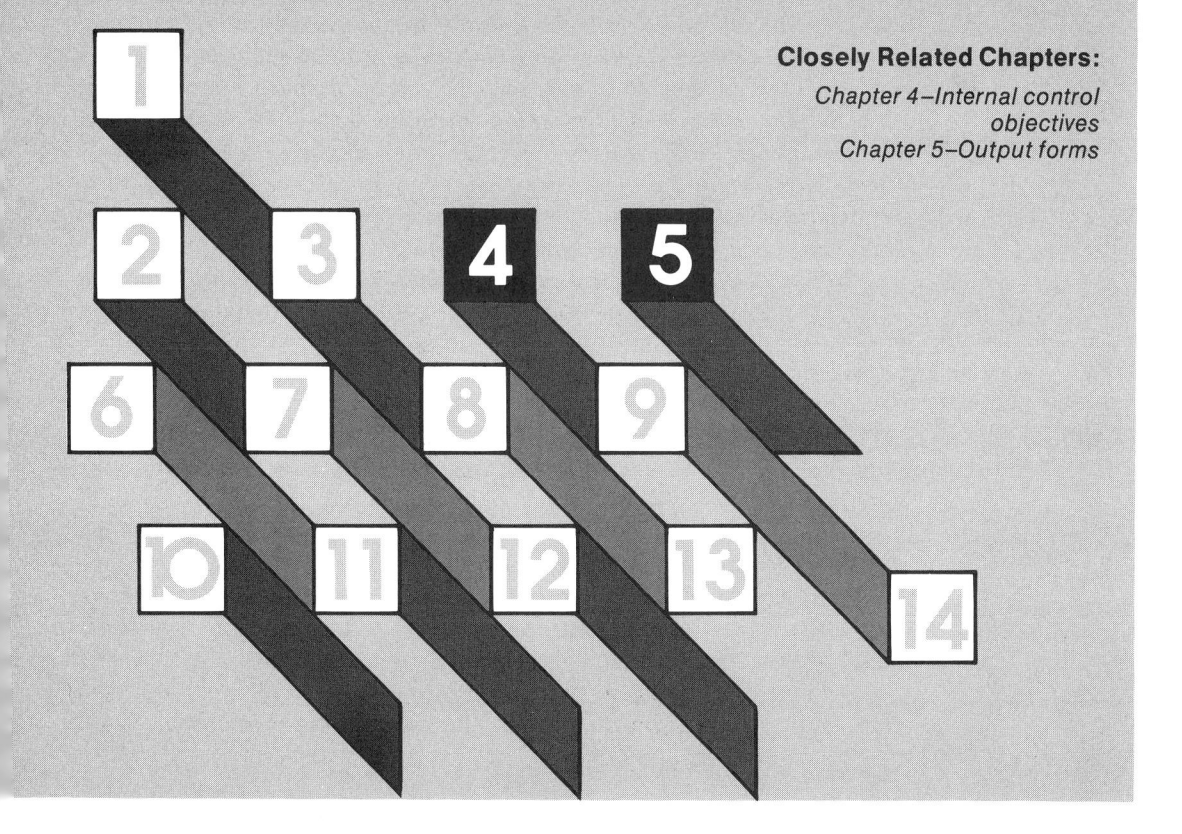

Closely Related Chapters:
Chapter 4−Internal control objectives
Chapter 5−Output forms

INTRODUCTION

The development of an information system implies the communication of data and information. The selection and design of the medium of transmission, the medium of display, the method of storage, and the format of the record or report is as important as the flow of information. In spite of this, the subject of data recording and information display is given cursory consideration in textbooks and in practice. In accounting, in particular, millions of transactions must be accurately recorded each year. These must be converted from one medium to another and manipulated many times to end up in a form useful to managers in making critical decisions for the company. In short, the success or failure of an AIS depends upon good forms design.

Before the advent of the electronic computer, the printed form was the basis of thousands of operations in the office. It has been so common in the past 100 years that it is difficult to conceive how business could be carried on without it. A printed form is simply a document with constant information printed on it and with space for the entry of variable data.

The starting point in systems design is the determination of information needs. As stated earlier, in Chapters 5 and 8, this is usually done by defining the reports that will serve as output from the system. Once we have determined the output requirements, we look for data sources and data collection instruments. As we identify a data source, we must find a method of capturing that data. Most often we will find that a form is necessary to document the data and control it through processing.

It should be apparent that the failure to capture all pertinent data relating to a transaction or event at the time the form is prepared will necessitate the recapture of some of the data at another point in time to aid in identifying the newly captured data elements. This double effort affords additional possibilities for errors and misclassification. Thus, the basic objective in form design is to provide a method of collecting data, one time, in complete enough detail to satisfy all reporting requirements.

Variety of "Forms"

In a modern, broad, and systems sense, *any standardized communication that is an essential link in an operating procedure is the equivalent of a form.* Illustrations of this concept are:

1. Preprinted forms on paper or cardboard
2. Formats stored for such computer outputs as printouts or video images
3. Punched tickets used for product and price coding in retailing
4. Edge punched forms such as McBee Keysort
5. OCR, Optical Character Recognition, forms for optical scanning and input to computers
6. MICR, Magnetic Ink Character Recognition forms commonly used for banking checks
7. Microfilm and microfiche as media for standardized recording
8. Standard formats for regular periodic narrative reports to managements
9. Wall charts and video displays in corporate management "war rooms."[1]

Examples of the above forms appear throughout this text in systems illustrations.

Forms are an Integral Part of Systems Design

The relationship between a particular procedure for a system and the communication processes utilizing forms is inseparable. Both procedure and form must be designed as an integral unit. In essence, when data are generated and/or communicated, the decision as to how to record and transmit the data must be made. Figure 10-1 shows this basic procedure/recording module.

---

[1] See, for example, "Corporate 'War Rooms' Plug Into the Computer," *Business Week,* August 23, 1976, pp. 66–67.

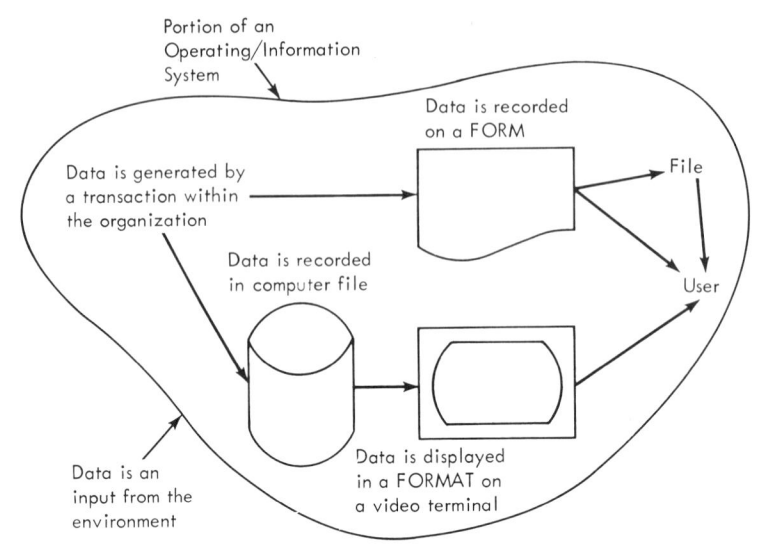

Fig. 10-1. Forms as Communications Devices in Information Systems

Forms may be designed as inputs to a particular information system, outputs from the same system, or intermediate records that remain within the system. The purpose of the form and the needs of users of the forms in these three cases obviously have important impact on the design of the form.

In summary, and for emphasis, we state that forms must be related to the design of both the operations and information systems. Forms and systems design must be an integrated process.

REASONS FOR USING FORMS

The basic reason for utilizing forms is to facilitate the flow, processing, and analysis of data by (a) arranging data, (b) minimizing recording time by elimination of constant data, and (c) providing control of operations. Arrangement of data in a standardized form makes it easier to enter, easier to read, and easier to check. The use of constant information positions data, identifies variable data, and allows shortcuts in entering data by such means as checking or circling items. Control of operations is provided by copies of the same form going to different people or different types of forms being brought to one person for comparison. (The computer, of course, may be the "controller" in some procedures.)

A detailed classification of functions is given as follows:

1. Acknowledge	20. Instruct
2. Agree	21. Lay out
3. Apply for	22. List
4. Approve	23. Notify
5. Assign	24. Offer
6. Attest	25. Order
7. Authorize	26. Pay
8. Bill	27. Purge
9. Cancel	28. Record
10. Change	29. Release
11. Certify	30. Report
12. Claim	31. Request
13. Classify	32. Research
14. Control	33. Route
15. Estimate	34. Schedule
16. Expedite	35. Terminate
17. Explain	36. Transfer
18. Follow up	37. Transmit
19. Identify	38. Verify

ESTABLISHING A FORMS MANAGEMENT PROGRAM

Need for Forms Management

The development of forms is part of systems *design* and systems *maintenance*. Responsibility for this activity must be centralized in one group or individual. Without such centralization, would-be Leonardo da Vinci's of forms design would be creating their masterpieces throughout the organization at great cost and confusion to the company. Even when responsibility has been clearly established, there is a need for the systems manager to be on the alert for "home-grown" forms throughout the organization.

Organization

The person responsible for forms management may be called a "forms specialist," a "forms controller," a "records manager," or a "systems manager." The position may be located within the controller's organiza-

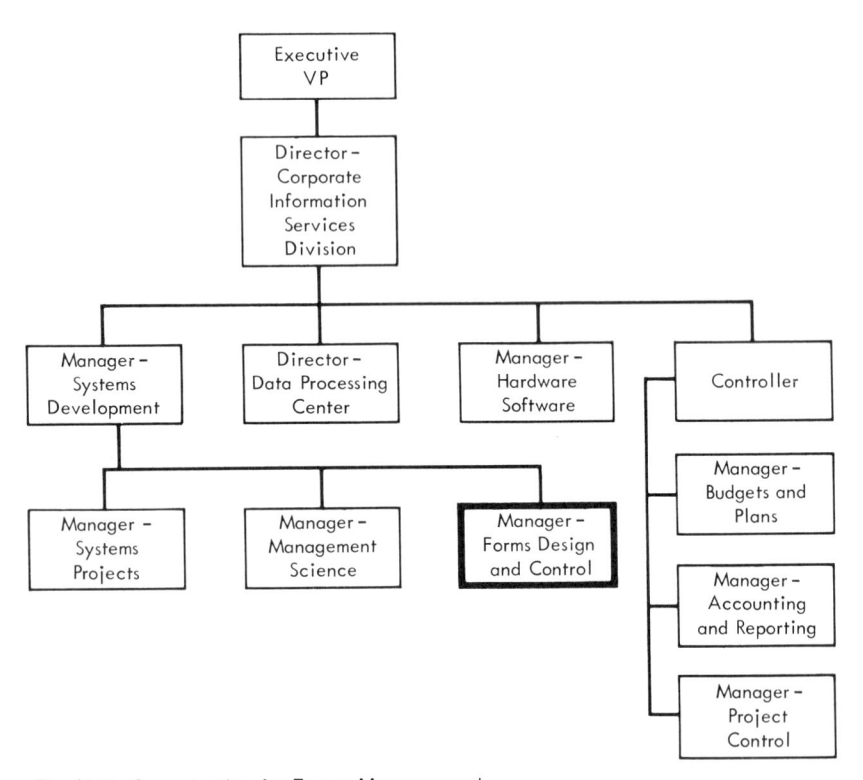

Fig. 10-2. Organization for Forms Management

tion, the systems organization, or the company's management services (administration division). An example of a position guide is given in Table 10-1.

In some companies, a forms committee made up of members from each functional organization reviews all proposed requests for new forms.

Possible organizational approaches to forms management are shown in Figures 10-2 and 10-3. As our previous discussion indicated, we feel that the responsibility for forms management should belong to the manager of systems development. A good argument, however, may be made for placing it with the controller.

Policies and Procedures

Once the position responsibility has been established, a policy (for the policy manual) should be prepared to clearly define this responsibility. Related to this, the procedure for initiating or revising a form should

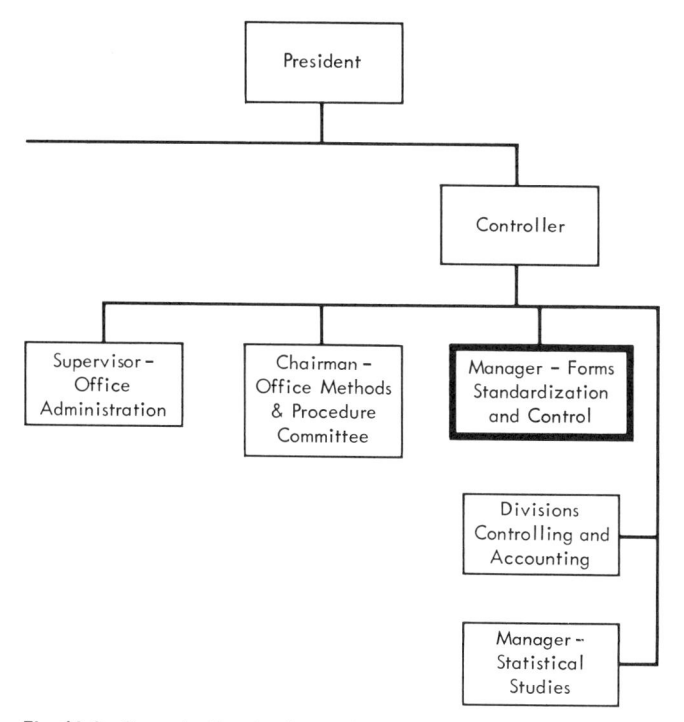

Fig. 10-3. Organization for Forms Management

also be prepared and distributed to all managers. Table 10-1 and Fig. 10-4 illustrate these concepts. The actual policies and procedures will, of course, vary widely from company to company.

Policies may also be developed on such topics as numbering and classification of forms, procurement and inventory of forms, issuance of forms, retention of forms, and maintenance of files of forms.

Stock Control of Forms

It is obviously not wise to order a ten-year supply of forms or to order new supplies of each form daily. In the first instance, money and storage space will be tied up over a long period. Equally important, the forms may become obsolete in a short time and have to be destroyed. In the second instance, the cost of ordering small amounts daily would be too expensive and time consuming.

A simple model to guide the forms controller in determining how many units (pads or boxes) of a form to order and when to order is based upon the diagram in Fig. 10-5.

Table 10-1. Position Guide for a Forms Controller

FORMS TECHNICIAN

Responsible to Director of Systems for development and implementation of the forms control and design function of the company.

Responsibility and Authority

  A. Operational

  1. Forms Design
     a. Set specifications for all company forms.
     b. Design all new company forms.
     c. Review and redesign all forms at reprint time as necessary.

  2. Forms Control
     a. Combine and eliminate forms as possible.
     b. Establish and maintain a criteria of basis to determine need for new forms.
     c. Identify changed API's and manuals and update them or cause them to be updated as a result of forms work.
     d. Set standards for consistency and uniformity in forms and maintain and implement these standards.
     e. Establish necessary records.

  3. Reporting
     a. Report on plans, programs and progress as required.

  B. Organizational
  None.

Relationships

  A. Within Company

  1. Direct contact with all supervisory and subordinate personnel as necessary to complete assignments. Particular emphasis should be placed on relations with Office Services personnel.

  B. Outside Company

  1. Attend meetings and seminars as required.

Outline of Responsibility and Authority of Forms Technician

Source: John Woychick, "Defining and Assigning the Forms Control Design Responsibility," Business Equipment Manufacturers' Association, *New Techniques in Office Operations,* Elmhurst, Ill.: The Business Press, 1968, p. 56.

In Fig. 10-5, we know or estimate the usage rate for a particular form as D units/month. We also know how long it takes to get delivery after we order as time T. When the inventory level reaches a level that will be used up during the delivery period, we would place our order. Therefore, recorder level is

$$L = DT$$

The next problem is to find how many units, Q, to order each time. To do this, we find the total cost for the inventory system and then find

		PRINTED IN THE USA
	APPROVED PRACTICE INSTRUCTIONS	
	GREEN GIANT COMPANY	
		API NUMBER 3

APL NO. 3	REVISION NO.	PAGE 1 OF 5	DATE ISSUED 8-1-67	DATE EFFECTIVE 8-1-67
SUBJECT	FORMS DESIGN AND CONTROL			

SUMMARY:

This API summarizes the procedure for creating, reviewing, revising and eliminating all company forms. The Systems Department is responsible for the Forms Design and Control Program, including forms coordination with API's and Manuals. Office Services Department is responsible for the procurement (make or buy), storage and inventory, and distribution of forms.

This procedure is divided into the following sections:

I. NEW FORM—ORIGIN AND ISSUE.
II. REPRINTED OR REVISION OF FORMS.
III. DISCONTINUED USE OF FORM.
IV. UPDATE API'S AND MANUALS.

POLICY:

All forms used within Green Giant Company must carry a form number. Other forms are unauthorized.

DEPARTMENTS AFFECTED:

All Departments.

DEFINITION OF TERMS:

A Form: A form is defined as a tool used by people to record or report company transactions. The final determination as to what is and what is not a form will be made as each request is processed by Systems Department.

PROCEDURE:

I NEW FORM—ORIGIN AND ISSUE

Originator:
1. Prepare rough draft or description of proposed form—include notations of company procedures or manuals affected.
2. Obtain his Department Director's approval signature on rough draft.
3. Forward approved rough draft to Systems Department.

ORIGINATED BY	ORIGINATED BY	APPROVED BY	APPROVED BY

Fig. 10-4. Policy on Forms Control

API NO. 3	REVISION NO	PAGE 2 OF 5	SUPERSEDES API 48-4, dated 6-5-63	DATED 8-1-67	DATE EFFECTIVE 8-1-67
SUBJECT	FORMS DESIGN AND CONTROL					

Systems Department:

4. Investigate use and need for proposed form.
5. Return disapproved proposed form to originator with reason.
6. Return proposal determined to be a worksheet and not a form to originator with approval for duplication.
7. Prepare drawing of approved proposed form.
8. Assign a form number and a functional number to the form.
9. Post these numbers to functional forms Record (46662).
10. Prepare Form's Specification Sheet (087) in triplicate.
11. Obtain using Department Director's approval of drawing of the form, and Form Specification Sheet.
12. Prepare Supplies Requisition (6161), in triplicate.
13. File third copy of Supplies Requisition and original of Form Specification Sheet in Master Forms File in a folder bearing the number of the new form.
14. Forward drawing of form, original and second copy of Supplies Requisition, and second and third copy of Form Specification Sheet to Office Services.

Office Services:

15. Determines if form should be printed internally or externally.

External Printing

(a) Send second copy of Form Specification Sheet, drawing of form, and original of supplies requisition to Purchasing for external printing.

(b) Determine low-order point of form, from information on Form Specification Sheet regarding quantity used annually and usage of forms.

(c) Note Form Number and loss order point quantity on form Inventory Control Card (46667).

Fig. 10-4 cont—page 2

API NO. 3	REVISION NO.	PAGE 3 of 5	SUPERSEDES API 48-1, dated 6-5-63	DATED 8-1-67	DATE EFFECTIVE 8-1-67
SUBJECT		FORMS DESIGN AND CONTROL			

        (d) Forward third copy of form specification Sheet to Supply Depot.

        (e) Retain copy of Purchase Order (6164) as a record of external printing.

  Internal Printing

        (a) Prepare and schedule form for internal printing.

        (b) Return original drawing of form to Systems Department.

        (c) Determine low-order point of form, from information on form Specification Sheet regarding quantity used annually and usage of form.

        (d) Post form number and low-order point quantity on form inventory Control Card (16467).

        (e) Forward second copy of Supplies Requisition, second copy of Form Specification sheet, and mat to Print Shop.

        (f) Forward third copy of Form Specification sheet to Supply Depot.

        (g) Retain original of Supplies Requisition as record of internal printing.

Purchasing:

16. Follow normal Purchasing procedure upon receipt of original Supplies Requisition, copy of Form Specification Sheet and drawing of new form.

Print Shop

17. Print forms according to specifications as shown on form Specification Sheet, and print shop procedures.

18. Forward printed forms to Supply Depot, with second copy of Supply Requisition and second copy of form Specification Sheet.

Supply Depot

19. Receive printed forms and check specifications according to third copy Form Specification Sheet.

20. Distribute initial supply of forms as per instructions on second copy of Supplies Requisition, store balance.

21. Destroy second copy of Form Specification Sheet.

Fig. 10-4 cont—page 3

API NO. 3	REVISION NO.	PAGE 4 OF 5	SUPERSEDES API 48-4, dated 6-5-63	DATED 8-1-67	DATE EFFECTIVE 8-1-67
SUBJECT: FORMS DESIGN AND CONTROL					

	22. Forward third copy of Form Specification Sheet to Office Services Supervisor in charge of Records Retention.
Office Services	23. File second copy of Supplies Requisition from Supply Depot.
	24. Destroy original of Supplies Requisition, on an internal print of a form.
Systems Department	25. Check copies of form against drawing and original forms Specification Sheet.
	26. File copies of form in Master Forms File with drawing and original Form Specification Sheet.

II. REVISION AND REPRINT OF FORMS

Revision Suggestions

Suggestor	1. Suggest revisions as forms are being used.
	2. Obtain department director's approval signature on proposed revisions.
	3. Forward proposed revisions to Systems Department.
Systems Department	4. Receive and review proposed revision, and file proposed revision in Master Form File until form is reprinted. (Circumstances may dictate immediate revision).

Reprint

Department with Total Supply	1. Write word "reprint" on face of form.
	2. Forward to Systems Department.
Supply Depot	3. Write word "reprint" on face of form that reaches low-order point.
	4. Forward to Systems Department.
Systems	5. Receive requests for reprint, and check Master Forms File for suggested revisions.
	6. Investigate need for revisions.
	7. Incorporate revisions in new design.
	8. Make copy of Form Specification Sheet.
	9. Prepare Supplies Requisition in triplicate.

Fig. 10-4 cont—page 4

API NO. 3	REVISION NO.	PAGE 5 OF 5	SUPERSEDES API 48-4, dated 6-5-63	DATED 8-1-67	DATE EFFECTIVE 8-1-67
SUBJECT: FORMS DESIGN AND CONTROL					

	10. Obtain using Department Director's approval of revised drawing of form and Form Specifications Sheet.
	11. Forward drawing of revised form, second and third copy of Form Specification Sheet, original and second copy of Supplies Requisition to Office Services. See Procedure 1, step 15.
III. DISCONTINUED USE OF FORMS	
Originator	1. Obtain Department Directors initials on form to be discontinued.
	2. Forward to Systems Department.
Systems Department	3. Originate 5-part Supplies Requisition.
	4. Place discontinued form folder in Out Forms File with third copy of Supplies Requisition.
	5. Post obsolete date to Functional Forms Record.
	6. Forward original and second copy of Supplier Requisition to Office Services.
Office Services	7. File original of Supplies Requisition.
	8. Forward second copy of Supplies Requisition to Supply Depot.
Supply Depot	9. Remove discontinued forms from supply as per second copy of Supplies Requisition.
	10. Forward second copy of Supplies Requisition to Office Services.
Office Services	11. Give original of Supplies Requisition to Office Services Supervisor in charge of Records Retention.
	12. File second copy of Supplies Requisition.
	13. Destroy Form Inventory Control Card for the discontinued form.
IV. UPDATE API's AND ORIGINAL	
Systems	1. Update any Approved Practice instructions or portions of company manuals that become obsolete as a result of a new, revised or discontinued form.

V. FORMS AFFECTED:

987	Form Specification Sheet
46652	Functional Forms Record
6161	Supplies Requisition
6164	Purchase Order

Fig. 10-4 cont—page 5

Source: John Woychick, "Defining and Assigning the Forms Control Design Responsibility," Business Equipment Manufacturers' Association, *New Techniques in Office Operations,* Elmhurst, Ill.: The Business Press, 1968, pp. 61–65.

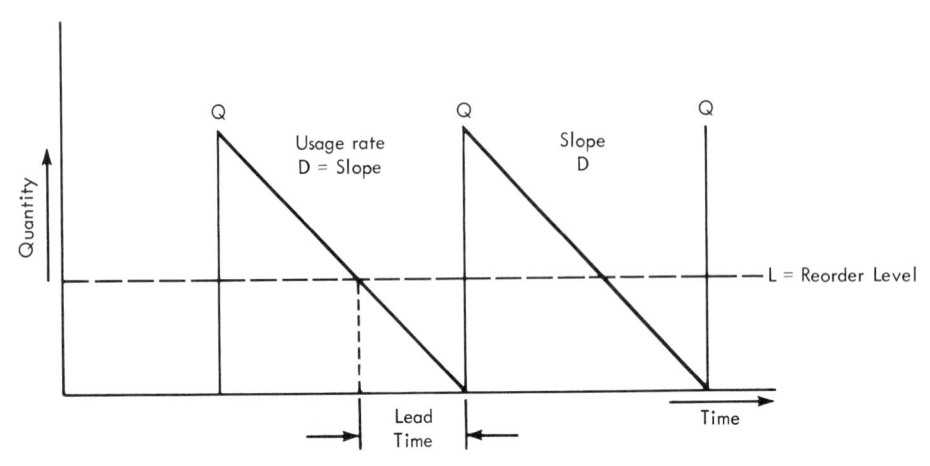

Fig. 10-5. Inventory Model

the value of Q that will minimize this cost. The system cost is:

Total System Cost Per Month = Cost of the forms purchased per month
+ Cost of processing purchases per month
+ Cost of storing forms for the month

$$TC = C_i D + C_p D/Q + C_h Q/2$$

where
C_i = cost of one unit of forms
C_p = cost of processing a single purchase
C_h = cost of stocking a unit of forms for one month
$Q/2$ = average inventory for a month
TC = total system cost per month

By setting the derivative of TC with respect to Q equal to zero and solving for Q, we find a simple formula for the "economic order quantity" to be:[2]

$$Q = \sqrt{\frac{2C_p D}{C_h}}$$

As an example, suppose that a box of forms, C_i, costs $80, the cost of placing an order, C_p, = $15, the cost of holding a box in inventory for one month is $.30, and demand, D, for the forms is 3 boxes per month. Then

[2] See W. J. Fabrycky and Paul E. Torgersen, *Operations Economy,* Englewood Cliffs, N.J.: Prentice-Hall, 1966, pp. 264–265, for a good exposition and derivation.

$$Q = \sqrt{\frac{2 \times \$15 \times 3}{\$.30}} = 17 \text{ boxes}$$

If it takes two months from the time the order is initiated until the forms arrive at the stock room, the reorder level is:

$$L = DT = 3 \times 2 = 6 \text{ boxes}$$

As a safety precaution, a buffer stock of three boxes may be kept in reserve so that if shipment is delayed, a month will elapse before the company faces the prospect of stockout.

Forms Files and Forms Classifications

The first step in effective control of forms is to gather copies of every printed document and every standard format displayed on computer peripheral equipment. Usually several copies are required, one for a numerical file, one for a form-title file, and one for either a subject, department, or function file, and in some cases, a file by media. The purpose of this is to permit a study of current forms, overlapping of forms, and obstacles to easy access of data. As an aid to studying current operations, such files are very valuable.

The numerical file is based upon an identification number assigned to each form. This number may be assigned in sequence in the order that forms arrive at forms control. For example, 215–77 may indicate that this is the 215th form to be issued and the year of issue was 1977. Alternatively, a block of numbers and the department or operations number may be assigned. Suppose that the marketing department has been assigned the account number 350 by the accounting department in order to accumulate costs. This number might also be used to identify forms originated and used by the marketing department. A block of numbers may also be made available to marketing to identify forms in sequence of their creation or to identify subsystems within marketing. As an illustration, form number 350-13-21 might indicate marketing, advertising, and form 21 as used by the advertising department.

The forms title file, if the titles are properly chosen, organizes the forms to some extent by procedure, operation, or subject. Thus this file serves a double purpose.

The classification of forms on the basis of department is usually one of the first methods tried to organize forms. One expert, at least, believes that this never works. Too many forms are used and needed by

Table 10-2. Index of Forms by Medium

0	Purchased outside the company
1	Printed by the company, up to 8½ × 13 inches, paper
2	Printed by the company, over 8½ × 13 inches, paper
3	Cardboard
4	Multilith printed forms
5	Mimeograph printed forms
6	Hecto printed forms
7	Envelopes
8	Tags
9	Labels
10	Edge punched cards
11	Punched cards
12	Microfilm
13	Microfiche
14	Format stored in the computer
A	Single Sheet
B	Multicarbon copy
C	Multicopy, no carbon required
D	Continuous strip
E	Pad

too many departments to permit such classification. A more useful classification is by function. A code number for each function may be printed on each form as part of the identification number, as well. We have listed earlier 38 functions which forms may serve as the basis for this file (p. 345).

The classification of forms according to media is sometimes useful. In Table 10-2, we show a possible list of media and a coding. With paper being replaced by video displays more and more, such an index may become very important for forms analysis.

In the case of forms used for reports, report frequency codes are also helpful for analysis. A typical coding might be as shown in Table 10-3.

Table 10-3. Frequency Index

1	Daily
2	Weekly
3	Biweekly
4	Monthly
5	Quarterly
6	Semiannually
7	Annually
8	Five years
A	Four-week rolling report
B	Three-month rolling report
C	Six-month rolling report
D	Five-year rolling report

A rolling report means that one period is dropped off and another added, each reporting period. For example, a three-month rolling budget report made monthly would cover a three-month period. Each month, the report would be issued for the next three months, so that an old month is dropped as a new one is added.

Line-Staff Relationship

The need for a new form or a revision may originate with either the line manager or the systems group. However, line management must make the final decision. The *authorship*, or contents of the form, is also a responsibility of line management. However, the *design* of the form is a technical skill, and design responsibility should be assigned to the forms specialist.

The design involves applications of both functional standards and physical standards. Functional standards apply to the organization of data on the form and the aesthetic appearance of the form. Physical standards apply to the production of the form—the use of computer output versus paper, the type of paper, the number of copies, and the type of printing production. It is the forms staff that is responsible for implementation of these standards.

Summary

The forms control function is vested in a staff group with the following responsibilities:

a. Gather and classify samples of all forms within the company.
b. Develop a master file or a set of files of all forms indexed in various ways for analysis.
c. Receive requests for new forms or revisions of forms and work with the requesting manager in the development of forms.
d. Initiate proposals for new or revised forms in the course of development of information systems.
e. Develop an inventory control system for forms covering quantity purchased, method of issuance, and record of inventory status.
f. Develop the design, including layout and productuion of all forms.
g. Develop policies and procedures, as approved by line management, to prevent development and use of unauthorized forms.
h. Provide for regular review of all forms.
i. Develop policies for retention of forms records.

FORMS ANALYSIS

Forms analysis overlaps both forms control and forms design. It has four objectives:

Determining the necessity of information
Preparing the information
Presenting the information
Storing the data

Forms in use should be analyzed to determine whether different data, fewer data, or more data are appropriate. The only data on the form should be those that are absolutely necessary. Too often, data that appear interesting are gathered without view to cost or usage. In addition, the entire form may be eliminated or consolidated with another form.

Analysis of the preparation of the material is concerned with finding the easiest and most economical way of getting the data. This requires a study of the entire operating and information system. Data may be collected in real time as transactions are performed, in batches after the transactions have been completed, or, in some cases, from forms prepared for other purposes. The systems specialist must take into account those people who fill in the data, those who handle the forms, and those who use the forms.

Data become information when somebody uses them to make decisions or take action. The information must be presented in a form that is clear, easy to understand, and current for the decision-maker. Cluttered forms, complex report formats, or computer printouts loaded with irrelevant data should be identified. With modern computerized data banks, well-designed formats may permit instant reporting to managers upon inquiry. Emphasis on information presented should not take precedence over the need to present the information in a form easily interpreted.

A study of the files and records is also a part of forms analysis. What forms are retained? How long has each form been retained? Have forms been converted to other media such as microfilm or computer tapes for storage? What is the condition of the stored data? In one instance, a tax accountant using a no-carbon-required form lost his entire file when the writing faded to a blank.

FORMS DESIGN

Forms analysis leads to form design or redesign. We will summarize the main points to consider in designing forms. The accountant who is knowledgeable concerning design may be of great assistance to the forms designer.

General Considerations in Forms Design

From the forms analysis, the need for specific data in accounting and management information systems has first been established. That is, we must first identify:

1. The function of a form;
2. When the form is used;
3. How many copies are used in a single cycle for the transaction, transmission, and storage;
4. Who fills out the form and who uses the form;
5. How many units of the form are required per year.

Principles of Forms Design

There are a number of specific factors that should be considered in forms design. These are presented below in the form of a check list:

1. After all of the following factors have been considered, the form should be attractive and easy to read.
2. Most forms should have a title. Examples of those that do not may be checks, labels, tags, and video displays (see Fig. 10-6). The title should be specific enough so that the function of the form may be determined, in most cases, without seeing the form. Table 10-4 shows a stores requisition form and a job cost sheet.
3. Forms should have an identification number with the date of issuance. For example, the Pitney Bowes service call form shown in Fig. 10-7 shows a form number 103-Y4/7-74 in the lower left corner. Note that this particular form does not have a title.
4. Group information into related areas on the form. Use a box design with captions printed in small distinct type in the upper left-hand corner of the boxes.
5. Arrange the items so that there is a logical flow from left to right and top to bottom in filling out the form. Reporting forms usually have summaries in the right columns and bottom rows. Shading may also be used to make report forms more readable, as shown in Fig. 10-8.
6. The use of box items to be checked or coded simplifies the readability of

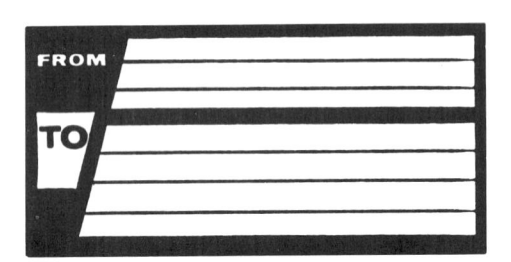

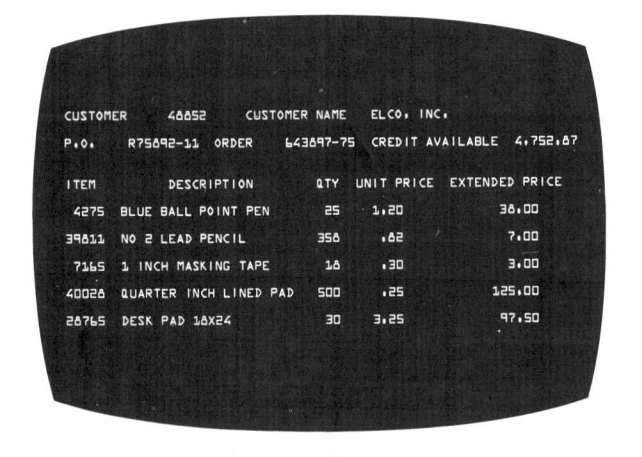

Fig. 10-6. Forms Without Titles

the design. When extreme emphasis is on accuracy, large boxes, heavily blocked sections, and lots of open space help, as shown in Fig. 10-9.

7. Provide sufficient space for entering data and do not bleed lines off the sides of the forms. If the horizontal lines stop short of the edge of the sheets, it is less likely that variable data will run off the edge.//
8. Consider colored ink for captions to make variable data stand out. Colored ink may also be used for serial identification numbers. In Fig. 10-10, (p. 365), the order number is in red on the actual form.
9. "Boiler plate" or standard contract information is often on the back of

Table 10-4. Stores Requisition

STORES REQUISITION			
Job No. _____			
Department _____		Date _____	
Debit Account _____			
Authorized by _____			
DESCRIPTION	QUANTITY	UNIT COST	AMOUNT

forms such as purchase orders. Alternatively, detailed instructions on how to fill out the form may be printed on the back.

10. Routing instructions for each copy may be indicated by using a different color of paper for each copy and printing routing instructions on the margin.

11. Type faces, the use of heavy and light lines, shaded areas, and color should be combined to provide an aesthetic form that makes the variable data stand out.

12. Standard form sizes should be used. These range from label sizes and shapes to the usual $8\frac{1}{2} \times 11''$ forms to $11 \times 17''$ foldouts. If forms are kept small, they may be cramped in appearance, difficult to handle, and awkward to file. On the other hand, cost savings may be realized since less paper or cardboard is required. Size is also related to the standard equipment available to process the forms, as for example, check sorters for checks in banks.

13. If the form is to be placed in a binder, leave adequate blank space at the top or sides.

14. If forms and envelopes are designed to match, the location of the address shown on the firm must show through the envelope window with normal folding.

15. When multiple copies of a form are desired, several alternatives are possible. Multiple copies with carbon interleaves are possible. Special no-carbon-required paper may be used to obtain copies. The form may be a ditto master and after the variable data has been added, copies may be run off. (This is appropriate for 5 or more copies.) Finally, a single copy of the form may be completed and then copies run off on an office copier.

16. Formats to be shown on video terminals should separate blocks of information adequately. If too much data is attempted in one display, it will be difficult to read. It is no problem to show a series of formats for clear presentation (see Fig. 10-11, p. 366).

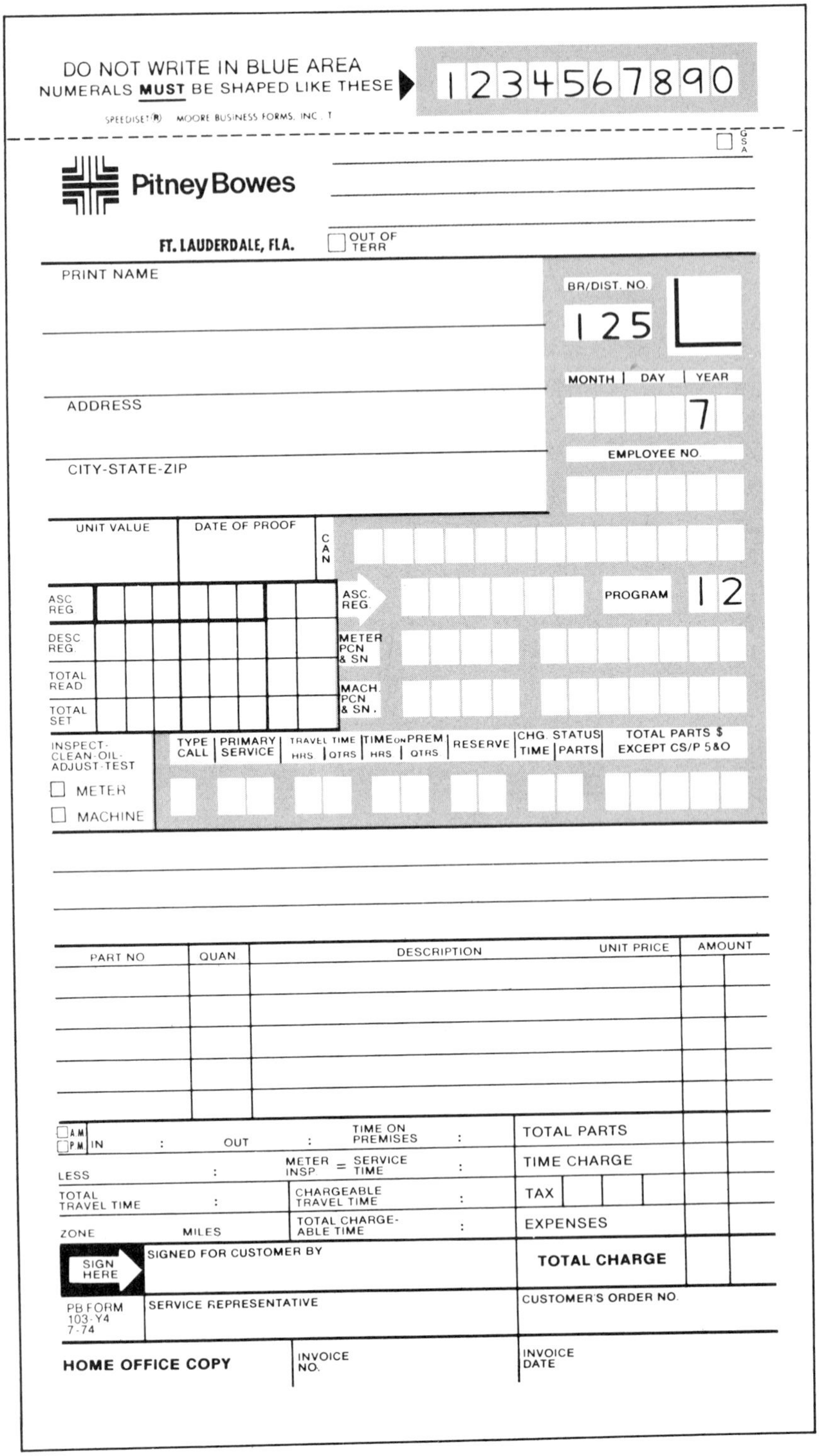

DO NOT WRITE IN BLUE AREA
NUMERALS **MUST** BE SHAPED LIKE THESE ▶ 1 2 3 4 5 6 7 8 9 0

SPEEDISET® MOORE BUSINESS FORMS, INC. T

GSA

Pitney Bowes

FT. LAUDERDALE, FLA. ☐ OUT OF TERR

PRINT NAME

BR/DIST. NO. 125 L

MONTH | DAY | YEAR 7

ADDRESS

EMPLOYEE NO.

CITY-STATE-ZIP

UNIT VALUE | DATE OF PROOF | CAN

ASC REG | ASC. REG. | PROGRAM 12

DESC REG | METER PCN & SN

TOTAL READ | MACH. PCN & SN.

TOTAL SET

INSPECT-CLEAN-OIL-ADJUST-TEST ☐ METER ☐ MACHINE

TYPE CALL | PRIMARY SERVICE | TRAVEL TIME HRS QTRS | TIME ON PREM HRS QTRS | RESERVE | CHG. STATUS TIME PARTS | TOTAL PARTS $ EXCEPT CS/P 5&O

PART NO	QUAN	DESCRIPTION	UNIT PRICE	AMOUNT

☐ AM ☐ PM IN : OUT : TIME ON PREMISES : | TOTAL PARTS
LESS : METER INSP. = SERVICE TIME : | TIME CHARGE
TOTAL TRAVEL TIME : CHARGEABLE TRAVEL TIME : | TAX
ZONE MILES TOTAL CHARGEABLE TIME : | EXPENSES

SIGN HERE ▶ SIGNED FOR CUSTOMER BY | **TOTAL CHARGE**

PB FORM 103-Y4 7-74 | SERVICE REPRESENTATIVE | CUSTOMER'S ORDER NO.

HOME OFFICE COPY | INVOICE NO. | INVOICE DATE

Fig. 10-7. Service Call Form

NOVEMBER 19

DISCHARGE ANALYSIS BY SERVICE
MEMORIAL HOSPITAL
ANYTOWN USA

CLASSIFICATION: SERVICE	TOTAL PATIENTS	% DISCHARGE	LENGTH OF STAY: TOTAL STAY	LENGTH OF STAY: AVG. STAY	CODE	LENGTH OF STAY IN SPECIAL CARE: ICU 1 CCU 2 ECF 3 BOARD 4 TOTAL STAY	ICU CCU ECF BRD AVG STAY	TOTAL EMERGENCY	DISCHARGE STATUS: ALIVE	DEAD: +48 HRS	DEAD: −48 HRS
MEDICINE-100											
GEN. MEDICINE	167	568	839	51		9	15	29	161	2	4
					2	18	26				
PEDIATRICS	32	109	112	35				6	32		
TOTAL MONTH	199	677	951	48	1	9	15	35	193	2	4
					2	18	26				
TOTAL Y.T.D.	383	659	1919	50	1	19		86	371	6	6
					2	31					
SURGERY-200											
GEN. SURGERY	51	173	397	78					51		
PEDIATRIC SUR	5	17	9	18				1	5		
TOTAL MONTH	56	190	406	73				1	56		
TOTAL Y.T.D.	109	188	738	68	1	2		3	109		
					2	2					
OBSTETRICS300											
GENERAL O.B.	18	61	44	24				1	18		
NOT DELIVERED	1	3	1	10					1		
CESARIAN SEC.	1	3	7	70		1					
TOTAL MONTH	20	68	52	26				1	20		
TOTAL Y.T.D.	46	79	117	25				2	46		
NEWBORN-400											
GENERAL N.B.	19	65	72	38	4	26	260		19		
TOTAL MONTH	19	65	72	38	4	26	260		19		
TOTAL Y.T.D.	43	74	159	37	4	62			43		
GRAND TOTAL MONTH	294		1481	50	1	9	15	37	288	2	4
					2	18	26				
					4	26	260				
Y.T.D.	581		2933	50	1	21		91	569	6	6
					2	33					
					4	62					

SERVICE	DEATHS: TOTAL DEATHS	% DEATHS	IN OR	POST OP	AUTOPSIES: % TOT	NO. +48	% +48	NO. −48	% −48	CORONER	XFUSIONS: TOTAL NO.	REACTIONS	COMPL.: CODE (INF. 1, CA 2, POD 3, OTH. 4)	CONSULTATIONS: TOTAL NO.	% DISCHARGE	NO. CONSULTANTS
GEN. MEDICINE	6	36			17			1		1						
PEDIATRICS																
TOTAL MONTH (MEDICINE)	6	30			17			1		1						
TOTAL Y.T.D. (MEDICINE)	12	31			8			1		1	3			2	50	
GEN. SURGERY											1			2	39	
PEDIATRIC SUR																
TOTAL MONTH (SURGERY)											1			2	36	
TOTAL Y.T.D. (SURGERY)											2			3	28	
GENERAL O.B.																
NOT DELIVERED																
CESARIAN SEC.																
TOTAL MONTH (OBSTETRICS)																
TOTAL Y.T.D. (OBSTETRICS)											2			3	65	
GENERAL N.B.																
TOTAL MONTH (NEWBORN)																
TOTAL Y.T.D. (NEWBORN)																
GRAND TOTAL MONTH	6	20			17			1		1	1			2	7	
Y.T.D.	12	21			8			1		1	7			13	22	

SERVICE	PRE-OP DAYS: TOTAL	PRE-OP DAYS: AVG.	AGE: 0-13	AGE: 13-64	AGE: 65+	MALE PATIENTS: NUMBER MALES	% MALES	MEDICARE MEDICAID PRIVATE AUTH ROOM	FINANCIAL: TOTAL CHARGES	AVG. CHG.	AVG. DAY
GEN. MEDICINE			4	122	41	70	42	5	56772	340	68
PEDIATRICS			31	1		17	53		6197	194	55
TOTAL MONTH (MEDICINE)			35	123	41	87	44	5	62969	316	66
TOTAL Y.T.D. (MEDICINE)			55	258	70	181	47	7	119637	313	62
GEN. SURGERY	72	150		47	4	14	27		27961	543	70
PEDIATRIC SUR	3	60	5			3	60		1031	206	115
TOTAL MONTH (SURGERY)	75	140	5	47	4	17	30		28992	518	71
TOTAL Y.T.D. (SURGERY)	84		5	90	14	31	28	2	51221	470	69
GENERAL O.B.				18					2938	163	67
NOT DELIVERED				1					27	27	27
CESARIAN SEC.									431	431	62
TOTAL MONTH (OBSTETRICS)				20					3396	170	65
TOTAL Y.T.D. (OBSTETRICS)				46					8179	178	70
GENERAL N.B.			19			9	47		1779	94	25
TOTAL MONTH (NEWBORN)			19			9	47		1779	94	25
TOTAL Y.T.D. (NEWBORN)			43			15	35		5008	116	31
GRAND TOTAL MONTH	75	14	59	190	45	113	38	5	97136	330	66
Y.T.D.	84		103	394	84	227	39	9	184045	317	63

50-1002 DISCHARGE ANALYSIS

Fig. 10-8.

Courtesy of Medical Dimensions, Inc.: Houston, Texas

snap

CASE ABSTRACT

CORRECTION

HOSPITAL CODE

PATIENT NAME ______

PATIENT NUMBER

SEX M F

AGE

RACE (1–9)

CENSUS AREA (1 – 99)

ADMISSION DATA

DATE MONTH DAY YEAR

DAY OF WEEK S M T W T F S

ATTENDING PHYSICIAN

EMERGENCY Y N

TYPE OF EXPECTED PAYMENT
(PRIMARY ONLY)

* MEDICARE 1
* MEDICAID 2

BLUE CROSS 3

GROUP INSURANCE 4

PRIVATE INSURANCE 5

NO INSURANCE 6

OTHER 7

DISCHARGE DATA

DATE MONTH DAY YEAR

HOSPITAL SERVICE

ALIVE 1

DEAD + 48 HRS. 2

DEAD – 48 HRS. 3

O.R. DEATH Y N

POST OP DEATH Y N

AUTOPSY Y N

CORONERS CASE Y N

SURGERY

PRIMARY SURGEON

THIRD SURGEON

PRIMARY SURGICAL PROCEDURE

SURGICAL PROCEDURES

SECONDARY SURGICAL PROCEDURES

HOSPITAL DAYS PRIOR TO EARLIEST SURGERY. IF LESS THAN 6 HOURS, USE 0

SECOND SURGEON

SURGICAL PROCEDURES

INFECTION Y N

CARDIAC ARREST Y N

POST-OP BLEEDING Y N

OTHER COMPLICATION Y N

DIAGNOSIS

PRIMARY

SECONDARY

CIRCLE DIAGNOSIS LISTED AS CAUSE OF DEATH

CONSULTANTS

TOTAL NUMBER OF CONSULTATIONS

SPECIAL CARE DAYS

ICU DAYS | CCU DAYS | ECF DAYS | (NEWBORN ONLY) BOARDER DAYS

TRANSFUSION

NUMBER OF UNITS

WHOLE BLOOD

REACTION

PACKED CELLS

SPECIAL

SPECIAL STUDY

OPTIONAL DATA

*IF PRIVATE ROOM AND MEDICARE OR MEDICAID, INDICATE WHETHER AUTHORIZED.

CHARGES

TOTAL BILL X X

(ROUND TO DOLLARS)

BY: ______

DATE ______

SHADED AREAS ARE NOT REQUIRED INFORMATION. FILL THEM IN ONLY AS NECESSARY TO PROVIDE STATISTICS WHICH YOUR HOSPITAL REQUIRES ON ITS REPORTS.

FORM NO. 1050

Fig. 10-9.

Source: Courtesy of Medical Dimensions, Inc., Houston, Texas

CMDC OR
SOURCE NAME
STREET ADDRESS
CITY, STATE &
ZIP CODE

Please enter our order for the following goods and ship according to General Shipping Directions. This is a purchase order if no contract has been entered into for the merchandise specified. If a Contract covering this merchandise has been entered into, this document constitutes shipping instructions to apply against such Contract.

SOURCE NO.

SHIP MERCHANDISE TO

SEARS, ROEBUCK AND CO.

STORE AND WAREHOUSE NO.

SEND INVOICE AND SHIPPING RECEIPT TO

SEARS, ROEBUCK AND CO. STORE NO.

(IF NO ADDRESS IS GIVEN IN THIS SPACE, SEND INVOICE TO ABOVE ADDRESS)

FOLD ON THIS LINE

TYPE OF ORDER

- ☐ BULK BILLING PURCHASE ORDER
- ☐ REQUISITION
- ☐ MASTER BILLING PURCHASE ORDER
- ☐ STORAGE SHIPPING ORDER
- ☐ REGULAR PURCHASE ORDER

ORDER NO. 576982

SHOW ORDER NO., ITEM NO., QUANTITY BY SIZE AND COLOR, AND THE FOLLOWING INFORMATION ON THE INVOICE, ON THE BILL OF LADING, AND ON OUTSIDE SHIPPING CONTAINERS.

EVENT ______ DIV | DEPT

STORE NO. ______

DATE OF ORDER	PARENT DEPT	ORDER GIVEN BY
SHIP ON	C. O. DEPT.	TRANS. ALLOW

RECEIVING NO.	NO. PACKAGES
DATE RECEIVED	RECEIVED BY

DATE MARKED	MARKED BY
MO DAY	

FOLD ON THIS LINE

IF YOU CANNOT SHIP ON DATE SPECIFIED, PLEASE ADVISE.

TERMS	TRADE DISCOUNT	F.O.B.	SHIP WITH P.O. #	TERRITORIAL ACCOUNTS PAYABLE CENTER

	ITEM NUMBER	SKU NO.	DESCRIPTION	SIZE/COLOR	PROMOTIONAL ESTIMATE	COST PRICE	UNIT	ORDERED QUANTITY	UNIT	QUANTITY RECEIVED		SELLING PRICE	UNIT	M/U CODE
1														
2														
3														
4														
5														
6														
7														
8														
9														
10														
11														
12														
13														
14														
15														
16														
17														
18														

IMPORTANT — BY ACCEPTING THIS ORDER, SELLER AGREES TO THE TERMS AND CONDITIONS SET FORTH ON THIS ORDER INCLUDING THE REVERSE SIDE OF THE NUMBER ONE COPY

TOTAL COST | TOTAL WEIGHT | **1** | TOTAL SELLING

NO. PIECES	PACK		B/L DESCRIPTION	WEIGHT
	BOX	BUNDLE		
	CRATE	CARTON		

ACTUAL SCALE SHIPPING WEIGHTS MUST BE SHOWN ON ALL B/L'S AND SHIPPING RECEIPTS. IF PARTIAL SHIPMENT IS MADE, INDICATE ON YOUR INVOICE THE APPROXIMATE DATE BALANCE OF THIS ORDER WILL BE SHIPPED.

14028 REV. 11/75

PICKER	CHECKER	PACKER

Fig. 10-10.

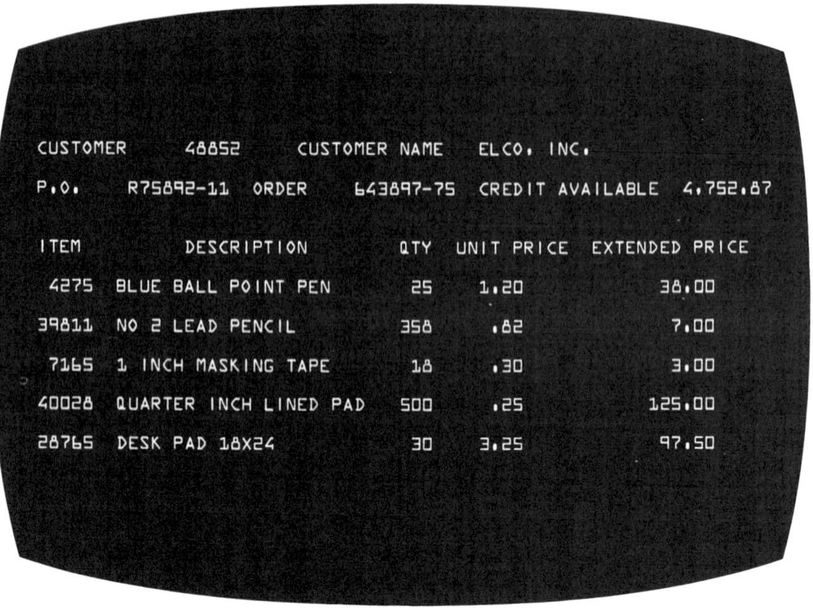

Fig. 10-11. Formats on Video Terminals

Source: IBM, *Communications Oriented Production Information and Control Systems,* Volume VII, 1972, p. 8. Courtesy of IBM Corporation.

RETENTION PERIOD

One of the most difficult and frustrating operating problems that a firm faces is the maintenance of records. Records obviously cannot be kept indefinitely. Each type of record must be retained for varying amounts of time, depending upon internal needs and external requirements. With the complexity and hazards of today's legal environment, the need for developing specific retention periods is essential. In Table 10-5 we have listed a number of sources to serve as guides to the system designer.

The designer may reduce the task by first dividing the total list of forms and records into two classes: intermediate forms or records, and input/output forms. The "intermediate" forms are those used simply to accomplish daily tasks and lead to formal or summary output records.

Summary

The accountant is vitally concerned with the design of forms as a user and as a controller of information flow in accounting information systems. He should be able to distinguish between good and poor forms

Table 10-5. Sources for Retention Periods

Fair Labor Standards Act

Armed Services Procurement Regulation

Interstate Commerce Commission

Industrial Security Manual (attachment to DD Form 441)

Prentice-Hall's *Payroll Guide*

Corporate tax department audit requirements

Corporate legal department

Internal Revenue Code

Corporate Records Retention (Requirements of State Governments)

Federal Register—Guide to Record Retention

Federal Insurance Compensation Act

Federal Reserve Operating Circular No. 20

Walsh-Healey Act

Revenue Ruling 71-20

---

designs relative to accounting information systems. In addition, he should be familiar with the broader concept of forms management.

In this chapter we have presented the elements of forms management. The basis for this discussion has been a broad definition of forms and formats in view of the role of the computer in data processing.

The development of the forms management program, the forms control, forms analysis, and forms design are discussed. Examples of forms in this chapter and throughout the text serve to illustrate the points made.

DISCUSSION QUESTIONS AND PROBLEMS

1. List at least ten forms used in business and discuss the information that each form is meant to communicate.
2. List and discuss several reasons for using forms.
3. Forms are designed to provide the maximum of variable information with the minimum of variable input. Discuss this statement and give examples.

4. It takes two months from the order date to receive a multipart, multicolor form from the printer. The firm uses 1,500 forms/month and pays $.10 for each. The carrying cost is $.15/pad and the order cost is $8.00. The forms are packed 100 to a pad. Compute the EOQ and reorder level.
5. List and discuss various methods of indexing forms.
6. List and discuss the principles of forms design.
7. Discuss the differences in format for CRT input displays and hard-copy forms.
8. Discuss the general considerations in forms design and relate each to the design of a purchase order.
9. Design a single form for the collection of data regarding the time spent on each client by the staff of a CPA firm. The form is to be filled out by each member of the firm on a weekly basis and will be used for both client billing and payroll. Staff members often work on several clients each week and also have several hours of non-billable time.
10. Identify the errors in the invoice shown in the figure.

Bibliography

Business Equipment Manufacturers Association, *New Techniques in Office Operations,* Elmhurst, Ill.: The Business Press, 1968.

CARRITHERS, WALLACE M., and ERNEST H. WEINWURM. *Business Information and Accounting Systems,* Columbus, Ohio: Charles E. Merrill Books, Inc., 1967.

CLARK, FRANK J., RONALD GALE, and ROBERT GRAY. *Business Systems and Data Processing Procedures,* Englewood Cliffs, N.J.: Prentice-Hall, 1972.

KAISER, JULIUS B. *Forms Design and Control,* New York: American Management Association, Inc., 1968.

KINDRED, ALTON R. *Data Systems and Management,* Englewood Cliffs, N.J.: Prentice-Hall, 1973.

LAZZARO, VICTOR (ed.). *Systems and Procedures* (2nd ed.), Englewood Cliffs, N.J.: Prentice-Hall, 1968.

LITTLEFIELD, CL. L., FRANK M. RACHEL, and DONALD L. CARUTH. *Office and Administrative Management* (3rd ed.), Englewood Cliffs, N.J.: Prentice-Hall, 1970.

MITCHELL, WILLIAM E. "Records Retention Schedule," *Journal of Systems Management,* August 1977.

MYERS, GIBBS. "Forms Management, Part 1: Why Forms Management?," *Journal of Systems Management,* September 1976.

MYERS, GIBBS. "Forms Management, Part 2: How to Design Business Forms," *Journal of Systems Management,* October 1976.

Preview:
EDP hardware and software are an integral part of any AIS. This chapter shows some of the basic hardware available and how it may be used in the AIS.

CHAPTER ELEVEN
hardware and software in AIS design

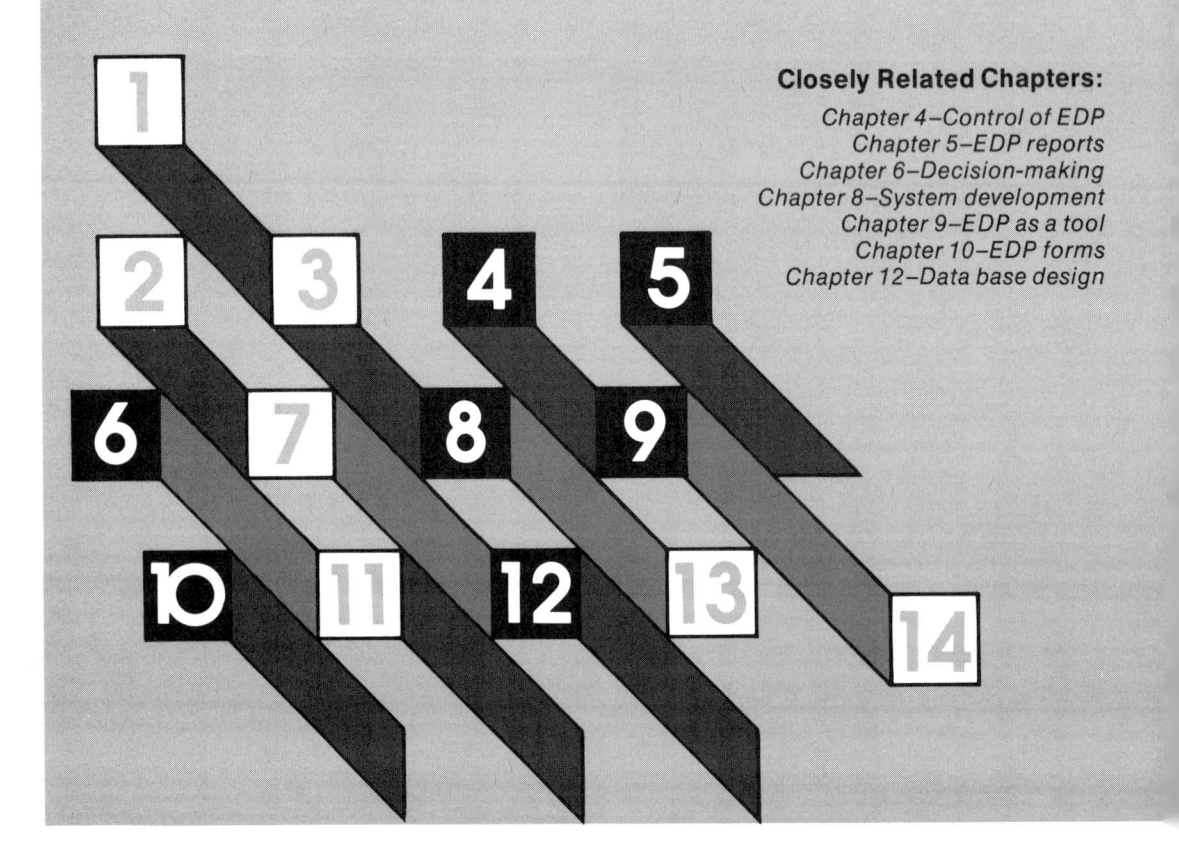

Closely Related Chapters:
Chapter 4–Control of EDP
Chapter 5–EDP reports
Chapter 6–Decision-making
Chapter 8–System development
Chapter 9–EDP as a tool
Chapter 10–EDP forms
Chapter 12–Data base design

"It works like a computer. I push the button . . . you show up with the answers."

Not since the invention of writing in about 3000 B.C. has there been such an advance in information processing as that provided by electronic computer equipment. Jumps in technology of computer equipment are occurring faster than textbooks can come off the press. While minicomputers are still newcomers on the scene, *micro*computers, which also give promise of matching early giant computers, are appearing.

Today, computers separated by great distances talk with each other. Computer output microfilmers translate data into readable language and microfilms at a rate 100 times faster than paper printers. Paper printers are not exactly slow, either, printing over 1000 lines per minute. A computer may store over 1 billion characters internally. On-line storage capacity may be expanded to nearly ½ *trillion* characters. In comparison, the average human, living 70 years, stores information equivalent to 1 trillion *words*.

According to a 1975 IBM advertisement, in 1952 it cost $1.26 to do 100,000 multiplications on an IBM computer; today it costs a penny. Multiplications have gone from 2,000 a second to more than two million a second over the same years. When we consider the millions of transactions involved in accounting systems in large firms, the impact of the computer on operations formerly performed manually is mind-boggling. Because so much of traditional accounting effort has been devoted to just trying to gather data, accountants have tended to focus on this aspect. Much of the promise of true AIS for managerial decision-making has been lost in the swamp of computerized data processing.

Accountants need not be computer experts in order to design or utilize AIS. In fact, the accountant who views the computer as a powerful but somewhat moronic helper will be able to concentrate on the major information needs and problems of the company. We therefore present only the basics of computer hardware and software so that the accountant, when called upon, can participate intelligently in the selection and use of these resources. Descriptions of specific hardware are obsolete by the time they are written about in books.

THE POSITION OF DATA PROCESSING IN THE ORGANIZATION

The data processing function in companies historically tended to be under the manager of accounting or the controller. This occurred because the computer was first conceived of as a substitute for clerical labor. Perhaps because accounting has the highest priority for computer usage in many smaller companies, the data processing manager reports to the controller in such cases. A survey of reporting relationships shows that almost one third of data processing managers report to the controller or financial office:

Data Processing Reports to:	
President, Owner, General Manager	25.7%
Vice President	23.9%
Financial, Controller	32.9%
Director of Management Services	3.5%
Director of Systems and Data Processing	1.7%
Director of Information	.9%
Director of MIS, Data Base	.5%
Others	11.0%

Source: Infosystems 6/76, p. 36. By permission.

DATA PROCESSING AND THE COMPUTER

As previously suggested, there are several prerequisites for a modern, effective computer-based management information system. The *first* of these is a *management* system: the organizational arrangements, the structure, and the procedures for adequate planning and control. *Second,* there must exist data and information: information about the company's goals, resources, environment, policies, operations, plans, and performance against plans. These types of information represent knowledge about the company's managerial and operational processes. *Third,* to process these data, it is necessary to have equipment that will (1) provide the capability for economic, rapid access to large-scale storage of retrievable data; (2) process the data economically and at high speed; and (3) enter information into the system and retrieve and display it.

These three activities are now often performed by special electronic communication devices and by today's computers and related hardware. *Fourth,* a final prerequisite to an effective computer-based management information system is an organization for designing, maintaining, and managing the required systems and procedures.

In this chapter we want to examine how information is stored, processed, transmitted and displayed, and retrieved by means of the electronic computer and related devices. The objective is to understand how the computer operates as the fundamental information processor and the essential element of a management information system.

COMPONENTS AND OPERATION OF A DATA PROCESSING SYSTEM

An information system is composed of five basic components, as shown in Fig. 11-1. In a manual system, human beings perform the five basic functions; in a computer based system, the functions are performed by equipment. In either type of system the basic functions are (1) entering data into the system; (2) processing the data (rearranging input data and processing files); (3) maintaining files and records; (4) developing procedures that tell what data are needed, when and where they are obtained, and how they are used, as well as providing instruction routines for the processor to follow; and (5) preparing report outputs.

Both manual and computer-based information systems have the elements and attributes of systems in general and can be described in terms of these elements: input, output, and processor. Our examination of computer systems in this chapter will proceed by analogy to make the transition from the easily understood manual system to a slightly more

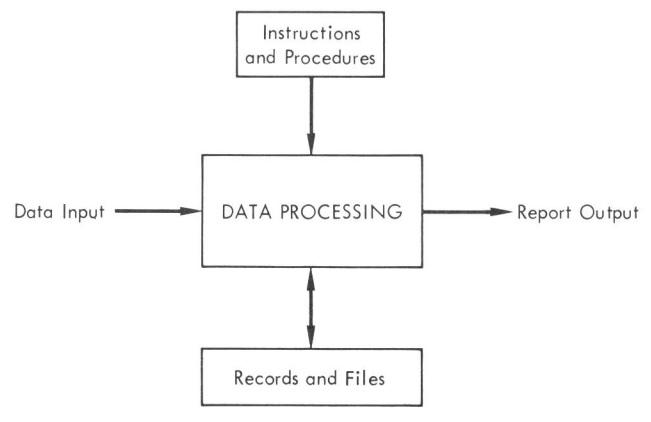

Fig. 11-1. Basic Components of an Information System.

complex computer-based system. The transition and analogy will accomplish two purposes. First, we shall be able to see how a computer-based data processing system can become a vital adjunct to management planning and control. Second, by examining the system through its components (input, output, processor), we shall be better able to understand how these components of an information system provide the framework for MIS design.

OPERATION OF A MANUAL INFORMATION SYSTEM

Humans are the most numerous data processors. Yet the human remains an unreliable data processor. On the other hand, where judgment and creativity are required, the human mind is indispensable.

All information systems were manual before the computer arrived; many of them still are. We shall describe a manual inventory system first and then compare it with a computerized inventory system. In each case, as in any company information system, the basic components of a system—input, processor, and output—are present.

In Fig. 11-2, we depict a manual inventory system. The components are described below.

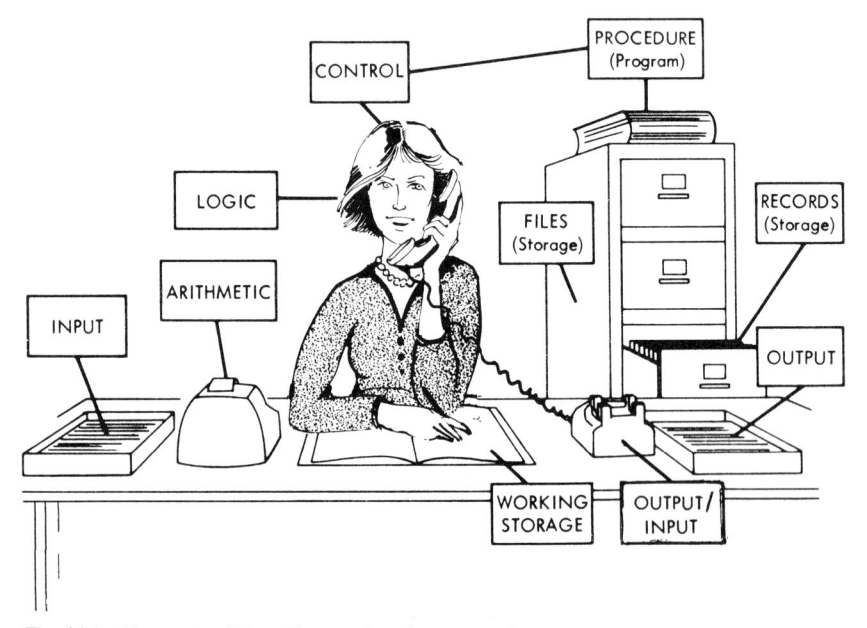

Fig. 11-2. Elements of Data Processing (Inventory System)

Input

We see that the *input device* for the manual inventory processing system is the in-basket of the inventory clerk. This device receives the *input data* to the system, which may be in various forms and media and is related to information surrounding inventory receipts and issues. Inventory records are updated with receipts on the one hand and reduced with orders for the item on the other. Receipts and issues may be recorded in writing by a storekeeper, stamped on an invoice by a mechanical device, or punched into a card. The resulting cards, invoices, receipt documents, issue papers, shipping documents, and a variety of other *input* information affecting the inventory system are entered into the in-basket for processing and ultimate preparation of output.

Processor

The processor consists of the storage, the arithmetic and logic elements, and the control elements.

The storage is made up of the *internal* (primary) memory. It is represented by the clerk's brain and the records being worked on. The *external* storage is the *file* of individual *records* for an item of inventory. The organization and structuring of this external storage is very important in both manual and computer-based systems.

The arithmetic and the logic elements are in the clerk's brain. The arithmetic unit adds, subtracts, multiplies, and divides. The logic unit compares two quantities to see if one is greater than, equal to, or less than the other in order to make a processing decision. Most people are surprised to learn that these five operations are all the manipulations that a computer can do.

The control element tells the clerk what data to enter into primary storage and when to enter them. It tells the arithmetic logic elements what operations to perform, where the data are to be found, and where to place results. It tells what files to enter. The control element in the manual system consists of the clerk's brain and the systems procedures manual.

The procedures manual may, for example, instruct the processor to "(1) multiply unit cost by units issued, (2) deduct units issued from balance on hand, and (3) deduct gross value of issue from dollar value of inventory." The clerk would then perform this processing on the input information, update the inventory balance (external storage), and prepare the required *output* report to go in the out-basket. Preparation of the *output* is the final step of the information processing system.

Output

Output may be (1) updated inventory records, (2) an inventory status report, and (3) other reports and documents related to inventory. The media are likely to be handwritten or typed reports. As we shall see, these limited media contrast greatly with the wide variety possible in computerized systems.

A schematic of the manual information system is shown in Fig. 11-3.

COMPONENTS OF A COMPUTER SYSTEM

Although many managers are awed or confused by the computer, its operation simply parallels that of the manual system we have just described. If we wish to convert our manual inventory system to a computerized equivalent, the input data would be the same. Only the *form* of the input would be different. The computer *processes* the data—hence the name electronic data processing (EDP).

The manual inventory control system previously discussed, when converted to computer application, might appear schematically as in Fig. 11-4, which illustrates the basic components of the computer system. Fig. 11-5 shows the actual hardware components of modern-generation computer systems. A discussion of the components follows.

Input

The function of entering data into the computer processor is performed by an input device. The input must be in a form acceptable to the computer as a machine. Normally this input form is a stack of punched cards, paper tape, magnetic tape, or electrical signal. An example of punched card input is shown in Fig. 11-6. The punches in a column may indicate any one of 26 letters, 10 numerals, or 25 special characters.

The input devices (machines) read or sense coded input data. Typical computer input/output devices are shown in Fig. 11-7. A list of

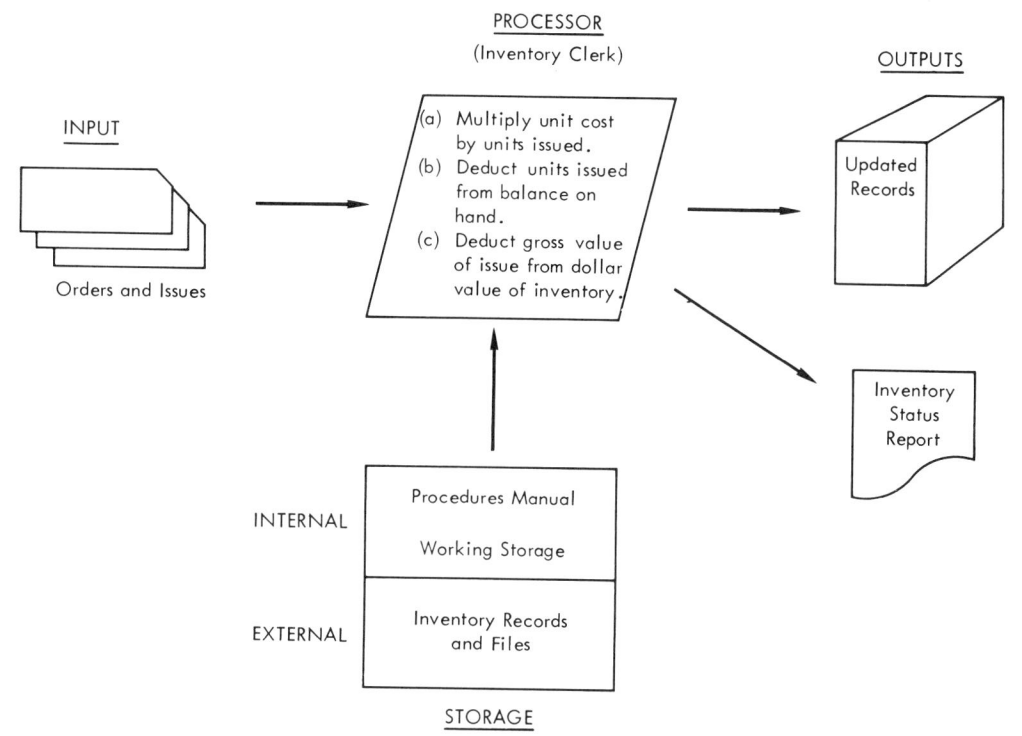

Fig. 11-3. Manual Inventory Accounting System.

input devices is as follows:

DEVICE	PRODUCT
Card punch	Punched cards
Perforator	Perforated cards
Paper tape punch	Paper tape record
Key-to-tape	Reel, cartridge, or cassette magnetic tape
Key-to-disk	Exchangeable disk or floppy disc record
Electric pen with CRT input	Internal storage
Teletype or typewriter input	Tape, disk, or internal storage
OCR (Optical character reader)	Tape or disc record or internal storage
MICR (magnetic ink character recognition)	Tape or disk record or internal storage
Terminal keyboard	Tape or disk records or internal storage
Special purpose devices such as sensors, plotters, etc.	Tape or disk records or internal storage

The Central Processor

The central processor is the most significant component of the computer. As in the case of our inventory control clerk in the manual system,

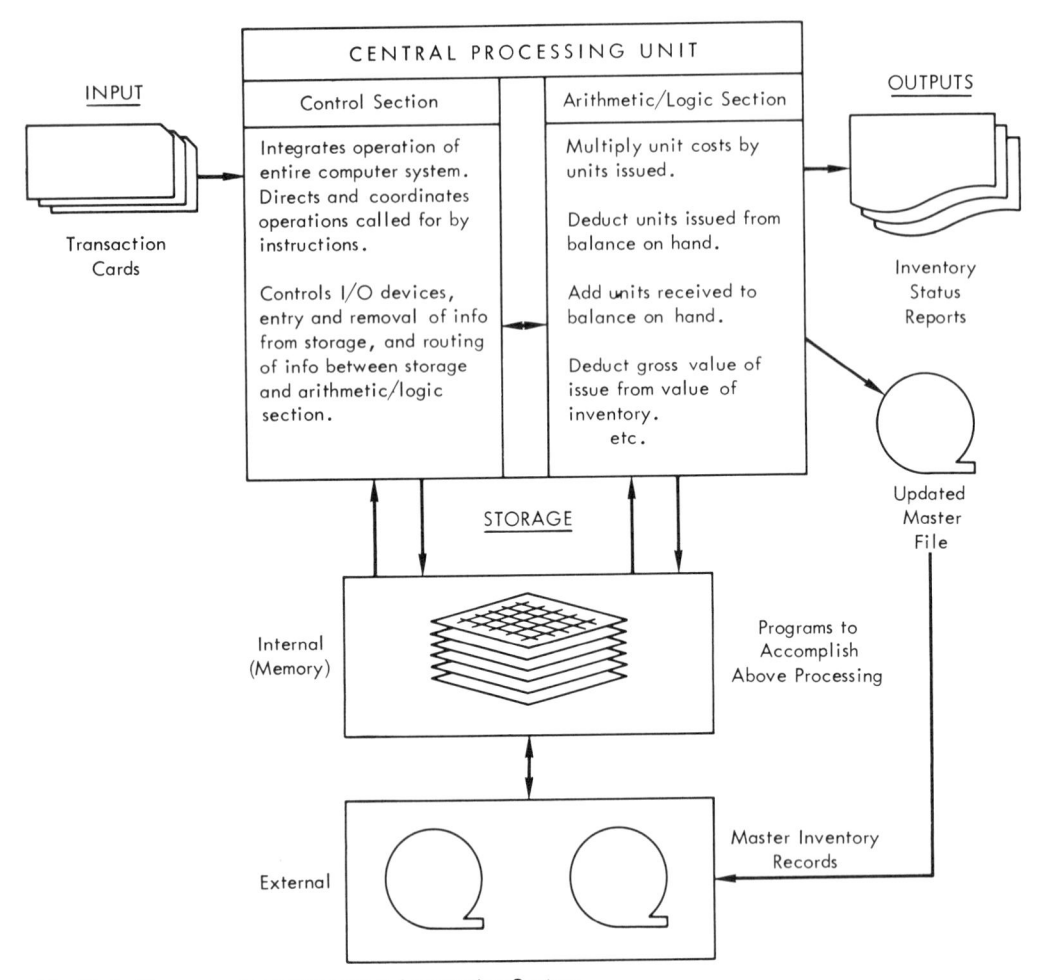

Fig. 11-4. Computer-based Inventory Accounting System.

it consists of a *control* section, which coordinates the system components, and the *arithmetic/logic* unit, which performs the same functions (add, subtract, multiply, divide, compare, shift, move, store) as the clerk-calculator combination of the manual system. However, the CPU (central processing unit) of the computer accomplishes these tasks at fantastically increased speed and accuracy. This meager processing logic, accompanied by the four simple functions, accounts for the almost infinite variety of tasks the computer can perform. Fig. 11-5 shows central processing units.

The control section of the CPU directs and coordinates all operations called for by the instructions (programs) to the system. It controls the input/output units and the arithmetic/logic unit, transferring data to and from storage, and routing information between storage and the

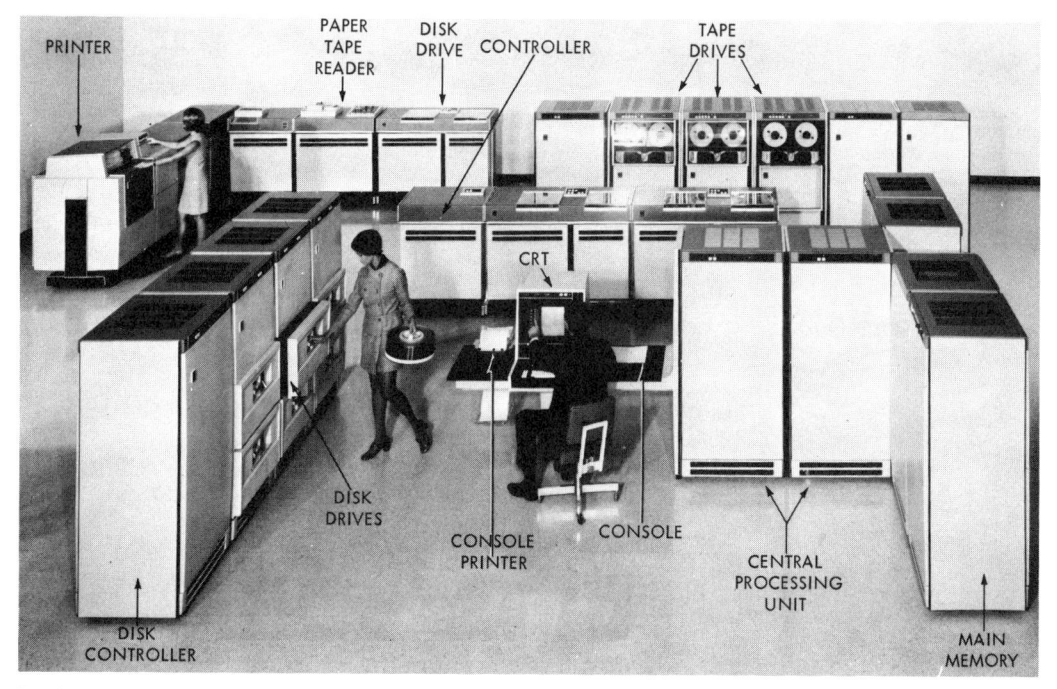

Fig. 11-5(a). Components of a Medium-to-large-scale Computer System (NCR Century 300).
Courtesy of the NCR Corporation.

Fig. 11-5(b). Components of a Small Computer System (NCR Century 101).
Courtesy of the NCR Corporation.

379

Fig. 11-5(c). Components of a Small Computer System (IBM system 3).
Courtesy of IBM Corporation.

arithmetic/logic unit. It is by means of the control section that automatic, and manual operation of the entire computer system is achieved.

Storage

Storage within the computer is somewhat like a huge electronic filing cabinet completely indexed and accessible instantly to the computer. All

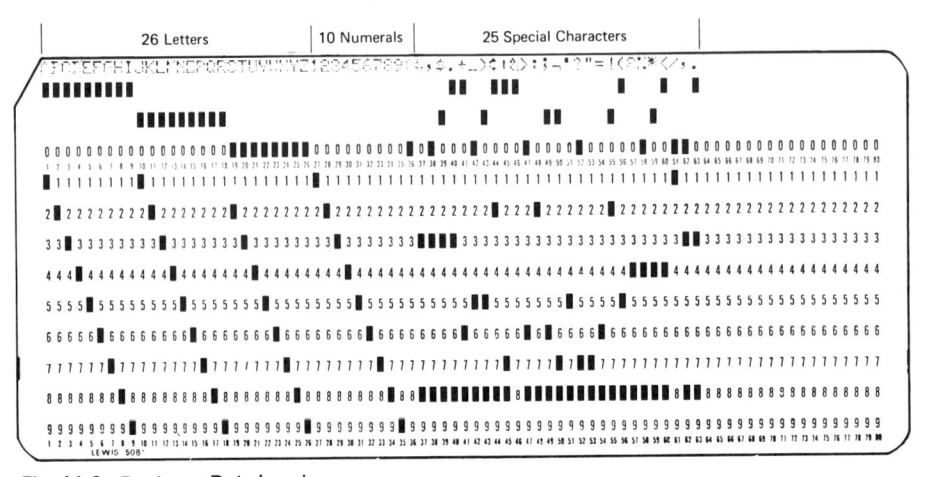

Fig. 11-6. Business Data Input.

IBM 1403 Printer

IBM 2540 Card Read Punch

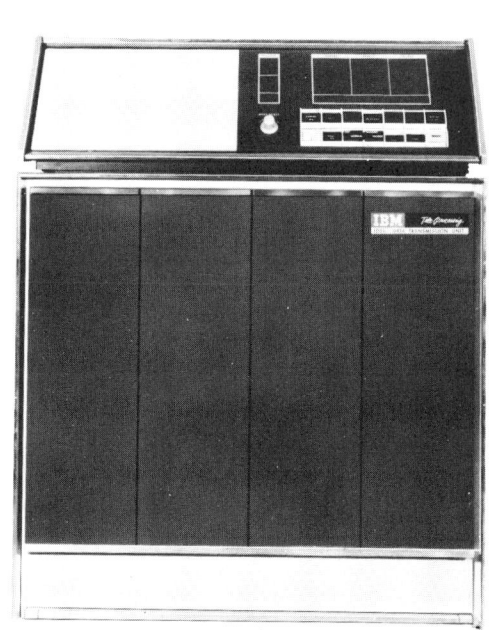

IBM 1009 Data Transmission Unit

Figure 11-7(a). Input/output Devices
Courtesy of IBM

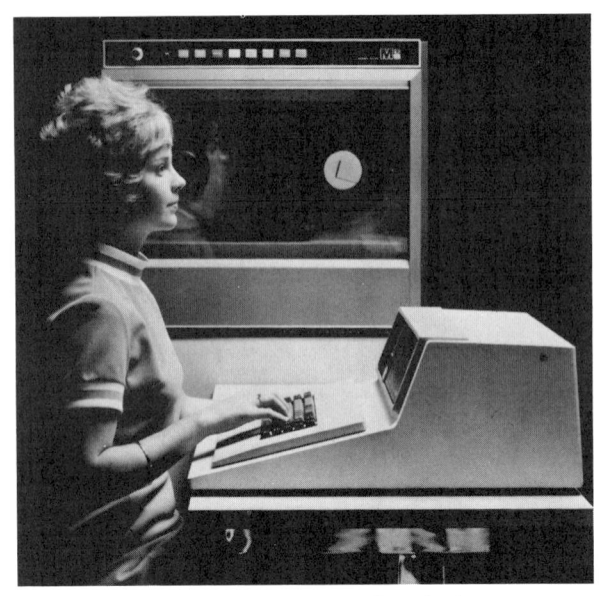

Fig. 11-7(b). Mohawk Data Sciences Terminal Key Station and Tape Drive.

Courtesy of Mohawk Data Sciences.

Fig. 11-7(c). Texas Instrument Silent 700 ASR Terminal with Mangetic Tape Casette Offline Storage.

Courtesy of Texas Instruments.

data must be placed in storage before being processed by the computer. Storage consists of *internal,* which is a part of the processing component, and *external.*

Note the similarity between manual and computer systems. Internal storage, frequently referred to as *memory,* is the characteristic that permits the computer to store, in electronic form, data from input devices as well as long series of instructions called *programs* that tell the machine what to do. These programs are similar to the procedures manual of the manual system. It is this memory facility that distinguishes the computer from devices such as calculators and bookkeeping machines, which, although they have input, output, and processing capabilities, cannot store programs internally within the processing unit. The program enables the computer to perform complex and lengthy calculations in order to process specific input data.

External storage (consisting of records and files, reference data, and other programs) is of two types:

1. *Direct access.* Disk, magnetic drum, and data cell devices providing random ordered mass storage that can be accessed without having to read from the beginning of the file to find the desired data.
2. *Sequential.* Magnetic tape that is sequentially ordered and must be read from the beginning in order to read or write a desired record.

To understand how programs of instructions permit the computer to process data, we must examine the concept of *computer memory* to see how information and instructions can be stored within the computer. The information can be (1) instructions (programs) to direct the processing unit, (2) data (input, in-process, or output), and (3) reference data associated with processing (tables, code charts, constant factors, etc.).

Output

Computer memory is made up of a certain number of magnetic cores. We want to be able to represent in memory 10 decimal digits, 26 alphabetic characters, and 25 special symbols (comma, dollar sign, etc.) (see Fig. 11-6). Binary schemes for representing these data vary, but all utilize a prearranged assignment of bits and groups of bits. This system of representation is important because of the need to arrange core storage and locate it by address.

Storage of computer memory is divided into locations, each with an assigned address. Each location holds a specific unit of data, which may be a character, a digit, an entire record, or a word. When a data item is desired, it is obtained from its known location in addressable storage units that are organized to provide data when wanted. There are several schemes for using the processor to assist the programmer in keeping track of the storage locations. These schemes provide *data names*, such as "update inventory" or "calculate net pay," to automatically refer to sections in the program designed to perform these calculations. Notice the similarity between these programs and the procedures manual of the manual inventory system described previously.

Output devices produce the final results of the data processing. They *record* information from the computer on a variety of media, such as cards, paper tape, and magnetic tape. They *print* information on paper. Additionally, output devices may generate signals for transmission over teleprocessing networks, produce graphic displays, microfilm images, and take a variety of special forms. As indicated in Fig. 11-4, the output from the inventory accounting system would be (1) a printout containing an inventory status report and (2) an updated inventory master file. Fig. 11-7 shows some typical output devices that are linked directly to the computer system.

Data Communications

No discussion of computer utilization would be complete without mention of data communications—the marriage of data processing and data transmission. The accelerating growth of this mode is reflected in the fact that in the period of time since the mid-1960s when only 1% of computers in use were linked to communication systems, it is expected that shortly over half of the existing computers will be so linked and that at least half of all communication transmitted over existing facilities will be nonlanguage, or data. To say it another way, the communications involved with computers "talking to each other" will exceed that of people talking to each other. Major users of data communications are listed in Table 11-1.

The data communications process generally requires at least six parts, tied together as shown in Fig. 11-8.

1. A transmitter or source of information. This is usually some type of input/output device such as a typewriter, keyboard, or cathode ray tube (CRT) terminal. These were shown in Fig. 11-5, 11-7, and 11-9.
2. A modem on the transmitting end. These modems convert the digital signals of your data transmission into analog signals for transmission over the dial-up network. Until recently these converters were almost always supplied by *common carriers*, such as AT&T or Western Union. A recent court decision has opened up a proliferation of these products by a variety of manufacturers.

Table 11-1. Major Users of Data Communications.

INDUSTRY	TYPE ORGANIZATION	TYPES OF APPLICATIONS
Transportation	Airlines, rail, truck and bus	Reservation system, traffic control & dispatching, MIS, Maintenance systems
Utilities	Public utilities, common carriers	Communications facilities, MIS
Manufacturing	All manufacturing	Shipping, order processing, internal time sharing, MIS
Industrial	Natural resources, metals, chemicals, machines, textiles, etc.	Warehouse control, shipping, process control, MIS
Retailing	All retailers	Point-of-sale systems, credit authorization, warehouse control, MIS
Service	Banks, financial, information services, warehousing, time sharing, insurance	Branch banking, money & securities transfers, time sharing, automated clerical operations, credit authorization, warehousing, quotation services
Government	Military & public administration	Communications, command & control, MIS, law enforcement, logistics, public health & education, postal automation

3. A transmission channel or carrier. Both the telephone companies and Western Union offer private-line teletypewriter-grade service at different speeds. TWX is the U.S. and Canadian exchange teletypewriter service, and TELEX is a worldwide exchange service offered by Western Union. Another illustration of line facilities is the WATS (Wide Area Telephone Service).

4. A modem on the receiving end. These modems conver the analog signal of the data link (transmission channel) back into a digital signal for computer use.

5. A receiver of transmitted information. This is the computer and a variety of input/output devices.

6. In addition, multiplexors or concentrators are often used to squeeze more input/output devices onto fewer communication channels, i.e., getting several messages through a channel at the same time. This is to reduce transmission costs.

Minicomputers

Minicomputers are "small" computers with all of the characteristics of large-scale computers but to a lesser degree. One authority defined them as central processors costing less than $23,000. However, the price keeps going down. Another definition is that a mini is small and inexpensive, with a primary storage of at least 4K words of from 8 to 24 bits.

The communications processor... why?

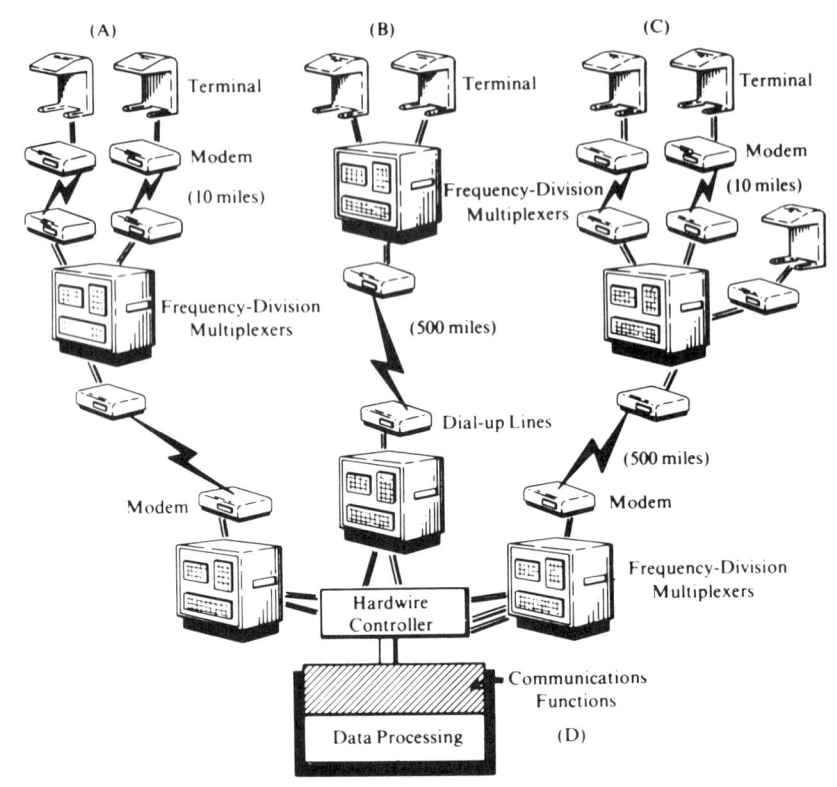

Fig. 11-8. This system has been configured without communications processors-relying on hardware multiplexing devices to realize efficiencies in transmission line utilization. The inefficiencies of the system are that (1) line costs are not minimized (especially when messages are switched from one terminal group to another and (2) a considerable portion of the host computer resources (central processing time and core memory utilization) is required to perform network control functions.

Source: Kenneth W. Ford, "About Communications Processors," *Infosystems,* February 1973, p. 47.

Minis are very useful for small companies who neither need nor can afford a large computer. In Fig. 11-9, a minicomputer is an integral part of a work station. This Data System 310 (Digital Equipment Corp.) has a core memory of 16K characters. Storage can be expanded to 1.34 million characters of disc storage. Warehouses, banks, insurance companies, and branch offices are typical users. A new trend is for companies to replace a large computer with a number of sophisticated minicomputers.

The growing sophistication of each generation of minicomputers has resulted in the development of *distributed computing.* In such systems, the power of computer hardware is distributed to the operating levels

Fig. 11-9.
Courtesy of Digital Equipment Corporation, Maynard, Massachusetts.

and work stations through use of minicomputers and their associated data storages. The central mainframe computer is remote and connected to the minicomputer computer system by means of teleprocessing.

SYSTEM ALTERNATIVES

Baffled by Snow Job

I've seen the ablest and toughest of executives insist on increased productivity by a plant manager, lean on accounting for improved performance, and lay it on purchasing in no uncertain terms to cut its staff. But when these same executives turn to EDP they stumble to an uncertain halt, baffled by the snow job and the blizzard of computer jargon. They accept the presumed sophistication and differences that are said to make EDP activities somehow immune from normal management demands. They are stopped by all this nonsense, uncertain about what's reasonable to expect, what they can insist upon. They become confused and then retreat, muttering about how to get a handle on this blasted situation.[1]

There is a very wide range of computer system configurations available to the user today. These range from a simple minicomputer system to huge multimainframe distributed computing systems. The particular configuration of a computer system for a given organization depends upon (a) the level of sophistication of the company's planning and control, (b) the average number of transactions per day, (c) storage and memory requirements, (d) speed of processing relative to rate of usage of information by users, and (e) degree of real-time and human-computer interaction involved. Finally, and by no means least, the cost/benefit ratio of the computer system is a dominant criterion.

One possible approach to developing the computer system is to list application requirements of the system as shown in Table 11-2. The file size, transaction rate, and run-times help to scope the computer needs.

Table 11-2. Applications Approach to Computer Configuration.

Application	Master File, Medium–Key	File Size, Records–Characters	Processing Frequency	Transactions Per Run	Average Run Time (hr)
Order entry	Disc–order no.	10,000–150	Daily	1,000	1
Sales analysis	Tape–cust. no.	2800–90	Weekly	7,000	1½
Inventory	Tape–prod. no.	2500–120	Daily	7,000	2
Distribution schedule	Network program	—	Daily	—	1
Production schedule	Linear program	—	Weekly	—	2
Payroll	Tape–employee no.	6000–100	Weekly	10,000	6
Accts receivable	Tape–cust. no.	3000–260	Daily	500	¾
Accts payable	Tape–vendor no.	3000–260	Daily	100	¼
Vendor analysis	Analysis program	—	Monthly	—	¼
General ledger	Tape–account	120–1000	Monthly	3,000	½
Purchasing	Disc–P.O. no.	600–200	Daily	600	½
(Other applications)					

The choice of a card system, tape system, or direct access system for each application must also be made. The general configuration of card or tape systems is pictured in Fig. 11-10, which a direct access system is presented in Fig. 11-11.

Typically, users are some distance from the mainframe computer and must communicate through a terminal connected to the main computer by wire, coaxial cable, or microwave. Figure 11-12 shows various configurations from simple networks to distributed computing.

[1]Harry T. Larson, "EDP, a 20-Year Ripoff," *Infosystems,* November 1974, p. 27.

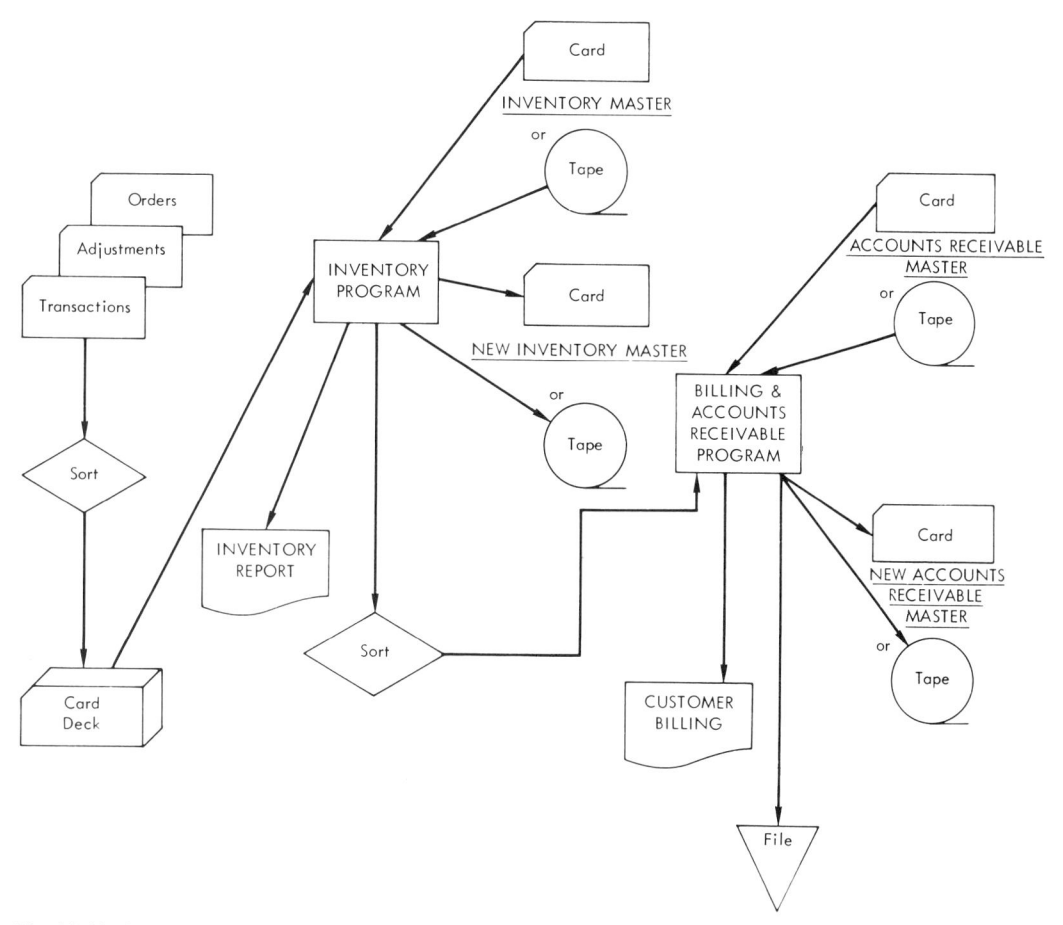

Fig. 11-10. Inventory and Accounts Receivable—Punch Card or Tape.

The computer configuration may be described in detail by means of a narrative description and a listing of equipment. Alternatively, a diagram (Fig. 11-13) or a pictorial presentation (Fig. 11-14) will serve.

The selection of a particular computer is aided by referring to current articles in computer periodicals which compare characteristics. The nature of characteristics considered important in one study is shown in Table 11-3.

THE PROCESS OF CONVERTING FROM A MANUAL TO A COMPUTER-BASED SYSTEM

To increase our understanding of computer hardware it is helpful to provide an elementary description of the basic steps involved in making

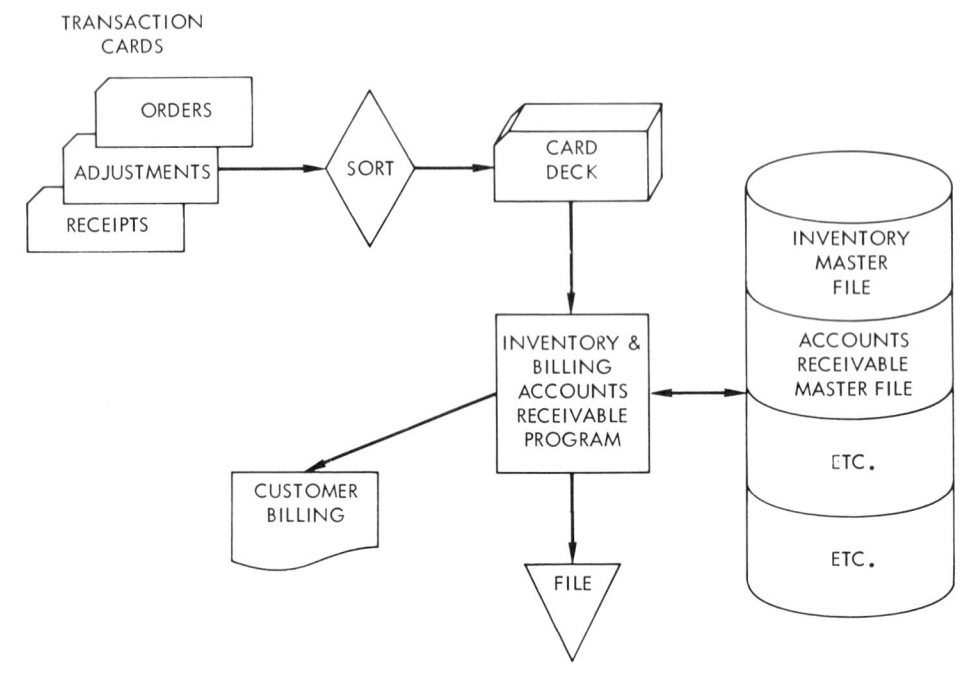

Fig. 11-11. Inventory and Accounts Receivable—Direct Access.

a simple one-for-one conversion from a manual to a computer system. In other words, we answer the question, "How do you get the system on the computer?"

The basic steps are:

1. System description.
2. Input documents.
3. Output documents.
4. File design.
5. The program.

System Description

The system description is usually prepared after preliminary investigation and definition of the problem. The description is essentially a statement of the major inputs, outputs, processing operations, and files needed. The purpose is to show the logical flow of information and the logical operations necessary to carry out the particular design alternative chosen. Systems descriptions are in both *narrative* and *flow-chart* form.

(a) Simple network

(b) Simple network with modems for use with common carrier lines

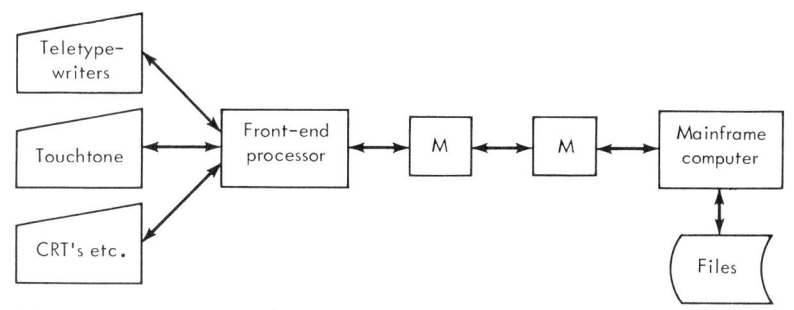

(c) Simple system with input/ouput and file multiplexors

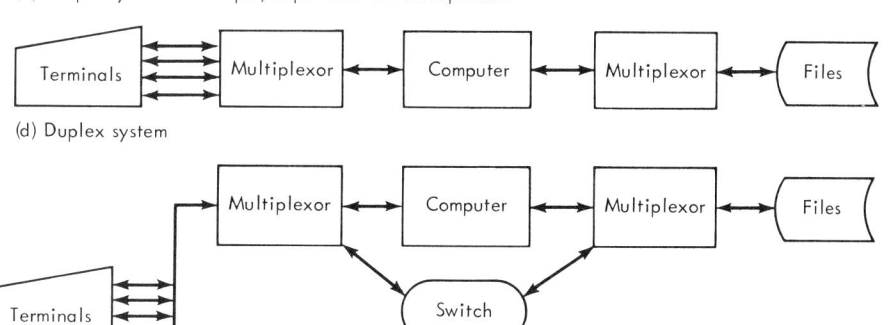

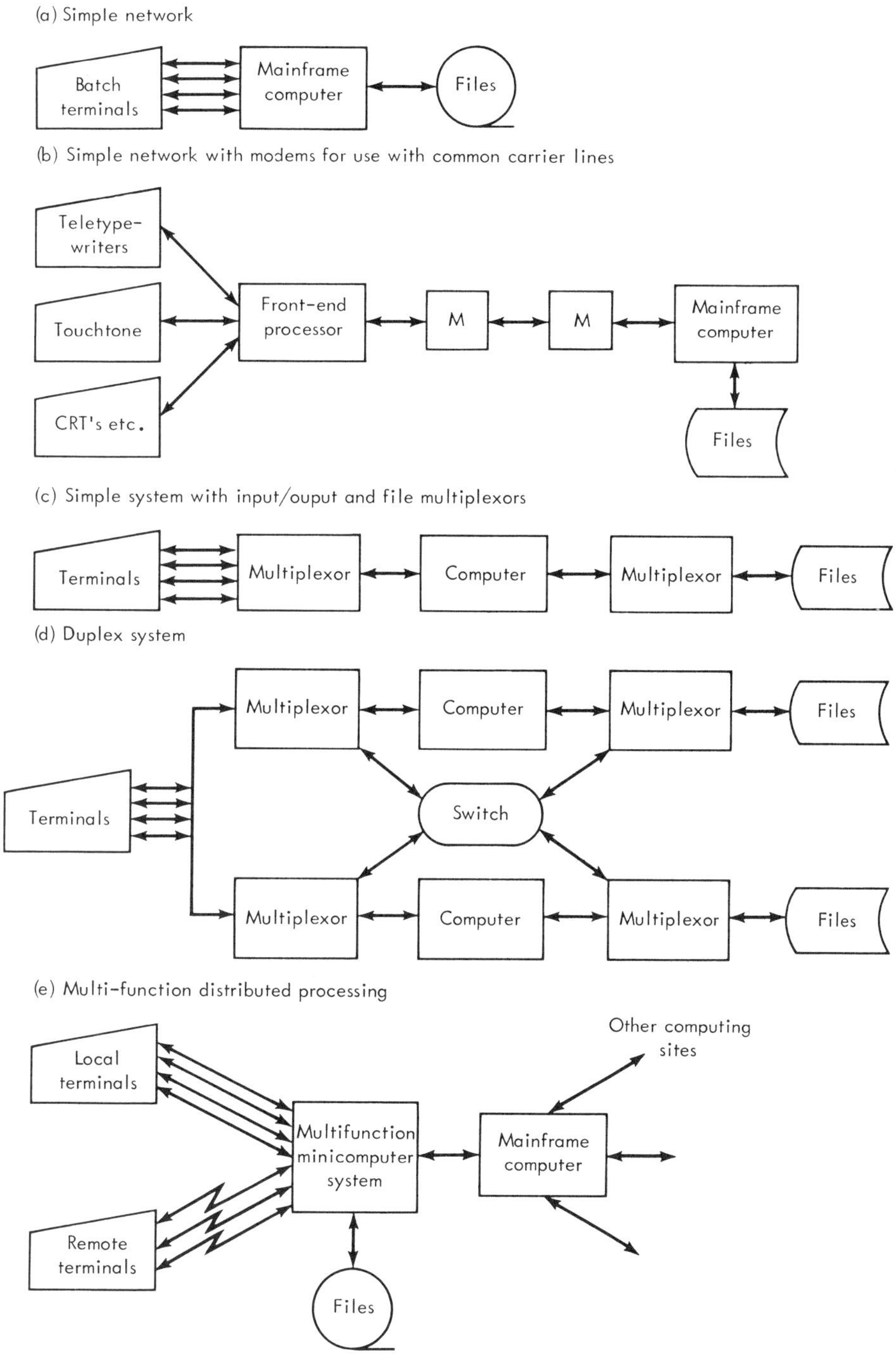

(d) Duplex system

(e) Multi-function distributed processing

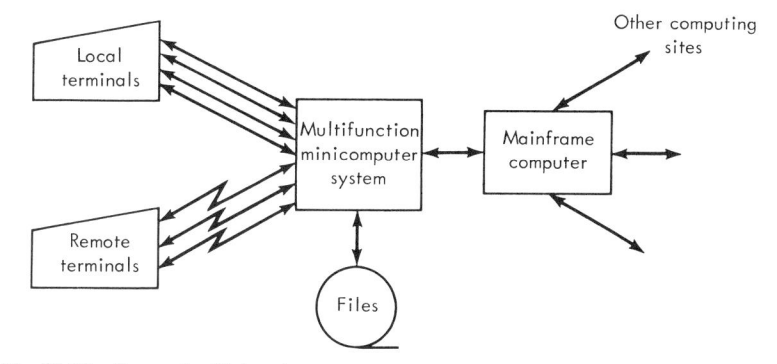

Fig. 11-12. Computer Networks

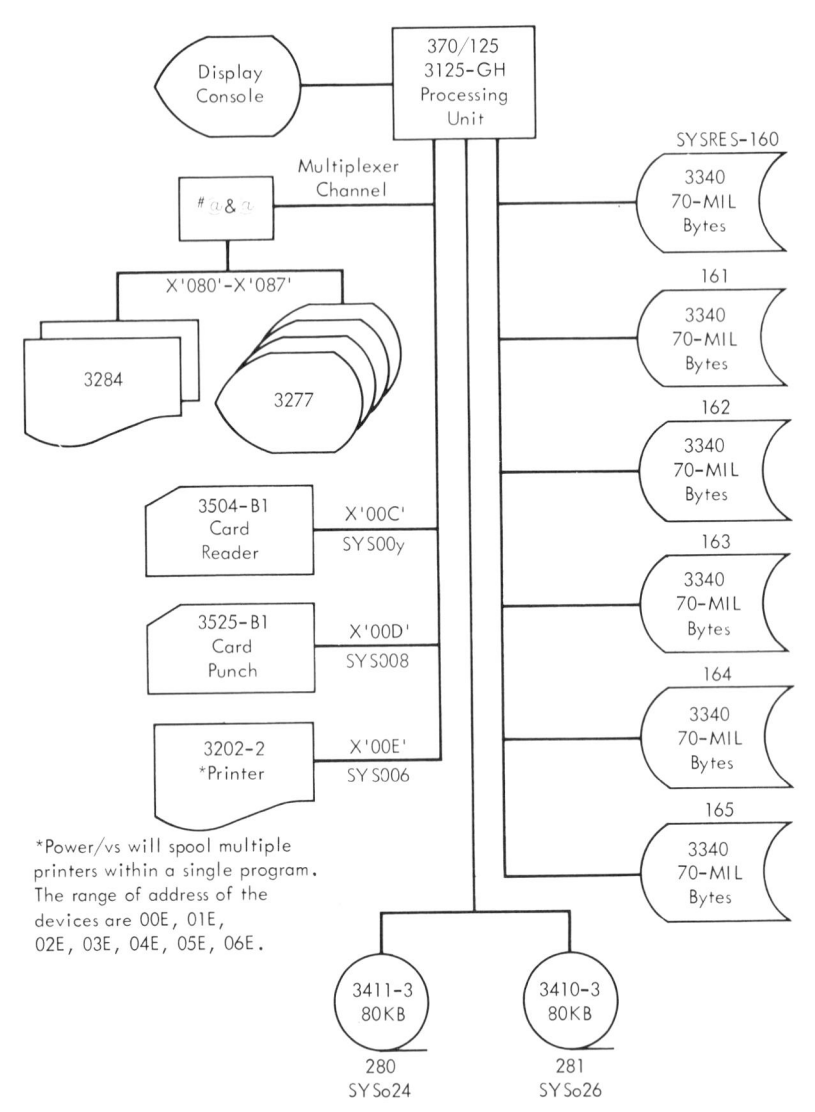

Fig. 11-13. System Configuration

The *narrative* description is an English language depiction of the operation of the system. It should describe inputs, outputs, files, and operations. It should be in that degree of detail that will allow users and computer technicians to understand the operation of the system and to utilize the narrative as a starting point for more detailed design. The narrative form of a simple inventory accounting system might take the following level of narration:

392

A 9119-1
96-Column Card
Reader
300 CPM

A 9122-1
Paper Tape
Reader
40 CPS

A 9222-1
Paper Tape
Punch
40 CPS

A 9419-6
96-Column
Multi-Purpose Card Unit
300/60/60 CPM

A 9480-12 4.6MB or
A 9481-12 9.2MB
Disk Drive

A 9114-1
80-Column Card
Reader
200 CPM

A 9419-2
96-Column Card
Reader/Punch/Data Recorder
300/60/60 CPM

B 9343-1 15.5"
Direct Entry
Console Printer

B 711 Processor
32 to 48KB

A 9491-2
Magnetic Tape Drive
10KB

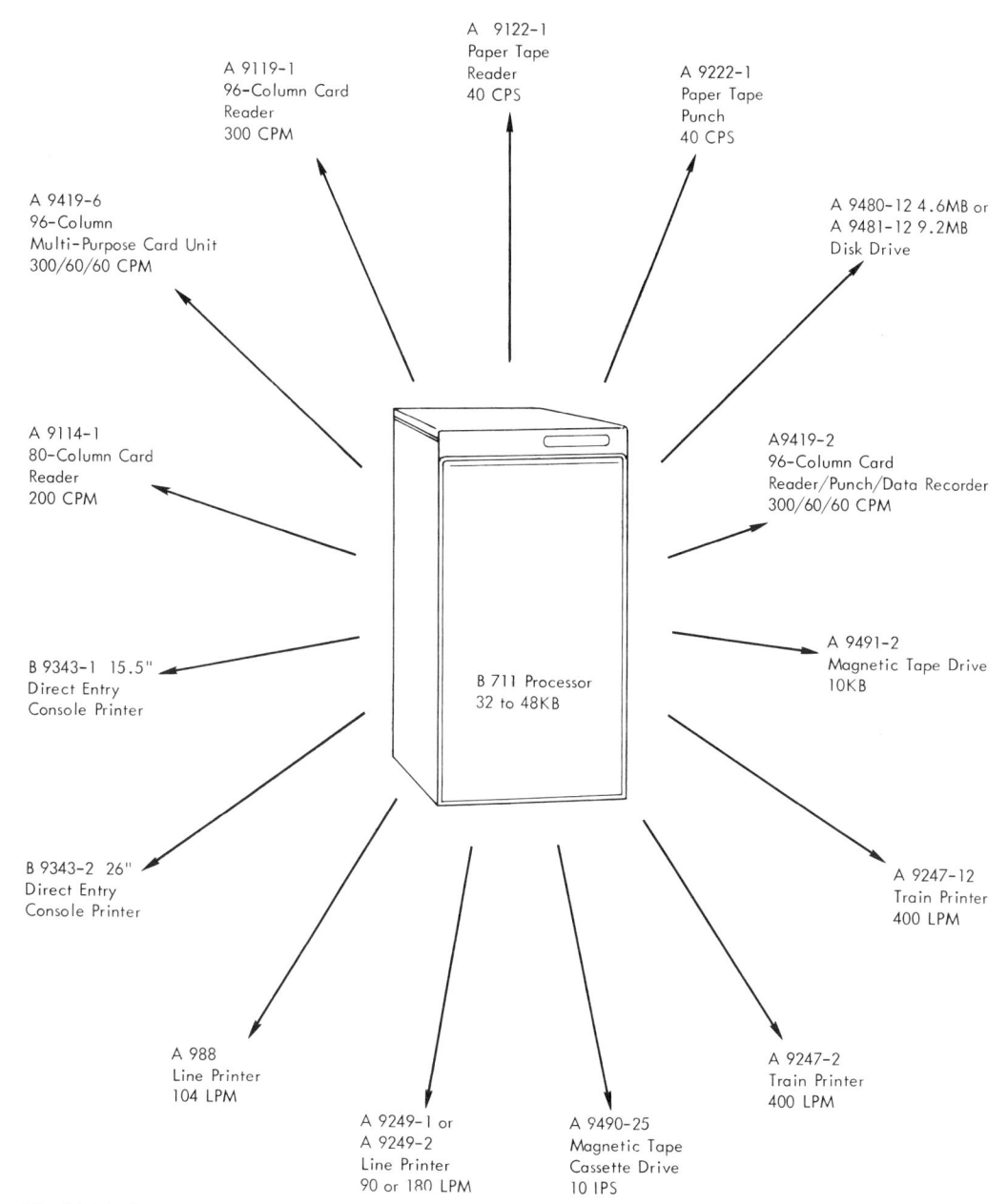

B 9343-2 26"
Direct Entry
Console Printer

A 9247-12
Train Printer
400 LPM

A 988
Line Printer
104 LPM

A 9249-1 or
A 9249-2
Line Printer
90 or 180 LPM

A 9490-25
Magnetic Tape
Cassette Drive
10 IPS

A 9247-2
Train Printer
400 LPM

Fig. 11-14. B 711 Processor Configuration

Table 11-3. Computer Characteristics

Manufacturer/ Model No.	Avg. Purchase Price ($1,000)	Avg. Rental Price ($/Mo.)	Speed (usec) CPU Cycle Time	Add Time*	Automatic Interrupt	Floating-Point Arith.	Memory Protection	Indirect Addressing	Editing Instructions	No. Index Registers	Medium**	Maximum Capacity (in characters)	Access Time (in usec)	Typewriter Console	No. CPU I/O Channels	Data Word Length***	Buffering	Data Collection	MICR	OCR
Honeywell Information Systems (cont.) — Circle 11																				
6040	1,155	22K	1.2	7.3	x	x	x	x		8	C DI	524K 2.13b	1.2 30ms	x	16	36	x		x	x
6050	1,966	39K	1.2	5.4	x	x	x	x		8	C DI	1,048K 2.13b	1.2 30ms	x	24	36	x		x	x
6060	2,035	40K	1.2	5.4	x	x	x	x		8	C DI	1,048K 2.13b	1.2 30ms	x	24	36	x		x	x
6070	2,740	55K	0.5	2.4	x	x	x	x		8	C DI	1,048K 2.13b	0.5 30ms	x	24	36	x		x	x
6080	2,823	56K	0.5	2.4	x	x	x	x		8	C DI	1,048K 2.13b	0.5 30ms	x	24	36	x		x	x
8200	2,900	40K 78K	0.75	3.12 128	x	x	x	x			C DR DI	2,096K 4.2m 300m	0.094 8.6ms 15ms	x	48-96		x		x	x
International Business Machines Corp. — Circle 12																				
System/3	136-298	3.2K-7.2K	1.52	35	x		x	x	x		C	128K	1.52m	x		B	x	x	x	x
System/3 Mod 6	48 (typical)		1.52	35	x			x	x	2	C	16K	1.52m	x	1	B	x			
System/3 Mod 10	57 189		1.52	35	x			x	x	2-4	C DI	48K 9.80ms	1.52m 153ms	x	1	B	x	x		

Printers		Magnetic Tape		Punched Cards		Punched Paper Tape		Data Communications	Software							
Lines Per Minute	List Per Minute	Plotter**** 7-Channel K/Char. Per Sec.	9-Channel K/Char. Per Sec.	Cards Per Minute Input	Cards Per Minute Output	Charac. Per Sec. Input	Charac. Per Sec. Output	No. Transmission Lines	Visual Display	Operating System	Time Share Capability	Multiprogram	Cobol	Fortran II, IV or VI	Utilities	Communications	Other
1,200		7.5-200	20-266	900	300			600	x	x	x	x	x	x	x	x
1,200		7.5-200	20-266	900	300			600	x	x	x	x	x	x	x	x
1,200		7.5-200	20-266	900	300			600	x	x	x	x	x	x	x	x
1,200		7.5-200	20-266	900	300			600	x	x	x	x	x	x	x	x
1,200		7.5-200	20-266	900	300			600	x	x	x	x	x	x	x	x
300-1,100	800-1,600	5.2-144	37.3-224	1,050	100-400	600	120	1-126	x	x	x		x	x	x	x
1,100				500/1,000	120/260			var	x	x		x	x	x	x	
				22	22			var	x	x		x	x	x	x	
1,100			80	250-500	60-120			var	x	x		x	x	x	x	

*this speed is the complete add time for two six digit numbers from memory to memory;
**C=core, DI=disc, DR=drum, IC=integrated circuit, PW=plated wire, TF=thin film;
***B=binary, D=decimal; K=thousand, m=million, b=billion, usec=microseconds, ms=milliseconds, ns=nanosecond, w=words, x=yes, mc=megacycle.

Source: "Computer Characteristics" *Infosystems,* May 1974, pp. 52–53.

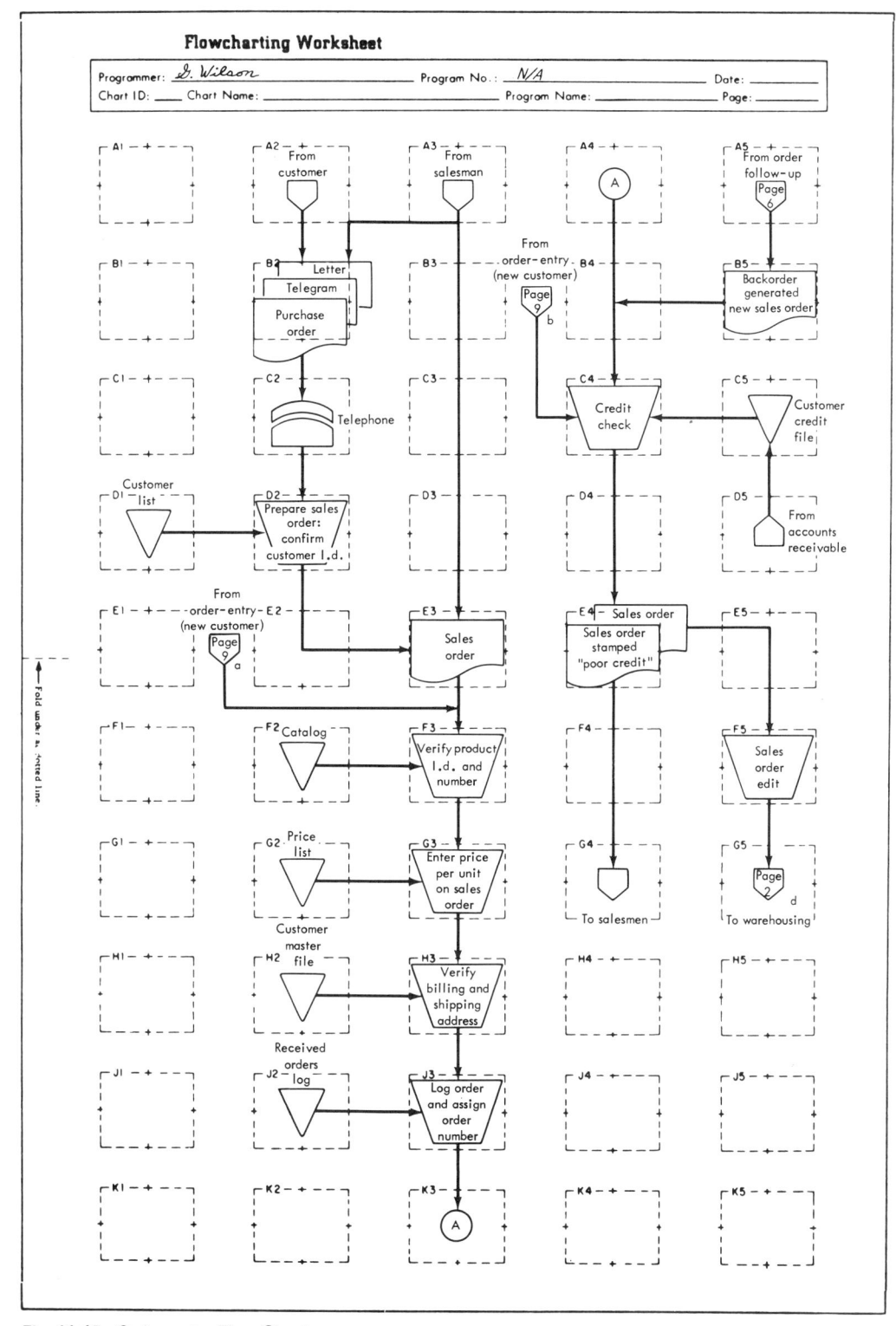

Fig. 11-15. Order-entry Flow Chart.
Courtesy of IBM Corporation.

The activity is concerned with an inventory control accounting system for finished goods inventory. Transactions (receipts and issues) are read from punched cards, the relevant magnetic tape master record is found and updated, and the new inventory status report is printed.

The *flow chart* puts in symbolic form what has been described in narrative form. It facilitates a quick analysis of the job being performed and provides a general symbolic overview of the entire operation. The flow chart for a typical order-entry system might appear as shown in Fig. 11-15.

Input Documents

After the system description is completed, it is necessary to specify how the information will be put into a form that is acceptable to the computer. Volume of information, frequency, accuracy and verification requirements, and the handling of the information are considerations in the selection of input format. Sometimes inputs have to be accepted in the form in which they are received from the outside. In this case, the task of conversion is merely one of preparing input to machine-usable form.

The exact layout of input documents is necessary because the computer program is an exact and precise sequence of steps that operates only when data are located in prescribed positions. In our example, the input format is determined to be punched cards. The holes in these cards are interpreted by the input device of the card reader, converted into computer-readable form, and stored in computer memory for processing.

The card input layout for our inventory accounting example is shown in Fig. 11-16. The item number of inventory is represented by an

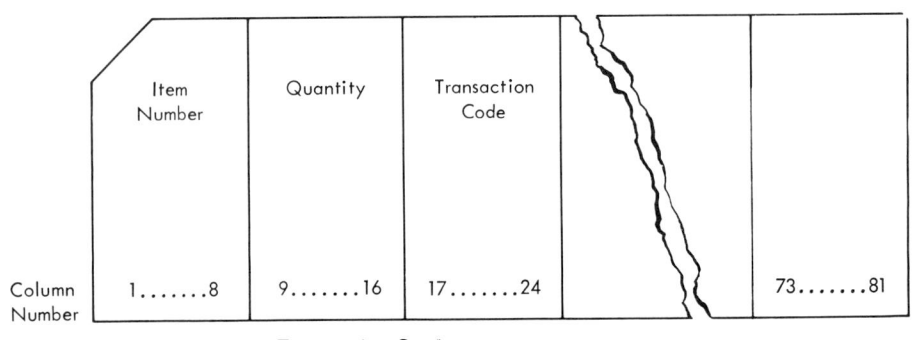

Fig. 11-16. Layout for Input Transaction Card.

eight-digit numeric field. A separate card is prepared for each transaction, with the quantity involved in the transaction represented by an eight-digit field and the nature of the transaction indicated by the last field on the card, which has an eight-digit code (this could be transaction by price, territory, customer, etc.).

Examination of the input document reveals that it provides all the relevant information contained in the system description. The typical *item description* normally associated with inventory is not contained in the input document because it is already filed in storage.

Output Documents

Outputs are subject to much the same considerations as input documents, but the output format should be treated with additional care because it represents the purpose or objective of the entire operation. It is the output document with which management is almost exclusively concerned, and because of its critical nature, care should be taken in its design.

The output layout of an inventory status report is shown in Fig. 11-17. Although the computer is capable of printing much more complex reports than our example, we show the minimum information required to meet the specifications of our system description and output requirements.

ITEM NO.	DESCRIPTION	QUANTITY ON HAND	QUANTITY ON ORDER	TRANSACTION QUANTITY	QUANTITY B/O	AVERAGE UNIT COST	EXTENDED COST	LAST RECEIPT	LAST ISSUE	MIN. BAL.	MAX. BAL.
411116	B500 TWINLITE SOCKET BLUE	458	500			.35	160.30			800	1600
	ADJUSTMENT			42		.35	14.70				
	RECEIPT			500		.37	185.00				
	ISSUE			50-		.36	18.00-				
		950*				.36	342.00	2/11/--	2/14/--		
411122	B506 SOCKET ADAPTER BROWN	325				.19	61.75			300	800
	ISSUE			20-		.19	3.80-				
	ISSUE			38-		.19	7.22-				
	ISSUE			10-		.19	1.90-				
		257*				.19	48.83	12/19/--	2/11/--	UNDER	
411173	C151C SILENT SWITCH IVORY	50	150			1.16	58.00			100	200
	RECEIPT			150		1.20	180.00				
		200*				1.19	238.00	2/10/--	2/03/--		
411254	A210 PULL CORD GOLD	62	75			2.25	139.50			80	165
	ISSUE			16		2.25	36.00				
	ISSUE			30		2.25	67.50				
		16*	75			2.25	36.00	11/17/--	2/10/--		
	FINAL TOTALS	BEG. INV		48295.26							
		CHANGE		700.08							
		NEW VALUE		48995.34							

Fig. 11-17. Inventory Status Report

Table 11-4. Layout for Magnetic Tape Records.

Frames	1.......8	9.......24	25.......32	
	Item Number	Item Description	Item Balance	End of Record Gap

File Design

The logic required to control the flow of data through the system is a part of systems design, and the flow is in turn dependent on the design of data files. These two steps are closely associated and should be considered in conjunction with considerations of type of equipment storage capacity, input and output media, and format.

The character-by-character contents of every record are specified by the file record layouts. Since magnetic tape files are already specified for our example, we are concerned with the tape input layout. This is shown in Table 11-4.

The Program

Steps involved in providing system instructions to the computer are:

1. Prepare the *program flow chart* to represent the detailed, logical sequence of *steps* for the computer to follow to accomplish a job.
2. Write the *translation instructions* in an *assembly language* or *compiler-level language* to be stored in the computer. The assembly language is one step above the binary (0, 1) language of the computer and uses a simple, easy-to-remember code for the numeric binary machine code. Compiler languages such as FORTRAN, COBOL, and PL/1 are higher-level languages that can incorporate several machine-level instructions into a single high-level instruction. Once a translation language is stored in the computer it is usually left there permanently.
3. Prepare the *computer program* by following the steps in the program flow chart to write computer instructions in the compiler language.

4. *Program storage* by the computer puts the program in the computer in binary form ready for processing data.
5. *Program operation* by the computer occurs when data are entered in the computer as called for by the program. The computer executes the instructions of the program in sequence until the program has been completed.

PITFALLS IN ACQUIRING COMPUTER HARDWARE

There are many kinds of mistakes possible in any expenditure of funds. There are, however, some very common and expensive mistakes associated with acquiring data processing hardware.

Pitfall 1: The Turnkey Operation

Some computer manufacturers and consultants may try to persuade you to buy a turnkey system. This is a hardware system designed, installed, and debugged ready for the buyer to push a button (turn a key) or start up.

The disadvantage is that you will have to spend a lot of time educating the seller or consultant in company operations. Second, installing the system without considerable orientation and training of your company's personnel is likely to result in chaos. Third, if you do not have a staff capable of designing your data processing systems, it is unlikely that the same staff can operate the turnkey system.

Borden, Inc. did some costly floundering around before developing some good computer systems. The vice president in charge concluded, "If you don't have an in-house staff doing the job of design and also available to maintain it, you are asking for trouble."

Summary: Systems are likely to be less expensive and to work better if you design them yourself.

Pitfall 2: Spending All Your Money on Hardware

A study showed that the average breakdown of each dollar of computer expenditures is:

Hardware	35 cents
Staff	30 cents
Updating present system	15 cents
New applications	20 cents

The money spent on new applications of the computer system is the only amount subject to significant short-term management control. Yet the impact of computer applications on future benefits and costs is enormous.

Summary: Spend more money on new applications and development than the average firm does.

Pitfall 3: Letting Computer Salesmen and Data Processing Managers Make Major Decisions About the Computer

The natural inclination of computer salesmen and data processing managers is "to sell you a Cadillac when you need a motorcycle." They want you to have the biggest and the best; they do not think of how to improve managing.

Summary: Just as wars are too important to be left to generals, computer hardware decisions are too important to be left to specialists.

Pitfall 4: Installing an MIS Without an MS

It is absurd to process data and call it an MIS instead of first developing a management system (MS). The management system is the basis for managing with selected information.

Summary: Do not waste computer power.

Pitfall 5: Underestimating the Time and Expense of Developing a System

The inclination of hardware managers is to underestimate the time required for hardware installation and debugging. Training of personnel and the great length of time required to generate needed software are often overlooked or optimistically planned.

Summary: Plan carefully the *total* design, installation, training, and software preparation. Double your time estimate and you will probably come close to this new end date.

Summary

In this chapter we have shown the close analogy between the manual process and the computerized process. This analogy explains the basic functions of the computer as (1) accepting input, (2) performing arithmetic, (3) storing data until they are needed, (4) controlling the sequence of its own operations, and (5) transmitting output.

The basic components of a computer system can also be matched with components of a manual system to show the similarity.

A wide variety of input and output devices exists for the central processing unit of the computer to make contact with the computer user. These devices are increasing steadily in type and sophistication. (We even have "intelligent terminals.")

Minicomputers are gaining in processing power and memory, challenging older giant computers or supporting the new ones. On the other hand, the transmission of data over long distances with ever-increasing efficiency makes possible the use of one central powerful computer.

Finally we have suggested several common and major pitfalls for management to avoid when hardware is being bought for an MIS.

DISCUSSION QUESTIONS AND PROBLEMS

1. What are the differences between problem-solving and data-processing uses of the computer?
2. a. What is the difference between internal and external storage?
   b. What is the function of internal storage?
   c. Where are the programs stored?
3. a. Differentiate between batch processing and on-line-real-time applications.
   b. In what type of applications would each be used?
4. List the basic steps involved in converting from a manual system to a computerized system.

5. a. Flowchart a manual subsystem (such as accounts payable).
   b. Flowchart the EDP application for the same subsystem.
6. a. Identify the major input devices.
   b. Identify the major output devices.
7. Define the attributes that you would consider in selecting a CPU.
8. What is the functional difference between a multiplexer and a concentrator?
9. What is the purpose for having a data communications system?
10. List data communication media.

Bibliography

BURCH, JOHN G., JR. and FELIX R. STRATER, JR. *Information Systems: Theory and Practice,* Santa Barbara, Cal.: Hamilton Publishing Company, 1974.

BURNETT, GERALD J. and RICHARD L. NOLAN, "At Last, Major Roles for Minicomputers, *Harvard Business Review,* May–June 1975.

"Data Communications Report," *Infosystems,* Part 1, February 1976 and Part 2, March 1976.

"Distributed Computing Report," *Infosystems,* November 1976.

JENNY, JOHN A. "The Crucial Element in Effective Computer Utilization is Man-Machine Interaction," *Automation,* May 1973.

KANTER, JEROME. *Management Guide to Computer Selection and Use,* Englewood Cliffs, N.J.: Prentice-Hall, 1970.

KINDRED, ALTON R. *Data Systems and Management,* Englewood Cliffs, N.J.: Prentice-Hall, 1973.

RADLEY, G. W. *Management Information Systems,* New York: Intext, 1974.

SCRIVEN, DONALD D. and STEPHEN F. HALLAM, "New Approaches to Computer Performance Evaluation," *Infosystems,* October 1976.

"Software Info," a regular feature of *Infosystems* which describes software packages as they appear on the market.

VOICH, DAN JR., HOMER J. MOTTICE, and WILLIAM A. SCHRODE. *Information Systems for Operations and Management,* Cincinnati: South-Western Publishing Co., 1975.

Preview:

This chapter shows the relationship of the data base to the AIS. We will look at the EDP portion of the AIS in terms of data files, programs, and personnel.

—Field definitions
—The programmer
—The librarian
—The data base administrator
—Role of the accountant

CHAPTER TWELVE
data base management systems

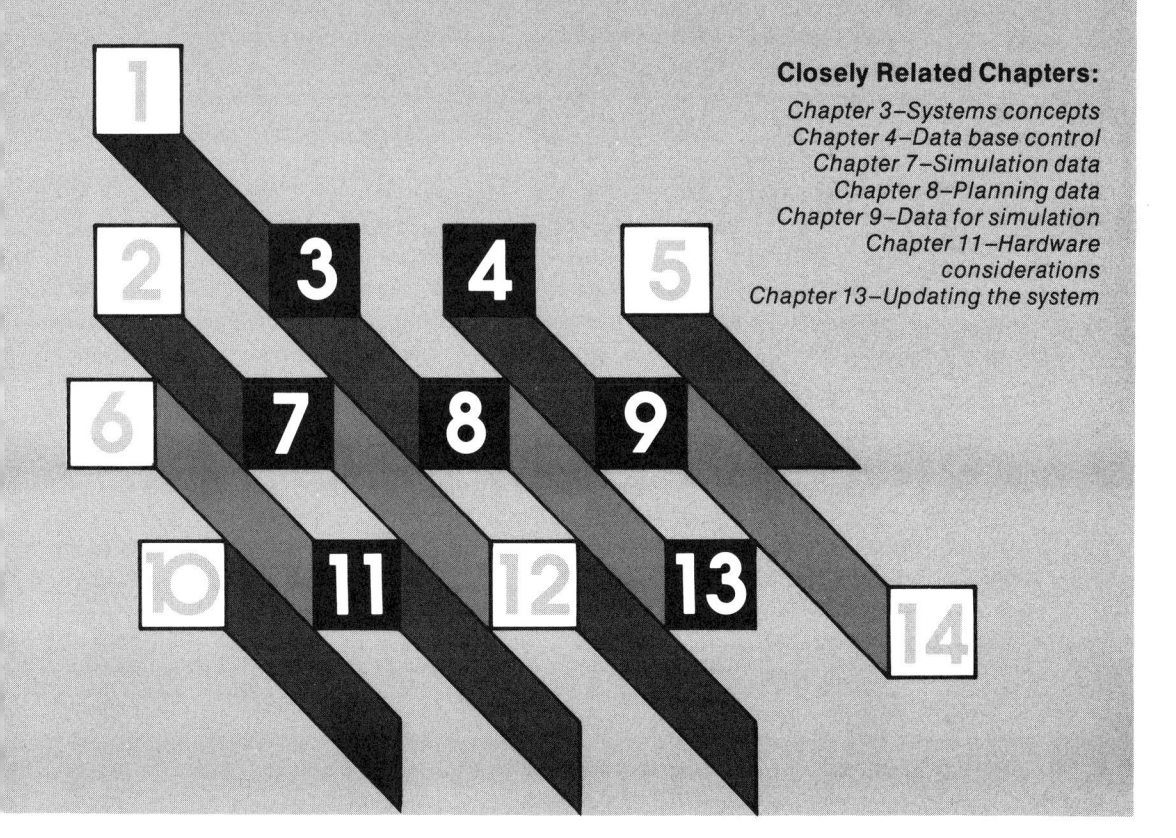

Closely Related Chapters:

Chapter 3—Systems concepts
Chapter 4—Data base control
Chapter 7—Simulation data
Chapter 8—Planning data
Chapter 9—Data for simulation
Chapter 11—Hardware considerations
Chapter 13—Updating the system

The term, data base, is the subject of some confusion. It sounds deceptively simple. A data base is not merely a collection of data nor may this term be accurately applied to any aggregate of data whether or not a computer is directly involved. To refer to a collection of computer files as a data base is rather on the order of calling a bookkeeper an accountant. It is imperative that accountants in particular know more precisely the concept of data base management because of the very dramatic impact that this field will have on basic accounting principles of the future. Future business enterprise will depend heavily on data base management systems. The development of these systems, in turn, will depend largely on the counsel of accountants. The very complexity of today's data processing systems has caused many segments of a business enterprise to retreat from the subject altogether with the claim that data processing is a rather technical activity and ought be left to the technical people that tend to be associated with computers.

What is this data base management? It is more of a philosophy of organization than it is a thing. To understand this philosophy we must first develop an historical perspective of basic data processing concepts, the vocabulary of data processing, and the people involved.

OBJECTIVES OF A DATA BASE MANAGEMENT SYSTEM

The essential objectives of a data base management system may be derived from the CODASYL group[1] and IBM's COPICS (Vol. VIII) as to:

[1]CODASYL, Conference on Data Systems Languages, is a voluntary group of people, supported by their respective organizations, who are interested in the development of the data base techniques and language.

*This chapter was specially prepared by Dr. John C. Munson, Florida Atlantic University

1. Provide instant system access to latest transactions related to an information system
2. Eliminate redundancy by data structuring suitable for all applications
3. Allow multiple concurrent updatings and retrievals
4. Provide a system that offers evolutionary growth by addition of data and programs
5. Provide a description of the data base not tied to any particular processing language
6. Reduce application program maintenance and provide on-line maintenance of data bases.

THE ROLE OF AN ACCOUNTANT IN DATA BASE MANAGEMENT

Basically, the data base will contain the necessary information for the day-to-day operation of the business enterprise and will serve as an extremely valuable tool for planning decisions. It is a repository for all

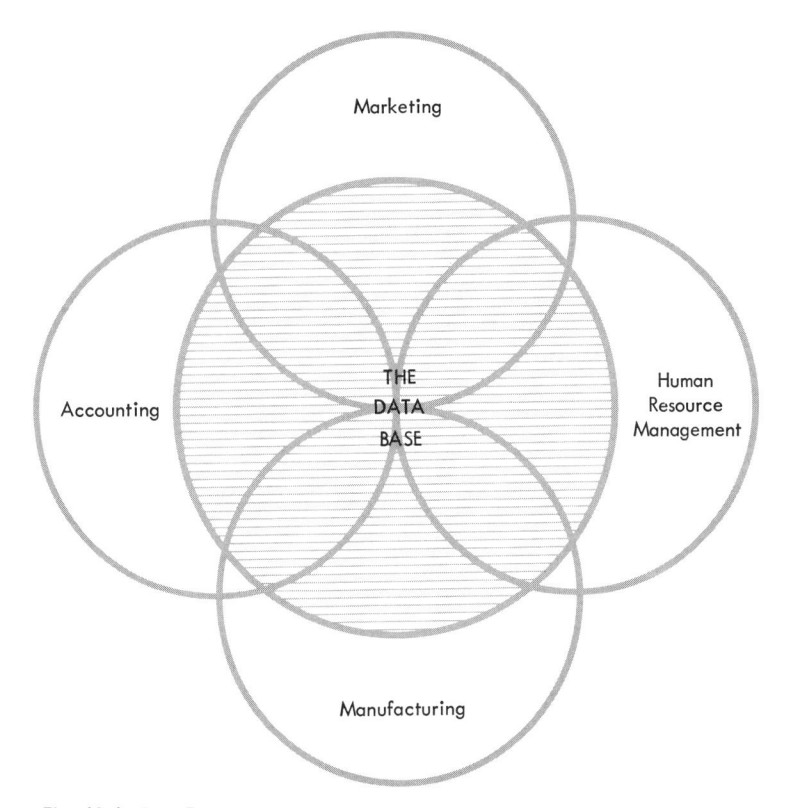

Fig. 12-1. The Relationship of the Data Base Management System to the Components of a Business

information pertaining to marketing, human resource management, manufacturing, and the accounting function. This concept is presented graphically in Fig. 12-1. In this figure we can see that the data base is the focus of the four areas of business activity. Representatives of each of these areas work very closely with the data base administrator to insure the integrity of their data and to develop the logical relationships of the data elements associated with their areas.

The role of the accountant in the data base management system is disproportionately greater than other segments of the business. This is so because the function of an accountant and the function of the data base administrator are very similar. Both function to define the logical relationships among data records. The data base administrator is concerned strictly with the integrity of the data and insuring that the necessary relationships among the data are preserved. Above and beyond these concerns the accountant must use these relationships to measure needs, demands, performance, and other criteria in terms of dollars. The close relationship between the accountant and the data base administrator greatly enhances this measurement function.

THE DATA BASE MANAGEMENT SYSTEM

The data base management system has five fundamental components as follows:

1. the *data base administrator*, who is responsible for the data base schema,
2. the *schema*, which describes the nature of logical and physical relationships among records in the data base,

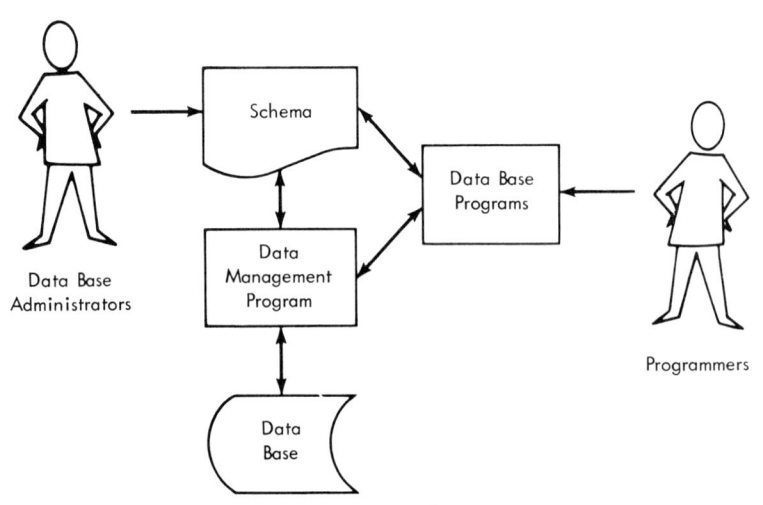

Fig. 12-2. Data Base Management System Components

3. the *data management program,* which creates all physical records in the data base and controls all subsequent record input and output activities of the data base,
4. the *data base,* which contains the physical records,
5. the *programmer,* who serves as a user interface to the data base system.

A graphical representation of this data base management system concept and its operation can be seen in Fig. 12-2. In this figure, we see that the data base administrator prepares the schema. The programmer writes a program, which accesses the schema to obtain a description of the necessary data record formats. Requests for data are made by the programs prepared by the programmer to the data management program.

A significant trend in data base management systems has been the effort to make access to the information in a data base relatively easy and uncomplicated. In an ideal data base system, a person with no particular computer skills should be able to construct requests for information from the data base in a computer language very similar to his own. Considerable effort is now being directed at this problem by vendors of data base system software. These programming systems are called *Query Languages.* Some existing query language processors are now in use and have demonstrated their usefulness, even though they now demand a fair level of programming sophistication to understand and use. On the whole, however, it is the intent of query languages to permit the end user to use the data base to assess the potential consequences and potentials of various alternatives that are being considered and to assess the consequences of decisions that have been made.

Future developments in query languages will ultimately determine the rate at which current file–oriented computer installations will convert to data base systems. Presently data base systems are very expensive, require massive amounts of computer processing and data overhead, and demand a massive conversion effort. Therefore it is simply not cost-effective for some computer installations to endure this conversion unless the ease of information access is sufficient to warrant this effort.

DATA AGGREGATES

Data Fields

To begin at the beginning we must understand that computers are very simple machines, and while they may appear to be intelligent, they are not very bright at all. Just exactly what is occurring in a computer and exactly how it works is not of interest to us in this chapter. This is a healthy attitude to take because no one can say with any degree of certainty exactly what is occurring in any one machine. For the moment we will regard a computer as a black box. We put data into the machine, and we get data out. Because a computer is not very smart, these data must be broken into the most simple possible pieces. For our purposes the most simple representation of data would be a character.

The English alphabet, for example, is composed of twenty-six characters, the letters A through Z. There are other sets of characters. Consider the numbers 0, 1, 2, ..., 9. Taken one at a time, each of these is said to be a numeric character. Another typical set of characters would be the uppercase characters on the top row of the typewriter keyboard: @#$%¢&*. Taken one at a time, each of these is said to be a special character. Another set of characters would be the lowercase letters in the alphabet. Another different set of characters would be the individual letters from the Hebrew alphabet.

Clearly, there are a large number of sets of characters in use throughout the world today. It would be very expensive to build a computer which would recognize any arbitrary character set. Thus, computers are typically built to recognize a rather limited set of characters. Unfortunately, not all computers even within the United States use exactly the same character set.

All a computer can do is read one character at a time. Similarly, it can print one character at a time. It is the responsibility of someone else to insure that characters are logically grouped and presented to a computer in a sensible fashion. When characters are grouped together in this fashion they constitute a data aggregate called a field.

Fields are usually composed of a fixed number of characters. For example, a field might be established to contain a telephone number (with an area code), making this field ten characters long. The fact that fields are usually a fixed length or contain a fixed number of characters raises a very important point. If a field were not composed of a fixed number of characters, then the field would have to carry a special character at its beginning and at its end, called a delimiter, which would serve to tell the computer where the field begins and where it ends. Further, the user program in the computer which is reading these characters would have to examine each character as it arrived to see if it were a delimiter. This process creates extra work for the computer which is not directly productive in solving a user problem. Computer time invested in this manner is called *overhead*.

Field Attributes

In addition to a length property, a field also has an attribute dimension. That is, only a certain type of character may be put in a particular field.

Consider a field set aside to contain social security numbers. It should be long enough to contain the full nine characters of a social security number. There will never be letters or even special characters in this field. It will only have numbers in it. Hence it is called a *numeric* field. On the other hand it may be useful to set up a field containing only letters. This is known as an *alphabetic* field. If the field can contain either alphabetic or numeric characters, it will be called *alphanumeric*. These are but three types of fields. As we progress with the discussion on data base design we will see the need for other types of fields.

As it turns out there is actually another attribute dimension to the concept of fields. There are exactly two types of characters which may be put in any field: correct ones and incorrect ones. There are two ways in which incorrect characters may be put in fields. To return to the example used earlier, that of the field containing social security numbers, it occasionally happens that well-intentioned computer users put dashes as characters between the third and fourth digits and the sixth and seventh digits of their social security numbers in what should have been a strictly numeric field. This constitutes an error in type and should be trapped as part of the input edit function. Another error which ultimately causes greater anguish to data processing people is logical error. In this case the user records the wrong social security number. This is a very costly error because it cannot be so readily diagnosed. Typically, it will be found only when Mr. 123456789 does not receive his monthly social security check because it has been sent to Mr. 123456788. Errors of this kind creates a very special type of grief in data base systems as will become apparent below.

Data Records

Fields may be grouped together to constitute the next type of data aggregate which is a record. A record is simply a collection of one or more fields. Clearly, the fields within each record must be ordered in some fashion such that a given field may always be found in the same place in each record. The physical organization of a record is called a record layout. A typical record layout for a time card application may be seen in Table 12-1. From this example we can see that a record is composed of three fields: the social security field of numeric characters, the name field of alphabetic characters, and the hours-worked field, which in turn is composed of five subfields for each day of the week. It is the programmer's function to prepare such a record layout for each type of record with which he will be working. For the programmmer's purposes this will be called a logical record.

An extremely important concept with respect to understanding data base concepts is the notion that a programmer is doing a lot more

Table 12-1. PAYROLL Record

Field Name	Field Format
SS-NO	9 Character Numeric
NAME	40 Character Alphabetic
HOURS-WORKED	
MON	3 Character Numeric
TUES	3 Character Numeric
WED	3 Character Numeric
THUR	3 Character Numeric
FRI	3 Character Numeric

than simply listing fields when he is preparing a record layout. He is forming a logical association between the fields of the record. This process is called *binding.* Thus, a programmer creates the fields SS-NO, NAME, and HOURS-WORKED, orders them, and thus binds them together into a larger data aggregate called a record. In this case this record would be given a name, probably PAYROLL, which would later serve to identify a set of employee records, all of type PAYROLL.

The record layout of Table 12-1 serves to describe a *logical* record of type PAYROLL. Sooner or later, there will have to be a physical representation of this record which the computer can read. Next the programmer will have to choose the appropriate medium for this type of record. He could choose to place these records on magnetic tape, on disk, on drum, and even on computer cards. When the appropriate choice has been made, the logical record description is transformed into a physical record description. Let us suppose that the programmer wishes to place these records on data cards. He must now take a description of the card in terms of its physical composition (a computer card is 80 characters long) and transform the record layout to the physical layout. An example of this physical record layout for the record PAYROLL can be seen in Fig. 12-3.

Thus we find that there are two types of records. First, there is the logical record, which is a description of the fields of the record and their relationship one to another. Second there is the physical record, which shows how the logical record will be represented, depending on the particular medium chosen to store that kind of record. As in the case of a logical record of type PAYROLL, it can be seen that the total record length is 64 characters. On the other hand, the physical record will be 80 characters long.

In the special case of records of type PAYROLL, there is a one-to-one correspondence between logical records and physical records. Sometimes more than one card per physical record is required. In this

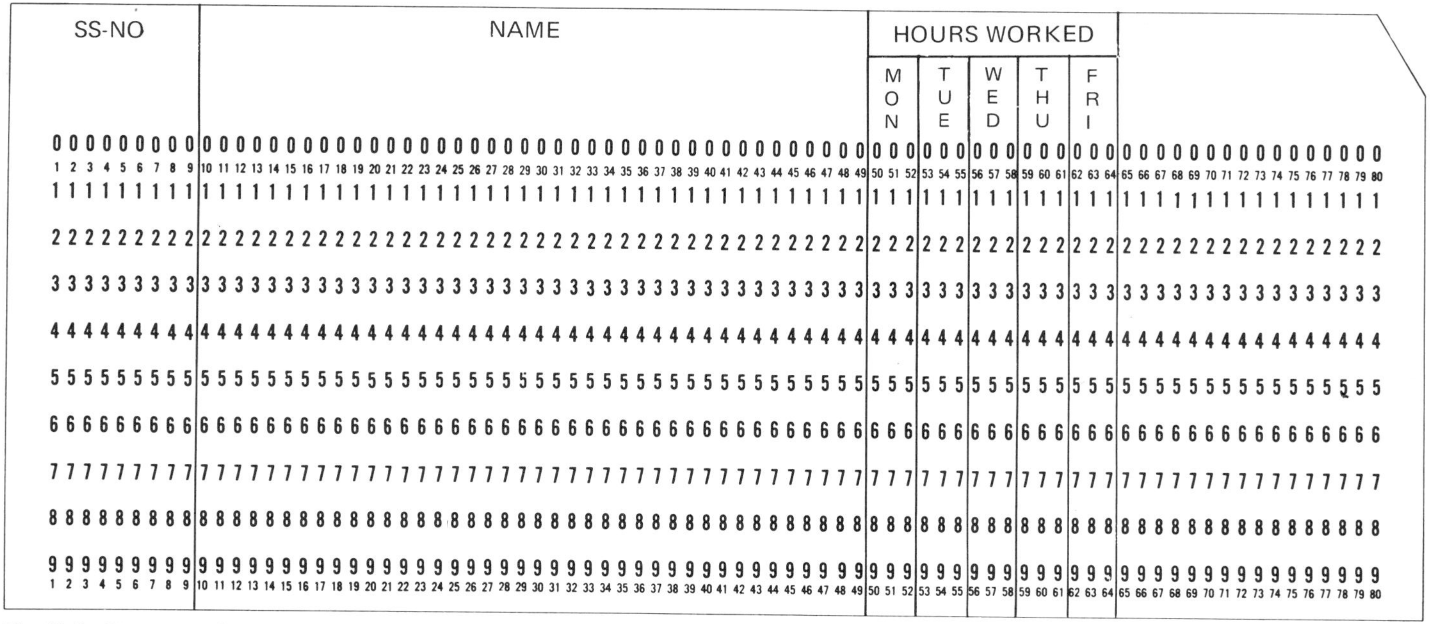

Fig. 12-3. Physical PAYROLL Record

case the logical record is said to be a *spanned* record. On the other hand, more than one logical record may be grouped in one physical record. (Clearly this would not be possible with the example above because the PAYROLL record is 64 characters long and a card is only 80 characters long.) Logical records grouped in this manner are said to be *blocked*. Where there is a one-to-one correspondence between the logical and the physical records, the logical records are said to be *unblocked*.

THE PROGRAMMER

In terms of our present discussion of records, we can now summarize the function of a programmer. He must

1. Establish fields and the necessary attributes for each of these fields,
2. Bind these fields into groups called records and order the fields within the records,
3. Choose the appropriate medium for the records to be represented on, and
4. Decide how the records must be blocked.

In the last analysis, the programmer will have very little choice in these matters. There is always a *best* way or an optimal way to represent records. Suboptimal solutions can be extremely expensive to financially ruinous.

Let us note at this point that records as described above contain only user–data. This will not always be the case.

DATA FILES

After the computer programmer has created the concept of a record, he then sets about to construct a computer program which will read a record organized according to the designated record layout. Presumably, there will be more than one record of the type specified in the record layout. That is, the programmer will write the program in such a fashion as to read a group of cards of the type PAYROLL from a card reader. This group of cards will be stacked one on top of another, placed into the card reader, and read one at a time by the card reader under control of the computer program. These cards will be presented to the computer program in a strictly sequential order.

This ordered collection of records is called a *sequential file*. Thus, a file is a group of records having the same format. In the particular case of the PAYROLL records, they are stored on the card medium. As such, they constitute a *card file*. These records could just as easily have been stored on magnetic tape or on disk. It is possible to construct sequential files on both magnetic tape and on disk.

One of the principal virtues of files constructed on disk units is that these files do not have to have the records placed in them in a strictly sequential order. Rather, records may be placed in disk files in a random order. As such, this type of file would be called a random access file. Each record in a random access file has associated with it a relative index number. Whenever a record is to be read from a random access file, a computer program must produce a relative index number for this record in order to locate the record in the file. One of the principal virtues of a file organized this way is that, to obtain the record # 100, we merely produce the number and use it directly to read the necessary record. Hence the term *direct access file* is sometimes used interchangably with the term random access file.

Consider now the problem of reading record number 100 from a file which has a sequential organization. We must read record number 1, read record number 2, read record number 3, and so forth until the necessary record is obtained. Thus to obtain one record we must read 100 records. This would seem to lead us to the conclusion that we should immediately abandon all magnetic tape files, card files, and sequential disk files in favor of a clearly superior random access file organization. This would be an extremely expensive conclusion to arrive at. Disk storage is one of the most expensive storage media available. Magnetic tape, on the other hand, is relatively inexpensive. Large volumes of data can be stored on sequential files on magnetic tape at the least possible cost.

This direct cost associated with storing records on disk files is not the entire problem associated with their use. With the introduction of third-generation computer hardware and software, the task of writing computer programs which would read directly from the various I/O devices associated with this new generation of computers becomes far too complex for even the more sophisticated programmers to manage. Consequently, most computer vendors supply a set of programs to people who purchase their machines which handle all of the input and output activities for each type of computer peripheral. When a programmer wishes to either read or write a record to a particular I/O device, his computer program will format the request in a particular manner and present it to the appropriate program supplied by the vendor. The vendor's program would then perform the action indicated by the user's program.

The particular set of programs provided by a computer manufacturer defines a set of *access methods* which serve to define the way in which records will be written or read from peripheral devices. The typical program provided by the vendor to perform a *sequential file access* is fairly simple and uncomplicated. The typical program provided by the vendor to perform a *random file access* is fairly complex and lengthy. Thus, if a file is organized as a random access file, every attempt to read from or write into this file causes the execution of a rather lengthy program to satisfy each request. While the computer is executing this access program it is not directly performing useful work for the user. Thus the user has increased the *overhead* associated with a given program activity by using random access file methods. This overhead might at first glance lead us to the conclusion that we should forego the use of direct access methods and disk files.

DATA FILES: AN EXAMPLE

In order to understand the circumstances which would force the use of direct access file methodology, let us invent a commercial bank. This bank has a small computer system complete with two magnetic tape transports and a MICR reader which will allow the computer to read the special magnetic ink characters recorded on the bottom of each check or deposit slip. This is a small bank. At the end of each business day, the bank employees will sort each of the day's checks and deposit slips into ascending order by account order. These employees will then turn on the power to the computer and put a magnetic tape on each of the tape units. One of these magnetic tapes contains a sequential file of records. Each record on this tape contains a field for account number, account balance, and a field for each transaction against this account number. The records are arranged in this file in ascending order by account number. The bank employees now cause a computer program to be loaded into computer memory. This program will read a MICR record which will be either a deposit or withdrawal. It will then read a record from the magnetic tape which contains current account information. As each account is updated it is written into a sequential tape file on the other tape unit. This new file will become the current account file for tomorrow. When the last account has been updated, the employees turn the computer off, put the tapes in the vault, and leave. If this bank were to replace its magnetic tape units and files with disk units and random access files, its costs would probably double because of the additional expense of the disk units and the overhead created by the random access files.

As long as the bank managers are happy with this approach, they probably have the best possible system. The business prospers, however, the number of accounts increase, the total check volume begins to rise, and the employees have to stay later each day to sort and process the checks. Finally it is decided that it would probably be better to equip each of the tellers with a terminal that was connected directly to the computer and process each transaction as it occurred. Now consider the problems involved with the use of sequential file methodology. A customer will approach a teller with a check to be cashed. The teller will key the number of the customer's account into the terminal, and the computer program will find the corresponding account on the magnetic tape, inform the teller as to the account balance, and process the transaction. Let us assume that the bank at this point in time has over one thousand such accounts and that the customer who just approached the teller has the fortune to have the highest account number yet assigned by the bank. Every single record on the magnetic tape will have to be read individually to check the account number to see if it matches the one sought by the teller. Clearly this is a waste. The customer will probably leave in disgust long before the necessary record is found.

What is important to this discussion is that this unnecessary record processing dictated by the sequential method of file processing is in itself a form of overhead. For this particular application, the tradeoff between sequential magnetic tape file and the expense and overhead induced by disk random access files is in favor of the disk files. Had disk files organized in random access fashion been used in the teller application above, the customer's account number could probably have been used directly to obtain the customer's account information without any unnecessary I/O. In this case, a savings, even in goodwill, will be realized through the use of expensive and high overhead file access methods.

There are many more different types of file access methods available to a programmer. Without loss of generality, these are but variants of the basic sequential and direct access methods. Each of these methods is tailored to a specific application. Thus we see that a programmer must, in addition to the duties outlined above (under "The Programmer");

5. Select the appropriate file access method for each file. As before, a bad decision on the programmer's part can simply be catastrophic.

THE LIBRARIAN

Most computer installations typically have a very large number of computer programs and files on magnetic tape and disk. These files constitute a centralized collection of data supporting a firm's business needs. As indicated above, this collection of files is not a data base. It is a very large collection of files which is in desperate need of management. As a result, a person is generally found in computer installations whose sole responsibility is to physically manage the collection of magnetic tapes. He or she is called a *librarian*.

The librarian's function is very similar to that of a librarian in a regular library. That is, he must classify the materials he is responsible for, know what these materials contain, and insure that they can be found or retrieved when requested. In addition to managing the physical magnetic tape reels, this librarian typically maintains a description of the record layout of each major type of file. He is also responsible for maintaining listings and documentation of all programs which process his files. For example, in the case of the PAYROLL file, the librarian would be responsible for all magnetic tapes containing the PAYROLL file, would have a description of the record layout for records of type PAYROLL, and would have documentation on programs which create the PAYROLL record, maintain them, or simply create reports from them. Specifically, then, the duties of a librarian are as follows:

a. Maintain the physical storage media containing the various files of a computer installation.
b. Control the access to these files to prevent unauthorized use of the information or the accidental destruction of data contained on them.
c. Maintain a description of the record layout or record layouts of a file.
d. Maintain a description of the file access method used to build the file.
e. Maintain the documentation of all programs which process these files.

As can be seen, the librarian's function is strictly one of maintenance. This maintenance function may be much more than any one person can handle for a big computer shop. Thus, in a larger computer installation we would expect to find a librarian whose function is to manage other librarians. These subordinate librarians would each manage a subset of library functions. There would be a tape librarian, a program librarian, and so forth. The number of librarians would depend directly on the size of the installation.

There is a very definite communication interface between the librarian and the programmer. As programs are modified or created, the programmer must keep the librarian informed. Also, should the record layout or access methodology of a file be altered by a programmer, the librarian must be informed. This is so because the librarian is the central source of information on data files. This timely interchange of information between the programmer and the librarian is also very necessary from another standpoint. The average tenure of a programmer at any one computer installation is approximately two years. A programmer's exit is usually rather rapid. He will often leave without doing any extra documentation. Thus, if programmer modifications to record formats and program are not captured immediately, it would be reasonable to expect to lose whole files because they can't be processed.

THE COMPUTER PROGRAM

It is now necessary to cultivate a greater understanding of exactly what a computer program is and what it does. As was discussed in Chapter 11, one view of a computer program is that it is a sequence of simple operations that are within the computer's ability to perform. With respect to basic data base concepts, a computer program does something in addition to causing a computer to act. That is, *a computer program is that entity which causes the contents of two or more files to be associated at some point in time.* It forms logical relationships among records. This is a key concept to the understanding of data base systems. To understand this concept of *binding*, consider the following example. Tables 12-2, 12-3, and 12-4 describe three separate record layouts.

We could write a computer program which would simply read SALARY records and extract from each SALARY record the EMPLOYEE-NO from that record. We could write a program which would read the employee number from the SALARY file and use that em-

Table 12-2. Salary Record

Field Name	Field Format
EMPLOYEE-NO	5 Character Alphanumeric
OFFICE-NO	3 Character Alphanumeric
WK-SALARY	5 Character Alphanumeric
NO-DEDUCT	2 Character Alphanumeric
JOB-CLASSIFICATION	3 Character Alphanumeric

Table 12-3. Weekly Record

Field Name	Field Format
EMPLOYEE-NO	5 Character Alphanumeric
SS-NO	9 Character Numeric
ANNUAL-LEAVE	3 Character Numeric
SICK-DAYS	3 Character Numeric
CREDIT-UNION	5 Character Numeric
FICA-TO-DATE	6 Character Numeric

Table 12-4. Employee Record

Field Name	Field Format
EMPLOYEE-NO	5 Character Alphanumeric
NAME	40 Character Alphabetic
SEX	1 Character Alphabetic
BIRTHDAY	6 Character Numeric
ADDRESS	40 Character Alphanumeric
MARITAL-ST	1 Character Numeric

ployee number to obtain a matching record from the WEEKLY file. This program would form a logical association between the SALARY file and the WEEKLY file.

Consider now the number of unique data fields (EMPLOYEE-NO occurs in all three record types). Even for this simple example, a program can be written to form logical associations among the various fields of records of these three files. It is important to note that whenever new associations are needed, a computer program must be written to make this association. Assume that we would like a report which listed by job classification the Social Security number, name, and sex of everyone occupying that job classification. A computer program would have to be written to produce that report. Writing a computer program is a very tedious and expensive process. Every time it is necessary to form a new logical relationship among files, a new program must be written to form the desired temporary relationship between files.

We will explore one mechanism designed to cut such programming overhead. We will incorporate the necessary logical relations into the records themselves. To show how this is done, consider the records of type SALARY from Table 12-2. We will assume that each of these records is in a direct access file. In order to process this file as it is, we will have to write a program which will systematically produce relative record numbers so that the appropriate access method can secure the appropriate record for us. Every time the program processes the file it

Table 12-5. Linked Salary Record

Field Name	Field Format
EMPLOYEE-NO	5 Character Alphanumeric
•	•
•	•
•	•
JOB-CLASSIFICATION	3 Character Numeric
NEXT-RECORD	5 Character Numeric

will have to produce the relative record numbers in precisely the same sequence. To relieve the program and the programmer of this function, let us create a new file withe the record layout as described in Table 12-5.

STRUCTURED RECORDS

The principal difference between the record SALARY in Table 12-2 and the new record SALARY of Table 12-5 is that the new record contains an additional field called NEXT-RECORD. In this field will be stored the relative record number of the next record. To process this file we will simply need to read the first record. From this first record we can obtain the next logical record from the field NEXT-RECORD. Hence, the logical or sequential relationship among the records of this file is built into the file structure. Records organized in this manner are said to form a *linked list*.

Figure 12-4 gives a graphical representation of records in a linked list. The records in the file might be organized in this list in order of EMPLOYEE-NO. Let us now suppose that we wish to read the SALARY file and print a report in order by the field JOB-CLASSIFICATION. To do this we cannot use the linked structure by NEXT-RECORD because to do so would present the records to us in order of EMPLOYEE-NO. Consequently, we would have to write a program to sort these records and present them in order of JOB-CLASSIFICATION. It is possible, assuming that the job classification order will occur rather frequently, for us to add yet another field to records of type SALARY. Let us call this new record field NEXT-JOB. The new record layout will be seen in Table 12-6.

After reading the first record of this new type SALARY we can get the next record by employee number by using the field NEXT-RECORD, or we can get the next record by job classification by using the contents of the field NEXT-JOB. A graphical representation of this new

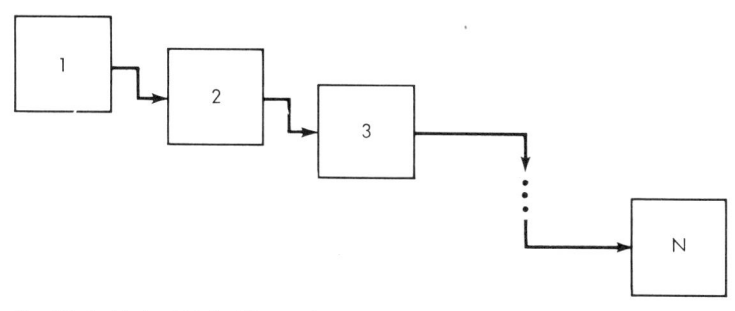

Fig. 12-4. Linked List of Records

Table 12-6. Keyed EMPLOYEE Record

Field Name	Field Format
EMPLOYEE-NO	5 Character Alphanumeric
•	•
•	•
•	•
NEXT-RECORD	5 Character Numeric
NEXT-JOB	5 Character Numeric

record structure can be seen in Fig. 12-5. This new structure of records is called a *keyed list*.

These new fields do not contain any data that directly relates to the employee whose record they occupy. Rather they serve to locate or point to the *next* record where "next" is a logical relationship established when the record was created. These new fields are called *pointer fields*. It is the function of these pointer fields to allow us to order in some logical fashion the records of a file without having to use a computer program or computer programmer to do this ordering function.

The use of pointer fields considerably reduces the programming overhead, but it also increases the total amount of computer storage required to store each occurrence of records of type SALARY. In a sense, we have traded off between programming and computer processing overhead for an increase in data overhead.

If we are willing to pay the price there are many different ways that records can be joined together. Another very useful linkage for a programmer to create would be to link records of different files together. To return to the record layouts of Tables 12-2, 12-3, and 12-4, we might want to link, for each employee, records of type SALARY to

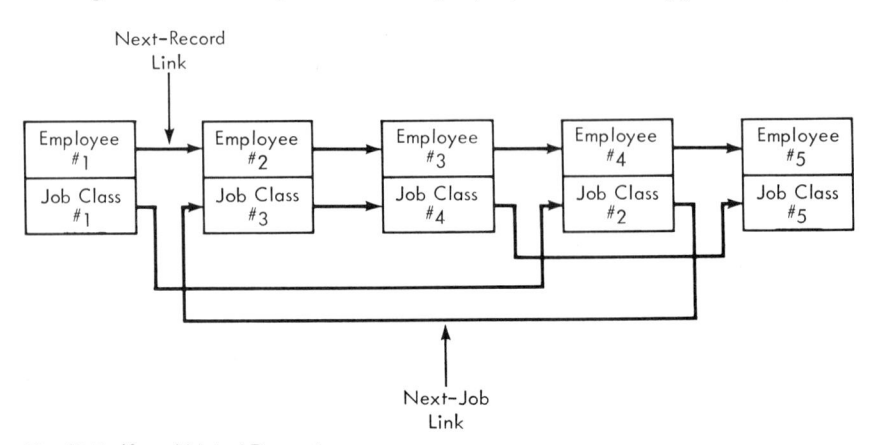

Fig. 12-5. Keyed List of Records

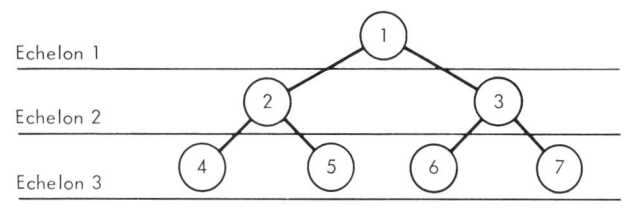

Fig. 12-6. Tree Structured Records

the corresponding record WEEKLY which would in turn be linked to a record of type EMPLOYEE. That is, for each particular employee number, we would form a linked list *across* files associating those records with the same number. With this arrangement of pointer fields, we could simply identify a particular employee in the SALARY file, and, having secured his record, we would have a pointer to his WEEKLY record. This would in turn have a pointer to his employee record. Normally, without the use of this linked structure, it would be the purpose of a computer program to perform this binding of all three record types. Through the use of pointer fields, however, we have preestablished the logical relationships of these different record types.

The number of possibilities of different types of record structures is limited only by the creativity of the computer programmer. Some of these data structures are more important to this discussion of data base systems than are others. Two of particular note are shown in Fig. 12-6 and 12-7. Figure 12-6 is a *tree* structure or *hierarchial* data structure. In this type of data arrangement, data records are organized into *echelons* or levels. To obtain a particular record from, say, the third echelon, we would first identify the appropriate *parent* or *owner* record at the second echelon, which would in turn be identified by the choice of a particular pointer from echelon 1.

Figure 12-7 is a representation of records associated in a *network* or

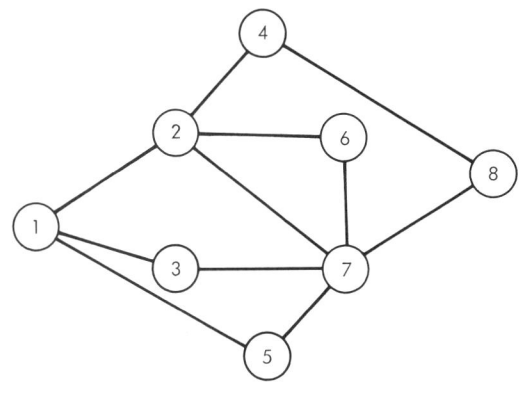

Fig. 12-7. Network Structured Records

421

plex fashion. Clearly, in a network the nature of associations which can be formed among the records which participate in it is indeed complex.

THE DATA BASE

A data base is an organized collection of records. Unlike records in a file-oriented data processing system, the logical relationships among records are not formed by programs or programmers. Rather, records in a data base are related one to another in an exceedingly complex fashion in advance of their creation. The description of the logical relationships is not characterized by the programs which process these records, nor are the physical descriptions of the records necessarily formed in programs. Instead, a *schema* is created. This schema describes the logical and the physical relationships among the records in the data base in a formal manner. It may be regarded as if it were a giant map showing all record types in the data base together with the name of the record and the fields it contains. These links between the nodes of the map are the logical record relationships, and the nodes themselves are the records.

The exact set of rules used to form associations among the various records in the system will determine the type of the data base. There are three major types of data base systems: relational data bases, network or plex data bases, and hierarchial data bases. Hierarchial data bases are composed of records organized in a tree structure as presented in Fig. 12-6. Network data bases have records organized as a system of networks as presented in Fig. 12-7. Relational data bases, on the other hand, work entirely with *flat* files or files which have been structured into tables as opposed to lists or trees. In this system, a file is said to be a relation and fields within the files or relations define domains of *tuples*. On the whole, relational approaches are rather more primitive with respect to the structure of the data. They depend heavily on a data management program to form logical associations.

THE DATA MANAGEMENT PROGRAM

The actual input/output operations in a data base system are far too complex for any individual to comprehend, let alone control. Thus, another fundamental constituent of a data base management system is the *data management program*. This data management program will control all access to and from the data base. Typically this program is the nucleus of a data base system and is provided by the computer manufacturer or a vendor of computer software as part of the total data base management system.

THE DATA BASE ADMINISTRATOR

A very important part of the total data base management system is a person and not a set of computer software. This person is called a *data base administrator*. The data base administrator performs a role very similar to that of an accountant. That is, he specifies the exact relationships among data records. He classifies and places these types of records according to established sets of rules. By the very nature of the way in which record relationships are made, the data base administrator can make the data base system extremely responsive to the data needs of his firm, or he can let the various sources of overhead grow in an uncontrolled manner until the data base management system is consuming the entire profit potential of a business.

As part of the overall system, the data base administrator is needed to provide standardization, organization, maintenance, and resolution of conflicts among users of the system. He performs such specific functions as:

1. Determining data needs of all users.
2. Determining the tradeoffs between data overhead and computer processing-programming overhead.
3. Publishing a directory of proposed data structures for review with potential users of the system.
4. Publishing data dictionaries containing basic information about the data stored in the data base (data field definition, format, editing rules, security considerations, etc.)
5. Resolving with all users special-purpose variations to the data base.
6. Setting up generalized methods for retrieval and a library of data base access programs.
7. Maintaining the data base, its integrity and completeness.
8. Providing and assigning privacy locks and security measures and monitoring for breaches of these.

As can be seen, this data base administrator has assumed a significant amount of the programmers' and the librarians' duties and responsibilities. Through the data base administrator, we have *central control* on and access to information in the data base. The programmer in a data base environment still prepares programs in the usual manner.

However, these programs will obtain the necessary record description information from the data base schema, and all access these programs make to the data base will be through the data management program. Both of these activities occur under the auspices of the data base administrator.

The alliance of the data base administrator and the accountant is a critical one in future business enterprises. Their functions within the business are totally interrelated and remarkably similar in terms of functions and responsibilities. Both serve to provide an important information base to assist a decision-maker for management decisions by virtue of their roles in data organization.

A DATA BASE SYSTEM MODEL

Let us now examine a model of a working data base system. Such a model may be seen in Fig. 12-8. On a regular basis, events occur which will influence the nature of the data in the data base. These events are called transactions. A typical transaction would be the arrival of a purchase order.

To process this transaction, we must submit the transaction to some type of *transaction interface program* which will check for errors in the various elementary fields, a process called editing. Once a transaction has been edited and approved, the change indicated by the transaction type is made to the data base and the edited transaction is recorded on a *transaction history file*. All edited transactions are recorded to provide backup for the data base system.

The entire data base is periodically copied in its entirety onto a series of backup files. Should the data base be destroyed accidently, it can be entirely recreated by restoring the most recent copy of the *data base save file* and reprocessing the transactions from the date of the last data base backup from the transaction history file. This very simple process provides almost complete data security. Also the transaction history, in addition to its role in data security, serves as a built-in audit trail.

Because information in a data base is never destroyed, hopefully, data bases grow predictably over a period of time. Standards must be set which determine the useful life of all of the various types of data records in a data base. Once these standards have been set, a program called an *archival program* will be run against the data base. This program will selectively, according to the established age criteria, remove records from the data base. These records will be placed on an *archive file*. Thus, we

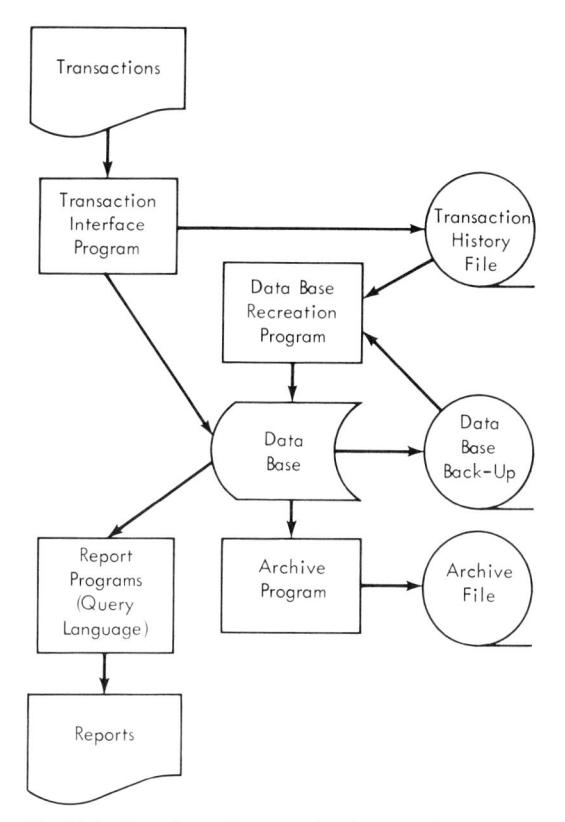

Fig. 12-8. Data Base System with Support Systems

see that there are three principal repositories of data in a data base system: the transaction history file, the data base proper, and the archive files.

Summary

The accountant is vitally concerned with the accuracy and integrity of the data base, particularly those items that affect accounting reports, budgets, and controls. While the development of a data base management requires a specialist, the accounting manager must be able to understand what the data base administrator is doing.

This chapter, has presented, therefore, the concepts of the data base management system and particularly the nature of data organization. The tasks of the data base administrator have also been sketched.

DISCUSSION QUESTIONS AND PROBLEMS

1. Define "data base management system."
2. List and discuss the objectives of a data base management system.
3. What is the role of the accountant in data base management?
4. Define the following terms and give examples of each:
   a. numeric field
   b. alphabetic field
   c. alphanumeric field
5. a. Differentiate between "data records" and "data files."
   b. Give an example of each
6. Discuss the differences between sequential file access and random file access.
7. a. List and discuss the functions of the EDP librarian.
   b. Describe the responsibilities of the librarian for customer files for each of the following:
      1. CPA client list
      2. Bank
      3. Manufacturing firm
      4. Department store
8. What is the function of a computer program?
9. a. Describe the functions of the data base administrator.
   b. Draw an organizational chart for a manufacturing company that would show the position of the data base administrator.
10. List and discuss the components of the Data Base Management System.
11. Define the following terms:
    a. linked list
    b. keyed list
    c. pointer field
12. Illustrate a keyed list for a mail-order firm customer listing which is defined by customer number and ZIP code. Use a diagram similar to Fig. 12-4 and explain.

Bibliography

BRUNN, ROY. "Trends in Database Management." *Infosystems*, June 1974.

CHOW, JOHN V. "What You Need to Know About DBMS," Parts 1 & 2, *Journal of Systems Management*, May and June 1975.

COHEN, LEO J. *Data Base Management Systems,* Wellesley, Mass.: Q.E.D. Information Sciences, Inc., 1975.

Communications Oriented Production Information and Control System, Vol. VIII, System Data Base. IBM Corp., 1972.

COUZZO, D. W. and J. F. KURTZ. "Building a Base for Data Base: A Management Perspective," *Datamation,* October 1973.

CURTICE, ROBERT M. "Some Tools for Data Base Development," *Datamation,* July 1974.

"Data Base Systems: A Mistake for Many," *Administrative Management,* May 1972.

DATE, C. J. *An Introduction to Database Systems,* Reading, Mass.: Addison-Wesley, 1974.

KINDRED, ALTON R. *Data Systems and Management,* Englewood Cliffs, N.J.: Prentice-Hall, 1973.

KROENKE, DAVID. *Database Processing,* Chicago, Ill.: Science Research Associates, Inc., 1977.

MARTIN, JAMES. *Computer Data-Base Organizations,* Englewood Cliffs, N. J.: Prentice-Hall, 1975.

———, *Principles of Data-Base Management,* Englewood Cliffs, N. J.: Prentice-Hall, 1976.

NOLAN, RICHARD L. "Computer Data Bases: the Future is Now," *Harvard Business Review,* September–October 1973.

OLLE, T. WILLIAM. "MIS: Data Bases," *Datamation,* November 15, 1970.

PALMER, IAN R. *Data Base Systems: A Practical Reference,* Wellesley, Mass.: Q.E.D. Information Sciences, Inc., 1975.

POWERS, VICTOR. "Implementing Generalized Data Base Management Systems," *Data Management,* May 1975.

PRICE, GERALD F. "The Ten Commandments of Data Base," *Data Management,* May 1972.

SCHUSSEL, GEORGE. "Scoring DP Performance," *Infosystems,* October 1974.

SNUGGS, MARY E., GERALD J. POPEK, and RONALD J. PETERSON. "Data Base System Objectives as Design Constraints," *Data Base,* Winter 1974.

TESTA, CHARLES J., and SHELDON J. LAUBE. "How Do You Choose a Data Base Management System? Carefully!," *Infosystems,* January 1975.

———, "Other Factors in DBMS Selection and Implementation," *Data Base,* Spring 1975.

TURN, REIN. "Cost Implications of Privacy Protection in Databank Systems," *Data Base,* Spring 1975.

VAZSONYI, ANDRES. *Information Systems in Management Science,* "Data Base Management Systems," INTERFACES, May 1975.

IV

CONTROL OF THE AIS

Preview:
Internal and external factors influence the AIS and as these factors change, the system must also change to meet new needs. This chapter shows many of these factors and how they may alter the system.
—Government
—Economic conditions
—Competition
—Technology
—Company policy

CHAPTER THIRTEEN
maintaining, controlling, and evaluating the AIS

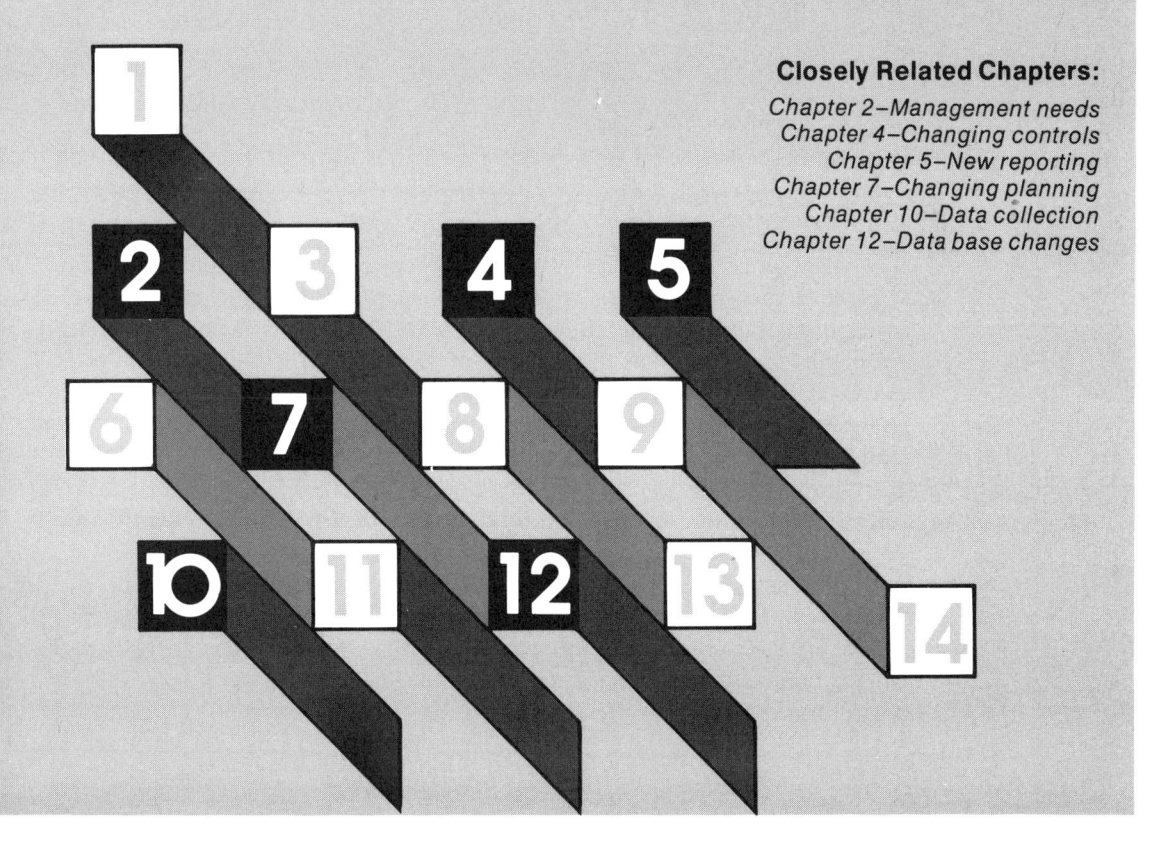

Closely Related Chapters:
Chapter 2—Management needs
Chapter 4—Changing controls
Chapter 5—New reporting
Chapter 7—Changing planning
Chapter 10—Data collection
Chapter 12—Data base changes

The AIS cannot simply be implemented and then forgotten. It requires constant updating, improving, monitoring, and evaluating. These are broad-ranging tasks which can only be covered briefly in a single chapter.

RESPONSIBILITY

The ultimate responsibility for the protection of the company's assets rests with the controller. His position description should clearly define his responsibility for the functioning of the AIS, for the accuracy and validity of its output, for the security of data and information within the system, and for periodic evaluations and improvement of the system. Although many of his tasks may be delegated to system managers and specialists, he personally is *accountable* for performance of the above responsibilities.

Organizationally, the maintenance function poses a problem. The controller, the MIS manager, and the EDP manager must coordinate the maintenance program. This is because management information of all kinds, accounting and financial information systems, and computer programs must be completely integrated. Some solutions place a coordinator for maintenance in the systems organization or in the controller's organization.

NEED FOR SYSTEM MAINTENANCE

As much as 40% of available programming resources are being used for system maintenance in many EDP installations.[1] When we add to this the effort involved in redesigning reports, inputs, forms, and work flow for the AIS in organizations, it is apparent that managements feel there is a great need for system maintenance.

System changes for maintenance fall into the following classifications:

1. Changes due to new government policy, regulations, and legislation;
2. Changes due to economic conditions;
3. Changes due to industry and competitive conditions;
4. Changes due to new technology;
5. Changes required by company major-policy decisions;
6. Extensions and improvements of existing AIS;
7. Change requests;
8. Error reports.

Obviously, priorities must be assigned to projects. Also some projects are long range and some very short range. The short range projects usually consist of emergency maintenance and routine maintenance. Emergency maintenance is required when the system malfunctions. A malfunctioning AIS in a bank, insurance company, or, in some instances, in manufacturing companies, requires immediate attention. Routine maintenance usually consists of minor changes from a technical view but important ones from an operating view. A change in payroll deductions because of a wage increase is an example.

Changes in Government Policies, Regulations, and Legislation

Most large companies require specialists or lawyers to keep management apprised of the numerous changes in reporting requirements, compliance requirements, and pressures for change. For example, banks must be aware of new regulations, maximum interest rates, interest rates established through Federal Reserve activities, minimum downpayments required on loans and mortgages, and mortgage acceptance rules. Manufacturing companies must be aware of changes in pension rules,

---

[1] Zafar Khan, "How To Tackle the Systems Maintenance Dilemma," *Canadian Datasystems*, March 1975, p. 30.

financial disclosure, and so on. Health care facilities must be aware of legislation and rulings with regard to state and federal government payments for the elderly, indigent, and so on. In other words, there is a continual flow of rules from government that requires constant updating of the AIS in a company.

Changes in Economic Conditions

Changes in general economic conditions play a major role in defining financial information systems. If the system is properly designed it should meet the needs of all users, not just the accounting and finance departments. General economic conditions dictate corporate policy in several areas, and the ability to internalize these changes is an important part of good systems design. As these changes are only partly predictable, the system should be evaluated periodically to ensure both proper inclusion and measurement of new conditions. Changes in the unemployment rate, both nationally and locally, could affect the direct labor cost and could also affect the time-frame for completion of planned projects. Changes in inflation and interest rates have even more far-reaching impacts. A rise in interest rates may hinder customers' attempting to obtain short-term credit to purchase a company's product. The same rise in interest rates may stop a company from expanding plant capacity, stockpiling inventories, or replacing and updating fixed assets. This list is not all inclusive but it should be noted that periodic systems evaluations will help ensure that these and similar items are included.

Industry and Competitive Conditions

Changes in industry conditions should be treated in the same manner as changes in economic conditions; however, the timing of reactions to these changes may be more important. The expansion or collapse of a market for a company's products is of such importance that failure to react on a timely basis may mean failure of the business as a whole. Competitive strategies, price policy, hiring, and capital budgeting are but a few of the areas affected by changes in business conditions. New technology, either in production of products or in the creation of alternative products, may impact even the basic concepts that form the corporate objectives.

New standards for measurement such as package sizes or the metric system may have great financial impact. Industry innovations in reporting or gathering data such as point of purchase data collection in retailing and video responses to stock price information in brokerage houses are other examples. These and the above changes require anything from routine to major changes in the AIS.

New Technology

The development of computer technology, applications programs, and management techniques has progressed at such a rate as to make farcical the articles of only five years ago suggesting that total information systems would always be myths. Data communication systems, interactive systems with video displays, tremendous storage capacities, and higher-speed computers are staggering to old line managers. This new technology is, however, being introduced and used by the flood of accounting and business graduates entering organizations each year. The aggressiveness of computer and software companies in promoting entire systems has also been a major factor. Thus, if nothing else changed, technological change alone requires continual system maintenance.

Company Policy and Organization

Company policies may change on a wide range of activities that relate to the AIS. For example, a change in inventory accounting from FIFO to LIFO, a change in pension benefits, a change to direct costing or in accounting for overhead, and capital budgeting evaluation procedures.

Staffing changes also have an impact. The appointment of new managers to old positions due to promotion and replacement usually requires different reports. That is, each manager has his or her individual style and will demand different kinds and forms of information.

When the company revises its organization structure, new managerial positions will appear and others will disappear. Since the AIS is tied into the organization for costing, planning, and controlling, the AIS will need to be modified.

Extensions and Improvements of the Existing AIS

Any business system or operation can be improved, and the AIS is no exception. When systems are designed originally, the scope is usually limited in order to control costs and achieve the major benefits promptly. Marginal benefits or unforeseen opportunities become part of the maintenance program to enhance the system. Refinement of reports, elimination of operations, and improved procedures and controls are examples of such enhancements. One particular area to which we give special attention in this chapter is the continual search for, and implementation of, improved security of the system and its data base.

Change Requests and Error Reports

A change request is a change initiated by a user rather than the accounting or systems designer. The designer must investigate such questions as:

> Is the change critical or merely desirable?
> Will any benefits be derived from the change? What will be the costs?
> What alternative maintenance could be performed with current resources?
> How will the change affect other parts of the system?

A standard form and procedure should be established for error reports. Normally, the initial debugging eliminates most errors. It is possible, however, for inputs falling outside the range of design to occur after long service of the system. A breakdown in procedures may also occur at any time. Thus, error reports should be investigated promptly to determine priority in maintenance.

MAINTAINING SECURITY

> *To impress his employer with the need for additional security, a programmer designed an undetectable program to automatically write payroll checks for several of his relatives, including a two year old girl. He ran the system for 3 months, keeping the checks in their unopened envelopes, then he dropped the entire collection of 30 checks on the security director's desk. He is now in charge of DP security.*[2]

In historical times people went to great lengths to protect their gold. In modern civilization, more companies are concerned with pro-

---

[2]"Computer Security . . . the Imperative Nuisance," *Infosystems*, February 1974, p. 27.

tecting their data. No system can be made 100% secure. The function of design and maintenance is to keep searching for ways to make the company's system and data base more secure. Since resources for this purpose, as for all others, are limited, a rule of thumb is to keep expenditures below 10% of total expenditures for design and maintenance.

System Threats on Order of Increasing Activism

Clark Weissman has structured a classification of system threats as follows:[3]

Accidental threats

1. Some user, employee, or outsider accidentally stumbles upon a loophole which makes the system or its data base accessible. Such loopholes are sometimes called "trapdoors."
2. Component failure invalidates a safeguard which protects the system from intrusion.
3. An error in application of the communication system leaks information improperly.
4. A component failure reveals or leaves vulnerable critical protection mechanisms. This differs from #2 in that the protection mechanism must still be overcome.

Passive threats

5. Electromagnetic pickup of system radiations such as those of microwave transmission.
6. Wire tapping of the communication subsystem of transmission is accomplished by wire or coaxial cable.
7. Exposure of critical system data to unauthorized persons. In a classic case, a college student retrieved guides, procedures, operating instructions, and forms in the trash cans outside the Pacific Telephone and Telegraph supply office. He learned enough to cut into the purchasing and invoice system and take away thousands of dollars of equipment.

Active threats

8. Employees, users, or computer operators may browse through system files for sensitive (unauthorized) data.

[3] Adapted from Clark Weissman, "Tradeoff Considerations in Security System Design," *Data Management*, April 1972.

9. An employee or outsider impersonates an authorized user. A knowledgeable outsider may call the computer center and ask that an entry code be used. He or she may then call back later using the new code as identification. There are a number of ways that access identification codes may be obtained.
10. "Between lines" entry. The system is used by an intruder when the user is on the system but inactive.
11. "Piggy-backing." An intruder intercepts the communication and substitutes for the original-user/system dialog.
12. Corrupt knowledgeable systems people. In the Equity Funding Corp. scandal (1973) over $120 million nonexistent assets were created by computers and about $2 billion in phony life insurance policies were sold to reinsurers.
13. Active search for and entry through trapdoors.
14. Data acquired from residual memory. When a program run has been completed, data may be left in memory (unless a special program clears it). Such data may be sensitive and readily available to any user.
15. The system, in the hands of a skilled programmer, may be used to ferret out its own weaknesses.

Protection of the AIS

There are a number of ways of developing the security of computerized information systems. One approach starts with the design of the system itself. We must find ways in both design and maintenance to minimize the probability that a breach can occur. We must design into the system the ability to audit data after the fact to detect and track violations. We would also like to deter people from attempting to breach the system. Finally, after all these means have made the risk of violating the system small, we may want to shift this risk to a third party.

Clark Weissman has identified successful protection strategies used in modern society as:[4]

1. *Isolate.* Protection is gained by isolating the valuable commodity and controlling access to it. History is filled with examples: the fortress, the jail, the bank vault, and the military shielded computer room (isolated from electromagnetic radiation). Most aspects of physical security embody this strategy.
2. *Confound.* Protection is gained by isolation (but not controlled access), based upon obfuscation. Valuables are hidden by removing them from view (e.g., buried dog bone), or by camouflage and disguise to confound and confuse search. Cryptography is the ultimate example of this strategy.

---
[4]*Ibid.*, p. 16.

3. *Deter.* Deterrence protects by making pilferage unprofitable. The profit/loss (gain/risk) equation is foremost. When gain is high and risk low, deterrence fails, and thievery is encouraged. To dissuade the interloper, risk or punishment must be high and always visible (legally or physically). Department of Defense security regulations and military and industrial espionage laws exploit this strategy.
4. *Wager.* As with deterrence, the profit/loss equation is again foremost; however, here it applies to the owner. Protection is in the form of a wager. Because the probability of loss is low, it is a good investment to hedge against loss by betting that such a loss *will* occur. If loss occurs, the owner wins the wager, which is usually adequate to replace the valuables lost. If the loss never occurs, as is most likely, the small premiums are less costly than other forms of protection or replacement. All in all, the wager is a better investment than other forms of purchased protection. The insurance industry is founded on this strategy. I predict that we shall see major use of this strategy to protect information as information systems become more pervasive in our society.
5. *Delgate.* Protection is achieved by shifting protection responsibility and liability to a second party, such as bank trusts, escrow agents, baby sitters, and police and fire departments. The strategy is most useful when the limited resources of many can be concentrated for the protection of the group. The second party protects by adopting one of the other strategies. One of the significant dampening factors in the current information utility boom is the failure of government and business to delegate protection of their "corporate data base" to the utility because of their lack of confidence in the privacy and security technology being employed. This factor is a distorting influence and has encouraged the proliferation and growth of private, dedicated, in-house systems.

Another approach to protecting the system is to examine hazards and preventative measures for each element of the system. These elements are hardware, software, personnel, procedures, and facilities. Table 13-1 summarizes this approach to security.

EVALUATING THE AIS IN OPERATION

The AIS is evaluated prior to the design of a new one. The same methods are used for the post-implementation review of a newly installed AIS. The evaluation provides the basis for continuing system maintenance for improvements.

Periodic system evaluation also supplements the standard audit as a means of internal control. SAS-1, Section 320, paragraph 34 points out several inherent limitations in internal control. These limitations are really reasons for continual monitoring of the system by management.

Table 13-1. Protection of Programs and Master Files

COMPUTER SYSTEM ELEMENTS	HAZARDS		
	Loss	Defects	Disclosure
Hardware	• Conscientious preventive maintenance.		• Hardware encoding of key information. • Protection against electronic eavesdropping or intrusion into remote access systems.
Software	• Careful program design, testing and maintenance to: 1. Ensure appropriate response to hardware malfunctions. 2. Limit entry of erroneous input data. 3. Detect and eliminate program bugs. 4. Minimize operator errors.		• Passwords, etc., to prevent outside access to programs and files of remote access systems. • Passwords, etc., to limit access to critical programs and files by in-house personnel. • Software encoding or other concealment of key information.
Personnel	• Proper training and qualification of personnel for key job positions.		• Pre-employment screening of personnel.
Procedures	• Adequate supervision and scheduling of work assignments. • Systematic copying of program and master files. • Controls over storage and use of programs and master files. • Separation of programming, data control, computer operation, and librarian functions. • Complete contingency plan, including loss prevention measures and provision for back-up facilities.	• Controls over data input and output, programs and master files. • Controls over program changes.	• Limited access to key areas. • Special supervision of key processing. • Careful disposal of printout, cards, tape, etc. • Good internal access control and supervision of personal belongings. • Controls over access to and use of programs, master files, and the computer.
Facilities	• Design and location of building to minimize exposure to fire, flooding, smoke, structural collapse, riot, sabotage, and vandalism. Safe storage facilities for programs, master files and documentation. • Off-site storage facilities.	• Good control of environment—air-conditioned room for prime power, and freedom from dirt contamination—to minimize hardware errors.	• Building design to permit adequate access control, and to minimize opportunities for intrusion.

Source: Robert V. Jacobson, "Providing Data Security," *Automation,* June, 1970, p. 88.

However, it should be remembered that management may override a system of controls, as in the Equity Funding Corp. case. An independent internal evaluation and audit staff is the first line of defense. The external auditor, if he or she performs his task according to new requirements, is the second line of defense against misuse of the system. The procedures for auditing computerized systems are covered in the next chapter. In this chapter we are concerned primarily with functioning of the AIS in terms of costs, benefits, and system protection.

Purposes of the AIS System Evaluation

The basic purposes of evaluating the AIS may be summarized as follows:

1. To evaluate the basic objectives and the concept of the AIS.
2. To evaluate the effectiveness of the AIS (degree to which objectives are achieved).
3. To evaluate the efficiency of the AIS (ratio of value of output to value of input) in operation.
4. To evaluate total life system costs. These are design, implementation, operating, and maintenance costs over the life of the system.

Problems in Evaluating the AIS

The development of methods for evaluating ongoing systems or for evaluating the cost/benefits of modifying or designing a new system is still in the research stage. The problems are (a) determination of criteria for evaluation, (b) the development of means to measure the variables for which criteria are established, and (c) the gathering of relevant data.

For example, a fundamental object of any AIS is to supply managers with information to assist their decision making. Some questions arise immediately. How do managers utilize information in making decisions? If specific information, as requested, is supplied, to what degree will this improve decision making? How do we know that a particular decision resulting is better than a decision based on a different kind of information? How much does it cost to prepare a particular report, in terms of total system cost? (Is it an allocation problem or an incremental cost problem?)

Functional Performance Measurement

The computerized AIS (and MIS) performs four different functions in the organization. At the lowest level, the AIS is directed toward improvement in clerical activities. Reduction in personnel, speedup in processing data, and improved accuracy are typical objectives. Criteria for measurement of improvements at this level are relatively easily established and measurements may be made.

The next higher level of application is the operational level. This is a higher level of aggregation, and we are concerned with evaluation subsystems and their characteristics. For example, how does the AIS improve the total cost of operating the inventory system? The accounts payable system? The standard cost system?

Middle and top management are concerned with tactical information supplied by the AIS. For example, what would the budget look like under assumptions concerning marketing campaigns? What incremental savings are achieved by transferring production from one plant to another, or buying instead of making components of products? To what degree is management decision making improved by the AIS? Some of these questions may be answered by establishment of criteria and subsequent measurement. Others may not.

The most complex functional performance of the AIS is at the strategic level. Here, much information is qualitative or probabilstic. Financial decisions are interrelated with the concept of the company five to twenty years hence. To what degree does the AIS improve strategic planning? This measurement may only be estimated roughly.

In Table 13-2, we note how one scholar analyzes the evaluation of the MIS/AIS from the functional view. Notice that many measures of effectiveness (MOE's) may be required to evaluate a functional level of the MIS. The table suggests only a few.

Hierarchy of Factors

What we really want to know is the value of the AIS or of a proposed maintenance program in terms of increased profits or increased return on investment. If we could hold all other factors constant and measure profits before and after the installation of the AIS, we would have our answer. In some stable business situations, it is possible to attribute changes in profits primarily to a newly installed AIS, but generally their approach is not practical. Too many other factors such as competitive

Table 13-2. Characteristic performance indicators*

ACTIVITY		DOMINANT ISSUES	EXAMPLE MOES
Clerical	Function:	cost displacement, task execution efficiency, speed of operation, economy	Units per labor hour, backlog
	System:		Throughput, capacity utilization, data preparation cost per unit
	Information:	accuracy	% error transactions
Operational	Function:	monitoring and control over activity and resources	Inventory level, yield rate, messages delivered/received, missed shipping dates
	System:	maintainability, sustainability, availability, sensitivity	% down time, time between failures, frequency of service, % requests with special handling
	Information:	timeliness, reliability	Response time
Tactical	Function:	decision quality, functional objectives	Return on investment, volume orders per district, unit cost, overtime/regular hours, % returned product, delivery time
	System:	auditability, compatibility, flexibility, security, scope	Actual users vs intended users, % service of total cost, reports returned vs delivered
	Information:	suficiency, conciseness, discovery	% file used when appropriate, volume of inquiries
Strategic	Function:	organizational mission, planning, outcome of decisions	Share of market, new products, earnings/share, change in risk, % R&D of total expense
	System:	user satisfaction**	Number of accesses per inquiry, time to formulate inquiry, % compliments vs complaints
	Information:	relevance	% responses appropriate

*W. A. Smith, Jr., *Effectiveness of Information Systems*. Bethlehem, Pa.: Lehigh University, Dept. of I.E. June 1972 (AD744027), National Technical Information Service.
**Access ease, available period, dependable source, suitability to purpose, personal convenience.

activities, changes in the company's marketing and its products, new markets, different economic conditions, and changes in management all interact with changes in the AIS.

Instead of looking at net earnings, we may look for specific costs that are changed and specific revenues that are increased due to the new AIS. This may provide at least a minimum or conservative evaluation of the subdivisions of profits.

If we cannot measure changes in costs and revenues, we may attempt to measure improvements in the performance of managerial functions which have great impact upon them. That is, we may attempt to measure improvement in the quality of planning and control attributable to the AIS. Continuing further down the hierarchy, we may consider measuring the quality of decisions that contribute to planning and control. It is apparent from Table 13-3 that developing such measures is not an easy task.

Surprisingly, the next lower level on the hierarchy of cost/benefits, the measurement of the value of information, may be better structured. Management science has provided us with quantitative measures, "the expected value of perfect information." In addition, there are numerous characteristics of information to which we may attach quantitative as well as qualitative measures as shown in Table 13-3.[5]

Finally, we may consider evaluating the improvement in system characteristics in terms of costs and crude estimates of benefits. Some ideas for this are suggested in Table 13-3, but we will deal with this in the following section.

AIS System and Subsystems Cost/Benefits

We may break the AIS down into its subsystems and attempt to evaluate specific advantages of each subsystem. A good summary form for this purpose is shown in Table 13-4. Another checklist format that is quite different is shown in Table 13-5. Both of these could be used simultaneously to advantage.

A broader managerial report deals with the entire AIS. Management would like to know the total life-cycle costs and benefits of the AIS in terms of dollars. Although some benefits may only be estimated, such a report would follow the format shown in Table 13-6. The development of such a report can be aided by a schedule such as that of Table 13-7.

Summary

Nothing is static in modern organizations; there is a continuing need to improve, control performance, evaluate, and repeat this cycle. In this chapter we have touched on external and internal factors which require continual maintenance of the AIS. We have introduced the major topic of security which is based both upon maintenance (enhancement) and control of the functioning of the total AIS. Finally, we have examined the problems of evaluating the AIS and presented several ap-

[5] See Gerald A. Feltham, *Information Evaluation* (Sarasota, Fla: American Accounting Association, 1972).

Table 13-3. Measurement Hierarchy

	HIERARCHY IN THE MIS	CHANGE THAT IS MEASURED
Level 1	Company Profit, Return on Investment	Dollars
Level 2	Company Costs, Revenues	Dollars
Level 3	Planning	Specificity, quantification, degree to which plans are achieved, time required to produce plans, number of alternative plans made available for consideration, cost.
	Control	Degree of control by exception, selection of activities to be controlled, forewarning of activities going beyond acceptable limits, managerial time required for control, automation of control of repetive situations, cost.
Level 4	Decisions	Quality of decisions, frequency of reversal of decisions by superiors in the organization, number of alternatives examined in arriving at decisions, sophistication of "what if...?" questions permitted, time required for decisions, number of decisions, automation of repetitive decision situations, cost.
Level 5	Information	Validity, accuracy, clarity, distribution, frequency, appropriateness of detail for each level of management, timeliness, format, availability on demand, selectivity of content, disposition method, retention time, cost.
Level 6	System characteristics	Number of people required, equipment and facilities, response time, frequency of breakdowns, inputs, outputs, number of forms, number of operations, number of storages, sizes and quality of data bank, size and quality of model bank, flexibility, simplicity, degree of automation, scope of business components that are related by the MIS, user satisfaction, error rates, persistent problem areas, ease of maintenance and modification, unplanned-for impact on company performance, savings, cost, etc.

Table 13-4. Evaluation Form for a Subsystem

SYSTEM CONCEPTS AND OBJECTIVES				
EXISTING PROBLEMS – ACCOUNTS PAYABLE SYSTEM		IMPROVEMENT PRIORITY		
^		TOP	MED	LOW
PRIMARY	The accounts payable cycle, from the receipt of the invoice, to the issuance of the payment requires 3-4 weeks. This is deemed to be excessive by 1 to 2 weeks. The existing processing method and resources cannot operate at an increased rate to reduce the time taken by the cycle.	X		
OTHERS	Excessive transcription of information – from invoice, to voucher and to subsidiary ledgers.		X	
	Excessive verification of clerical work (such as invoice extension).		X	
	Loss of discounts available for prompt payment.			X
	High volume of "rush" cheques due to complaints by suppliers.		X	
DESIRED SYSTEM OBJECTIVES	ACCEPTABLE SCORE – 70%	OBJECTIVES SATISFIED BY		MEASUREMENT OF RESULTS REPORTED BY
PRIMARY	Issue payments to suppliers within 2 weeks of receipt of invoice, while maintaining at least a 98% accuracy and not more than 2 man weeks of backlog.	Savings of 1-1/2 weeks of processing through: – Automation of A/P System to verify and pay supplier's invoices; – reduction of clerical processing; – simplification of payment authorization procedure; – automation of cheque preparation.		Payment Analysis report
SECONDARY	SERVICE/VOLUME 1) Processing priority accorded to invoice with cash discount terms. 2) Backlog from 1-2 man weeks maximum. 3) Payment priority to 50 key suppliers. QUALITY Error rate – volume 2% – value ± 1/2% invoice value	1) Priority programmed, manual procedures developed to comply. 2) Duplication of clerical effort elimination of unnecessary verifications and other improvements listed below. 3) As in 1) above. 1) Supervisory quality control cheque of work sample. 2) Computer edit; 100% key-verification.		1) Check Register 2) Payment Analysis Report (No. AH4) 3) Supervisory Check 1) Supervisor's Report 2) Edit Report (EDP) 3) Supplier complaint
OTHERS	COSTS/SAVINGS One time implementation costs not to exceed $35,000 including programming, forms and training. Reduce clerical workload from 4 to 2 clerks. FEASIBILITY OF IMPLEMENTATION With 3 months of start, parallel operations must cease.	Costs estimated at $38-45,000 1) Replacement of 100% clerical work verification with 95% confidence level random sample results in the saving of 1/2 clerk. 2) Elimination of manual posting of subsidiary ledgers result in the saving of 1 clerk. 3) Conversion of voucher and cheque typing to computer processing results in the saving of 1/2 clerk. System is planned to be fully implemented within 2 months after conversion.		Project Control System Transfer of an A/P Verifier clerk planned for 1 month after implementation and upon reorganization of jobs, 2nd clerk will be transferred (no later than 3 months after implementation).

Source: John P. Herzog, "System Evaluation Techniques for Users," *Journal of Systems Management*, May 1975, p. 32.

Table 13-5. Evaluation Guide for A/R and Sales Analysis Subsystems

ACCOUNTS RECEIVABLE EVALUATION GUIDE	INFONATIONAL	OTHER
1. Accounts receivable methods available to the company.		
a. Open item	Yes	
b. Balance forward	Yes	
c. Both intermixed	Yes	
2. Maximum number of divisions.	99	
3. Maximum number of departments.	9999	
4. Allows the company to process two accounting periods simultaneously and maintains the integrity of the data.	Yes	
5. Does the system allow the user to determine his own reporting cycle requirements as either daily, weekly, monthly, or as required?	Yes	
6. Does the system allow the company to establish his own discount terms?	Yes	
7. Based on the discount terms does the system automatically determine the discount due date, the invoice due date and the discount amount?	Yes	
8. Does the system automatically calculate discounts allowed?	Yes	
9. Can the company's standard terms be overridden at the customer or invoice level?	Yes	
10. Can a discount amount be entered as an override to any terms?	Yes	
11. Can sales, tax, freight and other invoice amounts be entered into the system?	Yes	
12. Does the system allow for the assignment of general ledger account numbers to all amount fields?	Yes	
13. Allows each company to use its own unique Chart-of-Accounts code and titles.	Yes	
14. Maximum number of characters in each Chart-of-Accounts code.	8	
15. Allows the use of alphanumeric Chart-of-Accounts code.	Yes	
16. Can the system be automatically interfaced into an automated general ledger system?	Yes	
17. Can the system be automatically interfaced into an automated sales analysis system?	Yes	
18. Are all transactions entering the system journalized for audit control?	Yes	
19. Is the total of all product sale amounts validated against the total sales amount of each invoice?	Yes	
20. Are total debits and credits matched at the journal level?	Yes	
21. Can the company correct accounting errors using a journal entry?	Yes	
22. Are there edits or audits on		
a. Company number?	Yes	
b. Customer number?	Yes	
c. Division number?	Yes	
d. Department number?	Yes	
e. Account number?	Yes	
f. Other fields?	Yes	
23. Does the edit identify multiple errors if they exist in the same transaction?	Yes	
24. What are the maximum number of digits on the following fields?		
a. Invoice amount	8	
b. Invoice number	6	
c. Customer number	7	
d. Quantities	5	
e. Purchase order number	10	
25. Can the company establish variable aging categories with a variable number of days?	Yes	
26. Can aging be performed based on		
a. Invoice date?	Yes	
b. Invoice due date?	Yes	

Table 13-5 (continued)

	ACCOUNTS RECEIVABLE EVALUATION GUIDE	INFONATIONAL	OTHER
27.	Can cash receipts be applied to		
	a. Cash on account?	Yes	
	b. Single invoice?	Yes	
	c. Consecutive block of invoices?	Yes	
	d. Multiple invoices in random sequence?	Yes	
	e. Service charges?	Yes	
	f. Any general ledger account including those not related to Accounts Receivable?	Yes	
28.	Can the system maintain a "cash on account" balance and provide a method to subsequently apply the cash to specific invoices?	Yes	
29.	Can the system accept partial payments to an invoice?	Yes	
30.	Can the system accept credit memos applied to specific invoices or to the customer balance?	Yes	
31.	Are the following reports available?		
	a. Sales Journal	Yes	
	b. Cash Receipts Journal	Yes	
	c. Sales Returns and Allowances Journal	Yes	
	d. Miscellaneous Adjustments Journal	Yes	
	e. Trial Balance and Aged Accounts Receivable Reports	Yes	
	1. Aged by Invoice Date	Yes	
	2. Aged by Invoice Due Date	Yes	
	f. Customer Credit Report	Yes	
	g. Credit Report	Yes	
	1. Aged by Invoice Date	Yes	
	2. Aged by Invoice Due Date	Yes	
	h. Accounts Receivable Recap Report	Yes	
	i. Customer Statements	Yes	
	j. Company Master File Listings	Yes	
	k. Customer Master File Listing	Yes	
	l. Update Audit Report	Yes	
	m. Edit Listings	Yes	
32.	Can reports be produced at any time reflecting the most current transactions and aging?	Yes	
33.	Can reports be requested on an "as needed basis"?	Yes	
34.	Are multi-levels of control available which provide totals by company, division, department and customer?	Yes	
35.	Are there flexible reporting options with variable reporting levels available?	Yes	
36.	Is there a single register to list all input for the current accounting period?	Yes	
37.	Are all transactions affecting an invoice printed until the invoice is fully paid for open item customers?	Yes	
38.	Do the statements feature aging of the customers balance?	Yes	
39.	Can statements be cycled by customer?	Yes	
40.	Up to how many copies of statements are available?	9	
41.	Can statements be run only for selected customers?	Yes	
42.	Can statements be produced which meet Federal Truth in Lending requirements?	Yes	
43.	Can variable service charges be applied by customer?	Yes	
44.	Are service charges applied to past due amounts according to the terms of each invoice?	Yes	
45.	Can dunning messages be applied selectively to past due amounts?	Yes	
46.	Can customers selectively be exempted from dunning?	Yes	
47.	Can adhesive labels for mailing be produced?	Yes	
48.	Is customer deletion possible only when he has a zero balance?	Yes	

Table 13-5 (continued)

	ACCOUNTS RECEIVABLE EVALUATION GUIDE	INFONATIONAL	OTHER
49.	Is the system compatible with the operational requirements of a Accounts Receivable Financing service?	Yes	
50.	Does the system maintain the following customer credit information?		
	Date account opened	Yes	
	Date of last sale	Yes	
	Date of last payment	Yes	
	Date of last statement	Yes	
	Y-T-D sales	Yes	
	Current month sales	Yes	
	Average collection period	Yes	
	Average age outstanding	Yes	
	Credit limit	Yes	
	Variance between outstanding balance and limit	Yes	
	High dollar amount	Yes	
	Credit type	Yes	
	Sales aging	Yes	
51.	Does the system have a single entry point simplifying operations procedures?	Yes	
52.	Is there a single output source allowing multiple company users to get all of one company's reports sorted together for ease of distribution?	Yes	
53.	Is the system immediately available?	Yes	
54.	Is the system warranted against programming errors?	Yes	
55.	Is on-site support, including personnel training, included in the purchase price?	Yes	
56.	Is the system coded one hundred percent in COBOL to allow smooth and easy transition to other equipment?	Yes	
57.	How much core space is required?	54K	
58.	Is the following documentation provided?		
	a. System flowchart	Yes	
	b. Logic diagram	Yes	
	c. Program listings	Yes	
	d. File layout	Yes	
	e. Input-output formats	Yes	
	f. Operator manuals	Yes	
	g. Input preparation procedure	Yes	
	h. Control technique	Yes	
	i. Sample output	Yes	
	j. Accounting department user's manual	Yes	
	k. General Systems narrative	Yes	
	l. Job Control Charts	Yes	
	m. Program run instructions	Yes	
	n. Keypunch procedures	Yes	
	o. Report layouts	Yes	

	SALES ANALYSIS EVALUATION GUIDE	INFONATIONAL	OTHER
1.	Maximum number of companies the system can handle in one processing cycle.	999	
2.	Maximum divisions in each company.	99	
3.	Maximum departments in each company.	9999	
4.	Does the Sales Analysis System automatically balance to the Accounts Receivable system controls?	Yes	
5.	Does the system carry salesmen's names and numbers?	Yes	

Table 13-5 (continued)

	SALES ANALYSIS EVALUATION GUIDE	INFONATIONAL	OTHER
6.	Does the system calculate and carry salesmen's commissions based on:		
	a. Customer sale amount?	Yes	
	b. Invoice sale amount?	Yes	
	c. Product sale amount?	Yes	
7.	Does the system carry descriptions for product categories and products?	Yes	
8.	Does the system provide the capability of carrying two years of historical information to the product level?	Yes	
9.	Can historical sales information be added when a company is converted to the system?	Yes	
10.	Maximum number of characters in the product number.	10	
11.	Is there edit validation of product extensions on the invoice?	Yes	
12.	Are the following reports available?		
	a. Commission Reports		
	1. By salesman	Yes	
	b. Gross Profit Reports		
	1. By salesman	Yes	
	2. By customer	Yes	
	3. By category/product	Yes	
	c. Comparative Analysis Report		
	1. By salesman	Yes	
	2. By customer	Yes	
	3. By category/product	Yes	
	d. Category/Product Master Listing	Yes	
13.	Does the system suspense invalid products and provide the capability to correct on subsequent processing cycles?	Yes	
14.	Are there flexible reporting options with variable reporting levels available?	Yes	
15.	Can actual performance be compared to historical data?	Yes	
16.	Is the following documentation provided?		
	a. System flowchart	Yes	
	b. Logic diagram	Yes	
	c. Program listings	Yes	
	d. File layout	Yes	
	e. Input-output formats	Yes	
	f. Operator manuals	Yes	
	g. Input preparation procedure	Yes	
	h. Control technique	Yes	
	i. Sample output	Yes	
	j. Accounting department user's manual	Yes	
	k. General Systems narrative	Yes	
	l. Job Control Charts	Yes	
	m. Program run instructions	Yes	
	n. Keypunch procedures	Yes	
	o. Report layouts	Yes	

Source: Accounting and Financial Reporting Evaluation Guide, San Diego, Cal.: Infonational, undated.

Table 13-6. MIS Evaluation Form

	PAGE		
	DATE		
MIS PROJECT NAME _____	NO.		

Initial Costs	1974	1975	1976	Total
1. Project planning	$5,000			$ 5,000
2. Gross design	1,000	$ 2,000		3,000
3. Detailed design		10,000	$ 23,000	33,000
4. Implementation			7,000	7,000
5. Testing			4,800	4,800
6. Special			600	600
TOTAL INITIAL COSTS	$6,000	$12,000	$ 35,400	$ 53,400

Capital Costs				
7. Computer center hardware		$10,300	$ 33,000	$ 43,300
8. Facilities		5,000	13,000	18,000
TOTAL CAPITAL COSTS		$15,300	$ 46,000	$ 61,300

Annual Operating Costs				
9. Computer and equipment lease		$ 5,000	$ 24,000	$ 29,000
10. Personnel		47,000	200,000	247,000
11. Overhead and supplies		10,000	20,000	30,000
TOTAL ANNUAL OPERATING COSTS		$62,000	$244,000	$306,000

Benefits				
12. Reduced salary and labor costs			$ 2,000	$ 2,000
13. Reduced inventory costs			97,000	97,000
14. Better strategic decisions (estimated impact)		$50,000	320,000	370,000
15. Freeing up of managerial time (estimated)		5,000	60,000	65,000
TOTAL BENEFITS		$55,000	$479,000	$534,000

Table 13-7. Important Cost Considerations

DESIGN ALTERNATIVES	Equipment	Programming	Personnel	Outside Services	Finance Charges	Other Applications	BENEFITS BEING SOUGHT
PRESENT SYSTEM	B	b	B	b		B	AVOIDANCE OF REPROGRAMMING COST
FINANCING ARRANGEMENTS							AVOIDANCE OF REPROGRAMMING COST
Third Party	d	n	n	n		n	Lower Monthly Costs
Purchase	d	n	n	n	I	n	Ownership & Lower Monthly Costs
Peripheral Replacement	d	n	n	n		n	Lower System Cost
MODIFYING EXISTING SYSTEM							AVOIDANCE OF REPROGRAMMING COST
New Channels Tapes, etc.	i	n	n	d		d	Making More Time Available
Reprogramming	n	i	n	d		d	Making More Time Available and Responsive
AUGMENTING EXISTING SYSTEM							AVOIDANCE OF REPROGRAMMING COST
Service Bureau	n	n	n	I		d	Ability to Process Complex Programs
Time Sharing Service	n	d	n	I		d	Ability to Handle Interactive Programs
Second (Like) System	I	i	I	d	I	D	Making More Time Available
NEW COMPUTER SYSTEM							INCREASED CAPABILITY
Sole Source	I	i	d	d		D	Multiple (time factor, vendor relationship)
Competitive Procurement	I	I	d	d		D	Multiple (Discounted System)
Second Hand	I	I	d	d		D	Multiple (Lower Costs Software Library)
Third Party	I	I	d	d		D	Multiple (Lower Costs)
Purchase	I	I	d	d	I	D	Multiple (Lower Costs)

Legend: b—Base for Comparison; i—Increased Costs Expected; d—Decreased Costs Expected; n—No Appreciable Costs Change. (The size of the letter indicates the importance of that cost item in that alternative.)
Source: Edward O. Joslin, "Costing the System Design Alternatives," *Data Management,* April, 1971, p. 25.

proaches. The accountant should keep in mind that some of the greatest benefits (improved managerial decision making, for example) are not those that are easily and commonly measured by accountants.

DISCUSSION QUESTIONS AND PROBLEMS

1. a. Define the controller's responsibility for system maintenance.
   b. Can this responsibility be shared with other managers?
2. List and discuss several types of internal and external changes that may require that changes be made to the systems.
3. List and discuss several types of threats to the security of a system.
4. List and discuss several protective strategies that may be employed to enhance system security.
5. a. Discuss the purposes of evaluating the AIS.
   b. What are the problems in developing an evaluation program?
6. a. Discuss the term "functional performance measurement."
   b. At what levels does it apply?
7. How may we measure the AIS in terms of dollars or "value"?

Bibliography

Accounting and Financial Reporting Evaluation Guide. San Diego, Cal.: Infonational (undated).

BERG, JOHN L. "Federal Privacy Act Countdown ... Is the Private Sector Ready?," *Infosystems,* July 1975.

BURCH, JOHN G., JR. and FELIX R. STRATER, JR. *Information Systems: Theory and Practice,* Santa Barbara, Cal.: Hamilton Publishing Co., 1974, pp. 370–374.

BURNS, KEVIN J., Cincom Systems, Inc., King of Prussia, Pa. "Security in a Data Base Environment," Paper presented at INFO 75, New York, September 8–11, 1975.

"Computer Security ... The Imperative Nuisance," *Infosystems,* February 1974.

FELTHAM, GERALD A. *Information Evaluation* (Studies in Accounting Research #5), Sarasota, Fla.: American Accounting Association, 1972.

HERZOG, JOHN P. "System Evaluation Technique for Users," *Journal of Systems Management,* May 1975.

JACOBSON, ROBERT V. "Providing Data Security," *Automation,* June 1970.

JOSLIN, EDWARD O. "Costing the System Design Alternatives," *Data Management,* April 1971.

KANTER, JEROME. *Management Guide to Computer System Selection and Use,* Englewood Cliffs, N.J.: Prentice-Hall, 1970. Chapter 7, "Maintenance and Modification."

Khan, Zafar. "How to Tackle the Systems Maintenance Dilemma," *Canadian Datasystems,* March 1975.

Murdick, Robert G., and Joel E. Ross. *Information Systems for Modern Management* (2nd ed.), Englewood Cliffs, N.J.: Prentice-Hall, 1975.

Parker, D. B. *Crime by Computer,* New York: Scribner, 1976.

Scriven, Donald D., and Stephen J. Hallam, "New Approaches to Computer Performance Evaluation," *Infosystems,* October 1976.

Shaw, John C., and William Atkins. *Managing Computer System Projects,* New York: McGraw-Hill, 1970. Chapter 14, "Post-implementation Review."

Smith, William A., Jr., and Ben L. Wechsler. *Planning Guide for Information Systems Evaluation Studies,* Atlanta, Ga.: American Institute of Industrial Engineers, 1973.

Weissman, Clark, "Trade-off Considerations in Security System Design," *Data Management,* April 1972.

Preview:
This chapter shows how auditors, both internal and external, deal with the AIS. We will look at how the auditors approach the system and some audit techniques for the computorized AIS.
–The auditor
–The audit approach
–EDP auditing
–AICPA statements

CHAPTER FOURTEEN
auditing the AIS

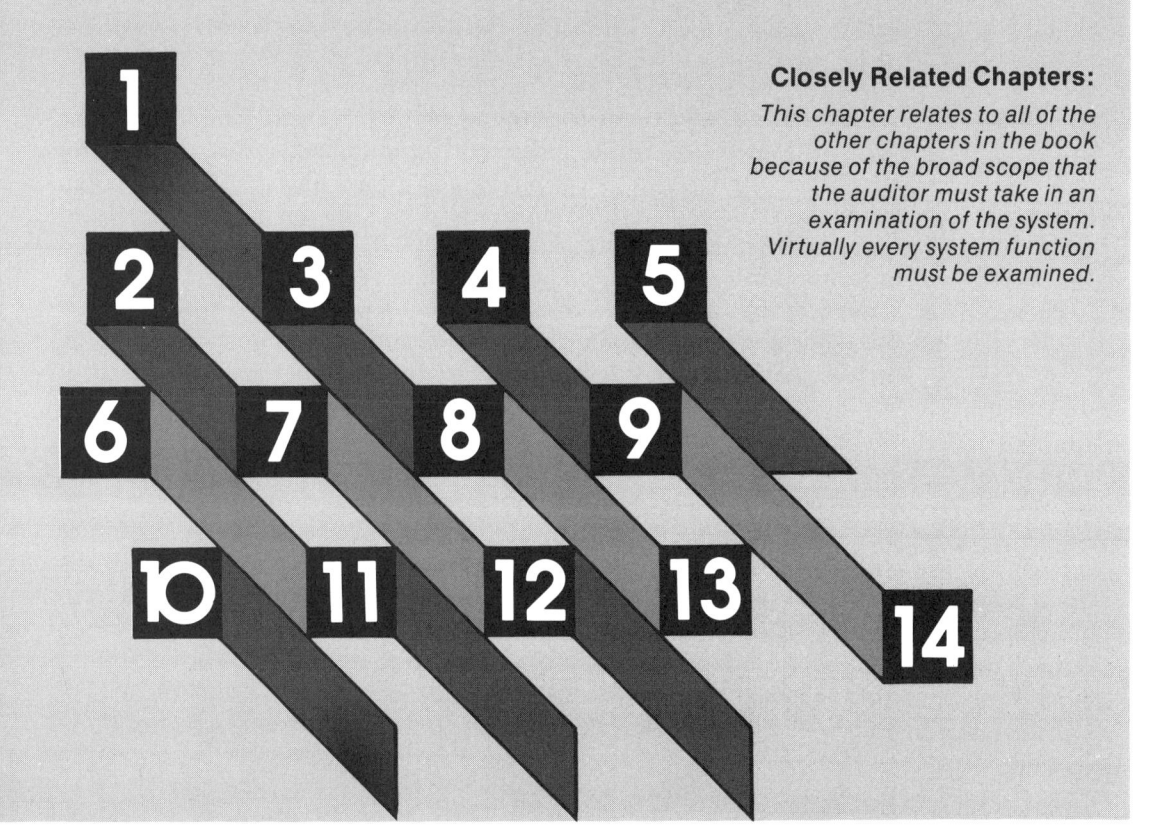

Closely Related Chapters:
This chapter relates to all of the other chapters in the book because of the broad scope that the auditor must take in an examination of the system. Virtually every system function must be examined.

Auditing is . . . "a systematic process of objectively obtaining assertions about economic actions and events to ascertain the degree of correspondence between those assertions and established criteria and communicating the results to interested users."

AMERICAN ACCOUNTING ASSOCIATION'S
COMMITTEE ON BASIC AUDITING CONCEPTS

With the advent of the computerized accounting information system, auditors have had to cope with the resulting increased complexity of the flow of information through the AIS. Traditional auditing procedures did not accommodate the sophisticated processing devices that often "hide the numbers" in the computerized AIS. As the design of the computerized AIS advanced from simple clerical automation to complicated integrated information systems, the auditor could no longer audit *to* the computer, but found it necessary to develop procedures to audit *through* the computer. Further, the "traditional" auditor was not trained in the special languages and devices used in the computerized AIS. Accordingly, a significant effort has been made in recent years in universities, internal audit departments, firms of certified public accountants, and professional organizations to educate the auditor to function effectively in a computerized accounting information system.[1]

The purpose of this chapter is first to describe the two general categories of auditors and the audit approach they take to accomplish the objectives of each category. Then we will consider the specific audit techniques used in the computerized AIS.

---

[1] The auditor must satisfy the Generally Accepted Auditing Standards established by the AICPA. The first of these standards says: "The examination is to be performed by a person or persons having adequate training and proficiency as an auditor."

AUDITING AND AUDITORS

There are two primary groups of auditors: (1) auditors who represent a separate department within the organization—*internal auditors* and (2) independent auditors who are engaged by the owners of the organization (or their representatives) to provide assurance that the output of the AIS is fairly stated—these are the *external auditors*.

Internal Auditors

The objectives of the internal auditor are to insure that assets are properly safeguarded and transactions are properly authorized, executed, and recorded in the accounts, thereby providing reasonable assurance as to the reliability of the AIS output. To attain these objectives, the internal auditor acts as a "mobile" form of internal control. This function is termed a mobile control because the internal auditor neither verifies each transaction in the system nor does he determine the proper safeguarding of each asset in the organization. Instead, the internal auditor develops an annual plan to *test* the operation of the AIS. The areas of the AIS that are either loosely controlled or critical to AIS output receive the most audit attention. Other areas of the system are audited to determine that internal controls are operating effectively and output is reliable.

As the output requirements of the AIS change or as the internal controls within the system are modified, the internal audit plan must be appropriately modified. The plan should also be modified periodically to avoid becoming predictable. The internal audit plan, as a truly mobile form of internal control, should be responsive to the reliability needs of the system, yet remain dynamic.

The internal audit department should be as independent as possible from the other departments in the organization. The department should report directly to the board of directors or to an audit committee established by the board of directors. Audit reports given to the board of directors should also be given to the appropriate department managers, except where such reports are sensitive in nature (such as where fraud or other defalcations are discovered). Additionally, procedures should be established to determine that deficiencies noted in these reports are subsequently corrected.

In a computerized AIS, the internal audit department must develop sufficient EDP auditing expertise. The can be done either by training existing audit personnel as computer audit specialists or by hiring an EDP specialist and training him in auditing techniques and procedures. Many internal audit departments have their own audit software packages to audit through the computer or use "test deck" procedures on a periodic basis to verify EDP software (these approaches are discussed later in this chapter). Organizations with limited or no internal audit activities often rely on the services of the external auditor to verify the proper operation of the computerized and manual elements of the AIS.

External Auditors

External auditors are usually engaged to certify that the financial statements generated by the AIS are fairly stated in accordance with generally accepted accounting principles. The purpose of this certification is to provide interested outsiders (such as banks, investors, and regulatory agencies) and the owners of the organization with an independent verification of the financial statements.

The objectives of the external auditor are similar to those of the internal auditor. However, the following clearly separate the two functions:

1. The external auditor is concerned with the form and content of the financial statements. The internal audit function usually stops short of this step.
2. The external auditor views the internal auditor as an important internal control to evaluate when planning the audit approach.
3. The external auditor is concerned with the interests of outsiders where the internal auditor is concerned with determining that transactions are carried out in accordance with management's policies.

Although the objectives of internal and external auditors may differ, the approach taken to audit the AIS is essentially the same for each group. Let us now consider the steps taken in a basic audit approach.

AUDIT APPROACH

The audit approach is a set of procedures designed to develop an audit program (a detailed list of auditing work to be done) to reach the stated audit objectives. The types of procedures used in an audit program vary primarily because of the variation in: (1) the extent of internal controls in the system, (2) the size of the organization, (3) the type of business in which the organization is engaged, and (4) the degree of computerization of the AIS. While all of these variables affect the type and extent of audit procedures, the approach taken to develop these procedures remains essentially the same for all organizations. The first step in this audit approach is to define the objectives of the audit and to develop a preliminary plan to attain these objectives.

Audit Objectives and Planning

As we previously discussed, the objective of the external auditor is usually to perform sufficient audit work to express an opinion on the organization's financial statements. The objectives of internal auditors are usually related to specific elements of the AIS as part of an annual audit plan. For example, one objective of internal audit may be to verify the proper operation of all computer software with particular emphasis on the manufacturing cost control element of the management information system. The external auditor would also be concerned with EDP software, however, his concern is primarily with software that affects the numbers on the financial statements.

Once the auditor has clearly defined the audit objectives, he can develop a plan to achieve these objectives. The audit plan depends to a great extent on the quality of internal controls in the AIS. A system with weak internal controls usually requires more extensive auditing procedures than a system with strong internal controls. Therefore the auditor must make a preliminary evaluation of the internal controls in the AIS to decide on a viable audit plan. This is usually accomplished by discussions with appropriate management and accounting personnel. This evaluation will determine the type of system documentation the auditor will require to design his audit procedures. If internal controls are strong, the auditor will need to obtain or prepare a detailed set of flowcharts or narratives of the system to properly identify the internal control strengths and weaknesses. If internal controls are weak, the auditor will still need to document the system, but will be more concerned with identifying critical areas of audit concern than with documenting internal control strengths that are completely negated by pervasive system weaknesses. After the system is documented, the auditor can make a more informed decision as to the extent of reliance he will place on internal controls in developing the detailed audit procedures.

Developing the Audit Program

The first step in developing the audit program is to identify the areas of audit concern. The auditor must identify those elements of the AIS that affect his audit objectives. Then, if the system has strong internal controls, the auditor will need to decide which of these controls: (1) relate to the areas of audit concern and (2) will be tested using compliance audit procedures and relied upon to limit the extent of substantive audit procedures. Substantive audit procedures are usually related to the verification of system output. An example of a substantive procedure would be the matching of vendor invoices with related cash disbursements, purchase orders, and receiving reports to test purchases. However if internal controls require the review of the purchase order, receiving report, and vendor invoice prior to payment, the auditor might perform a compliance test on this control to limit the extent of the substantive procedure. For example, the auditor might select a sample of these payments and verify that this "prepayment" review is made by inspecting the appropriate form for the initials of the reviewer.

Weaknesses in internal control must also be identified in each area of audit concern. Substantive audit procedures will need to be devised to test these areas. For example, if the EDP department does not provide for effective input and output controls, the auditor should consider selecting a sample of certain EDP output and reconciling control totals to user department input control totals. If the user department consistently performs this reconciliation, the auditor might consider performing a compliance test to determine that these reconciliations are being performed, thus limiting the extent of the substantive procedures.

One technique to relate the areas of audit concern and system control strengths and weaknesses to the detailed audit program is the use of a "bridging workpaper." This workpaper acts as a "bridge" between the system flowcharts and narratives and the audit program. The bridging workpaper should:

1. Identify internal control strengths, state their audit implications, and reference them to the related compliance testing procedures.

2. Identify internal control weaknesses, state their audit implication, and reference them to the related substantive testing procedures.

3. Identify any internal control weaknesses that are mitigated by internal control strengths, and conversely, any strengths that are negated by control weaknesses.

4. Reference all areas of audit concern to related substantive and compliance testing procedures.

Once developed, the audit program should not be static. It should be constantly updated for any new information obtained while performing the audit procedures.[2]

Performing Audit Program Steps and Reaching Conclusions

Compliance testing procedures are usually performed early in the audit. This way if internal control strengths relied on to limit substantive procedures prove to be faulty, the audit program can be modified to: (1) take advantage of other control strengths in the system or (2) to include more extensive substantive procedures. Consider the following examples of the control total reconciliation procedures discussed earlier:

> *One of the internal controls in the sales system for Company A is that all batches of sales invoices input into the EDP department are controlled by a separate EDP control group. This group accumulates control totals and reconciles all EDP output totals before distribution to the user departments. However, when the auditor was performing compliance tests to determine the existence of this control, it was discovered that the reconciliation for sales invoices was only done on a periodic basis. Therefore, the auditor modified the audit program to include substantive procedures for testing the batch control totals to EDP output totals.*
>
> *Assume the same situation as above for Company B, except here the auditor discovers that the user department (sales) also maintains control totals and reconciles all EDP output to these totals. Therefore, the auditor modifies the audit program to include compliance test procedures for the sales department instead of the EDP control group.*

As the substantive audit procedures are performed, the auditor should be alert for possible required audit program modifications. For example, during the testing of a bank's EDP software for calculating interest on certificates of deposit, the auditor verifies that the system is calculating the interest correctly, but notices numerous errors in the input documents. The auditor should then extend the scope of the substantive procedures planned to test the accuracy of user department input.

Once the audit procedures have been performed, the auditor should evaluate the results of the work and document his conclusions. For the internal auditor, this conclusion will normally be in the form of a detailed report of procedures performed and the results of those procedures. For the external auditor, these conclusions will be docu-

---

[2]Note: The appendix to Chapter 4 contains a typical EDP questionnaire used as part of this review of internal controls and audit program development.

mented for each area of audit concern which together support the overall opinion on the financial statements.

Figure 14-1 presents a summary of the audit approach. This diagram is an adaptation of the Systems Evaluation Approach used by Peat, Marwick, Mitchell & Co., the largest of the "Big Eight" certified public accounting firms.

The primary theme of this audit approach, regardless of the extent of computerization, is the *integration* of audit procedures into the system of internal controls. The extent of internal control in the AIS has a direct and significant effect of the types of audit procedures the auditor will perform to attain his audit objectives. A system with strong internal controls will usually lend itself to a combination of compliance and substantive audit procedures. A system with weak internal controls usually results in a totally substantive audit approach.

The types of audit procedures designed to perform these tests have a direct relationship to the extent of computerization present in the AIS. Specific audit procedures are available for auditing the computerized elements of the AIS. Let us now discuss these "high-powered" audit

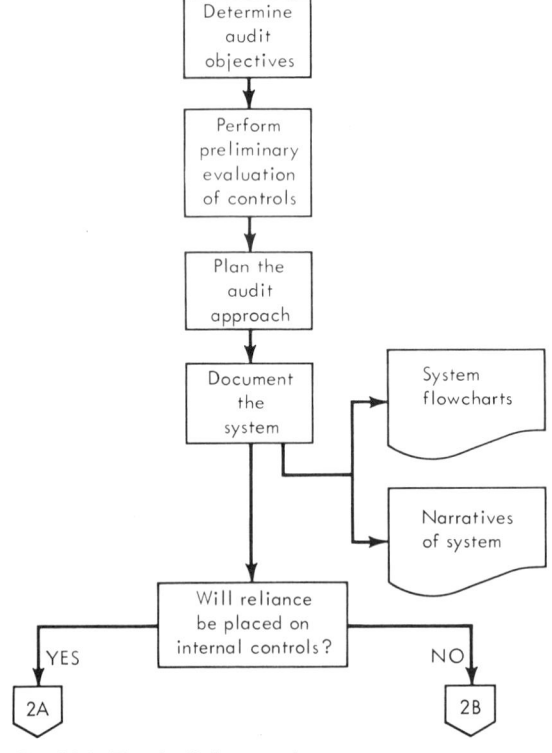

Fig. 14-1. The Audit Approach

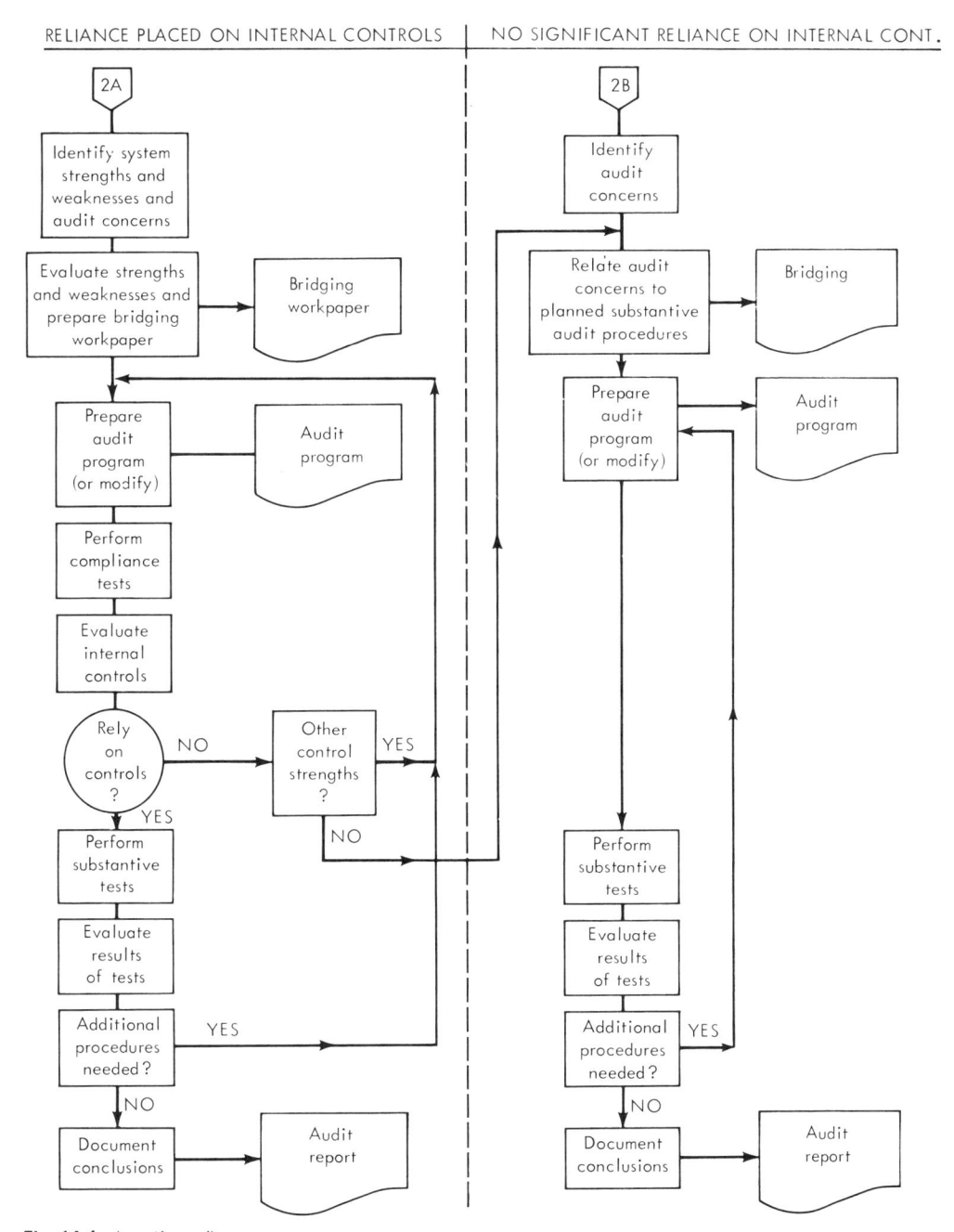

Fig. 14-1. (continued)

procedures that, when properly applied in the audit approach, facilitate attaining the audit objectives in a computerized AIS.

AUDIT PROCEDURES FOR THE COMPUTERIZED AIS

The use of the computer in the AIS usually results in a centralization of control procedures and accounting data. Additionally, many accounting records may no longer be produced in hard copy form. Thus the computerized AIS may have an important impact on the type of audit procedures to be performed. Usually this impact will relate to one or more of the following areas:

1. Sophisticated audit software packages may be used to test the proper operation of the system.
2. Advanced statistical auditing techniques (such as variables and attribute estimation) are more practical in a computerized environment.
3. Other procedures such as processing "test decks" through the various EDP applications and independent analysis of EDP software are often used.

Audit Software Packages

The most powerful tool available to the auditor in an EDP environment is the audit software package. Audit software can range from a simple computer program developed to test a particular EDP application to a separate programming language which allows the user to test and analyze any EDP application.

Specific Computer Audit Software

Two examples of a computer program developed to achieve a specific audit objective are:

During the audit of a bank, the auditor identifies the computation of interest on loans as a critical area of audit concern. Having a complete knowledge of COBOL, the software language used in the EDP installation, the auditor writes a COBOL program to achieve the following objectives:

(1) verify the amount of accrued interest receivable,
(2) verify the calculation of late penalty fees, and
(3) verify the amount of interest income.

Once the program is written, the auditor periodically processes his program against the EDP loan master file and compares his output with that of the EDP department for a given day.

During the audit of a large retail land sales company, the auditor identifies the calculation of deferred gross profit on land sales as a critical area of audit concern. He then writes a computer program to calculate the deferred gross profit on all sales on the master file in accordance with appropriate AICPA pronouncements. At the end of the accounting period, the auditor obtains from the EDP installation the final master file used to generate deferred gross profit for the financial statements. He then processes his own program against the master file to determine that the deferred gross profit presented on the financial statements was calculated correctly.

Time-sharing Audit Software

The problem with the specific audit software approach is that it assumes the auditor has a working knowledge of the necessary programming languages (or has access to someone independent of the EDP installation who has such knowledge). This, of course, is not always the case. To bypass this problem, at least to some extent, the auditor can use "time sharing" audit software to attain numerous audit objectives. Time-sharing programs are various types of audit software that are stored in an on-line system accessible through a terminal, usually on a rental basis. The auditor simply inputs the appropriate data in a predescribed format through a terminal and receives the output almost immediately. The time-sharing service then bills the auditor later for the computer time used. Several examples of time-sharing programs are:

1. Lease disclosure programs that perform rather complicated calculations related to long term leases in accordance with AICPA pronouncements.
2. Imputed interest programs that calculate the imputed interest on receivables and payables in accordance with AICPA pronouncements.
3. Cash flow programs that apply a "what if" analysis to cash flow projections to determine which assumptions used in these projections are most sensitive to change.

There are numerous other time-sharing applications, however the main point is that although these programs are quite standardized and not easily adaptable to unique situations, they eliminate the requirement for the auditor to be a computer programmer.

Table 14-1. Sample Uses of System 2170

CAPABILITY	AUDIT AREA		
	Investments	*Commercial Loans*	*Installment Loans*
Totals and Subtotals	• Original cost • Par value • Carrying value • Original discount or premium • Present discount or premium • Accrued interest • Amortization of discount or premium • Interest income	• Original balance • Current balance • Lines of credit • Unused lines of credit • Commitment fees • Accrued interest • Interest income • Participation amount • Undisbursed loan amount	• Original balance • Current balance • Original amount disbursed • Original unearned discount • Present unearned discount • Accrued interest • Cash or side collateral • Credit life insurance reserve • Dealer reserve
Computations	• Accrued interest • Interest income • Amortization of discount or premium • Remaining balance of discount or premium • Extended carrying value	• Accrued interest receivable • Commitment fees • Collateral valuation • Penalty fees • Interest income	• Original discount • Loan liquidation • Amortization of unearned discount • Remaining balance of unearned discount • Accrued interest • Penalty fees
File Edits and Tests of Controls and Policies	• Default codes accurate • Legal vs. nonlegal status • Investment maturities	• Loan officer lending limits • Disbursement instructions • Waivers of interest, etc. • Credit limits • Past due loans	• Write-off formula • Credit limits • Dunning status • No accrual codes
Information Retrieval— Analytical Review	• Dollar amount • Interest rate • Maturity • Investment rating • Industry • Physical location of security • Average yield	• Dollar amount • Interest rate • Maturity • Industry • Renewal status • Repayment terms • Collateralization • Credit officer • Guarantee • Average yield	• Dollar amount • Interest rate • Maturity • Type of goods financed • Branch office • Dealer • Potential runoff

Table 14-1 (continued)

AUDIT AREA			
Real Estate Loans	*Demand Deposits*	*Savings Deposits*	*Certificates of Deposit*
• Original balance • Current balance • Original cost • Carrying value • Original discount or premium • Present discount or premium • Replacement reserves • Commitments • Escrow deposits • Participations • Accrued interest	• Current balance • Available balance • Overdrafts • Overdraft limits • Dormant accounts • Automatic overdraft accounts	• Current balance • Available balance • Anticipated interest • Passbook loan balance • Dormant accounts	• Original balance • Current balance • Anticipated interest payable
• Amortization of discount or premium • Remaining balance of discount or premium • Commitment fees • Accrued interest • Servicing fees • Average life of portfolio	• Service charges • Overdraft charges	• Accrued interest • Interest expense	• Accrued interest • Interest expense
• Appraisal date • Inspection dates • Tax search dates	• Overdraft limits • Approval of large withdrawals • Employee accounts	• Approval of large withdrawals • Employee accounts	• Numerical control • Approval of large withdrawals • Interest instructions • Regulation Q
• Dollar amount • Interest rate • Maturity • Servicer • Branch office • Type of loan • Type of property mortgaged	• Dollar amount • Branch office • Type of depositor • Service charge code	• Dollar amount • Branch office • Type of depositor • Type of account • Interest rate	• Dollar amount • Branch office • Type of depositor • Maturity • Interest rate • Disposition on maturity

Table 14-1 (continued)

	AUDIT AREA		
Real Estate Loans	Demand Deposits	Savings Deposits	Certificates of Deposit
Information Retrieval— Selected Data for Audit Testing	• Security listing for physical count • Purchases and sales • Securities pledged • Securities loaned	• Listing of notes and agreements for inspection • Listing of collateral for physical count or confirmation • Loans to officers and directors • Loans charged-off	• Listing of notes and files for inspection • Loans charged-off • Repossessions • "No mail" tests
Confirmation	• Securities held elsewhere • Fails to receive or deliver • Securities loaned • Collateral	• Customer balances et al. • Documents held elsewhere • Collateral held elsewhere • Participations • Notes out for collection	• Customer balances et al.
Valuation	• Securities at market • Securities in default	• Liability ledger • Past due report • Principal reductions • Collateral valuation • Payment history	• Past due report • Collateral valuation • Loss experience by type
File Comparison			• Subsequent payments

Audit Program Languages

Advanced audit programming languages provide the best of both of the audit software approaches mentioned above. These languages are usually quite simplified and require only limited training time for the auditor. By only inputing a limited number of instructions, the auditor can use the audit programming language to have the computer generate a complicated computer program to achieve the audit objectives. Further, this audit software is typically quite flexible and able to perform varied audit tasks. For example, among many other applications, an advanced audit software package could be used to generate programs to:

1. Subtotal and total key amounts in a master file or transaction file.
2. Verify computations of EDP department software.
3. Perform edit routines and limit checks on files.
4. Retrieve information from the system and perform analytical reviews.

Table 14-1 (continued)

	AUDIT AREA		
Real Estate Loans	Demand Deposits	Savings Deposits	Certificates of Deposit
• Escrow overdraft • Satisfactions • Foreclosures • Arrearages • Document inspection control	• "No mail" tests • Service charges • Uncollected funds • Error corrections	• Dormant accounts • "No mail" tests • No passbook accounts • Error corrections	• "No mail" tests • Inspection of cancelled certificates • Issued to officers or employees • Regulation Q violations
• Customer balances et al. • Documents with attorneys • Participations	• Customer balances et al.	• Customer balances et al.	• Customer balances et al.
• Appraisal value vs. principal outstanding • Properties by location (geographic concentration)	• Age and list overdrafts	• Passbook loans in excess of deposit balance	
	• Clearance of overdrafts • Reciprocal accounts		• Maturity of certificates

5. Select data for other audit tests using sophisticated sampling techniques.
6. Select and print audit confirmations.

The extent of possible applications depends on the relative sophistication of the audit programming language. One of the most sophisticated audit programming languages is "System 2170" developed by the certified public accounting firm of Peat, Marwick, Mitchell & Co. After approximately one week of traning, the auditor can become proficient in using System 2170. Then, by using a set of only twenty-one System 2170 commands and completing certain predescribed input forms, the auditor can use the computer to generate a COBOL program to perform myriad audit tasks. Earlier we described the procedures an auditor might perform to develop specific audit software for verifying the calculation of interest on loans in a bank. Table 14-1 presents a list of computer audit applications through System 2170 for a bank. The key point here is that these extensive procedures can be accomplished by an auditor who need not be a computer programmer.

The advantages of such powerful audit programming languages are numerous, however the cost to develop such a system is significant. Appropriate cost versus benefit analytical techniques must be considered. In lieu of developing their own audit programming languages, many organizations make arrangements to use the audit package already developed by the firm's external auditors.

Audit Software Control Considerations

When using audit software to analyze EDP files, the auditor must ascertain that he is auditing the *actual files* used in the generation of AIS output. A clever computer operator/programmer could generate a bogus EDP file for the auditor's use to conceal possible defalcations. To avoid this potential problem, the auditor should consider: (1) EDP general controls, (2) accumulating control totals of key fields on the file and reconciling these totals to corresponding totals outside the EDP department (such as general ledger control accounts), and (3) requesting the use of EDP files on a surprise basis rather than giving the EDP department sufficient lead time to prepare a bogus file.

During processing it is possible for an EDP file to be erased or altered due to operator or program error. The EDP auditor should always work from a copy of the EDP files to avoid this problem. Usually this copy of the file is obtained subject to the same control procedures mentioned above for determining that the EDP file being used is genuine.

Finally, the auditor should not rely on the EDP department to process his audit software applications. Again, the operator (or operator/programmer) could alter the files or programs to conceal possible defalcations. Ideally, the audit programs should be processed at a separate EDP installation. However, strong EDP general controls, once tested and verified, may provide an acceptable environment for processing at the organization's EDP installation.

Statistical Auditing Techniques

Statistical auditing techniques are a valuable audit tool for examining any system—manual or computerized. However certain related procedures such as sample design, organization of data, sample selection, and evaluation of test results have proved to be too time consuming and complicated to be performed on a manual basis. With the introduction of the computer most of these problems related to statistical auditing techniques are solved. The computer easily organizes large volumes of data for subsequent testing. Sophisticated statistical sampling programs have been developed to design and select an *efficient* sample and evaluate test results. The two general categories of statistical auditing techniques are: (1) attribute estimation (which relates to compliance testing procedures) and (2) variables estimation (which relates to substantive testing procedures).

Attribute Estimation

The auditor performs compliance tests to evaluate the extent of compliance with internal controls. Traditionally the sample of items selected for such a test was based on a "judgmental" approach. An example of a judgmental approach would be as follows:

> *The auditor decides that the second-party review of sales invoices before sales are recorded is a key internal control. If this control is complied with, the auditor will limit other substantive audit procedures. The evidence of such a control is the initials of the reviewer on the invoice. The auditor selects every hundreth invoice (a sample) from the total of 10,000 invoices (the "population" to be tested) that were processed during the period being tested. This represents a judgmental sample that in the auditor's "judgment" will determine the extent of compliance with the internal control being evaluated. The auditor then examines the sample invoices for the evidence of the review. Finally, he evaluates the results of the test and decides whether or not the review is taking place.*

This is a very common audit approach. However, several questions remain unanswered: Was the auditor's judgment correct? Was the sample large enough to support his conclusion? Was the sample too large to be efficient, hence overaudited? Based on the answer to these questions, is the auditor's final evaluation valid? To avoid such questions, the auditor could modify the approach taken above to include statistical compliance test procedures or attribute estimation.

The attribute estimation approach requires (1) determination of sample size, (2) drawing of a random sample, and (3) an evaluation table. Modern audit software can perform all three of these functions. Many time-sharing programs have been developed for this purpose. For example, to perform the same compliance test discussed above, the sales invoice review evaluation, the auditor would:

1. Determine the extent of his reliance on the control being tested. This reliance is quantified by defining a precision limit (that defines the extent of possible error in the test at a given confidence level) and a confidence level (that defines the expectation that the results of the test will occur

within the precision limit).[3] A confidence level of 95% and an upper precision limit of 5% represents a standard configuration of these two factors where the auditor will place substantial reliance on the internal control being tested.
2. Input the upper precision limit and confidence level into the time-sharing program together with the beginning and ending number of the sales invoices processed during the year (such as invoice number 10,520 through 11,519).
3. Obtain from the computer a random sample of invoice numbers to be examined and obtain an evaluation table from the computer.
4. Examine the invoices selected, compare the results with the sample evaluation table produced by the computer, and document the conclusion.

The attribute estimation approach does not replace the need for audit judgment that was required by the judgmental sample approach. Indeed, the attribute estimation approach requires even more audit judgment to determine the appropriate precision limit and confidence level. However this approach quantifies the results of this judgment on a statistically valid basis. The attribute estimation approach points out the significant extent to which related audit software can be used to improve the quality of compliance testing procedures.

Variables Estimation

The auditor performs substantive testing procedures to verify the details of transactions and the resulting balances. For example, assume that the organization maintains a current master file of all accounts receivable. If the auditor wishes to verify the existence of the accounts receivable, he could select a judgmental sample of specific accounts and mail a confirmation (a form requesting the *customer* to verify the recorded balance) to the customer. This is an acceptable and commonly used procedure. However, with access to the appropriate audit software, the auditor could:

1. After inputting certain qualitative information (similar to that used in the attribute estimation approach) the computer could select a statistically valid sample from the accounts receivable master file.
2. The computer could then print the confirmations selected in the sample.

---

[3]The purpose here is not to present a complete discussion of sample selection techniques. This is an extremely complex area that requires a complete understanding of the principles involved. Such an understanding demands an extensive review of the contents of standard texts in attribute sampling, such as Volumes I, II, and IV of the AICPA series, *An Auditor's Approach To Statistical Sampling.*

3. Finally, after the results of the test are obtained, the computer could evaluate these results and verify a statistically valid balance in accounts receivable within the predescribed parameters set by the auditor.

As we noted earlier, statistical procedures require a clear understanding of all the principles involved. By using audit software, the mechanics of selecting and evaluating a statistical sample are reduced from an extremely complex and time-consuming manual task to a rapid, efficient, and accurate EDP calculation. This, of course, relieves the auditor of a significant amount of work, however it does *not* relieve the auditor of the ultimate responsibility for the validity of the test results. Just as the use of audit software requires the auditor to have sufficient knowledge of EDP concepts, the use of statistical audit techniques requires a thorough understanding of statistical concepts.

Test Decks and Analytical Review of EDP Software

The test deck approach has several advantages, not the least of which is simplicity. In this approach the auditor selects the critical elements of the EDP software being examined and prepares a set of input data that will produce a predescribed result. Then he processes this data through the EDP department and evaluates the output against these predescribed results.

This can be very useful approach when properly controlled. Such control is concerned with: (1) determining that the software tested is the same software used to test "live data," (2) determining that the computer operator does not alter the processing stream during the test to conceal possible defalcations, and (3) determining that the auditor performing the test has at least a basic understanding of the EDP software and hardware being tested. If the EDP installation has strong general and application controls (such as a librarian for files and software, clear separation of duties, documented "run books" to process the job stream, etc.), the auditor can compliance-test these controls and rely on them to some extent during the processing of the test deck. If controls are not strong, the auditor can perform other procedures to control the processing of the test deck. For example, he could:

1. Perform the test on a surprise basis, using the software presently in the system.
2. Have the operator process the test data under the direct supervision of the EDP manager or the supervisor of operators.
3. With the cooperation of the user departments, summarize "live" data and

compare the "live" output with the prescribed results without notifying the EDP department.

However, none of the general controls or other procedures employed relieves the auditor of his responsibility to be properly trained in EDP concepts and procedures. When auditing any system, regardless of the extent of computerization, one paramount standard is that the auditor have adequate technical training and proficiency to perform a quality audit.

An alternative to the test deck approach is a detailed analysis of the EDP software. This requires that a person knowledgable in the appropriate software language analyze the software and determine whether the desired controls are properly included. This approach is subject to the same control considerations mentioned for the test deck approach. When using this procedure, however, there is one additional control consideration: rarely will an auditor possess an adequate knowledge of the programming language to perform this analysis himself. He may have to rely on the expertise of another member of the audit "team" or secure the services of an outside specialist with appropriate EDP knowledge (discussed later in this chapter) to perform the analysis. The auditor should also consider the cost/benefit viewpoint because a detailed review of software is usually quite time-consuming and costly.

RELATED AICPA PRONOUNCEMENTS

The AICPA has issued numerous pronouncements pertaining to the function of auditing. Since the auditor in the computerized AIS is concerned with all critical elements of the AIS, manual and computerized, all of these pronouncements must be considered in the audit approach. Three of these pronouncements that closely relate to the key auditing concepts in a computerized AIS are: (1) Statements on Auditing Standards #3, "The Effects of EDP on the Auditor's Study and Evaluation of Internal Control," (2) Statement on Auditing Standards #11, "Using the Work of a Specialist," and (3) the AICPA audit guide: "Audits of Service-Center-Produced Records."

Statement on Auditing Standards #3 (SAS-3)

SAS-3 is a statement on auditing standards and is written in broad general terms. It is meant as a guideline and does not introduce specific procedures to be used in all audit situations. The auditor must avail himself of other relevant information to tailor an audit program to fit the particular requirements of an audit.

SAS-3 states that the auditor must make a determination as to whether a client's accounting system uses a computer in any significant accounting applications and, further, to determine if reliance can be placed on the internal controls. Upon completing a "preliminary review," the auditor must evaluate the controls and determine if such controls, once tested, can be relied upon to limit the extent of substantive audit tests.

The first step for conducting a preliminary review is to identify significant accounting applications. SAS-3 states "significant accounting applications are those that relate to accounting information that can materially affect the financial statements the auditor is examining." As we are only interested in the utilization of EDP with significant accounting applications, the auditor should next determine the type of processing that is involved with each application. The data gathered at this stage should be general in nature and should not be designed to provide an evaluation of the effectiveness of controls. If the auditor should determine that no significant accounting applications are involved with the computer, SAS-3 will not be applicable to the audit.

After evaluating the extent of internal controls in the system, the auditor can decide whether these controls appear to provide a basis for reliance thereon to limit the extent of substantive procedures. Then, the auditor must choose from three alternatives in determining the course of action for completing the audit:

1. The auditor may accept the controls as adequate and proceed with his detailed review and test of compliance.
2. The auditor may decide that controls over specific applications are weak or that the overall system of internal control is inadequate. In such cases the detailed review and related compliance tests are not necessary as other audit procedures will have to be used to attain the audit objectives.
3. The auditor may decide not to rely on the internal controls even though they appear to be adequate. Justification for this course of action should be based on the effectiveness and the efficiency of alternative audit procedures.

If the auditor decides to rely on controls, performs related compliance tests, and then discovers these controls are not operating effectively, he cannot rely on such controls to limit the extent of substantive procedures. If, however, these controls are found to be operative, the auditor can procede with the related substantive audit procedures.

Figure 14-2 summarizes the approach recommended by SAS-3. Note the similarity of this approach to the general audit approach taken for the audit of the entire AIS presented in Figure 14-1.

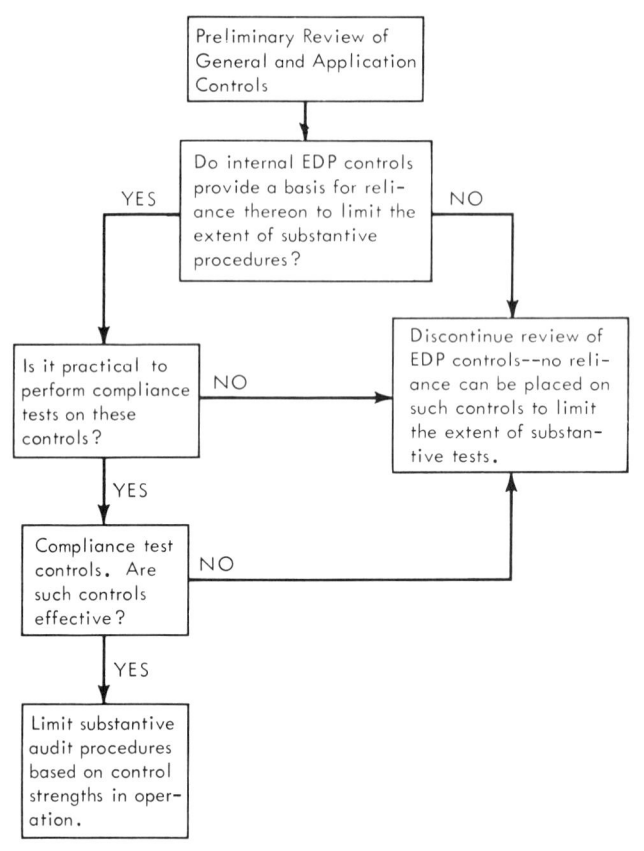

Fig. 14-2. Summary of Statement On Auditing Standards #3 (Section 321 of the SAS Codification)

Statement on Auditing Standards #11 (SAS-11)

As we noted earlier, many times the auditor will not possess particular EDP knowledge to effectively perform a segment of the audit (e.g., analysis of EDP software). In these cases, the auditor may secure the services of an outside expert to assist in the audit procedures. The use of an outside expert should conform to the guidelines set forth in SAS-11. In selecting the specialist, care should be taken to insure that the individual selected is indeed an expert. Some clues as to the determination of expertise follow:

1. The individual should be recognized as a professional by license, certification, or other public recognition.
2. The individual's reputation should be checked through reliable sources.

3. The qualifications, both academic and actual experience, should be verified.
4. The specialist, as the auditor, should be independent of the client.

Using an outside specialist should give the auditor a degree of additional confidence due to the objectivity the specialist is employing in the particular audit area. SAS-11, paragraph 7, states that an understanding should exist between the auditor, the organization, and the specialist as to the nature of the work to be performed by the specialist. Preferably, the understanding should be documented and should cover the following:

1. The objectives and scope of the specialist's work.
2. The specialist's representations as to his relationship, if any, to the organization.
3. The methods or assumptions to be used.
4. A comparison of the methods or assumptions to be used with those used in the preceding period.
5. The specialist's understanding of the auditor's corroborative use of the specialist's findings in relation to the representations in the financial statements or audit report.
6. The form and content of the specialist's report that would enable the auditor to make the evaluation described in paragraph 8 of SAS-11.

If the auditor has reason to doubt the results obtained from the report of the specialist, a second expert opinion may be necessary. If the matter cannot be resolved in this manner, the external auditor must look at the possibility that a qualification or disclaimer of opinion may be in order. The inability to resolve the problem is comparable to a scope limitation and should be disclosed accordingly.

The scope of the work to be performed by the specialist should be defined by the auditor and should conform to the standards he would require for his own work. When using outside specialists, care should be taken in explaining the nature of the examination and the criteria to be evaluated. The specialist should be advised of the particular internal control features that should be present and any alternative controls that would be satisfactory if the primary controls are lacking.

Audits of Service-Center-Produced Records

Rule 202 of the AICPA "Code of Professional Ethics" requires compliance with generally accepted auditing standards issued by the AICPA.

"Audits of Service-Center-Produced Records" is an *audit guide* and not subject to the provisions of Rule 202. However, the guide represents the opinion of the Committee on Computer Auditing of the AICPA, and therefore, departures from the provisions of the guide are not common and should be justified.

The audit guide defines a service center as "any organization that provides data processing functions for other organizations, including the actual processing function itself." The guide discusses the: (1) nature of service centers, (2) evaluating controls at service centers, (3) accumulation of evidential matter, and (4) third-party reviews of service centers. For the most part, the main points of this guide have already been discussed in this chapter and in Chapter 4 (Internal Control). Before proceeding with an audit of a system using a service center, the auditor should become familiar with all of the concepts presented in the audit guide.

Summary

The introduction of the computer into the AIS has had a significant effect on the types of procedures used by auditors, however the general audit approach remains essentially the same for all systems regardless of the extent of computerization. New techniques have been developed to audit *through* and not *to* the computer, yet evaluating internal controls and designing related compliance and substantive tests remains the basic framework of the audit approach. As this framework is modified to accommodate the audit procedures required in the computerized AIS, the auditor (whether he be an internal or external auditor) must be adequately trained in the use of EDP auditing techniques and related EDP principles.

DISCUSSION QUESTIONS AND PROBLEMS

1. a. Describe the functions of the internal auditors.
   b. How may the internal auditors be functionally independent?
2. a. Describe the functions of the external auditors.
   b. What factors influence the auditor's approach and procedures employed in an audit?
3. a. Define the purpose or objective of the external auditor's examination.

b. How will the evaluation of internal controls impact the auditor's plan?
4. a. Differentiate between compliance and substantive tests.
   b. Define "bridging workpapers."
5. How does computerization of the AIS impact the audit procedures?
6. a. Define "audit software packages."
   b. Define "audit program languages."
7. How may the auditor be certain that the EDP files examined during an audit are the files that were actually used during processing?
8. a. Describe the uses of statistical sampling in auditing.
   b. Define "attribute estimation."
   c. Define "variable estimation."
9. Describe the controls that would be necessary to properly use test checks to validate a systems operation.
10. a. Related to SAS-3, define "significant accounting applications."
    b. What is the auditor's responsibility when significant accounting applications are computerized?
    c. After evaluating the system, what are the auditor's alternatives?
11. List the minimum criteria that would be acceptable in choosing an EDP expert.
12. What types of supervision or control should the auditor exercise over the EDP specialist?
13. List the major audit areas for the following:
    a. manufacturing,
    b. hospital,
    c. retailer.
14. Related to Exhibit 14-2, develop a chart showing potential applications for System 2170 for a small manufacturing firm.
15. As part of his engagement, the external auditor may furnish management with an "Internal Control Memo." What value would this have to management regarding the following:
    a. purpose of the AIS,
    b. design of the AIS,
    c. operation of the AIS,
    d. validity of information generated by the AIS.

Bibliography

AICPA. *Codification of Statements on Auditing Standards,* New York, 1977.

AICPA Professional Development Division. *An Auditor's Approach to Statistical Sampling,* New York, 1967, and supplementary updating sections.

GORDON B. DAVIS, CPA, PhD. *Auditing and EDP*, AICPA, New York, 1968.
Peat, Marwick, Mitchell & Co. Technical Material.

APPENDIX
CPA EXAMINATION QUESTIONS

1. An internal administrative control that is sometimes used in connection with procedures to detect unauthorized or unexplained computer usage is
   a. Maintenance of a computer tape library.
   b. Use of file controls.
   c. Control over program tapes.

2. A company uses the account code 669 for maintenance expense. However, one of the company's clerks often codes maintenance expense as 996. The highest account code in the system is 750. What would be the best internal control check to build into the company's computer program to detect this error?
   a. A check for this type of error would have to be made before the information was transmitted to the EDP department.
   b. Valid-character test.
   c. Sequence check.
   d. Valid-code test.

3. For good internal control, the monthly bank statements should be reconciled by someone under the direction of the
   a. Credit manger.
   b. Controller.
   c. Cashier.
   d. Treasurer.

4. For good internal control, the person who should sign checks is the
   a. Person preparing the checks.
   b. Purchasing agent.
   c. Accounts-payable clerk.
   d. Treasurer.

5. For good internal control, the credit manager should be responsible to the
   a. Sales manager.
   b. Customer-service manager.
   c. Controller.
   d. Treasurer.

6. For good internal control, the billing department should be under the direction of the
   a. Controller.

b. Credit manager.
   c. Sales manager.
   d. Treasurer.
7. The authorization for write-off of accounts receivable should be the responsibility of the
   a. Credit manager.
   b. Controller.
   c. Accounts-receivable clerk.
   d. Treasurer.
8. The machine-language program that results when a symbolic-language program is translated is called a (an)
   a. Object program.
   b. Processor program.
   c. Source program.
   d. Wired program.
9. An advantage of manual processing is that human processors may note data errors and irregularities. To replace the human element of error detection associated with manual processing, a well-designed electronic data processing system should introduce
   a. Programmed limits.
   b. Dual circuitry.
   c. Echo checks.
   d. Read after write.
10. The real-time feature normally would be least useful when applied to accounting for a firm's
    a. Bank-account balances.
    b. Property and depreciation.
    c. Customer accounts receivable.
    d. Merchandise inventory.
11. A technique for controlling identification numbers (part number, man number, etc.) is
    a. Self-checking digits.
    b. Sequence checks.
    c. Parity control.
    d. File protection.
12. On magnetic disks, more than one file may be stored on a single disk. Likewise, in multiprogramming computer operations, several programs may be in core storage at one time. In both cases, it is important to prevent the intermixing or overlapping of data. This is accomplished by a technique known as
    a. Boundary protection.
    b. File integrity.
    c. Paging.
    d. Interleaving.

13. Echo checks and dual heads are both control devices for checking the transmission of recorded information. The major advantage of dual heads over echo check is that
    a. The cost is less.
    b. They require less time.
    c. They check the recorded information.
    d. They also check overflow.
14. If a trailer label is used on a magnetic-tape file, it is the last record and summarizes the file. Which of the following is information not typically found on a trailer label?
    a. Record count.
    b. Identification number.
    c. Control totals for one or more files.
    d. End-of-file or end-of-reel code.
15. A group of related records in a data-processing system is a
    a. Character.
    b. Field.
    c. Cluster.
    d. File.
16. Contact with banks for the purpose of opening company bank accounts should normally be the responsibility of the corporate.
    a. Board of Directors.
    b. Treasurer.
    c. Controller.
    d. Executive Committee.
17. Evaluation of the electronic data processing aspects of a system of accounting control should
    a. Not be a part of the auditor's evaluation of the system.
    b. Be a separate part of the auditor's evaluation of the system.
    c. Be an integral part of the auditor's evaluation of the system.
    d. Be coordinated with the auditor's evaluation of administrative control.
18. In comparison to the external auditor, an internal auditor is more likely to be concerned with
    a. Internal administrative control.
    b. Cost accounting procedures.
    c. Operational auditing.
    d. Internal accounting control.
19. Which of the following is not a problem associated with the use of test decks for computer-audit purposes?
    a. Auditing through the computer is more difficult than auditing around the computer.
    b. It is difficult to design test decks that incorporate all potential variations in transactions.

c. Test data may be commingled with live data causing operating problems for the client.
d. The program with which the test data are processed may differ from the one used in actual operations.

20. An auditor's investigation of a company's electronic data processing control procedures has disclosed the following four circumstances. Indicate which circumstance constitutes a weakness in internal control.
    a. Machine operators do not have access to the complete run manual.
    b. Machine operators are closely supervised by programmers.
    c. Programmers do not have the authorization to operate equipment.
    d. Only one generation of back-up files is stored in an off-premises location.

21. Which of the following is an example of application controls in electronic data processing systems?
    a. Input controls.
    b. Hardware controls.
    c. Documentation procedures.
    d. Controls over access to equipment and data files.

22. An auditor would be least likely to use a generalized computer-audit program for which of the following tasks?
    a. Selecting and printing accounts receivable confirmations.
    b. Listing accounts receivable confirmation exceptions for examination.
    c. Comparing accounts receivable subsidiary files to the general ledger.
    d. Investigating exceptions to accounts receivable confirmations.

23. Control totals are used as a basic method for detecting data errors. Which of the following is not a control figure used as a control total in EDP systems?
    a. Ledger totals.
    b. Check-digit totals.
    c. Hash totals.
    d. Document-count totals.

24. Program controls, in an electronic data processing system, are used as substitutes for human controls in a manual system. Which of the following is an example of a program control?
    a. Dual read.
    b. Echo check.
    c. Validity check.
    d. Limit and reasonableness test.

25. Which of the following best describes a fundamental control weakness often associated with electronic data processing systems?
    a. Electronic data processing equipment is more subject to systems error than manual processing is subject to human error.
    b. Electronic data processing equipment processes and records similar transactions in a similar manner.
    c. Electronic data processing procedures for detection of invalid and unusual transactions are less effective than manual control procedures.
    d. Functions that would normally be separated in a manual system are combined in the electronic data processing system.

26. A company has additional temporary funds to invest. The Board of Directors decided to purchase marketable securities and assigned the future purchase and sale decisions to a responsible financial executive. The best person(s) to make periodic reviews of the investment activity should be
    a. An investment committee of the Board of Directors.
    b. The chief operating officer.
    c. The corporate controller.
    d. The treasurer.

27. Data Corporation has just completely computerized its billing and accounts receivable recordkeeping. You want to make maximum use of the new computer in your audit of Data Corporation. Which of the following audit techniques could not be performed through a computer program?
    a. Tracing audited cash receipts to accounts receivable credits.
    b. Selecting on a random number basis accounts to be confirmed.
    c. Examining sales invoices for completeness, consistency between different items, valid conditions and reasonable amounts.
    d. Resolving differences reported by customers on confirmation requests.

28. Operating control over the check signature plate normally should be the responsibility of the
    a. Secretary.
    b. Chief accountant.
    c. Vice president of finance.
    d. Treasurer.

29. General and special computer programs have been developed for use in auditing EDP systems. When considering the use of these computer-audit programs, the auditor
    a. Should determine the audit efficiency of using a given computer program.
    b. Will find them ineffective for applications containing many records and requiring significant time for testing.

c. Should use them on a surprise basis in order for them to be effective.
d. Will find them economically feasible for any size EDP system.

30. The Smith Corporation has numerous small customers. A customer file is kept on disk storage. For each customer the file contains customer name, address, credit limit, and account balance. The auditor wishes to test this file to determine whether credit limits are being exceeded. Assuming that computer time is available, the best procedure for the auditor to follow would be to:
   a. Develop a test deck which would cause the account balance of certain accounts to be increased until the credit limit was exceeded to see if the system would react properly.
   b. Develop a program to compare credit limits with account balances and print out the details of any account with a balance exceeding its credit limit.
   c. Ask for a printout of all account balances so that they can be manually checked against the credit limits.
   d. Ask for a printout of a sample of account balances so that they can be individually checked against the credit limits.

31. In connection with the study of internal control, an auditor encounters the following flowcharting symbols:

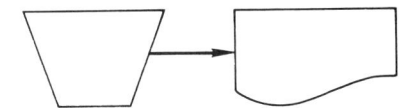

   The auditor would conclude that:
   a. A document has been generated by a manual operation.
   b. A master file has been created by a computer operation.
   c. A document has been generated by a computer operation.
   d. A master file has been created by a manual operation.

32. In its electronic data processing system a company might use self-checking numbers (check digits) to enable detection of which of the following errors?
   a. Assigning a valid identification code to the wrong customer.
   b. Recording an invalid customer's identification charge account number.
   c. Losing date between processing functions.
   d. Processing data arranged in the wrong order.

33. Which of the following statements relating to compliance tests is most accurate?
   a. Auditing procedures cannot concurrently provide both evidence of compliance with accounting control procedures and evidence required for substantive tests.

b. Compliance tests include physical and observations of the proper segregation of duties which ordinarily may be limited to the normal audit period.

c. Compliance tests should be based upon proper application of an appropriate statistical sampling plan.

d. Compliance tests ordinarily should be performed as of the balance sheet date or during the period subsequent to that date.

34. An auditor obtains a magnetic tape that contains the dollar amounts of all client inventory items by style number. The information on the tapes is in no particular sequence. The auditor can best ascertain that no consigned merchandise is included on the tape by using a computer program that:

a. Statistically selects samples of all amounts.

b. Excludes all amounts for items with particular style numbers that indicate consigned merchandise.

c. Mathematically calculates the extension of each style quantity by the unit price.

d. Prints on paper the information that is on the magnetic tape.

35. Effective internal control in a small company that has an insufficient number of employees to permit proper division of responsibilities can best be enhanced by:

a. Employment of temporary personnel to aid in the separation of duties.

b. Direct participation by the owner of the business in the record-keeping activities of the business.

c. Engaging a CPA to perform monthly "write-up" work.

d. Delegation of full, clear-cut responsibility to each employee for the functions assigned to each.

36. So that the essential accounting control features of client's electronic data processing system can be identified and evaluated, the auditor must, at a minimum, have:

a. A basic familiarity with the computer's internal supervisory system.

b. A sufficient understanding of the entire computer system.

c. An expertise in computer systems and analysis.

d. A background in programming procedures.

37. In connection with the study and evaluation of internal control during an examination of financial statements, the independent auditor

a. Gives equal weight to internal accounting and administrative control.

b. Emphasizes the internal administrative control.

c. Emphasizes the separation of duties of client personnel.

d. Emphasizes internal accounting control.

38. What is the computer process called when data processing is performed concurrently with a particular activity and the results are available soon enough to influence the particular course of action being taken or the decision being made?
    a. Realtime processing.
    b. Batch processing.
    c. Random access processing.
    d. Integrated data processing.
39. The grandfather-father-son approach to providing protection for important computer files is a concept that is most often found in
    a. On-line, real-time systems.
    b. Punched-card systems.
    c. Magnetic tape systems.
    d. Magnetic drum systems.
40. When auditing a computerized system, an auditor may use the "integrated test facility" technique, sometimes referred to as the minicompany approach, as an audit tool. This technique
    a. Is more applicable to independent audits than internal audits.
    b. Involves using test decks.
    c. Is the most commonly used audit tool for "auditing through the computer."
    d. Involves introducing simulated transactions into a system simultaneously with actual transactions.
41. The normal sequence of documents and operations on a well-prepared systems flowchart is
    a. Top to bottom and left to right.
    b. Bottom to top and left to right.
    c. Top to bottom and right to left.
    d. Bottom to top and right to left.
42. The auditor should be concerned about internal control on a data processing system because
    a. The auditor cannot follow the flow of information through the computer.
    b. Fraud is more common in an EDP system than a manual system.
    c. There is usually a high concentration of data processing activity and control in a small number of people in an EDP system.
    d. Auditors most often "audit around the computer."
43. A magnetic tape header label is used to warn the operator that
    a. The next processing step is about to begin.
    b. A wrong input tape has been mounted.
    c. An incorrect number of records have been processed.
    d. A different type of input or output device must be used.
44. Which of the following best describes the principal advantage of the use of flowcharts in reviewing internal control?

a. Standard flowcharts are available and can be effectively used for describing most company internal operations.
b. Flowcharts aid in the understanding of the sequence and relationships of activities and documents.
c. Working papers are not complete unless they include flowcharts as well as memoranda on internal control.
d. Flowcharting is the most efficient means available for summarizing internal control.

45. A customer inadvertently ordered part number 12368 rather than part number 12638. In processing this order, the error would be detected by the vendor with which of the following controls?
a. Batch total.
b. Key verifying.
c. Self-checking digit.
d. An internal consistency check.

46. (Estimated time—20 to 25 minutes)
Anthony, CPA, prepared the flowchart on the facing page which portrays the raw materials purchasing function of one of Anthony's clients, a medium-sized manufacturing company, from the preparation of initial documents through the vouching of invoices for payment in accounts payable. The flowchart was a portion of the work performed on the audit engagement to evaluate internal control.
Required:
Identify and explain the systems and control weaknesses evident from the flowchart on the facing page. Include the internal control weaknesses resulting from activities performed or not performed. All documents are prenumbered.

The following sales procedures were encountered during the regular annual audit of Marvel Wholesale Distributing Company.

Customer orders are received by the sales-order department. A clerk computes the dollar amount of the order and sends it to the credit department for approval. Credit approval is stamped on the order and returned to the sales-order department. An invoice is prepared in two copies and the order is filed in the "customer order" file.

The "customer copy" of the invoice is sent to the billing department and held in the "pending" file awaiting notification that the order was shipped.

The "shipping copy" of the invoice is routed through the warehouse and the shipping department as authority for the respective departments to release and ship the merchandise. Shipping-department personnel pack the order and prepare a three-copy bill of lading: the original copy is mailed to the customer, the

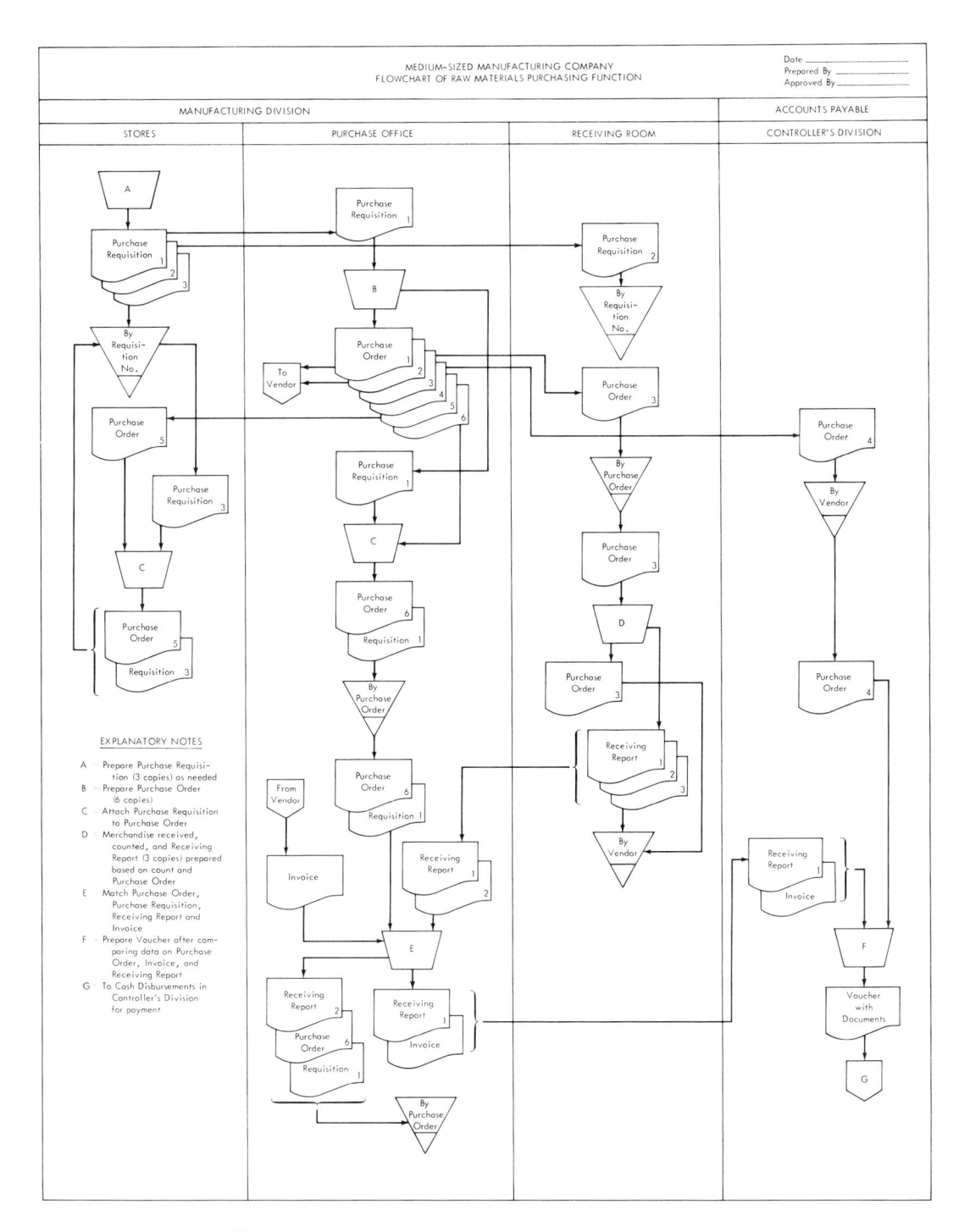

MEDIUM-SIZED MANUFACTURING COMPANY
FLOWCHART OF RAW MATERIALS PURCHASING FUNCTION

Date _____
Prepared By _____
Approved By _____

MANUFACTURING DIVISION			ACCOUNTS PAYABLE
STORES	PURCHASE OFFICE	RECEIVING ROOM	CONTROLLER'S DIVISION

EXPLANATORY NOTES

A — Prepare Purchase Requisition (3 copies) as needed
B — Prepare Purchase Order (6 copies)
C — Attach Purchase Requisition to Purchase Order
D — Merchandise received, counted, and Receiving Report (3 copies) prepared based on count and Purchase Order
E — Match Purchase Order, Purchase Requisition, Receiving Report and Invoice
F — Prepare Voucher after comparing data on Purchase Order, Invoice, and Receiving Report
G — To Cash Disbursements in Controller's Division for payment

489

second copy is sent with the shipment, and the other is filed in sequence in the "bill of lading" file. The invoice "shipping copy" is sent to the billing department.

The billing clerk matches the received "shipping copy" with the customer copy from the "pending" file. Both copies of the invoice are priced, extended, and footed. The customer copy is then mailed directly to the customer and the "shipping copy" is sent to the accounts-receivable clerk.

The accounts-receivable clerk enters the invoice data in a sales-accounts-receivable journal, posts the customer's account in the "subsidiary customer's accounts ledger," and files the "shipping copy" in the "sales invoice" file. The invoices are numbered and filed in sequence.

47. In order to gather audit evidence concerning the proper credit approval of sales, the auditor would select a sample of transaction documents from the population represented by the
    a. "Customer order" file.
    b. "Bill of lading" file.
    c. "Subsidiary customers' accounts ledger."
    d. "Sales invoice" file.

48. In order to determine whether the system of internal control operated effectively to minimize errors of failure to post invoices to customers' accounts ledger, the auditor would select a sample of transactions from the population represented by the
    a. "Customer order" file.
    b. "Bill of lading" file.
    c. "Subsidiary customers' accounts ledger."
    d. "Sales invoice" file.

49. Control operated effectively to minimize errors of balance to invoice a shipment, the auditor would select a sample of transactions from the population represented by the
    a. "Customer order" file.
    b. "Bill of lading" file.
    c. "Subsidiary customers' accounts ledger."
    d. "Sales invoice" file.

50. In order to gather audit evidence that uncollected items in customers' accounts represented valid trade receivables, the auditor would select a sample of items from the population represented by the
    a. "Customer order" file.
    b. "Bill of lading" file.
    c. "Subsidiary customers' accounts ledger."
    d. "Sales invoice" file.

51. You are reviewing audit work papers containing a narrative description of the Penney Corporation's factory payroll system. A portion of that narrative is as follows:

Factory employees punch time clock cards each day when entering or leaving the shop. At the end of each week the timekeeping department collects the time cards and prepares duplicate batch-control slips by department showing total hours and number of employees. The time cards and original batch-control slips are sent to the payroll accounting section. The second copies of the batch-control slips are filed by date.

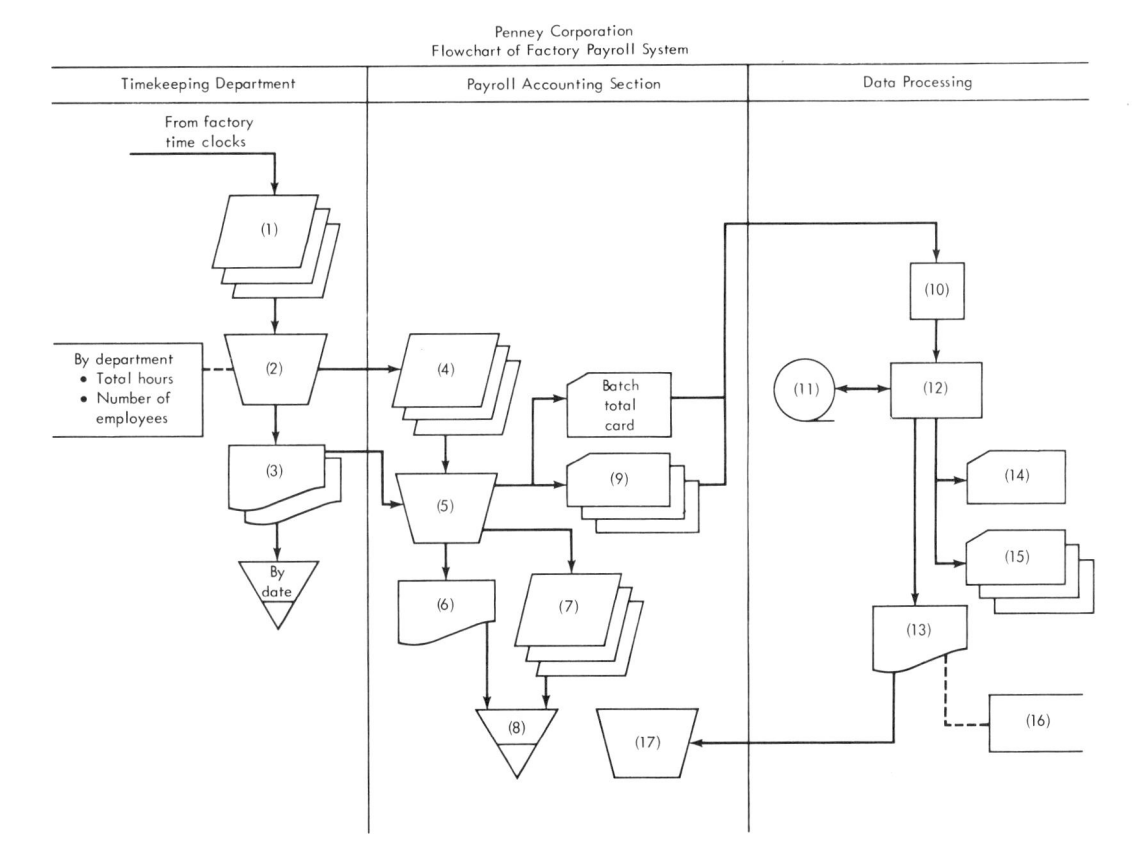

In the payroll accounting section, payroll transaction cards are keypunched from the information on the time cards, and a batch total card for each batch is keypunched from the batch-control slip. The time cards and batch-control slips are then filed by batch for possible reference. The payroll transaction cards and batch total card are sent to data processing where they are sorted by employee number within batch. Each batch is edited by a computer program which checks the validity of employee number against a master employee tape file and the total hours and number of employees against the batch total card. A detail printout by batch and employee number is produced which indicates batches that do not balance and invalid employee numbers. This printout is returned to payroll accounting to resolve all differences.

In searching for documentation you found a flowchart of the payroll system which included all appropriate symbols (American National Standards Institute, Inc.) but was only partially labeled. The portion of this flowchart described by the above narrative appears on page 491.

Required:
a. Number your answer 1 though 17. Next to the corresponding number of your answer, supply the appropriate labeling (document name, process description, or file order) applicable to each numbered symbol on the flowchart.
b. Flowcharts are one of the aids an auditor may use to determine and evaluate a client's internal central system. List advantages of using flowcharts in this context.

index

a

Access methods, 413–414
Accidental threats to system, 437
Accountants:
  data base management and, 405–406
  functions of, 15–22
  future role of, 22–23
  problem–solving and decision–making and, 200–201
  stereotypes, 7
Accounting control, 110, 112–113
Accounting information systems, 4–22, 81–105
  accounting functions and, 15–22
  accounts receivable system example, 86, 88–96
  auditing, *see* Audits
  computer–based, *see* Computer systems
  decision–making and, *see* Decision–making
  defined, 13–14
  design, *see* Systems design
  developments affecting, 9–10
  evaluation of, 439, 441–452
  future role of accountants in, 22–23
  internal control in, *see* Internal control
  maintenance function, 432–440
  operating systems and, 96–101
  reports, *see* Reports
  role of, 15–22
  security, 436–440
  statistical analyses, 101–105
  users of, 5–6
Accounts receivable system, 86, 88–96
Account tests, 126

Ackoff, Russell L., 189n
Acquisition, divestment, and merger (ADM) analysis, 225, 233
Active threats to system, 437–438
Activities analysis, 256, 260
Administrative control, 110, 111–112
Administrator, data base, 406, 423–424
Aguilar, Francis J., 37n
Airlines, reporting requirements of, 152–153
American Accounting Association (AAA), 4–5, 9n, 13, 192
American Institute of Certified Public Accountants (AICPA), 9n, 21, 110, 456n, 465, 474–478
Andrews, K. R., 39n
Application controls, 123–127
Archival program, 424
Archive file, 424–425
Arnoff, E. Leonard, 189n
Assembly language, 398
Attention–directing, 17
Attribute estimation, 471–472
Auditors, 457–458
Audits, 7, 18–20, 456–478
  AICPA and, 474–478
  analysis of EDP software, 474
  approach, 458–464
  external auditors, 457, 458
  internal auditors, 457–458
  software packages, 464–470
  statistical techniques, 470–473
  test decks, 474–475
Audit trails, 18, 127–128
Authority, delegation of, 52, 115

b

Banks:
   operations, 82
   statistical analyses for, 104
Bennis, Warren, 53–54
Binding, 410
Block diagrams, 298–300
Blocked logical records, 412
Bridging workpaper, 460
Brink, Victor Z., 53n
Budgeting, 212–213, 225–233, 276

c

Cannon, Thomas, 37n
Capital budgeting, 212–213, 225–233
Card files, 413
Centralized control, 53
Central processing unit (CPU), 378–380
Chain of operations, fundamental, 80–81
Change requests, 436
Christensen, C. R., 39n
Churchman, C. West, 189n
Civil Aeronautics Board, 152–153
Classical organization structure, 46, 48
Clerical automation, 18
COBOL, 398, 464
CODASYL group, 404–405
Codes, 126
Communications function of management, 29, 30
Company policy, changes in, 435
Company strengths and weaknesses, identification of, 37, 38
Compensation plans, 236–237
Competitive conditions, changes in, 434–435
Competitive edge, 37, 39, 45
Competitive information, 40, 43
Compiler–level language, 398
Completeness controls, 124–125, 129
Compliance tests, 466, 471
Computer capacity, 270
Computer programs, 383–384, 398–399, 417–419, 464–465
Computer systems, 371–401
   components of, 373–374, 376–387
   configurations, 387–394
   conversion from manual system to, 389–390, 392, 395–399
   data base, *see* Data base management systems
   impact of, 7–9
   internal controls in, 115–129
   pitfalls in acquiring hardware, 399–401
   prerequisites for, 372–373

Computer systems (cont.)
   security of, 436–440
   See also Audits
Consolidated profit plans, 218–220
Constraints, system, 268–271
Contract bidding, 235–236
Contribution analysis, 234
Contribution costs, 233
Control:
   of forms, 345–357
   internal, *see* Internal control
   managerial, 11, 29–32, 58–65
   project, 277–279, 291–296
Controllable costs, 233
Controller, role of, 161–162, 432
Controller's manual, 237–240
Control reports, 64
Control totals, 124–125
Cordiner, Ralph, 262
Corporate decisions, *see* Decision–making
Cost allocation, 233–234
Cost behavior, 233
Cost centers, 39, 233
Costs:
   segregation according to behavior, 204
   as system constraint, 270
CPM (Critical Path Method), 223, 292–296
Critical path network analysis, 220, 223, 275–276, 292–296
Cultural factors, decisions based on, 195–196
Customer departmentation, 47, 48, 49
Customers, as system constraint, 270

d

Data, distinguished from information, 12, 14
Data aggregates, 407–412
Data base, 404, 407, 422
Data base management systems, 280, 404–425
   components of, 406–407
   computer program, 417–419
   data aggregates, 407–412
   data base, 404, 407, 422
   data base administrator, 406, 423–424
   data files, 412–415
   data management program, 407, 422–423
   librarian, 415–417
   model of, 424–425
   objectives of, 404–405
   programmer, 407, 412, 416–417
   role of accountant in, 405–406
   structured records, 419–422
Data base relationships chart, 300, 305, 306
Data base save file, 424

Data communications, 384–386
Data fields, 407–409
Data files, 412–415
Data-flow matrices, 302, 305–306, 309–314
Data gathering, 323–327
Data management program, 407, 422–423
Data names, 384
Data processing:
  computerized, see Computer systems
  manual, 373–376
  position in organization, 372
Data processing cycle, 8
Data records, 409–412
Data relationship grid, 311
Decentralization, 52–53
Decision–making, 11, 29, 31–32, 64, 180–181, 209–240
  accountant's contribution to, 200–201
  controller's manual, 237–240
  defined, 180
  economic concepts and, 201–205
  operational planning, 213–223
  process of, see Decision process
  strategic planning, 209–213
  types of decisions, 223–237
  See also Problem–solving
Decision process, 191–200
  anatomy of choosing, 197–200
  factors shaping, 193–196
  information and, 192–193
Decision tables (DT), 318–323
Demographical information, 42
Departmentation, 47, 48–49
Department store, operations flowchart for, 80
Design, see Systems design
Design report, 285, 286
Detailed computer program flowchart, 300, 308
Detailed design, 280–283
  See also Systems design techniques and tools
Detailed system flowcharts, 300, 302
Development information, 63
Diminishing marginal productivity, 205
Direct access files, 413
Distributed computing, 386–387
Distribution-by-value report, 102, 103
Documentation, 122, 283–286, 334–337, 459
Documentation manual, 284–286, 336–337
Dual transmission controls, 129
Duties, segregation of, 114

e

Echelons, 421
Economic conditions, changes in, 434

Economic profit, 203–204
Economic trends, information about, 42
Electronic data processing, see Computer systems
Engineering information, 63
Environment, analysis of, 37, 38
Environmental information, 41–43
Equimarginal allocation, 205
Error reports, 436
Estimates, 324–325
Evaluation of system, 439, 441–452
Expected monetary value, 205
Extended entry decision table, 321
External auditors, 457, 458
External constraints, 270–271
External reports, 150–155
External storage, 383
External users of accounting information, 5, 6

f

Fabrycky, W. J., 236n
Federal Aviation Administration, 152
Federal Communications Commission, 152
Federal Power Commission, 152
Federal Trade Commission, 151
Feedback, 62, 64–65
Feedforward, 65
Feltham, Gerald A., 192n, 444n
File relationships charts, 300, 304
Files:
  data, 412–415
  design of, 398
  flat, 422
  forms, 355
  transaction, 126, 424
Financial Accounting Standards Board, 154
Financial Executives Institute, 9n
Financial plan, 44
Financial statements, 150–151
First–line management, 63
Flat files, 422
Flowcharting, 296–308
Flow chart system description, 392, 395, 396
Forms, 342–367
  analysis, 358
  design, 342, 357–366
  management program for, 345–357
  reasons for using, 344–345
  retention period, 366, 367
  systems design and, 343–344
  variety of, 343
Form flowcharts, 300, 303
FORTRAN, 331, 398
Functional departmentation, 47, 48

g

General controls, 117–123
Ghare, P. M., 236n
Government accountant, 21–22
Governmental information, 42
Government policies, regulations, and legislation, changes in, 433–434
Government restrictions, 270
GPSS (General Purpose Systems Simulation), 332
Gulf Energy and Environmental Systems, Inc., 211–212
Gunning, Robert, 278n

h

Hall, Arthur D., 195n
Hierarchical data structure, 421
Historical reporting, 101–105
Horngren, Charles T., 17, 235n
Hospitals:
 operations flowchart, 83
 report requirements of, 154
 statistical analyses for, 105

i

Ill-structured problems, 188
Incremental costs, 233
Incremental reasoning, 202–203
Individual problem-solving, 190–191
Industry conditions, changes in, 434–435
Information:
 control function of management and, 31, 32, 62–65
 decision-making and, 192–193
 distinguished from data, 12, 14
 organizing function of management and, 31, 32, 57–58
 planning function of management and, 31–32, 41–44
Information lag, 58
Information needs research, 260–265
Information systems, 4–5
 computerized, see Computer systems
 developments affecting, 9–10
 defined, 11–14
 manual, 373–376
Input:
 computer system, 376–377, 381
 manual system, 375
Input controls, 124–125
Input documents, 396–397
Insurance companies, report requirements of, 153–154
Integrated information system, 19–20

Internal auditors, 457–458
Internal constraints, 269–270
Internal control, 22, 108–129
 accounting control, 110, 112–113
 administrative control, 110, 111–112
 application controls, 123–127
 audit trails, 18, 127–128
 checklist, 132–148
 in computerized system, 115–129
 defined, 110–111
 EDP input and output control group, 120
 execution and recording of transactions, 113–114
 general controls, 117–123
 implementation, 120–123
 input controls, 124–125
 isolation of EDP department, 119
 in on-line systems, 128–129
 organizational control, 118–119
 output controls, 127
 for outside service bureau, 128
 preinstallation controls, 118
 processing controls, 125–126
 reasonable assurance, 114–115
 segregation of duties, 114
Internal information, 40, 43–44
Internal reports, 155–160
Internal storage, 383
Interviews, 324–327
Investigation questions, 327
Item descriptions, 397

j

Job station analysis, 306, 308, 310, 313, 315–318

k

Karger, D. W., 49n, 221n
Katz, Robert L., 37n, 39n
Keyed list, 420
Khan, Zafar, 433n
Kuhn, Alfred, 192n

l

Larson, Harry T., 388n
Learned, Edward P., 39n
Librarian, 120, 415–417
Limited entry decision table, 321
Limit tests, 126
"Line-of-Business" reports, 151
Line project management, 56

Linked list, 419
Logical record, 409–410, 412
Long–range planning, 211–213
Lowin, Aaron, 195n

m

Maintenance function, 432–440
Management:
 communications function of, 29, 30
 control function of, 11, 29–32, 58–65
 data base, *see* Data base management systems
 decision process and, 196–200
 defined, 11
 initiating function of, 29, 30
 objective–setting function of, 29, 30
 organizing function of, 11, 29–32, 46–58
 planning function of, 11, 29–32, 35–45
 systems approach to, *see* Systems approach to managerial processes
Management by objectives (MBO), 39
Management effectiveness, 266
Management Information System (MIS), defined, 11–13
Management services, 20–21
Management trails, 127–128
Managerial accounting, 15–17
Managerial style, information needs and, 264
Manpower needs, as system constraint, 269
Manual information systems, 373–376
 conversion to computer–based system, 389–390, 392, 395–399
Manufacturing information, 63
Manufacturing organization:
 operating system of, 79, 97–101
 statistical analysis for, 102–104
MAPI method, 225
Marginal costs, 233
Marketing information, 63
Marx, Karl, 7
Master Budget, 221–223
Master files, 120, 126, 128
Master Program Schedule (MPS), 276
Matrices, data–flow, 302, 305–306, 309–314
Matrix project management, 54–56
Measures of effectiveness (MOE's), 442, 443
Memory, computer, 383–384
Microcomputers, 371
Miller, George A., 192n
Minicomputers, 371, 385–387
Mixed entry decision table, 321
MMS Accounts Receivable System, 86, 89–96
Monetary measurements, 60
Money, time value of, 204–205

Morris, William T., 199–200
Murdick, R. G., 49n, 221n

n

Narrative system description, 390, 392, 396
National Association of Accountants (NAA), 8, 9n
Network analysis, 220, 223, 275–276, 292–296
Network diagram, 281, 282
Network structured records, 421–422
New product evaluation, 210, 211–212

o

Objectives, setting, 29, 30, 266–268
"One–man shop" system, 120–121
On–line systems, internal controls in, 128–129
Operational planning, 213–223
Operations flowchart, 80
Operations of organizations, fundamental, 78–81
Operations systems:
 fundamental chain of operations, 80–81
 in manufacturing organization, 79, 97–101
 relationships between accounting systems and, 96–101
Opportunities, identification of, 38
Opportunity cost, 203
Order processing system, 97
Organizational control, 118–119
Organizational environment, information needs and, 265
Organizational operating plans, 214, 217–218
Organizational problem–solving, 190–191
Organization structure:
 changes in, 435
 information needs and, 265
 as system constraint, 269
Organizing function of management, 11, 29–32, 46–58
Output:
 computer system, 383–384
 manual system, 376, 377
Output controls, 127
Output documents, 397
Overhead, 408, 414

p

Parent record, 421
Passive threats to system, 437

Peat, Marwick, Mitchell & Co., 462, 469
"People problems," 269–270
Performance/cost/time (P/C/T), control of, 277–278
Performance indicators, 442, 443
Performance specifications, 292
Performance standards, 11, 59–61, 64
Personnel availability, as system constraint, 269
Personnel information, 63
PERT (Program Evaluation Review Technique), 220, 292–296
Physical record, 410–412
Pl/1, 398
Planning:
  audit, 459
  managerial, 11, 29–32, 35–45
  operational, 213–223
  project, 220–221, 272–276, 291–296
  strategic, 36–40, 45, 209–213
Pointer fields, 420
Political information, 42
Position description, 308, 310, 315, 317
Pragmatic approach to problem solving, 186–187
Preinstallation controls, 118
Preliminary (gross) design, 279–280
Problem boundaries system, 268–271
Problem-solving, 17, 180–191
  accountant's contribution to, 200–201
  defined, 180
  formulation of problem, 182–185
  nature of problems, 181–182
  process of, 186–191
Process departmentation, 47, 48, 49
Process flowcharts, 300, 301
Processing controls, 125–126
Processor:
  computer system, 377–380
  manual system, 375–376
Product departmentation, 47, 48
Production factors, information about, 43
Product/market scope, definition of, 37, 38
Product set, 63
Profit centers, 39
Pro forma plans, 218–220
Program flow chart, 398
Program logic flowchart, 300, 307
Programmer, 407, 412, 416–417
Programs, computer, 383–384, 398–399, 417–419, 464–465
Project budgeting, 276
Project departmentation, 47, 48, 49
Project planning, 220–221, 272–276, 291–296
Project proposal, 271–272
Psychological factors, decisions based on, 194–195
Public accounting, 18–20
Purchase order, 114

q

Quality measures, 60
Quantity measures, 60
Query languages, 407
Questionnaires, 324

r

Random file access, 414
Rational factors, decisions based on, 194
Receiving report, 114
Relevancy, decision-making and, 201–202
Remote access terminals, 129
Reports, 150–162
  controller and, 161–162
  external, 150–155
  internal, 155–160
  project, 278
  samples of, 164–176
  treasurer and, 160–161
Research information, 63
Resource limitations, 270
Resources, assignment of, 37, 38, 39, 45
Resources set, 63
Restrictions, system, 268–271
Retailing organizations, statistical analyses for, 104
Retention of forms, 366, 367
Return on investment concept, 16
Risks, identification of, 38

s

Sales forecast, 44
Sampling, 324, 470–473
Schema, 404, 422
Scorecard, 17
Search process, 189–190
Securities and Exchange Commission reports, 151
Security, 436–440
Segment evaluation, 234–235
Self-checking numbers, 126
Self-imposed restrictions, 270
Sequence planning, 275–276
Sequential file, 412–413
Sequential file access, 413–414
Service bureau, internal controls for, 128
Service-center-produced records, audits of, 477–478
Short-range planning, 39, 45
Simon, Herbert, 195
SIMSCRIPT II, 332–334

Simulation, 328–334
Social factors, decisions based on, 195
Social trends, information about, 42
Software International, 86
Software packages, audit, 464–470
Spanned record, 412
Span of management, 49–51
Specific amount tests, 126
Specification, 335
Specification report, 285, 286
Staats, Elmer B., 21–22
Staffing changes, 435
Standardization, 335–336
Standards of performance, 11, 59–61, 64
Statistical analyses, 101–105
Statistical auditing techniques, 470–473
Statistical report, 61
Statistical sampling, 324, 470–473
Steiner, George, 35
Stock control of forms, 347–348, 354–355
Storage, computer system, 380, 383–384
Strategic planning, 36–40, 45, 209–213
Strategy, defined, 37
Structured records, 419–422
Subsystems, evaluation of, 444, 446–452
Suppliers, as system constraint, 271
Supply factors, 44
System, defined, 12–13
System description, 390, 392, 395–396
Systems approach to managerial processes, 28–35
   control, 62
   organizing, 52–57
   planning, 40, 41
Systems design, 248–286
   activities analysis, 256, 260
   components of AIS, 249, 253–261
   constraints, identification of, 268–271
   control, 277–279
   detailed design, 280–283
   forms, see Forms
   information needs research, 260–265
   organization for, 248–249
   preliminary design, 279–280
   project planning, 272–276, 291–296
   project proposal, 271–272
   reporting, 278
   setting objectives, 266–268
   techniques and tools, see Systems design techniques and tools
Systems design techniques and tools, 291–337
   critical path network analysis, 220, 223, 275–276, 292–296
   data–flow matrices, 302, 305–306, 309–314
   data gathering, 323–327
   decision tables, 318–323
   documentation, 283–286, 334–337
   flowcharting, 296–308

Systems design techniques and tools (cont.)
   job station analysis, 306, 308, 310, 313, 315–318
   simulation, 328–334
Systems view of managing, 28–30
System 2170, 466–469

t

Targets, specifications of, 37, 38, 39, 45
Tax planning, 236
Technological change, 435
Technological environment, information about, 43
Terborgh, George, 225*n*
Territory departmentation, 47, 48–49
Test decks, 473–474
Time–sharing audit software, 465
Time studies, 318
Title description, 308, 310
Top management personal values, 37, 38
Torgersen, P. E., 236*n*
Transaction files, 126
Transaction history file, 424
Transaction interface program, 424
Transactions, execution and recording of, 113–114
Translation instructions, 398
Trapdoors, 437
Treasurer, role of, 160–161
Tree structured records, 421
Turnkey system, 399

u

Unblocked logical records, 412
Uncontrollable costs, 233
Unions, as system constraint, 271
Utilities, reporting requirements of, 152

v

Variable estimation, 472–473
Venture teams, 56–57
Voucher requesting payment, 114

w

Wage control flowchart, 307
Weisman, Clark, 437–439
Work Breakdown Structure (WBS), 220, 273–275
Work sampling, 318